Butterworths New Law Guide to
the Family Procedure Rules 2010

JOHN FOY
9 GOUGH SQ.
LONDON
EC4A 3DE

Check up to date
Regulations etc.

Butterworths New Law Guide to the Family Procedure Rules 2010

Andrew Newbury,
Head of Family, Private Client & Wealth Management Division, Pannone LLP

His Honour Judge Yelton

Vicki McLynn,
Senior Associate, Pannone LLP

Clare Williams,
Solicitor, Pannone LLP

Members of the LexisNexis Group worldwide

United Kingdom	LexisNexis UK, a Division of Reed Elsevier (UK) Ltd, Halsbury House, 35 Chancery Lane, LONDON, WC2A 1EL, and 4 Hill Street, EDINBURGH EH2 3JZ
Argentina	LexisNexis Argentina, BUENOS AIRES
Australia	LexisNexis Butterworths, CHATSWOOD, New South Wales
Austria	LexisNexis Verlag ARD Orac GmbH & Co KG, VIENNA
Canada	LexisNexis Butterworths, MARKHAM, Ontario
Chile	LexisNexis Chile Ltda, SANTIAGO DE CHILE
Czech Republic	Orac sro, PRAGUE
France	Editions du Juris-Classeur SA, PARIS
Germany	LexisNexis Deutschland GmbH, FRANKFURT, MUNSTER
Hong Kong	LexisNexis Butterworths, HONG KONG
Hungary	HVG-Orac, BUDAPEST
India	LexisNexis Butterworths, NEW DELHI
Ireland	LexisNexis, DUBLIN
Italy	Editore, MILAN
Malaysia	Malayan Law Journal Sdn Bhd, KUALA LUMPUR
New Zealand	LexisNexis Butterworths, WELLINGTON
Poland	Wydawnictwo Prawnicze LexisNexis, WARSAW
Singapore	LexisNexis Butterworths, SINGAPORE
South Africa	LexisNexis Butterworths, DURBAN
Switzerland	mpfli Verlag AG, BERNE
USA	LexisNexis, DAYTON, Ohio

This book is published by Reed Elsevier (UK) Ltd trading as LexisNexis ('LexisNexis') and copyright in this collection is owned by LexisNexis.

© 2011 All rights reserved. However, the individual contributors own the copyright in their own contributions to this book and such contributions are published under licence from the contributors who, hereby, assert copyright in their materials. Such materials do not represent any views or other positions of LexisNexis. The views contained herein are those of the licensors solely. No part of this publication may be reproduced in any material form (including photocopying or storing it in any medium by electronic means and whether or not transiently or incidentally to some other use of this publication) without the written permission of the copyright owner except in accordance with the provisions of the Copyright, Designs and Patents Act 1988 or under the terms of a licence issued by the Copyright Licensing Agency Ltd, 90 Tottenham Court Road, London, England W1T 4LP. Applications for the copyright owner's written permission to reproduce any part of this publication should be addressed to the publisher.

Warning: The doing of an unauthorised act in relation to a copyright work may result in both a civil claim for damages and criminal prosecution.

Crown copyright material is reproduced with the permission of the Controller of HMSO and the Queen's Printer for Scotland. Any European material in this work which has been reproduced from EUR-lex, the official European Communities legislation website, is European Communities copyright.

A CIP Catalogue record for this book is available from the British Library.

ISBN 978-1-4057-6346-2

ISBN 9781405763462

Printed and bound in Great Britain by CPI Antony Rowe Ltd, Chippenham and Eastbourne

Visit LexisNexis UK at www.lexisnexis.co.uk

Authors

Andrew Newbury

Andrew Newbury is head of the Family, Private Client and Wealth Management division at Pannone, Manchester. He is a contributor to *Butterworths Family Law Service* and writes columns for the *Law Society Gazette*, *Family Law* and *Resolution Review*. Andrew is a Resolution trained collaborative lawyer, accredited specialist and chaired its training committee and Manchester region for 10 years. He continues to provide financial updates at Resolution's national conference. He's a fellow of the International Academy of Matrimonial Lawyers and comments frequently on family law matters on national radio, television and in the press.

His Honour Judge Yelton

Michael Yelton was called to the Bar in 1972 and practiced in Family and Civil Law from 1973 to 1998: between 1977 and 1981 he combined this with a Fellowship of Corpus Christi College, Cambridge, teaching Family and other subjects. In 1998 he was appointed to the Circuit Bench and has sat in Family and Civil since then, mainly in East Anglia. He has written extensively on a variety of topics, many non-legal.

Vicki McLynn

Vicki McLynn is a senior associate in the family department at Pannone, Manchester. She undertakes all aspects of family law with a particular focus on complex financial cases and those involving business interests. She has acted for a wide range of clients based nationally and internationally. Vicki is a Resolution accredited family specialist in financial provision and children cases. She is also a trained Collaborative Lawyer. Vicki lectures frequently to the legal profession. She has contributed to several legal titles and online services. Vicki has articles published regularly in magazines and professional journals on family law issues.

Clare Williams

Clare Williams is a solicitor in the family department at Pannone, Manchester. She advises on all aspects of family law. Clare is a regular contributor to Family Law Journal and the Resolution Review. She has also written extensively for LexisPSL on ancillary relief, the enforcement of financial orders and child maintenance.

Contents

List of Authors	v
Chapter 1 Introduction	1
Background, philosophy of the new rules, new terminology and case management – FPR 2010, Pts 1, 2 & 4	1
ADR and the pre-application protocol – FPR 2010, Pt 3	10
Transitional provisions: what comes into force and when – FPR 2010, Pt 36	13
Chapter 2 Matrimonial and Civil Partnership Proceedings	17
Divorce, civil partnership dissolution and nullity – FPR 2010, Pt 7	18
Applications for a financial remedy – FPR 2010, Pts 9 & 21	33
Chapter 3 Protection of Individuals	53
Applications for non-molestation, occupation and forced marriage protection orders – FPR 2010, Pts 10 and 11	53
Chapter 4 Children and Vulnerable Adults	57
Proceedings relating to children – FPR 2010, Pt 12	57
Applications for parental orders – FPR 2010, Pt 13	63
Adoption and placement applications – FPR 2010, Pt 14	64
Representation of children and protected parties – FPR 2010, Pts 15 & 16	64
Chapter 5 General Procedural Provisions	69
Practicalities, use of forms, service – FPR 2010, Pts 5, 6, 26 & 29	71
Evidence – FPR 2010, Pts 17 & 22–24	88
Experts – FPR 2010, Pt 25	106
Procedure on applications: Pts 18 and 19, miscellaneous forms of action and publicity – FPR 2010, Pts 8, 18, 19 & 27	122

Contents

Chapter 6	**Other**	**143**
	Interim remedies and security for costs – FPR 2010, Pt 20	144
	Costs – FPR 2010, Pt 28	155
	Appeals – FPR 2010, Pt 30	160
	Enforcement and registration of orders – FPR 2010, Pts 31–34	164
Appendix	**The Family Procedure Rules 2010**	**185**
Index		**705**

Chapter 1
INTRODUCTION
FPR 2010, Pts 1–4 and 36

Background	1.1
General philosophy behind the rules	1.1
The underlying principles	1.2
Changes in nomenclature	1.3
Case management	1.4
Civil restraint orders	1.5
Types of civil restraint orders	1.6
Alternative dispute resolution (ADR)	1.7
Protocol requirements	1.8
Exceptions related to mediation	1.9
Transitional provisions – what comes into force when?	1.10
Existing proceedings	1.11
Steps taken in existing proceedings	1.12
New proceedings	1.13
Costs	1.14

BACKGROUND

General philosophy behind the rules

1.1 The Ministry of Justice, in its explanatory memorandum on the Family Procedure Rules 2010, SI 2010/2955 (FPR 2010), lists four key objectives which underpin the entire scheme. They are:

(1) modernisation of language;
(2) streamlining of procedure and harmonisation with the Civil Procedure Rules 1998, SI 1998/3132);
(3) a single unified code of practice; and
(4) alignment in all levels of court.

The new rules, which are generally in force with effect from 6 April 2011, are thus an attempt to codify into one document the procedure to be used for nearly all family proceedings in the High Court, the county court and the magistrates' court. There are no changes in relation to procedure in the Court of Appeal, although there are extremely significant reforms to the way in which family appeals are to be dealt with, particularly within the county court. Thus for the first time other than in relation to adoption, the three levels of court exercising jurisdiction in relation to family matters are to be governed by what is essentially the same procedure. This is in itself a radical change: while the Family Proceedings Rules 1991, SI 1991/1247 (FPR 1991), applied both to the High Court and to the county court, proceedings before the magistrates were governed by an entirely separate and, in some ways, very different regime. In both cases, the procedure had been amended over the years so that while the FPR 1991 was originally a self-contained code, it gradually became

1.1 Introduction

more difficult to comprehend, because of the many additions and amendments to it, and it also lacked any coherent underlying philosophy. It is rather odd that although the rules deal with 'family proceedings', that term, unlike many others used, is not defined, whereas it was under the 1991 Rules. There is a statutory definition in the Courts Act 2003, s 75(3), which defines such proceedings as 'proceedings . . . which are defined by either (a) section 65 of the [Magistrates' Courts] . . . Act [1980] or (b) section 32 of the Matrimonial and Family Proceedings Act 1984'. Thus certain matters which may have a family element are excluded entirely from the new procedures, including, for example, proceedings under the Trusts of Land and Appointment of Trustees Act 1996, the Inheritance (Provision for Family and Dependants) Act 1975, and the like.

The models for the FPR 2010 are the Civil Procedure Rules 1998 (CPR) and the Family Procedure (Adoption) Rules 2005, SI 2005/2795. When the CPR were introduced, they commenced with a broad and ambitious statement of the rationale behind them and the general approach which courts should adopt in applying them. While they have themselves been subject to detailed criticism and have, of course, been amended and added to since their introduction, it is generally considered that the CPR have been successful, not least because, instead of bringing together a mishmash of regulations from different sources, they were designed specifically to act as a unified whole and to point in the same direction. A similar concept was used for the reform of the adoption procedure in 2005 and has now been used to mould the new FPR, and in particular many provisions in relation to civil procedure, which were incorporated into the FPR 1991 only referentially (by r 1.3), are now set out expressly in the FPR 2010. The preliminary provisions and the underlying philosophy expressed in the FPR 2010 are derived almost word for word from the 2005 Adoption Rules, which will be familiar to many family lawyers.

Another idea adopted from the CPR is the supplementation of the rules by practice directions (PDs), some of which are very lengthy. Some also, which have been in place for many years, are incorporated into the new system. Whether or not this use of practice directions as additional, but often very important, sources of information is helpful is debatable: it certainly detracts from the tidiness and symmetry of the new code. Some of the forms previously in use have been retained for further use.

The FPR 2010 adopt, precisely or with minor amendments, many of the concepts set out in Part 1 (Overriding Objective) of the CPR. These new statements of intent govern all family proceedings, rather than, as hitherto, only certain specific areas (such as ancillary relief, as it has been known to date) to which they were added on amendment, in for example FPR 1991, r 2.51D. Thus the principles applicable in relation to case management of any application or proceedings in the county court should now be governed by the same objectives.

The FPR begin with exactly the same statement as the CPR: 'These rules are a new procedural code . . . '. This is an important statement of principle. It sets out from the very beginning that the code is a novel one: therefore, although the court is dealing with similar factual situations to those with which it had to deal under the old codes, the new rules, which are designed to be more intelligible, should generally be interpreted as they stand and without undue reference to cases decided under the old provisions. The courts have adopted exactly that principle in dealing with the CPR.

In FPR 2010, SI 2010/2955, 1.2–1.4 it is made clear that it is the duty of the *court* to give effect to the overriding objective, that is of enabling the court to deal with cases justly, having regard to any welfare issues involved, and to seek to give effect to that objective when exercising any power given to it by the rules or interpreting any rule: on the other hand, the parties are required only to *help* the court to further the objective. In other words, the duty of the parties is secondary to that of the court and the duty of the court to deal with matters before it in accordance with the objective is paramount. FPR 2010, 1.4(1) states specifically that the court *must* further the overriding objective by actively managing cases. Although that reflects no more than is the current practice in many courts, the explicit statement of an imperative duty is of considerable importance.

The underlying principles

1.2 The steps involved in active case management are set out in FPR 2010, SI 2010/2955, 1.4(2) and 4.1(3) and are dealt with in detail below. They are very similar to those in the CPR, but with some relevant additions, such as the need to decide who should be a party to proceedings. There is a specific emphasis on encouragement to use alternative dispute resolution (ADR) (defined in 2.3(1) as 'methods of resolving a dispute, including mediation, other than through the normal court process'), and this is reiterated in FPR 2010, SI 2010/2955, Pt 3 and, more particularly and controversially, in FPR 2010, PD 3A: see further **1.7** below.

There is further emphasis on proportionality, in other words, considering the economic and emotional effects of taking particular steps on the parties and on any child involved. The court is encouraged to be pro-active in taking decisions as to the future conduct of cases, such as deciding the order in which issues are to be heard and assisting with the settlement of some parts of the case even if others are intractable.

These underlying principles are likely to be of considerable importance if, as appears likely, the number of unrepresented litigants increases very substantially following the withdrawal of legal aid in most cases. It will be the court's duty in appropriate cases to exercise firm and early control over attempts to litigate issues which a party may consider to be of importance but which in fact, on objective consideration, are secondary to the real decisions which have to be made.

The detail of the active case management which is commended to courts in FPR 2010, SI 2010/2955, 1.4 is set out in 1.4(2): the rule says only that it *includes* the steps then set out: they are therefore not the only steps which can be taken, but only illustrations of the very wide case management powers which the court has. Further, FPR 2010, 1.4 does not actually confer powers of case management upon the court: this is effected by FPR 2010, SI 2010/2955, Pt 4.

The new rules import from the CPR a number of other procedures, which have the advantage of having been tried and tested, albeit within a different context.

1.2 Introduction

These include civil restraint orders (dealt with in FPR 2010, PD 4B) and the striking out of statements of case (defined as including the whole or part of an application form or answer) in circumstances where they are found either to disclose no reasonable grounds for bringing or defending the application, to be an abuse of the process of the court or as otherwise obstructing the just disposal of the proceedings, or where there has been a failure to comply with an order or rule: see CPR 4.4 and FPR 2010, PD 4A. In relation to divorce proceedings and the like, the court may also so act where the parties agree: FPR 2010, 4.4(2). The provisions reflect an appreciation that it is necessary to exercise close control to prevent misuse of resources by those few but time-consuming litigants in family proceedings who become obsessed by real or imaginary grievances and continue to attempt to relitigate matters which have already been decided.

The emphasis on agreements and on disposing of all, or part, of cases amicably is reflected also in the new definition of a 'consent order' set out in FPR 2010, SI 2010/2955, 2.3. Under the 1991 Rules, this term had a very restricted and technical meaning. Under the 2010 Rules it is defined very widely as 'an order in the terms applied for to which the respondent agrees'.

The application and interpretation of the new FPR are dealt with in FPR 2010, Pt 2, and in addition in the glossary, which is another innovation in family matters and reproduces a device used in CPR. Apart from the word 'service' which applies very frequently throughout, words which are in the glossary are followed by a superscribed GL.

FPR 2010, Pt 2 also sets out directly a number of relevant general matters which previously were set out directly only in the CPR and were then applied referentially to the FPR 1991. Thus, FPR 2010, SI 2010/2955, 2.8 sets out that the court may deal with a case at any place that it considers appropriate. Computation of time is dealt with comprehensively in FPR 2010, 2.9. It is provided that:

(a) a period of time expressed as a number of days must be computed as clear days (FPR 2010, 2.9(2));
(b) the expression 'clear days' excludes the day on which the period in question begins and, if the end of a period is defined by reference to an event, also excludes the day on which that event occurs (FPR 2010, 2.9(3));
(c) where the specified period is seven days or less, any non-business day is not included in that period (FPR 2010, 2.9 (4));
(d) where the specified period for doing an act ends with a date upon which the court office is closed, the time is extended to the next day on which the office is open (FPR 2010, 2.9(5)).

Considerable clarity is also given to the enforceability of orders or to being able to decide whether sanctions bite by FPR 2010, 2.10. This provides that where a time limit is imposed by an order or direction of the court, the last date must wherever practicable be expressed as a calendar date (that is 'by 6 April 2011' instead of 'within 14 days') and should also include the time of day by which the act must be done.

Background **1.4**

Changes in nomenclature

1.3 The new rules bring with them also considerable changes in nomenclature, with some time-honoured expressions being superseded.

Petitions, which have been the vehicle for applying for decrees of divorce and nullity for many generations, and for decrees on dissolution of civil partnership for a rather shorter period, were to have been abolished together with decrees nisi and absolute, and have no part in the FPR 2010, but the forms and the Practice Detections retain the former names, as a consequence of a last-minute decision not to update the antiquated software used in courts. The FPR use the expression an 'application for a matrimonial order', a matrimonial order itself being defined only as a decree of divorce, nullity, or judicial separation, although a similar procedure is to be employed in relation to civil partnership orders and the rarely found decrees of presumption of death and dissolution of marriage.

One of the most important changes introduced by the new code is that all applications for ancillary relief, whichever Act they fall under, are to be dealt with under a common procedure, thus avoiding the need for multiple separate proceedings and applications. Thus the new definition of 'financial remedy' covers all manner of orders, including 'financial orders' which are separately defined as including those orders generally made in or before ancillary relief proceedings. Thus 'financial remedy' covers, for example, applications for financial provision for children under Sch 1 to the Children Act 1989. These are deal with in detail under FPR 2010, SI 2010/2955, Pt 9.

Other Latin phrases such as 'ex parte' disappear, the latter being replaced by 'without notice': there is no more 'leave to appeal', but rather 'permission to appeal'.

Case management

1.4 The powers of the court in relation to case management are laid out in FPR 2010, SI 2010/2955, Pt 4, which sets out that they are additional to any other powers which the court may have under any other provision. Although in the scheme of the rules the factors to be considered in pursuance of the duty actively to case manage proceedings (FPR 2010, SI 2010/2955, Pt 1) precede the statement of the general powers (FPR 2010, SI 2010/2955, Pt 4), logically the latter should be considered first.

The additional case management powers which the court is given are set out in FPR 2010, SI 2010/2955, 4.1(3). They are very similar to, but not a direct reproduction of, CPR 3.1(1). They are as follows:

(a) *To extend or shorten the time for compliance with any rule, practice direction or court order, even if the application is retrospective and is made after the time for compliance has expired.* This interacts with FPR 2010, SI 2010/2955, 4.6, which deals with relief from sanctions. In the civil case of *Robert v Momentum Services Ltd* [2003] EWCA Civ 299, the Court of Appeal held that where an application to extend time is made before the expiry of the time limit in question, the court did not need to go through the checklist in relation to relief from sanctions,

1.4 *Introduction*

contained in FPR 2010, SI 2010/2955, 4.6. The position appears to be different if the time limit has already expired, even though, strictly speaking, being unable to take a step because it is too late under the rules is not a sanction imposed: in those circumstances the checklist should be consulted, as set out in *Sayers v Clarke Walker* [2002] 1 WLR 3095.

(b) *Make such order for disclosure and inspection, including specific disclosure of documents, as is thought fit.* This is not a reflection of the CPR and makes the important point that a family court may in appropriate cases make orders for disclosure for a specific purpose, such as to facilitate the disposal of a particular application, without prejudice to the general duties of disclosure, which are set out in FPR 2010, SI 2010/2955, 21.1.

(c) *Adjourn or bring forward a hearing.* This requires little comment, save that the practice of relisting either to a nearer or a later date is perhaps found more frequently in family than in civil proceedings.

(d) *Require a party or a party's legal representative (which itself is defined in FPR 2010, SI 2010/2955, 2.3) to attend the court.* This is a salutary power, save that it is difficult to enforce if a party simply puts his head in the sand. However, it must be noted and stressed that there is no general power to order a non-party to attend and a witness summons is required.

(e) *Hold a hearing and receive evidence by telephone or by using any other method of direct oral communication.* While this enables courts to avoid the attendance of witnesses and especially experts who are overseas or some distance away, it can also be used for case management conferences and the like or straightforward applications, in a way that has not generally been done in family cases. In many cases there are obvious advantages in bringing the parties together under one roof, so that settlement or the narrowing of issues can take place.

(f) *Direct that part of any proceedings be dealt with as separate proceedings.* This enables (for example) orders to be made that a residence application between mother and father be tried first and then an application by a grandparent for contact be tried subsequently and separately, thus saving the time and costs of the grandparent applicant.

(g) *Stay the whole or part of any proceedings or judgment either generally or until a specified date or event.* This power, which previously was set out on in the civil procedure code and imported into the family procedure under the general provisions is frequently used in a variety of factual situations.

(h) *Consolidate proceedings.* The court can thus direct that any number of applications or issues raising similar or the same issues be tried together and so the evidence in one is automatically admissible in another. An order consolidating can be followed if required by one deconsolidating, if the facts so justify it.

(i) *Hear two or more applications on the same occasion.* This is an obvious course in many cases, and can be done without the necessity for a formal consolidation, as under (h) above.

(j) *Direct a separate hearing of any issue.* This is another obvious course in many cases, particularly where a preliminary issue will either decide or at any rate greatly influence the future course of proceedings.

Background 1.4

(k) *Decide the order in which issues are to be heard.* Again, this general provision is spelled out specifically, but it reminds courts of the need to consider this power, which can substantially reduce the time required for hearings.
(l) *Exclude an issue from consideration.* This is the corollary of the previous provisions and enables matters which a party regards as vital, but in fact are not, to be left while the court determines the real questions in dispute.
(m) *Dismiss or give a decision on an application after a decision on a preliminary issue.* This is likely to be less used than its equivalent in civil proceedings, but there remain circumstances in which the decision in a preliminary issue will effectively decide the principal application.
(n) *Direct any party to file and serve an estimate of costs.* This often salutary power enables the court to obtain material upon which it can act so as to ensure that proportionality is maintained: it can, of course, be used in advance of the hearing of an issue as well as after it.
(o) *Take any other step or make any other order for the purpose of managing the case and furthering the overriding objective.* This is a very wide catch-all, but the powers have still to be exercised in accordance with the spirit of the rules and to further the objective.

The remainder of FPR 2010, SI 2010/2955, 4.1 deals with ancillary provisions, some of considerable importance. It is set out in FPR 2010, 4.1(4) that the court may make any order subject to conditions, including a condition to pay a sum of money into court, and may also specify the consequence of a failure to comply either with the order or with the condition: so an order may read: 'Unless the respondent files a statement in support of his application [or pays £2,000 into court] by 4 pm by [4 pm on a specified date], the application be struck out'. It is then set out in FPR 2010, 4.1(6) that a power under the rules to make an order includes a power to revoke or vary the order, and this is further developed by FPR 2010, 4.1(7) which sets out that direction and/or dates can be varied.

'Unless' orders, as they are often called – more exactly orders with sanctions – are further governed by FPR 2010, SI 2010/2955, 4.5 and Pt 6. FPR 2010, 4.5(1) makes the general position clear, namely that where a party fails to comply with a rule, practice direction or court order, any sanction for that failure has effect unless the party in default applies for and obtains relief from the sanction. Where the sanction is the payment of costs, the only method of obtaining relief is to appeal. The parties cannot bind the court by agreeing to extend time, although, of course, a court will take into account any agreement between the parties in deciding whether or not to grant the extension (FPR 2010, 4.5(3)).

On hearing an application for relief from sanctions, the court has a checklist of factors to consider which are very similar to those as now used in civil proceedings. It is clear from a stream of authority in that jurisdiction that the list must be considered seriatim, although clearly the weight to be attached to different circumstances varies according to the facts. In each case the application for relief must be supported by evidence (FPR 2010, SI 2010/2955, 4.6(2)).

The circumstances to be taken specifically into account are as follows:

1.4 *Introduction*

(i) the interest of the administration of justice;
(ii) whether the application for relief has been made promptly;
(iii) whether the failure to comply was intentional;
(iv) whether there is a good explanation for the failure;
(v) the extent to which the party in default has complied with other rules, practice directions, court orders and protocols;
(vi) whether the failure to comply was caused by the party or the party's legal representative;
(vii) whether the hearing date or the likely hearing date can still be met if relief is granted;
(viii) the effect which the failure to comply had on each party;
(ix) the effect which the granting of relief would have on each party and on a child whose interest the court considers relevant.

The mention of the interests of any relevant children, in (ix) above, is not found in the CPR and may well be of importance in the family jurisdiction. It is easy to underestimate the stress suffered by children waiting to have their future decided and then learning that after all the decision has been deferred.

Another general provision not previously set out expressly in the FPR is in FPR 2010, SI 2010/2955, 4.2 which states that a court officer may consult the court before taking any step which he is to take and the court may then take that step if appropriate. It is suggested in FPR 2010, PD 4A that an appropriate use of this power would be when a court officer issues an application which may come within one of the categories which should be struck out: he can then consult a judge before serving the respondent or listing the matter, so that consideration can be given to striking it out.

Orders in family proceedings can be made either as a result of the parties making an application or on the initiative of the court (FPR 2010, 4.3(1)). It is likely that this latter power will be used more in the future as the number of parties who are legally represented decreases. The court has three choices: it can order that a hearing take place, it can give the parties likely to be affected by the order an opportunity in advance to make representations, or it can simply make the order without either hearing the parties or giving them the opportunity to make representations. In those circumstances a party must be given the opportunity to apply to set aside, vary or stay the order, generally within seven days of it being served upon him (FPR 2010, 4.3(2)–(6)).

It is provided in FPR 2010, SI 2010/2955, 4.7, in another importation from the CPR, that where there has been an error of procedure, that does not (unless the court so orders) invalidate any step taken, and the court may make an order to remedy the defect.

Civil restraint orders

1.5 The increased emphasis displayed in the new rules towards control of applications which have no merit is shown by the explicit importation of the power to strike out, in FPR 2010, SI 2010/2955, 4.4, which has already been mentioned. This is dealt with further in FPR 2010, PD 4A, where examples are given of applications which may be thought to fall within the provisions, including:

(a) those which set out no facts indicating what the application is about;
(b) those which are incoherent and make no sense; and
(c) those which contain a coherent set of facts disclose no application known to the law.

Other such cases include frivolous or scurrilous applications, or answers which consist of a mere denial.

However, in the case of striking out or dismissal of applications, including applications for permission to appeal, whether made of the court's own initiative or at a hearing, the court should consider whether the application is wholly without merit and should record the fact if it so finds: it should then go on to consider whether or not to make a civil restraint order (see FPR 2010, 4.3(7) where the court acts of its own initiative and FPR 2010, 4.4(5) where it acts on an application made to it): these provisions apply only to the High Court and to the county court. A court may also make a civil restraint order (CRO) after hearing an application made under FPR 2010, SI 2010/2955, Pt 18 (see FPR 2010, 18.13), or an application for permission to appeal (see FPR 2010, SI 2010/2955, 30.11(5)).

The circumstances in which a court should make a CRO are set out in FPR 2010, PD 4B. It is a salutary power which has led to considerable improvements in civil procedure, although in that sphere the circumstances are usually different. Many claimants in civil proceedings issue a multiplicity of claims against different defendants, often with some connection between them. In the family context, it is likely that it will be used against a party who continually issues applications within the same proceedings or against the same party, and it is thus likely to be easier for the court and the litigants affected to pick up on the conduct.

The court already possesses an important statutory power under the Children Act 1989, s 91(14), which enables it to restrict the making of specified applications in relation to children by providing that the leave of the court must be sought before any further such application is made. However, that power can be exercised, in accordance with the wealth of authorities which have grown up on it, not only to restrain a party who continually makes applications but also, in appropriate cases, where the welfare of a child so demands it.

The new powers to make civil restraint orders, provided by the FPR 2010, are expressly stated to be 'separate from and do not replace' the jurisdiction under s 91(14). The circumstances in which civil restraint orders may be made are tightly circumscribed, as in the case of their civil equivalents. Applications are made by the party aggrieved under FPR 2010, SI 2010/2955, Pt 18.

Types of civil restraint orders

1.6 There are three forms of civil restraint order.

(1) A limited civil restraint order may be made by a judge (including a district judge) in the High Court or the county court and prevents a party making further applications *in those proceedings only* without the permission of the court. Such an order can only be made where there have been two applications made by the party concerned which

1.6 *Introduction*

have been marked as totally without merit. Applications for permission are made in writing, notice is given to the other side, and are determined without a hearing, as are any appeals from refusal. It lasts for the duration of the particular proceedings. For the reasons set out above, it is likely that this will be the most common form of civil restraint order made in family proceedings.

(2) An extended civil restraint order may be made only by a High Court judge and prevents a party making further applications in any court relating in any way to the proceedings in which the application is made without permission. So an applicant may be prevented from issuing (for example) any further applications in relation to the residence of, or living arrangements for, or otherwise concerning, a child of the family. It can only be made if the party concerned has 'persistently made applications which are totally without merit'. Applications for permission are subject to similar provisions to those involved in relation to limited civil restraint orders. An order must not in the first instance exceed two years in duration.

(3) A general civil restraint order may also be made only by a High Court judge and prevents a party from making any application in any court without permission: this of course relates only to family proceedings as this is a separate jurisdiction from that in civil actions. A general order can only be made if the party in question 'persists in making applications which are totally without merit, in circumstances where an extended civil restraint order would not be sufficient or appropriate'. Applications for permission are subject to similar conditions to the other forms. It too lasts for not more than two years in the first instance.

ALTERNATIVE DISPUTE RESOLUTION (ADR)

1.7 The emphasis on ADR is set out in FPR 2010, SI 2010/2955, Pt 3, which is expressly subject to any practice direction: one of the most striking features of the new regime so far as practitioners and the parties are concerned is in the new FPR 2010, PD 3A, which, in practice, is likely to be more important than the rules onto which it is grafted. However, it can only be understood by reference to those rules.

Although the practice direction is concerned with disputes at an early stage, FPR 2010, SI 2010/2955, 3.2 makes it clear that the court has to consider *at every stage in proceedings* whether or not ADR is appropriate. If it comes to the conclusion that it is, then under FPR 2010, 3.3 the court may adjourn either the whole proceedings or a particular hearing for a period it considers appropriate in order to allow the parties to obtain information and advice about ADR and, where they agree, to enable such resolution to take place. ADR cannot therefore be imposed on parties who are unwilling to permit it to take place. The parties are to be given directions so that at the conclusion of the specified period, they inform the court of the outcome: if they do not, direction can be given.

The FPR 2010, PD 3A is of very wide scope: it also applies before an application is brought rather than after it comes before the court. By Annex B to the practice direction, it covers all situations (save those excepted

Alternative dispute resolution (ADR) **1.8**

specifically) where a person is *considering applying* within family proceedings for any order within:

(a) private law proceedings relating to children, save for enforcement proceedings and the like or where emergency proceedings in relation to the children in question have been brought and not been determined (these are defined in FPR 2010, SI 2010/2955, 12.2 and include applications for emergency protection orders and for disclosure of information about children and the like);
(b) proceedings for a financial remedy save for applications for an order preventing a disposition, for an avoidance of disposition order or for enforcement of any order made in financial remedy proceedings: the term 'financial remedy' is itself defined widely in FPR 2010, SI 2010/2955, 2.3 as already set out, to include all manner of applications.

There are further exceptions, set out in Annex C, which are easier discussed after the procedure prescribed is set out: this is in Annex A, described as the 'pre-application protocol'. The rationale is set out FPR 2010, PD 3A, para 3.1, where it is stated 'there is a general acknowledgement that an adversarial court process is not always best-suited to the resolution of family disputes, particularly private law disputes between parents related to children . . . ': that may well be correct, but resolution depends also on a party knowing what powers a court has and how it is likely to exercise those powers, which a party will not know without having legal advice, which in turn he or she will not receive in many circumstances until after mediation has been attempted. However, it is certainly the case that many cases are capable of settlement at a very early stage, particularly where children are involved or where the parties have no, or no substantial, financial assets.

Protocol requirements

1.8 In order to achieve that aim, all applicants are expected to have followed the steps set out in the protocol and the court is therefore expected to ask at the first hearing whether or not mediation has been considered: in considering conduct the court can take into account any failure to comply and may refer the parties at that stage to a mediator. Thus a failure to attend mediation or to engage with the protocol does not prevent an applicant issuing proceedings: however, it may be taken into account once the application is under way.

The protocol requires that:

(i) the potential applicant contacts a family mediator to arrange to attend a meeting about mediation or ADR, having obtained the address of that mediator from the local court or from the Community Legal Advice Helpline;
(ii) the potential applicant then provides the mediator with contact details in relation to the other party or parties so that they can be contacted for discussion;
(iii) the mediator should then arrange a meeting or separate meetings with the parties, described as a 'Mediation Information and Assessment Meeting';

1.8 *Introduction*

(iv) the mediator is to consider whether or not public funding should be available to the parties to cover the cost of the mediation, but if it is not, the cost must be met by the parties;
(v) if the party then does make an application to court, he or she must file a signed Form F1 (Family Mediation Information and Assessment Form) confirming either that a mediation meeting has taken place or the reasons why it has not taken place;
(vi) the F1 must be countersigned by the mediator where either the applicant has attended a mediation meeting or where the applicant has not attended and the mediator has concluded that mediation is not suitable.

The exceptions to this procedure are in fact quite far-reaching and are likely to apply to many applications which will become contentious. The exceptions fall into three categories, the first and third of which relate to the process of mediation and the second to a variety of circumstances in which it is considered that mediation is unsuitable.

Exceptions related to mediation

1.9 The exceptions related to mediation are as follows, using the numbering used in Annex C:

(1) The mediator is satisfied that mediation is not possible because the other party will not attend;
(2) The mediator determines that the case is not suitable for a meeting;
(3) A mediator has determined within the preceding four months that the case is not suitable for a meeting or for mediation;
(13) The applicant contacts three local mediators, none of whom can conduct a meeting within 15 working days of the date of contact.

The exceptions which do not relate to the process or availability of mediation are as follows, again using the numbering in Annex C:

(4) Any party has made an allegation of domestic violence against another party and that has either resulted in a police investigation or the issuing of civil proceedings for protection within the preceding 12 months;
(5) The dispute concerns financial matters and one party is bankrupt;
(6) The parties are in agreement and thus there is no dispute to mediate;
(7) The whereabouts of the other party are unknown to the applicant;
(8) The prospective application is for an order in continuing family proceedings which are already in existence (so that there is no obligation to go to mediation when a second or further application is made in the same proceedings);
(9) The prospective application is to be made without notice;

(10) The proposed application is urgent: this is defined as meaning either that (a) there is a risk to the life, liberty or physical safety of the applicant or his or her family or home, or (b) any delay caused by attending a mediation meeting would cause a risk of significant harm to a child, a significant risk of a miscarriage of justice, unreasonable hardship to the applicant or irretrievable problems in dealing with the dispute;

(11) There is current social services involvement in relation to child protection so far as any child who would be the subject of the prospective application is concerned;

(12) A child would be a party to the proposed application.

It will readily be appreciated that points (4), (10) and (11) above cover a very substantial number of the applications in relation to children which are brought before the courts.

It remains to be seen whether or not the attempt to make mediation compulsory in the majority of cases works, or whether it results in those cases settling which would have settled in any event.

TRANSITIONAL PROVISIONS – WHAT COMES INTO FORCE WHEN?

1.10 Rule 36.1 applies the provisions of FPR 2010, PD 36A. The practice direction is perhaps the first element of FPR 2010 that practitioners should get to know.

Existing proceedings

1.11 The aim is to apply the new rules to existing proceedings so far as is practicable but to apply the previous rules where it is not practicable (FPR 2010, PD 36A, para 2.1).

There then follows a list of situations in which the previous rules will apply.

(a) If a step in proceedings is initiated *before* 6 April 2011, especially where old forms and processes have been used, that part of the case at least will proceed in accordance with the previous rules (FPR 2010, PD 36A, para 3.1). Any response required of the respondent must be made in accordance with the previous rules (para 3.2).

EXAMPLES:
- A divorce petition is issued before 6 April 2011. The acknowledgment will be filed under the old procedure and, if the proceedings are undefended, the old special procedure documents will be used to bring the suit to a conclusion.
- A respondent receives an originating summons issued pre-6 April 2011. Originating summonses will be a thing of the past once the new rules are fully implemented. However, the respondent must still follow through the filing and other procedural requirements of the previous rules even if service is effected on or after 6 April 2011 (para 3.3).

1.12 *Introduction*

(b) Where a court order dated before 6 April 2011 has made directions that are inconsistent with the new rules, the court order takes precedence (para 3.4).
(c) Any steps taken before 6 April 2011 in accordance with the previous rules will be valid and no action is required to rectify a step already taken.

Steps taken in existing proceedings

1.12 The aim is that where a new step is taken in existing proceedings, the new rules should apply (FPR 2010, PD36A, para 4.1). The overriding objective will apply to *all* proceedings after 6 April 2011 (para 4.2).

In general, if an application is issued on or after 6 April 2011 it *must* be issued using the new forms and procedure, otherwise it will be returned unissued (para 4.3(1)).

There is an exception for urgent cases. If such an application is issued on an old form or in accordance with an old procedure, the court *may* direct that the application be issued as if it had been made under the new rules (para 4.3(2)). Practitioners should be very careful about placing too much reliance on this provision.

EXAMPLES:
- A Form A was issued in March 2011. The applicant now seeks an order for maintenance pending suit. The application should be made under FPR 2010, SI 2010/2955, 9.7 and in accordance with the FPR 2010, SI 2010/2955, Pt 18 procedure.
- An urgent application relating to the safety and wellbeing of a child is made using an old Form C2. It is unlikely that the court will reject the application.

New proceedings

1.13 If proceedings come before the court for the first time on or after 6 April 2011, the court has the power to disapply FPR 2010 if necessary. This applies to hearings *and* paperwork (FPR 2010, PD 36A, para 4.4(1)). However, the new rules will apply from then on unless the court directs otherwise (para 4.4(2)).

If an application has been issued on or after 6 April 2011, presume that matters will be decided having regard to FPR 2010 unless the court directs otherwise (para 4.4(3)).

If the first hearing on a substantive issue takes place on or after 6 April 2011, presume that that FPR 2010 will apply (para 4.4(4)).

EXAMPLES:
- An applicant seeks an order under Sch 1 to the Children Act 1989 in May 2011. The application must be in the new Form A1.

Transitional provisions **1.14**

- An application for directions is made in proceedings issued before 6 April 2011. The first time the case will be before the court is for the hearing of the application. The directions for the future conduct of the case will be made having regard to FPR 2010, save in so far as the respondent's compliance with an old process is required due to service upon them of an originating process issued before 6 April 2011.

Costs

1.14 The most succinct explanation of the application of the new rules in the context of costs is the practice direction itself at FPR 2010, PD36A, para 4.5:

'(1) Any assessment of costs that takes place on or after 6th April 2011 will be in accordance with FPR Part 28 and the provisions of the Civil Procedure Rules as applied by that Part.

(2) However, the general presumption is that no costs for work undertaken before 6th April 2011 will be disallowed if those costs would have been allowed on detailed assessment before that date.

(3) The decision as to whether to allow costs for work undertaken on or after 6th April 2011 will generally be taken in accordance with FPR Part 28 and the provisions of the Civil Procedure Rules as applied by that Part.'

Chapter 2

MATRIMONIAL AND CIVIL PARTNERSHIP PROCEEDINGS
FPR 2010, Pts 7 and 9

Procedure for applications in matrimonial and civil partnership proceedings	2.1
Overview	2.1
Application	2.2
Comparison table	2.3
Changes and Innovations	2.4
Documents	2.4
Procedure and good practice	2.11
Applications for a financial remedy – Pt 9	2.21
Application	2.22
Conversion table	2.23
Changes and Innovations	2.24
Documents	2.24
Consent orders	2.31
Undertakings	2.32
Statement of information	2.33
Procedure and good practice	2.34
Voluntary disclosure	2.34
Pensions	2.35
Where proceedings may be heard	2.40
First appointment	2.41
Financial Dispute Resolution (FDR)	2.42
Hearings	2.43
Absent parties	2.44
Bundles	2.45
Other applications and forms of action	2.46
Proceedings in the magistrates' court	2.46
Maintenance pending suit and other applications for interim provision	2.47
Orders for disclosure against a person not a party (formerly known as 'inspection appointments')	2.49
Application	2.50
Response	2.51
Further guidance	2.52
Application for a financial remedy after overseas proceedings	2.53
Which court?	2.54
Application	2.55
Procedure	2.56

17

2.1 *Matrimonial and Civil Partnership Proceedings*

PROCEDURE FOR APPLICATIONS IN MATRIMONIAL AND CIVIL PARTNERSHIP PROCEEDINGS

Overview

2.1 The rules for divorce, nullity, judicial separation and civil partnership proceedings are now all dealt with together in FPR 2010, SI 2010/2955, Pt 7. This is in keeping with the overriding objective to harmonise procedures.

An undefended application for an order of nullity can now, therefore, be dealt with under the special procedure.

The processes remain largely unchanged but some of the detailed procedural requirements are either simplified or moved elsewhere in the rules.

The major change is as to the format of the forms. These should now be much easier to complete, which will hopefully avoid those delays which arise as a result drafting issues.

Noteworthy also is that a respondent who wishes to make his or her own application for a matrimonial or civil partnership order must file a separate application rather than deal with this in their answer. This differs from the old rules where the answer and cross petition were contained in the same document.

Application

2.2 The rules use the term 'matrimonial order'[1] to refer to:

(a) a decree of divorce[2];
(b) a decree of nullity[3];
(c) a decree of presumption of death and dissolution of marriage[4]; and
(d) a decree of judicial separation[5].

The term 'civil partnership order'[6] refers to:

(i) a dissolution order;
(ii) a nullity order;
(iii) a presumption of death order; and
(iv) a separation order[7].

Rather than the 'issue of proceedings' the new rules refer to starting these processes as an 'application for a matrimonial or civil partnership order'.

[1] FPR 2010, SI 2010/2955, 2.3(1).
[2] Matrimonial Causes Act 1973 (MCA 1973), s 1.
[3] MCA 1973, ss 11 and 12.
[4] MCA 1973, s 19.
[5] MCA 1973, s 17.
[6] FPR 2010, SI 2010/2955, 2.3(1).
[7] Civil Partnership Act 2004 (CPA 2004), s 37.

Procedure for applications 2.3

Comparison table

2.3 The table below highlights how the new rules reflect the old and where procedures from the old rules can now be found.

FPR 1991		*FPR 2010*	
2.1	Application of Matrimonial and Civil Partnership Causes.	7.1	Application and interpretation. Rule 7.1(1) confirms that Pt 7 of the rules applies to matrimonial and civil partnership proceedings.
2.3	Contents of petition (information set out in detail at Appendix 2).		No equivalent to Appendix 2. The supporting notes for guidance on completing the petition (D8 (Notes), D8D (Notes) and D8N (Notes)) explain in great detail what must be included.
2.4	Civil Evidence Act 1968, s 11 or 12.		Mirrored in PD 7A, para 4.1 which states the information which must be set out in the application if the Petitioner wishes to rely on a conviction or finding of adultery or paternity.
2.5	Signing of petition.		The rules and PD 7A are silent as to who can sign the petition. The form merely states 'Signed' and it is assumed, therefore, that a solicitor may still sign on behalf of their client.
2.6	Presentation of petition and what documents need to be attached.	7.5	Starting proceedings. Where proceedings can be started remains the same: – in a divorce county court; – in a civil partnership proceedings court;
		7.6	Statement of reconciliation. New form D6 (Statement of reconciliation) must be filed if a solicitor is acting for the petitioner. PD 7A, para 3.1 sets out the documents which must be attached to the petition as proof of the marriage or civil partnership.

2.3 Matrimonial and Civil Partnership Proceedings

FPR 1991		*FPR 2010*	
		7.7	Limitation on applications in respect of the same marriage or civil partnership. The new rules mirror the old in stating that a petitioner can only issue one application in relation to the same marriage *unless* the other is dismissed or finally determined or the court gives permission. The exception being following a judicial separation application within one year of the marriage where the petitioner wants to apply for divorce or dissolution.
		7.8	Service of application The Respondent must still receive: – the petition; – a form for acknowledging service; – notice of proceedings; – statement of arrangements for children.
		7.14	How the respondent can make an application. A respondent can make their own application for a matrimonial or civil partnership order within 21 days beginning with the date on which his acknowledgement of service is due to be filed or with court's permission
2.6A	Petition for nullity on ground of issue of interim gender recognition certificate.	7.11 (1)–(3)	Nullity: interim and full gender recognition certificates. Identical grounds
2.6B	Petition for nullilty on ground that respondent's gender had become acquired gender at time of marriage or civil partnership.	7.11(4)	Identical grounds

20

Procedure for applications **2.3**

FPR 1991		*FPR 2010*	
2.7	Parties.	7.10	Who the parties are.
			Identical provision as to parties including who should be co-respondent and when they should or should not be named.
2.8	Discontinuance of cause before service.	7.9	Withdrawal of application before service.
			Notice in writing to the court at any time before service is all that is now required. No need for filing of a notice of discontinuance.
2.9	Service of petition.	7.8	Service of application.
			Confirms that the application must be served on respondent and co respondent.
			Service of the application is dealt with in rr 6.3–6.22.
		7.12	What the respondent and co respondent should do on receiving the application.
			This rule confirms that the acknowledgement of service must be returned within seven days subject to r 6.42 which deals with service outside the jurisdiction.
			The acknowledgement *must* be signed by respondent personally if admitting adultery or consenting to two years' separation.
2.9A	Acknowledgement of service petition for nullity brought on ground relating to gender recognition.		There is no longer a requirement for the respondent to file an interim or full certificate with acknowledgement.
2.10	Consent to grant of decree or civil partnership order.	7.12(12) & (13)	Mirrors.
2.11	Supplemental petition and amendment of petition.		There is no provision for a supplemental petition to be filed.

21

2.3 Matrimonial and Civil Partnership Proceedings

FPR 1991		FPR 2010	
		7.13	Amendments to the application and answer.
			It remains the position that a petition or answer can be amended at any time before an answer if filed. Thereafter either the court's permission or written consent of all other parties is needed.
2.12A	Answer praying for nullity on grounds of interim gender recognition certificate.		No corresponding provision.
2.12B	Answer praying for nullity re acquired gender.		No corresponding provision.
2.13	Filing of reply and subsequent pleadings.	7.14	Rule 7.14 provides that a respondent can make their own application for a matrimonial or civil partnership order. The rules then apply as though they were the applicant[1] so that the original applicant can file an answer to that application.
2.14	Filing and amending pleadings after directions for trial given.	7.13(4)	Amendments can be made to an application or answer after 21 days either with the courts permission or written consent of all parties.
2.15	Contents of answer.		Form D8B (Answer to a divorce/dissolution/(judicial) separation or nullity petition must be used. It recommends referring to notes to forms D8 and D8N for guidance as to contents.
2.16	Allegations against third person in pleading.	7.10	Mirrors.
2.17	Service of pleadings.	6.3–6.22	Also apply to applications by respondent (ie answer).
2.18	Supplemental answer and amendment of pleadings.		No corresponding provision.
2.19	Particulars.	7.15	Further information about the contents of the application and answer.
			Very similar provision for court to require a party to clarify or give additional information.

Procedure for applications 2.3

FPR 1991			FPR 2010	
2.20	Discovery of documents in defended causes. RSC Order 24.		Disclosure and inspection. Detailed provision as to compliance with an order for disclosure is set out in PD 7A, paras 7.1–7.6.	
2.21	Discovery by interrogatories in defended cause. RSC Order 26.		No provision for discovery by this means in the new rules.	
2.22	Medical examination in proceedings for nullity of marriage.	7.26	Medical examination in proceedings for nullity of marriage. The procedure is detailed in this rule and PD 7B deals with this issue.	
2.23	Conduct of medical examination.		It is simpler than under the old rules.	
2.24	Directions for trial.	7.19	Applications for a decree nisi or conditional order. New form D84 – Application for decree nisi/conditional order or judicial separation decree is used to make the application.	
		7.20	What the court will do on an application for a decree nisi, conditional order, decree of judicial separation or a separation order. Either grant a certificate, require further information or list a case management hearing.	
		7.22	What the court must do for the case management hearing.	
2.25	Determination of place of trial.		Deal at case management hearing[2].	
2.26	Directions as to behaviour allegations.		Deal at case management hearing[3].	
2.27	Stay under Domicile and Matrimonial Proceedings Act 1973.	7.27	Stay of proceedings. Simplified.	
2.27AA	Stay under the Family Proceedings (Civil Partnership: Staying of Proceedings) Rules 2005, SI 2005/2921.		Where there is a question as to whether the proceedings should be stayed the court must give directions for a hearing.	
2.28	Evidence at trial of cause.	22.2	Mirrors.	

23

2.3 Matrimonial and Civil Partnership Proceedings

FPR 1991		FPR 2010	
2.29	Evidence by deposition.	24.7	Mirrors.
2.30	Issue of witness summons or subpoena.	24.3	Contains new procedure.
2.31	Revoked.		
2.32	Mode and place of trial.	7.23	Where proceedings under this part may be heard. Largely same but simplified by use of a table.
		7.24	The circumstances in which proceedings may be transferred between courts.
2.33	Trial of issue.		No corresponding provision regarding dealing with trial of a specific issue. Assume to be considered at case management hearing.
2.34	Exercise of district judge's jurisdiction in causes set down for trial.		No corresponding provision re causes proceeding in the High Court.
2.35	Further provisions as to date of trial.		No corresponding provision re causes proceeding <10 days from date directions for trial given.
2.36	Disposal of causes in the special procedure list.	7.20	What the court will do on an application for a decree nisi, conditional order, decree of judicial separation or a separation order. Procedure unchanged – but special procedure now standard procedure for all undefended causes.
2.37	Right to be heard re question of costs.	7.21	Further provisions about costs. Any party may be heard on question of costs. A requirement to give two days' notice is introduced.
2.38	Respondent's statement of arrangements.	7.12(7)	Respondent retains right to file own statement of arrangements.
2.39	Procedure for complying with s 41 of MCA 1973, s 41 and CPA 2004, s 63.	7.25	The procedure for complying with MCA 1973, s 41 or CPA 2004, s 63.

Procedure for applications 2.3

FPR 1991		FPR 2010	
			Mirrors requirement for court to consider whether it needs to exercise its powers re any children.
2.40	Revoked.		
2.41	Restoration of matters adjourned at the hearing.		No corresponding provision.
2.42	Application for rehearing.		No corresponding provision.
2.43	Decrees and orders.		All orders to be drawn up by proper officer of designated court.
2.44	Application for recission of decree or conditional order.	7.16	General rule – hearing to be in public.
		7.16(4)	Application for recission by consent to be in private.
2.45	Application under of MCA 1973, s 10(2) or CPA 2004, s 48(2).	7.29	Applications under MCA 1973, s 10(2) or CPA 2004, s 48(2). Simplified.
2.46	Intervention to show cause by Queen's Proctor.	7.31(6)	Mirrors but simplifies.
2.45A/ 2.45B	Applications and orders under MCA 1973, s 10A(2).		No provision re application for an order that the decree not be made absolute until declaration from the parties produced to the court. It is assumed it would be made on new form D11 (Application notice).
		7.30	Orders under MCA 1973, s 10A(2) mirrors procedure to be followed and documents to be produced on applying for decree absolute where order made under s 10A(2).
2.46	Intervention to show cause by Queen's Proctor.	7.31	Applications to prevent decree nisi being made absolute or conditional orders being made final. Simplifies process.

25

2.4 Matrimonial and Civil Partnership Proceedings

FPR 1991		FPR 2010	
2.47	Intervention to show cause by person other than Queen's Proctor.	7.31	Applications to prevent decree nisi being made absolute or conditional orders being made final.
			Simplifies process if considered there is a reason why decree absolute should not be made. CPR Pt 18 applies.
2.48	Recission of decree nisi or conditional order by consent.	7.28	The circumstances in which an order may be set aside (recission).
			Provision same. Court cannot hear an application by a respondent for recission less than 14 days after service of the application.
2.49	Decree absolute or final order on lodging notice.	7.32	Making decrees nisi absolute or conditional orders final by giving notice.
			Procedure remains the same. The form of notice is not specified. Assume old form can continue to be used.
2.50	Decree absolute or final order on application.	7.33	Applications to make decrees nisi absolute or conditional orders final.
			Mirrors provision.
2.51/ 2.51A	Indorsement and certificate of decree absolute/final order.	7.34	What the court officer must do when a decree nisi is made absolute.
		7.35	what the court officer must do when a conditional order is made final.
			Mirrors provision.

[1] FPR 2010, SI 2010/2955, 7.4.
[2] FPR 2010, SI 2010/2955, 7.22(2).
[3] FPR 2010, SI 2010/2955, 7.22 (2).

Changes and Innovations

Documents

2.4 The new forms are as follows:

- Form D8 – Divorce/dissolution/(judicial) separation petition;
- Form D8D – Petition for presumption of death decree/order and the dissolution of a marriage/civil partnership; and
- Form D8N – Nullity petition.

Procedure for applications 2.4

Applications for Divorce, Dissolution or (judicial) separation must be made on new form D8.

Applications for a presumption of death decree/order and dissolution must be made on form D8D.

Applications for an annulment of either a marriage or civil partnership must be made on form D8N.

There are extremely comprehensive supporting notes for all three forms explaining how they are to be completed which should be read before using the forms for the first time and deal with many of the queries which might arise.

The content of the petitions is almost identical to the old petitions. The new forms, however, use a tick box format to aid completion.

The additional information now required on the form for both the petitioner and respondent is:

- date of birth; and
- gender.

The particulars are now called the statement of case. The notes to both petitions state one or two sentences will suffice when completing that section.

Where the fact relied on is unreasonable behaviour, the notes say no more than six examples of the more serious incidents and most recent should be necessary.

FPR 2010, PD 7A, para 2.1 specifically states that if relying on adultery or improper association the third party *should not* be named unless the petitioner believes the respondent may object to the application. The third party should not be under the age of 16 or alleged to have been raped by the respondent unless the court gives specific permission.

A continuation sheet can be used for the statement of case which must have at the top the petitioner's and the respondent's names and Part 6 statement of case.

If the petitioner wishes to omit his or her address, the petition is be completed excluding this information and a new Form D11 Application Notice completed setting out the reasons for wanting to exclude this information. This is to be submitted to court with the petition.

There is no explanation as to what to do if one wishes to leave out any other information. It is to be assumed that similarly a D11 application should be submitted with the petition.

Domicile and habitual residence are very helpfully and clearly explained in the Notes to the petitions.

'Domicile' is defined as being the country a person consider to be his or her permanent home. 'Habitual Residence' is defined as the country where a person lives voluntarily and for settled purposes – somewhere he or she must spend a substantial amount of time.

If the respondent is not, or may not, be habitually resident in England and Wales, it is recommended that all the grounds of jurisdiction which apply should be stated.

2.4 *Matrimonial and Civil Partnership Proceedings*

The gender of any children must now be stated and whether each child was born/adopted by both petitioner and respondent or is a child treated as child of family but only born to, or adopted by, one.

Details of children who are *not* children of the family are also now to be included in the petition.

The petitioner must state if he or she is represented or receiving advice from a solicitor.

Tick boxes at the end of the Notes confirm that what must be sent to court remains the same:

- three copies of the petition;
- original or certified marriage certificate;
- statement of arrangements for children; and
- appropriate fee – as to which see leaflet EX50 – Civil & Family Court Fees.

Form D8D in relation to presumption of death enables the petitioner at Part 5 to apply in the alternative for a divorce decree or dissolution order in the event that the respondent is still alive. If the petitioner selects this option, a completed D8 petition must be attached to the Form D8D.

Form D6 – Statement of reconciliation

2.5 This replaces the certificate as to reconciliation.

It is a tick box form which requires the solicitor acting to confirm as under the old rules whether they have, or have not, discussed reconciliation and whether they have given names to help.

Form D8A – Statement of arrangements for children

2.6 The notes to Forms D8 and D8N state that if there are children under the age of 16, or under 18 if they are at school, college or in training, a statement of arrangements for children form must be completed. This is form D8A. Old rules did not require the form itself to be used. The new rules say you *must* use this form.

The information required by Form D8A is largely the same as old Form M4 but in a different order.

Less detail is sought regarding housing and working hours.

A new question is included asking about any other court proceedings which might impact on the children, for example, non molestation orders or criminal proceedings for domestic violence.

Another new question asks the petitioner to confirm his or her intentions if arrangements for the children are not agreed.

The statement of arrangements is now to be signed by the petitioner using a statement of truth.

Form D8B – Answer to a divorce/dissolution/(judicial) separation or nullity petition

2.7 This form is to be used in all proceedings.

The Notes to Forms D8 or D8N are to be used as guidance for its completion.

It is stated on Form D8B that if the respondent wishes to issue his or her own petition this should be done on Form D8 or D8N. The cross petition, as it was known under the old rules, is therefore no longer included in the answer.

The answer *must* be filed and served within 21 days[1] (calculated in accordance with FPR 2010, SI 2010/2955, 2.9) beginning with the date by which acknowledgement of service due to be filed. There is no reference to leave being granted by court after 21 days.

FPR 2010, SI 2010/2955, 7.14 confirms that a respondent who wishes to make his or her own application for a matrimonial or civil proceedings order must do so within the same time frame, unless the court gives permission to make the application after that time has passed.

An answer can still be filed even if an intention to defend has not been indicated in the acknowledgement of service[2].

[1] FPR 2010, SI 2010/2955, 7.12(8).
[2] FPR 2010, SI 2010/2955, 7.12(10).

Form D13B – Affidavit in support of request to dispense with service of petition on the respondent

2.8 This is a new form to be used when the petitioner does not know the present whereabouts of the respondent. It is intended to satisfy the court that all reasonable enquiries have been made to trace the respondent. The affidavit requires:

- brief details of all enquiries made to trace the respondent;
- names of relatives/friends of the respondent known to the petitioner and enquiries made of them;
- name and address of respondents last known employer and enquiries made of them;
- bank or building society accounts the respondent held (enquiries made?);
- trade union or professional memberships held by the respondent (enquiries made?);
- any magistrates' court order for maintenance or child maintenance order in place. enquiries made as a result;
- documents in support to be attached;
- affidavit to be sworn or affirmed.

Form D84 – Application for decree nisi/conditional order or judicial separation decree

2.9 This is a tick box form.

2.9 Matrimonial and Civil Partnership Proceedings

The petitioner must indicate on the form whether the divorce is undefended or defended. FPR 2010, SI 2010/2955, 7.1 defines what are 'undefended' and 'defended' proceedings.

If undefended, the petitioner must lodge an affidavit in support with the application (FPR 2010, 7.19(4)).

If a defended divorce, the court must direct a case management hearing (FPR 2010, 7.20(4)).

Forms D80A to D80G – Affidavits in support

2.10 The questions on these new forms are identical to the old affidavits but are now in tick box form.

There is a separate form for each different fact.

The affidavit in support must still be sworn.

Procedure and good practice

Proof of marriage or civil partnership to accompany the application

2.11 FPR 2010, PD 7A, paras 3.1–3.4 set out in detail the evidence required to accompany the application. This consolidates and clarifies what appeared in the previous rules. In particular, what to do if a marriage certificate is not available and the requirements for foreign marriage certificates.

It is confirmed that a marriage or civil partnership does not have to be evidenced by producing the marriage certificate[1].

[1] Other authorised method or pursuant to the Evidence (Foreign, Dominion and Colonial Documents) Act 1933.

Amendments to application/answer

2.12 FPR 2010, PD 7A, para 5.2 sets out the procedure for applying for permission to amend an application or answer.

Notice of application should be made using new Form D11 and a copy of application or answer, showing the proposed amendments should be filed at court. The application may be dealt with at a hearing. There is no requirement for evidence in support.

The amended petition/answer must be re-served.

Supplemental petitions, supplemental answers and replies

2.13 The new rules contain no provision for the filing of supplemental petitions, supplemental answers or replies to answers. This supports the overriding objective of streamlining the procedure. No doubt, however, the court could give directions in respect of supplemental pleadings at the case management hearing.

Further information about the contents of the application and answer

2.14 The new rules set out the procedure for obtaining further information[1].

The court can order a party to clarify any matter in dispute in the proceedings or to give additional information, such information to be filed and served.

The court can direct that information provided can only be used for the specific purpose of those proceedings.

Before applying to court, the party requesting the information must first serve a written request for such information on the other party. Details of the format are set out in the practice direction.

[1] FPR 2010, SI 2010/2955, 7.15 and FPR 2010, PD 7A, paras 6.1–6.5.

Case management hearing

2.15 Directions for trial are replaced by case management hearings. Where there are defended divorce proceedings, the court must direct a case management hearing[1] and must at that hearing[2]:

(a) decide where the next hearing should take place;
(b) set a timetable for filing/service of evidence;
(c) make such order for disclosure/inspection of documents as is appropriate;
(d) give directions for conduct of hearing/attendance of witnesses.

In an undefended case, if the court is not satisfied that the petitioner is entitled to the decree nisi, conditional order or decree of (judicial) separation, the court can direct a case management hearing and at such hearing must[3]:

(i) consider what further evidence is required;
(ii) consider whether further evidence is required re the children;
(iii) give directions re further conduct.

[1] FPR 2010, SI 2010/2955, 7.20(4).
[2] FPR 2010, SI 2010/2955, 7.22(3).
[3] FPR 2010, SI 2010/2955, 7.22(3).

Disclosure and inspection

2.16 FPR 2010, PD 7A, paras 7.1–7.6 sets out the streamlined procedure for this process.

It is confirmed that the court can make an order for disclosure of documents under FPR 2010, SI 2010/2955, 7.22(2)(c). The disclosing party must make reasonable search for the documents required.

Documents should be disclosed in a list normally listing the documents in date order, numbering them consecutively and giving concise description. FPR 2010, PD 7A, para 7.5 sets out wording for the statement which must be contained in the list.

2.16 *Matrimonial and Civil Partnership Proceedings*

The obligation of disclosure order continues until proceedings end. A supplemental list is to be produced if further documents are discovered.

If a disclosing party wishes to withhold inspection it must be indicated in writing on the disclosure statement with grounds.

MEDICAL EXAMINATION IN PROCEEDINGS FOR NULLITY OF MARRIAGE

2.17 The FPR 2010 deal with this issue and set out a much simplified process.[1]

A medical examination will only be ordered if it is necessary for the proper disposal of the case. The examination must be carried out by a doctor of same gender as the person being examined.

The costs of the report are to be paid in the first instance by the party on whose application the medical inspector is appointed and either party is entitled to see the report.

[1] FPR 2010, SI 2010/2955, 7.26 and FPR 2010, PD 7B.

PROVISION ABOUT COSTS

2.18 FPR 2010, SI 2010/2955, 7.21 confirms that any party may be heard on question of costs.

If the case has been listed for a hearing for the decree nisi to be made then the party wishing to be heard on costs *must* not less than two days before that hearing serve on every other party written notice of their intention to attend the hearing and apply for, or oppose, a costs order.

This is a new requirement.

APPLICATIONS UNDER MCA 1973, S 10(2) OR CPA 2004, S 48(2)

2.19 FPR 2010, SI 2010/2955, 7.29 considerably simplifies the procedure in cases where decree absolute is pronounced on two or five years separation. The court must now simply make a written record of its reasons for deciding to make the order.

EXPEDITING DECREES ABSOLUTE AND FINAL ORDERS: NEED FOR EXPEDITION

2.20 FPR 2010, PD 7A sets out the procedure which should be followed where one party wishes to expedite the making of the decree absolute or final order.

This is helpful as it is not an uncommon situation for practitioners.

It is suggested that the party wishing to apply should seek directions for an early hearing. If this has not been possible, an application should be made to the judge making the decree nisi for the time between nisi and absolute to be shortened.

If the need for expedition only becomes apparent after decree nisi, an application should be made on notice using the FPR 2010, SI 2010/2955, Pt 18 procedure for an order shortening the time before the nisi can be made absolute.

The same procedure is to be followed where there is a need to shorten the time in civil partnership proceedings between the conditional order and the final order.

APPLICATIONS FOR A FINANCIAL REMEDY – PT 9

2.21 FPR 2010, SI 2010/2955, Pt 9 of the new rules brings about few substantive procedural changes. The main alterations are to terminology and layout and the introduction of some new forms. In common with the whole of FPR 2010, the use of sub-headings makes the text far easier to navigate. The familiar Pre-Application Protocol[1], which came in with the 'Ancillary Relief Rules' in 2000, is a welcome incorporation to the accompanying FPR 2010, PD 9A.

The rules relating to costs, evidence, experts, the conduct of hearings, procedure for interim applications and practical matters such as service are covered in separate sections and are dealt with elsewhere in this text.

[1] *Practice Direction (Ancillary Relief Procedure)* [2000] 1 FLR 997.

Application

2.22 The jargon term, 'ancillary relief', is replaced with 'financial order' which corresponds with all the familiar forms of ancillary relief within divorce, nullity and civil partnership dissolution proceedings, including an avoidance of disposition order, maintenance pending suit and an order to vary periodical payments[1].

Although the 'Ancillary Relief Rules'[2] applied to some other proceedings (both explicitly and by adoption), FPR 2010, SI 2010/2955, Pt 9 applies to any application for a 'financial remedy', which encompasses applications for:

- a financial order;
- an order under the Children Act 1989, Sch 1;
- an order under the Matrimonial and Family Proceedings 1984, Pt 3 or CPA 2004, Sch 7 (financial relief after an overseas divorce/dissolution);
- an order under MCA 1973, s 27 or CPA 2004, Sch 5, Pt 9 (financial provision in case of failure to maintain);
- an order under MCA 1973, s 35 or CPA 2004, Sch 5, para 69 (application to vary a maintenance agreement);
- an order under the Domestic Proceedings and Magistrates' Courts Act 1978, Pt 1 or CPA 2004, Sch 6 (applications for maintenance in the magistrates' court);
- an order under MCA 1973, s 10(2) or CPA 2004, s 48(2) (applications for the consideration of financial circumstances where the divorce/civil partnership dissolution is based on two or five years' separation)[3].

[1] FPR 2010, SI 2010/2955, 2.3.
[2] FPR 1991, rr 2.51B–2.71.
[3] FPR 2010, SI 2010/2955, 2.3.

2.23 *Matrimonial and Civil Partnership Proceedings*

Conversion table

2.23 The table below is a guide to where the material covered in FPR 1991 can be found in FPR 2010. Revoked/replaced rules from FPR 1991 have not been included, neither has the sprinkling of rules regarding gender recognition found amongst the Ancillary Relief Rules.

FPR 1991	*FPR 2010*
2.51B Application of ancillary relief rules.	See FPR 2010, SI 2010/2955, 9.1 'Application' and r 9.3 'Interpretation'.
2.51D The overriding objective.	See Pt 1, which applies to all proceedings, not just applications for a financial remedy.
2.52 Right [of the respondent] to be heard on ancillary questions.	There is no direct equivalent but r 9.4 provides that an application for a financial order can be made in Form A within or after the filing of an application for a matrimonial or civil partnership order, ie within the petition and/or afterwards by either party as under FPR 1991.
2.53 Application by petitioner or respondent for ancillary relief.	Again, see r 9.4 for the simplified explanation of when an application for a financial order can be made, ie within an application for a matrimonial/civil partnership order or at any time after an application has been made.
2.54 Application by parent, guardian etc for ancillary relief in respect of children.	See r 9.10, although the new rule refers to a financial remedy (rather than merely a financial order).
2.57 Children to be separately represented on certain applications.	Rule 9.11 is identical.
2.59 Evidence on application for property adjustment or avoidance of disposition order.	Rule 9.13 is virtually identical in effect.
2.60 Service of statements in answer.	The Form F has been retained to enable the court (as part of its general power of case management) to make an order that a form or document in financial remedy proceedings be served upon any person against whom an allegation of adultery or improper association is made. The Form F provides the person with notice that he/she can apply to be joined as a party.

Applications for a financial remedy – Pt 9 **2.23**

2.61	Information on application for consent order for financial relief.	See r 9.26 and FPR 2010, PD 5A. Note that the content and signature requirements for the Statement of Information have been changed (see below).
2.61A	Application for ancillary relief.	See r 9.5 'Where to start proceedings' —essentially in the same court as the divorce/dissolution/nullity proceedings whether the county court or in the High Court. For applications other than for a financial order, there is a table showing where proceedings should be started. See also r 9.12 which lists the obligations of the court to timetable the filing of Form E and first appointment etc. There is no substantive change. The contents of the Form A are prescribed within the form itself rather than within the body of the rule. Rule 9.12(2) allows the applicant to arrange for service of the application and notice of first appointment upon the respondent provided it notifies the court. The applicant must do this within four days and file a certificate of service.
2.61B	Procedure before the first appointment.	See r 9.14. The procedure is almost identical, save that the widely-disregarded 'ban' on documents other than those prescribed in Form E being attached to the financial statement is lifted so that documents needed to clarify the Form E can be attached. There are also some minor changes to the Form E itself (see **2.27** below).
2.61C	Expert evidence.	FPR 2010, SI 2010/2955, Pt 25 replaces the partial incorporation of CPR Pt 35. See Chapter 5 for full details, including changes to the time limits for putting questions to experts and new obligations upon parties seeking to instruct experts.
2.61D	The first appointment.	See rr 9.15 and 9.16. The procedure is virtually identical. However, the practice direction provides some useful additional guidance as to the court's expectations for good practice (see **2.41** below).

2.23 *Matrimonial and Civil Partnership Proceedings*

2.61E	The FDR appointment.	See r 9.17 for the virtually identical procedure. Again, the practice direction fleshes out the court's expectations for good practice (see **2.42** below).
2.61F	Costs (ie the obligation to provide estimates before each hearing and 14 days before any final hearing).	See r 9.27. The existing Forms H and H1 have changed very little.
2.62	Investigation by district judge of application for ancillary relief. The subparagraphs in force immediately before the implementation of FPR 2010 covered: (2) the simultaneous listing of an application for an avoidance of disposition order with the application for ancillary relief (where possible); (4) district judge's general power to investigate the case, take evidence oral, order the attendance of witnesses and order the disclosure and inspection of documents; (7)–(9) the procedure for inspection appointments.	FPR 1991, r 2.62(2) is not directly reproduced. FPR 1991, r 2.62(4) has no direct equivalent. However, various sections within FPR 2010 provide the court with its armoury of powers and procedures to dispose of applications justly. These include: – FPR 2010, SI 2010/2955, Pt 1 – overriding objective; – FPR 2010, SI 2010/2955, Pt 4 – general powers of case management; – FPR 2010, SI 2010/2955, Pt 22 – evidence; – FPR 2010, SI 2010/2955, Pt 24 – witnesses, together with FPR 2010, PD 24A, which covers the issuing of witness summons; – FPR 2010, SI 2010/2955, Pt 27 – hearings, together with FPR 2010, PD 27A, which incorporates the existing practice direction on the preparation of bundles. FPR 1991, r 2.62(7)–(9) becomes r 21.2 which covers orders for disclosure against non-parties (see below).

Applications for a financial remedy – Pt 9 **2.23**

2.64	Order on application for ancillary relief.	There is no direct equivalent to FPR 1991, r 2.64(1) which provided that after hearing an application the district judge should make 'such order as he thinks just'. The power to make 'an interim order on such terms as [the district judge] thinks just' under the old r 2.64(2) is replaced by Pt 20 ('Interim remedies and security for costs' – see Chapter 6). The new r 9.7 dictates that applications for maintenance pending suit, interim maintenance or the interim variation of maintenance are governed by the Pt 18 procedure (see Chapter 5). The old r 2.64(3) incorporated RSC Ord 31 (power to order sale of land) into family proceedings. This is replaced by r 9.24 'Power to order delivery up of possession', which sets out the court's power to order vacant possession pursuant to an order for sale of land.
2.65	Reference of application to judge.	There is no direct replacement for the power of the district judge to refer an application for ancillary relief or any question arising from such an application to a judge. However, selecting the appropriate level of judge will form part of the court's powers of case management conferred by FPR 2010, SI 2010/2955, Pt 4.
2.66	Arrangements for hearing of application etc by judge.	This rule complemented r 2.65 and is not therefore reproduced.
2.67	Request for periodical payments order at same rate as order for maintenance pending suit or outcome of proceedings.	See r 9.8 in the context of divorce or nullity of marriage and see r 9.9 in the context of dissolution or nullity of civil partnership. In both cases the application is made using the Pt 18 procedure (see Chapter 5).
2.68	Application for order under MCA 1973, s 37(2)(a) or CPA 2004, Sch 5, para 74(2).	By r 9.6 the FPR 2010, SI 2010/2955, Pt 18 procedure applies to an application for an order preventing disposition, commonly known as a 'section 37 injunction' (see Chapter 5).
2.69E	Open proposals.	Rule 9.28 is identical.

2.24 *Matrimonial and Civil Partnership Proceedings*

2.69F	Application for interim orders.	By r 9.7, the Pt 18 procedure applies to an application for maintenance pending suit/outcome of proceedings, interim periodical payments, an interim variation order or any other form of interim order (see **2.47** below).
2.70	Pensions.	Rules 9.29–9.37 (see **2.35–2.40** below).
2.70F	Pension Protection Fund.	Rules 9.38–9.45 (see **2.39** below).
2.71	Costs orders.	See FPR 2010, SI 2010/2955, Pt 28. Chapter 6 gives full details.

Changes and Innovations

Documents

APPLICATION FORMS

Form A

2.24 Applications for a financial order are made in Form A.

The same information is required and the structure of the form will be very familiar. There is a major new addition in the form of a tick box, asking 'Have you attended a mediation information/assessment meeting as suggested in the pre-action protocol and/or attached Form FM1?'.

Form FM1 is a creature of FPR 2010, PD 3A, entitled 'Pre-application Protocol for Mediation and Assessment' (see **1.7** above). It is unclear what consequences there will be for parties who make an application for a financial remedy without exploring the option of mediation in the absence of a prescribed excuse. However, from the wording of the Form FM1, the courts appear to be expecting the parties to have attended a mediation information/assessment meeting absent compelling reasons or urgent features. Under FPR 2010, SI 2010/2955, Pt 3, the court can only encourage the parties to obtain information about mediation and adjourn the proceedings to enable them to attend where this is agreed; it cannot force them to participate.

Form A1

2.25 This is the application form for High Court and county court applications for a financial remedy other than an application for a financial order (ie what used to be known as ancillary relief). At the top of the form, applicants are helpfully directed to alternative forms in the event that the A1 is not appropriate to the form of action contemplated.

It is very similar in appearance to the Form A but there are some differences, mainly geared towards applications under Sch 1 to the Children Act 1989:

- there are different tick box options to include applications for a settlement or transfer of property for the benefit of children but (sensibly) no opportunity to apply for a pension sharing order;
- there is a question to establish whether a Child Support Agency (CSA) maintenance calculation is in place and space to explain why an application is being pursued nevertheless;
- if the application does relate to financial provision for children, details of each child must be given;
- there is space to give details of any written agreements in relation to financial arrangements (eg an earlier consent order), which must be attached.

In common with the Form A, there is a requirement to file an FM1 and/or confirm prior attendance at a mediation information/assessment meeting.

Form A2

2.26 This is the application form for a financial remedy in the magistrates' court. It is similar in structure to Forms A and A1. There are similar tick boxes to establish jurisdiction to make an order for periodical payments for the benefit of a child and space to record details of any written agreements. There is the same requirement in relation to mediation.

It may be that in the fullness of time the courts may encourage the allocation of simple maintenance variation applications to the magistrates' court in an attempt to make best use of judicial expertise. This may be the reason for the production of a tailor-made form and the corresponding financial statement in Form E2 (see **[2.29]** below).

DISCLOSURE

Form E

2.27 Practitioners will be relieved to note that the new Form E is little changed, save in a few minor respects:
- the front page now contains an additional warning: 'If you are found to have been deliberately untruthful, criminal proceedings may be brought against you for fraud under the Fraud Act 2006';
- the formatting is different in that there are more tick boxes, in keeping with the general trend across the forms introduced/revamped by FPR 2010;
- some additional information is requested at section 2.13 where parties are entitled to Pension Protection Fund (PPF) compensation; and
- the boxes in the familiar section 5 entitled 'order sought' have been broken down to encourage parties to set out their intentions for the disposal of the family home, whether the case is suitable for a clean break, what (if any) form of pension order is sought and whether any other transfers or settlement of property are sought.

The Form E must still be sworn and the same prescribed documents must be attached.

2.28 *Matrimonial and Civil Partnership Proceedings*

Form E1

2.28 This is an adapted version of the Form E which follows on from the Form A1 in that it is to be used in High Court and county court applications other than for a financial order. It is anticipated that its main use will be in applications under Sch 1 to the Children Act 1989. In keeping with this purpose, the information it captures enables the court to see how the relevant children and other dependants fit into the family composition and whether any maintenance is being paid for their benefit.

Unlike the Form E, the form directs the employed, the unemployed, the self-employed and pensioners to different sections of the form. Rather than launching into the familiar routine of family home, followed by other properties, bank accounts etc, the form first asks parties for details of income then moves onto a section entitled 'capital', which will be very familiar to those used to completing a Form E.

There is then a pro forma section on income need and a small section to detail any financial resources of the relevant children.

Unlike the Form E, there is no narrative section. Presumably it is for parties to state their case at a later stage.

The attachments required by the E1 are virtually identical to those required by Form E.

The form must be sworn in the usual way.

Form E2

2.29 This is essentially a much simplified version of the Form E which follows on from the Form A2, to be used for applications for a financial remedy in the magistrates' court. Given the limited range of relief available in such proceedings, the form is commensurately limited in scope and approaches financial disclosure in more summary terms.

The form asks for a schedule of bank accounts, including 'average' balances over the last six months, which may cause some arithmetical fun and games. Only six months' duplicate statements are required. There is no requirement to disclose policies or investments other than bank accounts.

The form must be sworn in the usual way.

Replies

2.30 These must now be verified by a statement of truth, which can be signed by the party's legal representative (see FPR 2010, SI 2010/2955, Pts 17 and 22 and accompanying practice directions (see Chapter 5)). Unless otherwise directed, replies should not be filed with the court (FPR 2010, PD 9A, para 5.2).

Consent orders

2.31 FPR 2010, SI 2010/2955, 9.26 and FPR 2010, PD 9A, para 7 set out the requirements.

Applications for a financial remedy – Pt 9 **2.33**

As under FPR 1991, the applicant must file two copies of any draft order, one of which must be endorsed by a signed statement indicating the respondent's agreement. FPR 2010, PD 9A, para 7.1 confirms that a solicitor on record as acting for the respondent can sign on his or her behalf.

Undertakings

2.32 FPR 2010, PD 9A states that where the either or both parties give undertakings, a written statement should also be signed by the giver of any undertaking(s). The enforcement of undertakings has been reformed and is dealt with in FPR 2010, PD 33A. There is a prescribed form of words for undertakings in order to ensure that they are enforceable. There is also a prescribed form for the signed statement to accompany an order containing undertakings. See Chapter 6 for full details.

Statement of information

2.33 The parties must file a statement of information in Form D81 with a consent order. This has been changed substantially and it is essential that practitioners familiarise themselves with it to avoid difficulties in case of a 'last minute' consent application.

The form looks very different and is expanded from two pages to six pages in length. It asks for more detail than the old Form D81, including:

- date of marriage, separation, decree nisi and decree absolute, rather than the former 'duration of marriage' box;
- dates of birth of the parties and their children (not just their ages);
- a box to confirm how the agreement was reached (eg through direct discussions, mediation, collaborative law);
- a clearer but more prescriptive substantive financial disclosure section. Parties must confirm the combined values of property net of mortgage and 'other capital' to arrive at a figure for 'gross capital'. There is then space for liabilities and pensions to give totals including and excluding pension values, and finally, combined net income from all sources;
- a box for 'any other matters';
- details of where they and the children will live (as with the old form) plus an additional 'basis of occupation in property' box;
- any new relationships (ie (proposed) cohabitation or remarriage);
- a familiar series of tick boxes to establish that any mortgagees and pension arrangements (in the case of a pension attachment order) have been served, plus provision for Pension Protection Fund compensation sharing orders (see **2.39** below).

The form must be verified by a statement of truth and there are more stringent requirements for the exchange and execution of the form. There are two options:

(1) where a single form is filed, both parties must sign it to certify that they have read the contents of the other party's statement (FPR 2010, SI 2010/2955, 9.26(2));

2.33 *Matrimonial and Civil Partnership Proceedings*

(2) where separate forms are filed, the form of each party must be signed by the other party to certify that they have read it (FPR 2010, 9.26(3)).

Although solicitors can be authorised by their clients to complete the statement of truth, practitioners will need to factor in extra time to comply with the requirement for parties either to complete amd sogme a single D81 or certify that each party has read the D81 completed by the other.

Rule 9.26(5) preserves the court's discretion to dispense with the statement of information where the parties are in attendance, which it may also exercise where there are relatively recent Forms E on the court file.

Procedure and good practice

Voluntary disclosure

2.34 Annexed to FPR 2010, PD 9A is the Pre-application Protocol. It is a restatement of the Protocol annexed to *Practice Direction (Ancillary Relief Procedure)* [2000] 1 FLR 997, which was implemented with the then new 'Ancillary Relief Rules' in 2000. It will be familiar to practitioners due to its reproduction in Part 4 of the Law Society Family Law Protocol[1].

It bears re-reading, containing as it does recommendations for good practice in carrying out negotiations and disclosure prior to, or instead of, commencing an application for a financial remedy. Practitioners' fears about the role of financial remedy proceedings amid the promotion of alternative dispute resolution in FPR 2010 may be allayed by paragraph 2, which states

> 'In considering the options of pre-application disclosure and negotiation, solicitors should bear in mind the advantage of having a court timetable and court managed process'.

Commencing proceedings is not 'frowned upon' under FPR 2010 as solicitors are encouraged to consider the benefits of a court timetable in preference to a potentially unwieldy voluntary process. However, mediation and/or collaborative law are promoted as ways of preventing costly voluntary disclosure and negotiation.

The guidance on involving experts in voluntary disclosure has been removed from the Protocol and practitioners should refer to FPR 2010, SI 2010/2955, Pt 25 and its accompanying practice direction for the relevant guidance (see Chapter 5).

[1] *Family Law Protocol* (2nd edn, 2006), The Law Society, London.

Pensions

2.35 FPR 2010, SI 2010/2955, 9.29 confirms that this chapter of the rules applies where an application for a financial remedy has been made and either the application or the respondent has pension rights. The procedure will be familiar and changes to the relevant forms (Form P, P1 and P2) are cosmetic only.

Like FPR 1991, the FPR 2010 requires that upon the fixing of a first appointment, the party with pension rights must within seven days request

Applications for a financial remedy – Pt 9 2.37

from the pension arrangement the information referred to in reg 2(2) of the Pensions on Divorce etc (Provision of Information) Regulations 2000, SI 2000/1048, essentially a cash equivalent value (CEV)[1]. This information must be forwarded to the other party within seven days of receipt[2]. The requirement is relaxed where the party already has a 'relevant valuation' less than 12 months old[3].

The improved use of sub-headings in FPR 2010 makes it far easier to discern at a glance which procedural requirements apply to applications for pension sharing orders and pension attachment orders respectively.

[1] FPR 2010, SI 2010/2955, 9.30(1) and (2).
[2] FPR 2010, SI 2010/2955, 9.30(3).
[3] FPR 2010, SI 2010/2955, 9.30(4) and see definition of 'relevant valuation' at FPR 2010, SI 2010/2955, 9.3(1).

PENSION SHARING ORDER

2.36 Applications for a pension sharing order must still be served upon the pension scheme under FPR 2010, SI 2010/2955, 9.31. Due to the combined (and somewhat complex) effects of the Pensions on Divorce etc (Provision of Information) Regulations 2000, regs 2(7) and 4, the pension arrangement has 21 days in which to object or stipulate qualifications to the making of a pension sharing order.

The procedure to be followed where a pension sharing order is to be made by consent is set out in FPR 2010, 9.32. If the Form A has not been previously served upon the scheme and the information required by section C of the Pension Inquiry Form (Form P) has not been otherwise provided, the party with pension rights must request this information and upon receipt send it to the other party[1]. The information in question is a series of short and 'tick box' questions, the answers to which will enable the parties to check whether:

- the pension sharing order and annex is addressed correctly;
- any of the pension rights are not shareable; or
- there are any other matters standing in the way of implementation.

The pension arrangement has 21 days in which to provide this information[2]. Forms P are seldom served upon pension arrangements in practice and practitioners may well continue simply to send the consent order and pension sharing annex to the pension arrangement for checking before filing them with the court for approval.

[1] FPR 2010, SI 2010/2955, 9.32(1) and (2).
[2] Pensions on Divorce etc (Provision of Information) Regulations 2000, SI 2000/1048, reg 4(1)(a).

PENSION ATTACHMENT ORDERS

2.37 As under FPR 1991, the requirements are more onerous where a pension attachment order is contemplated. The Form A, the applicant's address for service and details of where payment should be made must be served upon making the application[1]. Within 21 days of service, the pension scheme can still request the relevant section of the Form E filed by the party with pension

2.37 *Matrimonial and Civil Partnership Proceedings*

rights, which they in turn must produce within 21 days or by the date for filing Form E if later[2]. The pension scheme also retains its right to provide a statement in response and be represented at the first appointment[3].

FPR 2010, SI 2010/2955, 9.34 provides an equivalent set of requirements where a pension attachment order is to be made by consent and service as not been effected as set out at **2.36** above. Like the old FPR 1991, r 2.70(11) and (12), the draft consent order, pension attachment annex containing addresses for service and payment details must be sent to the pension arrangement, which has 21 days in which to object[4].

[1] FPR 2010, SI 2010/2955, 9.33(1).
[2] FPR 2010, SI 2010/2955, 9.33(2)-(4).
[3] FPR 2010, SI 2010/2955, 9.33(5)-(6).
[4] FPR 2010, SI 2010/2955, 9.34.

IMPLEMENTATION

2.38 The filing requirements and time limits for implementation set out in FPR 1991, r 2.70(16) and (17) are reproduced with minor stylistic alterations in FPR 2010, SI 2010/2955, 9.36. The only change is the inclusion of provision for service of the sealed order, annex, decree/final order upon the Board of the Pension Protection Fund (see **2.39** below).

PENSION PROTECTION FUND COMPENSATION

2.39 The Pension Protection Fund (PPF) was established to provide members of qualifying defined benefit pension schemes with compensation where their employer has become insolvent and where the assets of the scheme are insufficient to pay out a set amount.

FPR 2010, SI 2010/2955, 9.37 reproduces almost exactly FPR 1991, r 2.70A which imposes obligations to provide information upon parties whose pension arrangements are, or are about to be, subject to PPF involvement.

FPR 2010, SI 2010/2955, 9.38–9.42 provide a detailed scheme for the sharing or attachment of PPF compensation. The Chapter mirrors the provisions applicable to 'normal' pension sharing and attachment orders with appropriate modifications.

Where proceedings may be heard

2.40 FPR 2010, SI 2010/2955, 9.25 does not have a direct forbear in FPR 1991. Sub-paragraphs (1) and (2) provide that applications for a financial order or for financial provision after an overseas divorce/dissolution must be tried in a designated divorce/civil partnership county court if it is proceeding in the county court, and either at the Royal Courts of Justice or court authorised to hold High Court sittings in the case of a High Court matter. By sub-paragraph (3), applications for financial provision in case of failure to maintain[1] must be heard in either a designated divorce/civil partnership county court or the High Court.

Applications for a financial remedy – Pt 9 **2.42**

Sub-paragraph (4) enables the court to transfer a case to another court (provided it has jurisdiction) either of its own motion or on the application of one of the parties if either:

(a) the parties consent;
(b) the court has held a hearing to determine the issue of transfer; or
(c) the court has notified the parties that it intends to transfer the case and neither party has requested that a hearing take place to determine the issue[2].

[1] Under MCA 1973, s 7 or CPA 2004, Pt 9, Sch 5.
[2] FPR 2010, SI 2010/2955, 9.25(5).

First appointment

2.41 FPR 2010, SI 2010/2955, Pt 9 makes few changes to the conduct of this hearing. The practice direction recommends that as well as complying with the familiar requirements to file a Form E and subsequently a statement of issues, chronology, questionnaire and Form G[1], the parties should file with the court and exchange:

- a summary of the case agreed between the parties;
- a schedule of assets agreed between the parties;
- details of any directions that they seek, including, where appropriate, the name of any expert they wish to be appointed.

Directions sought and experts' details should be made available at the first appointment if they have not been provided previously. This serves as a useful reminder of the need to be fully prepared for the first appointment, minimising correspondence (and costs) thereafter.

Practitioners should be aware of the additional obligations placed upon parties who seek to instruct experts. Full details are set out in Chapter 5.

[1] FPR 2010, SI 2010/2955, 9.14, formerly FPR 1991, r 2.61D.

Financial Dispute Resolution (FDR)

2.42 Again, FPR 2010, SI 2010/2955, Pt 9 does little to alter fundamental practice and preparation for the FDR. FPR 2010, PD 9A, para 6 confirms the purpose of the FDR – 'a meeting held for the purposes of discussion and negotiation'. It reiterates the importance and scope of the parties' obligations not to disclose the negotiations.[1]

Representatives are reminded that parties should:

- make offers and proposals;
- give offers proper consideration; and
- not seek to exclude any offers or proposals from consideration at the hearing, except those made in the context of alternative dispute resolution.

[1] See also Family Law Protocol, para 4.14.4.

2.43 *Matrimonial and Civil Partnership Proceedings*

Hearings

2.43 FPR 2010, SI 2010/2955, Pt 27 does not apply exclusively to applications for a financial remedy but it contains several provisions, which are likely to be of greatest relevance to such proceedings.

Absent parties

2.44 FPR 2010, SI 2010/2955, 27.4 deals with the consequences of a party's non-attendance. The court has wide powers to deal with applications in the absence of either party, subject to the availability of sufficient evidence to decide the matter and the court receiving satisfactory evidence that a defaulting respondent has received reasonable notice of the proceedings.

Parties can apply to have orders made in their absence set aside by making an application supported by evidence. They will need to show that they:

- acted promptly upon finding out that an order had been made;
- had a good reason for not attending;
- have a reasonable prospect of success.

This applies to directions appointments as well as hearings[1].

[1] FPR 2010, SI 2010/2955, 27.5.

Bundles

2.45 By FPR 2010, SI 2010/2955, 27.6, the FPR 2010, PD 27B applies in relation to the preparation of all bundles. This is a reproduction of the President's Direction of 27 July 2006, the importance of which was highlighted memorably by Munby J in *Re X (Bundles: Failure to Comply with Practice Direction)*[1].

The practice direction applies to all hearings in excess of one hour in length unless they are listed in a family proceedings court or are listed urgently so as to make compliance impossible.

The terms of the practice direction will be familiar to all family practitioners but a reminder of the salient points is always useful:

- the responsibility for preparing and paginating the bundle lies with the applicant unless they appear in person, in which case the first named respondent to be legally represented must take responsibility[2];
- the bundle must contain documents *relevant to the hearing* in chronological order, divided into sections. Recommended section headings are listed in the practice direction[3];
- preliminary documents should be inserted at the beginning of the bundle and should, include a one-page case summary, statement of issues, reading list and chronology[4]. It is, of course, open to the court to disapply or adapt such elements of this or any other requirement as it sees fit;
- the bundles should be presented in A4 ring binders, no longer than 350 pages each with the prescribed identifying information on the outside of each file[5];

Applications for a financial remedy – Pt 9 **2.47**

- the default time limit for lodging the bundle is two days before the hearing but the court is likely to insist on a longer time limit for final hearings[5].

[1] [2008] EWHC 2058 (Fam), [2008] 2 FLR. 2053.
[2] FPR 2010, PD 27A, para 3.
[3] FPR 2010, PD 27A, para 4.1.
[4] FPR 2010, PD 27A, para 4.2.
[5] FPR 2010, PD 27A, para 5.

Other applications and forms of action

Proceedings in the magistrates' court

2.46 FPR 2010, SI 2010/2955, 9.18–9.23 set out the procedure for applications made in the magistrates' court. It is anticipated that such applications will remain few and far between but it may be that, in future, the courts will encourage the allocation of simple variation applications to the magistrates' court to make best use of judicial resources.

Maintenance pending suit and other applications for interim provision

2.47 FPR 2010, SI 2010/2955, 9.7 provides that a party can apply at any stage for:

- an order for maintenance pending suit/outcome of proceedings;
- an order for interim periodical payments;
- an interim variation order;
- any other form of interim order[1].

The application is governed by the FPR 2010, SI 2010/2955, Pt 18 procedure and its accompanying practice direction (SI 2010/2955, PD 18A). Full details can be found in Chapter 5 below.

Where an interim application is made before the filing of Form E, the written evidence in support must:

(a) explain why the order is necessary; and
(b) give up-to-date information about that party's financial circumstances[2].

Unless the respondent has already filed a financial statement (Form E, E1 or E2), he or she must, at least seven days before the hearing of the application, file a statement of his or her means and serve it upon the applicant[3].

This is very little different to the procedure prescribed by the old FPR 1991, r 2.69F, save in relation to the introduction and application of the FPR 2010, SI 2010/2955, Pt 18 procedure. Applicants should be aware of the requirement of Pt 18 to attach a draft of the order sought to their application notice in Form A[4]. See Chapter 5 for full details of the Pt 18 procedure.

[1] FPR 2010, SI 2010/2955, 9.7(1).
[2] FPR 2010, SI 2010/2955, 9.7(3).
[3] FPR 2010, SI 2010/2955, 9.7(4).
[4] FPR 2010, SI 2010/2955, 18.7(2).

2.48 *Matrimonial and Civil Partnership Proceedings*

Costs

2.48 Practitioners are put on notice that the default presumption of no order for costs *does not* apply to applications for:

- an order for maintenance pending suit/outcome of proceedings;
- an order for interim periodical payments;
- any other form of interim order.

Somewhat bizarrely, the presumption of no order for costs *does* apply to an application for an interim variation (FPR 2010, SI 2010/2955, 28.3). See Chapter 6 for full details of the provisions relating to costs.

Orders for disclosure against a person not a party (formerly known as 'inspection appointments')

2.49 In certain cases this can be an extremely important step in the proceedings. It is therefore fitting that FPR 2010 devotes a whole part to it, as opposed to the almost cursory mention of the procedure at FPR 1991, r 2.62(7)–(9).

FPR 2010, SI 2010/2955, Pt 21 deals with the disclosure and inspection of documents. Disclosure was previously one of those issues in which the FPR 1991 sought to apply, with modifications, the CPR, so that anyone wishing to comply with his or her obligations in family proceedings had to look also at the civil rules. The former FPR 1991, r 2.20, dealing with disclosure of documents in defended causes, was a masterpiece of convoluted and incomprehensible draftsmanship.

The new rules have imported, with modifications and simplifications, parts of CPR Pt 31. The FPR 2010 now have a very clear definition of both disclosure and inspection. By FPR 2010, SI 2010/2955, 21.1(1), 'a party discloses a document by stating that the document exists or has existed'. By FPR 2010, 21.1(2), 'inspection of a document occurs when a party is permitted to inspect a document disclosed by another person'. FPR 2010, 21.1(3) makes clear that the word 'document' has an extended meaning to include electronic storage and the like.

Part 21 applies to all family proceedings but it is likely to be of greatest relevance to applications for a financial remedy.

Application

2.50 The application can be made without notice and must be supported by evidence (FPR 2010, SI 2010/2955, 21.2(2)). It is suggested that regard should be had to the FPR 2010, SI 2010/2955, Pt 18 procedure when making an application and that the application notice Form D11 should be used. In the absence of compelling reasons, such as a real risk that a relevant document is imminently to be destroyed, the application ought to be made on notice to the other party to the proceedings and the person against whom the order is sought.

FPR 2010, SI 2010/2955, 21.2(3) states, in similar terms to the old FPR 1991, r 2.62(7), that an order will only be made 'where disclosure is necessary in

Applications for a financial remedy – Pt 9 2.53

order to dispose fairly of the proceedings or to save costs'. The reasons for the application should therefore be clearly stated in any statement in support of the application.

FPR 2010, SI 2010/2955, 21.2(4) states that any order must specify the document or classes of documents, which must be disclosed and require the respondent to specify which of the documents are no longer in his control or in respect of which he claims a right or duty to withhold inspection. It is therefore essential that the application is precise as to what disclosure is sought.

Directions may also be given for the respondent to explain what has become of any missing documents and to prescribe arrangements for inspection (FPR 2010, 21.2(5)).

Response

2.51 At an on notice hearing, the respondent and/or other party to the proceedings will have an opportunity to make submissions as to why an order for disclosure and/or inspection should not be made.

However, any person may apply without notice for an order permitting that person to withhold disclosure on public interest grounds (FPR 2010, SI 2010/2955, 21.3(1)). In addition, any person who claims a right or duty to withhold a document must state in writing what that right or duty is and the grounds upon which it is claimed (FPR 2010, 21.3(3)). In deciding whether such a claim should be upheld, the court can require the applicant to produce the document to the court and invite *any* person to make representations (FPR 2010, 21.3(6)).

Further guidance

2.52 FPR 2010, PD 21A sets out the usual form of order for disclosure in non-financial remedy proceedings, which will be, in a phrase familiar to civil practitioners, an order for standard disclosure. This is a list of material documents in or formerly in a party's control[1].

In financial remedy proceedings, a more sophisticated and staged process of financial disclosure has been envisaged by the rules[2]. However, in any family proceedings the court may order parties to disclose or search for documents if necessary (ie an order for specific disclosure)[3].

[1] FPR 2010, PD 21A, para 2.1.
[2] FPR 2010, PD 21A, para 2.2.
[3] FPR 2010, PD 21A, para 2.4.

Application for a financial remedy after overseas proceedings

2.53 Following the decision in the (now leading) case of *Agbaje v Agbaje*[1], applications for a financial remedy after a foreign divorce, dissolution, decree of nullity or their overseas equivalents look set to become more and more prevalent.

2.53 Matrimonial and Civil Partnership Proceedings

The application is made under the Matrimonial and Family Proceedings Act 1984 (MFPA 1984), Pt III or the CPA 2004, Sch 7. It is a two-stage process. Any person who has validly obtained a divorce, dissolution or annulment overseas *may* apply for a financial remedy in England and Wales[2]. However, before doing so, they must first apply for permission[3]. This application must be made in Form D50E in accordance with the FPR 2010, SI 2010/2955, Pt 18 procedure. For detailed guidance, see Chapter 5.

Once the permission stage has been passed, the substantive application is termed an application for a financial remedy[4], and is therefore governed by FPR 2010, SI 2010/2955, Pt 9.

[1] [2010] UKSC 13, [2010] 1 FLR 1813.
[2] MFPA 1984, s 12; CPA 2004, Sch 7, paras 1–3.
[3] MFPA 1984, s 13; CPA 2004, Sch 7, para 4.
[4] See the interpretation section at FPR 2010, SI 2010/2955, 2.3.

Which court?

2.54 FPR 2010, SI 2010/2955, 8.24(1) dictates that the application for permission must be made in the principal registry. The same is true of the substantive application[1]. The only exception to this is where the application for permission and thereafter for a financial remedy is made by consent purely to obtain the court's approval of a financial agreement. This procedure is dealt with in Chapter 5[2].

[1] FPR 2010, SI 2010/2955, 9.5(2).
[2] See FPR 2010, SI 2010/2955, 8.24(2), 9.5(2) and 9.26(6).

Application

2.55 The application is made in Form D50F, which is not dissimilar to the Form M26 it replaces. The form asks for the names of the parties and the respondent's address for service. There is space to summarise the orders sought.

The applicant must then reference and attach the order granting permission or (in the case of a consent application for permission and a substantive order) evidence the respondent's consent. There is an opportunity to set out the grounds for jurisdiction, which will already have been explored in summary terms at the permission stage, unless this is a consent application.

The main simplification facilitated by the form is the removal from the rules of the prescribed contents of the statement in support of the application. These are instead listed clearly in the form. The statement in support must:

- state the facts relied on in support of the application with particular reference to the matters set out in the relevant Act relating to the appropriateness of England and Wales as a venue for the litigation[1];
- give particulars of the divorce/dissolution/nullity/separation proceedings and of the marriage;
- state the occupation and residence of the parties;
- give names and dates of birth for any children of the family (or that they are over the age of 18);

- state whether either party has subsequently married or formed a civil partnership;
- give an estimate in summary form of the appropriate amount or value of the capital resources and net income of each party and of any child of the family under the age of 18;
- the grounds on which it is alleged that the court has jurisdiction to entertain an application for an order for a financial remedy.

The application form and statement in support must be verified by a statement of truth.

[1] MFPA 1984, s 16(2) or CPA 2004, Sch 7, para 8(3).

Procedure

2.56 Once the court has received the application, it must fix a date for a first appointment in the usual way (FPR 2010, SI 2010/2955, 9.12) and the parties are channelled through the same procedure as those engaged in an application for a financial order.

MFPA 1984 and its civil partnership equivalent provides the full range of financial orders available after an application in Form A. In addition, there are equivalent provisions to obtain avoidance of disposition orders, orders for interim periodical payments and other interim orders. Again, the procedure is the same as though the application was made within 'home-grown' financial order proceedings.

However, there is a specialised application Form D50G for applications to prevent transactions intended to defeat prospective applications for financial relief.

Chapter 3
PROTECTION OF INDIVIDUALS
FPR 2010, Pts 10 and 11

Applications under Part 4 of the Family Law Act 1996 (injunctions)	3.1
Applications under Part 4A of the Family Law Act 1996 (forced marriage protection)	3.2

APPLICATIONS UNDER PART 4 OF THE FAMILY LAW ACT 1996 (INJUNCTIONS)

3.1 The effect of the new FPR 2010, SI 2010/2955 on the procedure in relation to applications for injunctions under Part 4 of the Family Law Act 1996 is much less profound than in other areas. However, the rules do effect a comprehensive tidying up and simplification of the procedure and, in common with other aspects of procedure, largely unify the system between the three levels of court. In practice, of course, most applications for non-molestation and occupation orders are brought in the county court.

The procedure under the old rules was set out in relation to the High Court and county court in FPR 1991, SI 1991/1247, rr 3.8 and 3.9 and in relation to the magistrates' court in the Family Proceedings Courts (Matrimonial Proceedings etc) Rules 1991, SI 1991/1991, r 3A. That under the reformed procedure is now set out in FPR 2010, SI 2010/2955, Pt 10 and in its associated FPR 2010, PD 10A.

An application for a non-molestation or occupation order must now be supported by a witness statement verified by a statement of truth (FPR 2010, 10.2(1)), as opposed to the previous position in which a sworn statement was required. As now, if an application is made without notice to the other party, then the statement should set out the reasons why notice has not been given. Under the previous procedure, there was a separate form for applications made by a child under the age of 16: under the new procedure this is dealt with in FPR 2010, PD 10A, para 2.1. Although no special form is now provided, the practice direction reminds the reader that leave is required and that the Allocation and Transfer of Proceedings Order 2008, SI 2008/2836 provides that an application for leave should be made in the county court.

The previous Form FL401 used for an application for a non molestation or occupation order remains in use, as do some of the other ancillary forms, such as Form FL403, used to vary, extend or discharge an injunction, and Form FL407, the application for a warrant of arrest.

A court can, of course, still make non-molestation orders of its own motion: see the Family Law Act 1996, s 42(2)(b): in that case the advance procedural matters provided for do not apply.

The provisions in relation to notice (two days) and service of the application on a respondent or on a mortgagee or landlord are restated in FPR 2010, SI

3.1 *Protection of Individuals*

2010/2955, 10.3(1)–(3), although first class post is no longer prescribed as the method of service on third parties, and any of the usual methods set out in FPR 2010, SI 2010/2955, Pt 6 can be used. The provision, rarely, if ever, used, which enables the third party mortgagee or landlord to make representations to the court after an order has been made remains in force but the hearing may now be before the injunction application is disposed of rather than necessarily being afterwards[1].

An application for a transfer of tenancy is no longer dealt with as if it were an application for a non-molestation or occupation order.

The previous provisions, detailing the need to serve on a respondent personally any order made and for the court to serve the respondent if the applicant acts in person, remain in force[2].

Under the former procedure, separate forms were prescribed for the issuing of non-molestation and occupation orders, and a yet further form was prescribed for the setting out of any provisions to which a power of arrest was added. One reason for the separate forms was that after the reforms in the law designed to give further protection for applicants, which involved removal of the power to attach a power of arrest to non-molestation orders, such powers could only be added to occupation orders. FPR 2010, SI 2010/2955, 10.9 simply provides that any provision in an occupation order which has attached to it a power of arrest should be set out separately from any provision which does not have a power so attached.

The previous provisions relating to service of a non-molestation order or of an occupation order containing a power of arrest on the police station which covers the area where the applicant lives remain in force, albeit redrafted to make them simpler[3].

The general rule in relation to applications in family proceedings is that they will be held in private[4]: this means that the general public has no right to be present. This general rule supersedes the specific rule previously in force whereby applications under Part 4 of the Family Law Act 1996 were to be heard 'in chambers' (former FPR 1991, r 3.9(1)). However, the new FPR 2010, PD 10A, para 3.1 provides that, if at a hearing in private at which a non-molestation order or an occupation order with a power of arrest is made, and the person to whom the order is addressed was not given notice of the order and was not present, then the terms of the order and the name of the person to whom it is addressed shall be announced in open court at the earliest opportunity (either later that day or on the next listed sitting of the court). It is not easy to see why this procedure is of any value and it is certainly novel.

An order under Part 4 can be enforced in various ways. Since the changes in the substantive law, there are very few occasions on which a person is arrested and brought before a court under a power of arrest, as these are now attached only to occupation orders. However, the procedure has still to be prescribed if such a sequence of events occurs. A further alternative is that the applicant applies, and the court grants, a warrant under the Family Law Act 1996, s 47(8), which again is a rarely found state of affairs. The procedure in relation to these two situations is assimilated.

The other procedure whereby injunctions granted under Part 4 can be enforced is by committal proceedings: this applies also to undertakings given to the court to compromise an application for an injunction.

The rules as now codified simplify the procedures for all forms of enforcement of orders under the Family Law Act 1996, ironically at a time when the number of such applications coming before the family courts has diminished very greatly.

FPR 2010, SI 2010/2955, 10.11 deals with the situation in which a person is arrested pursuant either to a power of arrest or to a warrant of arrest and is brought before the High Court or a county court: the procedure before the magistrates is, unusually for this code, set out separately in rules made under the Magistrates' Court Act 1980, s 144.

The substance of the provisions is unchanged, but the language is different. The court, when a person is arrested and brought before it, may either determine on that occasion whether or not the facts and circumstances which led to the arrest amounted to disobedience of the order or may adjourn the proceedings: unless the court otherwise directs, the matter must be dealt with within 14 days and the respondent must be given two days' notice of the hearing. However, if it is not possible to deal with the arrested person within that time scale, an application to commit for contempt may still be issued.

The FPR 2010, PD 10A, para 3.3 makes it clear that where a person arrested under a power of arrest cannot be brought before the appropriate court within 24 hours (as is required by the terms of the Act) then he may be brought before the 'relevant judicial authority' at 'any convenient place': this is in practice usually a police station.

FPR 2010, PD 10A, paras 5.1–5.3 then deals with the attendance of the officer concerned after a person is arrested under a power of arrest: the officer's presence is not generally required, unless he was a witness to the events leading to the arrest or the arrest is itself in issue.

FPR 2010, PD 10A, paras 6.1–6.5 deals with applications for bail when a person is arrested under a power of arrest or a warrant of arrest. This reproduces the earlier provisions set out in the former FPR 1991, r 3.10. The taking of recognizances under the Family Law Act 1996 is now dealt with in FPR 2010, SI 2010/2955, 10.17.

The new rules do not even now replace Order 29 of the County Court Rules, which has remained effective despite the Civil Procedure Rules 1998, SI 1998/3132 having now been in force for some 12 years. Both Rule 1 of that Order, dealing with applications to commit for breach of injunctions, and Rule 1A, the corresponding provision in relation to undertakings, remain in force, albeit modified as before so that any injunction has attached to it a notice of the consequences of disobedience.

The former power to adjourn after contempt has been proved and to restore if required, also continues[5], as does the procedure where a hospital order is made[6] and the procedure for notification where a transfer direction is given so that a person remanded in custody is moved to hospital[7]. The rules in relation to these ancillary provisions have been reordered but not altered in substance.

3.1 *Protection of Individuals*

FPR 2010, SI 2010/2955, 33.1(2) applies to family proceedings CPR Pt 50 and Schs 1 and 2. The consequence of that is that the civil Practice Direction 'RSC 52 and CCR 29 – Committal Applications' applies. The form to be used for a committal application is set out in that PD: where a committal application is made in existing proceedings, as will be the case when it is sought to enforce an injunction, an application notice under FPR 2010, SI 2010/2955, Pt 18 has to be issued (see further Chapter 5).

[1] FPR 2010, SI 2010/2955, 10.7.
[2] FPR 2010, SI 2010/2955, 10.6.
[3] FPR 2010, SI 2010/2955, 10.10.
[4] FPR 2010, SI 2010/2955, 27.10.
[5] FPR 2010, SI 2010/2955, 10.14.
[6] FPR 2010, 10.15.
[7] FPR 2010, 10.16.

APPLICATIONS UNDER PART 4A OF THE FAMILY LAW ACT 1996 (FORCED MARRIAGE PROTECTION)

3.2 Forced marriage protection is a subject which has attracted a great deal of attention, but applications under the legislation have been few. The primary legislation is contained in the Family Law Act 1996, Pt 4A, ss 63A–63S, as inserted by the Forced Marriage (Civil Protection) Act 2007. The procedure was previously set out in FPR 1991, rr 3.25–3.30 and 3.33–3.36. It is now in FPR 2010, SI 2010/2955, Pt 11. As with non-molestation and occupation orders, the same forms as were previously in use (FL401A, FL403A and FL407A) remain.

The new provisions are more expansive than those which were previously in use and provide a self-contained code for applications under the legislation. The use of prescribed forms for applications has been abandoned, as it has under Part 4 of the Act, and the general provisions in FPR 2010, SI 2010/2955, Pt 18 apply.

The basic provisions in relation to permission, service, transfer, parties, and the like remain as before. However, there is a new provision in FPR 2010, SI 2010/2955, 11.2 which makes clear that an application for a forced marriage protection order can be made without notice in appropriate circumstances and sets out that the statement in support must explain why notice has not been given.

It is provided specifically in FPR 2010, 11.7 that applications for forced marriage protection orders should be 'in private', as opposed to the previous 'in chambers'. The remaining provisions in FPR 2010, 11.7–11.19 set out the procedure in relation to forced marriage protection orders specifically and in parallel to the provisions already set out for orders under FPR 2010, SI 2010/2955, Pt 4, so that they are no longer incorporated by reference to those other provisions. Therefore, the rules become clearer, and the applicant has to look no further than Pt 11, although there are no changes of substance.

Chapter 4

CHILDREN AND VULNERABLE ADULTS
FPR 2010, Pts 12–16

Proceedings relating to children	4.1
General	4.1
Special provisions in relation to public law proceedings	4.2
Special provisions in relation to private law proceedings	4.3
Special provisions in relation to wardship and other inherent jurisdiction proceedings	4.4
Special provisions in relation to international child abduction proceedings and the like	4.5
Communication of information: proceedings relating to children	4.6
Proceedings under the Human Fertilisation and Embryology Act 2008, s 54	4.7
Applications in adoption, placement and related proceedings	4.8
Representation of protected parties	4.9
Representation of children	4.10

PROCEEDINGS RELATING TO CHILDREN

General

4.1 The procedural provisions in relation to applications involving children had, under the previous system, become extremely complicated, as a result of piecemeal amendments of, and additions to, the original rules. Further, the general matters applicable to both private and public law cases were set out in Pt IV of FPR 1991, SI 1991/1247, to wardship in Pt V, and to Child Abduction and Custody in Pt VI, to which were subsequently added provisions for parental orders under the Human Fertilisation and Embryology Act 2008, s 54, in Pt IVA.

The new procedure aims, ambitiously, to combine into Pt 12 of the FPR 2010, SI 2010/2955 provisions in relation to all proceedings relating to children except those very unusual applications involving parental orders under the Children and Young Persons Act 2008, which are now in Pt 13, and those involving applications in adoption, placement and similar proceedings, which are now in Pt 14. The provisions in relation to representation both of children and of other protected parties are set out in the new Pts 16 and 15 respectively.

FPR 2010, SI 2010/2955, Pt 12 also incorporates by practice direction not only new material but also a number of existing directions, some dating back many years. Thus FPR 2010, PD 12A, relating to public law applications, and FPR 2010, PD 12B, relating to private law proceedings, were both issued on 6 April 2010, but are in effect reissued with the new rules and tied in to them.

4.1 Children and Vulnerable Adults

A full list of the incorporated practice directions in relation to Part 12 is as follows:

- FPR 2010, PD 12A: Public Law Outline (6 April 2010);
- FPR 2010, PD 12B: Private Law Programme (6 April 2010);
- FPR 2010, PD 12C: Service of proceedings (new);
- FPR 2010, PD 12D: Inherent jurisdiction, including wardship (new);
- FPR 2010, PD 12E: Urgent business (new);
- FPR 2010, PD 12F: International Child Abduction (new);
- FPR 2010, PD 12G: Communication of Information tables (new);
- FPR 2010, PD 12H: Contribution orders (new);
- FPR 2010, PD 12I: Reporting Restriction Orders (8 March 2005);
- FPR 2010, PD 12J: Residence and Contact Orders: Domestic Violence and Harm (14 January 2009);
- FPR 2010, PD 12K: Children Act 1989: Exclusion Requirement (14 December 1997);
- FPR 2010, PD 12L: Children Act 1989: Risk Assessments (3 September 2007);
- FPR 2010, PD 12M: Family Assistance Orders (3 September 2007);
- FPR 2010, PD 12N: Enforcement of Contact Order: Disclosure (6 November 2008);
- FPR 2010, PD 12O: Children: Arrival by Air (18 January 1980);
- FPR 2010, PD 12P: Removal from Jurisdiction: Passports (15 May 1987).

It is, of course, also the case that in relation to many private law proceedings, the applicant will have to consider, prior to making any application in relation to a child, whether or not to apply for ADR in accordance with FPR 2010, SI 2010/2955, Pt 3, as already discussed (see **1.7** above).

The application of Pt 12 of the new rules is therefore very wide ranging. By FPR 2010, SI 2010/2955, 12.1(1) it applies to:

(a) emergency proceedings (defined in FPR 2010, 12.2, the definition section, but applying principally to emergency protection orders and orders for information about or recovery of a child);

(b) private law proceedings (again there defined and including all applications for section 8 orders, as might be expected);

(c) public law proceedings (applications for care or supervision orders and some applications in relation to children who are already the subject of care orders);

(d) proceedings relating to the exercise of the court's inherent jurisdiction (other than applications for permission to commence such proceedings, which are governed by the general provision of FPR 2010, SI 2010/2955, Pt 18);

(e) proceedings relating to child abduction and the recognition and enforcement of decisions relating to custody;

(f) proceedings relating to the Council Regulation or the 1996 Hague Convention in respect of children (which are governed also by the procedure set out in FPR 2010, SI 2010/2955, Pt 31 for recognition and enforcement of judgments under those provisions); and

(g) any other proceedings which may be referred to in a practice direction.

Proceedings relating to children **4.1**

There is a new and helpful table in FPR 2010, 12.3, which sets out in relation to all orders sought under Pt 12, who may be the applicant and who should be the respondent. This is too indigestible to be summarised here, but is of considerable value. FPR 2010, 12.4 deals with notice of proceedings to a person with foreign parental responsibility.

FPR 2010, 12.5 sets out clearly and succinctly the way in which a court will approach an application under Pt 12, which is in line with the general approach set out in FPR 2010, SI 2010/2955, Pt 1. When an application has been issued, the court is mandated to consider setting a date for one of a variety of form of directions hearing: these include a First Hearing Dispute Resolution Appointment, as set out in the existing direction in relation to private law proceedings, which is now to be FPR 2010, PD 12B, a First Appointment in care or supervision proceedings, as set out in the existing direction in relation to public law proceedings, which is now to be FPR 2010, PD 12A, a directions appointment, or a date for the hearing of the full application or for an interim order. Alternatively, the court may give directions, the subject of many of which are set out in FPR 2010, SI 2010/2955, 12.12, or do anything else which the practice direction allows. The directions set out include the general management of the case, the timetable, joining other parties, and other matters, and may be considered at any stage in the proceedings.

This part of the rules is new and demonstrates the importance of the court dealing promptly with applications before it, and of setting out from the very start a direction in which the application should proceed.

This is followed by FPR 2010, SI 2010/2955, 12.6, which states that as soon as possible after the issue or transfer of proceedings (ie at the same time as considering the application under FPR 2010, 12.5, thus either on issue or on the first appearance before the court), the court must appoint a children's guardian in specified proceedings (which are defined both by reference to the Children Act 1989, s 41(6) and which mainly consist of care proceedings, and to FPR 2010, SI 2010/2955, 12.27, which as in the previous FPR 1991, r 4.2(2), extends that definition) unless an appointment has already been made or is thought not to be necessary, and should also consider, where s 41(3) of the 1989 Act applies (ie where the child is competent to act on his or her own behalf) whether a solicitor should be appointed for the child and also to consider in every case whether advice should be sought from Cafcass or whether a report should be requested from that organisation or any other body. The appointment of guardians is dealt with in FPR 2010, SI 2010/2955, Pt 16 see **4.10** below.

The next step in the progress of the application is then for a court officer to return to the applicant the application and any relevant forms and then give notice to the applicant of any hearing set: FPR 2010, SI 2010/2955, 12.7.

The applicant then has to serve the application and any relevant documents on a range of respondents. FPR 2010, PD 12C sets out who is to be served and with what and within what time scale. In general terms applications are to be served a minimum of 14 days prior to any hearing, although other periods are set out: in care proceedings the time limit is three days, and in emergency proceedings one day. All these periods are subject to extension or shortening by the court.

4.1 Children and Vulnerable Adults

A further table in FPR 2010, PD 12C also sets out non-parties who should be served: these include, for example, a local authority which is accommodating a child, and in care proceedings a parent who is believed not to have parental responsibility. A parent with parental responsibility is automatically made a respondent. This, again, is a clear and comprehensive set of provisions which do not need further summary.

The circumstances in which without notice (formally ex parte) applications will be heard is dealt within FPR 2010, SI 2010/2955, 12.16, which reproduces, albeit with changes in terminology, the previous FPR 1991, r 4.4(4).

Timing is dealt with in FPR 2010, SI 2010/2955, 12.13. This is a stronger rewriting of the former FPR 1991, r 4.15, and makes it even clearer that if proceedings are not concluded, the court must, on postponing or adjourning an application, set a fixed date for the next hearing. This is one of key provisions in the modern approach to litigation and is designed to prevent applications drifting and from being dependent for their progress on both the parties' ability to organise themselves. However, it is also provided, in FPR 2010, 12.15, that if the parties agree proposals to manage the case, including the fixing of a final hearing, the court may approve those directions without a hearing.

The provisions in relation to the attendance of the parties is dealt with in FPR 2010, SI 2010/2955, 12.14, which is in similar terms to the previous FPR 1991, r 4.15, save that the provision which set out that all applications are normally heard in chambers is replaced by a new rule of more general application, FPR 2010, SI 2010/2955, 27.10, which lays out the proposition that all proceedings to which the FPR 2010 apply will be held in private, save where they themselves or any enactment provide otherwise or the court so orders.

FPR 2010, SI 2010/2955, 12.19 deals with evidence at the hearing in applications for a section 8 order or for a special guardianship order, and reproduces in part the former FPR 1991, r 4.17. It makes stronger the principle that a party must not file or serve a document other than in accordance with the rules or any practice direction, and introduces a new direction that a party may not file or serve any witness statement or other document on which he intends to rely at a hearing, as opposed to in advance of it. The court then has a discretion to prevent reliance on any statement or document sought to be relied upon but in respect of which the party has not complied with the provisions. In practice, in children cases, while 'ambushing' is discouraged, a court is unlikely to pay no regard to a statement which appears to be relevant to the welfare of a child.

However, the overriding principle remains that no person may cause a child to be medically or psychiatrically examined with a view to the preparation of expert evidence without the permission of the court: this is reproduced in FPR 2010, SI 2010/2955, 12.20.

There are slight changes to the procedure where, by the Children Act 1989, s 37, the court asks a local authority to carry out a report to consider whether or not care or supervision proceedings should be commenced in relation to a child. FPR 2010, SI 2010/2955, 12.17 no longer makes it mandatory to adjourn the proceedings when a direction to a local authority is made: rather

Proceedings relating to children **4.3**

the court now has a discretion as to whether so to act. The rule further provides that, unless the court otherwise orders, the local authority shall serve the report prepared under s 37 on the parties: ie the general rule is that it should be served.

The position in relation to special guardianship reports prepared by a local authority remains, by FPR 2010, SI 2010/2955, 12.18, as it was previously, namely that the court has to consider whether or not if they are disclosed to the parties, so they are not to be given to them until the court has had the opportunity of considering the contents and possibly of removing information from them.

Special provisions in relation to public law proceedings

4.2 FPR 2010, SI 2010/2955, Pt 12, Ch 12 deals with specific provisions relating to care and supervision proceedings and, so far as practicable, to other public law proceedings. This is new in form, but in fact the effect of the provisions is to tie in the Public Law Outline, as set out in what is now FPR 2010, PD 12A: this was previously done by FPR 1991, r 4.14A, but that related only to the timetable for the child. The new provisions make specific reference to the First Appointment, Case Management Conference (CMC) and Issues Resolution Hearing (IRH), in FPR 2010, SI 2010/2955, 12.25, although the detail is set out in the practice direction, and, of course, this is not new. However, FPR 2010, 12.26 places a duty on the court when directing a CMC or an IRH to direct an advocates' meeting to discuss a draft case management order and to consider any of the other matters set out in FPR 2010, PD 12A.

It is, however, interesting that the new FPR 2010, 12.24 sets out clearly that the court will direct the parties to monitor compliance with the court's directions and to inform the court of any failure to comply with a direction of the court or any other delay in the proceedings.

Procedure relating to exclusion orders made as part of an interim care or emergency protection order, as to certain forms of consent, and as to reports in secure accommodation cases are also now contained in this Part, having previously been in FPR 1991, rr 4.24A, 4.24 and 4.25 respectively, but have not been substantially amended.

Special provisions in relation to private law proceedings

4.3 As with the provisions relating to public law matters, FPR 2010, SI 2010/2955, Pt 12, Ch 4 ties in the Revised Private Law Programme, which is now FPR 2010, PD 12B. In particular, it is now set out in FPR 2010, SI 2010/2955, 12.31 that the court may set a date for the First Hearing Dispute Resolution Appointment after the proceedings are issued: this is a further attempt, following on from the referral to ADR prior to proceedings being issued, to get the parties to come to agreement over the children concerned, which may be attempted whether or not mediation has already been tried. The provision in FPR 2010, 12.32 that the respondent must file and serve an answer to the application within 14 days of being served replaces the previous provision in FPR 1991, r 4.9 that an acknowledgement should be filed but that

4.3 Children and Vulnerable Adults

the filing of an answer was optional. The problem, of course, is that since the introduction of the Children Act 1989, the emphasis has been on reducing the information in statements put before the court at an early stage, which has the laudable aim of preventing the exchange of inflammatory material when an application may be settled: the corollary of that is, of course, that the court is somewhat in the dark as to what the parties' cases actually are.

The new FPR 2010 leave almost untouched the provisions introduced in the practice direction exactly one year previously, which may be thought not yet to have had time to prove themselves one way or the other.

Special provisions in relation to wardship and other inherent jurisdiction proceedings

4.4 Wardship proceedings are now far less common than was once the case. They previously had their own Pt V in the FPR 1991, but although that set out some special provisions, now reproduced in the FPR 2010, it contained no statement of principle.

However, FPR 2010, PD 12D, which supplements the code, sets out, perhaps for the first time, a clear statement that 'it is the duty of the court under its inherent jurisdiction to ensure that a child who is the subject of proceedings is protected and properly taken care of'. However, it goes on to make it clear that wardship proceedings should not be commenced unless it is apparent that the issues concerning the child in question cannot be resolved under the Children Act 1989.

This new clarity is continued in FPR 2010, SI 2010/2955, 12.36, which sets out the general procedural provision immediately, namely that any application must be started in the High Court, but that wardship proceedings, except applications for an order that a child be made or cease to be made a ward of court, may thereafter be transferred in appropriate cases to the county court. Considerations which may affect the decision to transfer are set out in FPR 2010, PD 12D, Pt 2. The previous provisions which applied to the necessity of all parties informing the court as to the whereabouts of the ward (if known) are reproduced in simplified and more comprehensible form in FPR 2010, SI 2010/2955, 12.39.

However, there is now a further direction, in FPR 2010, PD 12D, para 3.1, that where a child is thought to be associating with an undesirable party (a classic ground for commencing wardship proceedings, albeit less commonly encountered now than was the case), that party should not be made a party to the main application, and should be joined only if there is an application for an injunction or the like against him: even then, he should be shown only the papers relating to the particular application and not the underlying material.

There is a new Form C66 which deals with applications made under the inherent jurisdiction.

Special provisions in relation to international child abduction proceedings and the like

4.5 FPR 2010, SI 2010/2955, Pt 12, Ch 6, supplemented by FPR 2010, PD 12F, deals with all manner of proceedings relating to the Hague Conventions, the European Convention, and the Council Regulation[1]: Section 1 refers to proceedings under the 1980 Hague Convention or the European Convention, and Section 2 to the Council Regulation and the 1996 Hague Convention. These are a specialised area of law which falls outside the expertise of most family lawyers, and one in which because of the subject matter and also the necessity to comply with the requirements of the various conventions, matters have to be dealt with expeditiously. They are all also issued in the High Court and save for minor procedural matters are to be dealt with by a High Court judge, not a deputy. There is a reproduced restriction, now in FPR 2010, SI 2010/2955, 12.51, that proceedings must not be adjourned for more than 21 days at a time.

The procedure is technical and prescriptive; however the new FPR 2010, PD 12F attempts to explain what should happen in clear non-technical language and appears, more than most of the other directions issued, to be aimed at the party in person. The procedure has been rewritten without substantial amendment, but the overall underpinning emphasis on case management is reinforced by the provisions of FPR 2010, SI 2010/2955, 12.48, which provides specifically that in any proceedings of this nature the court may give directions, and a specific list of matters which can be ordered is set out: they are not new, but they are a comprehensive restatement of the procedural steps which can be taken.

[1] Council Regulation (EC) No 2201/2003 concerning jurisdiction and the recognition and enforcement of judgments in matrimonial matters and the matters of parental responsibility.

COMMUNICATION OF INFORMATION: PROCEEDINGS RELATING TO CHILDREN

4.6 The provisions relating to the communication of information to third parties in relation to proceedings relating to children was formerly contained in FPR 1991, Pt XI. It is now brought within the general rules relating to children, but given its own separate Chapter 7, supplemented by FPR 2010, PD 12G. Although the previous material has been divided between the rules and the practice direction, there is in fact no substantial change.

PROCEEDINGS UNDER THE HUMAN FERTILISATION AND EMBRYOLOGY ACT 2008, S 54

4.7 The provisions of s 54 of the Act enable two parties to apply jointly for an order (a parental order) declaring that a child carried for them by a third party is to be treated as their child. This necessitated a code of procedure to be inserted in the previous FPR 1991 as Pt IVA and this is reproduced with some minor modifications in FPR 2010, SI 2010/2955, Pt 13: the new rules apply to all levels of court, whereas previously there were separate proceedings in

4.7 Children and Vulnerable Adults

relation to the High Court and county court on the one hand and the magistrates' court on the other. There are no substantive changes.

APPLICATIONS IN ADOPTION, PLACEMENT AND RELATED PROCEEDINGS

4.8 The Family Procedure (Adoption) Rules 2005, SI 2005/ 2795 were in many ways a test for the new ideas which have reached their fulfilment in the comprehensive restatement set out in the FPR 2010. They too applied to all levels of court, and they too had preliminary statements of intention, which were borrowed almost word for word for the wider reforms, tables showing who should be served with applications, and provisions for considering the future timetable at the first directions hearings, all devices incorporated into the new rules. The consequence of that is that the new rules simply repeat in Pt 14, in renumbered form, such provisions of the 2005 Adoption Rules as applied to the specific procedure in relation to adoption applications and the like. Those sections in the 2005 Rules which set out the general philosophy behind them and the overall procedural matters are now applied throughout in the FPR 2010 and do not therefore feature separately in the adoption section.

REPRESENTATION OF PROTECTED PARTIES

4.9 The previous FPR 1991, Pt IX dealt comprehensively with the representation and participation of both children and those who lacked capacity, within the meaning of the Mental Capacity Act 2005. Despite being modernised in order to take account of the 2005 Act, the section remained headed 'Disability'. The new rules apply different provisions on the one hand to those who lack capacity within the meaning of the 2005 Act, which are set out in FPR 2010, SI 2010/2955, Pt 15, and to children who are parties, which are set out in FPR 2010, SI 2010/2955, Pt 16.

This is a helpful distinction because although there are some common considerations and overlap, the two groups of potential parties raise different problems. These topics are dealt with under the general heading of children as many of the matters in which children are parties are matters in which their future is under discussion, although the rules in Pt 16 apply generally. The section on protected parties is dealt with here also, partly because it comes within the group of sections dealing with children, and partly because the provisions need to be contrasted with those relating to children. However, it needs to be reiterated that Pt 15 does not apply only to parties in proceedings involving children, but to those involved in any family proceedings.

FPR 2010, SI 2010/2955, Pt 15 uses the new terminology: a party now conducts proceedings, whether as applicant or respondent, by a litigation friend, rather than, as previously, bringing proceedings by next friend and responding to them by guardian ad litem. As in other aspects, the procedure and language is brought into line with the CPR 1998. FPR 2010, SI 2010/2955, 15.2 lays down clearly the general provision that 'A protected party must have a litigation friend to conduct proceedings on that party's behalf. FPR 2010, SI 2010/2955, 15.3 sets out the converse, namely that any step taken before a protected party has a litigation friend has no effect unless the court otherwise orders, and if a party ceases to have capacity during the course of the proceedings no party may take any step without the permission of the court until a litigation friend has been appointed. The title of the proceedings should be amended to show that the party in question conducts proceedings by litigation friend.

FPR 2010, 15.4–15.9 then deal with the appointment and, if required, removal of litigation friends, all of which mirrors the procedure in the CPR 1998 and in the former Family Procedure (Adoption) Rules 2005.

The general position is as follows:

(1) a person with authority as a deputy (of the Court of Protection) to conduct proceedings is entitled to be the litigation friend;

(2) if there is no such person, a person may act as litigation friend if he can fairly and competently conduct proceedings for the protected party, has no interest adverse to his, and, unless he is the Official Solicitor, undertakes to pay any costs incurred;

(3) the court may appoint either the Official Solicitor or another person to be the litigation friend of the party, either on its own initiative or on application, but the proposed appointee must of course consent;

(4) the court may direct that a particular person may not act as litigation friend, may terminate the appointment of a litigation friend, and may appoint a replacement litigation friend.

The procedure is further developed in FPR 2010, PD 15A, but this particular practice direction does little more than reiterate the terms of the rule in rather more simplified language.

REPRESENTATION OF CHILDREN

4.10 As already set out, children are now dealt with separately from protected parties, not least because the rule has also to deal with a distinct issue which surfaces in many proceedings, namely, whether or not a child should be made a party. A further issue is whether or not in certain circumstances the child can conduct proceedings without a litigation friend, in contradistinction to the position with protected parties, where there is a blanket prohibition on that course being adopted.

The new code draws together a variety of provisions which were found in different places in the former rules: so under the revised provisions the position of a children's guardian in specified (care) proceedings was dealt with under FPR 1991, r 4.10 and a guardian in other (generally private law) proceedings under FPR 1991, r 9.5: now the material is all in one area and is much simpler to follow.

The new rules draw a distinction between proceedings in which a child is a party to proceedings but is not the subject of those proceedings, and proceedings where the child is both a party to, and the subject of, proceedings.

In the former category, subject to the situation in which a child is found to be competent to conduct proceedings on his or her own behalf, the child must have a litigation friend: FPR 2010, SI 2010/2955, 16.5. In that situation,

4.10 Children and Vulnerable Adults

similar provisions apply by FPR 2010, SI 2010/2955, Pt 16, Ch 5 to those set out in Pt 15 in relation to protected parties.

In the second category, that is those cases where the child is the subject of the proceedings, a guardian rather than a litigation friend will be appointed. There are in this situation two distinct sub-categories:

(a) There are certain proceedings in which children are generally required to become parties: these are in relation to care, adoption, placement and the like. FPR 2010, SI 2010/2955, 16.3 provides that in those circumstances the court *must* appoint a guardian for a child 'unless it is satisfied that it is not necessary to do so to safeguard the interest of the child' (as previously set out in FPR 1991, r 4.10).

(b) However, FPR 2010, 16.2 says that in all other family proceedings: 'The court may make a child a party to proceedings if it considers it is in the best interests of the child to do so'. This is the same test as is set out in the former FPR 1991, r 9.5, but is more starkly expressed. Some of the considerations which apply in relation to the question of whether a child should be joined are set out in FPR 2010, PD 16A, Pt 4. The new FPR 2010, 16.4 says that where (a) a child is an applicant (save for where the child is applying for consent to marry under FPR 2010, SI 2010/2955, 8.42) or (b) has been made a party under FPR 2010, 16.2, then unless the child is found competent to represent himself or herself, again the court *must* appoint a guardian.

The circumstances in which a child may act without a guardian or litigation friend were previously set out in FPR 1991, r 9.2A. They are now clarified and set out in FPR 2010, SI 2010/2955, 16.6. The underlying conditions have not altered: the permission so to act may be given by the court, or alternatively a solicitor may give a certificate that the child is able to give instructions and has instructed him. However, it is now entirely clear (FPR 2010, 16.6(2)) that this provision does not apply in specified (care) or FPR 2010, SI 2010/2955, Pt 14 (adoption or placement proceedings): in those instances the child must have a guardian.

A guardian, within family proceedings, is in a wholly different position to a litigation friend. FPR 2010, SI 2010/2955, Pt 16, Ch 6 deals with children's guardians appointed under FPR 2010, 16.3 (ie in care and related proceedings): the old FPR 1991, r 4.10 excluded certain persons from being so appointed because of their connections with the local authority, but FPR 2010, 16.18 makes it clear that the appointment should be of a Cafcass officer or an officer of its Welsh equivalent, and thus no other person. The bar on former employees of the local authority is now moved to FPR 2010, 16.36 and refers only to adoption proceedings and the like. The position is now different where the appointment of a guardian is under FPR 2010, 16.4 (ie in private law and similar proceedings) where FPR 2010, 16.24 says that an officer of Cafcass or a Welsh family proceedings officer *may* be appointed, but so may the Official Solicitor or any other suitable person.

The duties of the guardian are, within the rules, streamlined and set out in FPR 2010, SI 2010/2955, 16.20, but are supplemented by FPR 2010, PD 16A: a new provision, FPR 2010, 16.20(6) makes it crystal clear that any report by the guardian is confidential. The duties of a solicitor for the child, previously in FPR 1991, r 4.12, are restated in similar terms in FPR 2010, 16.29.

Representation of children **4.10**

The new rule imports also the provisions of the Family Procedure (Adoption) Rules 2005 in relation to reporting officers, which are now in FPR 2010, 16.30–16.32 and are supplemented by FPR 2010, PD 16A, Pt 5.

A largely rewritten provision in the rules, FPR 2010, 16.33, deals with the duties of those asked to prepare reports under the Children Act 1989, s 7, whether they be Cafcass officers or employees of the local authority, who in this context are referred to as 'welfare officers'. The rule sets out the principle, also in s 7(5) of the 1989 Act, that it is the duty of the officer to comply with the request and to provide the court with such assistance as it may require. It is also specifically provided, as with a guardian, that any report so provided is confidential. Parallel provisions in relation to parental order reporters are set out in FPR 2010, 16.34–16.35. There are further provisions in relation to Cafcass officers in relation to the making of risk assessments, reporting on family assistance orders, dealing with enforcement orders, and the like in FPR 2010, 16.38–16.39. These provisions are further supplemented in FPR 2010, PD 16A, Pts 6–8.

Chapter 5

GENERAL PROCEDURAL PROVISIONS
FPR 2010, Pts 5, 6, 8, 17–19, 22–27, 29

Practicalities: case management, use of forms and service	5.1
Rule 5 – Forms and start of proceedings	5.1
Forms	5.1
Start of proceedings	5.2
Rule 6 – Service	5.3
Changes and innovations	5.4
Procedure and good practice	5.8
Part 26 – Change of solicitor	5.38
Notice of change	5.39
Order that solicitor has ceased to act	5.40
Removal of a solicitor who has ceased to act on application of another party	5.41
Part 29 – Miscellaneous	5.42
Personal details	5.43
Disclosure under the Child Support Act 1991	5.44
Giving notice	5.45
Withdrawal of applications	5.46
Human Rights Act 1998	5.47
Applications for relief precluded by the Child Support Act 1991	5.48
Documents in family proceedings concerning gender recognition	5.49
Sealing	5.50
Judgments and orders	5.51
Summary	5.52
Evidence – Pts 17, 22–24	5.53
Part 17 – Statements of truth	5.53
Which documents need a statement of truth?	5.54
What is a statement of truth?	5.56
Signing of the statement of truth	5.57
What if a person cannot read or sign the statement of truth?	5.57
What are the consequences of failing to verify a document?	5.58
Consequences of making false statements	5.59
Summary	5.60
Part 22 – Evidence (general rules)	5.61
Powers of the court	5.62
The general rule	5.63
What is a witness statement?	5.64
When should an affidavit be used as evidence?	5.65
Format of the affidavit/statement	5.66
Swearing of an affidavit or verifying a witness statement	5.67
Exhibiting documents	5.68
Filing of affidavits and witness statements	5.69
Service of witness statement for use at the final hearing	5.70

General Procedural Provisions

Cross examination	5.71
Witness summary	5.72
Notice to admit facts	5.73
Notice to admit or procure documents	5.74
Use of witness statements in other proceedings	5.75
Witness statements in Part 7 proceedings	5.76
Evidence by video link	5.77
Summary	5.78
Part 23 – Miscellaneous rules about evidence	5.79
Hearsay evidence	5.80
Use of plans, photographs, models etc as evidence	5.81
Evidence on foreign law	5.82
Evidence of consent of trustee to act	5.83
Evidence in magistrates' court	5.84
Part 24 – Witnesses, depositions generally and taking of evidence in EU Member States	5.85
Chapter 1 – Witnesses and depositions	5.85
Summary	5.97
Experts and assessors – Pt 25	5.98
Overview	5.98
Comparison table	5.99
Practice Direction 25A – Experts and assessors in family proceedings	5.100
Introduction	5.101
Permission to instruct an expert	5.102
When should the court be asked for permission?	5.103
Pre-application instruction of experts	5.104
Emergency and urgent cases	5.105
Service of orders upon experts	5.106
Adults who may be protected parties	5.107
The duties of experts	5.108
Content of the report	5.109
Proceedings relating to children	5.110
Proceedings other than those relating to children	5.116
Questions to the expert	5.117
Experts' discussion or meeting	5.118
Refusal by one party to be bound by the experts' agreement	5.119
Arrangements for experts to give evidence and experts attending at court	5.120
Action after the final hearing.	5.121
Appointment of assessors in family proceedings	5.122
Applications and miscellaneous procedure: Pts 18, 19 and 8	5.123
Part 18	5.124
Scope	5.125
Procedure	5.126
Part 19	5.133
Scope	5.134
Procedure	5.135
Part 8	5.139
Conversion table	5.140
Application for a corrected gender recognition certificate	5.141

Practicalities: case management, use of forms etc 5.1

Application for alteration of maintenance agreement after death of one party	5.142
Application for question as to property to be decided in summary way	5.143
Procedure	5.144
Declarations	5.149
General procedure	5.150
Specific procedure	5.155
Application for permission to apply for a financial remedy after overseas proceedings	5.159
Application for the transfer of a tenancy under section 53 of, and schedule 7 to, the 1996 Act	5.164
Applications for orders preventing avoidance under section 32L of the Child Support Act 1991	5.171
Application for consent to marriage of a child or to registration of civil partnership of a child	5.172
Publicity	5.173

PRACTICALITIES: CASE MANAGEMENT, USE OF FORMS AND SERVICE

Rule 5 – Forms and start of proceedings

Forms

5.1 One of the most significant changes made by FPR 2010, SI 2010/2955, is to the forms to be used in family proceedings.

Although not all the forms have been changed, many have been updated to make them more user friendly which should help to ensure that all of the information required is included.

FPR 2010, SI 2010/2955, 5.1 states that the form referred to in the practice direction 'shall' be used although can be varied if 'required by the circumstances of a particular case'. The form must not be varied, however, so as to leave out:

- any information or guidance which it gives to the recipient; or
- any other essential information.

The forms can be expanded (FPR 2010, PD 5A, para 1.2(b)) to include additional pages but such pages must be verified by a statement of truth if this is required of the document itself.

Any documents referred to in the form must be attached.

FPR 2010, PD 5A sets out the forms to be used in proceedings under the rules in two separate tables identified by name and number.

Table 1 lists the forms against the part of the rules to which they relate. Table 2 lists the forms individually and provides a description of each.

5.2 General Procedural Provisions

Start of proceedings

5.2 FPR 2010, SI 2010/2955, 5.3 confirms that proceedings are considered to have started when a date is entered on the application form by a court officer. This is also the date of issue.

FPR 2010, SI 2010/2955, 29.7 requires an application form to be authenticated by a stamp of the court when issued.

Rule 6 – Service

5.3 Provision for service of all documentation within family proceedings is now dealt with in one place – FPR 2010, SI 2010/2955, Pt 6. This mirrors very closely CPR Pt 6.

The rule is divided into three main parts, which will be dealt with in turn below, being:

- service of an application for a matrimonial or civil partnership order[1];
- service of other proceedings within the UK[2]; and
- service outside the UK[3].

The rule itself is far easier to follow and is supported by two very comprehensive practice directions which contain further guidance:

- FPR 2010, PD 6A – Service within the jurisdiction; and
- FPR 2010, PD 6B – Service out of the jurisdiction.

Methods and proof of service in respect of matrimonial or civil partnership proceedings are largely unchanged. New methods of serving other proceedings are, however, introduced including by way of fax or other electronic means.

[1] FPR 2010, SI 2010/2955, Pt 6, Ch 2.
[2] FPR 2010, SI 2010/2955, Pt 6, Ch 3.
[3] FPR 2010, SI 2010/2955, Pt 6, Ch 4.

Changes and innovations

FORMS

5.4 FPR 2010, SI 2010/2955, Pt 6 introduces two new forms: Forms FP6 and D89.

FP6 – Certificate of service

5.5 This is a tick box form to be used when stipulated by the rules (see **5.11** below) to confirm that service has been effected. It contains a statement of truth.

It replaces in most cases the requirement for an affidavit of service.

FPR 2010, SI 2010/2955, 6.37 sets out the detail which must be contained in the certificate depending on the method of service used.

The certificate of service is, unless otherwise directed, to be filed at the earlier

Practicalities: case management, use of forms etc 5.10

of the first directions appointment, or first hearing in, the proceedings[1].

[1] FPR 2010, 6.37(2).

D89 – Request for personal service by a court bailiff

5.6 Any request for service by the court bailiff must be made on Form D89 with a photograph of the person to be served if available.

ALTERNATIVE MEANS OF SERVICE

5.7 The methods by which service can be effected have been widened and are far more innovative in respect of documents other than applications for matrimonial or civil partnership orders. The rules specifically provide for service by way of fax, email and other electronic means and also envisage that in some cases the use of short message service (SMS) or voicemail may be appropriate.

Procedure and good practice

(1) SERVICE OF PETITION

5.8 FPR 2010, SI 2010/2955, 6.3–6.22, supplemented by FPR 2010, PD 6A, deal with provision for service within the jurisdiction of an application for a matrimonial order or civil partnership order made under Pt 7 of the rules. This includes an application by the respondent[1].

This replaces the provision previously contained at FPR 1991, r 2.9 and sets out the various options in a much clearer and more methodical manner.

[1] FPR 2010, SI 2010/2955, 7.14.

Methods of service

5.9 In addition to personal and postal service if a solicitor has agreed to accept service then the petition can now be served by Document Exchange (DX)[1].

An application can be served either by the court or the applicant[2]. Personal service must still not be by the applicant themselves[3].

[1] FPR 2010, SI 2010/2955, 6.4.
[2] FPR 2010, SI 2010/2955, 6.5(1).
[3] FPR 2010, SI 2010/2955, 6.5(3).

Alternative address

5.10 Under FPR 2010, SI 2010/2955, 6.8(2), where the court has failed to serve the respondent the applicant may request the court officer to serve him at an alternative address.

5.11 *General Procedural Provisions*

Bailiff service

5.11 The applicant can request that service be by way of bailiff. FPR 2010, PD 6A sets out at paras 11.1–11.3 the procedure which must be followed.

The request for bailiff service should be made on Form D89 (request for personal service by a court bailiff) and the relevant fee paid. It must be accompanied by either:

- evidence that postal service has been attempted and failed; or
- if postal service has not been attempted, an explanation as to why it is not considered appropriate.

FPR 2010, PD 6A, para 11.4 specifically states that if the applicant is legally represented a request for bailiff service will rarely be granted and the representative would need to show why a bailiff was more appropriate than a process server.

Once service has been effected or attempted, the bailiff must file Form FP6 certificate of service.

Service on a solicitor

5.12 The rules now contain specific provision for service of a petition on a solicitor[1].

Where a solicitor acting for a respondent has notified the applicant in writing that they are instructed to accept service, the petition can be served at the business address of that solicitor, and this can be done by DX. This extends to solicitors in EEA States[2].

[1] FPR 2010, SI 2010/2955, 6.11.
[2] As defined in the Interpretation Act 1978, Sch 1.

Service where no address is given by the respondent

5.13 FPR 2010, SI 2010/2955, 6.13 confirms that the respondent must be served at his usual or last known address unless the applicant has reason to believe that the respondent no longer resides at that property.

If the applicant is able to ascertain the respondent's current address the application must be served at that address[1].

If the applicant cannot ascertain the current address then he or she must consider an alternative place or method for service and make application under FPR 2010, 6.19, which provides for service by an alternative method or at an alternative place[2].

[1] FPR 2010, SI 2010/2955, 6.13(4)(a).
[2] FPR 2010, SI 2010/2955, 6.13(5).

Service on children and protected parties

5.14 This no longer has to be done through the applicant. FPR 2010, SI 2010/2955, 6.14, however, mirrors FPR 1991, r 9.3 (service on a child or protected party) and sets out on whom service should be effected where the respondent is a child or protected party.

FPR 2010, 6.14(5) now allows an application for service on someone other than one of the specified persons to be made without notice.

The notice which must be endorsed on all documents served in accordance with FPR 2010, 6.14 is set out in FPR 2010, PD 6A, para 9.1 (which is taken from the unchanged Form D5).

Unless the Official Solicitor is acting, the person on whom the application was served must file a witness statement confirming whether (and, if not, why not) the contents of the application form, or the purpose and intention of the application has been communicated to the child or protected party. This largely mirrors FPR 1991 save for the use of a witness statement rather than an affidavit under the old rules.

Deemed service

5.15 The provision remains the same as under FPR 1991 so that the petition can be deemed served if:

(a) the acknowledgement of service has been returned signed by the respondent or his or her solicitor[1]; or
(b) the court is satisfied that the respondent has received the application, eg letter from the respondent's solicitor confirming he or she has seen a copy[2].

[1] FPR 2010, SI 2010/2955, 6.15(1).
[2] FPR 2010, SI 2010/2955, 6.16.

Proof of personal service

5.16 There is no longer a requirement for an affidavit of service.

The person who has effected service must instead file a certificate of service[1] (Form FP6 – see **5.5** above).

If the person being served was the other party to the marriage, the certificate of service must show the means by which the person serving the application knew the identity of the party served[2].

[1] FPR 2010, SI 2010/2955, 6.17(2).
[2] FPR 2010, SI 2010/2955, 6.17(3).

Service by alternative method or at an alternative place

5.17 FPR 2010, SI 2010/2955, 6.19 replaces what was referred to under the old rules as 'substituted service' with much simplified requirements.

If there is 'good reason' the court can direct service by an alternative method or by an alternative means[1].

The court can of its own volition, when hearing an application under this rule, find that previous steps taken to serve constitute good service[2].

5.17 General Procedural Provisions

Any direction for an alternative method or place of service given under FPR 2010, 6.19(3) must specify the following:

(a)   method or place of service;
(b)   date on which application form deemed served; and
(c)   period for filing the acknowledgement of service or answer.

FPR 2010, PD 6A, paras 6.1–6.4 provides further detail as to how an application should be made under this rule and must be read if a practitioner is applying under this rule. Particular points to note from the practice direction are as follows:

- the application can be made without notice;
- it must be supported by evidence setting out the reasons for the application;
- the alternative method/place proposed must be stated and why the applicant considers it likely that such application will by this means reach the person to be served; and
- if steps have been taken previously to serve these must also be set out.

FPR 2010, PD 6A, para 6.4 contains useful examples of alternative methods of service which include the use of SMS and voicemail.

[1]   FPR 2010, SI 2010/2955, 6.19(1).
[2]   FPR 2010, SI 2010/2955, 6.19(2).

Dispensing with service

5.18 The only ground for dispensing with service under the new rules is contained in FPR 2010, SI 2010/2955, 6.20, which states that it is 'impracticable to serve the application by any method provided for' by the rules. The grounds of necessity and expedience are gone.

Under FPR 2010, 6.20(2) the application to dispense with service must be supported by evidence. The form of such evidence is not stipulated but it is anticipated that a witness statement detailing all attempts at service made would be needed. The rules indicate that attendance by an applicant may be required when the court decides the issues[1].

[1]   FPR 2010, 6.20(3).

(2) SERVICE OF DOCUMENTS (OTHER THAN APPLICATIONS UNDER PT 7) – WITHIN THE UK

5.19 FPR 2010, SI 2010/2955, 6.23–6.39, supplemented by FPR 2010, PD 6A contain all the provision for service of documents within the jurisdiction other than service of the petition itself.

Method of service

5.20 Documents are to be served, as directed by FPR 2010, SI 2010/2955, 6.23 and FPR 2010, PD 6A, by one of the following means:

(a)   personal service;

(b) first class post, document exchange or other service providing next day delivery;
(c) leaving it at a specified place;
(d) fax or other electronic communication.

Unless otherwise directed by the rules, practice direction, or court the party to the proceedings will serve the document[1].

[1] FPR 2010, 6.24.

Personal service

5.21 A document is deemed personally served by leaving it with the individual[1].

Any document can be personally served unless the person to be served has given an address for service[2].

[1] FPR 2010, SI 2010/2955, 6.25.
[2] FPR 2010, SI 2010/2955, 25(2).

Address for service

5.22 A party to proceedings must give an address for service which must be either[1]:

(a) a business address of a solicitor within the UK or EEA; or
(b) where no solicitor is acting, an address within the UK where the party resides or carries on business.

If neither of the above apply, the party must give an address for service in the UK[2].

If the party has indicated they will accept service by fax, the fax number must be at the address for service[3].

If, however, the party has been served outside the UK and, apart for acknowledging service need not take part in the proceedings, under FPR 2010, 6.26(4) they do not need to provide an address.

Any document to be served must be sent to, transmitted to or left at the address for service unless the rules or court direct personal service[4].

Where a party changes address, notice must be given in writing as soon as it has taken place to the court and to every party[5].

[1] FPR 2010, SI 2010/2955, 6.26(1), (2).
[2] FPR 2010, SI 2010/2955, 6.26(3).
[3] FPR 2010, SI 2010/2955, 6.26.
[4] FPR 2010, SI 2010/2955, 6.26(5).
[5] FPR 2010, SI 2010/2955, 6.27.

Service by document exchange (DX)

5.23 FPR 2010, PD 6A specifically provides that the DX may be used for service where:

5.23 *General Procedural Provisions*

- the address provided by the party for service includes a DX numbers; or
- the writing paper of the party or his solicitor gives a DX number; and
- the party or solicitor has *not* indicated that they are unwilling to accept service by DX.

The onus is, therefore, on the party or their solicitor to state that they will *not* accept service by DX.

Effecting service by post, DX or other alternative service provider

5.24 Service is effected in accordance with FPR 2010, PD 6A, para 3.1 by:

(a) placing the document in a post box;
(b) leaving the document with or delivering it to the relevant service provider; or
(c) having the document collected by the relevant service provider.

Service by fax or other electronic means (including email)

5.25 FPR 2010, PD 6A, paras 4.1–4.4 set out the circumstances in which service can be effected by fax or other electronic means.

The party to be served, or his or her solicitor, must previously have indicated in writing that he or she was willing to accept service by fax or other electronic means *and* provided details of the fax number, email address or other electronic identification.

A fax number on the writing paper of the solicitor acting for the party to be served is sufficient indication for these purposes.

If an email address appears on the writing paper, this can only be taken as an indication of willingness to accept service by this means if it specifically states that the email address may be used for service.

An email address, fax number or other electronic identification set out on a statement of case, or on an answer to a claim, which is filed at court will also be deemed sufficient indication of a willingness to accept service by this means.

Where service is to be by electronic means other than fax, the serving party must check with the person being served as to whether there are any limitations (eg size or format) which apply.

No hard copy need follow the electronic transmission.

Service on children and protected parties

5.26 FPR 2010, SI 2010/2955, 6.28–6.33 deal with service on children and protected parties.

The rules which apply to service of the petition (see **5.15** above) are to be applied to service of any other application form for commencing proceedings on a child or protected party.

If a litigation friend or guardian has been appointed, any other document must be served on, or by, the litigation friend or guardian[1]. If the guardian has been

Practicalities: case management, use of forms etc 5.29

appointed pursuant to FPR 2010, 16.3 then the document must also be served on the solicitor appointed.

The court can, however, direct that service should be on someone other than those stated above[2].

FPR 2010, 6.33 specifically provides that, in children proceedings pursuant to FPR 2010, SI 2010/2955, Pt 12, where a rule requires that:

- a document to be served on a party;
- a party to be notified of any matter; or
- a party to be supplied with a copy of any document,

in addition to those people set out above, the following must also receive copies/notice:

- children's guardian;
- welfare officer;
- children and family reporter;
- officer of service, Welsh family proceedings officer or local authority officer;
- local authority, if preparing a section 14A report[3].

[1] FPR 2010, SI 2010/2955, 6.29 and 6.30.
[2] FPR 2010, SI 2010/2955, 6.32.
[3] Under the Children Act 1989.

Deemed service

5.27 FPR 2010, SI 2010/2955, 6.34 sets out in a very clear table when documents are deemed served by the various methods permitted under the rules.

Further clarification as to the calculation of time under this rule is given in FPR 2010, PD 6A, paras 8.1–8.5 by way of specific examples of each method of service. There really can be no excuse for not being able to calculate when service is deemed to have taken place.

Service by alternative method or at an alternative place

5.28 FPR 2010, SI 2010/2955, 6.35 confirms that r 6.19 (see **5.17** above) applies also to any other documents in family proceedings which are to be served.

Dispensing with service

5.29 FPR 2010, SI 2010/2955, 6.36 states simply that the court may dispense with service of any document. This gives the court, therefore, much wider scope than in respect of service of the petition. Such application can be made without notice[1]. Although no form is stipulated it is anticipated that the general application form D11 should be used. A witness statement in support

5.29 *General Procedural Provisions*

would be advisable detailing all attempts made to serve.

[1] FPR 2010, PD 6A, para 7.1.

(3) SERVICE OUT OF THE JURISDICTION

5.30 FPR 2010, SI 2010/2955, 6.40–6.48 and FPR 2010, PD 6B deal with service of all documents in family proceedings out of the jurisdiction[1], *including* applications for matrimonial or civil partnership orders.

It remains the case that documents can be served out of the jurisdiction without the leave of the court[2].

[1] 'Jurisdiction' is defined in FPR 2010, SI 2010/2955, 2.3.
[2] FPR 2010, SI 2010/2955, 2.3.

Period for acknowledging service/responding to an application

5.31 Where an application is served outside the jurisdiction, FPR 2010, SI 2010/2955, 6.42 states that the period for acknowledging service or filing an answer is extended to 21 days where the person served is in:

(a) Scotland;
(b) Ireland;
(c) a Member State of the European Union; or
(d) a Hague Convention[1] country within Europe.

If the person served is in a Hague Convention country outside Europe, that period is extended to 31 days after service[2].

If the person served falls into none of the categories above, FPR 2010, PD 6B contains a table setting out the number of days the person has to respond.

[1] Convention on the service abroad of judicial and extrajudicial documents in civil or commercial matters signed at the Hague on 15 November 1965.
[2] FPR 2010, SI 2010/2955, 6.42(3).

Methods of service

5.32 Where the party to be served is in Scotland or Northern Ireland, the application or document must be served by one of the methods permitted by FPR 2010, SI 2010/2955, Pt 6, Ch 2 or 3[1].

Service in any other jurisdiction may be:

(a) in accordance with the Service Regulation[2]; or
(b) through foreign governments, judicial authorities and British Consular authorities; or
(c) by a method permitted by the law of the country in which it is to be served[3].

[1] See FPR 2010, SI 2010/2955, 6.43(2).
[2] Regulation (EC) No 1393/2007 of the European Parliament.
[3] FPR 2010, SI 2010/2955, 6.43(3).

Service in accordance with the Service Regulation

5.33 FPR 2010, PD 6B confirms that where service is to be effected in another Member State of the European Union the Service Regulation applies. The Service Regulation is annexed to PD 6B.

This Regulation has applied to service on Member States, excluding Denmark, since November 2008 and the procedure its not changed by these rules. Important points to note from the Regulation are as follows:

- all Member States are required to have in place a body whose responsibility it is to deal with transmission of documents to and from other Member States for service;
- when documents are sent by one agency to another for service they must be accompanied by the form annexed to the Regulation completed in the language of the Member State to whom the papers are being sent for service;
- the document to be served should also be translated into that language;
- on receipt of the document for service the receiving agency should acknowledge receipt to the agency of the submitting Member State within seven days on the form, also annexed to the Regulation;
- service should then be affected as soon as possible and within one month;.
- the method of service shall either be in accordance with the Member State or as requested by the transmitting agency;
- if service is not possible the receiving agency should advise the transmitting agency by means of the certificate annexed to the Regulation while still trying to carry out service;
- the date on which the document will be considered served is the date on which it was served in accordance with the law of the Member State where service took place;
- a certificate of completed service, in the form annexed to the Regulation, should be returned to the transmitting agency duly completed in the language of the transmitting agency.

Service through foreign governments, judicial authorities and British Consular authorities

5.34 Under FPR 2010, SI 2010/2955, 6.45(1), where the person to be served is in a country which is party to the Hague Convention, the application form or other document may be served:

(a) through the authority designated under the Hague Convention for that country; or
(b) if the law to that country permits, through the judicial authorities of that country, or through a British Consular authority in that country.

If the person to be served is in a non Hague country they may be served, if the law of that country permits, by the government of that country or a British Consular authority in that country[1].

Where service is to take place in:

- any commonwealth state not party to Hague;
- the Isle of Man or Channel Islands; or

5.34 *General Procedural Provisions*

- any British Overseas Territory,

service cannot be effected through the judicial authority of that country or British Consular authority[2]. It should, therefore, be done by a means permitted by the law of that country.

The exception is where the country is one of the commonwealth countries listed in FPR 2010, PD 6B, paras 4.1 and 4.2 which require service through the judicial authority in that country.

FPR 2010, 6.46 sets out the detailed procedure to be followed by a person wishing to have an application or documents served through the foreign government, judicial authority or British Consular.

The applicant must file:

- a request for service and the method requested;
- a copy of the document to be served;
- any other documents as required by FPR 2010, PD 6B;
- any translation required by FPR 2010, 6.47.

The court of issue will seal the documents and forward them to the senior master of the Queen's Bench Division, who will in turn send to either:

(a) the authority designated under the Hague Convention; or
(b) in any other case to the Foreign and Commonwealth Office with a request that it arranges service.

The person who wishes service to be affected must undertake to be responsible for all of the expenses of the Foreign and Commonwealth Office or foreign judicial authority[3].

[1] FPR 2010, SI 2010/2955, 6.45(2).
[2] FPR 2010, SI 2010/2955, 6.45(3).
[3] FPR 2010, SI 2010/2955, 6.48.

Translations

5.35 Unless an exception applies all documents to be served pursuant to FPR 2010, SI 2010/2955, 6.45 by a foreign government, judicial authority or British Consular must be accompanied by a translation[1].

The translation must be in the language of the country in which it is to be served or, where more than one language is used, the more appropriate[2].

Every translation must be accompanied by a statement by the person making the translation that it is correct. The statement should include the person's name, address and qualifications for providing the translation[3].

Under FPR 2010, 6.47(4) a translation is not required if English is the official language of the country in which it is to be served or where the person to be served:

(a) is able to read and understand English; and
(b) is to be served directly.

[1] FPR 2010, SI 2010/2955, 6.47(1).
[2] FPR 2010, SI 2010/2955, 6.47(2).

[3] FPR 2010, SI 2010/2955, 6.47(3).

Service on members of the Regular Forces and United States Air Force

5.36 Detailed provision for service on this category of person is contained in the Annex to FPR 2010, PD 6B.

In order to ascertain where the person to be served is serving the legal representative of the person wishing to effect service must write to one of the authorities set out at para 10 of the Annex giving as much information as possible about the person to be served. The letter must contain an undertaking by the legal representative that the address, if given, will be used for the sole purpose of issuing and serving documents.

Usually the address will then be provided and can be used as the address for service by post where such method is allowed by the rules.

Where service must be affected personally an appointment will have to be sought through the commanding officer for the document server to attend. If this is not appropriate the commanding officer may offer arrangements for the person to be served to attend at a place in the vicinity for the purpose of being served.

If suitable arrangements cannot be made the legal representative should have evidence to support an application for service by an alternative method.

If a member of the US Air Force is be served there is also specific provision made in FPR 2010, PD 6B.

SUMMARY

5.37 The provisions for service which apply depend on whether you are serving within or outside the jurisdiction and whether they relate to a FPR 2010, SI 2010/2955, Pt 7 application.

The procedure is very clear and detailed which, together with the additional options now available for service, should ensure that service can be progressed more effectively and with greater certainty within family proceedings.

Part 26 – Change of solicitor

5.38 FPR 2010, SI 2010/2955, 26.1–26.4, together with the comprehensive FPR 2010, PD 26A – change of solicitor, set out the procedure to be followed when there is a change of solicitor or a solicitor ceases to act for a person.

Notice of change

5.39 Where the address for service of a party is the business address of his or her solicitor, that solicitor will be considered as acting until the steps set out under FPR 2010, SI 2010/2955, 26.1 have been fulfilled.

5.39 *General Procedural Provisions*

Under FPR 2010, 26.2(2) where a party appoints a solicitor, a new solicitor or chooses to act in person, that party, or his or her solicitor must file service notice of the change on:

(a) all parties; and
(b) the former solicitor (if applicable).

Notice must be on new Form FP8 – Notification of change of solicitor, and must include a new address for service[1] and confirmation that the relevant people have been served. The form must be filed in the court office in which the application is proceeding[2].

Form FP8 is very clearly set out with boxes to tick and complete. If new solicitors have been appointed then their full details should be included where indicated.

Where a party has been receiving legal aid and his or her certificate is withdrawn, the solicitor he or she then appoints must comply with the requirement to file a notice, even if he or she was previously acting under the legal aid certificate[3].

In addition, where a party or solicitor changes their address for service a notice of that change must be filed and served on every party[4].

[1] FPR 2010, SI 2010/2955, 26.2(3).
[2] FPR 2010, PD 26A, para 2.6.
[3] FPR 2010, SI 2010/2955, 26.2(6).
[4] FPR 2010, PD 26A, para 2.4.

Order that solicitor has ceased to act

5.40 A solicitor may apply for an order that he or she has ceased acting for a party or children's guardian. The application is to be made in accordance with FPR 2010, SI 2010/2955, Pt 18 and FPR 2010, PD 18A[1].

Notice of the application must be given to the party or guardian, unless directed otherwise and the application must be supported by evidence[2].

If an order is made it must be served by the court on every party to the proceedings[3].

[1] FPR 2010, SI 2010/2955, 26.3(1).
[2] FPR 2010, 26.3(2).
[3] FPR 2010, 26.3(3).

Removal of a solicitor who has ceased to act on application of another party

5.41 FPR 2010, SI 2010/2955, 26.4 contains the detailed procedure to be followed where a solicitor has died, become bankrupt, ceased to practise or cannot be found, and the party has not given notice of a change or intention to act in person[1].

In such circumstance any other party may apply for an order that the solicitor has ceased to act. Such application must similarly be made in accordance with FPR 2010, SI 2010/2955, Pt 18 and must be supported by evidence[2].

Practicalities: case management, use of forms etc **5.46**

Notice of the application must be given to the party for whom the solicitor acted, unless the court directs otherwise. Any order will be served by the court on all parties[3].

[1]   FPR 2010, SI 2010/2955, 26.4(1)(a).
[2]   FPR 2010, PD 26A, para 4.2.
[3]   FPR 2010, SI 2010/2955, 26.4(3).

Part 29 – Miscellaneous

5.42 This part of the rules covers, as it suggests, various miscellaneous procedural matters not dealt with elsewhere in the rules.

Most of this part mirrors exactly rules found in FPR 1991, Pt X, some rules are, however, new to the FPR 2010.

Personal details

5.43 As under FPR 1991, r 10.21, a party[1] is not required to reveal his or her home address or contact details, or the address or contact details of any child. Further, the party need not reveal the name of the person with whom a child is living or the proposed new surname of that child, in an application to change such name.

The details must, however, be given to the court, but will not be revealed unless the court directs otherwise.

Any change of home address during proceedings must be notified to the court.

[1]   FPR 2010, SI 2010/2955, 29.1.

Disclosure under the Child Support Act 1991

5.44 FPR 2010, SI 2010/2955, 29.2 repeats FPR 1991, r 10.21A so that nothing in FPR 2010 will prevent a person providing information or evidence to the Child Support Agency (CSA).

The detail regarding contempt has, however, been removed to simplify the rule.

Giving notice

5.45 Under FPR 2010, SI 2010/2955, 29.3, notice must still be given in writing unless directed otherwise and served in accordance with FPR 2010, SI 2010/2955, Pt 6.

Withdrawal of applications

5.46 FPR 2010, SI 2010/2955, 29.4 draws together and harmonises the provision for withdrawing applications:

- under FPR 2010, SI 2010/2955, Pt 7 (applications for matrimonial and civil partnership orders);

5.46 *General Procedural Provisions*

- under FPR 2010, SI 2010/2955, Pts 10–14 or any other parts relating to welfare or upbringing of a child;
- where either party is a protected party.

An application in such a case can only be withdrawn with the court's permission, and such permission must be sought in writing with reasons. The court will then notify the other parties.

The court can deal with the matter without a hearing if the other parties have had the opportunity to make representations in writing[1]. The request can be made orally if all parties are present[2].

[1] FPR 2010, SI 2010/2955, 29.4(6).
[2] FPR 2010, SI 2010/2955, 29.4(4).

Human Rights Act 1998

5.47 The procedure to be followed where a party seeks to rely on any provision arising under the Human Rights Act 1998 (HRA 1998) is largely unchanged from that set out previously in FPR 1991, r 10.26, although its language has been simplified and the rules streamlined.

Under the new rules the procedure can be found in FPR 2010, SI 2010/2955, 29.5 and FPR 2010, PD 29A – Human Rights Act, joining the Crown.

A party seeking to rely on any provision under the HRA 1998 must inform the court in writing[1]:

(a) of the alleged infringement; and
(b) the relief sought – and whether this includes a declaration of incompatibility.

The notice will be in such form as the court directs and will also be served on all parties. The court can ask the parties to assist in preparing the notice[2].

It is anticipated that the court will deal with these issues at a directions hearing.

The court may, at any time such issues are raised, consider giving notice to the Crown but there must not be a declaration of incompatibility unless 21 days' notice has been given to the Crown, although the court may vary that timeframe[3].

If the Minister or other permitted person wishes to be joined, having received the notice, they must give notice of their intention to the court and every party, accompanied by a written nomination[4].

If the appropriate person on behalf of the Crown does not apply within the 21 days, the court can join them in any event[5].

Where a claim is made under the HRA 1998, s 7(1) (claim that a public authority acted unlawfully), the claim must be set out in the application form or appeal notice, with details of the judicial act and notice must be given to the Crown[6].

If there is an application under this provision concerning a committal order and the court concludes that a person's convention rights have been breached this should be recorded in the judgment or order[7].

Practicalities: case management, use of forms etc **5.51**

FPR 2010, 29.5(8) confirms that the appropriate officer can discharge duties such as making a witness statement on behalf of the Crown.

[1]   FPR 2010, SI 2010/2955, 29.5(2).
[2]   FPR 2010, PD 29A, paras 1.4 and 1.5.
[3]   FPR 2010, PD 29A, para 1.1.
[4]   FPR 2010, PD 29A, para 1.6.
[5]   FPR 2010, SI 2010/2955, 29.5(6).
[6]   FPR 2010, SI 2010/2955, 29.5(5).
[7]   FPR 2010, SI 2010/2955, 29.5(7).

Applications for relief precluded by the Child Support Act 1991

5.48 FPR 2010, SI 2010/2955, 29.8 repeats almost in identical terms the procedure set out in FPR 1991, r 10.24 where an application is made for an order which the court is of the opinion it is prevented from making under s 8 or 9 of the Child Support Act 1991. Those are the sections which prevent any court from making, varying or reviving any orders for periodical payments for children and from varying any agreement for child maintenance.

FPR 2010, 29.9 contains the modifications for r 29.8 where the application for such provision is not free-standing, and is, therefore, contained in another document which contains material extrinsic to the application.

Documents in family proceedings concerning gender recognition

5.49 FPR 2010, SI 2010/2955, 29.6 repeats exactly the requirement of FPR 1991, r 10.21B for the court to keep in a place of special security documents relating to proceedings in the specified proceedings.

Sealing

5.50 FPR 2010, SI 2010/2955, 29.7 details which documents should be sealed by the court on issuing and practically how they should be sealed.

Judgments and orders

5.51 FPR 2010, SI 2010/2955, 29.10 confirms that every judgment or order must state on it:

- the name and judicial title of the person who made it;
- the date it was made; and
- be sealed.

Such judgments or orders will be drawn up by the court unless the court or rules direct otherwise[1].

FPR 2010, 29.11 now specifically confirms that the court can direct that a judgment or order be checked by the court before sealing or that before such judgment or order is drawn the parties must file an agreed statement of its terms.

5.51 *General Procedural Provisions*

Where an order is to be drawn by a party it must be filed no later than seven days after the date on which the court ordered or gave permission for it to be drawn[2].

If this is not done, FPR 2010, 29.11(3)(b) now states that any other party may draw it up and file it.

FPR 2010, 29.13 and 29.14 repeat the provision in FPR 1991, r 10.17 for service of judgments and orders by the court.

So that there can no longer be any doubt, FPR 2010, 29.15 specifically states that a judgment or order takes effect from the day it is given or made, or such other later date as the court may specify.

The 'slip rule' is now contained at FPR 2010, 29.16 which states that the court may correct an accidental slip or omission in a judgment and that an application for such correction can be made without notice.

[1] FPR 2010, SI 2010/2955, 29.11(1).
[2] FPR 2010, SI 2010/2955, 29.11(3)(a).

Summary

5.52 FPR 2010, SI 2010/2955, Pt 29 does not contain any substantive changes or innovations. It draws together miscellaneous provisions from the old rules relating to procedure so that they can be readily identified when such matters arise.

EVIDENCE – PTS 17, 22–24

Part 17 – Statements of truth

5.53 Under the new rules a statement of truth becomes the more usual means of verifying documents within family proceedings on which a party seeks to rely, although affidavits are still required for certain purposes.

Which documents need a statement of truth?

5.54 FPR 2010, SI 2010/2955, 17.2 sets out which documents are to be verified by a statement of truth. This includes any document where required by a rule or practice direction together with:

- a statement of case[1] (including any amendments[2]);
- a witness statement;
- an acknowledgement of service under Pt 19 procedure;
- a certificate of service;
- a statement of arrangements for children;
- a statement of information pursuant of FPR 2010, SI 2010/2955, 9.26(1)(b);
- application form or notice where the applicant wishes to rely on the contents as evidence[3];
- expert's report[4];

- application notice for a third party debt order, hardship payment order or charging order[5];
- notice of objections to an account taken by the court unless verified by affidavit or witness statement[6].

[1] Within the meaning given by FPR 2010, SI 2010/2955, Pt 4.
[2] FPR 2010, SI 2010/2955,17.2(2).
[3] FPR 2010, SI 2010/2955,17.2(3).
[4] FPR 2010, PD 25A.
[5] FPR 2010, PD 17A, para 1.4(b).
[6] FPR 2010, PD 17A, para 1.4(b).

What is a statement of truth?

5.55 FPR 2010, SI 2010/2955,17.2(4) confirms that 'a statement of truth' is a statement that the party putting forward the document believes the facts to be true.

The wording for the statement of truth is set out in FPR 2010, PD 17A, paras 2.1–2.3. The form of wording differs depending on whether the statement of truth is being used to verify a statement of case, application notice or witness statement.

The statement of truth can be contained in the document it verifies or a separate document[1]. If the latter, there is alternative wording as set out in PD 17A at para 2.3.

[1] FPR 2010, PD 17A, para 1.5.

Signing of the statement of truth

5.56 Under FPR 2010, SI 2010/2955, 17.2(6)(a), if the statement of truth is being used to verify a statement of case it must be signed by either:

(a) the party or litigation friend; or
(b) the legal representative of the party or litigation friend.

It can also be made by two parties jointly[1].

In the case of a witness statement or statement of arrangements it must be signed by the maker of the statement[2].

Where a document is being verified on behalf of a company or corporation, the statement of truth must be signed by a person holding a senior position[3]. FPR 2010, PD 17A then goes on to confirm who such a senior person would include as:

- director;
- treasurer;
- secretary;
- chief executive;
- manager;
- chairman;
- president; or
- other similar officer.

5.56 General Procedural Provisions

In the case of a partnership, one of the partners or a person having the management or control of the partnership business can sign the statement of truth[4].

In all such cases the person signing must state the office or position they hold[5].

A legal representative signing must refer to their client's belief in the truth, not his or her own, state the capacity in which he/she sign and the name of his/her firm[6].

Signature by a legal representative will be taken by the court as confirmation that the advisor[7]:

- is authorised to sign the statement of truth;
- has explained the meaning of the statement of truth to the client – in particular that the legal representative by signing is confirming the *client's* belief in the truth of the document;
- informed the client of the possible consequences if the client did not have an honest belief in the truth.

An individual signing a statement of truth must sign in his or her own name and not that of a firm or employer.

FPR 2010, PD 17A, para 3.11 helpfully provides specific examples of who may sign in particular cases.

[1] FPR 2010, SI 2010/2955, 17.2(8).
[2] FPR 2010, SI 2010/2955, 17.2(6).
[3] FPR 2010, PD 17A, para 3.4.
[4] FPR 2010, PD 17A, para 3.6.
[5] FPR 2010, PD 17A, para 3.4.
[6] FPR 2010, PD 17A, para 3.7.
[7] FPR 2010, PD 17A, para 3.8.

What if a person cannot read or sign the statement of truth?

5.57 FPR 2010, PD 17A, paras 4.1–4.4 set out the procedure to be followed where a person cannot read or sign the statement of truth.

The document must contain a certificate, in the form annexed to the practice direction, made by an authorised person confirming that:

- the document has been read to the person signing;
- the person appeared to understand and approve its contents to be accurate;
- the declaration of truth has been read to that person;
- the person appeared to understand the declaration and consequences of it being made falsely;
- the person has signed or made his mark in the presence of the authorised person.

An authorised person is one able to administer oaths and take affidavits. They need *not* be independent of the parties of representatives[1].

[1] FPR 2010, PD 17A, para 4.4.

What are the consequences of failing to verify a document?

5.58 A statement of case which is not verified by statement of truth will remain effective unless struck out. A party will not, however, be able to rely on it's contents as evidence until it has been verified by a statement of truth[1].

The court can order a statement of case be struck out by reason of it not being verified by a statement of truth and any party can apply to the court for such an order[2].

The court may direct that a witness statement which has not been verified by a statement of truth shall not be admissible as evidence[3].

FPR 2010, SI 2010/2955, 17.5 gives the court the power to order that a person who has failed to verify a document be required to do so, and any party may apply for such an order.

[1] FPR 2010, SI 2010/2955, 17.3(1).
[2] FPR 2010, SI 2010/2955, 17.3(2), (3).
[3] FPR 2010, SI 2010/2955, 17.4.

Consequences of making false statements

5.59 FPR 2010, SI 2010/2955, 17.6 confirms that proceedings for contempt of court can be brought against a person who makes or causes to be made a false statement in a document verified by a statement of truth without an honest belief in its truth.

If a party believes that a statement of truth is false the allegation must be referred to the court dealing with the proceedings[1].

The court can initiate steps to consider if there is contempt of court and, where there is, punish in accordance with the provisions of the RSC Ord 52 and CCR Ord 29.

Alternatively, the court can direct that the complaining party refer the matter to the Attorney General. The detailed procedure to be followed is set out at FPR 2010, PD 17A, para 6.3.

[1] FPR 2010, PD 17A, para 6.1.

Summary

5.60 Most applications or statements within family proceedings will now be verified by statement of truth. Care needs to be taken, however, to ensure that the correct wording is used to ensure documents can be relied upon.

Part 22 – Evidence (general rules)

5.61 The rules on evidence in FPR 2010, SI 2010/2955, Pt 22 are drawn largely from the CPR 1998.

There is now detailed guidance in FPR 2010, PD 22A, paras 6.1–6.5 as to the contents and format of a witness statement and affidavit including how documents should be exhibited and how they should be sworn.

5.61 *General Procedural Provisions*

The concept of witness summaries is introduced where a party is required to serve a witness statement but is unable to obtain one[1]. A notice to admit facts may also now be used in family proceedings[2].

FPR 2010, PD 22A contains full instructions as to how video conferencing should be conducted.

[1] FPR 2010, SI 2010/2955, 22.9.
[2] FPR 2010, SI 2010/2955, 22.15.

Powers of the court

5.62 The family court's overall discretion in respect of evidence within family proceedings is maintained by FPR 2010, SI 2010/2955, 22.1. This confirms that the court may control evidence in such proceedings by giving directions as to:

(a) the issues on which it requires evidence;
(b) the nature of the evidence it requires;
(c) the way that evidence is to be placed before the court.

The general rule

5.63 The general rule at FPR 2010, SI 2010/2955, 22.2 is that any fact to be proved by the evidence of witnesses is to be proved at a final hearing, by their oral evidence, or at any other hearing by their evidence in writing. Such evidence in writing will normally be by witness statement[1], unless the court, or any other rule or enactment requires otherwise[2].

At a hearing other than a final hearing a party can rely on matters set out in their application form, application notice or answer if verified by a statement of truth[3].

[1] FPR 2010, PD 22A.
[2] FPR 2010, SI 2010/2955, r 22.7(1).
[3] FPR 2010, SI 2010/2955, 22.7(2).

What is a witness statement?

5.64 FPR 2010, SI 2010/2955, 22.4(1) defines a witness statement as being a written statement signed by a person containing the evidence which that person would be allowed to give orally.

Such statement must comply with the detailed requirements of FPR 2010, PD 22A.

When should an affidavit be used as evidence?

5.65 FPR 2010, PD 22A, paras 1.4–1.6 confirms that an affidavit must be used where required by any rules or enactments, and in any application for alleged contempt of court. The court can direct that evidence be given by affidavit of its own volition or on the application of either party.

Format of the affidavit/statement

5.66 Extremely detailed guidance as to the layout and content of any affidavit/witness statement to be used in family proceedings is set out at FPR 2010, PD 22A, paras 3.1–4.5.

Where an affidavit, witness statement, or exhibit does not comply with the requirements of this practice direction or Pt 22 the court may refuse to admit it as evidence or to allow costs to be claimed in relation to its preparation[1]. Permission can, however, be sought from the court to file it defectively if the matter is proceeding.

It will be very important therefore for practitioners to be familiar with the detailed provision of FPR 2010, PD 22A, paras 3.1–4.5 as to the format of an affidavit/witness statement. This includes:

- description as to the heading of the document;
- information to be contained in the top right corner;
- paper to be used;
- must be single sided;
- numbered pages and paragraphs required;
- all numbers and dates in figures;
- reference to other documents in the margin or in bold text in the main body;
- expressed in the first person;
- it should identify statements made from the maker's own knowledge and those which are matters of information and belief – confirming the source of such information or belief;
- follow a chronological sequence (where convenient) with each paragraph confined to a distinct portion of the subject.

The standard wording to be used at the commencement of an affidavit or statement is set out at PD 22A, para 4.1 and how to refer to exhibits at para 4.5.

If evidence is being given in a professional or occupational capacity, such occupation must be stated together with the maker's employer's details and address.

Any alterations to a witness statement must be initialled by the maker and, in the case of an affidavit, also by the person before whom it is sworn.

If alterations have not been made in accordance with FPR 2010, PD 22A then the affidavit/statement may be filed or used in evidence only with the court's permission.

[1] FPR 2010, PD 22A, para 4.1.

Swearing of an affidavit or verifying a witness statement

5.67 The contents of the jurat to an affidavit in family proceedings are set out in FPR 2010, PD 22A, para 6.2. It must follow on immediately from the text and not be put on a separate page. The person before whom the oath is taken must print his or her name, qualification and address. Those people able to administer an oath and take an affidavit are listed at para 6.3.

5.67 General Procedural Provisions

An affidavit can be affirmed rather than sworn and the alternative wording is found at FPR 2010, PD 22A, para 15.1. All other rules apply to an affirmed affidavit in the same manner as to one which is sworn.

A witness statement must include a statement of truth in accordance with FPR 2010, SI 2010/2955, Pt 17 (see **5.53** et seq above).

Where an affidavit is sworn by a deponent who is unable to read or sign it, the person before whom it is made must certify in the jurat that:

(a)   the person read the affidavit to the deponent;
(b)   the deponent appeared to understand it; and
(c)   the deponent signed or made his mark in that person's presence.

Annex 1 to PD 22A sets out the format of that certificate.

FPR 2010, PD 22A repeats at para 7.4 the procedure set out in FPR 2010, PD 17A, paras 4.1–4.4 where a witness statement is being made by someone unable to read or sign that statement. Annex 2 to PD 22A sets out the form of certificate to be used with a witness statement in such circumstance.

Exhibiting documents

5.68 FPR 2010, PD 22A, paras 9.1–9.4 set out detailed instruction as to how documents should be exhibited to affidavits and statements. It is highly prescriptive and should be read carefully before attempting to exhibit documents to an affidavit or statement under the new rules.

Points of particular importance to note from these paragraphs are as follows:

- Documents used in conjunction with an affidavit/statement should be shown to and verified by the maker and remain separate from the affidavit/statement.
- They should be identified by a declaration from the person before whom it was made.
- The declaration should be headed with the proceedings in the same manner as the statement/affidavit.
- The numbering of the exhibits should run consecutively throughout and where more than one statement/affidavit is made by the same person not start again with each affidavit/statement.
- Where letters are exhibited they should be collected into chronological order, earliest on top and exhibited together numbered consecutively. The front page should state that the bundle consists of original letters and copies.
- Photocopies of other documents may be exhibited if the original can be made available for inspection by the parties before the hearing and by the court at the hearing.
- Court documents must not be exhibited.
- Where an exhibit contains more than one document, a front page should be attached setting out a list of the documents contained in the exhibit with their dates.
- Small items may be placed in a container which is appropriately marked.

- Where an exhibit contains more than one document it should not be stapled but should be securely fastened in such as way as reading is not hindered. The pages should be numbered consecutively at bottom centre.
- Typed copies of illegible documents should be included paginated with 'a' numbers.
- Where affidavits/statements and exhibits have become numerous they should be put in separate bundles and the pages numbered consecutively throughout.
- If bulk makes service of certain exhibits impracticable directions should be sought from the court.

Filing of affidavits and witness statements

5.69 If the court directs an affidavit or witness statement to be filed this must be done at the court where the matter is or will proceed. If it is in a foreign language it must be translated and have filed with it the foreign language affidavit/statement. The translator must sign the translation to certify it is accurate[1].

[1] FPR 2010, PD 22A, paras 8.1 and 8.2.

Service of witness statement for use at the final hearing

5.70 FPR 2010, SI 2010/2955, 22.5 confirms that the court may give directions as to the service of any witness statement of oral evidence on which a party intends to rely in relation to any issue to be decided at the final hearing. This includes directions as to the order of service and of filing.

If the witness statement is not served in accordance with such directions the witness may not be called to give oral evidence unless the court give permission[1].

If a witness statement has been served on which a party wishes to rely at final hearing, the witness must be called to give oral evidence unless the court directs otherwise or the statement is put in as hearsay evidence[2].

The witness statement is to stand as evidence in chief unless the court directs otherwise. A witness may, however, with the court's permission expand on his or her witness statement and given evidence in relation to new matters which have arisen since the witness statement was served[3].

If a party who has served a witness statement does not call that party to give evidence at the final hearing any other party may put the witness statement in as hearsay evidence[4].

[1] FPR 2010, SI 2010/2955, 22.10.
[2] FPR 2010, SI 2010/2955, 22.6(1) and see Part 23 at **5.79** et seq below.
[3] FPR 2010, SI 2010/2955, 22.6(3), (4).
[4] FPR 2010, SI 2010/2955, 22.6(5).

5.71 General Procedural Provisions

Cross examination

5.71 Where at a hearing other than a final hearing evidence is given in writing, any party may apply for permission to cross examine the person giving the evidence. If the court grants permission but the person does not attend to be questioned, FPR 2010, SI 2010/2955, 22.8 provides that the person's evidence may not be used unless the court directs otherwise.

At a final hearing a witness can be cross examined on any aspect of the witness statement – whether referred to in evidence in chief or not[1].

[1] FPR 2010, 22.11.

Witness summary

5.72 A witness summary is a summary of the evidence, if known, which would otherwise be included in a witness statement, or the matters about which the party serving the witness summary proposes to question the witness[1].

Permission to serve a witness summary can be obtained by a party who is required to serve a witness statement but is unable to obtain one[2].

[1] FPR 2010, SI 2010/2955, 22.9(2).
[2] FPR 2010, SI 2010/2955, 22.9(1).

Notice to admit facts

5.73 Under FPR 2010, SI 2010/2955, 22.15, a party may serve notice on another party requiring him or her to admit facts, or part of the case, specified in the notice. It must be served no later than 21 days before the final hearing.

Notice to admit or procure documents

5.74 Unless notice is served by a party, that he or she wishes a document to be proved at final hearing, he/she is deemed to admit the authenticity of any document disclosed to him/her[1].

A notice to prove must be served by the latest date for serving witness statements, or within seven days beginning with the date of service of the document, whichever is later.

[1] FPR 2010, SI 2010/2955, 22.16.

Use of witness statements in other proceedings

5.75 A witness statement in FPR 2010, SI 2010/2955, Pt 7 or Pt 9 proceedings may be used only for the purpose of the proceedings in which it is served unless:

- the court directs otherwise; or
- the witness statement has been put in evidence at a hearing in public[1].

[1] FPR 2010, SI 2010/2955, 22.20.

Witness statements in Pt 7 proceedings

5.76 The court can in limited circumstances, as specified by FPR 2010, SI 2010/2955, 22.19(4), direct that a witness statement which stands as evidence in chief at a final hearing under FPR 2010, SI 2010/2955, Pt 7 not be open to inspection.

Evidence by video link

5.77 FPR 2010, SI 2010/2955, 22.3 gives the court power to allow evidence by video link or other means.

Annex 3 to FPR 2010, PD 22A then sets out very detailed guidance as to the use of video conferencing (VCF) in the family courts. This must be read carefully by any practitioner involved in a case in which VCF is to be used, particularly if they have made the request for such facility and, therefore, have responsibility for the practical arrangements.

The guidance covers situations where the VCF equipment is in the courtroom but also where it is in a separate conference room/studio, potentially at a remote location.

Much of the guidance is common sense but the following points should in particular be noted:

- the objective is to make the VCF session as close as possible to the usual practice in court;
- the court's permission is required for any part of any proceedings to be dealt with in this way;
- before seeking a direction for the use of VCF the applicant should liaise with the appropriate court officers as to the availability of the equipment on a particular day;
- if all parties consent to a direction for the use of VCF permission from the court can be sought by letter, fax or email;
- ordinarily the party seeking permission will be responsible for practical arrangements;
- in the first instance, subject to contrary agreement or direction, all costs associated with the VCF will be the responsibility of the arranging party;
- the site of the VCF should be the court room if possible;
- if a remote site is to be used, details should be provided to the listing officer or other appropriate court officer;
- it is recommended that all parties should arrive at their respective VCF sites about 20 minutes prior to transmission starting;
- the judge will determine who is to sit where;
- if appropriate, a reasonable number of members of the public should be able to attend at the remote site;
- if possible, the arranging party should ensure the Royal coat of arms is placed above the judge's seat if the VCF is to take place at a remote site;
- the arranging party must ensure that the equipment is such that the evidence can be recorded;
- equipment should be set up and tested before the hearing begins;
- a back-up recording may be appropriate;

5.77 General Procedural Provisions

- if evidence is being given from abroad it should be considered that some countries may require the oath/affirmation to be taken in accordance with local customs rather than English requirements. The arranging party should make the necessary enquiry in this regard;
- the arranging party must ensure the necessary holy book is available at the site;
- consideration will need to be given as to what documents need to be available for the witness during the VCF and usually a bundle of documents sent by the arranging party to the remote site;
- if additional documents are introduced during the hearing the arranging party must ensure there is a facility for these to be transmitted to the remote site;
- the procedure will be controlled by the judge who will probably wish to introduce himself or herself and the advocates to the witness. He may want to give directions as to seating at the remote site;
- during examination the witness must be able to see the legal representative asking the questions and any other person making any statements in regard to their evidence;
- it will usually be most practical for everyone to remain seated throughout the transmission.

The Annex setting out this guidance runs to four pages and must be read carefully and in full if the issue of evidence being given in this format arises in a case in which a practitioner is involved.

Summary

5.78 The detailed provision contained in FPR 2010, SI 2010/2955, Pt 22 in respect of written and video evidence requires careful scrutiny to ensure compliance and avoid evidence being deemed inadmissible.

The language of the rule and practice direction is very practical and clear and should assist practitioners in preparing in particular witness statements and affidavits.

Part 23 – Miscellaneous rules about evidence

5.79 FPR 2010, SI 2010/2955, Pt 23 sets out the rules in respect of discrete issues of evidence not covered elsewhere in the rules, and is taken almost entirely from the CPR 1998.

Hearsay evidence

5.80 Where a party intends to rely on hearsay evidence at the *final hearing*, either by a witness giving oral evidence, or in a witness statement of someone not attending court, a witness statement must be filed on the other parties in accordance with the court's directions[1] to comply with the Civil Evidence Act 1985.

If the witness is not to attend the other party must be informed when the witness statement is served as to the reasons why the witness will not be called[2].

In all other cases compliance with the Civil Evidence Act 1985 is achieved, where a party intends to rely on hearsay evidence at a final hearing, by the serving of a hearsay notice on the other parties identifying the hearsay and why the witness will not be called. This notice must be filed no later than the latest date for serving witness statements[3].

There is no duty to give notice of intention to rely on hearsay evidence:

(a) at hearings other than final hearings;
(b) where the requirement is excluded by a practice direction[4].

If a party proposes to rely on hearsay evidence but does not intend to call the witness the other party can apply to the court to call the maker of the statement to be cross examined[5]. Such application must be made within 14 days beginning with the date a notice of intention to rely on hearsay evidence was served[6].

If a party intends to rely on hearsay evidence but is not calling the maker of the statement, the other party may call evidence to attack the credibility of the person who made the original statement.

The other party must give notice of their intention to the person intending to rely on the hearsay within 14 days after the hearsay notice was served.

[1] FPR 2010, SI 2010/2955, 23.2.
[2] FPR 2010, SI 2010/2955, 23.2(2).
[3] FPR 2010, SI 2010/2955, 23.2(3), (4).
[4] FPR 2010, SI 2010/2955, 23.3.
[5] FPR 2010, SI 2010/2955, 23.4(1).
[6] FPR 2010, SI 2010/2955, 23.4(2).

Use of plans, photographs, models etc as evidence

5.81 The provision at FPR 2010, SI 2010/2955, 23.6 is intended to cover use of such items in evidence where they are not contained in a witness statement, affidavit or expert's bundles or is not to be given orally at the final hearing.

FPR 2010, 23.6(3) confirms that such evidence can't be relied upon at a final hearing unless it has been served on the other party or an invitation to inspect the original been served, not later than the latest date for serving witness statements if it is to be used as evidence of any fact.

Where the evidence forms part of expert evidence, however, it must be served when the expert's report is served[1].

If the evidence is being produced for any reason other than as part of factual or expert evidence it must be served at least 21 days before the hearing at which it will be relied upon[2].

The court can direct that every other party be given the opportunity to inspect the evidence and to agree to its admission without further proof.

[1] FPR 2010, SI 2010/2955, 23.6(6).

5.81 *General Procedural Provisions*

[2] FPR 2010, SI 2010/2955, 23.6(7).

Evidence on foreign law

5.82 FPR 2010, SI 2010/2955, 23.7 set out the procedure to be followed regarding questions of foreign law.

If a party wishes to put in evidence a finding on a question of foreign law that party must give any other party notice not later that the latest date for serving witness statements or not less than 21 days the hearing, if there are no witness statements.

The notice must specify the question on which the finding was made and enclose a copy of a document where it is reported or recorded.

Evidence of consent of trustee to act

5.83 Within FPR 2010, SI 2010/2955, Pt 9 proceedings a document containing the written consent of a person to act as trustee and to bear that person's signature verified by some other person is evidence of such consent in accordance with FPR 2010, SI 2010/2955, 23.8.

Evidence in magistrates' court

5.84 FPR 2010, SI 2010/2955, 23.9 requires that the justice's clerk or the court is to keep a note of the substance of oral evidence given at directions appointments or hearings of any proceedings.

Part 24 – Witnesses, depositions generally and taking of evidence in EU Member States

Chapter 1 – Witnesses and depositions

5.85 FPR 2010, SI 2010/2955, Pt 24, Ch 1 deals with the circumstances in which a person can be required to attend at court to give evidence or to produce a document and also for a party to obtain evidence for use at a hearing.

The rules in respect of witness summons are now incorporated in full in the family rules.

The possibility of obtaining evidence by deposition is introduced which enables a witness to be examined in advance of a hearing. The written evidence taken of the examination can then be used at a hearing, if the correct procedures are followed.

WITNESS SUMMONSES

5.86 A witness summons is a document issued by the court *requiring* a witness to:

- attend at court to give evidence; or
- produce documents to the court[1]; or

- do both,

on either a date fixed or such date as the court may direct.

FPR 2010, PD 24A, para 1.2 confirms that two copies of the witness summons are to be filed with court for sealing with one retained on the court file. They must be issued at either the court where the case is proceeding or where the hearing in question is to be heard[2].

A separate witness summons is required for each witness[3].

The court's permission is not required to obtain a witness summons unless a party wishes[4]:

- a summons to be issued less than seven days before the date of the final hearing; or
- to have a witness attend or produce documents on a date other than that fixed for final hearing; or
- to have a witness attend at or produce documents for a hearing other than a final hearing.

Generally, a witness summons is binding if served at least seven days before the date on which the witness is required to attend at court, although that can be reduced by the court[5].

The party issuing the summons will be responsible for its service unless the court is asked by him or her in writing at the time of issue to serve it instead[6]. The exception is in proceedings to which FPR 2010, SI 2010/2955, Pt 14 applies where the court will serve unless it directs otherwise[7].

If the court is to serve then the money to be offered to the witness must be deposited with the court office[8].

[1] FPR 2010, SI 2010/2955, 24.2(1).
[2] FPR 2010, SI 2010/2955, 24.2(3).
[3] FPR 2010, SI 2010/2955, 24.2(3).
[4] FPR 2010, SI 2010/2955, 24.2(3).
[5] FPR 2010, SI 2010/2955, 24.4(1), (2).
[6] FPR 2010, SI 2010/2955, 24.5(1).
[7] FPR 2010, SI 2010/2955, 24.5(2).
[8] FPR 2010, SI 2010/2955, 24.5(3).

TRAVELLING EXPENSES AND COMPENSATION FOR LOSS OF TIME

5.87 FPR 2010, SI 2010/2955, 24.6 states that the witness *must* be offered or paid, at the time the summons is served, a sum reasonably sufficient to cover travel to and from court and compensation for loss of time.

FPR 2010, PD 24A confirms that the compensation for loss of time should be such sum as the witness will lose as a result of attendance at court in answer to the witness summons. This is to be based on the sums payable to witnesses attending the Crown Court[1].

[1] Fixed pursuant to Prosecution of Offences Act 1985 and Costs in Criminal Cases (General) Regulations 1986, SI 1986/1335.

5.88 *General Procedural Provisions*

Magistrates' court

5.88 FPR 2010, PD 24A states at paras 2.1 and 2.2 that an application for issue of a summons or warrant is to be made in writing to the court officer by the applicant or his legal representative.

Depositions

5.89 A party may now apply, pursuant to FPR 2010, SI 2010/2955, 24.7, for a person to be examined before the hearing takes place. Such evidence is referred to as a 'deposition' and the person giving the evidence a 'deponent'. It is a concept taken directly from the CPR 1998.

The deponent will be examined on oath before a judge, examiner of the court or other person appointed by the court[1].

[1] FPR 2010, 24.7(3).

Order for examination

5.90 Under FPR 2010, SI 2010/2955, 24.7(4) and (5), the order for examination must state the time, date and place of the examination and can require the production of any documentation. At the time of service of the order for examination the deponent must be offered or paid a sum reasonably sufficient to cover travel to and from the place of examination and by way of compensation for loss of time.

At the time of making the order for examination the court can also order the party who obtained the order to serve a witness statement or summary in relation to the evidence to be given by the deponent[1].

[1] FPR 2010, 24.7(7).

Examination

5.91 The examination should be conducted in the same way as if the witness were giving evidence at a final hearing. If all parties are present and consent, a person not named in the order for examination can be examined[1].

The examination will be in private unless this is not appropriate[2] and FPR 2010, PD 24A contains further practical steps in respect of the hearing and format of the deposition.

The court or examiner may permit the deposition to be recorded on audio or video tape. It must also, always be recorded in writing by the examiner or competent shorthand writer/stenographer. It must contain, as nearly as may be, the statement of the deponent and the examiner may record word for word any particular questions and answers which appear to have special importance[3].

If the deponent objects to answering any questions the examiner must record in the deposition the question, grounds for objection and any answer given.

The examiner must also record his or her view as to the validity of the objection[4].

Any documents or exhibits to a deposition should have an identifying number or letter and be preserved by the party or legal representative who obtained the order for examination[5].

The examiner may put any question to the deponent as to the meaning of his answers or any other matters arising in the course of the examination[6].

If the deponent:

- fails to attend; or
- refuses to answer to be sworn; or
- refuses to answer any lawful question; or
- refuses to produce any document,

then FPR 2010, 24.9 states that the examiner must sign a certificate to be filed by the party requiring the deposition. The certificate can include comment by the examiner as to the conduct of the deponent[7] or anyone at the examination. The party who obtained the order can apply for an order requiring the deponent attend, be sworn or answer a particular question. Such application can be made without notice. The court can order the person against whom the order is made to pay any costs resulting from his or her failure or refusal[8].

A person who wilfully refuses to obey such an order may be proceeded against for contempt[9].

The deposition must be:

(a) signed by the examiner with any amendments initialled by the examiner and deponent;
(b) endorsed by the examiner with statement of time occupied by the examination;
(c) record any refusal by the deponent to sign the deposition, with their reasons.

A copy of the deposition must be sent by the examiner to the person who obtained the order for examination and to the court where the case is proceeding. The court will give directions as to service on the other parties[10].

[1] FPR 2010, SI 2010/2955, 24.8(1), (2).
[2] FPR 2010, SI 2010/2955, 24.8(4).
[3] FPR 2010, PD 24A, paras 4.3 and 4.4.
[4] FPR 2010, PD 24A, para 4.5.
[5] FPR 2010, PD 24A, para 4.6.
[6] FPR 2010, PD 24A, para 4.7.
[7] FPR 2010, PD 24A, para 4.8.
[8] FPR 2010, SI 2010/2955, 24.9(4).
[9] FPR 2010, PD 24A, para 4.11.
[10] FPR 2010, SI 2010/2955, 24.8(7).

Use of deposition at hearing

5.92 Unless the court directs otherwise, a deposition obtained under FPR 2010, SI 2010/2955, 24.10 may be given in evidence.

5.92 *General Procedural Provisions*

A party intending to rely on a deposition must file a notice of intention on the court who will give direction about serving notice on every other party. Such notice must be filed at least 21 days before the date fixed for the hearing[1]. The court may still require a deponent to attend the hearing to give evidence orally[2].

Where a deposition has been obtained for the purposes of FPR 2010, SI 2010/2955, Pt 7 or Pt 9 proceedings for the purpose of any hearing other than the final hearing, the deposition may only be used for the purpose of those proceedings in which the order was made[3].

It may, however, be used for some other purpose[4]:

- by the party examined;
- if the party examined agrees; or
- if the court gives permission.

[1] FPR 2010, SI 2010/2955, 24.10(3).
[2] FPR 2010, SI 2010/2955, 24.10(4).
[3] FPR 2010, SI 2010/2955, 24.11(1), (2).
[4] FPR 2010, SI 2010/2955, 24.11(3).

Examiners of the court

5.93 FPR 2010, SI 2010/2955, 24.14 confirms that these will be appointed by the Lord Chancellor and have been practising barristers or solicitor-advocates for not less than three years.

FPR 2010, 24.13(1) and (2) states that the examiner of the court may charge a fee for the examination and need not send the deposition to court unless the fee is paid by the party who obtained the order for examination. Non payment of fees can be reported by the examiner to the court who may order the party who obtained the order to deposit in court a specified sum in respect of such fees[1].

[1] FPR 2010, 24.13(5).

DEPOSITION FROM A PERSON OUT OF THE JURISDICTION

5.94 The provision to be applied in respect of deposition evidence from a person outside the jurisdiction depends on whether the person is, or is not, in a Member State[1].

[1] As defined in the Council Regulation (EC) No 1206/2001 of 28 May 2001 on cooperation between the courts of the Member States in the taking of evidence in civil or commercial matters.

Non Member State

5.95 FPR 2010, SI 2010/2955, 24.12 applies where the person is not residing in a Member State. This confirms that a party can apply for an order that the High Court issue a letter of request to a judicial authority in the country where the proposed deponent lives requesting that authority to take, or arrange to have taken, that person's evidence. FPR 2010, 24.12(4) confirms that the High Court can make such an order under this rule in respect of county court proceedings.

FPR 2010, PD 24A confirms that when applying for such an order the party must file the documents set out in FPR 2010, 24.12(7) being:

- a draft letter of request in the form set out in annex A to FPR 2010, PD 24A;
- a statement of issues relevant to the proceedings;
- a list of questions or the subject of the questions to be put to the proposed deponent;
- a translation, if appropriate, of any of the above;
- an undertaking to be responsible for the expenses of the Secretary of State;
- draft order.

The address for filing of these documents is set out at FPR 2010, PD 24A, para 5.4.

if the government of a country allows a person to be appointed, the High Court may make an order appointing a special examiner for that purpose[1]. PD 24A, para 5.8 confirms that such person may be the British Consul or the Consul-General or his deputy.

The provisions for taking of depositions as set out in FPR 2010, PD 24A, paras 4.1–4.12 apply in the same way to depositions to be taken out of the jurisdiction[2].

[1] FPR 2010, SI 2010/2955, 24.12(5).
[2] FPR 2010, PD 24A, para 5.9.

Member State

5.96 The rules which apply where the deponent is located in a Member State (excluding Denmark) are based on the Taking of Evidence Regulation (see **5.94** above).

FPR 2010, SI 2010/2955, 24.16(2) states that the court in this jurisdiction may order the issue of a request to a designated court in the Member State where the proposed deponent is located. The form of that request is to be as prescribed in Annex A to FPR 2010, PD 24A.

Each Member State has prepared a list of courts competent to take evidence in accordance with the Taking of Evidence Regulation and the designated court for the purposes of FPR 2010, 24.16 will be the one from that list which is most appropriate to the application in hand[1].

Each Member State must under the Taking of Evidence Regulation nominate a central body responsible for:

- supplying information to the courts;
- seeking solutions if any difficulties arise;
- forwarding in exceptional cases requests to the competent court.

5.96 *General Procedural Provisions*

When applying for an order pursuant to FPR 2010, 24.16 the party applying must file:

- a draft form of request in the form set out at Annex A to FPR 2010, PD 24A;
- a translation of the form (unless English is the official language or a language which the Member State accepts);
- an undertaking to be responsible for costs sought by the court in the Member State regarding:
  (a) experts, interpreters and the use of special procedures or technology; and
  (b) court's expenses.

If the court grants the order the request will be sent direct to the designated court.

Article 17 of the Taking of Evidence Regulation permits the court where proceedings are taking place to take evidence directly from the deponent if the evidence is given voluntarily. The court can make an order for submission in accordance with that article pursuant to FPR 2010, 24.16(5). The application should be made in the form annexed to the Regulation and be accompanied by a translation and undertaking to be responsible for court expenses.

[1] FPR 2010, PD 24A, para 7.2.

Summary

5.97 The clarity with which the procedure for serving a witness summons is set out should make this process less daunting for practitioners.

The option to obtain evidence by deposition is a very exciting one with family proceedings. It could be extremely useful in cases with large numbers of witnesses where it can prove difficult to schedule a hearing date and also when witnesses live a long distance away, or indeed abroad.

Practitioners will find the detail of the provision for obtaining and using depositions in evidence very helpful and reassuring.

EXPERTS AND ASSESSORS – PT 25

Overview

5.98 Part 25 itself largely replicates CPR Pt 35. The provisions are cross-referenced in the table below.

By contrast, the practice direction, FPR 2010, PD 25A – Experts and Assessors in Family Proceedings, provides detailed changes to practice in respect of the instruction of experts and assessors.

Comparison table

5.99 The table below shows how CPR Pt 35 has been incorporated into the new FPR 2010, SI 2010/2955, Pt 25:

Experts and assessors – Pt 25 5.99

CPR 1998		*FPR 2010*	
35.1	Duty to restrict expert evidence.	25.1	Same provision.
35.2	Interpretation and definitions.	25.2	Identical, save that an 'expert' in this Part does not include:
			(i) a person who is within a prescribed description for the purposes of the Adoption and Children Act 2002, s 94(1); or
			(ii) an officer of the Service or a Welsh family proceedings officer when acting in that capacity.
35.3	Overriding duty of experts to the court.	25.3	Identical.
35.4	Court's power to restrict expert evidence. NB – r 35.4(3A) did not apply to family proceedings in any event.	25.4	Identical.
35.5	Requirement for expert evidence to be given in a written report. NB – r 35.5(2) did not apply to family proceedings by virtue of FPR 1991, r 2.61C.	25.5	Identical, save for the insertion of a new provision at 25.5(2) – the court will not direct an expert to attend a hearing unless it is necessary to do so in the interests of justice.
35.6	Written questions to experts	25.6	Identical, save that r 25.6(2)(b) provides that questions must be put within 10 days beginning with the date on which the expert's report was served. By contrast, under CPR Pt 35 the deadline was 28 days. By virtue of r 25.6(2)(c)(i) the 10-day deadline will not apply if the court directs otherwise. Accordingly, in practice it will be sensible to seek a direction for a longer deadline for questions to be put to the expert.
35.7	Court's power to direct that evidence is to be given by a single joint expert.	25.7	Identical.

107

5.99 General Procedural Provisions

CPR 1998		FPR 2010	
35.8	Instructions to a single joint expert. NB – by virtue of FPR 1991, r 2.61C, r 35.8(4)(b) did not apply to family proceedings.	25.8	Same as CPR 35.8 with the exception of paras (1) and (2) which are replaced with the following:
	Under r 35.8(1) any relevant party was entitled to give instructions to the expert. Under r 35.8(2), when a party gives instructions to the expert, that party must, at the same time, send a copy to the other relevant party.	25.8(1)	Where the court gives a direction for a single joint expert to be used, the instructions are to be contained in a jointly agreed letter, unless the court directs otherwise.
		25.8(2)	Where the instructions are to be contained in a jointly agreed letter, in default of agreement, the instructions may be determined by the court on the written request of any relevant party copied to the other relevant parties.
		25.8(3)	Where the court permits the relevant parties to give separate instructions to a single joint expert, each instructing party must, when giving instructions to the expert, at the same time send a copy of the instructions to the other relevant parties.
35.9	Power of court to direct the party to provide information.	25.9	Identical, save for inclusion of new r 2.59(2) which relates to proceedings under FPR 2010, SI 2010/2955, Pt 14 (Applications in Adoptions, Placement and Related Proceedings) and which provides that a court officer will send a copy of the document to the other party.
35.10	Contents of the report.	25.10	The basic rule is the same save that:

Experts and assessors – Pt 25 5.100

CPR 1998		FPR 2010	
			– by virtue of r 25.10(1), an expert's report must comply with the extensive requirements set out in the new PD 25A and which is considered in detail at **5.100** below.
			– under r 25.10(3) – the instructions to the expert are not privileged against disclosure. Disclosure is considered in detail in FPR 2010, SI 2010/2955, 21.1.
35.11	Use by one party of expert's report disclosed by another.	25.11	Identical.
35.12	Discussions between experts.	25.12	Identical, save that r 25.12(4) and (5) are not carried over to the new rules.
35.13	Consequences of failure to disclose expert's report.		No equivalent rule appears in the new FPR.
35.14	Expert's right to ask the court for directions.	25.13	Identical.
35.15	Assessors.	25.14	Identical, save for the provisions relating to the payment of an assessor at paragraph (5).

Practice Direction 25A – Experts and assessors in family proceedings

5.100 The new practice direction provides extensive and detailed new provisions relating to the instruction of experts and is broken down as follows:

- introduction;
- general matters, including pre-application and instruction of experts and emergency and urgent cases;
- duties of experts, including the contents of the expert's report;
- proceedings relating to children;
- proceedings other than those relating to children;
- the court's control of expert evidence, including questions to experts and experts' discussion or meetings;
- arrangements for experts to give evidence and action to be taken after the final hearing;
- finally, there is an Annex drafted by the Family Justice Council setting out suggested questions to experts in certain Children Act 1989 proceedings.

Throughout the practice direction reference is made to it being a 'guidance'.

5.101 *General Procedural Provisions*

Introduction

5.101 FPR 2010, PD 25A incorporates and supersedes the Practice Direction on Experts in Family Proceedings Relating to Children – 1 April 2008 and all other relevant guidance.

Paragraph 1.2 specifically states that the phrase 'proceedings relating to children' is merely a description and is not a legal term of art. In the guidance the phrase covers:

- placement and adoption proceedings;
- family proceedings which relate to the inherent jurisdiction of the High Court with respect to children;
- family proceedings brought under the Children Act 1989 in any family court;
- family proceedings brought in the High Court and county court and otherwise relate wholly or mainly to the maintenance or upbringing of a minor;

Paragraph 1.3 states that the aim of the guidance is:

- to provide the court with early information to determine whether expert evidence is required
- To help the court and the parties narrow the issues and encourage agreement where possible
- To enable the parties and the court to get expert evidence on an issue that is not within the expertise of the court
- To encourage early identification of questions that need to be answered by an expert
- To encourage full and frank information between the parties, the court and the expert.

Permission to instruct an expert

5.102 FPR 2010, PD 25A, para 1.5 – by virtue of FPR 2010, SI 2010/2955, 25.4(1) the court's permission is required to call an expert or put in evidence an expert's report; however, in relation to children proceedings, the court's permission is also required to instruct an expert[1].

As stated at PD 25A, para 1.6, particular care must be taken with regard to the disclosure of information in proceedings concerning children. Disclosure of information and documents relating to such proceedings may amount to a contempt of court. Information may only be communicated to an expert in accordance with paras 1.7 and 1.8 or whose instruction by a party has been permitted by the court. In children proceedings to which FPR 2010, SI 2010/2955, Pt 12 applies, the court's permission is required for a child to be medically or psychiatrically examined or otherwise assessed. Where the court's permission has not been given, no evidence arising out of such an examination may be adduced without the court's permission.

In accordance with PD 25A, para 1.8, before permission is sought from the court to instruct an expert in proceedings relating to children, it will be necessary to make enquiries of the expert in order to provide the court with information to enable the court to decide whether to give permission. In practice, enquiries may need to be made of more than one potential expert and that will in turn require the potential expert to be given sufficient information to enable them to assess whether they are in a position to accept the instructions. Such preliminary enquiries and the disclosure of information about the case which is a necessary part of such enquiries will not require the court's permission and will therefore not amount to a contempt of court.

[1] FPR 2010, SI 2010/2955, 12.74(1).

When should the court be asked for permission?

5.103 By reference to FPR 2010, PD 25A, 1.11, any application for permission to instruct an expert should be raised with the court and with the other parties as soon as possible. This will normally mean the following:

- in public law proceedings under Children Act 1989 – by or at the Case Management Conference[1];
- in private law proceedings under Children Act 1989 – by or at the First Hearing Dispute Resolution Appointment[2];
- in placement and adoption proceedings – by or at the First Directions Appointment[3];
- in financial proceedings – by or at the First Appointment[4];
- In defended matrimonial and civil partnership proceedings – by or at the Case Management Hearing[5];

By virtue of FPR 2010, PD 25A, para 2.2, the guidance does not apply to proceedings issued before 6 April 2011, but in such proceedings the court may direct that the guidance will apply either wholly or partly.

[1] FPR 2010, SI 2010/2955, 12.25.
[2] FPR 2010, SI 2010/2955, 12.31.
[3] FPR 2010, SI 2010/2955, 14.8.
[4] FPR 2010, SI 2010/2955, 9.15.
[5] FPR 2010, SI 2010/2955, 7.20 and 7.22.

Pre-application instruction of experts

5.104 Under FPR 2010, PD 25A, para 2.3, if experts' reports are commissioned prior to the issued proceedings, it should be made clear to that expert that he or she may in due course be reporting to the court and therefore should consider themselves bound by the guidance. For example, a prospective party to family proceedings relating to children should always state in a letter of instruction whether the request is within proceedings or pre-proceedings. In any event, the letter should conform to the principles set out in the guidance.

Emergency and urgent cases

5.105 Under FPR 2010, PD 25A, para 2.4, in emergency or urgent cases a party may wish to call expert evidence without having complied with all or any part of the guidance. In those circumstances, the party wishing to call the expert evidence must apply forthwith to the court, where possible, on notice to the other parties, for directions as to the future steps to be taken in respect of the expert evidence in question.

5.106 *General Procedural Provisions*

Service of orders upon experts

5.106 Under FPR 2010, PD 25A, para 2.5, where an order or direction requires an act to be done by an expert, or otherwise affects an expert, the party instructing that expert, or in the case of a jointly instructed expert, the lead solicitor, must serve a copy of the order or direction on the expert forthwith upon receiving the order from the court.

Adults who may be protected parties

5.107 FPR 2010, PD 25A, paras 2.6–2.9 deal with this issue. Under para 2.8, where the adult is a protected party, that party's representative should be involved in any instruction of an expert, including the instruction of an expert to assess whether the adult is competent to give evidence.

Paragraph 2.10 deals with children who are a party to the proceedings and nearing the age of 18 and who may be considered likely to lack capacity to conduct the proceedings upon reaching 18.

The duties of experts

5.108 The overriding duty of the expert set out in FPR 2010, SI 2010/2955, 25.3 is re-stated at FPR 2010, PD 25A, para 3.1 of the guidance.

By virtue of para 3.2, an expert shall have regard to the following duties:

(a) to assist the court in accordance with the overriding duty;
(b) to provide advice to the court which conforms to the best practice of the expert's profession;
(c) to provide an opinion which is independent of the parties;
(d) to confine the opinion to questions that are within the expert's expertise and material to the issues between the parties;
(e) where a question falls outside of the expert's expertise, to state at the earliest opportunity that this is the case and to volunteer an opinion as to whether another expert is required to deal with that issue;
(f) in expressing an opinion, to take into consideration all of the material facts which may include factors arising from ethnic, cultural, religious or linguistic contexts;
(g) to inform those instructing the expert immediately of any change in the opinion and of the reason for the change.

Content of the report

5.109 FPR 2010, PD 25A, para 3.3 sets out what should be included in the report. Paragraph 3.3 also emphasises that the report must be addressed to the court and filed in accordance with the court's timetable. Paragraph 3.3 provides that the report must contain the following:

(a) Details of the expert's qualifications and experience.

Experts and assessors – Pt 25 5.109

(b) A statement identifying the documents containing the material instructions and the substance of any oral instructions. As far as it is necessary to explain any opinions or conclusions in the report, a summary of the facts and instructions which are material to the conclusions and opinions expressed.
(c) State who carried out any test, examination or interview which has been used for the report. The expert should also state whether or not the test, examination or interview was carried out under the expert's supervision.
(d) Give details of the qualifications of any person who carried out the test, examination or interview.
(e) In expressing an opinion to the court, the expert must:
  (i) take into consideration all of the material facts and any other material the expert has relied upon;
  (ii) describe their own professional risk assessment process, highlighting any factual assumptions and any unusual or contradictory features of the case;
  (iii) indicate whether any proposition in the report is an hypothesis or an opinion deduced with a tested technique or research accepted as a consensus in the scientific community;
  (iv) if appropriate, indicate whether the opinion is provisional or qualified and stating the reason for that. In such circumstances, the expert must identify what further information is required to give an opinion without qualification.
(f) Where there is a range of opinion on any question to be answered, the expert must:
  (i) summarise the range of the opinion;
  (ii) identify and explain within the range of opinions any unknown element;
  (iii) give reasons for any opinion expressed. The use of a balance sheet to weigh up the factors which support or undermine the opinion can be of great assistance to the court.
(g) The report must contain a summary of the expert's conclusions and opinions.
(h) The report must contain a statement from the expert including the following:
  (i) the expert has no conflict of interest, otherwise than as identified in the report;
  (ii) the expert does not consider that any such interest disclosed affects his or her suitability as an expert witness;
  (iii) the expert will advise the instructing party if between the date of the report and the final hearing there is any change of circumstances which affects his or her answers regarding any conflict of interest;
  (iv) the expert understands his or her duty to the court and has complied with that duty;
  (v) the expert is aware of the requirements of FPR 2010, SI 2010/2955, Pt 25 and the practice direction.
(i) Finally, the statement of truth to be included in the expert's report must be as follows:

5.110 *General Procedural Provisions*

> 'I confirm that I have made clear which facts and matters referred to in this report are within my own knowledge and which are not. Those that are within my own knowledge I confirm to be true. The opinions I have expressed represent my true and complete professional opinions on the matters to which they refer'.

Proceedings relating to children

5.110 Extensive guidance is given in relation to the instruction of experts in proceedings relating to children at FPR 2010, PD 25A, paras 4.1–4.7.

INITIAL ENQUIRIES OF PROPOSED EXPERTS

5.111 FPR 2010, PD 25A, para 4.1 deals with preliminary enquiries of the expert before he or she is instructed. The paragraph emphasises that an approach must be made to the proposed experts in good time for the information requested to be available for the relevant hearing or for the advocates' meeting or discussion prior to the relevant hearing. The expert shall be approached with the following information:

(a) the nature of the proceedings and issues likely to require determination by the court;
(b) the questions about which the expert is to be asked to give an opinion;
(c) the date when the court is to be asked to give permission for the instruction. In the unusual event that permission has already been given, the date and details of that order must be given to the proposed expert;
(d) whether permission is to be asked of the court for the instruction of another expert in the same or any related field;
(e) the volume of reading which the expert will have to undertake;
(f) whether permission has been applied for or given for the expert to examine a child;
(g) whether or not it will be necessary for the expert to conduct interviews. if so, with whom;
(h) the likely timetable of legal and social work steps;
(i) in care and supervision proceedings, any dates in the timetable for the child which would be relevant to the proposed timetable for the assessment;
(j) when the expert's report is likely to be required;
(k) whether any date has been fixed by the court for a hearing at which the expert will be required to give evidence and whether it will be possible for the expert to give that evidence by telephone conference or video link;
(l) the possibility of the expert making representations to the court about being named or otherwise identified in any public judgment given by the court.

There needs to be proper co-ordination between the court and the expert when drawing up the case management timetable. That is particularly the case where an expert carries out forensic work which is an adjunct to his or her main professional duties.

Experts' response to enquiries

5.112 FPR 2010, PD 25A, para 4.2 deals with the expert's response to preliminary enquiries. In good time for the relevant hearing, advocates' meeting or discussion, where one is to take place before the relevant hearing, the solicitors intending to instruct the expert shall obtain confirmation of the following from the expert:

(a) acceptance of the proposed instructions will not involve any conflict of interest;
(b) the work is within the expert's expertise;
(c) the expert is available to do the work within the suggested timescale;
(d) when the expert is available to give evidence and any dates or times to avoid;
(e) the expert's costs including hourly or other charging rates and the likely hours to be spent by the expert; and
(f) any representations which the expert may wish to make to the court about being named or otherwise identified in any public judgment.

Where the parties have not agreed upon the appointment of a single joint expert, they should obtain the above confirmation set out at points (a)–(f) above in respect of all the experts whom they intend to put to the court for the purpose of FPR 2010, SI 2010/2955, 25.7(2)(a).

Proposal to instruct an expert – information to be filed and served

5.113 Under FPR 2010, PD 25A, para 4.3, any party who proposes to seek permission from the court to instruct an expert shall file and serve a written proposal by 11.00am on the business day before the relevant hearing. That proposal must include the following detail:

(a) name, discipline, qualifications and expertise of the expert. A CV should be provided where possible;
(b) the expert's availability to undertake the work;
(c) the relevance of the expert evidence to the issues in the proceedings and the specific questions upon which it is proposed that the expert should give an opinion;
(d) the proposed timetable for the report;
(e) the responsibility for instruction;
(f) whether or not the expert evidence can properly be obtained by the joint instruction of the expert by two or more of the parties;
(g) whether the expert evidence can properly be obtained by only one party;
(h) why the expert evidence proposed cannot be given by Social Services undertaking a core assessment with the Children's Guardian in accordance with their respective statutory duties;
(i) the likely cost of the report on an hourly or other charging basis. Where possible, the expert's terms of instruction should be made available to the court; and

5.113 *General Procedural Provisions*

(j) the proposed apportionment of any jointly instructed expert's fee, including when it needs to be paid and, if applicable, whether public funding has been approved.

DRAFT ORDER

5.114 As well as filing and serving the written proposal in accordance with FPR 2010, PD 25A, para 4.3 above, by virtue of para 4.4, by 11.00am on the business day before the relevant hearing, any party proposing to instruct an expert shall submit to the court a draft order for directions dealing in particular with:

(a) the party who is to be responsible for drafting the letter of instruction and providing the documents to the expert;
(b) the issues identified by the court and the questions about which the expert is to give an opinion;
(c) the timetable for the report being prepared, filed and served;
(d) the disclosure of the report to the parties and any other expert;
(e) the organisation of, preparation for and conduct of, an expert's discussion;
(f) the preparation of a statement of agreement/disagreement by the experts following on from such a discussion;
(g) making available to the court at an early opportunity the reports in electronic form;
(h) the attendance of the expert at court to give oral evidence (or in writing or by video link), whether at the final hearing or at any hearing, unless agreement about the opinions given by the expert is reached at, or before, the Issues Resolution Hearing (IRH) or, if there is to be no IRH, by a specified date.

LETTER OF INSTRUCTION

5.115 FPR 2010, PD 25A, para 4.5 deals with the contents of the letter of instruction. The provisions of para 4.5 should be read in conjunction with the Annex to the practice direction which sets out the following:

- suggested questions in letters of instruction to a child mental health professional or paediatrician in Children Act 1989 proceedings; and
- suggested questions in letters of instruction to adult psychiatrists and applied psychologists in Children Act 1989 proceedings.

FPR 2010, PD 25A, para 4.5 states that the solicitor or party instructing the expert shall within five business days after the relevant hearing prepare, file and serve a letter of instruction to the expert. That letter should be prepared in agreement with the other parties where appropriate. The letter shall contain the following:

(a) Set out the context in which the opinion in sought, to include any ethnic, cultural, religious or linguistic context.

(b) Set out the specific questions which the expert is required to answer, but ensuring that they are within the ambit of the expert's expertise, do not contain unnecessary detail, are kept to a manageable number and are clear, focused and direct and reflect what the expert has been requested to do by the court.
(c) List the documents provided, or provide for the expert an indexed and paginated bundle which must include a copy of the order, an agreed list of essential reading and a copy of the guidance.
(d) Identify any materials provided to the expert which have not been produced either as original records or in response to an instruction from a party.
(e) Identify all requests to third parties for disclosure and their responses.
(f) Identify the relevant people concerned with the proceedings and advise the expert of their right to talk to them, provided that an accurate record is made of the discussions.
(g) Identify any other expert instructed and advise the expert of their right to talk to other experts, provided that an accurate record is made of the discussions.
(h) Subject to any public funding requirements, define the contractual basis upon which the expert is retained and in particular the funding mechanism, including how much the expert will be paid, when the expert will be paid and what limitation there might be on the amount the expert can charge for the work which they will do.

On occasions, there may be a disagreement regarding the contents of a letter of instruction to a single joint expert. Under FPR 2010, PD 25A, para 4.6, the written request for the court to consider the letter in accordance with FPR 2010, SI 2010/2955, 25.8(2) should be set out in an email to the court and copied by email to the other parties. The request should be sent to the relevant court, or, by prior arrangement only, directly to the judge dealing with the matter. In the magistrates' court, the request should be sent to the legal adviser who will refer it to the appropriate judge or justices, if necessary. The court will usually settle a letter of instruction without a hearing, to avoid delay. The court will then send the settled letter to the lead solicitor for transmission forthwith to the expert and copy it to the other instructing parties for information.

In accordance with FPR 2010, PD 25A, para 4.7, the expert should be provided promptly with any new document filed at court, together with an updated document list or bundle index.

Proceedings other than those relating to children

5.116 The provisions for the instruction of experts in proceedings other than those relating to children are far less detailed, although as it can be seen below, some of the provisions for the instruction of experts in proceedings relating to children are repeated wholesale in this section of the guidance.

FPR 2010, PD 25A, para 5.1 repeats the principle that, wherever possible, expert evidence should be obtained from a single joint expert. Accordingly, a party wishing to instruct an expert should first give to the other party a list of names of one or more experts in the relevant speciality he or she considers to

5.116 General Procedural Provisions

be suitable. The guidance does not specify the number of experts which should be suggested, although common practice is to submit three names.

Under para 5.2, within 10 days after receipt of the list, the other party or parties should indicate any objection to one or more of the names. If so, they should supply the names of one or more experts whom they consider to be suitable.

Paragraph 5.3 provides that each party should disclose whether they have already consulted any of the proposed experts about the issues in question.

Paragraph 5.4 states that if the parties cannot agree upon the identity of a suitable single joint expert, then they should think carefully about instructing their own expert in view of the costs implications. Where there is a dispute over the identity of the suitable expert, then such issues should be managed by the court in the context of an application for directions. Where the dispute is in the context of financial proceedings, such dispute may therefore precipitate an application for financial remedy.

In the event that the parties agree to instruct their own separate experts, para 5.5 states that they should agree in advance that the reports will be disclosed and should also agree their instructions to each expert should comply with FPR 2010, PD 25A, paras 4.5 to 4.7.

Under para 5.6, where the parties have agreed to instruct a single joint expert, before instructions are given to the expert, the parties should:

(a) as far as appropriate, comply with the guidance in FPR 2010, PD 25A, paras 4.1, regarding preliminary enquires of the expert, and 4.2 regarding the expert's confirmation in response to those preliminary enquiries;
(b) have agreed in what proportion the single joint expert's fee is to be shared between them, at least in first instance, and when it is to be paid;
(c) if applicable, to have obtained agreement for public funding.

In accordance with para 5.7, the instructions to the single joint expert should comply with FPR 2010, PD 25A, paras 4.5–4.7, so far as is appropriate for proceedings which do not concern children. Paragraph 5.9 imposes the same requirement where experts are instructed pursuant to a court direction.

Where the parties are seeking the court's directions for the use of a single joint expert, in accordance with FPR 2010, PD 25A, para 5.8 they should comply, so far as is appropriate, with FPR 2010, PD 25A, paras 4.1 to 4.4 as discussed above.

Questions to the expert

5.117 FPR 2010, SI 2010/2955, 25.6 is silent as to the deadline for an expert responding to questions. In accordance with FPR 2010, PD 25A, para 6.1(a), where written questions are put to an expert, the court will specify the timetable according to which the expert is to answer the written questions. By virtue of para 6.1(b) of the guidance, where a party sends questions under FPR 2010, 25.6 to an expert, the copy of the questions must, at the same time, be sent to the other party or parties.

Experts' discussion or meeting

5.118 FPR 2010, SI 2010/2955, 25.12 provides that the court may direct a discussion or meeting taking place between experts. FPR 2010, PD 25A, para 6.2 provides that the issues discussed will include: the reasons for disagreement on any expert question and what action needs to be taken to resolve any outstanding disagreement or question; and an explanation of existing evidence or additional evidence in order to assist the court to determine the issues. One of the aims of specifying the issues for discussion is to limit, wherever possible, the need for experts to attend court to give oral evidence.

Paragraph 6.3 of the guidance provides details on arrangements for experts' discussion or meeting. Subject to the directions given by the court under FPR 2010, SI 2010/2955, 25.12, the solicitor given responsibility by the court (defined in the guidance as 'the nominated professional') shall within 15 days after the experts' reports have been filed and copied to the other parties, make arrangements for the experts to meet or communicate. Subject to any further direction by the court as to issues which the experts must discuss under FPR 2010, 25.10(2), the following matters should be considered, as appropriate:

(a) Where there has been permission for the instruction of experts from different disciplines, there may be a global discussion relating to those questions which concern all or most of them.

(b) Separate discussions may have to be held between experts from the same or related disciplines. Care should, however, be taken to ensure that the discussions complement each other so that related questions are discussed by all relevant experts.

(c) Five days prior to the discussion or meeting, the nominated professional should formulate an agenda, including a list of questions for consideration. That agenda should focus on questions intended to clarify areas of agreement or disagreement, but questions which repeat questions asked in the letter of instruction or which seek to rehearse issues for cross-examination should be rejected as likely to defeat the purpose of the meeting. The agenda could take the form of a list of questions to be circulated amongst the other parties in advance. The agenda and list of questions should be sent to each of the experts no later than two business days before the discussion or meeting.

(d) The nominated professional may exercise his or her discretion to accept further questions after the agenda has been circulated to the parties. Only in exceptional circumstances should questions be added to the agenda within the two-day period. Under no circumstances should any question received on the day of, or during, the meeting be accepted. That does not, however, preclude questions arising during the meeting for the purposes of clarification.

(e) The discussion should be chaired by the nominated professional. A minute must be taken of the questions answered by the experts. Where the court has made an appropriate direction under FPR 2010, SI 2010/2955, 25.12(3), a Statement of Agreement and Disagreement must be prepared and which should be agreed and signed by each of the experts who participated in the discussion/meeting. It must also contain

5.118 *General Procedural Provisions*

a summary of experts' reasons for disagreeing. The statement must be filed and served no later than five business days after the discussion or meeting has taken place.

(f) Consideration should be given as to whether some or all of the experts may participate in the meeting by telephone conference or video link to ensure that costs are minimised and that there is minimum disruption to their professional schedules.

By reference to FPR 2010, PD 25A, para 6.4, single joint experts should not attend any meeting or conference which is not a joint one, unless all the parties have agreed in writing or the court has directed that such a meeting may be held and that it has also been agreed or directed who is to pay the expert's fees for the meeting or conference.

In public law Children Act proceedings, in accordance with para 6.5, where the court directs that the meeting shall take place between a local authority and any relevant experts for the purpose of providing assistance to the local authority in formulating plans or proposals for the child, that meeting shall be arranged, chaired and minuted in accordance with directions given by the court.

Refusal by one party to be bound by the experts' agreement

5.119 In accordance with FPR 2010, PD 25A, para 7.1, where a party refuses to be bound by an agreement reached by experts, that party must inform the court and the other parties in writing within 10 business days after the discussion or meeting, or where an IRH is to be held, not less than five business days before the IRH of his or her reasons for refusing to accept the agreement.

Arrangements for experts to give evidence and experts attending at court

5.120 In accordance with FPR 2010, PD 25A, para 8.1, where the court has directed the attendance of an expert witness, the party who is responsible for his or her instruction shall by the specified date, or where an IRH is to be held, by the IRH ensure that:

(a) a date and time, which should be convenient to the expert, are fixed for the court to hear the expert's evidence. That date and time must be fixed substantially in advance of the hearing at which the expert is to give evidence and no later than a specified date prior to that hearing, or where an IRH is to be held, no later than the IRH;

(b) in the event that the expert's oral evidence is not required, they must be notified as soon as possible;

(c) the witness template must accurately indicate how long the expert is likely to be giving evidence, in order to avoid the inconvenience of the expert being delayed at court;

(d) consideration must be given as to whether some or all of the experts may participate by way of telephone conference or video link or may submit their evidence in writing with a view to minimising costs and ensuring there is minimum disruption to their professional schedules.

Experts and assessors – Pt 25 **5.122**

In accordance with FPR 2010, PD 25A, para 8.2, where expert witnesses are to be called to give evidence, all parties shall by the specified date, or where an IRH is to be held, by the IRH, ensure that:

- the parties' advocates have identified the issues which the experts are to address;
- where possible, a logical sequence to the evidence is arranged, with experts of the same discipline giving evidence on the same day;
- the court is informed of any circumstance where the experts agree, but a party does not accept the agreed opinion. This will enable the court to give directions for the proper consideration of the experts' evidence and of the parties' reasons for not accepting the agreed opinion and
- in exceptional cases, the court is informed of the need for a witness summons.

Action after the final hearing.

5.121 An interesting new development places an obligation upon solicitors to advise the expert of the outcome of the case. In the past, experts were often left in the dark regarding the implications of their evidence and the final judgment of the trial judge.

FPR 2010, PD 25A, para 9.1 provides that within 10 business days after the final hearing, the solicitor instructing the expert shall inform the expert in writing of the outcome of the case and also how the court used the expert's opinion.

Paragraph 9.2 provides that where the court directs the preparation of a transcript, it may also direct that the solicitor instructing the expert shall send a copy of the transcript to the expert within 10 business days after receiving the transcript.

After a final hearing in the family proceedings court, the lead solicitor instructing the expert shall send the expert a copy of the court's written reasons for its decision within 10 business days after receiving those written reasons.

Appointment of assessors in family proceedings

5.122 The provisions of FPR 2010, PD 25A, paras 10.1–10.4 are to be read in conjunction with FPR 2010, SI 2010/2955, 25.14. By virtue of para 10.2, not less than 21 days before the making of the appointment of an assessor, the court will notify each party in writing of the name of the proposed assessor, of the matter in respect of which the assistance of the assessor is sought and the qualifications of the assessor.

FPR 2010, PD 25A, paras 10.3 and 10.4 deal with any objections to the proposed appointment. Such objections must be made in writing and filed and served within seven business days of receipt of the notification from the court of the proposed appointment. Those objections will be taken into account by the court in deciding whether or not to make the appointment.

5.123 General Procedural Provisions

APPLICATIONS AND MISCELLANEOUS PROCEDURE: PTS 18, 19 AND 8

5.123 As well as providing detailed guidance on the conduct of specific types of proceedings, FPR 2010 sets out a comprehensive scheme for the making of all other applications within family proceedings. FPR 2010, SI 2010/2955, Pt 18 covers the procedure for making applications within existing proceedings and in certain other circumstances and FPR 2010, SI 2010/2955, Pt 19 deals with applications involving no substantive factual dispute. FPR 2010, SI 2010/2955, Pt 8 sets out the rules to be followed in some of the more unusual family proceedings and channels applicants to either the Pt 18 or Pt 19 procedure. Other parts of FPR 2010 direct applicants to either the Pt 18 or Pt 19 procedure as necessary.

The advantage of structuring the rules in this way is that it sets down two broad frameworks for making applications across various types of proceedings.

Part 18

5.124 The best description of the application of Pt 18 is found in its accompanying practice direction[1]:

> 'Part 18 makes general provision for a procedure for making applications. All applications for the court's permission should be made under this Part, with the exception of applications for permission for which specific provision is made in other Parts of the FPR, in which case the application should be made under the specific provision'.

Practitioners should familiarise themselves with the contents of the practice direction because it contains detailed and useful guidance as to what the court expects of applicants and how all parties can assist in the furtherance of the overriding objective.

[1] FPR 2010, PD 18A at para 1.1.

Scope

5.125 FPR 2010, SI 2010/2955, Pt 18 is of wide and frequent application and practitioners will need to become acquainted with it.

Part 18 may be used if an application is made:

- in the course of existing proceedings;
- to start proceedings except where some other Part prescribes the procedure;
- in connection with proceedings which have been concluded[1].

Elsewhere in the rules, it is prescribed that Pt 18 should be followed in applications for:

- an order to prevent decrees nisi being made absolute or conditional orders being made final[2];
- an order under the Married Women's Property Act 1882[3] within existing financial order proceedings[4];
- permission to apply for a financial remedy after overseas proceedings[5];

Applications & misc procedure: Pts 18, 19, 8 **5.125**

- an order preventing a disposition[6];
- an interim order within financial remedy proceedings, being:
  (a) an order for maintenance pending suit/outcome of proceedings;
  (b) an order for interim periodical payments;
  (c) an interim variation order;
  (d) any other form of interim order[7];
- periodical payments order at the same rate as an order for maintenance pending suit/outcome of proceedings[8];
- permission to make an application in respect of a child where permission is required;
- the holder of foreign parental responsibility to be joined to proceedings taking place in this jurisdiction[9];
- an order transferring proceedings from the magistrates' court following refusal of such a request[10];
- permission to start proceedings in connection with the adoption of a child who is a ward of court[11];
- the stay or transfer of proceedings relating to a child under the Hague Convention or the Council Regulation[12];
- permission to adduce evidence following the registration of a Scottish maintenance order[13];
- the cancellation of the registration of, or enforcement of a Scottish order or a Northern Irish order in the High Court[14];
- an order relating to the provision of evidence in a mediated cross-border dispute[15].

Even where the use of FPR 2010, SI 2010/2955, Pt 18 is not prescribed, the general Pt 18 application notice (Form FP2) must be used in certain other applications[16] and, more importantly, FPR 2010, PD 18 guidance contains guidance on making applications generally, which will be of relevance in the absence of specific guidance elsewhere in the rules.

[1] FPR 2010, SI 2010/2955, 18.1(2).
[2] FPR 2010, SI 2010/2955, 7.31(2).
[3] Or its equivalent, the Civil Partnership Act 2004 (CPA 2004), s 66.
[4] FPR 2010, SI 2010/2955, 8.13.
[5] FPR 2010, SI 2010/2955, 8.24(3).
[6] FPR 2010, SI 2010/2955, 9.6(1).
[7] FPR 2010, SI 2010/2955, 9.7(2).
[8] FPR 2010, SI 2010/2955, 9.8(2) or 9.9(2).
[9] FPR 2010, SI 2010/2955, 12.4(5), 13.4(5) (equivalent provision in parental order proceedings) and 14.4(5) (equivalent provision in placement and adoption order proceedings).
[10] FPR 2010, SI 2010/2955, 12.10(2).
[11] FPR 2010, SI 2010/2955, 12.42.
[12] FPR 2010, SI 2010/2955, 12.62(2).
[13] FPR 2010, SI 2010/2955, 32.8.
[14] FPR 2010, SI 2010/2955, 32.10 or 32.11.
[15] FPR 2010, SI 2010/2955, 35.3(1).
[16] Applications for certain permissions with applications for a forced marriage protection order. See FPR 2010, SI 2010/2955, 11.3(1) and 11.6(1).

5.126 *General Procedural Provisions*

Procedure

APPLICATION

5.126 Applicants must file an application notice unless the court dispenses with this direction or a rule or practice direction permits it[1]. Many of the applications to which FPR 2010, SI 2010/2955, Pt 18 applies have specialised application forms, as set out in the relevant chapters of this work. For example, the application for permission to apply for a financial remedy after an overseas divorce is made in Form D50E (see **2.53** above).

FPR 2010, PD 5A should always be consulted before making an application to see whether a specific form exists (see **5.1** et seq above). However, where it does not, applicants appear to have three choices. In light of the contents of the various forms, it is submitted that they should be utilised as follows:

- Form C2 (familiar but revamped and expanded) – use in Children Act 1989 applications:
  (a) for permission to start proceedings;
  (b) for an order or directions in existing proceedings;
  (c) to be joined as, or cease to be, a party in existing proceedings.
- Form D11 (familiar but, again, revamped and expanded) – use for:
  (a) interlocutory and interim applications in financial remedy proceedings;
  (b) interlocutory applications in matrimonial or civil partnership proceedings.
- Form FP2 (new):
  (a) interlocutory applications in other proceedings under FPR 2010;
  (b) applications for permission where no prescribed form exists.

The respondents will be the parties in the case of existing proceedings. Where there are no existing proceedings and permission to make an application is sought, the respondents will be those who *would* be parties *were* permission granted. The court also has power to direct that any other person should be a respondent[2].

The application notice must state what order the applicant is seeking and the reasons why[3]. A draft of the order sought *must* also be attached[4]. Both the Form D11 and Form FP2 prompt the applicant for this information. Where permission is sought to make an application under certain parts of the Children Act 1989, the application must also include a draft of the order sought were permission to be granted[5].

Service must be effected on each respondent or other persons as prescribed by the rule or practice direction specific to the application contemplated unless a rule, practice direction or the court permits otherwise[6].

[1] FPR 2010, SI 2010/2955, 18.4.
[2] FPR 2010, SI 2010/2955, 18.3(1).
[3] FPR 2010, SI 2010/2955, 18.7(1).
[4] FPR 2010, SI 2010/2955, 18.7(2).
[5] FPR 2010, PD 18A, paras 3.5 and 3.6.
[6] FPR 2010, SI 2010/2955, 18.5.

SERVICE

5.127 The application notice must be served on each respondent in accordance with FPR 2010, SI 2010/2955, Pt 6 (Service). This must happen 'as soon as practicable after it is filed' but there are prescribed time limits:

- fourteen days in the case of an application for an interim order in financial remedy proceedings (eg maintenance pending suit, interim variation order); or
- seven days in the case of all other applications[1].

There will be situations in which this is not possible and the court has the power to direct that a shorter period than that required by the rules amounts to sufficient notice to the respondent[2]. For example, a hearing may already have been fixed and a party may wish to make an application at it but does not have time to make and serve it within the prescribed timescale. The practice direction anticipates this situation and recommends that the party 'inform the court (if possible in writing) and, if possible, the other parties of the nature of the application and the reason for it. That party should then make the application orally at the hearing'[3]. Where service cannot be effected within the prescribed timeframe, applicants should make every effort to give the parties at least informal notice of any application[4].

Applications can be made without filing an application notice in cases of exceptional urgency, if the court gives permission or the parties consent, in the circumstances set out immediately above or if a rule or practice direction permits it[5]. The court has the power to exercise great flexibility where the overriding objective demands it but this should not be taken as a general licence to make speculative or last-minute applications.

[1] FPR 2010, SI 2010/2955, 18.8(1).
[2] FPR 2010, SI 2010/2955, 18.8(4)(b).
[3] FPR 2010, PD18A, para 4.9.
[4] FPR 2010, PD18A, para 6.2.
[5] FPR 2010, PD18A, para 5.1.

EVIDENCE IN SUPPORT

5.128 FPR 2010, SI 2010/2955, 18.8(2) does not require a statement in support of the application to be filed unless another rule requires the particular application to be supported by a statement. However, if a statement is filed it must be served upon the respondent(s) at the same time as the application notice.

HEARINGS

5.129 The court has discretion whether to list the application for a hearing. If it considers that a hearing would not be appropriate or if all parties agree to the terms of the order sought, the court can make an order without hearing the parties[1]. In the case of consent orders, the court will need sufficient information in order to decide whether to grant the application in the absence of the parties. Subject to the contents of any other rule or practice direction, a letter explaining the circumstances will normally be sufficient[2].

5.129 General Procedural Provisions

If the court considers that an application can be dealt with without a hearing, but needs further information before doing so, it can make directions for the filing of further evidence[3]. Conversely, where a hearing is required, the court can make directions for the filing of further evidence in advance of the hearing[4].

FPR 2010, PD 18A, para 3.2 prescribes that, amongst other things, the application must include a request that it be disposed of either with or without a hearing. There is space for this in the Form D11.

Applicants must state whether a specific judge or level of judge is needed to hear the application (see Form D11)[5]. District judges considering applications have a general power to refer the matter to a judge who can either dispose of the application or refer it back to a district judge[6].

This may seem obvious, but the practice direction reminds us that at every hearing in a case the parties should be prepared for the court to review the overall conduct of the matter and make such directions as it sees fit for the management of the case[7]. FPR 2010, PD 18A recommends that applications made under Pt 18 should be listed for hearing at existing directions or other hearings wherever possible[8].

Where permission is sought to make an application in proceedings under the Children Act 1989, and the court exercises its discretion to refuse the application without a hearing, the court must, upon the applicant's request, list the application for a hearing[9]. It is therefore important that applicants falling into this category take the initiative to ask the court to fix a hearing following a refusal in these circumstances. This does not apply to magistrates' courts[10].

[1] FPR 2010, SI 2010/2955, 18.9(1).
[2] FPR 2010, PD 18A, para 12.1.
[3] FPR 2010, PD 18A, para 4.3.
[4] FPR 2010, PD 18A, para 4.4.
[5] FPR 2010, PD 18A, para 4.5.
[6] FPR 2010, PD 18A, para 2.1.
[7] FPR 2010, PD 18A, para 4.8.
[8] FPR 2010, PD 18A, para 4.7.
[9] FPR 2010, PD 18A, 18.9(2).
[10] FPR 2010, PD 18A, 18.9(3).

Telephone hearings and video conferencing

5.130 Telephone hearings are commonplace in civil litigation but unusual in family proceedings. The benefits in terms of time saved and the greater likelihood of being heard at a specified time are substantial though it remains to be seen whether the provision for telephone hearings in these rules will make them more widespread.

The court may direct that an application made under FPR 2010, SI 2010/2955, Pt 18 may be heard on the telephone and, indeed, the Form D11 asks parties to state whether there are any reasons why it *should not*. A telephone hearing will only be directed if at least one party is legally represented and, normally, where all parties consent[1]. It may therefore be sensible for the party seeking a telephone hearing to consult with the other parties beforehand to obtain their consent.

Applications & misc procedure: Pts 18, 19, 8 **5.132**

Once a direction for a telephone hearing has been made, it is the responsibility of the applicant's legal representative to arrange it, not the court. FPR 2010, PD 18A contains detailed guidance for conduct of telephone hearings[2]. The following in particular should be remembered:

- a telecommunications provider approved by Her Majesty's Courts Service (HMCS) *must* be used, currently BT or Legal Connect;
- the appointment will need to be booked in advance with the provider once the time and date of the hearing are known;
- the applicant's representative must obtain the correct telephone numbers for all persons who need to participate;
- at the appointed time, the applicant's representative should be connected first, followed by the representatives of any respondents and finally the court;
- unless all parties consent, no representative may attend at court where a hearing is to take place by telephone;
- the costs of the telephone conference will form part of the applicant's overall claim for costs.

If a video conference is required, for example, where a party to the proceedings is in prison, the applicant must check that the necessary facilities are available at the relevant court and then seek a direction that a particular party or witness be permitted to appear via video link[3].

[1] FPR 2010, PD 18A, paras 8.1–8.3.
[2] FPR 2010, PD 18A, para 8.
[3] See FPR 2010, PD 18A, para 9.

ORDERS MADE WITHOUT NOTICE

5.131 Under FPR 2010, SI 2010/2955, 18.10.2, the application notice, evidence in support and the order must be served on all the parties in the proceedings. Importantly, any order made without notice must contain a statement of the right to make an application to vary or set aside the order[1].

The variation/set aside procedure is set out in FPR 2010, SI 2010/2955, 18.11. The application must be made within seven days of service of the order and in accordance with Pt 18.

[1] FPR 2010, SI 2010/2955, 18.10(3).

ABSENT PARTIES AND APPLICATIONS WITHOUT MERIT

5.132 The court can proceed in the absence of any party. If an order is made and any party fails to attend, the court retains discretion to relist the application upon an application or on its own initiative.[1]

If an application in the High Court or county court is dismissed and the court considers it to be 'totally without merit', the court's order must record the fact and the court must give consideration to making a civil restraint order. This is part of the court's general power of case management conferred by FPR 2010, SI 2010/2955, Pt 4. Regard should be had to FPR 2010, SI 2010/2955, 4.8 and

5.132 *General Procedural Provisions*

FPR 2010, PD 4B.

[1] FPR 2010, SI 2010/2955, 18.13.

Part 19

5.133 This Part's closest living relative is CPR Pt 8 in that it is to be used where:

- there is no form available for the type of application contemplated;
- a decision is sought, which is unlikely to involve a substantial dispute of fact; or
- a rule or practice direction requires or permits the use of the FPR 2010, SI 2010/2955, Pt 19 procedure[1].

It is therefore a catch-all provision for situations where no other procedure is specified or where the issue for the court to decide will not necessitate the consideration of a large volume of evidence.

[1] FPR 2010, SI 2010/2955, 19.1(2) and (5).

Scope

5.134 According to FPR 2010, SI 2010/2955, Pt 19 itself, the procedure must be used for applications under:

- Adoption and Children Act 2002, s 60(3) (an order to prevent disclosure of information to an adopted person);
- Adoption and Children Act 2002, s 79(4) (order for Registrar General to give any information making a connection between original birth and adoption records); and
- FPR 2010, SI 2010/2955, 14.21 (application to consider whether a father without parental responsibility should be given notice of the intention to place a child for adoption)[1].

Part 19 must also be used for:

- all the applications listed in FPR 2010, SI 2010/2955, Pt 8 (see **5.139** below) except an application under the Married Women's Property Act 1882 within existing financial order proceedings[2] and applications for permission to apply for a financial remedy after overseas proceedings, both of which are to be made under FPR 2010, SI 2010/2955, Pt 18 (see **5.124** above)[3];
- applications under the Family Law Act 1986, s 28(2) (an application to cancel the registration of a child custody order in another jurisdiction within the United Kingdom)[4].

Part 19 will be an option where all the potential respondents to an application consent to the making of an order and the only purpose of making the application is to obtain the court's approval of the agreement[5]. However, if this situation arises within existing proceedings, the Pt 18 procedure should be followed.

If another practice direction permits or requires the use of the Pt 19 procedure it may disapply or modify elements of it. In this eventuality, the provisions of the other practice direction take precedence over FPR 2010, PD 19A[6].

[1] FPR 2010, SI 2010/2955, 19.2(1).
[2] Or its civil partnership equivalent, CPA 2004, s 66.
[3] FPR 2010, SI 2010/2955, 8.1.
[4] FPR 2010, SI 2010/2955, 32.28.
[5] See FPR 2010, PD 19A, para 1.5.
[6] FPR 2010, PD 19A, para 1.4.

Procedure

APPLICATION

5.135 The application is made in Form FP1 which must be verified by a statement of truth[1]. Like proceedings under CPR Pt 8, FPR 2010, SI 2010/2955, Pt 19 proceedings are 'front-loaded' with evidence. The Form FP1 must specify:

- that Pt 19 applies;
- either, the question the applicant wants the court to decide, or the order the applicant seeks, together with its legal basis;
- if the application is made under an enactment, what that enactment is;
- if the applicant is applying in a representative capacity, what that capacity is; and
- if the respondent appears or is to appear in a representative capacity, what that capacity is[2].

At the same time as filing the application, the applicant must file the written evidence on which he or she intends to rely[3]. This must be served on the respondent(s) with the application[4]. There is a certificate of service in Form FP6 for the applicant to complete.

[1] See FPR 2010, SI 2010/2955, Pt 17.
[2] FPR 2010, SI 2010/2955, 19.3(a)–(e).
[3] FPR 2010, SI 2010/2955, 19.7(1).
[4] FPR 2010, SI 2010/2955, 19.7(2).

RESPONSE

5.136 There are circumstances in which a respondent need not be named. Such circumstances can be specified in a practice direction[1]. This includes applications under FPR 2010, SI 2010/2955, 14.21 and the Adoption and Children Act 2002, s 60(3)[2] mentioned at **5.134** above. This will also include applications for permission to apply for an order where specified by a practice direction[3].

If a respondent is named, their deadline for filing an acknowledgment of service is tight – 14 days beginning with the date on which the application is served[4]. The acknowledgment should be in Form FP5, which contains boxes asking the respondent to confirm:

- whether they contest the application;

5.136 *General Procedural Provisions*

- if they seek a different order from the one sought, what that is;
- whether they intend to dispute the court's jurisdiction; and
- whether they object to the applicant using the FPR 2010, SI 2010/2955, Pt 19 procedure (which will trigger the court to make directions for the future management of the case)[5].

A less formal acknowledgment than the Form FP5, such as a letter, is also permissible[6].

Under FPR 2010, SI 2010/2955, 19.6, the consequence of failing to acknowledge the application within the 14 days is serious; the respondent may attend the hearing but can only take part in it with the court's permission.

When acknowledging, the respondent must file and serve any written evidence on which they wish to rely[7]. Within 14 days of receiving the acknowledgement and evidence in support, the applicant may file and serve further written evidence in reply[8].

[1] FPR 2010, SI 2010/2955, 19.4(1).
[2] FPR 2010, PD 19A, para 2.2.
[3] FPR 2010, SI 2010/2955, 19.4(2)–(4).
[4] FPR 2010, SI 2010/2955, 19.5(1).
[5] See FPR 2010, SI 2010/2955, 19.5(3) and 19.9
[6] FPR 2010, PD 19A, para 3.1.
[7] FPR 2010, SI 2010/2955, 19.7(3) and (4)
[8] FPR 2010, SI 2010/2955, 19.7(5) and (6).

EVIDENCE

5.137 FPR 2010, PD 19A, para 5.2 anticipates that most written evidence will be in the form of a statement but the applicant may simply rely on the matters set out in the application form provided it is verified by a statement of truth.

CASE MANAGEMENT AND HEARINGS

5.138 FPR 2010, SI 2010/2955, Pt 19 proceedings are designed to be limited in scope and the court therefore keeps a tight rein on the introduction of further evidence. No further written evidence can be relied upon unless the court gives permission[1]. The court may require or permit a party to give oral evidence at a hearing and it may give directions requiring any witness who has given written evidence to attend for cross-examination[2].

An application for an extension of time to file and serve evidence in support or response can be made as well as an application for permission to file and serve additional evidence. Practitioners are directed to FPR 2010, SI 2010/2955, Pt 18 for the rules on making applications[3]. Extensions can be agreed between the parties in writing[4]. If this relates to the respondent's evidence, the agreement must be filed with the acknowledgment and the time for filing cannot be extended more than 17 days after the date for the acknowledgment[5]. The parties cannot agree an extension for the applicant's evidence in reply of more than 28 days after service of the respondent's evidence[6].

A hearing may or may not be required and the court has discretion to fix hearings and give directions for the disposal of the application as it sees fit. If it has not already fixed a hearing, the court must give directions as soon as is

Applications & misc procedure: Pts 18, 19, 8 **5.140**

practicable after the filing of an acknowledgment or after the time for filing one has expired[7]. Hearings can be listed either for the disposal of the application or the giving of case management directions[8].

[1] FPR 2010, SI 2010/2955, 19.8(1).
[2] FPR 2010, SI 2010/2955, 19.8(2) and (3).
[3] FPR 2010, PD 19A, para 5.5.
[4] FPR 2010, PD 19A, para 5.6.
[5] FPR 2010, PD 19A, para 5.7.
[6] FPR 2010, PD 19A, para 5.8.
[7] FPR 2010, PD 19A, para 4.
[8] FPR 2010, PD 19A, para 6.

Part 8

5.139 This Part contains the specific procedure to be used in a variety of miscellaneous applications not dealt with elsewhere. The procedural provisions common to each application are found within FPR 2010, SI 2010/2955, Pt 19, except in the case of applications under the Married Women's Property Act 1882 within existing financial order proceedings[1] and applications for permission to apply for a financial remedy after overseas proceedings, which are found in FPR 2010, SI 2010/2955, Pt 18[2]. This ensures that there is a unified procedural framework for many diverse forms of action.

There is no practice direction to accompany FPR 2010, SI 2010/2955, Pt 8 but regard must be had to those accompanying Pts 18 and 19 where relevant as to general procedural matters.

[1] Or its civil partnership equivalent, CPA 2004, s 66.
[2] FPR 2010, SI 2010/2955, 8.1, 8.13 and 8.24.

Conversion table

5.140 The table below shows the various forms of action covered in each chapter of FPR 2010, SI 2010/2955, Pt 8 and where the relevant procedure was covered in FPR 1991.

FPR 2010	*FPR 1991*
Ch 2 – Application for corrected gender recognition certificate.	FPR 1991, r 2.51C
Ch 3 – Application for alteration of maintenance agreement after death of one party.	FPR 1991, r 3.3
Ch 4 – Application for question as to property to be decided in summary way.	FPR 1991, rr 3.6 and 3.7
Ch 5 – Declarations.	Marital status – FPR 1991, rr 3.12–3.12A Parentage – FPR 1991, r 3.13 Legitimacy/legitimation – FPR 1991, r 3.14

5.140 *General Procedural Provisions*

FPR 2010	*FPR 1991*
	As to adoption effected overseas – FPR 1991, r 3.15
	General procedure – FPR 1991, r 3.16
Ch 6 – Application for permission to apply for a financial remedy after overseas proceedings.	FPR 1991, r 3.18
Ch 7 – Application for the transfer of a tenancy under the Family Law Act 1996, s 53 and Sch 7.	FPR 1991, r 3.8(12)–(15), applying r 3.6(7)–(9)
Ch 8 – Application for order preventing avoidance under the Child Support Act 1991, s 32L.	FPR 1991, rr 3A.1–3A.7
Ch 9 – Application for consent to marriage of a child or to registration of civil partnership of a child.	FPR 1991, rr 3.20 and 3.20A

The chapters of Pt 8 follow a common format as far as possible, setting out:

- the scope of the chapter;
- where to start proceedings;
- who the parties are; and
- any issues specific to the relevant application.

Application for a corrected gender recognition certificate

5.141 FPR 2010, SI 2010/2955, 8.2–8.5 are identical to their FPR 1991 equivalent (r 2.51C). Either the recipient of the certificate or the Secretary of State can make an application under FPR 2010, SI 2010/2955, Pt 19 to correct a gender recognition certificate which contains an error[1].

[1] An application under the Gender Recognition Act 2004, s 6(1).

Application for alteration of maintenance agreement after death of one party

5.142 FPR 2010, SI 2010/2955, 8.6–8.11 dictate the procedure for applying for an order to vary a maintenance agreement[1] following the death of one of the parties if the agreement makes provision for the continuation of payments thereafter[2]. Given the relative scarcity of maintenance agreements, such applications will be rare.

The application is made in Form D50D. Rather than repeating the prescribed contents within the text, the form shows what must be included in a typical (and sensible) simplifying move. Regard must, of course, be had to the provisions of FPR 2010, SI 2010/2955, Pt 19 when filing the application and evidence in support.

In addition to the acknowledgment of service, any personal representative who is a respondent to the application must file a statement setting out:

- full particulars of the deceased's estate net of funeral expenses, liabilities and tax;
- the beneficiaries or classes of beneficiaries who have an interest in the estate[3].

Respondents have 28 days within which to file an acknowledgment of service and any statement required by the rule, as opposed to the usual 14-day period cited in Pt 19[4].

[1] As defined by MCA 1973, s 34(2) or its equivalent, CPA 2004, Sch 5, para 67(1).
[2] See MCA 1973, s 36 or its equivalent, CPA 2004, Sch 5, para 73.
[3] FPR 2010, SI 2010/2955, 8.10(1).
[4] FPR 2010, SI 2010/2955, 8.10(2).

Application for question as to property to be decided in summary way

5.143 Applications under the Married Women's Property Act 1882, s 17 or their equivalent under the CPA 2004, s 66 are unusual but not unheard of. The court has jurisdiction to give and enforce a declaratory judgment as to any question 'as to title or possession of property'.

Few spouses or civil partners will avail themselves of this option due to the comprehensive scheme of provision available under MCA 1973, Part II and CPA 2004, Sch 5. However, these proceedings may be used helpfully where a declaratory judgment is needed to establish beneficial interests in case of a spouse or civil partner's impending bankruptcy. Section 2(2) of the Law Reform (Miscellaneous Provisions) Act 1970 extends the application of the statute to engaged couples. Practitioners may recall the 2004 case of *Cox v Jones*[1] in which two formerly engaged barristers sought judgment as to their respective entitlements to a flat, a house and (memorably) a £10,000 engagement ring.

[1] [2004] EWHC 1486 (Ch), [2004] 2 FLR 1010.

Procedure

5.144 Applications must be made in accordance with the FPR 2010, SI 2010/2955, Pt 18 procedure if they are made 'in any proceedings for a financial order'[1]. Freestanding applications should therefore be made in accordance with FPR 2010, SI 2010/2955, Pt 19.

[1] FPR 2010, SI 2010/2955, 8.13.

WHICH COURT?

5.145 Under FPR 2010, SI 2010/2955, 8.14(1), applications must be made in the High Court or county court. If the application is made in a county court, then this must either be the same county court in which any matrimonial or civil partnership proceedings have been, or are intended to be, started by the applicant or the county court of the district in which either party resides (FPR 2010, 8.14(2). Where there are existing or contemplated proceedings in the principal registry, the application can be started there (FPR 2010, 8.14(3)).

5.146 *General Procedural Provisions*

APPLICATION

5.146 The application must be made in Form D50B. In contrast with FPR 1991, r 3.6, which lists contents of the application in the body of the rule, the necessary information is prescribed by the various boxes in Form D50B. The form prompts the applicant to attach a statement in support and, if the application concerns title to land, state whether it is registered (giving the title number(s)) or unregistered and give details of any mortgage or third party interest. The D50B must be verified by a statement of truth[1].

If particulars of a mortgage are given in the application, the applicant must serve a copy of the application upon the mortgagee who may, within 14 days of receipt, file an acknowledgment of service in Form D50A and may be heard on the hearing of the application[2]. If a mortgagee requests to become a party to the proceedings, the court must make them a party[3].

[1] FPR 2010, SI 2010/2955, 17.2(3).
[2] FPR 2010, SI 2010/2955, 8.15(1).
[3] FPR 2010, SI 2010/2955, 8.15(2).

RESPONSE

5.147 The Form D50B contains a notice to the respondent, stating that:

- they must complete the accompanying acknowledgement of service in Form D50A and send it so as to reach the court within eight days after receiving the application;
- if they wish to oppose the application they must file a statement in answer within 14 days after the time allowed for sending the acknowledgement of service.

This modifies the requirements of FPR 2010, SI 2010/2955, Pts 18 and 19 slightly.

Like D50B, the Form D50A is used for several different types of proceedings. There is a guide for the respondent highlighting what information must be submitted in the case of each form of action.

CASE MANAGEMENT AND HEARING

5.148 The old FPR 1991, r 3.6(10)–(11) applied certain sections of the pre-2000 provisions covering ancillary relief proceedings to applications under the Married Women's Property Act 1882. Under FPR 2010, the court's powers to give directions to take the matter forward and dispose of it as it sees fit are conferred by the relevant sections of either FPR 2010, SI 2010/2955, Pt 18 or Pt 19.

The court can grant an injunction ancillary or incidental to the main application[1]. For example, if the applicant could establish that there was a risk that either an asset in which they asserted a beneficial interest was about to be disposed of or that a third party had colluded in a course of conduct designed to defeat their claim, an injunction may be granted. However, this is not a licence to obtain injunctive relief by the back door. The procedure for making such an application is set out in FPR 2010, SI 2010/2955, 20.4 ('How to apply for an interim remedy')[2].

[1] FPR 2010, SI 2010/2955, 8.16(1).
[2] FPR 2010, SI 2010/2955, 8.16(2).

Declarations

5.149 There are circumstances in which a party will require a declaration of status. This could be an application for a declaration of marital status to demonstrate to an overseas authority that a marriage was valid at its inception or that a civil partnership has been validly dissolved. Although most applications concerning children will be made within existing proceedings, a declaration of parentage may be needed to establish child maintenance liability or entitlement to an inheritance.

Previously, declarations were sought by filing a petition[1]. The old rules set out at length the prescribed contents of each petition. Happily, this content has been removed from the body of the rules and confined to the form specific to each kind of declaration. The new procedure is broadly equivalent to the old and the information that must be given to the court at each stage is very similar. However, the old FPR 1991, r 3.16(12) which provided that the proceedings should follow the procedure applicable to petitions for divorce, dissolution and nullity (with the necessary modifications) has not been reproduced in FPR 2010.

Like most forms of action described in FPR 2010, SI 2010/2955, Pt 8, applications for a declaration proceed in accordance with FPR 2010, SI 2010/2955, Pt 19 with specific modifications. The prescribed forms are:

- marital or civil partnership status – Form D70;
- parentage – Form C63;
- legitimacy or legitimation – Form C64; and
- as to overseas adoptions – Form C65.

[1] See FPR 1991, rr 3.12(1), 3.12A(1), 3.13(1), 3.14(1), and 3.15.

General procedure

WHICH COURT?

5.150 Proceedings can be started in either the High Court, county court or (in the case of declarations of parentage) magistrates' court.

PARTIES

5.151 FPR 2010, SI 2010/2955, 8.20(1) provides a table (reproduced below) showing who will be the respondent(s) to each application.

5.151 *General Procedural Provisions*

Proceedings	Respondent
Applications for declarations as to marital or civil partnership status.	The other party to the marriage or civil partnership in question or, where the applicant is a third party, both parties to the marriage or civil partnership.
Applications for declarations of parentage.	The person whose parentage is in issue or any person who is or is alleged to be the parent of the person whose parentage is in issue.
Applications for declarations of legitimacy or legitimation.	The applicant's father and mother or the survivor of them.
Applications for declarations as to adoption effected overseas.	The person(s) whom the applicant is claiming are or are not the applicant's adoptive parents.

In addition to the information requested in each application form, the applicant must include in his or her application particulars of every person whose interest may be affected by the proceedings and his or her relationship to the applicant (FPR 2010, SI 2010/2955, 8.20).

RESPONSE

5.152 In the acknowledgment of service the respondent must give details of anyone they consider should be made a party or be given notice of the application. It is submitted that this information should be included as part of the written evidence accompanying the acknowledgment of service (Form FP5)[1].

Upon receipt of the completed FP5, the court must give directions as to whether any other persons should be made a respondent or given notice of the application[2]. Any party receiving notice of proceedings pursuant to such a direction has 21 days in which to make an application to be joined as a party and no further directions can be given until the expiry of this period[3].

[1] FPR 2010, SI 2010/2955, 19.7(3).
[2] FPR 2010, SI 2010/2955, 8.20(4).
[3] FPR 2010, SI 2010/2955, 8.20(4) and (5).

CASE MANAGEMENT

5.153 Under the general provisions of FPR 2010, SI 2010/2955, Pt 19, the court has the power to dispose of the application as it sees fit, subject to the specific requirements of the relevant section of FPR 2010, SI 2010/2955, Pt 8. This may include the giving of directions to file further evidence or expert reports, listing directions appointments and listing a hearing in order to decide the application.

ROLE OF THE ATTORNEY GENERAL

5.154 In common with the old FPR 1991, r 3.16(4), copies of all applications for declarations, except for declarations of parentage, must be sent to the Attorney General[1] at least one month *before* the application is made[2]. When giving directions as to what other parties should be made a respondent or notified of the proceedings, the court must consider whether to ask the Attorney General to argue any question relating to the proceedings.

Service upon the Attorney General enables the state to make representations where the making of a declaration would be contrary to public policy or where a declaration is sought for fraudulent purposes, such as the unlawful obtaining of British citizenship.

[1] As to the role of the Attorney General, see the Family Law Act 1986, (FLA 1996) s 59.
[2] FPR 2010, SI 2010/2955, 8.21(1).

Specific procedure

DECLARATIONS AS TO MARITAL OR CIVIL PARTNERSHIP STATUS

5.155 The application is made in Form D70. This captures information about the applicant, their status in relation to the couple whose status is in question and details about the marriage/civil partnership[1]. A certified copy of any marriage certificate must be attached to the application and a translation provided 'by a person authorised to provide translations' if the certificate is not in English or Welsh. There are further boxes to complete in order to establish whether the marriage/civil partnership has been dissolved or a decree of separation granted. Again, a certified copy of any decree must be attached with a proper translation if it is not in English or Welsh. The form provides a series of tick boxes to establish jurisdiction and a space for summary details of why the application should be granted. The application form must be verified by a statement of truth.

[1] See FLA 1986, s 55 and CPA 2004, s 58.

DECLARATIONS OF PARENTAGE

5.156 In respect of declarations of parentage[1], the application is made in Form C63. It is similar in layout to the Form C100 required to commence private law Children Act proceedings. Personal information, including addresses for the previous five years is required for the applicant and each respondent and there is an opportunity for the applicant to provide summary details of the reasons why they believe they are entitled to a declaration. There is a section to establish jurisdiction which asks questions about the domicile and habitual residence of the person whose parentage is in question. The application form must be verified by a statement of truth.

If the applicant/person whose parentage is in issue is known by a name other than that appearing on his or her birth certificate, then that other name must be stated in any order and declaration of parentage[2].

Within 21 days of a declaration of parentage being made, the court must send

5.156 General Procedural Provisions

a copy to the Registrar General[3].

[1] See FLA 1986, s 55A.
[2] FPR 2010, SI 2010/2955, 8.22(1).
[3] FPR 2010, SI 2010/2955, 8.22(2).

DECLARATIONS OF LEGITIMACY OR LEGITIMATION

5.157 Declarations of legitimacy or legitimation[1] are unusual and would only be required if, for example, an overseas jurisdiction only conferred certain rights upon persons who are the legitimate offspring of their parents or have been 'legitimated' and that status is in doubt.

The application is made in Form C64. Like the other declaration application forms, information is sought about the applicant (ie the person(s) whose status is in question), any respondents (the mother and the father), jurisdiction and the reasons for applying. The applicant's birth certificate must be attached. The application form must be verified by a statement of truth.

[1] See FLA 1986, s 56.

DECLARATIONS AS TO ADOPTION EFFECTED OVERSEAS

5.158 A declaration can be obtained where a person has been adopted by either a Convention adoption, overseas adoption or an adoption recognised by the law of England and Wales[1]. This will confirm that their status as an adopted person.

The application is made in Form C65. Information must be given about the child, the (alleged) adoptive parents, the purported adoption (attaching certified copies of the document evidencing the adoption with a translation where is it not in English or Welsh), jurisdiction and the applicant's reasons for applying. The application form must be verified by a statement of truth.

[1] See FLA 1986, s 57.

Application for permission to apply for a financial remedy after overseas proceedings

5.159 The essential elements of the old procedure have been retained. However, under FPR 2010, SI 2010/2955, 8.24(3) the application must be made in accordance with the FPR 2010, SI 2010/2955, Pt 18 procedure (see above).

PROCEDURE UPON AN APPLICATION

5.160 The application is made in Form D50E, which is very similar to the Form M25 it replaces. It is a very simple form which has space for details of the applicant, his or her solicitors, the date and time for the hearing (to be completed by the court office), and an opportunity to record the respondent's consent to the application if he or she has consented.

Which court?

5.161 The application must be made in the principal registry[1]. However, if the parties have agreed a settlement and simply seek the court's approval, the application for permission can be lodged at the same time as the consent order at any divorce county court[2]. The application for permission can then be heard at the same time as the application for the approval of the consent order.

Whether the application is to be heard with or without notice (see **5.162** below), the court officer must fix a hearing date upon receipt of the application before a judge (not a district judge), and give notice to the applicant[3].

[1] FPR 2010, SI 2010/2955,, r 8.24(1).
[2] See FPR 2010, SI 2010/2955, 8.24(2), 9.5(2) and 9.26(6).
[3] FPR 2010, SI 2010/2955, 8.26.

Hearing

5.162 Under FPR 2010, SI 2010/2955, 8.25(1), the application can be granted without notice to the respondent if there are good reasons for not giving notice. The applicant must state these reasons in the statement in support of the application[1]. This may include applications in which the applicant clearly has the 'substantial ground' required by the Matrimonial and Family Proceedings Act 1984, s 13[2], ie there is obviously jurisdiction to entertain the application by virtue of s 15[3] and it is clear that England and Wales is an 'appropriate venue' for the application in accordance with s 16[4]. This would also include applications with merit, to which the respondent consents.

Otherwise, the case will be listed for hearing. It is submitted that such hearings should be relatively brief and dealt with on the basis of submissions only. In *Agbaje v Agbaje* [2009] EWCA Civ 1 the Supreme Court made clear that the purpose of the permission stage was to weed out weak applications rather than to consider the merits of the application in any great depth. Whether an application was granted with or without notice, respondents should focus their energies on the substantive application for a financial remedy, rather than on seeking to set aside the grant of permission[5].

[1] FPR 2010, SI 2010/2955, 8.25(2).
[2] or CPA 2004, Sch 7, para 4.
[3] Or CPA 2004, Sch 7, para 7.
[4] Or CPA 2004, Sch 7, para 8.
[5] Per Ward LJ at para 31.

The substantive application

5.163 Once permission to make an application has been granted, an application should be made in Form D50F. This application can be heard by either a judge or a district judge of the principal registry (FPR 2010, SI 2010/2955, 8.28).

The relevant procedure is set out in FPR 2010, SI 2010/2955, Pt 9 and readers are referred to Chapter 2 on applications for a financial remedy.

5.164 *General Procedural Provisions*

Application for the transfer of a tenancy under section 53 of, and schedule 7 to, the 1996 Act

5.164 Under the Family Law Act 1996, s 53, the court has the power to transfer certain types of tenancy from one party to another or from joint names into one party's sole name. Applications are likely to be made in conjunction with an application for a non-molestation and/or occupation order under FLA 1996.

The provision applies to protected tenancies under the Rent Act 1977, certain agricultural holdings and tenancies granted by Registered Social Landlords. It covers (former) spouses, (former) civil partners and cohabitants. The most common form of private sector arrangement – the assured shorthold tenancy – is not included and all transfers are subject to the landlord's right to make representations as to the suitability of the parties as tenants.

The essential character of the procedure is little different from that provided by FPR 1991, r 3.8(11)–(15).

PROCEDURE

5.165 The application is made in Form D50B and in accordance with FPR 2010, SI 2010/2955, Pt 19. Regard must be had to the general filing and service requirements of this part.

WHICH COURT?

5.166 Under FPR 2010, SI 2010/2955, 8.30(1), the application must be made to either the High Court or a county court. If there are already divorce, dissolution or nullity proceedings pending between the parties, the application must be made to the court in which they are taking place[1].

[1] FPR 2010, 8.30(2).

SERVICE

5.167 Under FPR 2010, SI 2010/2955, 8.31(1), the court will effect service upon the respondent and the landlord unless it directs that the applicant must do so. If the applicant effects service upon the respondent, he or she must file a certificate of service[1], which will be in Form FP6.

[1] FPR 2010, 8.31(2).

RESPONSE

5.168 The Form D50B contains a notice to the respondent, stating that:

- they must complete the accompanying acknowledgement of service in Form D50A and send it so as to reach the court within eight days after receiving the application;

Applications & misc procedure: Pts 18, 19, 8 **5.171**

- if they wish to oppose the application they must file a statement in answer within 14 days after the time allowed for sending the acknowledgement of service.

This modifies the requirements of FPR 2010, SI 2010/2955, Pts 18 and 19 slightly.

Like D50B, the Form D50A is used for several different types of proceedings. There is a guide for the respondent highlighting what information must be submitted in the case of each form of action.

The landlord will be made a party to the proceedings if they request to be one[1].

[1] FPR 2010, SI 2010/2955, 8.32.

CASE MANAGEMENT

5.169 The court's powers to give directions to take the matter forward and dispose of it as it sees fit are conferred by the relevant sections of FPR 2010, SI 2010/2955, Pt 19.

INJUNCTIONS

5.170 FPR 2010, SI 2010/2955, 8.34 enables the court to grant an injunction 'only if the injunction is ancillary or incidental to the assistance sought by the applicant'. The relevant procedure is set out at FPR 2010, SI 2010/2955, 20.4. This is most likely to arise where there is a risk that one party will surrender either a tenancy in their sole name or in joint names (which they can do unilaterally[1]).

[1] See *Hammersmith and Fulham LBC v Monk* [1992] 1 FLR 465, [1992] 1 AC 478.

Applications for orders preventing avoidance under section 32L of the Child Support Act 1991

5.171 The Child Maintenance Enforcement Commission can apply for an avoidance of disposition order as part of process of enforcing arrears of child maintenance. This application is similar to an application to prevent or reverse a disposition of property under MCA 1973, s 37 or CPA 2004, Sch 5, para 74.

FPR 2010, SI 2010/2955, 8.35–8.40 replace the recently-implemented FPR 1991, rr 3A.1–3A.7 and, consequently, little has changed. By the old r 3A.3, applications were to be made under CPR Pt 8 so the migration to FPR 2010, SI 2010/2955, Pt 19 will make very little practical difference.

The now-familiar process of simplification brought about by FPR 2010 means that the prescribed contents of the application are no longer listed within the rules and are instead set out in a user-friendly format on the application form (D50J).

5.172 *General Procedural Provisions*

Application for consent to marriage of a child or to registration of civil partnership of a child

5.172 If a person aged over 16 but under 18 wishes to marry or register a civil partnership, he or she must obtain the consent of any parent or guardian who has parental responsibility for him or her or other relevant person (eg prospective adopter, special guardian). If such consent is refused or if one or all of the persons required to give consent are either untraceable or under a disability, an application can be made to the court to enable the marriage/registration to take place[1].

The procedure is similar to that prescribed by the old FPR 1991, rr 3.20 and 3.20A. The application must be made in accordance with the FPR 2010, SI 2010/2955, Pt 19 procedure.

The child can make the application without the need for a children's guardian unless the court directs otherwise[2]. If the application is made because of a refusal of a relevant person to give consent, then every person who has refused must be a respondent to the application[3].

As there is no application form prescribed in FPR 2010, PD 5A for an application of this nature, the general Pt 19 application form (FP1) should be used.

[1] Marriage Act 1949, s 3 or CPA 2004, Sch 2, paras 3,4 or 10.
[2] FPR 2010, SI 2010/2955, 8.42.
[3] FPR 2010, SI 2010/2955, 8.43.

PUBLICITY

5.173 The provisions of the former FPR 1991, r 10.28 regulated attendance at private hearings. The new FPR 2010, SI 2010/2955, 27.10 makes it clear that unless otherwise provided (such as, for example, committal proceedings), proceedings to which the FPR apply will be held in private, that is, the general public have no right to be present.

The right to be present is regulated by FPR 2010, SI 2010/2955, 27.11 and it reproduces almost exactly the words of the previous rule, save that it makes it clear that the exclusion of the press is absolute not only in cases involving judicially assisted conciliation or negotiation, but also all matters within FPR 2010, SI 2010/2955, Pt 13 (parental orders) and FPR 2010, SI 2010/2955, Pt 14 (adoption, placement and the like).

Chapter 6

OTHER
FPR 2010, Pts 20, 28 and 30–34

Interim remedies and security for costs – Pt 20	6.1
Overview	6.1
Orders for interim remedies	6.2
Scope and jurisdiction	6.3
Time when an order for an interim remedy may be made	6.4
Procedure for applying for an interim remedy	6.5
Evidence in support of an application	6.6
Urgent applications and applications without notice	6.7
Interim injunction to cease if application is stayed	6.8
Orders for injunctions	6.9
Search orders	6.10
Delivery up orders	6.11
Injunctions against third parties	6.12
Security for costs	6.13
Position prior to FPR 2010	6.13
Security for costs under Pt 20	6.14
Costs – Pt 28	6.15
Overview	6.15
Applications	6.16
Application of Civil Procedure Rules	6.17
Costs in financial remedy proceedings	6.18
(1) Definition of financial remedy proceedings	6.19
(2) Applications for interim orders	6.20
(3) FPR 2010, PD 28A and orders for costs within financial remedy proceedings	6.21
Appeals – Pt 30	6.22
General	6.22
Permissions	6.23
Notice of appeal	6.24
Grounds for appeal	6.25
Enforcement and registration of orders – Pts 31–34	6.26
Enforcement – Pt 33	6.26
Enforcement – general provisions	6.27
Methods of enforcement	6.28
Registration of orders under the Council Regulation, the Civil Partnership (Jurisdiction and Recognition of Judgments) Regulations 2005 and under the Hague Convention 1996 – Pt 31	6.58
Venue	6.59
Forms	6.60
Procedure	6.61
Registration and enforcement of orders – Pt 32: The wider UK context	6.62
Chapter 1 – Scope and interpretation of this Part	6.62
Chapter 2 – Registration etc of orders under the 1950 Act	6.63

6.1 *Other*

Chapter 3 – Registration of maintenance orders under the 1958 Act (registration in the magistrates' court)	6.64
Chapter 4 – Registration and enforcement of custody orders under the 1986 Act	6.65
Reciprocal enforcement of maintenance orders – Pt 34	6.66

INTERIM REMEDIES AND SECURITY FOR COSTS – PT 20

Overview

6.1 FPR 2010, SI 2010/2955, 20.2 sets out a whole raft of interim remedies and orders which may be made by the court. FPR 2010, SI 2010/2955, Pt 20 and FPR 2010, PD 20A largely replicate CPR Pt 25 and its accompanying practice direction[1]. Of particular note is the court's new power to order the sale of 'relevant property', which is either of perishable nature 'or which for any other good reason it is desirable to sell quickly'.

Part 20 also provides guidance on the time when an application for an order for an interim remedy may be made and how such an application may be made. Further detail is also set out in FPR 2010, PD 20A.

Part 20 also deals with security for costs which were not covered in FPR 1991.

Finally, it should be noted that by virtue of FPR 2010, SI 2010/2955, 20.1, Pt 20 does not apply to proceedings in the magistrates' court.

[1] Civil Procedure Rules 1998 (CPR).

Orders for interim remedies

6.2 FPR 2010, SI 2010/2955, 20.2 sets out the courts' extensive powers to grant interim remedies under this Part, but little further guidance is given in the accompanying FPR 2010, PD 20A. To a large extent, the list in FPR 2010, r 20.2 is a consolidation of the courts' existing powers, but in some significant areas, the power of the family court appears to have been significantly widened. The list under FPR 2010, r 20.2 provides as follows:

(1) The power to grant 'an interim injunction' (FPR 2010, 20.2(1)(a)). This is not further defined save that in the glossary an injunction is simply stated as being, 'a court order prohibiting a person from doing something or requiring a person to do something'. As the definition of injunction is not therefore limited by the rules or the accompanying practice direction, it would therefore appear to broaden the court's powers. By way of example, the court had limited powers dealing with the attendance of a party at business premises or being involved in the running of a family business pending the conclusion of proceedings. The court's powers under s 37 of the Matrimonial Causes Act 1973 (MCA 1973) or Pt IV of the Family Law Act 1996 (FLA 1996), were of limited application in such circumstances, although some protection was provided under the County Court Remedies Regulations 1991, SI 1991/1222.

(2) An interim declaration[1]. In financial proceedings, an interim declaration may be appropriate regarding the ownership of property.

(3)　　FPR 2010, 20.2(1)(c) lists available orders as follows:
　　(i)　　for the detention, custody or preservation of relevant property;
　　(ii)　　for the inspection of relevant property;
　　(iii)　　for the taking of a sample of relevant property;
　　(iv)　　for the carrying out of an experiment on or with relevant property;
　　(v)　　for the sale of relevant property which is of a perishable nature or which for any other good reason it is desirable to sell quickly; and
　　(vi)　　for the payment of income from relevant property until an application is decided.

Of these, the most important is the court's power to sell property if desirable to sell quickly. Since *Wicks v Wicks* [1998] 1 FLR 470, CA it has been clear that the court does not have the power to order an interim lump sum or sale of property, although in the more recent decision of *Miller-Smith v Miller-Smith* [2009] EWCA Civ 1297, the Court of Appeal held that a husband was entitled to pursue an interim order for sale of the family home under the Trusts of Land and Appointment of Trustees Act 1996 where there was no power for such an order to be made under the MCA 1973. Such an order was viewed as appropriate in *Miller-Smith* as the husband was having to service a mortgage debt of £7m which he could not afford. Arguably, the provision in FPR 2010, 20.2(c)(v) therefore clarifies the approach adopted by the Court of Appeal in *Miller-Smith*. It should, however, be noted that FPR 2010, Pt 20 does not include any provision for the proceeds of sale to be paid to either party on an interim basis.

(4)　　Under FPR 2010, 20.2(1)(d), an order authorising a person to enter any land or buildings in the possession of a party to the proceedings for the purposes of carrying out an order under sub-paragraph (c), ie the list set out at points (i)–(vi) above.

(5)　　Under FPR 2010, 20.2(1)(e), an order under the Torts (Interference with Goods) Act 1977, s 4 to deliver up goods.

(6)　　Under FPR 2010, 20.2.(1)(f), an order either restraining a party from removing from the jurisdiction assets located there, or restraining a part from dealing with any assets whether located within the jurisdiction or not. This is referred to as a 'freezing injunction'. By virtue of FPR 2010, PD 20A, para 1.2, freezing injunctions may be made by High Court judges and any other judge duly authorised. This provision therefore reflects the power of the court to grant freezing order, otherwise known as Mareva injunctions.

(7)　　Under FPR 2010, 20.2(1)(g), an order directing a party to provide information about the location of relevant property or assets or to provide information about relevant property or assets which are or may be the subject of an application for a freezing injunction. This is in addition to the court's power to order disclosure within proceedings.

(8)　　Under FPR 2010, 20.2(1)(h), an order under the Civil Procedure Act 1997, s 7, ie an order requiring a party to admit another party to premises for the purpose of preserving evidence etc. This is otherwise known as a search order, or historically, an Anton Piller Order. By virtue of FPR 2010, PD 20A, para 1.2, such orders may be made by

6.2 *Other*

High Court judges and any other judge duly authorised. Extensive guidance regarding applications for search orders is contained at FPR 2010, PD 20A, paras 6.1–6.9 and is considered further at **6.10** below.

(9) Under FPR 2010, 20.2(1)(i) an order under the Senior Courts Act 1981, s 34 or the County Courts Act 1984, s 53, ie an order for disclosure of documents or inspection of property against a non-party. This is in addition to the court's power to order disclosure against a person who is not a party under FPR 2010, 21.2.

(10) An order for a specified fund to be paid into court or otherwise secured, where there is a dispute over a party's right to that fund[1].

(11) An order permitting a party seeking to recover personal property to pay money into court pending the outcome of the proceedings and directing that, if money is paid into court, the property must be given up to that party[2].

(12) An order directing a party to prepare and file accounts relating to the dispute (FPR 2010, 20.2(1)(l)).

(13) An order directing any account to be taken or enquiry to be made by the court (FPR 2010, 20.2(1)(m)).

With reference to FPR 2010, 20.2(1)(c) and (g), 'relevant property' means any property, including land, which is the subject of an application or as to which any question may arise on the application.

[1] FPR 2010, 20.2(1)(b).
[1] FPR 2010, 20.2(1)(j).
[2] FPR 2010, 20.2(1)(k).

Scope and jurisdiction

6.3 FPR 2010, PD 20A, para 1.1 specifically states that the practice direction does not apply to orders under the following:

- Children Act 1989, s 48 (power to assist in discovery of children who may be in need of emergency protection);
- Children Act 1989, s 50 (recovery of abducted children);
- Family Law Act 1986, s 33 (power to order disclosure of a child's whereabouts);
- Family Law Act 1986, s 33 (power to order recovery of a child).

FPR 2010, SI 2010/2955, 20.2(3) states that the fact a particular kind of interim remedy is not listed in sub-para (1) of that rule does not affect any power that the court may have to grant that remedy.

FPR 2010, PD 20A, para 1.2 states that High Court judges and any other judge duly authorised may grant freezing injunctions (Mareva orders) under FPR 2010, 20.2(1)(f) and search orders (Anton Piller orders) under FPR 2010, 20.2(1)(h).

Under FPR 2010, PD 20A, para 1.3, in High Court proceedings, district judges have the power to grant injunctions as follows: by consent; in connection with charging orders and appointment of receivers; and in aid of execution of judgments.

In any other case, any judge who has the jurisdiction to conduct the hearing of the proceedings, has the power to grant an injunction in those proceedings[1].

A district judge has the power to vary or discharge an injunction granted by any judge with the consent of all the parties[2].

[1] FPR 2010, PD 20A, para 1.4.
[2] FPR 2010, PD 20A, para 1.5.

Time when an order for an interim remedy may be made

6.4 The power of the court is broad. An order for an interim remedy may be made at any time, including before proceedings are started and after judgment has been given[1]. Under FPR 2010, SI 2010/2955, 2.3, 'proceedings' means, unless the context requires otherwise, family proceedings as defined in the Courts Act 2003, s 75(3).

FPR 2010, 20.3(1) is, however, subject to the provisos in FPR 2010, 20.3(2) as follows:

(a) the rule is subject to any rule, practice direction or other enactment which provides otherwise; and
(b) The court may grant an interim remedy before an application has been started only if the matter is urgent, or it is otherwise desirable to do so in the interests of justice.

By virtue of FPR 2010, 20.3(3), where the court does grant an interim remedy before an application has been started, it will give directions regarding an application to be issued. An exception to this rule is under FPR 2010, 20.3(4) – the court need not direct that an application be started where the interim order made before the issue of proceedings is for disclosure or inspection of documents or property under the Senior Courts Act 1981, s 33 or the County Courts Act 1984, s 52.

[1] FPR 2010, SI 2010/2955, 20.3(1).

Procedure for applying for an interim remedy

6.5 The procedure is set out in FPR 2010, SI 2010/2955, 20.4 and FPR 2010, PD 20A, paras 2.1–2.4. Further rules regarding urgent applications/applications without notice are set out in FPR 2010, PD 20A, paras 4.1–4.5. Rules in respect of applications for orders for injunctions are dealt with at FPR 2010, PD 20A, paras 5.1–5.4, and applications for search orders are covered at FPR 2010, PD 20A, paras 6.1–6.9.

FPR 2010, SI 2010/2955, 20.4 provides as follows:

(a) under FPR 2010, 20.4(1), the court may grant an interim remedy without notice if it appears there is good reason for not giving notice;
(b) FPR 2010, 20.4(2) – an application for an interim remedy must be supported by evidence, unless the court orders otherwise;

6.5 *Other*

(c) FPR 2010, 20.4(3) – if the applicant makes an application without notice, the evidence in support of the application must state why notice has not been given.

These rules must, however, be read in the context of FPR 2010, SI 2010/2955, Pt 4 which deals with general case management powers of the court (see Chapter 1) and FPR 2010, SI 2010/2955, Pt 18 which contains general rules about making an application (see further Chapter 5).

In addition to the provisions of FPR 2010, 20.4, the practice direction provides as follows:

(i) FPR 2010, PD 20A, para 2.1 provides that the application notice must state the order sought and the date, time and place of the hearing.
(ii) FPR 2010, PD 20A, para 2.2 provides that the notice and evidence must be served as soon as possible and in any event not less than seven days before the court is due to hear the application, unless the court directs otherwise. By reference to FPR 2010, SI 2010/2955, 2.9(4), periods of seven days or less do not include non-business days.
(iii) Where the court is to serve the application, sufficient copies of the notice and evidence for the court and each respondent should be filed for issue and service.
(iv) Under FPR 2010, PD 20A, para 2.4, where possible a draft of the order should be filed with the notice. An electronic version of the draft order should also be available to the court in a format compatible with the word processing software used by the court.

Evidence in support of an application

6.6 FPR 2010, PD 20A, paras 3.1–3.4 deal with evidential requirements. A distinction is drawn between applications for search orders and freezing injunctions and applications for other interim injunctions. An application for search orders and freezing injunctions must be supported by affidavit evidence (para 3.1), although applications for other interim injunctions must be supported by evidence set out in either a witness statement or the application notice, provided that it is verified by a statement of truth, unless the court, an Act or a rule in the FPR or practice direction requires evidence by affidavit (para 3.2).

FPR 2010, PD 20A, para 3.3 provides that the evidence must set out the facts upon which the applicant relies for the application, including all material facts of which the court should be made aware.

FPR 2010, PD 20A, para 3.4 reflects FPR 2010, SI 2010/2955, 20.4(3) – where an application is made without notice, the evidence must also set out why notice was not given.

In addition to the above, please also see FPR 2010, SI 2010/2955, Pt 22 and the practice direction that supplements it for information about evidence. (See further Chapter 5 at **5.61** et seq.)

Urgent applications and applications without notice

6.7 FPR 2010, SI 2010/2955, 20.4(3) and FPR 2010, PD 20A, para 3.4 states that where an application is made without notice, the evidence must set out why notice has not been given.

FPR 2010, PD 20A, paras 4.1–4.5 provide specific detail regarding urgent applications and applications without notice. The provisions are as follows:

(1) These are defined under FPR 2010, PD 20A, para 4.1 as falling into two categories; applications where an application in proceedings has already been issued, and applications where proceedings have not yet been issued. In both cases, where notice of the application has not been given to the respondent.

(2) Under FPR 2010, PD 20A, para 4.2, such applications will normally be dealt with at a court hearing, but in cases of extreme urgency, they may be dealt with by telephone.

(3) FPR 2010, PD 20A, para 4.3 deals with the procedure for issuing applications to be dealt with at a court hearing after the issue of an 'application form'. 'Application form' is defined in FPR 2010, SI 2010/2955, 2.3 as being for an application other than under FPR 2010, SI 2010/2955, Pt 18. The procedure is as follows:

  (a) the application, evidence in support and draft order should be filed with the court two hours before the hearing, wherever possible;

  (b) if the application is made before the actual 'application notice' (defined in FPR 2010, SI 2010/2955, 2.3 as an application to which FPR 2010, SI 2010/2955, Pt 18 applies – interim applications etc) has been issued, then a draft order should be provided at the hearing, and the application notice and evidence in support must be filed with the court on the same day or the next working day, or as ordered by the court;

  (c) with the exception of cases where it is essential that the respondent must not be aware of the application, the applicant should take steps to notify the respondent informally of the application.

(4) FPR 2010, PD 20A, para 4.4 deals with applications made before the issue of a substantive application as follows:

  (a) in addition to the provisions set out at para 4.3 above, unless the court directs otherwise, either the applicant must undertake to the court to issue an application immediately, or the court will give directions for the commencement of the application in accordance with FPR 2010, SI 2010/2955, 20.3(3).

  (b) where possible, the application should be served with the order before the injunction;

  (c) where an order is made before the issue of an application, it should state in the title after the names of the applicant and respondent 'the Applicant and Respondent in Intended Proceedings'.

(5) FPR 2010, PD 20A, para 4.5 deals with urgent applications which are made outside normal working hours as follows:

6.8 *Other*

(a) the applicant should telephone the Royal Courts of Justice on 020 7947 6000 and speak to the clerk to the appropriate duty judge in the High Court, or the appropriate area circuit judge where known. Alternatively, the applicant should telephone the Urgent Court Business Officer of the appropriate Circuit who will then contact the local duty judge;

(b) where the facility is available, it is anticipated that the judge will require a draft order to be faxed to him or her;

(c) the application notice and evidence in support must be filed with the court on the same or next working day or as ordered, together with two copies of the order for sealing;

(d) injunctions will be heard by telephone only where the applicant is acting by counsel or solicitors.

Interim injunction to cease if application is stayed

6.8 By virtue of FPR 2010, SI 2010/2955, 20.5, if the court has granted an interim injunction, other than a freezing injunction, and if the substantive application is stayed, other than by agreement between the parties, then the interim injunction will be set aside, unless the court orders that it should continue to have effect even though the application is stayed.

Orders for injunctions

6.9 FPR 2010, PD 20A, paras 5.1–5.4 set out specific rules relating to orders for injunctions. These rules extend beyond freezing injunctions under FPR 2010, SI 2010/2955, 20.2(1)(f) and extend to any form of injunction granted under Pt 20. The practice direction provides as follows:

(1) By virtue of FPR 2010, PD 20A, para 5.1, any order for an injunction must contain the following, unless the court orders otherwise:

(a) an undertaking by the applicant to the court to pay damages to the respondent which he sustains by virtue of the injunction and which the court considers the applicant should pay;

(b) where the order is made without notice, an undertaking by the applicant to the court to serve on the respondent the application notice, evidence in support and any order as soon as practicable;

(c) where the order is made without notice, a return date for a further hearing at which the other party can be present;

(d) where the order is made before filing the application notice (ie the application for the injunction), an undertaking to file the application and pay the appropriate fee on the same or next working day; and

(e) where the order is made before the issue of an application in proceedings, an undertaking to issue and pay the appropriate fee on the same or next working day, or directions for the commencement of the application.

(2) In addition to the undertaking from the applicant required in accordance with FPR 2010, PD 20A, para 5.1(a), the court should also consider whether an undertaking is required from the applicant to pay

Interim remedies and security for costs – Pt 20 **6.10**

(3) By virtue of FPR 2010, PD 20A, para 5.3, where an order for an injunction is made in the presence of all parties who are to be bound by it, or made it a hearing of which they have had notice, that order may state that it is to be effective until final hearing or further order.
(4) Under FPR 2010, PD 20A, para 5.4, any order for an injunction must clearly set out what the respondent must, or must not, do.

Search orders

6.10 FPR 2010, PD 20A provides extensive guidance and detail in respect of search orders, which by virtue of FPR 2010, PD 20A, para 6.1, is not just limited to orders for the preservation of evidence and property. The practice direction provides as follows:

Under FPR 2010, PD 20A, para 6.2, the Supervising Solicitor must be experienced in the operation of search orders. A Supervising Solicitor can be contacted either through the Law Society or through the London Solicitors Litigation Association for search orders in the London area.

FPR 2010, PD 20A, para 6.3 deals with the provision of evidence. The affidavit in support of the application must state the name, firm and its address and the experience of the Supervising Solicitor. It must also specify the address of the premises and whether it is a private or business address. In addition, the affidavit must disclose very fully the reason the order is sought, including the probability that relevant material would disappear if the order were not made.

FPR 2010, PD 20A, para 6.4 deals with service as follows:

(a) Under para 6.4(1), unless the court otherwise directs, the order must be served personally by the Supervising Solicitor. It must be accompanied by the evidence in support and any documents capable of being copied.
(b) Under para 6.4(2), confidential exhibits need not be served, but must be made available for inspection by the respondent in the presence of the applicant's solicitors whilst the order is carried out. Such documents may be retained by the respondent's solicitors on their undertaking not to permit the respondent to see the documents, or copies of them, except in their presence, and not to permit the respondent to make or take away any note or record of them.
(c) Under para 6.4(3), the Supervising Solicitor may only be accompanied by the persons mentioned in the order.
(d) Under paragraph 6.4(4), there is an obligation upon the Supervising Solicitor to explain the terms and effect of the order to the respondent in everyday language. He or she must advise the respondent of their right to take legal advice and to apply to vary or discharge the order. They must also advise the respondent that they may be entitled to rely upon legal professional privilege and privilege against self-incrimination.

6.10 Other

(e) Under para 6.4(5), in the event that the Supervising Solicitor is a man and the respondent is likely to be an unaccompanied woman, at least one other person named in the order must be a woman and must accompany the Supervising Solicitor.

(f) Under para 6.4(6), the order may only be served between 9.30am and 5.30pm, Monday to Friday unless the court directs otherwise.

FPR 2010, PD 20A, para 6.5 sets out detailed rules regarding the implementation of search orders as follows:

- para 6.5(1) – no material shall be removed, unless clearly covered by the order;
- para 6.5(2) – the premises may only be searched and items removed in the presence of the respondent, or a person who appears to be a responsible employee of the respondent;
- para 6.5(3) – where copies of documents which are sought, the documents should be retained for no more than two days before they are returned to the owner;
- para 6.5(4) – in the event that it is material that is in dispute that is removed pending a hearing, in such circumstances the applicant's solicitors should place it in the custody of the respondent's solicitors who should undertake to retain it in safe keeping and produce it to the court when required;
- para 6.5(5) – where appropriate, the applicant should insure the material held in the respondent's solicitors' custody;
- para 6.5(6) – it is the duty of the Supervising Solicitor to make a list of all material removed and supply a copy of the list to the respondent;
- para 6.5(7) – no material shall be removed until the respondent has had reasonable time to check the list;
- para 6.5(8) – where any of the listed items exist only in computer readable form, the respondent must immediately give the applicant's solicitors access to the computers. That will include providing all necessary passwords to enable the computers to be searched and cause the listed items to be printed out;
- para 6.5(9) – it is the responsibility of the applicant to take all reasonable steps to ensure that no damage is done to any computer or data;
- para 6.5(10) – neither the applicant nor his representatives may themselves search the respondent's computers, unless they have sufficient expertise to do so without damaging the respondent's system;
- para 6.5(11) – the Supervising Solicitor shall provide a report on the carrying out of the order to the applicant's solicitors;
- para 6.5(12) – as soon as that report is received by the applicant's solicitors, they shall serve a copy of it on the respondent and file a copy of it with the court;
- para 6.5(13) – in the event that the Supervising Solicitor is satisfied that full compliance with paragraphs 6.5(7) and (8) is impracticable, he or she may permit the search to proceed and the items be removed without compliance with the impractical requirements.

Other general provisions relating to search orders contained in the practice direction are as follows:

(i) under FPR 2010, PD 20A, para 6.6, the Supervising Solicitor must not be an employee or member of the applicant's firm of solicitors;
(ii) under FPR 2010, PD 20A, para 6.7, in the event that the court orders that the order need not be served by the Supervising Solicitor, the reasons for so ordering must be detailed in the order;
(iii) under FPR 2010, PD 20A, para 6.8, the search order must not be carried out at the same time as a police search warrant;
(iv) under FPR 2010, PD 20A, para 6.9, there is no privilege against self incrimination in proceedings in which a court is hearing an application for an order under FPR 2010, SI 2010/2955, Pts 4 or 5 – Children Act 1989 (see the Children Act 1989, s 98).

Delivery up orders

6.11 FPR 2010, PD 20A, paras 7.1 and 7.2 apply to orders, other than search orders, for the delivery up or preservation of evidence or property where it is likely that such an order will be executed at the premises of the respondent or a third party. The court must consider whether to include in the order similar provisions to those specified above in relation to injunctions and search orders for the benefit or protection of the parties.

Injunctions against third parties

6.12 FPR 2010, PD 20A, paras 8.1 and 8.2 set out specific provisions where injunctions are made against third parties.

Paragraph 8.1 states that the provision is to apply to third parties who did not attend the hearing at which the order was made and who have been served with the order. In accordance with para 8.2, where a third party is served with the order and if they request a notice of hearing or a copy of any materials read by the court, including material prepared after the hearing at the direction of the court or in compliance with the order, the applicant or his or her legal representative must comply promptly with the request, unless the court directs otherwise.

Security for costs

Position prior to FPR 2010

6.13 Although FPR 1991 included no specific provision for security for costs, it has been possible for the family court to make an order for security for costs, although that power was only to cover costs impending proceedings; no such order could be made to guard against costs which have already been incurred – *Penny v Penny*[1]. The court's power depended upon the nature of the proceedings as follows:

- proceedings in the county court were governed by County Court Rules 1981, Pt 13, r 8;

6.13 *Other*

- proceedings in the High Court were governed by RSC Ord 23[2], the criteria of which was wider than the corresponding provision in the County Court Rules (CCR)[3].
- appeals were not covered by the Family Proceedings Rules, and therefore by extension CCR and RSC, and were in any event covered by CPR Pt 26.

[1] [1997] 1 FCR 126, [1996] 1FLR 646, CA.
[2] Rules of the Supreme Court 1965, SI 965/1776 (RSC).
[3] SI 1981/1687.

Security for costs under Pt 20

6.14 FPR 2010, SI 2010/2955, 20.6 deals with the substantive rules for applications as follows:

(a) the application may be made by a respondent (but not an applicant) to any application, but see FPR 2010, SI 2010/2955, 20.8 below regarding appeals;
(b) the application for security must be supported by written evidence;
(c) where the court makes an order it will determine the amount of security and also direct the manner in which, and the time within which, the security must be given.

FPR 2010, SI 2010/2955, 20.7 sets out the conditions to be satisfied for the court to make an order for security for costs:

(i) Under FPR 2010, 20.7(1), the court may make an order for security for costs under FPR 2010, 20.6 if the following conditions are satisfied:
- it is satisfied that it is just to make such an order, having regard to all the circumstances of the case; and
- either one or more of the conditions in FPR 2010, 20.7(2) applies, or an enactment permits the court to require security for costs.

(ii) The conditions to be satisfied under FPR 2010, SI 2010/2955, 20.7(2) are all of the following:
- the applicant is resident out of the jurisdiction, but is not resident in any of the following:
  (a) a Brussels Contracting State;
  (b) a Lugano Contracting State;
  (c) a Regulation State as defined in the Civil Jurisdiction and Judgements Act 1982, s 1(3);
  (d) a Member State bound by the Council Regulation;
- the applicant has changed address since the application was started with a view to evading the consequences of the litigation;
- the applicant failed to give an address in the application form, or gave an incorrect address in that form;
- the applicant has taken steps in relation to the assets that would make it difficult to enforce an order for costs against him.

(iii) The court may not, however, make an order for security for costs under FPR 2010, SI 2010/2955, 20.6 in relation to the costs of proceedings under the Hague Convention 1980.

(iv)   In respect of appeals, FPR 2010, SI 2010/2955, 20.8 provides that the court may order security for costs of an appeal against either an appellant or a respondent who appeals, on the same grounds as it may order security for costs against an applicant under Pt 20.

COSTS – PT 28

Overview

6.15 There are relatively few substantive changes to the rules on costs. The general rule remains that the court will not make an order as to costs within financial remedy proceedings; however, specifically excluded from that presumption are maintenance pending suit and interim periodical payments applications.

In addition, there are changes as to detail in so far as the relevant parts of the Civil Procedure Rules on costs apply in family proceedings.

Applications

6.16 FPR 2010, SI 2010/2955, Pt 28 covers four areas as follows:

(1)   **General principle**
Under FPR 2010, SI 2010/2955, 28.1, 'the court may at any time make such order as to costs as it thinks just'. This is a clear statement of the court's discretion as to costs, but must be read subject to the specific provisions in Pt 28.

(2)   **Application of other rules**
FPR 2010, SI 2010/2955, 28.2 specifically deals with the application of the appropriate parts of the Civil Procedure Rules to the Family Procedure Rules. These are addressed in detail at **6.17** et seq below.

(3)   **Costs in financial remedy proceedings**
FPR 2010, SI 2010/2955, 28.3 deals specifically with financial remedy proceedings and re-states the presumption set out in FPR 1991, r 2.71 that the court will not make an order as to costs, although there is a specific exemption with regards to applications for maintenance pending suit/interim periodical payments. A table showing a comparison of the changes to the rules is set out below.

(4)   **Wasted costs orders in the magistrates' court**
FPR 2010, SI 2010/2955, 28.4 simply provides that a legal or other representative against whom a wasted costs order is made in the magistrates' court may appeal to the Crown Court.

Application of Civil Procedure Rules

6.17 By virtue of FPR 2010, SI 2010/2955, 28.2, the Civil Procedure Rules on costs apply to costs in proceedings (as defined in FPR 2010, SI 2010/2955, 2.3 – see Chapter 1 at **1.14** above) as follows:

(a)   CPR Pt 43 in its entirety.

6.17 *Other*

(b) CPR Pt 4, with the following exceptions; which do not apply to proceedings:
- CPR 44.3(2) and (3). In addition, FPR 2010, SI 2010/2955, 28.3 also means that CPR 44.3(1), (4) and (5) do not apply to financial remedy proceedings. This therefore mirrors FPR 1991, r 2.71(1) which stated that CPR 44.3(1)–(5) shall not apply to ancillary relief proceedings. (Note that CPR 44.3C does not apply to proceedings in a magistrates' court. Under CPR 43.2(1)(c)(ii), 'district judge' includes a district judge of the Principal Registry);
- CPR 44.9–44.12C;
- CPR 44.13(1A) and (1B);
- CPR 44.18–44.20.

(c) CPR 45.6 (note this rule does not apply to proceedings in a magistrates' court);

(d) CPR Pt 47 (note that Pt 47 does not apply to proceedings in a magistrates' court).

(e) CPR Pt 48, save that:
- by virtue of FPR 2010, PD 28A, in CPR 48.1(1)(b) after paragraph (ii) there should be inserted '(iii) Section 68A of the Magistrates' Court Act 1980'.
- in CPR 48.7(1) after 'section 51(6) of the Senior Courts Act 1981' insert 'or section 145A of the Magistrates' Courts Act 1980(a)'.

By virtue of FPR 2010, PD 28A, para 2.4, the practice direction about costs which supplements CPR Pts 43–48 (known as 'the Costs Practice Direction') applies to proceedings as follows:

(i) to family proceedings generally, other than in the magistrates' courts, with the exception of sections 6, 15, 16, 17 and 23A of the Costs Practice Direction;

(ii) to family proceedings generally, in magistrates' courts only, with the exception of sections 6, 15, 16, 17, 23A and sections 28-49A of the Costs Practice Direction;

(iii) to financial remedy proceedings, other than in magistrates' courts, with the exception of section 6, paragraphs 8.1 to 8.4 of section 8 and sections 15, 16, 17 and 23A of the Costs Practice Direction;

(iv) to financial remedy proceedings in magistrates' courts only, with the exception of section 6, paragraphs 8.1 to 8.4 of section 8, sections 15, 16, 17, 23A and sections 28 – 49A of the Costs Practice Direction.

Furthermore, by virtue of FPR 2010, PD 28A, para 2.7, paragraph 1.4 of section 1 of the Costs Practice Direction shall be modified in the definition of 'counsel' for 'High Court or in the county court' substitute 'High Court, county court or in a magistrates' court'.

Finally, on the issue of interpretation:
- by virtue of FPR 2010, PD 28A, para 3.1, references to 'claimant' and 'defendant' in the CPR Costs Practice Direction shall be read as references to similar terms to which the Family Procedure Rules apply.

Costs – Pt 28 6.18

- under para 3.2, where there is reference in CPR Pts 43–48 to other rules or other Parts of the CPR, and where there is an equivalent rule or Part in the Family Proceedings Rules, those references should be read as referring to the equivalent rule or Part in the Family Proceedings Rules.

Costs in financial remedy proceedings

6.18 The table below highlights the differences between the FPR 1991 rules and the new FPR 2010, SI 2010/2955, 28.3:

FPR 1991		*FPR 2010*	
2.71(1)	CPR 44.3(1)–(5) shall not apply to ancillary relief proceedings.	28.3(2)	CPR 44.3(1), (4) and (5) do not apply to financial remedy proceedings. By virtue of r 28.2, CPR 44.3(2) and (3) do not apply either.
2.71(2)	CPR 44.3(6)–(9) apply to an order made under this rule as they apply to an order made under CPR 44.3.	28.3(3)	Identical provision.
2.71(3)	'Costs' has the same meaning as in CPR 33.2(1)(a) and includes the costs payable by a client to his or her solicitor.	28.3(4)(a)	Identical provision, save that there is no reference to including the costs payable by a client to his solicitor.
2.71(4)(a)	General rule in ancillary relief proceedings is that the court will not make an order requiring one party to pay the costs of another party.	28.3(5)	Same provision, save that the new rule refers to 'financial remedy proceedings' which are specifically defined under r 28.3(4)(b) – see **6.19** below.
2.71(4)(b)	The court may make a costs order at any stage in the proceedings where it considers it appropriate to do so because of the conduct of a party in relation to those proceedings, whether before or during them.	28.3(6)	Identical provision.
2.71(5)	Issues to which the court must have regard in deciding what costs order, if any, it is to make by virtue of r 2.71(4)(b).	28.3(7)	Identical provision.

6.18 *Other*

FPR 1991		FPR 2010	
2.71(6)	No offer to settle, which was not an open offer, shall be admissible at any stage of the proceedings, save as provided for by r 2.61(E), ie filing of offers for FDR hearings.	28.3(8)	Identical provision, save that the corresponding rule in respect of filing of offers for FDR is FPR 2010, SI 2010/2955, 9.17.

The three principal areas to note in respect of costs in financial remedy proceedings are as follows:

(1) *Definition of financial remedy proceedings*

6.19 By virtue of FPR 2010, SI 2010/2955, 28.3(4)(b) 'financial remedy proceedings' are specifically defined as being limited to the following:

- proceedings for a financial order, save in respect of interim orders (see further **6.20** below);
- an order under Pt III of the 1984 Act, ie for financial relief in England and Wales after an overseas divorce under the Matrimonial and Family Proceedings Act 1984;
- an order under the Civil Partnership Act 2004, s 48(2) and Sch 7.
- an order under Section 10(2) of the Matrimonial Causes Act 1973.

For a comparison of the definition of a 'financial order' under the FPR 2010 and 'ancillary relief' under the FPR 1991, see Chapter 2 at **2.22**.

By way of further clarification, FPR 2010, PD 28A specifically provides that FPR 2010, SI 2010/2955, 28.3 does not apply to an application for any of the following financial remedies:

(a) an order under the Children Act 1989 Sch 1;
(b) an order under the Matrimonial Causes Act 1973, s 27 or the Civil Partnership Act 2004, Sch 5, Pt 9;
(c) an order under the Matrimonial Causes Act 1973, s 35 or paragraph 69 of Schedule 5 Civil Partnership Act 2004; or
(d) an order under the Domestic Proceedings and Magistrates' Courts Act 1978, Pt 1 or the Civil Partnership Act 2004, Sch 6.

(2) *Applications for interim orders*

6.20 By virtue of FPR 2010, SI 2010/2955, 28.3(4)(b)(i), the specific rules relating to costs in financial remedy proceedings as set out in FPR 2010, 28.3 do not apply to the following forms of application for interim orders:

- an application for an order for maintenance pending suit;
- an application for an order for maintenance pending outcome of proceedings;
- an interim periodical payments order;
- any other form of interim order for the purposes of FPR 2010, SI 2010/2955, 9.7(1)(a)–(c) and (e).

In summary, FPR 2010, SI 2010/2955, 9.7(1) provides that a party may apply at any stage of the proceedings for:

(a)   an order for maintenance pending suit;
(b)   an order for maintenance pending outcome of proceedings;
(c)   an order for interim periodical payments;
(d)   an interim variation order; or
(e)   any other form of interim order.

A few points to note:

- Applications for an interim variation order are not caught by the exclusion and therefore the general rule of no order as to costs under FPR 2010, 28.3 applies to applications to vary interim orders.
- 'Any other form of interim order' under FPR 2010, SI 2010/2955, 9.7(1)(e). Applications for interim orders generally are covered by FPR 2010, SI 2010/2955, Pt 20 and are considered in Chapter 5.

(3) *FPR 2010, PD 28A and orders for costs within financial remedy proceedings*

6.21 In determining whether and how to make an order for costs within financial remedy proceedings, the judge must have regard to the list of factors set out in FPR 2010, SI 2010/2955, 28.3(7), but cannot take into account any offers to settle marked 'without prejudice' or 'without prejudice save as to costs'.

In considering the conduct of the parties in that context, the court will have regard to the obligation of the party to help the court to further the overriding objective under FPR 2010, SI 2010/2955, 1.1 and 1.3 and will take into account the nature, importance and complexity of the issues in the case. This may be particularly significant in applications for variation orders and interim variation orders or other cases where there is a risk of the costs becoming disproportionate to the amount in dispute.

Where a party intends to seek a costs order under FPR 2010, SI 2010/2955, 28.3, that should ordinarily be made plain in open correspondence or in skeleton arguments prior to the hearing. Where a summary assessment of costs is appropriate, the parties must file a statement of costs in CPR Form N260.

An interim financial order which includes an element to enable a party to pay legal fees is an order under the Matrimonial Causes Act 1973, s 22/Civil Partnership Act 2004, Sch 5, para 38 and is not a 'costs order' within the meaning of FPR 2010, 28.3.

Where FPR 2010, 28.3 does not apply, by virtue of FPR 2010, 28.2(1), the exercise of the court's discretion as to costs is governed by the relevant provisions of CPR as set out above.

6.22 *Other*

APPEALS – PT 30

General

6.22 One of the most important series of changes introduced by the FPR 2010 relates to the treatment of appeals, particularly appeals from district judges to circuit judges in the county court, the so called 'internal appeals'.

One of the most successful innovations which was introduced by the CPR 1998 was the general need to obtain permission to appeal, either from the court below or the court to which the appeal is to be brought. Thus a meritless application for permission to appeal from a district judge can be determined by the circuit judge without the proposed respondent having to incur any costs, and save in wholly exceptional circumstances there is no further appeal against the refusal of permission to appeal.

On the other hand, the system in relation to family proceedings did not hitherto restrict appeals from the district judge, although in practice there appear to have been relatively few. It is likely that with the expected rise in the number of litigants in person, attempts to appeal by the dissatisfied will increase. Further, the system as it has developed was unnecessarily complicated, with different considerations being applied to ancillary relief appeals from those in children appeals, and so on. The provisions of FPR 1991, r 8.1, which applied to ancillary relief appeals, were significantly different from those set out in r 8.2 and following, which applied to appeals in relation to children, injunctions and various other orders.

The new system introduces a much needed simplification and uniformity to family appeals. It imports a similar system to that which has proved itself over the last 12 years in civil proceedings. However, the FPR 2010 are, as it were, grafted on to the CPR: the FPR provisions are set out in FPR 2010, SI 2010/2955, Pt 30 and FPR 2010, PD 30A, and they govern appeals to the High Court and to the county court: they do not affect or alter the provisions in relation to appeals to the Court of Appeal, which are set out in the CPR. FPR 2010, Pt 30 also applies in relation to appeals from the magistrates' court, which are also now heard in the county court, in place of the earlier system of appeal by case stated to the High Court, and to date appear to have been relatively uncommon: the appeal can only be brought on the grounds that the decision below was wrong in law or in excess of jurisdiction (Magistrates' Court Act 1980, s 111A). It also applies to deduction order appeals from the Child Maintenance and Enforcement Commission, which have their own procedure, set out in FPR 2010, PD30A.

Permissions

6.23 The only immediate problem with the new system is that the relatively short and clear Pt 30 is supplemented by a very lengthy and complicated practice direction, FPR 2010, PD 30A.

The substance of the new procedure is set out in FPR 2010, 30.3(1): this provides that a party, whether appellant or respondent, needs *permission to appeal*:

(a) against a decision in proceedings where the decision appealed against was made by a district judge or a costs judge;
(b) as provided in FPR 2010, PD 30A: at present there are no provisions extending the principle in the practice direction.

Those general principles are subject to exceptions: permission to appeal is not required against a committal order or a secure accommodation order made pursuant to the Children Act 1989, s 25.

The effect of FPR 2010, 30.3 is therefore that a party wishing to appeal from the decision of a district judge to the circuit judge in the county court, or from a district judge of the High Court or the Principal Registry to a High Court judge, requires permission to appeal. However, a party wishing to appeal from the magistrates' court, whether the proceedings were heard by lay justices or a district judge (magistrates' court) retains the right of appeal without having to seek permission. The new procedure does not affect the substantive law: in other words, it does not affect the destination of appeals, but rather affects the way in which they are regulated and imposes filters in certain cases. FPR 2010, PD 30A, para 2.1, sets out a helpful table of routes of appeal in family proceedings.

An application for permission to appeal may be made either to the lower court at which the decision was made which is sought to be appealed, or to the higher court to which the appeal is assigned. If the lower court refuses permission to appeal, that application can then be renewed to the higher court.

The general procedure in the High Court and the county court in relation to applications for permission to appeal in civil proceedings is that the judge either grants or refuses permission on paper: he or she can, of course, order that the application be heard in court, with or without notice to the respondent, or that it be heard on notice with the substantive appeal to follow if permission be given, in which case notice will have to be given to the respondent. This practice is introduced in relation to family proceedings by FPR 2010, PD 30A, paras 4.10–4.21. It is specifically provided in PD 30A 4.17 that where an appellant is funded by the Legal Services Commission (LSC), and permission to appeal is refused without a hearing, the reasons given by the appeal court have to be given to the Commission, and the court may enquire whether this has been done if there is then a renewed oral application for permission.

If the judge refuses permission on paper, the appellant may request that that decision be reconsidered at an oral hearing: such request must be made within seven days of service of the notice refusing permission: see FPR 2010, SI 2010/2955, 30.3(6).

By FPR 2010, 30.3(7) permission to appeal can only be given where:

(a) the court considers that the appeal would have a real prospect of success; or
(b) there is some other compelling reason why the appeal should be heard.

However, if given, permission may be (i) limited to certain issues or (ii) subject to conditions.

'A real prospect of success' may be considered as an entirely straightforward expression: it has however been the subject of decisions under the CPR, which

6.23 *Other*

seem certain to be followed, to the effect that what is required is a realistic, as opposed to a fanciful, chance of success.

Notice of appeal

6.24 All appeals, are brought by notice ('an appellant's notice'): any application for permission to appeal must be brought within such period as the lower court directs, or in default within 21 days of the decision under appeal: FPR 2010, 30.4(2). The appeal court may vary the time limit, but the parties cannot agree so to do[1]. This again is a simplification and making uniform of the previous provisions, which varied in the time prescribed.

The only exception to that general provision is in relation to appeals against the making of orders for interim care or supervision orders under the Children Act 1989, s 38(1). In that case, under FPR 2010, 30.4(3), the notice must be filed within seven days of the decision, and the lower court cannot extend or shorten that period. This is not a new provision and is designed to ensure that appeals against interim care orders in particular, which can be drastic in their effect, are heard as soon as possible. There is a further special provision in FPR 2010, 30.5(7) which prevents a respondent to an appeal in relation to an order made under s 38(1) from himself appealing or from inviting the appellate tribunal to uphold the order of the court below on grounds different from or additional to those given by that court: this again is not entirely novel, but is more far reaching and clearer than the provisions it replaces.

The FPR 2010 also provides specifically for the service of notices of appeal not only on the respondent but also on any children's guardian, Cafcass officer or the like, a local authority which has prepared a Special Guardianship report or a placement report, a local authority or adoption agency which has prepared a report on the suitability of an applicant to adopt, and, where the appeal is from the magistrates, the officer designated for that court under the Courts Act 2003, s 37(1): FPR 30.4(5). This is a longer and more comprehensive list than was set out in FPR 1991, r 8.2A.

A respondent, unless the appeal is against an order made under the Children Act 1989, s 38(1) in respect of which there are special provisions as set out above, may file a notice ('a respondent's notice') if he seeks to appeal or to uphold the decision of the lower court on different grounds. There are elaborate provisions as to the time for filing of such a notice, but in essence in most cases it should be done 14 days after the respondent is told that permission to appeal has been granted to the other party.

As before, an appeal notice does not operate as a stay unless an order is given to that effect: FPR 2010, SI 2010/2955, 30.8.

[1] FPR 2010, 30.7(1) and (2).

Grounds for appeal

6.25 The general theme that wasteful litigation should be avoided is continued in relation to the provisions relating to appeals. An appeal notice has to set out the grounds of the appeal[1]. It can only be amended with permission of the appeal court[2]. At the hearing of the appeal, the appellant cannot rely on any matter not contained in the appeal notice without the permission of the appeal court[3]. However, where there is 'a compelling reason for doing so' the appeal court may strike out the whole or part of an appeal notice and may set aside permission to appeal or impose conditions upon such permission[4]. On refusing an application for permission to appeal, striking out an appellant's notice, or dismissing an appeal, the appeal court should consider whether to exercise its new power to record that the matter is wholly without merit and should then go on if necessary to use its powers to make a civil restraint order.

FPR 2010, PD 30A, para 4.5 also lays down distinctly the important proposition that 'There is no appeal from a decision of the appeal court to allow or refuse permission to appeal to that court': that is, of course, after an oral hearing has been held. This is one of the most important provisions in controlling the litigation.

The powers of the court in hearing an appeal are again imported from the CPR: the important point for the family practitioner is that they now apply to all appeals in the family jurisdiction which come before either the High Court or the county court. The court may affirm, set aside or vary any order or judgment made below, refer any application or issue for determination below, order a new hearing, or make orders for the payment of interest or for costs[5] and may exercise those powers as appropriate in relation to the whole or any part of the order of the lower court.

The general rule in relation to the scope of appeals, which modifies that set out for certain purposes in the former FPR 1991, r 8.2G, is now clear, and is set out in FPR 2010, SI 2010/2955, 30.12(1). It provides that:

'Every appeal will be limited to a review of the decision of the lower court unless . . . [there is a specific provision to the contrary] or (b) the court considers that in the circumstances of an individual appeal it would be in the interests of justice to hold a re-hearing'.

In other words it is not normally appropriate to hold a rehearing, but the court can so order. It is further provided that the appeal court will not, unless it orders otherwise, receive either oral evidence or evidence which was not before the lower court. It may well be that this general principle will be much less strictly applied in cases where children are concerned than is the case with financial matters. However, the general principle is very clear: the appeal court is to consider the decision below and ask whether it should be reviewed: it should not consider the matter afresh.

The court, in all the cases covered by the new rule, is to allow an appeal where the decision of the lower court was either (a) wrong or (b) unjust because of a serious or other irregularity in the proceedings in the lower court: FPR 2010, SI 2010/2955, 30.12(3). The PD says that the grounds of appeal should 'set out clearly the reasons why . . . (a) or (b) is said to apply' and should also set out whether each ground of appeal is on a point of law or is an appeal against a finding of fact.

It is also of importance that FPR 2010, PD 30A, para 14.1 makes it clear that Pt 30 and the practice direction itself apply in relation to consent orders as well as orders made after a hearing. The direction continues: 'An appeal is the only way in which a consent order can be challenged'. This is a clear statement of

6.25 *Other*

principle which should settle the long controversy as to whether application should be made to set aside, as opposed to appeal, a consent order where one party says that he did not give true consent to it, or was subject to undue influence or the like. Henceforth the position appears free from doubt.

A court other than the magistrates' court from which, or to which, an appeal is brought may transfer the appeal to the Court of Appeal if satisfied that it raises an important point of principle or practice or if there is some other compelling reason for the Court of Appeal to hear it: FPR 2010, SI 2010/2955, 30.13. It is likely that this power will be exercised only in rare cases: it is new so far as family proceedings are concerned. FPR 2010, PD 30A, para 2.2 lays down that where the decision to be appealed is an application on a point of law where there was no substantial dispute of fact, the court to which the appeal lies should consider whether to use its power under FPR 2010, SI 2010/2955, 30.13.

[1] FPR 2010, SI 2010/2955, 30.6.
[2] FPR 2010, SI 2010/2955, 30.9.
[3] FPR 2010, SI 2010/2955, 30.12(5).
[4] FPR 2010, SI 2010/2955, 30.10.
[5] FPR 2010, SI 2010/2955, 30.11(2).

ENFORCEMENT AND REGISTRATION OF ORDERS – PTS 31–34

Enforcement – Pt 33

6.26 The procedure for enforcing orders has been complicated due to the partial survival of the RSC and CCR for the purposes of family proceedings[1]. This is because the CPR 1998 do not (and will continue not to) apply to family proceedings except in a few instances[2]. Family practitioners have therefore had to rely on the somewhat antiquated provisions of the RSC and CCR for the enforcement of orders, unable to benefit from the more streamlined provisions of the CPR. FPR 2010 goes a long way to improving the position by incorporating Pts 50 and 69–73 and Schs 1 and 2 of the CPR, with some sensible modifications to take account of the specificities of family proceedings. Parts of the CCR survive (as they do in CPR 1998) but this is stated clearly where applicable[3]. FPR 2010, SI 2010/2955, Pt 33 is therefore close to being a 'one-stop shop' for enforcement.

The main benefit is the harmonisation of enforcement proceedings in civil and family proceedings. The major innovation of FPR 2010 is the introduction of a general application notice in Form D50K, which can either specify the form of enforcement sought or ask for 'such method of enforcement as the court may consider appropriate'[4].

FPR 2010, PD 33A puts undertakings on an equal footing with orders, provided they are drafted correctly and consented to in the proper way (see below).

[1] See **6.13** above.
[2] See CPR 2.1(2).
[3] Note that the retention of parts of the CCR by FPR 2010 correlates with their retention by CPR 1998. See CPR Pt 50, which is incorporated by FPR 2010, SI 2010/2955, 33.1(2).
[4] FPR 2010, SI 2010/2955, 33.3(2).

Enforcement – general provisions

APPLICATION

6.27 All applications for enforcement must be made in a notice of application with a statement in support. This statement must specify the amount owed and show how that figure has been arrived at and be verified by a statement of truth[1]. For example, if interest is claimed, it would be helpful to attach a schedule to the statement showing the working upon which the calculation is based. This is little different from the requirements of the old FPR 1991, r 7.1.

The notice of application can either be the form specific to a particular method of enforcement or the general application form D50K, which actually contains a pro forma calculation.

FPR 2010, 33.2 incorporates CPR Pt 70 with modifications. CPR Pt 70 introduces the (hopefully familiar) terms, judgment debtor and judgment creditor and specifically includes an order for costs within the definition of 'judgment or order for the payment of money'.

[1] FPR 2010, SI 2010/2955, 33.3.

VENUE

6.28 Both CPR 70.3 and FPR 2010, SI 2010/2955, 33.4 make provision for the transfer of proceedings between the High Court and the county court. This may be needed where, for example, the enforcement of a High Court order can be dealt with just as well by a county court. Either way, the application to transfer is made without notice and must be supported by a statement specifying the amount owed and how that figure has been arrived at (FPR 2010, 33.4(2)). Regard should be had to FPR 2010, SI 2010/2955, Pt 18 for guidance on making applications. FPR 2010, 33.4 does not apply to orders for periodical payments or the recovery of arrears.

FORM D50K

6.29 This form is the complement of FPR 2010, SI 2010/2955, 33.3(2)(b) whereby instead of specifying a method of enforcement, an applicant can apply 'for an order for such method of enforcement as the court may consider appropriate'. Where the parties have been out of contact for a long time or if the defaulting party's financial position is opaque, this could be a useful alternative to committing early to a particular method.

The form is very straightforward and asks for the details of both parties, the order and the default. Page 2 is effectively a pro forma statement in support confirming/quantifying the nature of the default, which will satisfy the requirement to file a statement verified by a statement of truth showing how the amount sought has been calculated (FPR 2010, 33.3(1)). However, applicants may wish to submit a separate witness statement, which will give the court the background it needs to establish which means of enforcement will be most appropriate.

6.29 *Other*

The effect of an application in Form D50K is that an order will be made for the debtor to attend court, triggering the procedure for obtaining information from a debtor, which is set out in more detail at **6.31** below. Following this initial hearing, the court will issue an order for 'such method of enforcement as it considers to be appropriate'.

It will be interesting to see what the take up of this new procedure is. It certainly offers an alternative to litigants who may previously have been deterred by having to 'put all their eggs in one basket'.

Methods of enforcement

6.30 The practice direction accompanying CPR Pt 70 lists the more common forms of enforcement[1]. The table below lists them together with some other methods which may be needed to enforce an order in family proceedings and which are covered by FPR 2010, alongside the relevant parts of FPR 2010, CPR 1998 and/or the RSC/CCR, and the form to be used in each case.

Method	*Form*	*References:* FPR 2010	CPR 1998	RSC/CCR
Committal	N40B or PF103, 104 or 105	33.5–33.8	–	RSC Ord 52; CCR Ord 29
Committal by way of judgment summons	D62	33.9–33.18	–	CCR Ord 28 (of limited application)
Attachment of earnings order	N337	33.19[2]	–	CCR Ord 27
Warrant of execution	N323	33.20–33.21	–	RSC Ords 46, 47; CCR Ord 26
Appointment of a receiver	N356	33.22	Pt 69	–
Orders to obtain information from a judgment debtor	N446	33.23	Pt 71	–
Third party debt order (formerly a garnishee order)	N349	33.24	Pt 72	–
Charging order (or stop order or stop notice)	N379 – land N380 – securities	33.25	Pt 73	–

Taking some of the more common methods of enforcement in turn, these are discussed below.

[1] CPR PD 70, para 1.1.

²   Enabling the enforcement of an order of the principal registry.

Committal by way of judgment summons

6.31 Under the Debtors Act 1869, s 5 (as amended to comply with the Human Rights Act 1998), the court can imprison for up to six weeks a judgment debtor who is in default and can be shown to have, or have had, since the date of the relevant order the means to pay but refuses or neglects to do so. Because the judgment debtor's liberty is at stake, an application for judgment summons has a quasi-criminal character. As a result, the judgment debtor is protected against self-incrimination, which puts the onus upon the judgment creditor to prove to the requisite standard both that the judgment debtor has/had means and has nevertheless refused to pay. A corollary of this is that judgment creditors considering this course of action must be very confident as to the cogency of their evidence and comply with the various procedural requirements to the letter.

FPR 2010, SI 2010/2955, 33.9–33.18 replace the old FPR 1991 rr 7.4–7.6 but there is very little change to the procedure which was updated in 2003 to take account of the decision in *Mubarak v Mubarak*[1].

[1]   [2001] 1 FLR 698.

Application

6.32 The application is made in Form D62 and accompanied by a statement which:

- sets out the amount owed and how it has been calculated;
- contains all the evidence on which the judgment creditor relies; and
- exhibits a copy of the order (ie the order made in family proceedings for the payment of money)[1].

If the debtor is in default under a committal order arising from a judgment summons relating to the same original order, no application can be made without the permission of the court[2].

[1]   FPR 2010, SI 2010/2955, 33.10(2) and see definitions at 33.9.
[2]   FPR 2010, SI 2010/2955, 33.11(1).

Which court?

6.33 Applications relating to High Court orders can be made in either the principal registry, a district registry or a county court. Where the original order was made in a county court, the application may be made in a convenient county court. In both cases, regard must be had to where the debtor lives or carries on business wherever the original order was made[1].

[1]   FPR 2010, SI 2010/2955, 33.10(1).

6.34 Other

Service

6.34 The judgment summons generated by the court and statement in support must be personally served on the debtor not less than 14 days before the hearing[1]. The debtor must be paid or offered 'a sum reasonably sufficient' to enable him or her to travel to and from court[2].

The debtor must also be personally served with notice of any adjourned hearing arising from their non-attendance at the original hearing[3].

[1] FPR 2010, SI 2010/2955, 33.11(2).
[2] FPR 2010, 33.11(3).
[3] FPR 2010, 33.13.

Committal

6.35 The judgment debtor can be committed to prison if[1]:

- he or she has failed to attend the initial hearing to which he/she was summonsed and then fail to attend the adjourned hearing; or
- the creditor proves that he or she:
  (a) has, or has had, means to pay; and
  (b) has refused or neglected, or refuse or neglect, to pay the sum due.

As previously, the court has the power to make a new order for payment of the amount due under the original order, together with the costs of the judgment summons, either as a lump sum or in instalments[2]. An order of committal can be suspended on terms that the debtor will pay the creditor the amount due, plus costs and any interest[3].

[1] FPR 2010, SI 2010/2955, 33.14.
[2] FPR 2010, SI 2010/2955, 33.16(1).
[3] FPR 2010, 33.16(2).

ATTACHMENT OF EARNINGS ORDER

6.36 This is a simple and effective means of enforcement where a paying party in default is in salaried employment. It is best suited to the enforcement of maintenance orders. However, a wide range of money orders in family proceedings can form the basis of an attachment of earnings order, including lump sums[1]. An attachment of earnings order cannot be used to secure payment of a sum less than £50[2].

In common with attachment of earnings orders made in the context of civil proceedings, the procedure is governed by CCR Ord 27. The only involvement of FPR 2010 in the process is by virtue of FPR 2010, SI 2010/2955, 33.19, which reproduces word for word the old FPR 1991, r 7.1(4) and enables the enforcement of orders made in the principal registry.

[1] Attachment of Earnings Act 1971, Sch 1.
[2] CCR Ord 27, r 7(9).

Application

6.37 The process is largely administrative and much of CCR Ord 27 is directed towards court staff who must keep an index of all debtors in their local area who are subject to attachment of earnings orders. This is relevant to a creditor who suspects a debtor may reside in the district covered by a particular court. The creditor can make an application for a search of the index in Form N336 to find out whether there are any other attachment of earnings orders in force that may affect their decision whether or not to apply.

An application for an attachment of earnings order is made in Form N337. This captures details about the original order and the nature of the default. In accordance with FPR 2010, SI 2010/2955, 33.3(1), the application form must be accompanied by a statement setting out the amount due and how the figure has been arrived at.

Which court?

6.38 The application can be made to the court for the district in which the debtor lives. If he or she is not resident in England or Wales or the creditor does not know where the debtor lives, the application can be made to the court that made the original order[1].

[1] CCR Ord 27, r 3.

Service

6.39 The court will normally effect service of the application[1]. The debtor then has eight days in which to file a reply in Form N56 unless he pays the sum(s) due within that timescale[2].

[1] CCR Ord 27, r 5(1).
[2] CCR Ord 27, r 5(2), (2A).

Case management and hearings

6.40 If upon receipt of the reply the court office has sufficient information to make an attachment of earnings order it may do so. This order is sent by the court to the debtor's employer[1]. The employer is under a duty, enforceable by criminal sanctions, to give effect to the order: Attachment of Earnings Act 1971, s 23(3).

Either the debtor or the creditor can make an application on notice for the order to be reconsidered within 14 days of receiving it[2]. Provided the time limits and any other requirements set out in CCR Ord 27 are complied with, it would be appropriate for regard also to be had to the provisions of FPR 2010, SI 2010/2955, Pt 18 when making such an application.

[1] CCR Ord 27, r 7(1)
[2] CCR Ord 27, r 7(3)

6.41 *Other*

ORDER TO OBTAIN INFORMATION FROM A JUDGMENT DEBTOR

6.41 Formerly known as 'oral examination of debtor', which was governed by CCR Ord 25, r 3, this can be useful where details of the debtor's means (and consequently what is the most effective form of enforcement) are unclear, especially if the prospect of cross-examination is likely to force the debtor's hand.

Family orders are now on the same footing as those made within civil proceedings by the wholesale incorporation of CPR Pt 71 into the rules by virtue of FPR 2010, SI 2010/2955, 33.23.

It is envisaged that applicants may use the new Form D50K to make an application for 'such method of enforcement as the court sees fit'. The court will conduct an enquiry in accordance with the CPR Pt 71 procedure set out at **6.44** below, which should then reveal which form of enforcement is appropriate to the debtor's financial circumstances.

Application

6.42 The application is made Form N316 for the discrete procedure or Form D50K if the creditor wishes to initiate the generic enforcement procedure alluded to above. The application must contain the information specified in CPR PD 71[1]. This information is captured by the application form and includes details of both creditor and debtor, the relevant order and whether the examination can be carried out by a court officer or whether a judge will be required. The form itself states that '[q]uestioning will be by a court officer unless a judge agrees there are compelling reasons for questioning to take place before a judge'. It is anticipated that all but the most straightforward family cases will need to be referred to a judge as there may be technical questions around the interpretation of the original order, large sums of money involved or the prospect of a cross-application (for example) to vary maintenance and/or remit arrears[2].

If the creditor requires any specific questions to be asked of the debtor or the debtor to produce any particular documents, lists must be attached to the Form N316. This is particularly important where the judge, rather than the court officer, will be carrying out the examination as there are no set questions or standard forms and it is therefore up to the judgment creditor to set the questions (see **6.44** below).

In addition to completing the Form N316, a statement in support identifying the amount owed and how that figure has been calculated should be attached in accordance with FPR 2010, SI 2010/2955,33.3(1). While it may be arguable that CPR Pt 71 constitutes a rule or practice direction stating otherwise, a statement in support will enable the court to determine the correct level of official to conduct the examination and provide further background information beyond the limited details contained in the Form N316. If the order to be enforced is other than an order for the payment of money, the creditor should identify the matters about which the debtor should be questioned[3].

[1] CPR 71.2(3).
[2] Under MCA 1973, s 31/CPA 2004, Sch 5, Pt 11.

[3] CPR PD 71, para 1.2(7).

Which court?

6.43 The application must be issued in the court that made the original order unless the proceedings have been transferred. The court will usually make an order for the debtor to attend in the court of the district where he lives or carries on business[1].

[1] CPR PD 71, para 2.1.

Service

6.44 The application can be made without notice and it is suggested that this will be the norm[1]. The court officer can deal with the application without the need for a hearing[2].

The order to attend court must specify when and where the debtor must attend, the documents he or she must produce and notify him/her that he/she must answer on oath such questions as the court may require[3]. The order requiring the debtor's attendance must contain a penal notice in the form: 'You must obey this order. If you do not, you may be sent to prison for contempt of court'[4].

The order must be personally served upon the debtor at least 14 days before the hearing. If the order is served by the creditor (and it seems unlikely that the court would involve itself in serving orders of this nature) he must notify the court at least seven days before the hearing if he has been unable to effect service[5]. The debtor may request his *reasonable* travelling expenses to attend court within seven days of being served with the order and the creditor must pay[6].

Two days before the hearing (or at the hearing) the creditor must file an affidavit by the person who served the order, giving details of where and how it was served, and (either in the same, or a subsequent, affidavit) confirm whether the debtor requested his travelling expenses and, if so, that they were paid. The creditor must also specify in the same or a subsequent affidavit how much of the judgment debt remains unpaid[7].

It is vital that the creditor complies with his obligations to offer/pay travelling expenses and files the required affidavit(s) otherwise the debtor cannot be committed in case of non-compliance or non-attendance[8].

[1] CPR 71.2(2)(a).
[2] CPR 71.2(4).
[3] CPR 71.2(6).
[4] CPR 71.2(7).
[5] CPR 71.3.
[6] CPR 71.4.
[7] CPR 71.5.
[8] CPR 71.8(3).

6.45 *Other*

Case management and hearings

6.45 Whether a court officer or judge officiates, the debtor must answer questions on oath[1].

There is a standard form of enquiry (Form EX140), which will only be used if a court officer is to carry out the examination[2]. This is similar in appearance to a Form E, albeit that it asks more searching questions about the debtor's assets and current monthly outgoings. In the order requiring his attendance, the debtor will be asked to produce relevant documents, including but not limited to: pay slips, bank statements, building society books, share certificates, rent book/mortgage statement, hire purchase and similar agreements, court orders, any other outstanding bills, electricity, gas, water and council tax bills for the past year. The debtor will also be required to give details of his or her business, including financial statements. The creditor may attend the examination and ask questions[3].

If the hearing is to be conducted by a judge, the judgment creditor must attend the examination and conduct the questioning. No written record will be kept by the court when the examination takes place, in contrast to the position when a court officer officiates[4]. The responsibility for setting the questions and identifying what documents must be produced lies with the creditor and the standard form will not be used, though it may be a useful starting point for the creditor when formulating his questions[5].

If the debtor either fails to attend the hearing or comply with any directions to produce information or documents, the matter must be referred to a circuit or High Court judge who will consider whether an order for the debtor's committal should be made[6].

[1] CPR 71.6.
[2] CPR PD 71, para 4.1
[3] CPR 4.2.
[4] CPR PD 71, paras 4.3 and 5.2.
[5] CPR PD 71, para 5.1.
[6] CPR 71.8(1), (2).

THIRD PARTY DEBT ORDER

6.46 Known to the pre-CPR/pre-FPR 2010 world as a garnishee order, a third party debt order enables a judgment creditor to enforce payment by obtaining an order that a third party who is indebted to the debtor pay back the creditor instead. The main application of this is to compel a bank which holds an account (with a positive balance) on behalf of the debtor to pay some or all of that balance to the creditor in full or part satisfaction of the judgment debt.

CPR Pt 72 is imported into the new rules by FPR 2010, SI 2010/2955, 33.24, the only modifications being minor changes to wording and the disapplication of the provisions concerning the diversion of monies held in court.

Application

6.47 The application is made in Form N349, which captures information about the creditor, debtor, the original order and the third party debt, including precise details to enable bank accounts to be identified (if relevant).

Enforcement and registration of orders – Pts 31–34 6.49

It is important that the creditor is sure of the details of the relevant debt. The practice direction warns applicants against making speculative applications and, where a bank account is concerned, the Form N349 *must* contain details evidencing the creditor's belief that the debtor holds an account with the institution cited[1].

In accordance with FPR 2010, SI 2010/2955, 33.3(1), the application form should be supplemented by a statement setting out the amount due to the creditor and how that figure has been arrived at.

The application can be made without notice[2]. The application will initially be considered by the court without a hearing[3]. Provided the court is satisfied as to the contents of the application, it must first make an interim third party debt order[4]. This order will fix a hearing and direct that the third party shall not reduce the amount owed to the debtor to less than the amount specified in the order[5]. The amount specified will be the amount owed by debtor plus the creditor's fixed costs[6].

[1] CPR PD 72, para 1.3.
[2] CPR 72.3(1)(a).
[3] CPR 72.4(1).
[4] CPR 72.2(2).
[5] CPR 72.4(2).
[6] CPR 72.4(3).

Which court?

6.48 The application must be issued in the court that made the original order unless the proceedings have been transferred[1]. Upon the application of a debtor opposing the making of an order, the court can make an order for the proceedings to be transferred to the court of the district where the debtor lives or carries on business[2].

[1] CPR 72.3(b)(i).
[2] CPR PD 72, para 4.

Service

6.49 The interim order is binding as soon as it is served on the third party[1]. It must be served upon the third party at least 21 days before the date fixed for the hearing and upon the debtor within seven days after service upon the third party and seven days before the date of the hearing[2]. After obtaining an interim order and hearing date, the creditor should sit down with a calendar and schedule the dates for service to avoid errors, particularly the debtor being put on notice of (proposed) service upon the third party and taking steps to close a relevant bank account.

The creditor must file a certificate of service either at or two days before the hearing[3]. Form N215 can be used for this purpose.

After service, the third party has obligations to give effect to the interim order and notify the court and the creditor if the basis of the order is mistaken[4].

[1] CPR 72.4(4).

6.49 *Other*

[2] CPR 72.5(1).
[3] CPR 72.5(2).
[4] CPR 72.6.

Hardship orders

6.50 There is provision for a debtor suffering 'hardship' as a result of the making of an interim third party debt order to make an application for the court to allow the third party to make a 'hardship payment order'. This must be served upon the creditor at least two days before the hearing[1]. The debtor upon such an application must give details of his financial position with documentary evidence in support[2].

[1] CPR 72.7.
[2] CPR PD 72, para 5.6.

Further evidence and hearings

6.51 In the event that the third party has given notice to the creditor under CPR 72.6 that they owe less to the debtor than stated or nothing at all and the creditor wishes to dispute this, he must serve written evidence if he disputes this. This must be served as soon as possible but at least three days before the hearing. Similar provisions apply where the debtor or third party believes another person has a claim to the money stated to be owed[1].

At the hearing the court can:

- make a final third party debt order;
- discharge the interim third party debt order and dismiss the application;
- decide any issues in dispute between the parties, or between any of the parties and any other person who has a claim to the money specified in the interim order; or
- direct a trial of any such issues, and if necessary give directions[2].

If a final third party debt order is made it is enforceable in the same way as a money order and relieves the third party of his obligations to the debtor to the extent of the sum forwarded to the creditor[3].

[1] CPR 72.8(1)–(5).
[2] CPR 72.8(6).
[3] CPR 72.8(6).

CHARGING ORDER

6.52 Charging orders create a security for a sum owed under a court order. A charge can be obtained over land in which the debtor has an interest or other assets such as securities. The order will be satisfied by payment of the judgment debt, or if the relevant asset is sold either voluntarily or following the enforcement of the charge via an order for sale. The procedure for obtaining an order for sale pursuant to a charging order is beyond the scope of this text.

A charging order is not necessarily the quickest route to receipt of sums owed under an order. Attachment of earnings or third party debt orders may provide

Enforcement and registration of orders – Pts 31–34 **6.54**

swifter satisfaction if the debtor's financial position allows it. They are a useful option where the debtor is self-employed or if the details required to obtain a third party debt order cannot be ascertained. However, charging orders can be of particular assistance where a debtor depends upon the sale or remortgaging of property to conduct business.

The ability of the court to make charging orders in respect of an ascertainable sum derives from the Charging Orders Act 1979. FPR 2010, SI 2010/2955, 33.25 incorporates a modified version of the civil procedure at CPR Pt 73 into family proceedings. The modifications make a few minor changes of terminology, disapply the provisions relating to funds/securities held in court and remove references to other regulations not applicable to family proceedings.

CPR Pt 73 also covers the procedure for making an application for a stop order or stop notice which prevent certain steps being taken in relation to securities.

Application

6.53 The procedure is very similar to the procedure for obtaining a third party debt order, namely a without notice application is made, which, if successful, results in an interim charging order, followed by a final charging order.

The application is made in Form N379 (land) or Form N380 (securities). Form N379 captures details of the creditor, debtor, original order and the land to be charged, including the title number. The creditor must also specify the nature of the debtor's interest in the land and state whether there are any other creditors of the debtor (to the best of his or her knowledge) or third party interests in the land, such as co-owners and/or mortgagees. Form N380 captures analogous information.

The application notice can cover multiple assets but if a final order is made, there will be a separate order in relation to each asset[1].

In accordance with FPR 2010, SI 2010/2955, 33.3(1), the application form should be supplemented by a statement setting out the amount due to the creditor and how that figure has been arrived at.

The application will initially be dealt with by the court without a hearing and (provided the basis of the application is correct) an interim charging order will be made and a date fixed for a hearing[2].

[1] CPR PD 73, para 1.3.
[2] CPR 73.4.

Which court?

6.54 The application must be issued in the court that made the original order unless the proceedings have been transferred[1]. Upon the application of a debtor opposing the making of an order, the court can make an order for the proceedings to be transferred to the court of the district where the debtor lives or carries on business[2].

[1] CPR 73.3(2).

6.54 *Other*

[2] CPR PD 73, para 3.

Service

6.55 It is very important that care is taken to effect service of the application notice and interim charging order upon the necessary persons. No less than 21 days before the hearing, the application notice, interim charging order and any documents filed in support must be served upon:

- the judgment debtor;
- such other creditors as the court directs, which may or may not include mortgage lenders;
- trustees as directed by the court, which will include any co-owners if relevant;
- various other relevant individuals in the case of securities[1].

The creditor must file a certificate of service (in Form N215) two days before or at the hearing[2].

Any disposal of securities following service upon the debtor of an interim charging order will be invalid as against the creditor[3]. In the case of an order in respect of registered land, the appropriate application should be made to the Land Registry to ensure that any relevant titles contain a notice or restriction recording the making of the interim order.

[1] CPR 73.5(1).
[2] CPR 73.5(2).
[3] CPR 73.6.

Further evidence and hearings

6.56 If any person (including the debtor) objects to the making of a final charging order, they must file and serve upon the applicant evidence of their grounds for objecting no less than seven days before the hearing[1].

At the hearing, the court can:

- make a final charging order confirming that the charge imposed by the interim charging order shall continue, with or without modification;
- discharge the interim charging order and dismiss the application;
- decide any issues in dispute between the parties, or between any of the parties and any other person who objects to the court making a final charging order; or
- direct a trial of any such issues, and if necessary give directions.

In the case of registered land, the applicant should make an application to the Land Registry to update the entries registered in respect of the interim charging order once a final order has been made.

[1] CPR 73.8(1).

Enforcement of undertakings

6.57 A welcome development is the application of the enforcement provisions of FPR 2010 to undertakings, which unambiguously enables undertakings to be enforced in the same way as orders (with the necessary modifications)[1]. In particular, undertakings for the payment of money achieve an analogous status to orders made under MCA 1973, Part II/CPA 2004, Sch 5 and can be enforced in the same way[2].

To ensure that undertakings are fully enforceable, certain formalities must be complied with. This must be taken into consideration when drafting consent orders in financial remedy proceedings to make certain that beneficiaries of undertakings are afforded maximum protection.

Orders containing undertakings to do or abstain from doing any act:

- must be endorsed with a notice as follows:

    'You may be sent to prison for contempt of court if you break the promises that you have given to the court';

- the person giving the undertaking must make a signed statement as follows:

    'I understand the undertaking that I have given, and that if I break any of my promises to the court I may be sent to prison for contempt of court';

- the giver of the undertaking does not need to be present in court. However, the requirement to file a signed statement must be borne in mind when filing any form of consent order containing undertakings[3].

There is an adapted notice for orders containing undertakings to pay a sum of money:

'If you fail to pay any sum of money which you have promised the court that you would pay, a person entitled to enforce the undertaking may apply to the court for an order. If it is proved that you have had the means to pay the sum but you have refused or neglected to pay that sum, you may be sent to prison'.

The signed statement is also slightly different:

'I understand the undertaking that I have given, and that if I break my promise to the court to pay any sum of money, I may be sent to prison'.

Again, the giver of the undertaking need not be present in court[4].

The option of enforcing an undertaking or other direction endorsed with a penal notice by making an application for the contemnor's committal remains. The procedure is still governed by CCR Ord 29, with modifications[5].

---

[1] FPR 2010, PD 33A, para 1.3.
[2] FPR 2010, PD 33A, para 2.1.
[3] FPR 2010, PD 33A, paras 1.4–1.6.
[4] FPR 2010, PD 33A, paras 2.1–2.4.
[5] See FPR 2010, SI 2010/2955, 33.5–33.8.

6.58 *Other*

Registration of orders under the Council Regulation, the Civil Partnership (Jurisdiction and Recognition of Judgments) Regulations 2005 and under the Hague Convention 1996 – Pt 31

6.58 FPR 2010, SI 2010/2955, Pt 31 offers a complete reworking of the material covered by FPR 1991, rr 7.40–7.55. The conduct of family proceedings with an international element is a complex and specialised discipline and detailed consideration of the new framework is outside the scope of this text. However, the following paragraphs are intended to act as signposts.

Venue

6.59 All applications made under this Part must be made in the principal registry, except for an application for a certified copy of a judgment or for rectification of a certificate issued under Articles 41 and 42. However, this rule does not prevent any other court deciding an incidental question concerning the recognition of a judgment in other proceedings[1].

[1] FPR 2010, SI 2010/2955, 31.3.

Forms

6.60 FPR 2010, PD 5A prescribes the use of five forms for proceedings under this Part:

- C60: Certificate referred to in Article 39 of Council Regulation (EC) No 2201/2003 of 27 November 2003 concerning judgments on parental responsibility (already in use);
- C61: Certificate referred to in Article 41(1) of Council Regulation (EC) No 2201/2003 of 27 November 2003 concerning judgments on rights of access (already in use);
- C62: Certificate referred to in Article 42(1) of Council Regulation (EC) No 2201/2003 of 27 November 2003 concerning the return of the child (already in use);
- C69: Application for registration, recognition or non recognition of a judgment under Council Regulation (EC) 2201/2003 (new);
- D180: Certificate referred to in Article 39 of Council Regulation (EC) No 2201/2003 of 27 November 2003 concerning judgments in matrimonial matters (already in use).

Procedure

6.61 Under FPR 2010, SI 2010/2955, 31.4, applications for the registration, recognition or non-recognition of a judgment are to be made in accordance with the FPR 2010, SI 2010/2955, Pt 19 procedure, as modified by FPR 2010, PD 31A, para 31.8–31.14[1].

Any documents that are required to be produced and are not in English must translated and certified by a notary public or supported by a sworn statement confirming that the translation is accurate[2].

[1] See PD 31A, para 1.1.

[2] PD 31A, para 2.3.

Registration and enforcement of orders – Pt 32: The wider UK context

Chapter 1 – Scope and interpretation of this Part

6.62 This chapter confirms the application of FPR 2010, SI 2010/2955, Pt 32 and confirms a few definitions, none of which are new. The Part applies to:

- the mutual recognition of maintenance orders made in England and Wales, Scotland and Northern Ireland and provisions for their registration;
- the registration of a maintenance order in a magistrates' court for the purposes of enforcement;
- the mutual recognition of child custody orders made in different parts of the United Kingdom, the Isle of Man and Jersey and provisions for their registration.

FPR 2010 makes no substantive changes to the existing procedure but the presentation of the rules is better.

Chapter 2 – Registration etc of orders under the 1950 Act

6.63 The '1950 Act' is a reference to the Maintenance Orders Act 1950, Pt II of which provides for the mutual recognition and enforcement of maintenance orders made in England and Wales, Scotland and Northern Ireland. The term 'maintenance order' includes orders for maintenance payments made pursuant to MCA 1973 and the Children Act 1989, Sch 1[1].

An application to register an English maintenance order in Scotland or Northern Ireland is made by sending to the court officer of the court that made the original order a certified copy of the relevant order and a statement setting out various particulars, including the reason why it is convenient for the order to be enforced in Scotland or Northern Ireland[2]. If the court is satisfied that the payer does indeed reside in Scotland or Northern Ireland and agrees that it is convenient for the order to be enforced there, the court officer will send the order and application to the appropriate person in the other jurisdiction[3].

There are complementary provisions addressed to court officers on the receiving end of incoming orders from Scotland or Northern Ireland[4], which can then be enforced in the High Court[5].

The table below shows how the old provisions have been replaced and notes any changes beyond restructuring of the subparagraphs and improved clarity of language.

FPR 2010		*FPR 1991*
32.2	Interpretation	7.18
32.3	Registration of High Court order	7.19(1)–(3)
32.4	Notice of variation etc of a High Court order	7.19(4)

6.63 *Other*

FPR 2010		*FPR 1991*
32.5	Cancellation of registration of a High Court order	7.19(5)
32.6	Application of this Chapter to a county court order	7.19(6)
32.7	Registration of Scottish and Northern Irish orders	7.20(1), (2)
32.8	– Application to adduce evidence before High Court	7.20(3)
	A payer can make an application to the High Court to adduce such evidence as he would be entitled to put before the court that made the original order for its variation or discharge[6]. This application must be made in accordance with the FPR 2010, SI 2010/2955, Pt 18 procedure.	
32.9	Notice of variation etc. of Scottish and Northern Irish orders	7.20(4)
32.10	Cancellation of registration of Scottish and Northern Irish orders	7.20(5)
	An application to cancel registration can be made by the payee[7]. It must be made in accordance with the FPR 2010, Pt 18 procedure without notice to the payer.	
32.11	Enforcement	7.20(6)
	The application to enforce an order registered in the High Court can be made in accordance with the FPR 2010, Pt 18 procedure, with or without notice to the payer.	
32.12	Inspection of register and copies of order	7.21

[1] For a full list, see Maintenance Orders Act 1950, s 16(2).
[2] FPR 2010, SI 2010/2955, 32.3(1).
[3] FPR 2010, SI 2010/2955, 32.3(2).
[4] FPR 2010, SI 2010/2955, 32.7, 32.9 and 32.10.
[5] FPR 2010, SI 2010/2955, 32.11.
[6] Under the Maintenance Orders Act 1950, s 21(2).
[7] Under the Maintenance Orders Act 1950, s 24(1).

Chapter 3 – Registration of maintenance orders under the 1958 Act (registration in the magistrates' court)

6.64 Orders for periodical payments made in the High Court or a county court can be registered in a magistrates' court[1]. This includes maintenance orders made under MCA 1973 or the Children Act 1989, Sch 1[2].

The advantage of registration in the magistrates' court is that the process of enforcing payment is taken out of the hands of the payee, which keeps his or her costs to a minimum. The court will keep a full record of payments received so that there can be no ambiguity as to the level of arrears and payment history.

Enforcement and registration of orders – Pts 31–34 **6.64**

Beyond the updating of certain words and phrases and improved structuring of the sub-paragraphs, the application process is unchanged by FPR 2010.

The application is still made by filing two copies of Form D151, the appearance of which has been updated in keeping with the format of other forms created for the new rules. The applicant must give basic information about the parties, the order (attaching a certified copy), the payment history and level of arrears, and why he or she wishes it to be registered. The applicant must also confirm whether there are any other enforcement proceedings and that the order is not registered elsewhere. Applicants should be aware that as soon as the court that made the original order grants the application to register the order in the magistrates' court, any attachment of earnings order made by the original court will cease to have effect[3].

As with the old rules, many of the provisions concern the keeping of records and communication between the different levels of court involved in the registration process and the procedure for updating the registration upon variation or discharge.

The table below shows how the old provisions have been replaced.

FPR 2010		*FPR 1991*
32.13	Interpretation	7.22
32.14	Registration of orders – prescribed period	7.23(2)
32.15	Application for registration of a maintenance order in a magistrates' court	7.23(1), (3), (4)
	The new rule clarifies that the application should be sent to the court officer at the court which made the order.	
32.16	Registration in a magistrates' court of an order registered in the High Court	7.24
32.17	Registration in the High Court of a magistrates' court order	7.25
32.18	Registration in the High Court of an order registered in a magistrates' court	7.26
32.19	Variation or discharge of an order registered in a magistrates' court	7.27(1), (2)
32.20	Variation or discharge or an order registered in the High Court	7.27(3)
32.21	Cancellation of registration – orders registered in the High Court	7.29(1), (3), (5)
32.22	Cancellation of registration – orders registered in a magistrates' court	7.29(2), (4)

[1] Maintenance Orders Act 1958, s 1(1).
[2] For a full list, see the Administration of Justice Act 1970, Sch 8.
[3] Attachment of Earnings Act 1972, s 11(1)(a).

6.65 *Other*

Chapter 4 – Registration and enforcement of custody orders under the 1986 Act

6.65 Section 25 of the Family Law Act 1986 provides for the mutual recognition of orders relating to the upbringing of children[1] made in the different parts of the United Kingdom, the Isle of Man or Jersey[2]. Section 27 of the Act provides a framework for the registration of such orders to enable their enforcement and the updating of the registration in case of variation or discharge.

FPR 2010 makes only cosmetic changes to the existing procedure. The table below shows how the old provisions have been replaced and makes a note of any alterations beyond the restructuring of the subparagraphs and improvements to clarity.

FPR 2010		FPR 1991
32.23	Interpretation	7.7(1)
32.24	Prescribed offer and functions of the court	7.7(2)
33.25	Application for the registration of an order made by the High Court or a county court	7.8
	Rather than filing an affidavit in support of the application (old FPR 1991, r 7.8(2)), a statement in support verified by a statement of truth is required instead (new FPR 2010, 32.5(1)(c)).	
33.26	Registration of order made in Scotland, Northern Ireland or a specified dependent territory	7.9
32.27	Revocation and variation of an order made in the High Court or a county court	7.10
32.28	Registration of varied, revoked or recalled orders made in Scotland, Northern Ireland or a specified dependent territory	7.11
	Applications to cancel the registration of an order are to be made in accordance with the FPR 2010, SI 2010/2955, Pt 19 procedure (see Chapter 5) rather than by summons (new FPR 2010, 32.28(3)).	
32.29	Interim directions	7.12
32.30	Staying and dismissal of enforcement proceedings	7.13
32.31	Particulars of other proceedings	7.14
32.32	Inspection of register	7.15

[1] For a full list, see the definition of a 'Part I order' in FLA 1986, s 1(1), which includes s 8 orders, special guardianship orders and certain orders made under the inherent jurisdiction.
[2] Schedule 1 to the Family Law Act 1986 (Dependent Territories) Order 1991, SI 1991/1723.

Reciprocal enforcement of maintenance orders – Pt 34

6.66 The ability to enforce a maintenance order in an overseas country will depend on a number of factors, including:

(a) general considerations as to the financial position and traceability of the payer which would be applicable to any application for enforcement;
(b) the nature of the reciprocal relationship between this jurisdiction and the overseas country in question, which falls into four broad categories:
- Commonwealth countries which are not reciprocating countries under the Maintenance Orders (Reciprocal Enforcement) Act 1972 and are therefore covered by the residual jurisdiction of the Maintenance Orders (Facilities for Enforcement) Act 1920;
- reciprocating countries covered by Maintenance Orders (Reciprocal Enforcement) Act 1972;
- EEA countries covered by the various European regulations and conventions;
- countries where there is no reciprocal relationship.

(c) local conditions and the consequent feasibility of enforcing an order (eg some countries have tight restrictions on the amount of money that can be sent out of the country).

The approach to the foreign state is made by the UK authorities to the central authority in the relevant country and vice versa in the case of 'inward' applications, not by the applicant. The administration of the various reciprocal arrangements is delegated by the Lord Chancellor to the Official Solicitor in the guise of the REMO Unit[1].

FPR 2010 brings together the procedure applicable to applications under the 1920 Act, the 1972 Act and European legislation/conventions. Much of the contents will be familiar from the procedure for applications under the 1972 Act contained in FPR 1991, rr 7.30–7.39. There is a lengthy practice direction[2] accompanying the Part. This contains detailed guidance and modifications to the general procedure in the case of countries falling into the various subcategories, including the USA and Republic of Ireland. This should be consulted carefully before making an application.

Forms REMO1 and REMO2 have been developed for use in conjunction with FPR 2010, SI 2010/2955, Pt 34 applications.

[1] At http://www.courtfunds.gov.uk/os/remo_role.htm.
[2] FPR 2010, PD 34A.

APPENDIX – THE FAMILY PROCEDURE RULES 2010

FAMILY PROCEDURE RULES 2010
SI 2010/2955

Made - - - - 13th December 2010
Laid before Parliament 17th December 2010
Coming into force - - 6th April 2011

CONTENTS

PART 1
OVERRIDING OBJECTIVE

1.1.	The overriding objective
1.2.	Application by the court of the overriding objective
1.3.	Duty of the parties
1.4.	Court's duty to manage cases

PART 2
APPLICATION AND INTERPRETATION OF THE RULES

2.1.	Application of these Rules
2.2.	The glossary
2.3.	Interpretation
2.4.	Modification of rules in application to serial numbers etc.
2.5.	Power to perform functions conferred on the court by these rules and practice directions
2.6.	Powers of the single justice to perform functions under the 1989 Act, the 1996 Act, the 2002 Act and the Childcare Act 2006
2.7.	Single justice's power to refer to a magistrates' court
2.8.	Court's discretion as to where it deals with cases
2.9.	Computation of time
2.10.	Dates for compliance to be calendar dates and to include time of day
	Practice Direction 2A Functions of the court in the Family Procedure Rules 2010 and Practice Directions which may be performed by a single justice of the peace

PART 3
ALTERNATIVE DISPUTE RESOLUTION: THE COURT'S POWERS

3.1.	Scope of this Part
3.2.	Court's duty to consider alternative dispute resolution
3.3.	When the court will adjourn proceedings or a hearing in proceedings
	Practice Direction 3A Pre-Application Protocol for Mediation Information and Assessment

PART 4
GENERAL CASE MANAGEMENT POWERS

4.1.	The court's general powers of management
4.2.	Court officer's power to refer to the court
4.3.	Court's power to make order of its own initiative
4.4.	Power to strike out a statement of case

The Family Procedure Rules 2010

4.5.	Sanctions have effect unless defaulting party obtains relief
4.6.	Relief from sanctions
4.7.	General power of the court to rectify matters where there has been an error of procedure
4.8.	Power of the court to make civil restraint orders
	Practice Direction 4A Striking Out a Statement of Case
	Practice Direction 4B Civil Restraint Orders

PART 5
FORMS AND START OF PROCEEDINGS

5.1.	Forms
5.2.	Documents to be attached to a form
5.3.	Proceedings are started by issue of application form
	Practice Direction 5A Forms

PART 6
SERVICE

CHAPTER 1
SCOPE OF THIS PART AND INTERPRETATION

6.1.	Part 6 rules about service apply generally
6.2.	Interpretation

CHAPTER 2
SERVICE OF THE APPLICATION FOR A MATRIMONIAL ORDER OR CIVIL PARTNERSHIP ORDER IN THE JURISDICTION

6.3.	Interpretation
6.4.	Methods of service
6.5.	Who is to serve the application
6.6.	Every respondent to be served
6.7.	Personal service
6.8.	Service of application by the court
6.9.	Service by the bailiff
6.10.	Where to serve the application – general provisions
6.11.	Service of the application on a solicitor within the jurisdiction or in any EEA state
6.12.	Service of the application where the respondent gives an address at which the respondent may be served
6.13.	Service of the application where the respondent does not give an address at which the respondent may be served
6.14.	Service of the application on children and protected parties
6.15.	Deemed service – receipt of acknowledgment of service
6.16.	Deemed service by post or alternative service where no acknowledgment of service filed
6.17.	Proof of personal service where no acknowledgment of service filed
6.18.	Proof of service by the court etc.
6.19.	Service of the application by an alternative method or at an alternative place
6.20.	Power of the court to dispense with service of the application
6.21.	Notification of failure of service by the court
6.22.	Notice of non-service by bailiff

CHAPTER 3
SERVICE OF DOCUMENTS OTHER THAN AN APPLICATION FOR A MATRIMONIAL ORDER OR CIVIL PARTNERSHIP ORDER IN THE UNITED KINGDOM

6.23.	Method of service
6.24.	Who is to serve
6.25.	Personal service
6.26.	Address for service
6.27.	Change of address for service

Family Procedure Rules 2010

6.28.	Service of an application form commencing proceedings on children and protected parties
6.29.	Service of other documents on or by children and protected parties where a litigation friend has been or will be appointed
6.30.	Service on or by children where a children's guardian has been or will be appointed under rule 16.4
6.31.	Service on or by children where a children's guardian has been appointed under rule 16.3
6.32.	Supplementary provisions relating to service on children and protected parties
6.33.	Supplementary provision relating to service on children
6.34.	Deemed service
6.35.	Service by an alternative method or at an alternative place
6.36.	Power to dispense with service
6.37.	Certificate of service
6.38.	Notification of outcome of service by the court
6.39.	Notification of non-service by bailiff

CHAPTER 4
SERVICE OUT OF THE JURISDICTION

6.40.	Scope and interpretation
6.41.	Permission to serve not required
6.42.	Period for acknowledging service or responding to application where application is served out of the jurisdiction
6.43.	Method of service – general provisions
6.44.	Service in accordance with the Service Regulation
6.45.	Service through foreign governments, judicial authorities and British Consular authorities
6.46.	Procedure where service is to be through foreign governments, judicial authorities and British Consular authorities
6.47.	Translation of application form or other document
6.48.	Undertaking to be responsible for expenses of the Foreign and Commonwealth Office
	Practice Direction 6A Service within the Jurisdiction
	Practice Direction 6B Service out of the Jurisdiction
	Practice Direction 6C Practice Direction (Disclosure of Addresses by Government Departments)

PART 7
PROCEDURE FOR APPLICATIONS IN MATRIMONIAL AND CIVIL PARTNERSHIP PROCEEDINGS

CHAPTER 1
APPLICATION AND INTERPRETATION

7.1.	Application and interpretation
7.2.	District Registries
7.3.	Principal Registry
7.4.	References to respondents

CHAPTER 2
RULES ABOUT STARTING AND RESPONDING TO PROCEEDINGS

7.5.	Starting proceedings
7.6.	Statement of reconciliation
7.7.	Limitation on applications in respect of same marriage or civil partnership
7.8.	Service of application
7.9.	Withdrawal of application before service
7.10.	Who the parties are
7.11.	Nullity: Interim and full gender recognition certificates

The Family Procedure Rules 2010

7.12.	What the respondent and co-respondent should do on receiving the application
7.13.	Amendments to the application and the answer
7.14.	How the respondent can make an application
7.15.	Further information about the contents of the application and the answer

CHAPTER 3
HOW THE COURT DETERMINES MATRIMONIAL AND CIVIL PARTNERSHIP PROCEEDINGS

7.16.	General rule – hearing to be in public
7.17.	Exercise of jurisdiction in cases heard at place other than the court in which the case is proceeding
7.18.	Notice of hearing
7.19.	Applications for a decree nisi or a conditional order
7.20.	What the court will do on an application for a decree nisi, a conditional order, a decree of judicial separation or a separation order
7.21.	Further provisions about costs
7.22.	What the court must do for the case management hearing
7.23.	Where proceedings under this Part may be heard
7.24.	The circumstances in which proceedings may be transferred between courts
7.25.	The procedure for complying with section 41 of 1973 Act or section 63 of 2004 Act
7.26.	Medical examinations in proceedings for nullity of marriage
7.27.	Stay of proceedings

CHAPTER 4
COURT ORDERS

7.28.	The circumstances in which an order may be set aside (rescission)
7.29.	Applications under section 10(2) of 1973 Act or section 48(2) of 2004 Act
7.30.	Orders under section 10A(2) of the 1973 Act
7.31.	Applications to prevent decrees nisi being made absolute or conditional orders being made final
7.32.	Making decrees nisi absolute or conditional orders final by giving notice
7.33.	Applications to make decrees nisi absolute or conditional orders final
7.34.	What the court officer must do when a decree nisi is made absolute
7.35.	What the court officer must do when a conditional order is made final
7.36.	Records of decrees absolute and final orders
	Practice Direction 7A Procedure on Applications in Matrimonial and Civil Partnership Proceedings
	Practice Direction 7B Medical Examinations on Applications for Annulment of a Marriage
	Practice Direction 7C Polygamous Marriages
	Practice Direction 7D Gender Recognition Act 2004

PART 8
PROCEDURE FOR MISCELLANEOUS APPLICATIONS

CHAPTER 1
PROCEDURE

8.1.	Procedure

CHAPTER 2
APPLICATION FOR CORRECTED GENDER RECOGNITION CERTIFICATE

8.2.	Scope of this Chapter
8.3.	Where to start proceedings
8.4.	Who the parties are
8.5.	Delivery of copy certificate to Secretary of State

CHAPTER 3
APPLICATION FOR ALTERATION OF MAINTENANCE AGREEMENT AFTER DEATH OF ONE PARTY

8.6.	Scope of this Chapter
8.7.	Where to start proceedings
8.8.	Who the parties are
8.9.	Representative parties
8.10.	Acknowledgment of service
8.11.	Hearings may be in private

CHAPTER 4
APPLICATION FOR QUESTION AS TO PROPERTY TO BE DECIDED IN SUMMARY WAY

8.12.	Scope of this Chapter
8.13.	Procedure
8.14.	Where to start proceedings
8.15.	Mortgagees as parties
8.16.	Injunctions
8.17.	Application of other rules

CHAPTER 5
DECLARATIONS

8.18.	Scope of this Chapter
8.19.	Where to start proceedings
8.20.	Who the parties are
8.21.	The role of the Attorney General
8.22.	Declarations of parentage

CHAPTER 6
APPLICATION FOR PERMISSION TO APPLY FOR A FINANCIAL REMEDY AFTER OVERSEAS PROCEEDINGS

8.23.	Scope of this Chapter
8.24.	Where and how to start proceedings
8.25.	Application to be made without notice
8.26.	Notification of hearing date
8.27.	Hearings to be in private unless the court directs otherwise
8.28.	Direction that application be dealt with by a district judge of the principal registry

CHAPTER 7
APPLICATION FOR THE TRANSFER OF A TENANCY UNDER SECTION 53 OF, AND SCHEDULE 7 TO, THE 1996 ACT

8.29.	Scope of this Chapter
8.30.	Where to start proceedings
8.31.	Service of the application
8.32.	Who the parties are
8.33.	Orders for disclosure
8.34.	Injunctions

CHAPTER 8
APPLICATIONS FOR ORDERS PREVENTING AVOIDANCE UNDER SECTION 32L OF THE CHILD SUPPORT ACT 1991

8.35.	Scope of this Chapter
8.36.	Interpretation
8.37.	Where to start proceedings
8.38.	Who the parties are
8.39.	Service of the application
8.40.	Applications without notice

The Family Procedure Rules 2010

CHAPTER 9
APPLICATION FOR CONSENT TO MARRIAGE OF A CHILD OR TO REGISTRATION OF CIVIL PARTNERSHIP OF A CHILD

8.41.	Scope of this Chapter
8.42.	Child acting without a children's guardian
8.43.	Who the respondents are

PART 9
APPLICATIONS FOR A FINANCIAL REMEDY

CHAPTER 1
APPLICATION AND INTERPRETATION

9.1.	Application
9.2.	Application of Magistrates' Courts Rules 1981
9.3.	Interpretation

CHAPTER 2
PROCEDURE FOR APPLICATIONS

9.4.	When an Application for a financial order may be made
9.5.	Where to start proceedings
9.6.	Application for an order preventing a disposition
9.7.	Application for interim orders
9.8.	Application for periodical payments order at same rate as an order for maintenance pending suit
9.9.	Application for periodical payments order at same rate as an order for maintenance pending outcome of proceedings

CHAPTER 3
APPLICATIONS FOR FINANCIAL REMEDIES FOR CHILDREN

9.10.	Application by parent, guardian etc for financial remedy in respect of children
9.11.	Children to be separately represented on certain applications

CHAPTER 4
PROCEDURE IN THE HIGH COURT AND COUNTY COURT AFTER FILING AN APPLICATION

9.12.	Duties of the court and the applicant upon issuing an application
9.13.	Service of application on mortgagees, trustees etc
9.14.	Procedure before the first appointment
9.15.	Duties of the court at the first appointment
9.16.	After the first appointment
9.17.	The FDR appointment

CHAPTER 5
PROCEDURE IN THE MAGISTRATES' COURT AFTER FILING AN APPLICATION

9.18.	Duties of the court and the applicant upon filing an application
9.19.	Procedure before the first hearing
9.20.	Power of the court to direct filing of evidence and set dates for further hearings
9.21.	Who the respondent is on an application under section 20 or section 20A of the 1978 Act or Part 6 of Schedule 6 to the 2004 Act
9.22.	Proceedings by or against a person outside England and Wales for orders under section 20 of the 1978 Act or paragraphs 30 to 34 of Schedule 6 to the 2004 Act other than proceedings for variation of orders
9.23.	Duty to make entries in the court's register

CHAPTER 6
GENERAL PROCEDURE

9.24.	Power to order delivery up of possession etc.
9.25.	Where proceedings may be heard

9.26.	Applications for consent orders for financial remedy

CHAPTER 7
ESTIMATES OF COSTS

9.27.	Estimates of Costs
9.28.	Duty to make open proposals

CHAPTER 8
PENSIONS

9.29.	Application and interpretation of this Chapter
9.30.	What the party with pension rights must do when the court fixes a first appointment
9.31.	Applications for pension sharing orders
9.32.	Applications for consent orders for pension sharing
9.33.	Applications for pension attachment orders
9.34.	Applications for consent orders for pension attachment
9.35.	Pension sharing orders or pension attachment orders
9.36.	Duty of the court upon making a pension sharing order or a pension attachment order
9.37.	Procedure where Pension Protection Fund becomes involved with the pension scheme

CHAPTER 9
PENSION PROTECTION FUND COMPENSATION

9.38.	Application and interpretation of this Chapter
9.39.	What the party with compensation rights must do when the court fixes a first appointment
9.40.	Applications for pension compensation sharing orders
9.41.	Applications for consent orders for pension compensation sharing
9.42.	Applications for pension compensation attachment orders
9.43.	Applications for consent orders for pension compensation attachment
9.44.	Pension compensation sharing orders or pension compensation attachment orders
9.45.	Duty of the court upon making a pension compensation sharing order or a pension compensation attachment order

Practice Direction 9A Applications for a Financial Remedy

PART 10
APPLICATIONS UNDER PART 4 OF THE FAMILY LAW ACT 1996

10.1.	Scope and interpretation of this Part
10.2.	Applications for an occupation order or a non-molestation order
10.3.	Service of the application
10.4.	Transfer of pending proceedings to another court
10.5.	Privacy
10.6.	Service of an order
10.7.	Representations made by a mortgagee or landlord
10.8.	Applications to vary, extend or discharge an order
10.9.	Orders containing provisions to which a power of arrest is attached
10.10.	Service of an order on the officer for the time being in charge of a police station
10.11.	Proceedings following arrest in a county court or the High Court
10.12.	Enforcement of an order in a county court
10.13.	Enforcement of an undertaking in a county court
10.14.	Power to adjourn the hearing for consideration of the penalty
10.15.	Hospital orders or guardianship orders under the Mental Health Act 1983
10.16.	Transfer directions under section 48 of the Mental Health Act 1983
10.17.	Recognizances

Practice Direction 10A Part 4 of the Family Law Act 1996

The Family Procedure Rules 2010

PART 11
APPLICATIONS UNDER PART 4A OF THE FAMILY LAW ACT 1996

11.1.	Scope and interpretation
11.2.	Applications
11.3.	Permission to apply
11.4.	Service of applications on notice
11.5.	Transfer of proceedings
11.6.	Parties
11.7.	Hearings and service of orders
11.8.	Orders made by the court of its own initiative
11.9.	Representations in respect of orders
11.10.	Applications to vary, extend or discharge an order
11.11.	Orders containing provisions to which a power of arrest is attached
11.12.	Service where order contains a power of arrest
11.13.	Application for issue of warrant for arrest
11.14.	Proceedings following arrest
11.15.	Enforcement of orders
11.16.	Power to adjourn the hearing for consideration of the penalty
11.17.	Hospital orders or guardianship orders under the Mental Health Act 1983
11.18.	Transfer directions under section 48 of the Mental Health Act 1983
11.19.	Recognizances

PART 12
PROCEEDINGS RELATING TO CHILDREN EXCEPT PARENTAL ORDER PROCEEDINGS AND PROCEEDINGS FOR APPLICATIONS IN ADOPTION, PLACEMENT AND RELATED

CHAPTER 1
INTERPRETATION AND APPLICATION OF THIS PART

12.1.	Application of this Part
12.2.	Interpretation

CHAPTER 2
GENERAL RULES

12.3.	Who the parties are
12.4.	Notice of proceedings to person with foreign parental responsibility
12.5.	What the court will do when the application has been issued
12.6.	Children's guardian, solicitor and reports under section 7 of the 1989 Act
12.7.	What a court officer will do
12.8.	Service of the application
12.9.	Request for transfer from magistrates' court to county court or to another magistrates' court
12.10.	Procedure following refusal of magistrates' court to order transfer
12.11.	Transfer of proceedings from one court to another court
12.12.	Directions
12.13.	Setting dates for hearings and setting or confirming the timetable and date for the final hearing
12.14.	Attendance at hearings
12.15.	Steps taken by the parties
12.16.	Applications without notice
12.17.	Investigation under section 37 of the 1989 Act
12.18.	Disclosure of a report under section 14A(8) or (9) of the 1989 Act
12.19.	Additional evidence
12.20.	Expert evidence-examination of child
12.21.	Hearings

Family Procedure Rules 2010

CHAPTER 3
SPECIAL PROVISIONS ABOUT PUBLIC LAW PROCEEDINGS

12.22.	Application of rules 12.23 to 12.26
12.23.	Timetable for the Child
12.24.	Directions
12.25.	First Appointment, Case Management Conference and Issues Resolution Hearing
12.26.	Discussion between advocates
12.27.	Matters prescribed for the purposes of the Act
12.28.	Exclusion requirements: interim care orders and emergency protection orders
12.29.	Notification of consent
12.30.	Proceedings for secure accommodation orders: copies of reports

CHAPTER 4
SPECIAL PROVISIONS ABOUT PRIVATE LAW PROCEEDINGS

12.31.	The First Hearing Dispute Resolution Appointment
12.32.	Answer
12.33.	Applications for warning notices or applications to amend enforcement orders by reason of change of residence
12.34.	Service of a risk assessment
12.35.	Service of enforcement orders or orders amending or revoking enforcement orders

CHAPTER 5
SPECIAL PROVISIONS ABOUT INHERENT JURISDICTION PROCEEDINGS

12.36.	Where to start proceedings
12.37.	Child as respondent to wardship proceedings
12.38.	Registration requirements
12.39.	Notice of child's whereabouts
12.40.	Enforcement of orders in wardship proceedings
12.41.	Child ceasing to be ward of court
12.42.	Adoption of a child who is a ward of court

CHAPTER 6
PROCEEDINGS UNDER THE 1980 HAGUE CONVENTION, THE EUROPEAN CONVENTION, THE COUNCIL REGULATION, AND THE 1996 HAGUE CONVENTION

12.43.	Scope
Section 1	Proceedings under the 1980 Hague Convention or the European Convention
12.44.	Interpretation
12.45.	Where to start proceedings
12.46.	Evidence in support of application
12.47.	Without-notice applications
12.48.	Directions
12.49.	Answer
12.50.	Filing and serving written evidence
12.51.	Adjournment
12.52.	Stay of proceedings upon notification of wrongful removal etc.
12.53.	Stay of proceedings where application made under s.16 of the 1985 Act (registration of decisions under the European Convention)
12.54.	Transfer of proceedings
12.55.	Revocation and variation of registered decisions
12.56.	The central index of decisions registered under the 1985 Act
12.57.	Disclosure of information in proceedings under the European Convention

The Family Procedure Rules 2010

Section 2	Applications relating to the Council Regulation and the 1996 Hague Convention
12.58.	Interpretation
12.59.	Procedure under Article 11(6) of the Council Regulation where the court makes a non-return order under Article 13 of the 1980 Hague Convention
12.60.	Procedure under Article 11(7) of the Council Regulation where the court receives a non-return order made under Article 13 of the 1980 Hague Convention by a court in another Member State
12.61.	Transfer of proceedings under Article 15 of the Council Regulation or under Article 8 of the 1996 Hague Convention
12.62.	Application by a party for transfer of the proceedings
12.63.	Application by a court of another Member State or another Contracting State for transfer of the proceedings
12.64.	Exercise by the court of its own initiative of powers to seek to transfer the proceedings
12.65.	Application to High Court to make request under Article 15 of the Council Regulation or Article 9 of the 1996 Hague Convention to request transfer of jurisdiction
12.66.	Procedure where the court receives a request from the authorities of another Member State or Contracting State to assume jurisdiction in a matter concerning a child
12.67.	Service of the court's order or request relating to transfer of jurisdiction under the Council Regulation or the 1996 Hague Convention
12.68.	Questions as to the court's jurisdiction or whether the proceedings should be stayed
12.69.	Request for consultation as to contemplated placement of child in England and Wales
12.70.	Request made by court in England and Wales for consultation as to contemplated placement of child in another Member State or Contracting State
12.71.	Application for a declaration as to the extent, or existence, of parental responsibility in relation to a child under Article 16 of the 1996 Hague Convention

CHAPTER 7
COMMUNICATION OF INFORMATION: PROCEEDINGS RELATING TO CHILDREN

12.72.	Interpretation
12.73.	Communication of information: general
12.74.	Instruction of experts
12.75.	Communication of information for purposes connected with the proceedings
	Practice Direction 12A Public Proceedings Guide to Case Management: April 2010
	Practice Direction 12B Revised Private Law Programme
	Practice Direction 12C Service of Application in Certain Proceedings Relating to Children
	Practice Direction 12D Inherent Jurisdiction (including Wardship) Proceedings
	Practice Direction 12E Urgent Business
	Practice Direction 12F International Child Abduction
	Practice Direction 12G Communication of Information
	Practice Direction 12H Contribution Orders
	Practice Direction 12I Applications for Reporting Restriction Orders
	Practice Direction 12J Residence and Contact Orders: Domestic Violence and Harm
	Practice Direction 12K President's Direction (Children Act 1989: Exclusion Requirement)
	Practice Direction 12L Children Act 1989: Risk Assessments under Section 16A
	Practice Direction 12M Family Assistance Orders: Consultation

Family Procedure Rules 2010

Practice Direction 12N Enforcement of Children Act 1989 Contact Orders: Disclosure of Information to Officers of the National Probation Service (High Court and county court)
Practice Direction 12O Practice Direction (Arrival of Child in England by Air)
Practice Direction 12P Registrar's Direction (Removal from jurisdiction: issue of Passports)

PART 13
PROCEEDINGS UNDER SECTION 54 OF THE HUMAN FERTILISATION AND EMBRYOLOGY ACT 2008

13.1.	Interpretation and application
13.2.	Application of Part 12
13.3.	Who the parties are
13.4.	Notice of proceedings to person with foreign parental responsibility
13.5.	What the court or a court officer will do when the application has been issued
13.6.	Service of the application and other documents
13.7.	Acknowledgement
13.8.	Date for first directions hearing
13.9.	The first directions hearing
13.10.	Where the agreement of the other parent or the woman who carried the child is not required
13.11.	Agreement
13.12.	Reports of the parental order reporter and disclosure to the parties
13.13.	Notice of final hearing
13.14.	The final hearing
13.15.	Proof of identity of the child
13.16.	Disclosing information to an adult who was subject to a parental order
13.17.	Application for recovery orders
13.18.	Keeping of registers, custody, inspection and disclosure of documents and information
13.19.	Documents held by the court not to be inspected or copied without the court's permission
13.20.	Orders
13.21.	Copies of orders
13.22.	Amendment and revocation of orders

PART 14
PROCEDURE FOR APPLICATIONS IN ADOPTION, PLACEMENT AND RELATED PROCEEDINGS

14.1.	Application of this Part and interpretation
14.2.	Application for a serial number
14.3.	Who the parties are
14.4.	Notice of proceedings to person with foreign parental responsibility
14.5.	Who is to serve
14.6.	What the court or a court officer will do when the application has been issued
14.7.	Date for first directions hearing
14.8.	The first directions hearing
14.9.	Requesting the court to dispense with the consent of any parent or guardian
14.10.	Consent
14.11.	Reports by the adoption agency or local authority
14.12.	Health reports
14.13.	Confidential reports to the court and disclosure to the parties
14.14.	Communication of information relating to proceedings
14.15.	Notice of final hearing
14.16.	The final hearing

The Family Procedure Rules 2010

14.17.	Proof of identity of the child
14.18.	Disclosing information to an adopted adult
14.19.	Translation of documents
14.20.	Application for recovery orders
14.21.	Inherent jurisdiction and fathers without parental responsibility
14.22.	Timing of applications for section 89 order
14.23.	Custody of documents
14.24.	Documents held by the court not to be inspected or copied without the court's permission
14.25.	Orders
14.26.	Copies of orders
14.27.	Amendment and revocation of orders
14.28.	Keeping registers in the family proceedings court
	Practice Direction 14A Who Receives a Copy of the Application Form for Orders in Proceedings
	Practice Direction 14B The First Directions Hearing — Adoptions with a Foreign Element
	Practice Direction 14C Reports by the Adoption Agency or Local Authority
	Practice Direction 14D Reports by a Registered Medical Practitioner ("Health Reports")
	Practice Direction 14E Communication of Information Relating to the Proceedings
	Practice Direction 14F Disclosing Information to an Adopted Adult

PART 15
REPRESENTATION OF PROTECTED PARTIES

15.1.	Application of this Part
15.2.	Requirement for litigation friend in proceedings
15.3.	Stage of proceedings at which a litigation friend becomes necessary
15.4.	Who may be a litigation friend for a protected party without a court order
15.5.	How a person becomes a litigation friend without a court order
15.6.	How a person becomes a litigation friend by court order
15.7.	Court's power to change litigation friend and to prevent person acting as litigation friend
15.8.	Appointment of litigation friend by court order – supplementary
15.9.	Procedure where appointment of litigation friend comes to an end
	Practice Direction 15A Protected Parties

PART 16
REPRESENTATION OF CHILDREN AND REPORTS IN PROCEEDINGS INVOLVING CHILDREN

CHAPTER 1
APPLICATION OF THIS PART

16.1.	Application of this Part

CHAPTER 2
CHILD AS PARTY IN FAMILY PROCEEDINGS

16.2.	When the court may make a child a party to proceedings

CHAPTER 3
WHEN A CHILDREN'S GUARDIAN OR LITIGATION FRIEND WILL BE APPOINTED

16.3.	Appointment of a children's guardian in specified proceedings or proceedings to which Part 14 applies
16.4.	Appointment of a children's guardian in proceedings not being specified proceedings or proceedings to which Part 14 applies
16.5.	Requirement for a litigation friend

CHAPTER 4
WHERE A CHILDREN'S GUARDIAN OR LITIGATION FRIEND IS NOT REQUIRED

16.6. Circumstances in which a child does not need a children's guardian or litigation friend

CHAPTER 5
LITIGATION FRIEND

16.7. Application of this Chapter
16.8. Stage of proceedings at which a litigation friend becomes necessary
16.9. Who may be a litigation friend for a child without a court order
16.10. How a person becomes a litigation friend without a court order
16.11. Appointment of litigation friend by the court
16.12. Court's power to change litigation friend and to prevent person acting as litigation friend
16.13. Appointment of litigation friend by court order – supplementary
16.14. Powers and duties of litigation friend
16.15. Procedure where appointment of litigation friend comes to an end

CHAPTER 6
CHILDREN'S GUARDIAN APPOINTED UNDER RULE 16.3

16.16. Application of this Chapter
16.17. Who may be a children's guardian
16.18. What the court or a court officer will do once the court has made a decision about appointing a children's guardian
16.19. Termination of the appointment of the children's guardian
16.20. Powers and duties of the children's guardian
16.21. Where the child instructs a solicitor or conducts proceedings on the child's own behalf

CHAPTER 7
CHILDREN'S GUARDIAN APPOINTED UNDER RULE 16.4

16.22. Application of this Chapter
16.23. Stage of proceedings at which a children's guardian becomes necessary
16.24. Appointment of a children's guardian
16.25. Court's power to change children's guardian and to prevent person acting as children's guardian
16.26. Appointment of children's guardian by court order – supplementary
16.27. Powers and duties of children's guardian
16.28. Procedure where appointment of children's guardian comes to an end

CHAPTER 8
DUTIES OF SOLICITOR ACTING FOR THE CHILD

16.29. Solicitor for child

CHAPTER 9
REPORTING OFFICER

16.30. When the court appoints a reporting officer
16.31. Appointment of the same reporting officer in respect of two or more parents or guardians
16.32. The duties of the reporting officer

CHAPTER 10
CHILDREN AND FAMILY REPORTER AND WELFARE OFFICER

16.33. Request by court for a welfare report in respect of the child

CHAPTER 11
PARENTAL ORDER REPORTER

16.34. When the court appoints a parental order reporter
16.35. Powers and duties of the parental order reporter

The Family Procedure Rules 2010

CHAPTER 12
SUPPLEMENTARY APPOINTMENT PROVISIONS

16.36. Persons who may not be appointed as children's guardian, reporting officer or children and family reporter
16.37. Appointment of the same person as children's guardian, reporting officer and children and family reporter

CHAPTER 13
OFFICERS OF THE SERVICE, WELSH FAMILY PROCEEDINGS OFFICERS AND LOCAL AUTHORITY OFFICERS: FURTHER DUTIES

16.38. Officers of the Service, Welsh family proceedings officers and local authority officers acting under certain duties

CHAPTER 14
ENFORCEMENT ORDERS AND FINANCIAL COMPENSATION ORDERS: PERSONS NOTIFIED

16.39. Application for enforcement orders and financial compensation orders: duties of the person notified
Practice Direction 16A Representation of Children

PART 17
STATEMENTS OF TRUTH

17.1. Interpretation
17.2. Documents to be verified by a statement of truth
17.3. Failure to verify a statement of case
17.4. Failure to verify a witness statement
17.5. Power of the court to require a document to be verified
17.6. False statements
Practice Direction 17A Statements of Truth

PART 18
PROCEDURE FOR OTHER APPLICATIONS IN PROCEEDINGS

18.1. Types of application for which Part 18 procedure may be followed
18.2. Applications for permission to start proceedings
18.3. Respondents to applications under this Part
18.4. Application notice to be filed
18.5. Notice of an application
18.6. Time when an application is made
18.7. What an application notice must include
18.8. Service of a copy of an application notice
18.9. Applications which may be dealt with without a hearing
18.10. Service of application notice following court order where application made without notice
18.11. Application to set aside or vary order made without notice
18.12. Power of the court to proceed in the absence of a party
18.13. Dismissal of totally without merit applications
Practice Direction 18A Other Applications in Proceedings

PART 19
ALTERNATIVE PROCEDURE FOR APPLICATIONS

19.1. Types of application for which Part 19 procedure may be followed
19.2. Applications for which the Part 19 procedure must be followed
19.3. Contents of the application
19.4. Issue of application without naming respondents
19.5. Acknowledgment of service
19.6. Consequence of not filing an acknowledgment of service
19.7. Filing and serving written evidence
19.8. Evidence – general
19.9. Procedure where respondent objects to use of the Part 19 procedure
Practice Direction 19A Alternative Procedure for Applications

PART 20
INTERIM REMEDIES AND SECURITY FOR COSTS

CHAPTER 1
INTERIM REMEDIES

20.1.	Scope of this Part
20.2.	Orders for interim remedies
20.3.	Time when an order for an interim remedy may be made
20.4.	How to apply for an interim remedy
20.5.	Interim injunction to cease if application is stayed

CHAPTER 2
SECURITY FOR COSTS

20.6.	Security for costs
20.7.	Conditions to be satisfied
20.8.	Security for costs of an appeal
	Practice Direction 20A Interim Remedies

PART 21
MISCELLANEOUS RULES ABOUT DISCLOSURE AND INSPECTION OF DOCUMENTS

21.1.	Interpretation
21.2.	Orders for disclosure against a person not a party
21.3.	Claim to withhold inspection or disclosure of a document
	Practice Direction 21A Disclosure and Inspection

PART 22
EVIDENCE

CHAPTER 1
GENERAL RULES

22.1.	Power of court to control evidence
22.2.	Evidence of witnesses – general rule
22.3.	Evidence by video link or other means
22.4.	Witness statements
22.5.	Service of witness statements for use at the final hearing
22.6.	Use at the final hearing of witness statements which have been served
22.7.	Evidence at hearings other than the final hearing
22.8.	Order for cross-examination
22.9.	Witness summaries
22.10.	Consequence of failure to serve witness statement
22.11.	Cross-examination on a witness statement
22.12.	Affidavit evidence
22.13.	Form of affidavit
22.14.	Affidavit made outside the jurisdiction
22.15.	Notice to admit facts
22.16.	Notice to admit or produce documents
22.17.	Notarial acts and instruments

CHAPTER 2
RULES APPLYING ONLY TO PARTICULAR PROCEEDINGS

22.18.	Scope of this Chapter
22.19.	Availability of witness statements for inspection during the final hearing
22.20.	Use of witness statements for other purposes
	Practice Direction 22A Written Evidence

PART 23
MISCELLANEOUS RULES ABOUT EVIDENCE

23.1.	Scope and interpretation of this Part
23.2.	Notice of intention to rely on hearsay evidence
23.3.	Circumstances in which notice of intention to rely on hearsay evidence is not required

The Family Procedure Rules 2010

23.4.	Power to call witness for cross-examination on hearsay evidence
23.5.	Credibility
23.6.	Use of plans, photographs and models etc as evidence
23.7.	Evidence of finding on question of foreign law
23.8.	Evidence of consent of trustee to act
23.9.	Note of oral evidence in magistrates' courts

PART 24
WITNESSES, DEPOSITIONS GENERALLY AND TAKING OF EVIDENCE IN MEMBER STATES OF THE EUROPEAN UNION

CHAPTER 1
WITNESSES AND DEPOSITIONS

24.1.	Scope of this Chapter
24.2.	Witness summonses
24.3.	Issue of a witness summons
24.4.	Time for serving a witness summons
24.5.	Who is to serve a witness summons
24.6.	Right of witness to travelling expenses and compensation for loss of time
24.7.	Evidence by deposition
24.8.	Conduct of examination
24.9.	Enforcing attendance of witness
24.10.	Use of deposition at a hearing
24.11.	Restrictions on subsequent use of deposition taken for the purpose of any hearing except the final hearing
24.12.	Where a person to be examined is out of the jurisdiction – letter of request
24.13.	Fees and expenses of examiner of the court
24.14.	Examiners of the court

CHAPTER 2
TAKING OF EVIDENCE – MEMBER STATES OF THE EUROPEAN UNION

24.15.	Interpretation
24.16.	Where a person to be examined is in another Regulation State
	Practice Direction 24A Witnesses, Depositions and Taking of Evidence in Member States of the European Union

PART 25
EXPERTS AND ASSESSORS

25.1.	Duty to restrict expert evidence
25.2.	Interpretation
25.3.	Experts- overriding duty to the court
25.4.	Court's power to restrict expert evidence
25.5.	General requirement for expert evidence to be given in a written report
25.6.	Written questions to experts
25.7.	Court's power to direct that evidence is to be given by a single joint expert
25.8.	Instructions to a single joint expert
25.9.	Power of court to direct a party to provide information
25.10.	Contents of report
25.11.	Use by one party of expert's report disclosed by another
25.12.	Discussions between experts
25.13.	Expert's right to ask court for directions
25.14.	Assessors
	Practice Direction 25A Experts and Assessors in Family Proceedings

PART 26
CHANGE OF SOLICITOR

26.1.	Solicitor acting for a party

26.2.	Change of solicitor – duty to give notice
26.3.	Order that a solicitor has ceased to act
26.4.	Removal of solicitor who has ceased to act on application of another party
	Practice Direction 26A Change of Solicitor

PART 27
HEARINGS AND DIRECTIONS APPOINTMENTS

27.1.	Application of this Part
27.2.	Reasons for a decision of the magistrates' courts
27.3.	Attendance at hearing or directions appointment
27.4.	Proceedings in the absence of a party
27.5.	Application to set aside judgment or order following failure to attend
27.6.	Court bundles and place of filing of documents and bundles
27.7.	Representation of companies or other corporations
27.8.	Impounded documents
27.9.	Official shorthand note etc of proceedings
27.10.	Hearings in private
27.11.	Attendance at private hearings
	Practice Direction 27A Family Proceedings: Court Bundles (Universal Practice to be applied in All Courts other than the Family Proceedings Court)
	Practice Direction 27B Attendance of Media Representatives in Family Proceedings (High Court and county courts)
	Practice Direction 27C Attendance of Media Representatives in Family Proceedings (Family Proceedings Court)

PART 28
COSTS

28.1.	Costs
28.2.	Application of other rules
28.3.	Costs in financial remedy proceedings
28.4.	Wasted costs orders in the magistrates' court: appeals
	Practice Direction 28A Costs

PART 29
MISCELLANEOUS

29.1.	Personal details
29.2.	Disclosure of information under the 1991 Act
29.3.	Method of giving notice
29.4.	Withdrawal of applications in proceedings
29.5.	The Human Rights Act 1998
29.6.	Documents in proceedings concerning gender recognition
29.7.	Stamping or sealing court documents
29.8.	Applications for relief which is precluded by the 1991 Act
29.9.	Modification of rule 29.8 where the application is not freestanding
29.10.	Standard requirements
29.11.	Drawing up and filing of judgments and orders
29.12.	Copies of orders made in open court
29.13.	Service of judgments and orders
29.14.	Power to require judgment or order to be served on a party as well as the party's solicitor
29.15.	When judgment or order takes effect
29.16.	Correction of errors in judgments and orders
	Practice Direction 29A Human Rights, Joining the Crown
	Practice Direction 29B Human Rights Act 1988

PART 30
APPEALS

30.1.	Scope and interpretation

The Family Procedure Rules 2010

30.2.	Parties to comply with the practice direction
30.3.	Permission
30.4.	Appellant's notice
30.5.	Respondent's notice
30.6.	Grounds of appeal
30.7.	Variation of time
30.8.	Stay
30.9.	Amendment of appeal notice
30.10.	Striking out appeal notices and setting aside or imposing conditions on permission to appeal
30.11.	Appeal court's powers
30.12.	Hearing of appeals
30.13.	Assignment of appeals to the Court of Appeal
30.14.	Reopening of final appeals
	Practice Direction 30A Appeals

PART 31
REGISTRATION OF ORDERS UNDER THE COUNCIL REGULATION, THE CIVIL PARTNERSHIP (JURISDICTION AND RECOGNITION OF JUDGMENTS) REGULATIONS 2005 AND UNDER THE HAGUE CONVENTION 1996

31.1.	Scope
31.2.	Interpretation
31.3.	Where to start proceedings
31.4.	Application for registration, recognition or non-recognition of a judgment
31.5.	Documents – supplementary
31.6.	Directions
31.7.	Recognition and enforcement under the Council Regulation of a judgment given in another Member State relating to rights of access or under Article 11(8) for the return of the child to that State
31.8.	Registration for enforcement or order for non-recognition of a judgment
31.9.	Stay of recognition proceedings by reason of an appeal
31.10.	Effect of refusal of application for a decision that a judgment should not be recognised
31.11.	Notification of the court's decision on an application for registration or non-recognition
31.12.	Effect of registration under rule 31.11
31.13.	The central index of judgments registered under rule 31.11
31.14.	Decision on recognition of a judgment only
31.15.	Appeal against the court's decision under rules 31.10, 31.11 or 31.14
31.16.	Stay of enforcement where appeal pending in state of origin
31.17.	Enforcement of judgments registered under rule 31.11
31.18.	Request for a certificate or a certified copy of a judgment
31.19.	Certificates issued in England and Wales under Articles 41 and 42 of the Council Regulation
31.20.	Rectification of certificate issued under Article 41 or 42 of the Council Regulation
31.21.	Authentic instruments and agreements under Article 46 of the Council Regulation
31.22.	Application for provisional, including protective measures.
	Practice Direction 31A Registration of Orders under the Council regulation, The Civil Partnership (Jurisdiction and recognition of Judgments) Regulations 2005 and under the 1986 Hague Convention

Family Procedure Rules 2010

PART 32
REGISTRATION AND ENFORCEMENT OF ORDERS

CHAPTER 1
SCOPE AND INTERPRETATION OF THIS PART

32.1. Scope and interpretation

CHAPTER 2
REGISTRATION ETC. OF ORDERS UNDER THE 1950 ACT

Section 1 Interpretation of this Chapter
32.2. Interpretation

Section 2 Registration etc of High Court and county court orders
32.3. Registration of a High Court order
32.4. Notice of Variation etc. of a High Court order
32.5. Cancellation of registration of a High Court order
32.6. Application of this Chapter to a county court order

Section 3 Registration etc. of Scottish and Northern Irish orders
32.7. Registration of Scottish and Northern Irish orders
32.8. Application to adduce evidence before High Court
32.9. Notice of variation etc. of Scottish and Northern Irish orders
32.10. Cancellation of registration of Scottish and Northern Irish orders
32.11. Enforcement
32.12. Inspection of register and copies of order

CHAPTER 3
REGISTRATION OF MAINTENANCE ORDERS UNDER THE 1958 ACT

32.13. Interpretation
32.14. Registration of orders – prescribed period
32.15. Application for registration of a maintenance order in a magistrates' court
32.16. Registration in a magistrates' court of an order registered in the High Court
32.17. Registration in the High Court of a magistrates' court order
32.18. Registration in the High Court of an order registered in a magistrates' court
32.19. Variation or discharge of an order registered in a magistrates' court
32.20. Variation or discharge of an order registered in the High Court
32.21. Cancellation of registration – orders registered in the High Court
32.22. Cancellation of registration – orders registered in a magistrates' court

CHAPTER 4
REGISTRATION AND ENFORCEMENT OF CUSTODY ORDERS UNDER THE 1986 ACT

32.23. Interpretation
32.24. Prescribed officer and functions of the court
32.25. Application for the registration of an order made by the High Court or a county court
32.26. Registration of orders made in Scotland, Northern Ireland or a specified dependent territory
32.27. Revocation and variation of an order made in the High Court or a county court
32.28. Registration of varied, revoked or recalled orders made in Scotland, Northern Ireland or a specified dependent territory
32.29. Interim directions
32.30. Staying and dismissal of enforcement proceedings
32.31. Particulars of other proceedings
32.32. Inspection of register

The Family Procedure Rules 2010

PART 33
ENFORCEMENT

CHAPTER 1
GENERAL RULES

33.1. Application

Section 1	Enforcement of orders for the payment of money
33.2.	Application of the Civil Procedure Rules
33.3.	How to apply
33.4.	Transfer of orders
Section 2	Committal and injunction
33.5.	General rule — committal hearings to be in public
33.6.	Proceedings in the principal registry treated as pending in a designated county court
33.7.	Specific modifications of the CCR
33.8.	Section 118 County Courts Act 1984 and the tipstaff

CHAPTER 2
COMMITTAL BY WAY OF JUDGMENT SUMMONS

33.9.	Interpretation
33.10.	Application
33.11.	Judgment summons
33.12.	Successive judgment summonses
33.13.	Requirement for personal service
33.14.	Committal on application for judgment summons
33.15.	Orders for the benefit of different persons
33.16.	Hearing of judgment summons
33.17.	Special provisions as to judgment summonses in the High Court
33.18.	Special provisions as to judgment summonses in designated county courts

CHAPTER 3
ATTACHMENT OF EARNINGS

33.19. Proceedings in the Principal Registry

CHAPTER 4
WARRANT OF EXECUTION

33.20.	Applications to vary existing orders
33.21.	Section 103 County Courts Act 1984

CHAPTER 5
COURT'S POWER TO APPOINT A RECEIVER

33.22. Application of the CPR

CHAPTER 6
ORDERS TO OBTAIN INFORMATION FROM JUDGMENT DEBTORS

33.23. Application of the CPR

CHAPTER 7
THIRD PARTY DEBT ORDERS

33.24. Application of the CPR

CHAPTER 8
CHARGING ORDER, STOP ORDER, STOP NOTICE

33.25. Application of the CPR
Practice Direction 33A Enforcement of Undertakings

PART 34
RECIPROCAL ENFORCEMENT OF MAINTENANCE ORDERS

34.1. Scope and interpretation of this Part

Family Procedure Rules 2010

34.2.	Meaning of prescribed officer in a magistrates' court
34.3.	Registration of maintenance orders in magistrates' courts in England and Wales

CHAPTER 1
ENFORCEMENT OF MAINTENANCE ORDERS UNDER THE MAINTENANCE ORDERS (FACILITIES FOR ENFORCEMENT) ACT 1920

34.4.	Interpretation
34.5.	Confirmation of provisional orders made in a reciprocating country
34.6.	Payment of sums due under registered orders
34.7.	Enforcement of sums due under registered orders
34.8.	Prescribed notice for the taking of further evidence
34.9.	Transmission of maintenance orders made in a reciprocating country to the High Court
34.10.	Transmission of maintenance orders made in the High Court to a reciprocating country
34.11.	Inspection of the register in the High Court

CHAPTER 2
ENFORCEMENT OF MAINTENANCE ORDERS UNDER PART 1 OF THE 1972 ACT

34.12.	Interpretation
34.13.	Scope
Section 1	Reciprocal enforcement of maintenance orders under Part 1 of the 1972 Act
34.14.	Application for transmission of maintenance order to reciprocating country
34.15.	Certification of evidence given on provisional orders
34.16.	Confirmation of a provisional order made in a reciprocating country
34.17.	Consideration of revocation of a provisional order made by a magistrates' court
34.18.	Notification of variation or revocation of a maintenance order by the High Court or a county court
34.19.	Notification of confirmation or revocation of a maintenance order by a magistrates' court
34.20.	Taking of evidence for court in reciprocating country
34.21.	Request for the taking of evidence by a court in a reciprocating country
34.22.	Transmission of documents
34.23.	Method of payment under registered orders
34.24.	Enforcement of payments under registered orders
34.25.	Notification of registration and cancellation
Section 2	Modification of rules in Section 1 of this Chapter
34.26.	Application of Section 1 of this Chapter to the Republic of Ireland
34.27.	Application of Section 1 of this Chapter to the Hague Convention Countries
34.28.	Application of Section 1 of this Chapter to the United States of America

CHAPTER 3
ENFORCEMENT OF MAINTENANCE ORDERS UNDER THE CIVIL JURISDICTION AND JUDGMENTS ACT 1982, THE JUDGMENTS REGULATION AND THE LUGANO CONVENTION

Section 1	Registration and Enforcement in a Magistrates' Court of Maintenance Orders made in a Contracting State to the 1968 Convention, a Contracting State to the 1988 Convention, a Regulation State or a State bound by the Lugano Convention
34.29.	Interpretation
34.30.	Registration of maintenance orders

The Family Procedure Rules 2010

34.31.	Appeal from a decision relating to registration
34.32.	Payment of sums due under a registered order
34.33.	Enforcement of payments under registered orders
34.34.	Variation and revocation of registered orders
34.35.	Transfer of registered order
34.36.	Cancellation of registered orders
Section 2	Reciprocal enforcement in a Contracting State or Regulation State of Orders of a court in England and Wales
34.37.	Application in a magistrates' court for a maintenance order, or revocation of a maintenance order, to which the 1982 Act, the Judgments Regulations or the Lugano Convention applies
34.38.	Admissibility of Documents
34.39.	Enforcement of orders of a magistrates' court
	Practice Direction 34A Reciprocal Enforcement of Maintenance Orders
	Practice Direction 34B Practice Note Tracing Payers Overseas

PART 35
MEDIATION DIRECTIVE

35.1.	Scope and Interpretation
35.2.	Relevant disputes: applications for consent orders in respect of financial remedies
35.3.	Mediation evidence: disclosure and inspection
35.4.	Mediation evidence: witnesses and depositions
	Practice Direction 35A Mediation Directive

PART 36
TRANSITIONAL ARRANGEMENTS AND PILOT SCHEMES

36.1.	Transitional provisions
36.2.	Pilot schemes
	Practice Direction 36A Transitional Arrangements
	Practice Direction Relating to Family Proceedings in force before 6th April 2011 which support the Family Procedure Rules 2011

The principal forms listed in PD 5A Forms will be reproduced in due course.

PART 1

OVERRIDING OBJECTIVE

1.1.— The overriding objective

(1) These rules are a new procedural code with the overriding objective of enabling the court to deal with cases justly, having regard to any welfare issues involved.

    (2) Dealing with a case justly includes, so far as is practicable—
        (a) ensuring that it is dealt with expeditiously and fairly;
        (b) dealing with the case in ways which are proportionate to the nature, importance and complexity of the issues;
        (c) ensuring that the parties are on an equal footing;
        (d) saving expense; and
        (e) allotting to it an appropriate share of the court's resources, while taking into account the need to allot resources to other cases.

1.2. Application by the court of the overriding objective
The court must seek to give effect to the overriding objective when it—
        (a) exercises any power given to it by these rules; or
        (b) interprets any rule.

1.3. Duty of the parties
The parties are required to help the court to further the overriding objective.

1.4.— Court's duty to manage cases
(1) The court must further the overriding objective by actively managing cases.
(2) Active case management includes—
  (a) encouraging the parties to co-operate with each other in the conduct of the proceedings;
  (b) identifying at an early stage—
    (i) the issues; and
    (ii) who should be a party to the proceedings;
  (c) deciding promptly—
    (i) which issues need full investigation and hearing and which do not; and
    (ii) the procedure to be followed in the case;
  (d) deciding the order in which issues are to be resolved;
  (e) encouraging the parties to use an alternative dispute resolution procedure if the court considers that appropriate and facilitating the use of such procedure;
  (f) helping the parties to settle the whole or part of the case;
  (g) fixing timetables or otherwise controlling the progress of the case;
  (h) considering whether the likely benefits of taking a particular step justify the cost of taking it;
  (i) dealing with as many aspects of the case as it can on the same occasion;
  (j) dealing with the case without the parties needing to attend at court;
  (k) making use of technology; and
  (l) giving directions to ensure that the case proceeds quickly and efficiently.

PART 1 ANNOTATIONS

No Practice Direction accompanies Part 1.

Part 1 sets out that the rules are a new procedural code so decisions and interpretations of previous rules will not necessarily be relevant to these rules. Rule 1.1 brings together (with modifications) the overriding objectives hitherto applied to children proceedings (in the Public Law Outline and Private Law Programme), adoption and placement proceedings (in the 2005 Rules) and financial proceedings (in FPR 1991, r 2.51D). It now applies to the conduct of all family proceedings.

As with the equivalent provisions of the CPR, by r 1.3 the parties are required to help the court to further the overriding objective. This places an express obligation on parties and their legal representatives to co-operate in the expeditious, fair and proportionate conduct of proceedings.

The court's duty to manage proceedings set out at r 1.4 requires the court to engage in strategic case planning.

It has been suggested by Hughes LJ in *Goldstone v Goldstone* [2011] EWCA Civ 39, that joinder applications will fall to be dealt with under the case management powers, and in particular r 1.4 (b)(ii) – the duty to identify at an early stage who should be a party to the proceedings. The rules say nothing about the principles on which an application to join a third parties should be exercised.

PART 2

APPLICATION AND INTERPRETATION OF THE RULES

2.1.— Application of these Rules

(1) Unless the context otherwise requires, these rules apply to family proceedings in—
   (a) the High Court;
   (b) a county court; and
   (c) a magistrates' court.

(2) Nothing in these rules is to be construed as—
   (a) purporting to apply to proceedings in a magistrates' court which are not family proceedings within the meaning of section 65 of the Magistrates' Courts Act 1980 or
   (b) conferring upon a magistrate a function which a magistrate is not permitted by statute to perform.

2.2.— The glossary

(1) The glossary at the end of these rules is a guide to the meaning of certain legal expressions used in the rules, but is not to be taken as giving those expressions any meaning in the rules which they do not have in the law generally.

(2) Subject to paragraph (3), words in these rules which are included in the glossary are followed by "GL".

(3) The word "service", which appears frequently in the rules, is included in the glossary but is not followed by "GL".

2.3.— Interpretation

(1) In these rules—

"the 1973 Act" means the Matrimonial Causes Act 1973;

"the 1978 Act" means the Domestic Proceedings and Magistrates' Courts Act 1978;

"the 1980 Hague Convention" means the Convention on the Civil Aspects of International Child Abduction which was signed at The Hague on 25 October 1980;

"the 1984 Act" means the Matrimonial and Family Proceedings Act 1984;

"the 1986 Act" means the Family Law Act 1986;

"the 1989 Act" means the Children Act 1989;

"the 1990 Act" means the Human Fertilisation and Embryology Act 1990;

"the 1991 Act" means the Child Support Act 1991;

"the 1996 Act" means the Family Law Act 1996;

"the 1996 Hague Convention" means the Convention on Jurisdiction, Applicable Law, Recognition, Enforcement and Co-Operation in Respect of Parental Responsibility and Measures for the Protection of Children;

"the 2002 Act" means the Adoption and Children Act 2002;

"the 2004 Act" means the Civil Partnership Act 2004;

"the 2005 Act" means the Mental Capacity Act 2005;

"the 2008 Act" means the Human Fertilisation and Embryology Act 2008;

"adoption proceedings" means proceedings for an adoption order under the 2002 Act;

"Allocation Order" means any order made by the Lord Chancellor under Part 1 of Schedule 11 to the 1989 Act;

"alternative dispute resolution" means methods of resolving a dispute, including mediation, other than through the normal court process;

"application form" means a document in which the applicant states his intention to seek a court order other than in accordance with the Part 18 procedure;

"application notice" means a document in which the applicant states his intention to seek a court order in accordance with the Part 18 procedure;

"Assembly" means the National Assembly for Wales;

"bank holiday" means a bank holiday under the Banking and Financial Dealings Act 1971

(a) for the purpose of service of a document within the United Kingdom, in the part of the United Kingdom where service is to take place; and

(b) for all other purposes, in England and Wales.

"business day" means any day other than—

(a) a Saturday, Sunday, Christmas Day or Good Friday; or

(b) a bank holiday;

"care order" has the meaning assigned to it by section 31(11) of the 1989 Act;

"CCR" means the County Court Rules 1981, as they appear in Schedule 2 to the CPR;

"child" means a person under the age of 18 years who is the subject of the proceedings; except that—

(a) in adoption proceedings, it also includes a person who has attained the age of 18 years before the proceedings are concluded; and

(b) in proceedings brought under the Council Regulation, the 1980 Hague Convention or the European Convention, it means a person under the age of 16 years who is the subject of the proceedings;

"child of the family" has the meaning given to it by section 105(1) of the 1989 Act;

"children and family reporter" means an officer of the Service or a Welsh family proceedings officer who has been asked to prepare a welfare report under section 7(1)(a) of the 1989 Act or section 102(3)(b) of the 2002 Act;

"children's guardian" means—

(a) in relation to a child who is the subject of and a party to specified proceedings or proceedings to which Part 14 applies, the person appointed in accordance with rule 16.3(1); and

(b) in any other case, the person appointed in accordance with rule 16.4;

"civil partnership order" means one of the orders mentioned in section 37 of the 2004 Act;

"civil partnership proceedings" means proceedings for a civil partnership order;

"civil partnership proceedings county court" means a county court so designated by the Lord Chancellor under section 36A of the 1984 Act;

"civil restraint order" means an order restraining a party—

(a) from making any further applications in current proceedings (a limited civil restraint order);

(b) from making certain applications in specified courts (an extended civil restraint order); or

(c) from making any application in specified courts (a general civil restraint order);

"Commission" means the Child Maintenance and Enforcement Commission;

"consent order" means an order in the terms applied for to which the respondent agrees;

"contact order" has the meaning assigned to it by section 8(1) of the 1989 Act;

"the Council Regulation" means Council Regulation (EC) No 2201/2003 of 27 November 2003 on jurisdiction and the recognition and enforcement of judgments in matrimonial matters and in matters of parental responsibility;

"court" means, subject to any rule or other enactment which provides otherwise, the High Court, a county court or a magistrates' court;

(rule 2.5 relates to the power to perform functions of the court.)

"court of trial" means—

(a) in proceedings under the 1973 Act, a divorce county court designated by the Lord Chancellor as a court of trial pursuant to section 33(1) of the 1984 Act; or

(b) in proceedings under the 2004 Act, a civil partnership proceedings county court designated by the Lord Chancellor as a court of trial pursuant to section 36A(1)(b) of the 1984 Act; and

in proceedings under the 1973 Act pending in a divorce county court or proceedings under the 2004 Act pending in a civil partnership proceedings county court, the principal registry is treated as a court of trial having its place of sitting at the Royal Courts of Justice;

"court officer" means—

(a) in the High Court or in a county court, a member of court staff; and

The Family Procedure Rules 2010

  (b) in a magistrates' court, the designated officer;
    ("designated officer" is defined in section 37(1) of the Courts Act 2003.)
"CPR" means the Civil Procedure Rules 1998;
"deputy" has the meaning given in section 16(2)(b) of the 2005 Act;
"designated county court" means a court designated as—
  (a) a divorce county court;
  (b) a civil partnership proceedings county court; or
  (c) both a divorce county court and a civil partnership proceedings county court;
"detailed assessment proceedings" means the procedure by which the amount of costs is decided in accordance with Part 47 of the CPR;
"directions appointment" means a hearing for directions;
"district judge"—
  (a) in relation to proceedings in the High Court, includes a district judge of the principal registry and in relation to proceedings in a county court, includes a district judge of the principal registry when the principal registry is treated as if it were a county court;
  (b) in relation to proceedings in a district registry or a county court, means the district judge or one of the district judges of that registry or county court, as the case may be;
"district registry" means—
  (a) in proceedings under the 1973 Act, any district registry having a divorce county court within its district;
  (b) in proceedings under the 2004 Act, any district registry having a civil partnership proceedings county court within its district; and
  (c) in any other case, any district registry having a designated county court within its district;
"divorce county court" means a county court so designated by the Lord Chancellor pursuant to section 33(1) of the 1984 Act, including the principal registry when it is treated as a divorce county court;
"the European Convention" means the European Convention on Recognition and Enforcement of Decisions concerning Custody of Children and on the Restoration of Custody of Children which was signed in Luxembourg on 20 May 1980;
"filing", in relation to a document, means delivering it, by post or otherwise, to the court office;
"financial order" means—
  (a) an avoidance of disposition order;
  (b) an order for maintenance pending suit;
  (c) an order for maintenance pending outcome of proceedings;
  (d) an order for periodical payments or lump sum provision as mentioned in section 21(1) of the 1973 Act, except an order under section 27(6) of that Act;
  (e) an order for periodical payments or lump sum provision as mentioned in paragraph 2(1) of Schedule 5 to the 2004 Act, made under Part 1 of Schedule 5 to that Act;
  (f) a property adjustment order;
  (g) a variation order;
  (h) a pension sharing order; or
  (i) a pension compensation sharing order;
    ("variation order", "pension compensation sharing order" and "pension sharing order" are defined in rule 9.3.)
"financial remedy" means—
  (a) a financial order;
  (b) an order under Schedule 1 to the 1989 Act;
  (c) an order under Part 3 of the 1984 Act;

(d) an order under Schedule 7 to the 2004 Act;
(e) an order under section 27 of the 1973 Act;
(f) an order under Part 9 of Schedule 5 to the 2004 Act;
(g) an order under section 35 of the 1973 Act;
(h) an order under paragraph 69 of Schedule 5 to the 2004 Act;
(i) an order under Part 1 of the 1978 Act;
(j) an order under Schedule 6 to the 2004 Act;
(k) an order under section 10(2) of the 1973 Act; or
(l) an order under section 48(2) of the 2004 Act;

"hearing" includes a directions appointment;

"hearsay" means a statement made, otherwise than by a person while giving oral evidence in proceedings, which is tendered as evidence of the matters stated, and references to hearsay include hearsay of whatever degree;

"inherent jurisdiction" means the High Court's power to make any order or determine any issue in respect of a child, including in wardship proceedings, where it would be just and equitable to do so unless restricted by legislation or case law;

(Practice Direction 12D (Inherent Jurisdiction (including Wardship Proceedings)) provides examples of inherent jurisdiction proceedings.)

"judge", in the High Court or a county court, means, unless the context requires otherwise, a judge, district judge or a person authorised to act as such;

"jurisdiction" means, unless the context requires otherwise, England and Wales and any part of the territorial waters of the United Kingdom adjoining England and Wales;

"justices' clerk" has the meaning assigned to it by section 27(1) of the Courts Act 2003;

"legal representative" means a—
(a) barrister;
(b) solicitor;
(c) solicitor's employee;
(d) manager of a body recognised under section 9 of the Administration of Justice Act 1985; or
(e) person who, for the purposes of the Legal Services Act 2007, is an authorised person in relation to an activity which constitutes the conduct of litigation (within the meaning of the Act),

who has been instructed to act for a party in relation to proceedings;

"litigation friend" has the meaning given—
(a) in relation to a protected party, by Part 15; and
(b) in relation to a child, by Part 16;

"matrimonial cause" means proceedings for a matrimonial order;

"matrimonial order" means—
(a) a decree of divorce made under section 1 of the 1973 Act;
(b) a decree of nullity made on one of the grounds set out in sections 11 or 12 of the 1973 Act;
(c) a decree of judicial separation made under section 17 of the 1973 Act;

"note" includes a record made by mechanical means;

"officer of the Service" has the meaning given by section 11(3) of the Criminal Justice and Court Services Act 2000;

"order" includes directions of the court;

"order for maintenance pending outcome of proceedings" means an order under paragraph 38 of Schedule 5 to the 2004 Act;

"order for maintenance pending suit" means an order under section 22 of the 1973 Act;

"parental order proceedings" has the meaning assigned to it by rule 13.1;

"parental responsibility" has the meaning assigned to it by section 3 of the 1989 Act;

"placement proceedings" means proceedings for the making, varying or revoking of a placement order under the 2002 Act;

"principal registry" means the principal registry of the Family Division of the High Court;

The Family Procedure Rules 2010

"proceedings" means, unless the context requires otherwise, family proceedings as defined in section 75(3) of the Courts Act 2003;

"professional acting in furtherance of the protection of children" includes—
- (a) an officer of a local authority exercising child protection functions;
- (b) a police officer who is—
  - (i) exercising powers under section 46 of the Act of 1989; or
  - (ii) serving in a child protection unit or a paedophile unit of a police force;
- (c) any professional person attending a child protection conference or review in relation to a child who is the subject of the proceedings to which the information regarding the proceedings held in private relates; or
- (d) an officer of the National Society for the Prevention of Cruelty to Children;

"professional legal adviser" means a—
- (a) barrister;
- (b) solicitor;
- (c) solicitor's employee;
- (d) manager of a body recognised under section 9 of the Administration of Justice Act 1985; or
- (e) person who, for the purposes of the Legal Services Act 2007, is an authorised person in relation to an activity which constitutes the conduct of litigation (within the meaning of that Act),

who is providing advice to a party but is not instructed to represent that party in the proceedings;

"property adjustment order" means—
- (a) in proceedings under the 1973 Act, any of the orders mentioned in section 21(2) of that Act;
- (b) in proceedings under the 1984 Act, an order under section 17(1)(a)(ii) of that Act;
- (c) in proceedings under Schedule 5 to the 2004 Act, any of the orders mentioned in paragraph 7(1); or
- (d) in proceedings under Schedule 7 to the 2004 Act, an order for property adjustment under paragraph 9(2) or (3);

"protected party" means a party, or an intended party, who lacks capacity (within the meaning of the 2005 Act) to conduct proceedings;

"reporting officer" means an officer of the Service or a Welsh family proceedings officer appointed to witness the documents which signify a parent's or guardian's consent to the placing of the child for adoption or to the making of an adoption order or a section 84 order;

"risk assessment" has the meaning assigned to it by section 16A(3) of the 1989 Act;

"Royal Courts of Justice", in relation to matrimonial proceedings pending in a divorce county court or civil partnership proceedings pending in a civil partnership proceedings county court, means such place as may be specified in directions given by the Lord Chancellor pursuant to section 42(2)(a) of the 1984 Act;

"RSC" means the Rules of the Supreme Court 1965 as they appear in Schedule 1 to the CPR;

"section 8 order" has the meaning assigned to it by section 8(2) of the 1989 Act;

"section 84 order" means an order made by the High Court under section 84 of the 2002 Act giving parental responsibility prior to adoption abroad;

"section 89 order" means an order made by the High Court under section 89 of the 2002 Act—
- (a) annulling a Convention adoption or Convention adoption order;
- (b) providing for an overseas adoption or determination under section 91 of the 2002 Act to cease to be valid; or
- (c) deciding the extent, if any, to which a determination under section 91 of the 2002 Act has been affected by a subsequent determination under that section;

"Service" has the meaning given by section 11 of the Criminal Justice and Court Services Act 2000;

"the Service Regulation" means Regulation (EC) No. 1393/2007 of the European Parliament and of the Council of 13 November 2007 on the service in the Member States of judicial and extrajudicial documents in civil or commercial matters (service of documents), and repealing Council Regulation (EC) No. 1348/2000, as amended from time to time and as applied by the Agreement made on 19 October 2005 between the European Community and the Kingdom of Denmark on the service of judicial and extrajudicial documents in civil and commercial matters;

"specified proceedings" has the meaning assigned to it by section 41(6) of the 1989 Act and rule 12.27;

"welfare officer" means a person who has been asked to prepare a report under section 7(1)(b) of the 1989 Act;

"Welsh family proceedings officer" has the meaning given by section 35(4) of the Children Act 2004.

(2) In these rules a reference to —
- (a) an application for a matrimonial order or a civil partnership order is to be read as a reference to a petition for—
  - (i) a matrimonial order;
  - (ii) a decree of presumption of death and dissolution of marriage made under section 19 of the 1973 Act; or
  - (iii) a civil partnership order,

and includes a petition by a respondent asking for such an order;
- (b) "financial order" in matrimonial proceedings is to be read as a reference to "ancillary relief";
- (c) "matrimonial proceedings" is to be read as a reference to a matrimonial cause or proceedings for an application for a decree of presumption of death and dissolution of marriage made under section 19 of the 1973 Act.

(3) Where these rules apply the CPR, they apply the CPR as amended from time to time.

2.4. Modification of rules in application to serial numbers etc.

If a serial number has been assigned under rule 14.2 or the name or other contact details of a party is not being revealed in accordance with rule 29.1—
- (a) any rule requiring any party to serve any document will not apply; and
- (b) the court will give directions about serving any document on the other parties.

2.5.— Power to perform functions conferred on the court by these rules and practice directions

(1) Where these rules or a practice direction provide for the court to perform any function then, except where any rule or practice direction, any other enactment or any directions made by the President of the Family Division under section 9 of the Courts and Legal Services Act 1990, provides otherwise, that function may be performed—
- (a) in relation to proceedings in the High Court or in a district registry, by any judge or district judge of that Court including a district judge of the principal registry;
- (b) in relation to proceedings in a county court, by any judge or district judge including a district judge of the principal registry when the principal registry is treated as if it were a county court; and
- (c) in relation to proceedings in a magistrates' court—
  - (i) by any family proceedings court constituted in accordance with sections 66 and 67 of the Magistrates' Courts Act 1980; or
  - (ii) by a single justice of the peace who is a member of the family panel in accordance with Practice Direction 2A.

(The Justices' Clerks Rules 2005 make provision for a justices' clerk or assistant clerk to carry out certain functions of a single justice of the peace.)

The Family Procedure Rules 2010

(2) A deputy High Court judge and a district judge, including a district judge of the principal registry, may not try a claim for a declaration of incompatibility in accordance with section 4 of the Human Rights Act 1998.

2.6.— **Powers of the single justice to perform functions under the 1989 Act, the 1996 Act, the 2002 Act and the Childcare Act 2006**

(1) A single justice who is a member of the family panel may perform the functions of a magistrates' court—

- (a) where an application without notice is made under sections 10, 44(1), 48(9), 50(4) and 102(1) of the 1989 Act;
- (b) subject to paragraph (2), under sections 11(3) or 38(1) of the 1989 Act;
- (c) under sections 4(3)(b), 4A(3)(b), 4ZA(6)(b), 7, 34(3)(b), 41, 44(9)(b) and (11)(b)(iii), 48(4), 91(15) or (17) or paragraph 11(4) of Schedule 14 of the 1989 Act;
- (d) in accordance with the Allocation Order;
- (e) where an application without notice is made under section 41(2) of the 2002 Act (recovery orders);
- (f) where an application without notice is made for an occupation order or a non molestation order under Part 4 of the 1996 Act; or
- (g) where an application is made for a warrant under section 79 of the Childcare Act 2006;

(2) A single justice of the peace may make an order under section 11(3) or 38(1) of the 1989 Act where—

- (a) a previous such order has been made in the same proceedings;
- (b) the terms of the order sought are the same as those of the last such order made; and
- (c) a written request for such an order has been made and —
    - (i) the other parties and any children's guardian consent to the request and they or their legal representatives have signed the request; or
    - (ii) at least one of the other parties and any children's guardian consent to the request and they or their legal representatives have signed the request, and the remaining parties have not indicated that they either consent to or oppose the making of the order.

(3) The proceedings referred to in paragraph (1)(a), (c) and (d) are proceedings which are prescribed for the purposes of section 93(2)(i) of the 1989 Act.

2.7. Single justice's power to refer to a magistrates' court

Where a single justice —

- (a) is performing the function of a magistrates' court in accordance with rules 2.5(1)(c)(ii) and 2.6(1) and (2); and
- (b) considers, for whatever reason, that it is inappropriate to perform the function,

the single justice must refer the matter to a magistrates' court which may perform the function.

2.8. Court's discretion as to where it deals with cases

The court may deal with a case at any place that it considers appropriate.

2.9.— Computation of time

(1) This rule shows how to calculate any period of time for doing any act which is specified—

- (a) by these rules;
- (b) by a practice direction; or
- (c) by a direction or order of the court.

(2) A period of time expressed as a number of days must be computed as clear days.

(3) In this rule "clear days" means that in computing the numbers of days—

- (a) the day on which the period begins; and

(b) if the end of the period is defined by reference to an event, the day on which that event occurs,

are not included.

(4) Where the specified period is 7 days or less and includes a day which is not a business day, that day does not count.

(5) When the period specified—
  (a) by these rules or a practice direction; or
  (b) by any direction or order of the court,

for doing any act at the court office ends on a day on which the office is closed, that act will be in time if done on the next day on which the court office is open.

2.10.— Dates for compliance to be calendar dates and to include time of day

(1) Where the court makes an order or gives a direction which imposes a time limit for doing any act, the last date for compliance must, wherever practicable—
  (a) be expressed as a calendar date; and
  (b) include the time of day by which the act must be done.

(2) Where the date by which an act must be done is inserted in any document, the date must, wherever practicable, be expressed as a calendar date.

(3) Where "month" occurs in any order, direction or other document, it means a calendar month.

PART 2 COMMENTARY

Part 2 is supplemented by PD2A as to the functions of the court in these rules and practice directions which can be performed by a single justice of the peace, r 2.5(1)(c)(ii).

Part 2 contains the provisions for the application of and the interpreting of the rules.

Rule 2.1 sets out the universal application of these rules to family proceedings save that by r 2.1(2)(b) it is recorded that they do no confer powers upon a magistrate which a magistrate is not permitted by statute to perform. The term 'family proceedings' for the purpose of the rules means those proceedings which are so defined:

(a) in the High Court and county courts, by the Matrimonial and Family Proceedings Act 1984, s 32 and the Senior Courts Act 1981, s 61, Sch 1; and
(b) in the magistrates' court, under the Magistrates' Courts Act 1980, s 65.

The main provisions about interpretation are contained in r 2.3 but there is further a short glossary at the end of the rules. Of note in r 2.3 is:

(a) 'children's guardian', which now refers not only to a Cafcass officer appointed under r 16.3(1) in specified (public law and adoption) proceedings, but also to a person appointed under r 16.4 to represent a subject child in other proceedings (formerly a 'guardian ad litem');
(b) 'financial order', which broadly replaces the term 'ancillary relief' under the FPR 1991;
(c) 'financial remedy', which includes a financial order and a range of other financial applications (see under Part 9 below);
(d) 'inherent jurisdiction', which is defined in rules of court for the first time (example of inherent jurisdiction proceedings are given in PD12D);

The Family Procedure Rules 2010

(e) 'litigation friend' who is a person acting for a protected party under Part 15 or a non-subject child party under Part 16;
(f) 'matrimonial orders' and 'civil partnership orders' means decrees of divorce and dissolution; and
(g) 'RSC' and 'CCR' mean the Rules of the Supreme Court 1965 and the County Court Rules 1981 as they respectively appear in Schs 1 and 2 to the CPR.

Rule 2.5 sets out that in general, where the rules or a PD provide for the court to perform any function, it may be performed:

(a) in the High Court or a county court by a judge or district judge (including a district judge of the PRFD); and
(b) in the magistrates' court, by a family proceedings court or a single justice.

This is subject to any other provision limiting the powers, including Allocation Directions made under the Courts and Legal Services Act 1990, s 9: see r 2.5(1).

Rule 2.6 contains provisions about the delegations of certain functions of a magistrates' court to a single justice.

Rule 2.9 deals with the computation of time.

Rule 2.10 provides that a date for compliance with an order or direction should where practicable be a calendar date and include a time of day.

PRACTICE DIRECTION 2A — FUNCTIONS OF THE COURT IN THE FAMILY PROCEDURE RULES 2010 AND PRACTICE DIRECTIONS WHICH MAY BE PERFORMED BY A SINGLE JUSTICE OF THE PEACE

This Practice Direction comes into force on 6th April 2011

This Practice Direction supplements FPR Part 2, rule 2.5(1)(c)(ii) (Power to perform functions conferred on the court by these rules and practice directions)

1.1 Where the FPR or a practice direction provide for the court to perform any function, that function may be performed by a single justice of the peace who is a member of a family panel except that such a justice cannot perform the functions listed in:

(a) column 2 of Table 1 in accordance with the rules listed in column 1; and
(b) column 2 of Table 2 in accordance with the paragraph of the practice direction listed in column 1.

1.2 For the avoidance of doubt, unless a rule, practice direction or other enactment provides otherwise, a single justice cannot make the decision of a magistrates' court at the final hearing of an application for a substantive order. For example, a single justice cannot make a residence order on notice, placement order, adoption or care order. However, a single justice can discharge the functions of a family proceedings court under the statutory provisions listed in rule 2.6 of the FPR.

FPR 2010, Practice Direction 2A

Table 1

Rule	Nature of function
4.1(3)(g)	Stay the whole or part of any proceedings or judgment either generally or until a specified date or event.
4.1(3)(l)	Exclude an issue from consideration.
4.1(3)(m)	Dismiss or give a decision on an application after a decision on a preliminary issue.
4.1(4)(a)	When the court makes an order, making that order subject to conditions.
4.1(6)	Varying and revoking an order (other than directions which the court has made).
4.3(1)	Ability of the court to make orders (other than directions) of its own initiative.
4.4, 4.5 and 4.6	All the powers of a magistrates' court under these rules (power to strike out statement of case, sanctions have effect unless defaulting party obtains relief from sanctions).
8.20(4)	A direction that a child should be made a respondent to the application for a declaration of parentage under section 55A of the Family Law Act 1986, except where the parties consent to the child being made a respondent.
9.11 (2)	Direction that a child be separately represented on an application.
9.22	All the powers of a magistrates' court under this rule (relating to proceedings by or against a person outside England and Wales for variation or revocation of orders under section 20 of the 1978 Act or paragraphs 30 to 34 of Schedule 6 to the 2004 Act).
12.3(2)	Where the person with parental responsibility is a child, a direction for that child be made a party, except where the parties consent to that child being made a party.
12.3(3)	Direction that a child be made a party to proceedings or that a child who is a party be removed, except where the parties consent to the child being made a party or to the removal of that party.
12.3(4)	Consequential directions following the addition or removal of a party except where a single justice is able to make such a direction under rule 12.3(2) and (3).
12.61(1) and (2)	Considering the transfer of proceedings to the court of another member state, directions in relation to the manner in which parties may make representations and power to deal with question of transfer without a hearing with the consent of parties.
12.64(1)	Exercising court's powers under Article 15 of the Council Regulation or Article 8 of the 1996 Hague Convention.
12.68(1)	Staying the proceedings.
12.68(3)	Giving reasons for the court's decision, making a finding of fact and stating a finding of fact where such a finding has been made.
12.70(1)	Contemplating the placement of a child in another member state.

The Family Procedure Rules 2010

Rule	Nature of function
12.70(3)	Sending request directly to the central authority or other authority having jurisdiction in the other Member State.
12.70(4)	Sending request to Central Authority for England and Wales for onward transmission.
12.70(5)	Considering the documents which should accompany the request.
13.3(3)	Where the person with parental responsibility is a child, a direction for that child be made a party, except where the parties consent to that child being made a party.
13.3(4)	Direction that a child be made a party to proceedings or that a child who is a party be removed, except where the parties consent to the child being made a party or to the removal of that party.
13.3(5)	Consequential directions following the addition or removal of a party except where a single justice is able to make such a direction under rule 13.3(3) and (4).
13.9(7)	Variation or revocation of direction following transfer, except where a single justice would be able to make the direction in question under rule 13.9(1).
13.15(3)	Determination of the probable date of the child's birth.
13.20(1)	Specifying a later date by which a parental order takes effect.
14.3(2)	Direction that a child be made a respondent, except where the parties consent to the child being made a respondent.
14.3(3)(b)	Direction that a child who is a party be removed, except where the parties consent to the child being made a respondent.
14.3(4)	Consequential directions following the addition or removal of a party except where a single justice is able to make such a direction under rule 14.3(2) and (3)
14.8(3)	Any of the directions listed in PD14B in proceedings for- (a) a Convention adoption order (b) a section 84 order (c) a section 88 direction (d) a section 89 order; or (e) an adoption order where section 83(1) of the 2002 Act applies (restriction on bringing children in)
14.16(8)	Making an adoption order under section 50 of the 2002 Act after personal attendance of one only of the applicants if there are special circumstances.
14.16(9)	Not making a placement order unless the legal representative of the applicant attends the final hearing.
14.17(4)	Determination of the probable date of the child's birth.
14.25(1)	Specifying a later date by which an order takes effect.
15.3(1)	Permission to a person to take steps before the protected party has a litigation friend.

FPR 2010, Practice Direction 2A

Rule	Nature of function
15.3(2)	Permission to a party to take steps (where during proceedings a person lacks capacity to continue to conduct proceedings) before the protected party has a litigation friend.
15.3(3)	Making an order that a step taken before a protected party has a litigation friend has effect.
15.6(1)	Making an order appointing a person as a litigation friend.
15.6(6)	Court may not appoint a litigation friend unless it is satisfied that the person complies with the conditions in rule 15.4(3).
15.7	Direction that a person may not act as a litigation friend, termination of an appointment, appointment of a litigation friend in substitution for an existing one.
16.2	Power of court to make a child a party to proceedings if it considers it is in the best interests of the child to do so.
16.6(3)(a)	Permission to a child to conduct proceedings without a children's guardian or litigation friend.
16.6(6)	Power of the court to grant an application under paragraph (3)(a) or (5) if the court considers that the child has sufficient understanding to conduct the proceedings.
16.6(7)	Power of the court to require the litigation friend or children's guardian to take such part in proceedings (referred to in paragraph (6)) as the court directs.
16.6(8)	Power of the court to revoke permission granted under paragraph (3) in specified circumstances.
16.6(10)	Power of the court, in specified circumstances, to appoint a person to be the child's litigation friend or children's guardian.
16.8(2)	Permission to a person to take steps before the child has a litigation friend.
16.8(3)	Making an order that a step taken before the child has a litigation friend has effect.
16.11(1)	Making an order appointing a person as a litigation friend.
16.12	Direction that a person may not act as a litigation friend, termination of an appointment, appointment of a litigation friend in substitution for an existing one.
16.23(2)	Permission to a person to take steps before the child has a children's guardian.
18.3(1)(c)	Direction that a child be a respondent to an application under Part 18.
18.9(1)(a)	Power of court to deal with a Part 18 application without a hearing.
18.12	Power of the court to proceed in absence of a party, except where a single justice has the power to make the relevant order applied for.
19.8(2)	The court's power to require or permit a party to give oral evidence at the hearing.
21.3	Power of court relating to withholding inspection or disclosure of a document.

The Family Procedure Rules 2010

Rule	Nature of function
22.1(2) to (4)	Power to exclude evidence that would otherwise be admissible, power to permit a party to adduce evidence, or to seek to rely on a document, in respect of which that party has failed to comply with requirements of Part 22 and power to limit cross examination.
22.6	Court's powers relating to use at final hearing of witness statements which have been served.
22.12	Power of court to require evidence by affidavit instead of or in addition to a witness statement.
22.15(4)	Permission for a party to amend or withdraw any admission made by that party on such terms as the court thinks just.
22.20(3)(a)	Permission for a witness statement in proceedings in the magistrates' court under Part 9 to be used for a purpose other than the proceedings in which it is served.
24.16(2)	Ordering the issue of a request to a designated court.
24.16(5)	Order for the submission of a request under article 17 of the Taking of Evidence Regulation.
27.10(1)(b)	Direction that proceedings to which the Rules apply will not be held in private, expect that a single justice may give such a direction in relation to a hearing which that single justice is conducting.
27.11(2)(g)	Power of the court to permit any other person to be present during any hearing, except that a single justice may give such permission in relation to a hearing which that single justice is conducting.
27.11(3)	Direction that persons within rule 27.11(2)(f) shall not attend the proceedings or any part of them.
Part 28	Powers of the court to make costs orders including wasted costs orders under section 145A of the Magistrates' Courts Act 1980.
29.8(1)	Court's opinion that it would be prevented by section 8 or 9 of the Child Support Act 1991 from making an order.
29.8(2)	Court's consideration of the matter without a hearing.
29.8(10)	Power of the court to determine that it would be prevented by sections 8 or 9 of the 1991 Act from making an order, and to dismiss the application.
29.8(11)	The court must give written reasons for its decision.
29.9(2)	Direction that the document will be treated as if it contained the application and directions as the court considers appropriate as to the subsequent conduct of the proceedings.
29.13(1)	Direction for a court officer not to serve a copy of an order (other than directions that the single justice has made) to every party affected by it.
29.15	Specifying alternative date for an order to take effect, except an order which the single justice has made.
29.16	Correcting an accidental slip or omission in an order, except where that order was made by a single justice.

FPR 2010, Practice Direction 2A

Rule	Nature of function
Part 30	Any power of the magistrates' court (where it is the lower court) to grant or refuse permission to appeal, except where a single justice has the power to make the order which is subject to the appeal.
31.9	Power for court to stay the proceedings.

Table 1

Practice Direction: Family Assistance Orders dated 3 September 2007- Paragraphs 2, 3, and 5	
	Under paragraph 2 the court must have obtained the opinion of the appropriate officer about whether it would be in the best interests of the child in question for a family assistance order to be made and, if so, how the family assistance order could operate and for what period.
	Under paragraph 3 the court decides on the category of officer required to be made available under the family assistance order.
	Under paragraph 5 the court must give to the person it proposes to name in the order an opportunity to comment.
Public Law Proceedings Guide to Case Management: 6th April 2010- Paragraphs 8.1 to 8.5	Under paragraphs 8.1 to 8.5 determination by the court of issues as to whether an adult party or intended party to proceedings lacks capacity.
Practice Direction: Residence and Contact Orders: Domestic Violence and Harm: 14 January 2009- Paragraphs 17, 18, 21 to 23, 28 and 29	Under paragraph 17 the court will consider whether a child who is the subject of an application should be made a party to proceedings.
	Under paragraph 18 the court will consider whether an interim order for residence or contact is in the best interests of the child.
	Under paragraphs 21-23, 27, 28 and 29 determinations of the court at fact finding hearings, in cases where a finding of domestic violence is made consideration of the conduct of the parents and where there has been a finding of domestic violence court directions or conditions on orders.
Practice Direction: Attendance of Media Representatives at Hearings in Family Proceedings dated 6 April 2009	Generally –court's discretion to exclude media representatives from attending hearings or part of hearings for "relevant proceedings" as defined in rule 1 of the Family Proceedings Courts (Children Act 1989) Rules 1991 (other than where a Single Justice or Justice's Clerk is conducting the hearing)
PD 14B-The First Directions Hearing- adoptions with a Foreign Element- Paragraph 2	Under paragraph 2 the court's consideration of:- (a) whether the requirements of the Adoption and Children Act 2002 and the Adoptions with a Foreign Element Regulations 2005 (S.I. 2005/392) appear to have been complied with and, if not, consider whether or not it is appropriate to transfer the case to the High Court;

	(b) whether all relevant documents are translated into English and, if not, fix a timetable for translating any outstanding documents;
	(c) whether the applicant needs to file an affidavit setting out the full details of the circumstances in which the child was brought to the United Kingdom, of the attitude of the parents to the application and confirming compliance with the requirements of The Adoptions with a Foreign Element Regulations 2005; and
	(d) give directions about:
	(i) the production of the child's passport and visa;
	(ii) the need for the Official Solicitor and a representative of the Home office to attend future hearings; and
	(iii) personal service on the parents (via the Central Authority in the case of an application for a Convention Adoption Order) including information about the role of the Official Solicitor and availability of legal aid to be represented within the proceedings; and
	(e) consider fixing a further directions no later than 6 weeks after the date of the first directions appointment and timetable a date by which the Official Solicitor should file an interim report in advance of that further appointment.
PD 15A- Protected Parties- Paragraph 4.2(b)	Under paragraph 4.2 (b) court directions on service on protected party.
PD16A- Representation of Children- Paragraphs 6.8 and 7.5	Under paragraph 6.8 the children's guardian must—
	(a) unless the court otherwise directs, file a written report advising on the interests of the child in accordance with the timetable set by the court; and
	(b) in proceedings to which Part 14 applies, where practicable, notify any person the joining of whom as a party to those proceedings would be likely, in the opinion of the children's guardian, to safeguard the interests of the child, of the court's power to join that person as a party under rule 14.3 and must inform the court
	(i) of any notification;
	(ii) of anyone whom the child's guardian attempted to notify under this paragraph but was unable to contact; and
	(iii) of anyone whom the children's guardian believes may wish to be joined to the proceedings
	Under paragraph 7.5 the court may, at the same time as deciding whether to join the child as a party, consider whether the proceedings should be transferred to another court taking into account the provisions of Part 3 of the Allocation and Transfer of Proceedings Order 2008.
PD18A – Other Applications in Proceedings	Under paragraph 4.1 on receipt of an application notice containing a request for a hearing, unless the court considers that the application is suitable for consideration without a hearing, the court officer will, if serving a copy of the application notice, notify the applicant of the time and date fixed for the hearing of the application.

Paragraphs 4.1 to 4.4(a)	Under paragraph 4.2 on receipt of an application notice containing a request that the application be dealt with without a hearing, the court will decide whether the application is suitable for consideration without a hearing.
	Under paragraph 4.3 where the court considers that the application is suitable for consideration without a hearing but is not satisfied that it has sufficient material to decide the application immediately it may give directions for the filing of evidence and will inform the applicant and the respondent(s) of its decision.
	Under paragraph 4.4 (a) where the court does not consider that the application is suitable for consideration without a hearing it may give directions as to the filing of evidence.
PD22A-Written Evidence	Under paragraph 1.6 the court may give a direction under rule 22.12 that evidence shall be given by affidavit instead of or in addition to a witness statement on its own initiative; or after any party has applied to the court for such a direction.
Paragraphs 1.6, 14.1 and 14.2	Under paragraph 14.1 where an affidavit, a witness statement or an exhibit to either an affidavit or a witness statement does not comply with Part 22 or PD 22A in relation to its form, the court may refuse to admit it as evidence and may refuse to allow the costs arising from its preparation.
	Under paragraph 14.2 permission to file a defective affidavit or witness statement or to use a defective exhibit may be obtained from the court where the case is proceeding.
PD 24A- Witnesses, Depositions and Taking of Evidence in Member States of the European Union- Paragraph 9.1 and 9.6	Under paragraph 9.1 where a person wishes to take a deposition from a person in another Regulation State, the court where proceedings are taking place may order the issue of a request to the designated court in the Regulation State (rule 24.16(2)). The form of request is prescribed as Form A in the Taking of Evidence Regulation.
	Under paragraph 9.6 Article 17 permits the court where proceedings are taking place to take evidence directly from a deponent in another Regulation State if the conditions of the article are satisfied. Direct taking of evidence can only take place of evidence is given voluntarily without the need for coercive measures. Rule 24.16(5) provides for the court to make an order for the submission of a request to take evidence directly. The form of request is Form I annexed to the Taking of Evidence Regulation and rule 24.16(6) makes provision for a draft of this form to be filed by the a party seeking the order. An application for an order under rule 24.16(5) should be by application notice in accordance with Part 18.

....

The Right Honourable

Sir Nicholas Wall

The President of the Family Division

Signed by authority of the Lord Chancellor:

The Family Procedure Rules 2010

....

Parliamentary Under Secretary of State Ministry of Justice

PART 3

ALTERNATIVE DISPUTE RESOLUTION: THE COURT'S POWERS

3.1.— Scope of this Part

(1) This Part contains the court's powers to encourage the parties to use alternative dispute resolution and to facilitate its use.

(2) The powers in this Part are subject to any powers given to the court by any other rule or practice direction or by any other enactment or any powers it may otherwise have.

3.2. Court's duty to consider alternative dispute resolution

The court must consider, at every stage in proceedings, whether alternative dispute resolution is appropriate.

3.3.— When the court will adjourn proceedings or a hearing in proceedings

(1) If the court considers that alternative dispute resolution is appropriate, the court may direct that the proceedings, or a hearing in the proceedings, be adjourned for such specified period as it considers appropriate—
  (a) to enable the parties to obtain information and advice about alternative dispute resolution; and
  (b) where the parties agree, to enable alternative dispute resolution to take place.

(2) The court may give directions under this rule on an application or of its own initiative.

(3) Where the court directs an adjournment under this rule, it will give directions about the timing and method by which the parties must tell the court if any of the issues in the proceedings have been resolved.

(4) If the parties do not tell the court if any of the issues have been resolved as directed under paragraph (3), the court will give such directions as to the management of the case as it considers appropriate.

(5) The court or court officer will—
  (a) record the making of an order under this rule; and
  (b) arrange for a copy of the order to be served as soon as practicable on the parties.

(6) Where the court proposes to exercise its powers of its own initiative, the procedure set out in rule 4.3(2) to (6) applies.

(By rule 4.1(7), any direction given under this rule may be varied or revoked.)

PART 3 COMMENTARY

Part 3 is supplemented by PD3A which contains a pre-application protocol on Mediation Information and Assessment.

PD3A sets out, at Annex A, a pre-application protocol for Mediation Information and Assessment. The protocol, which applies where a person intends to make an application to the court in private law Children Act proceedings or for a financial remedy provides that the prospective applicant should first contact a mediator for the purposes of obtaining information about mediation and should attend a Mediation Information and Assessment Meeting. The other party to the dispute is also expected to attend a meeting (which may be held separately), if invited to do so. The parties will not be expected to attend a meeting if, in certain specified circumstances (set out in

FPR 2010, Practice Direction 3A

Annex C, including where there has been an allegation of domestic violence, or where there is urgency, restrictively defined), it would be inappropriate to do so.

It is provided in para 4 of PD3A, that where an application is made to the court in cases to which the practice direction applies, the court will wish to know whether mediation has been considered and in considering the conduct of the proceedings will take into account any failure to comply with the protocol. This may include referring the parties to a meeting with a mediator before the proceedings continue further.

Form FM1 Family Mediation and assessment form is to be used for filed at court with an application confirming attendance at a Mediation Information and Assessment Meeting or giving the reasons for not attending in certain circumstances signed by the mediator (PD 3A, Annex A, The Pre Application Protocol, paras 8, 9, 10).

Part 3 sets out the court's powers to encourage the parties to use ADR and facilitate its use. The court must consider at every stage whether ADR is appropriate and may adjourn the proceedings to enable the parties to obtain information about ADR or, where agreed, for ADR to take place.

The Form FM1 – Family Mediation Information and Assessment Form applies to Part 3.

PRACTICE DIRECTION 3A – PRE-APPLICATION PROTOCOL FOR MEDIATION INFORMATION AND ASSESSMENT

This Practice Direction supplementing the Family Procedure Rules 2010 is made by the President of the Family Division under the powers delegated to him by the Lord Chief Justice under Schedule 2, Part 1, paragraph 2(2) of the Constitutional Reform Act 2005, and is approved by the Parliamentary Under Secretary of State, by authority of the Lord Chancellor.

This Practice Direction comes into force on 6th April 2011.

This Practice Direction supplements FPR Part 3

1. INTRODUCTION

1.1 This Practice Direction applies where a person is considering applying for an order in family proceedings of a type specified in Annex B (referred to in this Direction as "relevant family proceedings").

1.2 Terms used in this Practice Direction and the accompanying Pre-action Protocol have the same meaning as in the FPR.

1.3 This Practice Direction is supplemented by the following Annexes:

(i) Annex A: The Pre-application Protocol ("the Protocol"), which sets out steps which the court will normally expect an applicant to follow before an application is made to the court in relevant family proceedings;
(ii) Annex B: Proceedings which are "relevant family proceedings" for the purposes of this Practice Direction; and
(iii) Annex C: Circumstances in which attendance at a Mediation Information and Assessment Meeting is not expected.

2. AIMS

2.1 The purpose of this Practice Direction and the accompanying Protocol is to:

The Family Procedure Rules 2010

(a) supplement the court's powers in Part 3 of the FPR to encourage and facilitate the use of alternative dispute resolution;
(b) set out good practice to be followed by any person who is considering making an application to court for an order in relevant family proceedings; and
(c) ensure, as far as possible, that all parties have considered mediation as an alternative means of resolving their disputes.

3. RATIONALE

3.1 There is a general acknowledgement that an adversarial court process is not always best-suited to the resolution of family disputes, particularly private law disputes between parents relating to children, with such disputes often best resolved through discussion and agreement, where that can be managed safely and appropriately.

3.2 Litigants who seek public funding for certain types of family proceedings are (subject to some exceptions) already required to attend a meeting with a mediator as a pre-condition of receiving public funding.

3.3 There is growing recognition of the benefits of early information and advice about mediation and of the need for those wishing to make an application to court, whether publicly-funded or otherwise, to consider alternative means of resolving their disputes, as appropriate.

3.4 In private law proceedings relating to children, the court is actively involved in helping parties to explore ways of resolving their dispute. The Private Law Programme, set out in Practice Direction 12B, provides for a first hearing dispute resolution appointment ('FHDRA'), at which the judge, legal advisor or magistrates, accompanied by an officer from Cafcass (the Children and Family Court Advisory and Support Service), will discuss with parties both the nature of their dispute and whether it could be resolved by mediation or other alternative means and can give the parties information about services which may be available to assist them. The court should also have information obtained through safeguarding checks carried out by Cafcass, to ensure that any agreement between the parties, or any dispute resolution process selected, is in the interests of the child and safe for all concerned.

3.5 Against that background, it is likely to save court time and expense if the parties take steps to resolve their dispute without pursuing court proceedings. Parties will therefore be expected to explore the scope for resolving their dispute through mediation before embarking on the court process.

4. THE PRE-APPLICATION PROTOCOL

4.1 To encourage this approach, all potential applicants for a court order in relevant family proceedings will be expected, before making their application, to have followed the steps set out in the Protocol. This requires a potential applicant, except in certain specified circumstances, to consider with a mediator whether the dispute may be capable of being resolved through mediation. The court will expect all applicants to have complied with the Protocol before commencing proceedings and (except where any of the circumstances in Annex C applies) will expect any respondent to have attended a Mediation Information and Assessment Meeting, if invited to do so. If court proceedings are taken, the court will wish to know at the first hearing whether mediation has been considered by the parties. In considering the conduct of any relevant family proceedings, the court will take into account any failure to comply with the Protocol and may refer the parties to a meeting with a mediator before the proceedings continue further.

4.2 Nothing in the Protocol is to be read as affecting the operation of the Private Law Programme, set out in Practice Direction 12B, or the role of the court at the first hearing in any relevant family proceedings.

Signed   President of the Family Division
                                                                                        Date

FPR 2010, Practice Direction 3A

Signed   Parliamentary Under Secretary of State

                                                        Date

ANNEX A THE PRE-APPLICATION PROTOCOL

(1) This Protocol applies where a person ("the applicant") is considering making an application to the court for an order in relevant family proceedings.

(2) Before an applicant makes an application to the court for an order in relevant family proceedings, the applicant (or the applicant's legal representative) should contact a family mediator to arrange for the applicant to attend an information meeting about family mediation and other forms of alternative dispute resolution (referred to in this Protocol as "a Mediation Information and Assessment Meeting").

(3) An applicant is not expected to attend a Mediation Information and Assessment Meeting where any of the circumstances set out in Annex C applies.

(4) Information on how to find a family mediator may be obtained from local family courts, from the Community Legal Advice Helpline – CLA Direct (0845 345 4345) or at http://www.direct.gov.uk.

(5) The applicant (or the applicant's legal representative) should provide the mediator with contact details for the other party or parties to the dispute ("the respondent(s)"), so that the mediator can contact the respondent(s) to discuss that party's willingness and availability to attend a Mediation Information and Assessment Meeting.

(6) The applicant should then attend a Mediation Information and Assessment Meeting arranged by the mediator. If the parties are willing to attend together, the meeting may be conducted jointly, but where necessary separate meetings may be held. If the applicant and respondent(s) do not attend a joint meeting, the mediator will invite the respondent(s) to a separate meeting unless any of the circumstances set out in Annex C applies.

(7) A mediator who arranges a Mediation Information and Assessment Meeting with one or more parties to a dispute should consider with the party or parties concerned whether public funding may be available to meet the cost of the meeting and any subsequent mediation. Where none of the parties is eligible for, or wishes to seek, public funding, any charge made by the mediator for the Mediation Information and Assessment Meeting will be the responsibility of the party or parties attending, in accordance with any agreement made with the mediator.

(8) If the applicant then makes an application to the court in respect of the dispute, the applicant should at the same time file a completed Family Mediation Information and Assessment Form (Form FM1) confirming attendance at a Mediation Information and Assessment Meeting or giving the reasons for not attending.

(9) The Form FM1, must be completed and signed by the mediator, and counter-signed by the applicant or the applicant's legal representative, where either
    (a) the applicant has attended a Mediation Information and Assessment Meeting; or
    (b) the applicant has not attended a Mediation Information and Assessment Meeting and
        (i) the mediator is satisfied that mediation is not suitable because another party to the dispute is unwilling to attend a Mediation Information and Assessment Meeting and consider mediation;
        (ii) the mediator determines that the case is not suitable for a Mediation Information and Assessment Meeting; or

(iii) a mediator has made a determination within the previous four months that the case is not suitable for a Mediation Information and Assessment Meeting or for mediation.
(10) In all other circumstances, the Form FM1 must be completed and signed by the applicant or the applicant's legal representative.
(11) The form may be obtained from magistrates' courts, county courts or the High Court or from http:www.direct.gov.uk.

ANNEX B PROCEEDINGS WHICH ARE "RELEVANT FAMILY PROCEEDINGS" FOR THE PURPOSES OF THIS PRACTICE DIRECTION

(1) Private law proceedings relating to children, except:
- proceedings for an enforcement order, a financial compensation order or an order under paragraph 9 or Part 2 of Schedule A1 to the Children Act 1989;
- any other proceedings for enforcement of an order made in private law proceedings; or
- where emergency proceedings have been brought in respect of the same child(ren) and have not been determined.

("Private law proceedings" and "emergency proceedings" are defined in Rule 12.2)

(2) Proceedings for a financial remedy, except:
- Proceedings for an avoidance of disposition order or an order preventing a disposition;
- Proceedings for enforcement of any order made in financial remedy proceedings.

("Financial remedy" is defined in Rule 2.3(1) and "avoidance of disposition order" and "order preventing a disposition" are defined in Rule 9.3(1))

ANNEX C A PERSON CONSIDERING MAKING AN APPLICATION TO THE COURT IN RELEVANT FAMILY PROCEEDINGS IS NOT EXPECTED TO ATTEND A MEDIATION INFORMATION AND ASSESSMENT MEETING BEFORE DOING SO IF ANY OF THE FOLLOWING CIRCUMSTANCES APPLIES:

(1) The mediator is satisfied that mediation is not suitable because another party to the dispute is unwilling to attend a Mediation Information and Assessment Meeting and consider mediation.
(2) The mediator determines that the case is not suitable for a Mediation Information and Assessment Meeting.
(3) A mediator has made a determination within the previous four months that the case is not suitable for a Mediation Information and Assessment Meeting or for mediation.
(4) *Domestic abuse*
Any party has, to the applicant's knowledge, made an allegation of domestic Violence against another party and this has resulted in a police investigation or the issuing of civil proceedings for the protection of any party within the last 12 months.
(5) *Bankruptcy*
The dispute concerns financial issues and the applicant or another party is bankrupt.
(6) The parties are in agreement and there is no dispute to mediate.
(7) The whereabouts of the other party are unknown to the applicant.
(8) The prospective application is for an order in relevant family proceedings which are already in existence and are continuing.
(9) The prospective application is to be made without notice to the other party.

(10) Urgency
The prospective application is urgent, meaning:
(a) there is a risk to the life, liberty or physical safety of the applicant or his or her family or his or her home; or
(b) any delay caused by attending a Mediation Information and Assessment Meeting would cause a risk of significant harm to a child, a significant risk of a miscarriage of justice, unreasonable hardship to the applicant or irretrievable problems in dealing with the dispute (such as an irretrievable loss of significant evidence).
(11) There is current social services involvement as a result of child protection concerns in respect of any child who would be the subject of the prospective application.
(12) A child would be a party to the prospective application by virtue of Rule 12.3(1).
(13) The applicant (or the applicant's legal representative) contacts three mediators within 15 miles of the applicant's home and none is able to conduct a Mediation Information and Assessment Meeting within 15 working days of the date of contact.

PART 4

GENERAL CASE MANAGEMENT POWERS

4.1.— The court's general powers of management

(1) In this Part, "statement of case" means the whole or part of, an application form or answer.

(2) The list of powers in this rule is in addition to any powers given to the court by any other rule or practice direction or by any other enactment or any powers it may otherwise have.

(3) Except where these rules provide otherwise, the court may—
(a) extend or shorten the time for compliance with any rule, practice direction or court order (even if an application for extension is made after the time for compliance has expired);
(b) make such order for disclosure and inspection, including specific disclosure of documents, as it thinks fit;
(c) adjourn or bring forward a hearing;
(d) require a party or a party's legal representative to attend the court;
(e) hold a hearing and receive evidence by telephone or by using any other method of direct oral communication;
(f) direct that part of any proceedings be dealt with as separate proceedings;
(g) stay$^{(GL)}$ the whole or part of any proceedings or judgment either generally or until a specified date or event;
(h) consolidate proceedings;
(i) hear two or more applications on the same occasion;
(j) direct a separate hearing of any issue;
(k) decide the order in which issues are to be heard;
(l) exclude an issue from consideration;
(m) dismiss or give a decision on an application after a decision on a preliminary issue;
(n) direct any party to file and serve an estimate of costs; and
(o) take any other step or make any other order for the purpose of managing the case and furthering the overriding objective.

(Rule 21.1 explains what is meant by disclosure and inspection.)

(4) When the court makes an order, it may—

(a) make it subject to conditions, including a condition to pay a sum of money into court; and
(b) specify the consequence of failure to comply with the order or a condition.

(5) Where the court gives directions it will take into account whether or not a party has complied with any relevant pre-action protocol$^{(GL)}$.

(6) A power of the court under these rules to make an order includes a power to vary or revoke the order.

(7) Any provision in these rules—
(a) requiring or permitting directions to be given by the court is to be taken as including provision for such directions to be varied or revoked; and
(b) requiring or permitting a date to be set is to be taken as including provision for that date to be changed or cancelled.

(8) The court may not extend the period within which a section 89 order must be made.

4.2. Court officer's power to refer to the court

Where a step is to be taken by a court officer—
(a) the court officer may consult the court before taking that step;
(b) the step may be taken by the court instead of the court officer.

4.3.— Court's power to make order of its own initiative

(1) Except where an enactment provides otherwise, the court may exercise its powers on an application or of its own initiative.
(Part 18 sets out the procedure for making an application.)

(2) Where the court proposes to make an order of its own initiative—
(a) it may give any person likely to be affected by the order an opportunity to make representations; and
(b) where it does so it must specify the time by and the manner in which the representations must be made.

(3) Where the court proposes—
(a) to make an order of its own initiative; and
(b) to hold a hearing to decide whether to make the order,
it must give each party likely to be affected by the order at least 5 days' notice of the hearing.

(4) The court may make an order of its own initiative without hearing the parties or giving them an opportunity to make representations.

(5) Where the court has made an order under paragraph (4)—
(a) a party affected by the order may apply to have it set aside$^{(GL)}$, varied or stayed$^{(GL)}$; and
(b) the order must contain a statement of the right to make such an application.

(6) An application under paragraph (5)(a) must be made—
(a) within such period as may be specified by the court; or
(b) if the court does not specify a period, within 7 days beginning with the date on which the order was served on the party making the application.

(7) If the High Court or a county court of its own initiative strikes out a statement of case or dismisses an application (including an application for permission to appeal) and it considers that the application is totally without merit—
(a) the court's order must record that fact; and
(b) the court must at the same time consider whether it is appropriate to make a civil restraint order.

4.4.— Power to strike out a statement of case

(1) Except in proceedings to which Parts 12 to 14 apply, the court may strike out$^{(GL)}$ a statement of case if it appears to the court—
(a) that the statement of case discloses no reasonable grounds for bringing or defending the application;

- (b) that the statement of case is an abuse of the court's process or is otherwise likely to obstruct the just disposal of the proceedings;
- (c) that there has been a failure to comply with a rule, practice direction or court order; or
- (d) in relation to applications for matrimonial and civil partnership orders and answers to such applications, that the parties to the proceedings consent.

(2) When the court strikes out a statement of case it may make any consequential order it considers appropriate.

(3) Where—
- (a) the court has struck out an applicant's statement of case;
- (b) the applicant has been ordered to pay costs to the respondent; and
- (c) before paying those costs, the applicant starts another application against the same respondent, arising out of facts which are the same or substantially the same as those relating to the application in which the statement of case was struck out,

the court may, on the application of the respondent, stay$^{(GL)}$ that other application until the costs of the first application have been paid.

(4) Paragraph (1) does not limit any other power of the court to strike out $^{(GL)}$ a statement of case.

(5) If the High Court or a county court strikes out an applicant's statement of case and it considers that the application is totally without merit—
- (a) the court's order must record that fact; and
- (b) the court must at the same time consider whether it is appropriate to make a civil restraint order.

4.5.— Sanctions have effect unless defaulting party obtains relief

(1) Where a party has failed to comply with a rule, practice direction or court order, any sanction for failure to comply imposed by the rule, practice direction or court order has effect unless the party in default applies for and obtains relief from the sanction.

(Rule 4.6 sets out the circumstances which the court may consider on an application to grant relief from a sanction.)

(2) Where the sanction is the payment of costs, the party in default may only obtain relief by appealing against the order for costs.

(3) Where a rule, practice direction or court order—
- (a) requires a party to do something within a specified time; and
- (b) specifies the consequence of failure to comply,

the time for doing the act in question may not be extended by agreement between the parties.

4.6.— Relief from sanctions

(1) On an application for relief from any sanction imposed for a failure to comply with any rule, practice direction or court order the court will consider all the circumstances including—
- (a) the interests of the administration of justice;
- (b) whether the application for relief has been made promptly;
- (c) whether the failure to comply was intentional;
- (d) whether there is a good explanation for the failure;
- (e) the extent to which the party in default has complied with other rules, practice directions, court orders and any relevant pre-action protocol$^{(GL)}$;
- (f) whether the failure to comply was caused by the party or the party's legal representative;
- (g) whether the hearing date or the likely hearing date can still be met if relief is granted;
- (h) the effect which the failure to comply had on each party; and
- (i) the effect which the granting of relief would have on each party or a child whose interest the court considers relevant.

The Family Procedure Rules 2010

(2) An application for relief must be supported by evidence.

4.7. General power of the court to rectify matters where there has been an error of procedure

Where there has been an error of procedure such as a failure to comply with a rule or practice direction—

    (a)   the error does not invalidate any step taken in the proceedings unless the court so orders; and

    (b)   the court may make an order to remedy the error.

4.8. Power of the court to make civil restraint orders

Practice Direction 4B sets out—

    (a)   the circumstances in which the High Court or a county court has the power to make a civil restraint order against a party to proceedings;

    (b)   the procedure where a party applies for a civil restraint order against another party; and

    (c)   the consequences of the court making a civil restraint order.

PART 4 COMMENTARY

Part 4 is supplemented by two practice directions: 4A – Striking out a Statement of Case and 4B – Civil Restraint Orders.

Part 4 contains the general case management powers. Rule 4.1 contains a comprehensive list of powers including power to: extend or shorten time for compliance with any rule, practice directions or court order (even if an application for extension is made after the time for compliance has expired) (r 4.1(3)(a)); make orders for disclosure and inspection (r 4.1(3)(b)); receive evidence on the telephone (r 4.1(3)(e)); exclude an issue from consideration (r 4.1(3)(l)); give a decision on an application after a decision on a preliminary issue (r 4.1 (3)(m)); and to specify sanctions if there is failure to comply with an order (r 4.1(4)) (but see r 4.6 for relief from those sanctions).

Rule 4.3 mirrors r 3.3 of the CPR. It makes provision for the court to make a decision of its own initiative with or without taking submissions and provides a default period of seven days for the order to be set aside if it has made a decision without hearing representations from the parties.

Rule 4.4 mirrors r 3.4 of the CPR and gives the court the power to strike out a 'statement of case' (which is defined in r 4.1 as the whole or part of, an application form or answer) except in specified children proceedings. The power is to be exercised where there is no reasonable grounds for bringing or defending the application, there is an abuse of the process of the court, a failure to comply with a rule, practice direction or order, and in relation to matrimonial and civil partnership orders, where there is consent of the parties. The procedure to be followed on an application to strike out is set out in PD4B. If the High Court or county court strikes out and considers that an application is totally without merit it is required to record that fact on the order and consider whether it is appropriate to make a civil restraint order (r 4.4(5)). This provision is expressed in very similar terms to CPR r 23.12.

Rule 4.8 together with PD4B set out the circumstances, procedure and consequence of a civil restraint order.

FPR 2010, Practice Direction 4A

PRACTICE DIRECTION 4A – STRIKING OUT A STATEMENT OF CASE

This Practice Direction supplements FPR Part 4, rule 4.4 (Power to strike out a statement of case)

INTRODUCTION

1.1 Rule 4.4 enables the court to strike out the whole or part of a statement of case which discloses no reasonable grounds for bringing or defending the application (rule 4.4 (1)(a)), or which is an abuse of the process of the court or otherwise likely to obstruct the just disposal of the proceedings (rule 4.4(1)(b)). These powers may be exercised on an application by a party or on the court's own initiative.

1.2 This practice direction sets out the procedure a party should follow to make an application for an order under rule 4.4.

EXAMPLES OF CASES WITHIN THE RULE

2.1 The following are examples of cases where the court may conclude that an application falls within rule 4.4(1)(a)—

(a) those which set out no facts indicating what the application is about;
(b) those which are incoherent and make no sense;
(c) those which contain a coherent set of facts but those facts, even if true, do not disclose any legally recognisable application against the respondent.

2.2 An application may fall within rule 4.4(1)(b) where it cannot be justified, for example because it is frivolous, scurrilous or obviously ill-founded.

2.3 An answer may fall within rule 4.4(1)(a) where it consists of a bare denial or otherwise sets out no coherent statement of facts.

2.4 A party may believe that it can be shown without the need for a hearing that an opponent's case has no real prospect of success on the facts, or that the case is bound to succeed or fail, as the case may be, because of a point of law (including the construction of a document). In such a case the party concerned may make an application under rule 4.4.

2.5 The examples set out above are intended only as illustrations.

2.6 Where a rule, practice direction or order states 'shall be struck out or dismissed' or 'will be struck out or dismissed' this means that the order striking out or dismissing the proceedings will itself bring the proceedings to an end and that no further order of the court is required.

APPLICATIONS WHICH APPEAR TO FALL WITHIN RULE 4.4(1)(A) OR (B)

3.1 A court officer who is asked to issue an application form but believes the application may fall within rule 4.4(1)(a) or (b) should issue the application form, but may then consult the court (under rule 4.2) before returning the form to the applicant or taking any other step to serve the respondent. The court may of its own initiative make an immediate order designed to ensure that the application is disposed of or (as the case may be) proceeds in a way that accords with the rules.

3.2 The court may allow the applicant a hearing before deciding whether to make such an order.

3.3 Orders the court may make include—

(a) an order that the application be stayed until further order;
(b) an order that the application form be retained by the court and not served until the stay is lifted;
(c) an order that no application by the applicant to lift the stay be heard unless the applicant files such further documents (for example a witness statement or an amended application form) as may be specified in the order.

3.4 Where the court makes any such order or, subsequently, an order lifting the stay,

The Family Procedure Rules 2010

it may give directions about the service on the respondent of the order and any other documents on the court file.

3.5 The fact that the court allows an application referred to it by a court officer to proceed does not prejudice the right of any party to apply for any order against the applicant.

ANSWERS WHICH APPEAR TO FALL WITHIN RULE 4.4(1)(A) OR (B)

4.1 A court officer may similarly consult the court about any document filed which purports to be an answer and which the officer believes may fall within rule 4.4 (1)(a) or (b).

4.2 If the court decides that the document falls within rule 4.4(1)(a) or (b) it may on its own initiative make an order striking it out. Where the court does so it may extend the time for the respondent to file a proper answer.

4.3 The court may allow the respondent a hearing before deciding whether to make such an order.

4.4 Alternatively the court may make an order requiring the respondent within a stated time to clarify the answer or to give additional information about it. The order may provide that the answer will be struck out if the respondent does not comply.

4.5 The fact that the court does not strike out an answer on its own initiative does not prejudice the right of the applicant to apply for any order against the respondent.

GENERAL PROVISIONS

5.1 The court may exercise its powers under rule 4.4(1)(a) or (b) on application by a party to the proceedings or on its own initiative at any time.

5.2 Where the court at a hearing strikes out all or part of a party's statement of case it may enter such judgment for the other party as that party appears entitled to.

APPLICATIONS FOR ORDERS UNDER RULE 4.4(1)

6.1 Attention is drawn to Part 18 (Procedure for Other Applications in Proceedings) and to the practice direction that supplements it. The practice direction requires all applications to be made as soon as possible.

6.2 While many applications under rule 4.4(1) can be made without evidence in support, the applicant should consider whether facts need to be proved and, if so, whether evidence in support should be filed and served.

PRACTICE DIRECTION 4B – CIVIL RESTRAINT ORDERS

This Practice Direction supplements FPR rule 4.8

INTRODUCTION

1.1 This practice direction applies where the court is considering whether to make—

(a) a limited civil restraint order;
(b) an extended civil restraint order; or
(c) a general civil restraint order,

against a party who has made applications which are totally without merit.

Rules 4.3(7), 4.4(5) and 18.13 provide that where a statement of case or application is struck out or dismissed and is totally without merit, the court order must specify that fact and the court must consider whether to make a civil restraint order. Rule 30.11(5) makes similar provision where the appeal court refuses an application for permission to appeal, strikes out an appellant's notice or dismisses an appeal.

The powers of the court to make civil restraint orders are separate from and do not replace the powers given to the court by section 91(14) of the Children Act 1989.

LIMITED CIVIL RESTRAINT ORDERS

2.1 A limited civil restraint order may be made by a judge of the High Court or a county court where a party has made 2 or more applications which are totally without merit.

2.2 Where the court makes a limited civil restraint order, the party against whom the order is made—

(a) will be restrained from making any further applications in the proceedings in which the order is made without first obtaining the permission of a judge identified in the order;
(b) may apply for amendment or discharge of the order, but only with the permission of a judge identified in the order; and
(c) may apply for permission to appeal the order and if permission is granted, may appeal the order.

2.3 Where a party who is subject to a limited civil restraint order—

(a) makes a further application in the proceedings in which the order is made without first obtaining the permission of a judge identified in the order, such application will automatically be dismissed—
   (i) without the judge having to make any further order; and
   (ii) without the need for the other party to respond to it; and
(b) repeatedly makes applications for permission pursuant to that order which are totally without merit, the court may direct that if the party makes any further application for permission which is totally without merit, the decision to dismiss the application will be final and there will be no right of appeal, unless the judge who refused permission grants permission to appeal.

2.4 A party who is subject to a limited civil restraint order may not make an application for permission under paragraphs 2.2(a) or (b) without first serving notice of the application on the other party in accordance with paragraph 2.5.

2.5 A notice under paragraph 2.4 must—

(a) set out the nature and grounds of the application; and
(b) provide the other party with at least 7 days within which to respond.

2.6 An application for permission under paragraphs 2.2(a) or (b)—

(a) must be made in writing;
(b) must include the other party's written response, if any, to the notice served under paragraph 2.4; and
(c) will be determined without a hearing.

2.7 An order under paragraph 2.3(b) may only be made by a High Court judge but not a district judge.

2.8 Where a party makes an application for permission under paragraphs 2.2(a) or (b) and permission is refused, any application for permission to appeal—

(a) must be made in writing; and
(b) will be determined without a hearing.

2.9 A limited civil restraint order—

(a) is limited to the particular proceedings in which it is made;
(b) will remain in effect for the duration of the proceedings in which it is made, unless the court orders otherwise; and
(c) must identify the judge or judges to whom an application for permission under paragraphs 2.2(a), 2.2(b) or 2.8 should be made.

The Family Procedure Rules 2010

EXTENDED CIVIL RESTRAINT ORDERS

3.1 An extended civil restraint order may be made by a judge of the High Court but not a district judge where a party has persistently made applications which are totally without merit.

3.2 Unless the court orders otherwise, where the court makes an extended civil restraint order, the party against whom the order is made—

(a) will be restrained from making applications in any court concerning any matter involving or relating to or touching upon or leading to the proceedings in which the order is made without first obtaining the permission of a judge identified in the order;
(b) may apply for amendment or discharge of the order, but only with the permission of a judge identified in the order; and
(c) may apply for permission to appeal the order and if permission is granted, may appeal the order.

3.3 Where a party who is subject to an extended civil restraint order—

(a) makes an application in a court identified in the order concerning any matter involving or relating to or touching upon or leading to the proceedings in which the order is made without first obtaining the permission of a judge identified in the order, the application will automatically be struck out or dismissed—
    (i) without the judge having to make any further order; and
    (ii) without the need for the other party to respond to it; and
(b) repeatedly makes applications for permission pursuant to that order which are totally without merit, the court may direct that if the party makes any further application for permission which is totally without merit, the decision to dismiss the application will be final and there will be no right of appeal, unless the judge who refused permission grants permission to appeal.

3.4 A party who is subject to an extended civil restraint order may not make an application for permission under paragraphs 3.2(a) or (b) without first serving notice of the application on the other party in accordance with paragraph 3.5.

3.5 A notice under paragraph 3.4 must—

(a) set out the nature and grounds of the application; and
(b) provide the other party with at least 7 days within which to respond.

3.6 An application for permission under paragraphs 3.2(a) or (b)—

(a) must be made in writing;
(b) must include the other party's written response, if any, to the notice served under paragraph 3.4; and
(c) will be determined without a hearing.

3.7 An order under paragraph 3.3(b) may only be made by a High Court judge but not a district judge.

3.8 Where a party makes an application for permission under paragraphs 3.2(a) or (b) and permission is refused, any application for permission to appeal-

(a) must be made in writing; and
(b) will be determined without a hearing.

3.9 An extended civil restraint order-

(a) will be made for a specified period not exceeding 2 years;
(b) must identify the courts in which the party against whom the order is made is restrained from making applications; and
(c) must identify the judge or judges to whom an application for permission under paragraphs 3.2(a), 3.2(b) or 3.8 should be made.

3.10 The court may extend the duration of an extended civil restraint order, if it considers it appropriate to do so, but the duration of the order must not be extended for a period greater than 2 years on any given occasion.

GENERAL CIVIL RESTRAINT ORDERS

4.1 A general civil restraint order may be made by a judge of the High Court but not a district judge where, the party against whom the order is made persists in making applications which are totally without merit, in circumstances where an extended civil restraint order would not be sufficient or appropriate.

4.2 Unless the court otherwise orders, where the court makes a general civil restraint order, the party against whom the order is made—

(a) will be restrained from making any application in any court without first obtaining the permission of a judge identified in the order;
(b) may apply for amendment or discharge of the order, but only with the permission of a judge identified in the order; and
(c) may apply for permission to appeal the order and if permission is granted, may appeal the order.

4.3 Where a party who is subject to a general civil restraint order—

(a) makes an application in any court without first obtaining the permission of a judge identified in the order, the application will automatically be struck out or dismissed—
   (i) without the judge having to make any further order; and
   (ii) without the need for the other party to respond to it; and
(b) repeatedly makes applications for permission pursuant to that order which are totally without merit, the court may direct that if the party makes any further application for permission which is totally without merit, the decision to dismiss that application will be final and there will be no right of appeal, unless the judge who refused permission grants permission to appeal.

4.4 A party who is subject to a general civil restraint order may not make an application for permission under paragraphs 4.2(a) or (b) without first serving notice of the application on the other party in accordance with paragraph 4.5.

4.5 A notice under paragraph 4.4 must—

(a) set out the nature and grounds of the application; and
(b) provide the other party with at least 7 days within which to respond.

4.6 An application for permission under paragraphs 4.2(a) or (b)—

(a) must be made in writing;
(b) must include the other party's written response, if any, to the notice served under paragraph 4.4; and
(c) will be determined without a hearing.

4.7 An order under paragraph 4.3(b) may only be made by a High Court judge but not a district judge.

4.8 Where a party makes an application for permission under paragraphs 4.2(a) or (b) and permission is refused, any application for permission to appeal—

(a) must be made in writing; and
(b) will be determined without a hearing.

4.9 A general civil restraint order-

(a) will be made for a specified period not exceeding 2 years;
(b) must identify the courts in which the party against whom the order is made is restrained from making applications; and
(c) must identify the judge or judges to whom an application for permission under paragraphs 4.2(a), 4.2(b) or 4.8 should be made.

4.10 The court may extend the duration of a general civil restraint order, if it considers it appropriate to do so, but he duration of the order must not be extended for

The Family Procedure Rules 2010

a period greater than 2 years on any given occasion.

GENERAL

5.1 The other party or parties to the proceedings may apply for any civil restraint order.

5.2 An application under paragraph 5.1 must be made using the procedure in Part 18 unless the court otherwise directs and the application must specify which type of civil restraint order is sought.

PART 5

FORMS AND START OF PROCEEDINGS

5.1.— Forms

(1) Subject to rule 14.10(2) and (3), the forms referred to in a practice direction, shall be used in the cases to which they apply.

(2) A form may be varied by the court or a party if the variation is required by the circumstances of a particular case.

(3) A form must not be varied so as to leave out any information or guidance which the form gives to the recipient.

(4) Where these rules require a form to be sent by the court or by a party for another party to use, it must be sent without any variation except such as is required by the circumstances of the particular case.

5.2. Documents to be attached to a form

Subject to any rule or practice direction, unless the court directs otherwise, a form must have attached to it any documents which, in the form, are—

    (a) stated to be required; or
    (b) referred to.

5.3.— Proceedings are started by issue of application form

(1) Proceedings are started when a court officer issues an application at the request of the applicant.

(2) An application is issued on the date entered in the application form by the court officer.

(Rule 29.7 requires an application form to be authenticated with the stamp of the court when it is issued)

PART 5 COMMENTARY

Part 5 is supplemented by PD5A. This contains a table of the forms applicable to each type of proceedings and a list of all the forms and their description. Particular provision is made at paragraph 2.1 of the text for committal applications: where they are taking place in existing proceedings an application notice under those proceedings is to be filed, otherwise there is to be a Part 19 application notice (FP1).

Part 5 sets out that the appropriate forms should be used (r 5.1) but the form may be varied if variation is required by the circumstances of a particular case (r 5.1(2)) so long as no information or guidance which the form gives is left out (r 5.1(3)). Such documents should be attached as are required to be attached or referred to in the form (r 5.2). Proceedings are started when the court officer issues an application (r 5.3).

FPR 2010, Practice Direction 5A

PRACTICE DIRECTION 5A—FORMS

This Practice Direction is made by the President of the Family Division under the powers delegated to him by the Lord Chief Justice under Schedule 2, Part 1, paragraph 2(2) of the Constitutional Reform Act 2005, and is approved by the Parliamentary Under Secretary of State, by authority of the Lord Chancellor and comes into force on 6th April 2011

This Practice Direction supplements FPR Part 5, rule 5.1 (Forms)

SCOPE AND INTERPRETATION

1.1 This Practice Direction lists the forms to be used in family proceedings on or after 6th April 2011. Table 1 lists the forms against the part of the FPR to which they are relevant, and Table 2 lists the forms individually with their description.

1.2 The forms may be—

(a) modified as the circumstances require, provided that all essential information, especially information or guidance which the form gives to the recipient, is included;
(b) expanded to include additional pages where that may be necessary, provided that any additional pages are also verified by a statement of truth.

1.3 Any reference in family proceedings forms to a Part, rule or Practice Direction is to be read as a reference to the equivalent Part, rule or Practice Direction in the FPR and any reference to a Practice Direction in any CPR form used in family proceedings is to be read as a reference to the equivalent Practice Direction in the FPR.

FORMS FOR COMMITTAL APPLICATIONS

2.1 Rule 33.1(2) applies Part 50 of, and Schedules 1 and 2 to the CPR, in so far as they are relevant and with necessary modification (including the modification referred to in rule 33.7), to an application made in the High Court and a county court to enforce an order made in family proceedings. The CPR Practice Direction "RSC52 and CCR 29-Committal Applications" therefore applies with necessary modifications to the enforcement of such an order. The form to be used for a committal application is set out in that Practice Direction. Accordingly, where a committal application is made in existing proceedings, it must be commenced by filing an application notice under Part 18 in those proceedings (a form C2 where there are existing proceedings under the Children Act 1989, a form D11 where the existing proceedings are matrimonial or civil partnership proceedings, financial remedy proceedings and proceedings under Part 8 or otherwise a form FP2).Otherwise a committal application must be commenced by the issue of a Part 19 application notice (a form FP1).

OTHER FORMS

3.1 Other forms may be authorised by practice directions.

Table 1
Index to forms

FPR Part	Forms
Part 3 Alternative Dispute Resolution (Family Mediation)	FM1
Part 6 Service	C9, D5, D89, FL415, FP6

The Family Procedure Rules 2010

FPR Part	Forms
Part 7 Matrimonial and Civil Partnership Proceedings	C60, D6, D8, D8 Notes, D8A, D8B, D8D, D8D Notes, D8N, D8N Notes, D11, D13B, D20, D36, D80A, D80B, D80C, D80D, D80E, D80F, D80G, D81, D84,
Part 8 Miscellaneous Applications	D50, D50A, D50B, D50C, D50D, D50E, D50F, D50G, D50H, D50J, D50K
Part 8 Chapter 5 Applications for declarations	C63, C64, C65, D70
Part 9 Applications for a Financial Remedy	Form A, Form A1, Form A2, Form B, Form E, Form E Notes, Form E1, Form E2, Form F, Form I, Form P, Form P1, Form P2, Form PPF, Form PPF1, Form PPF2
Part 10 Applications under Part 4 of the Family Law Act 1996	FL401, FL403, FL407, FL415
Part 11 Applications under Part 4A of the Family Law Act 1996	FL401A, FL403A, FL407A, FL430, FL431
Part 12 Applications in respect of children	C1, C1A, C2, C3, C4, C5, C8, C9, C11, C12, C13, C13A, C14, C15, C16, C17, C17A, C18, C19, C20, C61, C62, C66, C67, C68, C78, C79, C100, C110, C(PRA1), C(PRA2) C(PRA3), PLO1, PLO2, PLO3, PLO4, PLO5, PLO6, PLO8, PLO9, PLP10
Part 13 Applications under section 54 of Human Fertilisation and Embryology Act 2008	C51, C52, A64A, A101A
Part 14 Adoption	A4, A5, A50, A51, A52, A53, A54, A55, A56, A57 A58, A59, A60, A61, A62, A63, A50 Notes, A51 Notes, A52 Notes, A53 Notes, A54 Notes, A55 Notes, A56 Notes, A57 Notes, A58 Notes, A59 Notes, A60 Notes, A61 Notes, A 62 Notes, A63 Notes, A64, A65, A100, A101, A102, A103, A104, A105, A106, A107
Part 15 Representation of Protected Parties	FP9
Part 16 Representation of children	FP9
Part 18 Applications in proceedings	C2, D11, FP2

FPR 2010, Practice Direction 5A

FPR Part	Forms
Part 19 Alternative Procedure for applications	FP1, FP1A, FP1B, FP3, FP5
Part 22 Evidence	N285
Part 24 Witnesses	FP25
Part 26 Notification of change of solicitor	FP8
Part 28 Costs	D252, D254, D258, D258A, D258B, D258C, D259, Form H, Form H1, N260
Part 30 Appeals	N161, N161A, N161B, N162, N162A, N162, N164
Part 31 Registration of Orders under the Council Regulation, The Civil Partnership (Jurisdiction and Recognition of Judgements) Regulations 2005 and under the Hague Convention 1996	C60, C61, C62, C69, D180
Part 32 Registration and Enforcement of Orders	D151
Part 33 Enforcement	D62, N56, N323, N336, N337, N349, N379, N380
Part 34 Reciprocal Enforcement of Maintenance Orders	REMO 1, REMO 2

Table 2
List of Forms

Number	Name
A4	Application For Revocation Of An Order Freeing A Child For Adoption
A5	Application For Substitution Of One Adoption Agency For Another
A50	Application for a placement order Section 22 Adoption and Children Act 2002
A51	Application for variation of a placement order Section 23 Adoption and Children Act 2002
A52	Application for revocation of a placement order Section 24 Adoption and Children Act 2002
A53	Application for a contact order Section 26 Adoption and Children Act 2002
A54	Application for variation or revocation of a contact order Section 27(1)(b) Adoption and Children Act 2002

The Family Procedure Rules 2010

Number	Name
A55	Application for permission to change a child's surname Section 28 Adoption and Children Act 2002
A56	Application for permission to remove a child from the United Kingdom Section 28 Adoption and Children Act 2002
A57	Application for a recovery order Section 41 Adoption and Children Act 2002
A58	Application for an adoption order Section 46 Adoption and Children Act 2002
A59	Application for a Convention adoption order Section 46 Adoption and Children Act 2002
A60	Application for an adoption order (excluding a Convention adoption order) where the child is habitually resident outside the British Islands and is brought into the United Kingdom for the purposes of adoption Section 46 Adoption and Children Act 2002
A61	Application for an order for parental responsibility prior to adoption abroad Section 84 Adoption and Children Act 2002
A62	Application for a direction under section 88(1) of the Adoption and Children Act 2002
A63	Application for an order to annul a Convention adoption or Convention adoption order or for an overseas adoption or determination under section 91 to cease to be valid Section 89 Adoption and Children Act 2002
A50 Notes	Application for a placement order Section 22 Adoption and Children Act 2002 – Notes on completing the form
A51 Notes	Application for variation of a placement order Section 23 Adoption and Children Act 2002 – Notes on completing the form
A52 Notes	Application for revocation of a placement order Section 24 Adoption and Children Act 2002 – Notes on completing the form
A53 Notes	Application for a contact order Section 26 Adoption and Children Act 2002 – Notes on completing the form
A54 Notes	Application for variation or revocation of a contact order Section 27(1)(b) Adoption and Children Act 2002 – Notes on completing the form
A55 Notes	Application for permission to change a child's surname Section 28 Adoption and Children Act 2002 – Notes on completing the form
A56 Notes	Application for permission to remove a child from the United Kingdom Section 28 Adoption and Children Act 2002 – Notes on completing the form
A57 Notes	Application for a recovery order Section 41 Adoption and Children Act 2002 – Notes on completing the form
A58 Notes	Application for an adoption order Section 46 Adoption and Children Act 2002 – Notes on completing the form
A59 Notes	Application for a Convention adoption order Section 46 Adoption and Children Act 2002 – Notes on completing the form
A60 Notes	Application for an adoption order (excluding a Convention adoption order) where the child is habitually resident outside the British Islands and is brought into the United Kingdom for the purposes of adoption Section 46 Adoption and Children Act 2002 – Notes on completing the form
A61 Notes	Application for an order for parental responsibility prior to adoption abroad Section 84 Adoption and Children Act 2002 – Notes on completing the form

Number	Name
A62 Notes	Application for a direction under section 88(1) of the Adoption and Children Act 2002 – Notes on completing the form
A63 Notes	Application for an order to annul a Convention adoption or Convention adoption order or for an overseas adoption or determination under section 91 to cease to be valid Section 89 Adoption and Children Act 2002 – Notes on completing the form
A64	Application to receive information from court records Section 60(4) Adoption and Children Act 2002
A64A	Application to receive information from court records about a parental order Section 60(4) Adoption and Children Act 2002
A65	Confidential information
A100	Consent to the placement of my child for adoption with any prospective adopters chosen by the Adoption Agency Section 19 of the Adoption and Children Act 2002
A101	Consent to the placement of my child for adoption with identified prospective adopters Section 19 of the Adoption and Children Act 2002
A101A	Agreement to the making of a parental order in respect of my child Section 54 of the Human Fertilisation and Embryology Act 2008
A102	Consent to the placement of my child for adoption with identified prospective adopter(s) and, if the placement breaks down, with any prospective adopter(s) chosen by the adoption agency Section 19 of the Adoption and Children Act 2002
A103	Advance Consent to Adoption Section 20 of the Adoption and Children Act 2002
A104	Consent to Adoption The Adoption and Children Act 2002
A105	Consent to the making of an Order under Section 84 of the Adoption and Children Act 2002
A106	Withdrawal of Consent Sections 19 and 20 of the Adoption and Children Act 2002
A107	Consent by the child's parent to adoption by their partner The Adoption and Children Act 2002
C1	Application for an Order
C1A	Allegations of harm and domestic violence (Supplemental information form)
C2	Application • For permission to start proceedings • For an order or directions in existing proceedings • To be joined as, or cease to be, a party in existing family proceedings under the Children Act 1989
C3	Application for an order authorising search for, taking charge of and delivery of child
C4	Application for an order for disclosure of a child's whereabouts
C5	Local Authority application concerning the registration of a childminder or a provider of day care
C8	Confidential contact details
C9	Statement of service
C11	Supplement for an application for an Emergency Protection Order
C12	Supplement for an application for a warrant to assist a person authorised by an Emergency Protection Order
C13	Supplement for an application for a Care or Supervision Order

The Family Procedure Rules 2010

Number	Name
C13A	Supplement for an application for a Special Guardianship Order Section 14A Children Act 1989
C14	Supplement for an application for authority to refuse contact with a child in care
C15	Supplement for an application for contact with a child in care
C16	Supplement for an application for a Child Assessment Order
C17	Supplement for an application for Education Supervision Order
C17A	Supplement for an application for an extension of an Education Supervision Order
C18	Supplement for an application for a Recovery Order
C19	Application for a warrant of assistance
C20	Supplement for an application for an order to hold a child in Secure Accommodation
C51	Application for a Parental Order Section 54 Human Fertilisation and Embryology Act 2008
C52	Acknowledgement of an application for a Parental Order
C60	Certificate referred to in Article 39 of Council Regulation (EC) No. 2201/2003 of 27 November 2003 concerning judgments on parental responsibility
C61	Certificate referred to in Article 41(1) of Council Regulation (EC) No. 2201/2003 of 27 November 2003 concerning judgments on rights of access
C62	Certificate referred to in Article 42(1) of Council Regulation (EC) No. 2201/2003 of 27 November 2003 concerning the return of the child
C63	Application for declaration of parentage under section 55A of the Family Law Act 1986
C64	Application for declaration of legitimacy or legitimation under section 56 (1) (b) and (2) of the Family Law Act 1986
C65	Application for declaration as to adoption effected overseas under section 57 of the Family Law Act 1986
C66	Application for inherent jurisdiction order in relation to children
C67	Application under the Child Abduction and Custody Act 1985 or Article 11 of Council Regulation (EC) 2201/2003
C68	Application for international transfer of jurisdiction to or from England and Wales
C69	Application for registration, recognition or non recognition of a judgment under Council Regulation (EC) 2201/2003
C78	Application for attachment of a warning notice to a contact order
C79	Application related to enforcement of a contact order
C100	Application under the Children Act 1989 for a residence, contact, prohibited steps, specific issue section 8 order or to vary or discharge a section 8 order
C110	Application under the Children Act 1989 for a care or supervision order
C(PRA1)	Parental Responsibility Agreement
C(PRA2)	Step Parent Parental Responsibility Agreement
C(PRA3)	Parental Responsibility Agreement Section 4ZA Children Act 1989 (Acquisition of parental responsibility by second female parent)
D5	Notice to be indorsed on documents served in accordance with rule 6.14

FPR 2010, Practice Direction 5A

Number	Name
D6	Statement of Reconciliation
D8	Divorce/dissolution/(judicial) separation petition
D8 Notes	Supporting notes for guidance on completing a divorce/dissolution/(judicial) separation petition
D8A	Statement of arrangements for children
D8B	Answer to a divorce/dissolution/(judicial) separation or nullity petition
D8D	Petition for a presumption of death decree/order and the dissolution of a marriage/civil partnership
D8D Notes	Supporting notes for guidance on completing a petition for a presumption of death decree/order and the dissolution of a marriage/civil partnership
D8N	Nullity petition
D8N Notes	Supporting notes for guidance on completing a nullity petition
D11	Application Notice
D13B	Affidavit in support of a request to dispense with service of the divorce/dissolution/nullity (judicial) separation petition on the Respondent
D20	Medical Examination: statement of parties & inspector
D36	Notice of Application for Decree Nisi to be made Absolute or Conditional Order to be made final
D50	Notice of application on ground of failure to provide maintenance or for alteration of maintenance agreement during parties' lifetime
D50A	Notice of proceedings and acknowledgement of service - maintenance/property proceedings
D50B	Application under Section 17 of the Married Women's Property Act 1882/Section 67 of the Civil Partnership Act 2004/Application to transfer a tenancy under the Family Law Act 1996 Part IV
D50C	Application on ground of failure to provide maintenance
D50D	Application for alteration of maintenance agreement after the death of one of the parties
D50E	Application for permission to apply for financial relief after overseas divorce/dissolution etc under section 13 of the Matrimonial and Family Proceedings Act 1984/paragraph 4 of Schedule 7 to the Civil Partnership Act 2004
D50F	Application for financial relief after overseas divorce etc under section 12 of the Matrimonial and Family Proceedings Act 1984/paragraph 4 to Schedule 7 to the Civil Partnership Act 2004
D50G	Application to prevent transactions intended to defeat prospective applications for financial relief
D50H	Application for alteration of maintenance agreement during parties lifetime
D50J	Application for an order preventing avoidance under section 32L of the Child Support Act 1991
D50K	Notice of Application for Enforcement by such method of enforcement as the court may consider appropriate
D62	Request for issue of Judgment Summons
D70	Application for Declaration of Marital/Civil Partnership Status
D80A	Affidavit in Support of divorce/(judicial) separation - adultery

The Family Procedure Rules 2010

Number	Name
D80B	Affidavit in Support of divorce/dissolution (judicial) separation - unreasonable behaviour
D80C	Affidavit in Support of divorce/dissolution/(judicial) separation – desertion
D80D	Affidavit in Support of divorce/dissolution/(judicial) separation - 2 years consent
D80E	Affidavit in Support of divorce/dissolution/(judicial) separation - 5 years separation
D80F	Affidavit in Support of annulment -void marriage/civil partnership
D80G	Affidavit in support of annulment – voidable marriage/civil partnership
D81	Statement of information for a Consent Order in relation to a financial remedy
D84	Application for a decree nisi/conditional order or (judicial) separation decree/order
D89	Request for personal service by a court bailiff
D151	Application for registration of maintenance order in a magistrates' court
D180	Concerning judgements in matrimonial matters
D252	Notice of commencement of assessment of bill of costs.
D254	Request for a default costs certificate
D258	Request for a detailed assessment of hearing
D258A	Request for detailed assessment (legal aid only)
D258B	Request for detailed assessment (Costs payable out of a fund other than the Community Legal Service Fund)
D258C	Request for detailed assessment hearing pursuant to an order under Part III of the Solicitors Act 1974
D259	Notice of appeal against a detailed assessment (divorce)
FL401	Application for a non molestation order/an occupation order
FL401A	Application for a Forced Marriage Protection Order
FL403	Application to vary, extend or discharge
FL403A	Application to vary, extend or discharge Forced Marriage Protection Orders
FL407	Applications for warrant of Arrest
FL407A	Application for warrant of arrest for a Forced Marriage Protection Order
FL415	Statement of service
FL430	Application for leave to apply for a Forced Marriage Protection Order
FL431	Application to join / cease as a party to Forced Marriage Protection Proceedings
FM1	Family Mediation Information and Assessment Form FM1
Form A	Notice of [intention to proceed with] an application for a financial order (**NOTE: This form should be used whether the applicant is proceeding with an application in the petition or making a free standing application**)
Form A1	Notice of [intention to proceed with] an application for a financial remedy (other than a financial order) in the county or high court
Form A2	Notice of [intention to proceed with] an application for a financial remedy in the magistrates court

FPR 2010, Practice Direction 5A

Number	Name
Form B	Notice of an application to consider the financial position of the Respondent after the divorce/dissolution
Form E	Financial Statement for a financial order or for financial relief after an over seas divorce or dissolution etc
Form E Notes	Form E (Financial Statement for a financial order or for financial relief after an overseas divorce or dissolution etc) Notes for guidance
Form E1	Financial Statement for a financial remedy (other than a financial order or financial relief after an overseas divorce/dissolution etc) in the county or high court
Form E2	Financial Statement for a financial remedy in the magistrates court
Form F	Notice of allegation in proceedings for financial remedy
Form H	Estimate of costs (financial remedy)
Form H1	Statement of Costs (financial remedy)
Form I	Notice of request for periodical payments order at the same rate as order for interim maintenance pending outcome of proceeding
Form P	Pension inquiry form
Form P1	Pension sharing annex
Form P2	Pension attachment annex
Form PPF	Pension Protection Fund Inquiry Form
Form PPF 1	Pension Protection Fund sharing annex
Form PPF 2	Pension Protection Fund attachment annex
FP1	Application under Part 19 of the Family Procedure Rules 2010
FP1A	Application under Part 19 of the Family Procedure Rules 2010 Notes for applicant on completing the application (Form FP1)
FP1B	Application under Part 19 of the Family Procedure Rules 2010 Notes for respondent
FP2	Application notice Part 18 of the Family Procedure Rules 2010
FP3	Application for injunction (General form)
FP5	Acknowledgment of service Application under Part 19 of the Family Procedure Rules 2010
FP6	Certificate of service
FP8	Notice of change of solicitor
FP9	Certificate of suitability of litigation friend
FP25	Witness Summons
N56	**Form for replying to an attachment of earnings application (statement of means)**
N161	**Appellant's Notice**
N161A	**Guidance Notes on Completing the Appellant's Notice**
N161B	**Important Notes for Respondents**
N162	**Respondent's Notice**
N162A	**Guidance Notes for Completing the Respondent's Notice**
N163	**Skeleton Argument**
N164	**Appellant's Notice**
N260	Statement of costs (summary assessment)
N285	General Affidavit
N323	**Request for Warrant of Execution**

The Family Procedure Rules 2010

Number	Name
N336	**Request and result of search in the attachment of earnings index**
N337	**Request for attachment of earnings order**
N349	Application for a third party debt order
N379	**Application for a charging order on land or property**
N380	**Application for charging order on securities**
PLO1	Application for a care order or supervision order: Supplementary form
PLO2	The local authority's case summary
PLO3	Draft case management order
PLO4	Allocation record and timetable for the child(ren)
PLO5	Directions and allocation on issue of proceedings
PLO6	Directions and allocation at first appointment
PLO8	Standard Directions on Issue
PLO9	Standard Directions at First Appointment
PLP10	Order Menu - Directions Revised Private Law Programme
REMO 1	Notice of Registration
REMO 2	Notice of Refusal of Registration.

The Right Honourable

Sir Nicholas Wall

The President of the Family Division

Signed by authority of the Lord Chancellor:

Parliamentary Under Secretary of State

Ministry of Justice

PART 6

SERVICE

CHAPTER 1

Scope of this part and interpretation

6.1. Part 6 rules about service apply generally

This Part applies to the service of documents, except where—
- (a) another Part, any other enactment or a practice direction makes a different provision; or
- (b) the court directs otherwise.

6.2. Interpretation

In this Part "solicitor" includes any person who, for the purposes of the Legal Services Act 2007, is an authorised person in relation to an activity which constitutes the conduct of litigation (within the meaning of that Act).

CHAPTER 2

SERVICE OF THE APPLICATION FOR A MATRIMONIAL ORDER OR CIVIL PARTNERSHIP ORDER IN THE JURISDICTION

6.3. Interpretation

In this Chapter, unless the context otherwise requires, a reference to an application—
- (a) is a reference to an application for a matrimonial or civil partnership order; and
- (b) includes an application by a respondent as referred to in rule 7.4.

(Part 7 deals with applications in matrimonial or civil partnership proceedings.)

6.4. Methods of service

An application may be served by any of the following methods—
- (a) personal service in accordance with rule 6.7;
- (b) first class post, or other service which provides for delivery on the next business day, in accordance with Practice Direction 6A; or
- (c) where rule 6.11 applies, document exchange.

6.5.— Who is to serve the application

(1) Subject to the provisions of this rule, an application may be served by—
- (a) the applicant; or
- (b) a court officer, if so requested by the applicant.

(2) A court officer will not serve the application if the party to be served is a child or protected party.

(3) An application must not be served personally by the applicant himself or herself.

(Rule 6.14 deals with service of the application on children and protected parties.)

6.6. Every respondent to be served

The application must be served on every respondent.

6.7. Personal service

An application is served personally on a respondent by leaving it with that respondent.

6.8.— Service of application by the court

(1) Where the application is to be served by a court officer, the applicant must give the court officer an address at which the respondent is to be served in accordance with rule 6.4.

(2) Where the court officer has sent a notification of failure of service to the applicant in accordance with rule 6.21, the applicant may request the court officer to serve the document on the respondent at an alternative address.

6.9.— Service by the bailiff

(1) An applicant may request that an application be served by a bailiff delivering a copy of the application to the respondent personally.

(2) The request must be made in accordance with Practice Direction 6A.

(3) Where the bailiff is unable to serve the application, the applicant may apply to the court for an order under rule 6.19 (service by an alternative method or at an alternative place).

(Practice Direction 6A contains provision about when a request under this rule is appropriate.)

(Rule 6.22 provides for notice of non-service by a bailiff.)

6.10.— Where to serve the application – general provisions

(1) The application must be served within the jurisdiction except as provided for by Chapter 4 of this Part (service out of the jurisdiction).

(2) The applicant must include in the application an address at which the respondent may be served.

The Family Procedure Rules 2010

(3) Paragraph (2) does not apply where an order made by the court under rule 6.19 (service by an alternative method or at an alternative place) specifies the place or method of service of the application.

6.11.— Service of the application on a solicitor within the jurisdiction or in any EEA state

(1) Where a solicitor acting for the respondent has notified the applicant in writing that the solicitor is instructed by the respondent to accept service of the application on behalf of the respondent at a business address within the jurisdiction, the application must be served at the business address of that solicitor.

(2) Subject to the provisions of Chapter 4 of this Part, where a solicitor acting for the respondent has notified the applicant in writing that the solicitor is instructed by the respondent to accept service of the application on behalf of the respondent at a business address within any EEA state, the application must be served at the business address of that solicitor.

("Solicitor" has the extended meaning set out in rule 6.2 and "EEA state" is defined in Schedule 1 to the Interpretation Act 1978.)

6.12. Service of the application where the respondent gives an address at which the respondent may be served

Subject to rule 6.13, the respondent may be served with the application at an address within the jurisdiction which the respondent has given for the purpose of being served with the proceedings.

6.13.— Service of the application where the respondent does not give an address at which the respondent may be served

(1) This rule applies where—
   (a) rule 6.11 (service of application on solicitor); and
   (b) rule 6.12 (respondent gives address at which respondent may be served),

do not apply and the applicant does not wish the application to be served personally under rule 6.7.

(2) Subject to paragraphs (3) to (5) the application must be served on the respondent at his usual or last known address.

(3) Where the applicant has reason to believe that the respondent no longer resides at his usual or last known address, the applicant must take reasonable steps to ascertain the current address of the respondent.

(4) Where, having taken the reasonable steps required by paragraph (3), the applicant—
   (a) ascertains the respondent's current address, the application must be served at that address; or
   (b) is unable to ascertain the respondent's current address, the applicant must consider whether there is—
       (i) an alternative place where; or
       (ii) an alternative method by which,
       service may be effected.

(5) If, under paragraph (4)(b), there is such a place where or a method by which service could be effected, the applicant must make an application under rule 6.19.

6.14.— Service of the application on children and protected parties

(1) Where the respondent is a child, the application form must be served on—
   (a) one of the child's parents or guardians; or
   (b) if there is no parent or guardian, an adult with whom the child resides or in whose care the child is.

(2) Where the respondent is a protected party, the application must be served on—
   (a) one of the following persons with authority in relation to the protected party—
       (i) the attorney under a registered enduring power of attorney;
       (ii) the donee of a lasting power of attorney; or

(iii) the deputy appointed by the Court of Protection; or
(b) if there is no such person, an adult with whom the protected party resides or in whose care the protected party is.

(3) Any reference in this Chapter to a respondent or party to be served includes the person to be served with the application form on behalf of a child or protected party under paragraph (1) or (2).

(4) The court may make an order permitting an application form to be served on a child or protected party, or on a person other than the person specified in paragraph (1) or (2).

(5) An application for an order under paragraph (4) may be made without notice.

(6) The court may order that, although an application form has been sent or given to someone other than the person specified in paragraph (1) or (2), it is to be treated as if it had been properly served.

(7) Where a document is served in accordance with this rule—
(a) it must be endorsed with the notice set out in Practice Direction 6A; and
(b) the person commencing the proceedings must file a witness statement by the person on whom the application form was served stating whether—
(i) the contents of the application form; or
(ii) the purpose and intention of the application,
were communicated to the child or protected party and, if not, why not.

(8) Paragraph (7)(b) does not apply where the Official Solicitor is, as the case may be—
(a) the litigation friend of the protected party; or
(b) the litigation friend or children's guardian of the child.

6.15.— Deemed service – receipt of acknowledgment of service

(1) Subject to paragraph (2), an application is deemed to be served if the acknowledgment of service, signed by the party served or the solicitor acting on that party's behalf, is returned to the court office.

(2) Where the signature on the acknowledgment of service purports to be that of the other party to the marriage or civil partnership, the applicant must prove that it is the signature of that party by—
(a) giving oral evidence to that effect at the hearing; or
(b) if the application is undefended, confirming it to be so in the affidavit the applicant files under rule 7.19(4).

6.16.— Deemed service by post or alternative service where no acknowledgment of service filed

(1) Subject to paragraph (2), if—
(a) an application has been served on a respondent by post or other service which provides for delivery on the next business day;
(b) no acknowledgment of service has been returned to the court office; and
(c) the court is satisfied that the respondent has received the application,
the district judge may direct that the application is deemed to be served.

(2) Where—
(a) the application alleges 2 years' separation and the respondent consents to a matrimonial or civil partnership order being granted; and
(b) none of the other facts mentioned in section 1(2) of the 1973 Act or section 44(5) of the 2004 Act, as the case may be, is alleged,
paragraph (1) applies only if—
(i) the court is satisfied that the respondent has received notice of the proceedings; and
(ii) the applicant produces a written statement, signed by the respondent, containing the respondent's consent to the grant of an order.

6.17.— Proof of personal service where no acknowledgment of service filed

(1) This rule applies where—
(a) an application has been served on a respondent personally; and

The Family Procedure Rules 2010

(b) no acknowledgment of service has been returned to the court office.

(2) The person serving the application must file a certificate of service stating the date and time of personal service.

(Practice Direction 6A makes provision for a certificate of service by a bailiff.)

(3) If the respondent served was the other party to the marriage or civil partnership, the certificate of service must show the means by which the person serving the application knows the identity of the party served.

6.18.— Proof of service by the court etc.

(1) Where a court officer serves an application by post, or other service which provides for delivery on the next business day, the court officer must note in the court records the date of—

    (a) posting; or

    (b) leaving with, delivering to or collection by the relevant service provider.

(2) A record made in accordance with paragraph (1) is evidence of the facts stated in it.

(3) This rule does not affect the operation of section 133 of the County Courts Act 1984.

(Section 133 of the County Courts Act 1984 provides that where a summons or other process issued from a county court is served by an officer of a court, service may be proved by a certificate in a prescribed form.)

6.19.— Service of the application by an alternative method or at an alternative place

(1) Where it appears to the court that there is a good reason to authorise service by a method or at a place not otherwise permitted by this Part, the court may direct that service is effected by an alternative method or at an alternative place.

(2) On an application under this rule, the court may direct that steps already taken to bring the application form to the attention of the respondent by an alternative method or at an alternative place is good service.

(3) A direction under this rule must specify—

    (a) the method or place of service;

    (b) the date on which the application form is deemed served; and

    (c) the period for filing an acknowledgment of service or answer.

6.20.— Power of the court to dispense with service of the application

(1) The court may dispense with service of the application where it is impracticable to serve the application by any method provided for by this Part.

(2) An application for an order to dispense with service may be made at any time and must be supported by evidence.

(3) The court may require the applicant to attend when it decides the application.

6.21. Notification of failure of service by the court

Where—

    (a) the court serves the application by post or other service which provides for delivery on the next business day; and

    (b) the application is returned to the court,

the court will send notification to the applicant that the application has been returned.

6.22. Notice of non-service by bailiff

Where—

    (a) the bailiff is to serve an application; and

    (b) the bailiff is unable to serve it on the respondent,

the court officer will send notification to the applicant.

CHAPTER 3

Service of documents other than an application for a matrimonial order or civil partnership order in the United Kingdom

6.23. Method of service

A document may be served by any of the following methods—
- (a) personal service, in accordance with rule 6.25;
- (b) first class post, document exchange or other service which provides for delivery on the next business day, in accordance with Practice Direction 6A;
- (c) leaving it at a place specified in rule 6.26; or
- (d) fax or other means of electronic communication in accordance with Practice Direction 6A.

(Rule 6.35 provides for the court to permit service by an alternative method or at an alternative place.)

6.24.— Who is to serve

(1) A party to proceedings will serve a document which that party has prepared, or which the court has prepared or issued on behalf of that party, except where—
- (a) a rule or practice direction provides that the court will serve the document; or
- (b) the court directs otherwise.

(2) Where a court officer is to serve a document, it is for the court to decide which method of service is to be used.

(3) Where the court officer is to serve a document prepared by a party, that party must provide a copy for the court and for each party to be served.

6.25.— Personal service

(1) Where required by another Part, any other enactment, a practice direction or a court order, a document must be served personally.

(2) In other cases, a document may be served personally except where the party to be served has given an address for service under rule 6.26(2)(a).

(3) A document is served personally on an individual by leaving it with that individual.

6.26.— Address for service

(1) A party to proceedings must give an address at which that party may be served with documents relating to those proceedings.

(2) Subject to paragraph (4), a party's address for service must be—
- (a) the business address either within the United Kingdom or any other EEA state of a solicitor acting for the party to be served; or
- (b) where there is no solicitor acting for the party to be served, an address within the United Kingdom at which the party resides or carries on business.

("EEA state" is defined in Schedule 1 to the Interpretation Act 1978.)

(3) Where there is no solicitor acting for the party to be served and the party does not have an address within the United Kingdom at which that party resides or carries on business, the party must, subject to paragraph (4), give an address for service within the United Kingdom.

(4) A party who—
- (a) has been served with an application for a matrimonial or civil partnership order outside the United Kingdom; and
- (b) apart from acknowledging service of the application, does not take part in the proceedings,

need not give an address for service within the United Kingdom.

(5) Any document to be served in proceedings must be sent, or transmitted to, or left at, the party's address for service unless it is to be served personally or the court orders otherwise.

(6) Where, in accordance with Practice Direction 6A, a party indicates or is deemed to have indicated that they will accept service by fax, the fax number given by that party must be at the address for service.

(7) Where a party indicates in accordance with Practice Direction 6A, that they will accept service by electronic means other than fax, the e-mail address or electronic identification given by that party will be deemed to be at the address for service.

(8) This rule does not apply where an order made by the court under rule 6.35 (service by an alternative method or at an alternative place) specifies where a document may be served.

6.27. Change of address for service
Where the address for service of a party changes, that party must give notice in writing of the change, as soon as it has taken place, to the court and every other party.

6.28.— Service of an application form commencing proceedings on children and protected parties
(1) This rule applies to the service of an application form commencing proceedings other than an application for a matrimonial or civil partnership order.

(2) An application form commencing proceedings which would otherwise be served on a child or protected party must be served—
    (a) where the respondent is a child, in accordance with rule 6.14(1); and
    (b) where the respondent is a protected party, in accordance with rule 6.14(2).

6.29.— Service of other documents on or by children and protected parties where a litigation friend has been or will be appointed
(1) This rule applies to—
    (a) a protected party; or
    (b) a child to whom the provisions of rule 16.5 and Chapter 5 of Part 16 apply (litigation friends).

(2) An application for an order appointing a litigation friend where a protected party or child has no litigation friend must be served in accordance with rule 15.8 or rule 16.13 as the case may be.

(3) Any other document which would otherwise be served on or by a child or protected party must be served on or by the litigation friend conducting the proceedings on behalf of the child or protected party.

6.30.— Service on or by children where a children's guardian has been or will be appointed under rule 16.4
(1) This rule applies to a child to whom the provisions of rule 16.4 and Chapter 7 apply.

(2) An application for an order appointing a children's guardian where a child has no children's guardian must be served in accordance with rule 16.26.

(3) Any other document which would otherwise be served on or by a child must be served on or by the children's guardian conducting the proceedings on behalf of the child.

6.31.— Service on or by children where a children's guardian has been appointed under rule 16.3
(1) This rule applies where a children's guardian has been appointed for a child in accordance with rule 16.3.

(2) Any document which would otherwise be served on the child must be served on—
    (a) the solicitor appointed by the court in accordance with section 41(3) of the 1989 Act; and
    (b) the children's guardian.

(3) Any document which would otherwise be served by the child must be served by—
    (a) the solicitor appointed by the court in accordance with section 41(3) of the 1989 Act or by the children's guardian; or
    (b) if no solicitor has been appointed as mentioned in paragraph (a), the children's guardian.

6.32.— Supplementary provisions relating to service on children and protected parties

(1) The court may direct that a document be served on a protected party or child or on some person other than a person upon whom it would be served under rules 6.28 to 6.31 above.

(2) The court may direct that, although a document has been sent or given to someone other than a person upon whom it should be served under rules 6.28 to 6.31 above, the document is to be treated as if it had been properly served.

(3) This rule and rules 6.28 to 6.31 do not apply where the court has made an order under rule 16.6 allowing a child to conduct proceedings without a children's guardian or litigation friend.

6.33.— Supplementary provision relating to service on children

(1) This rule applies to proceedings to which Part 12 applies.

(2) Where a rule requires—
- (a) a document to be served on a party;
- (b) a party to be notified of any matter; or
- (c) a party to be supplied with a copy of a document,

in addition to the persons to be served in accordance with rules 6.28 to 6.32, the persons or bodies mentioned in paragraph (3) must be served, notified or supplied with a copy of a document, as applicable, unless the court directs otherwise.

(3) The persons or bodies referred to in paragraph (2) are—
- (a) such of the following who are appointed in the proceedings—
    - (i) the children's guardian (if the children's guardian is not otherwise to be served);
    - (ii) the welfare officer;
    - (iii) the children and family reporter;
    - (iv) the officer of the Service, Welsh family proceedings officer or local authority officer acting under a duty referred to in rule 16.38; and
- (b) a local authority preparing a report under section 14A(8) or (9) of the 1989 Act.

6.34. Deemed service

A document, other than an application for a matrimonial or civil partnership order, served in accordance with these rules or a practice direction is deemed to be served on the day shown in the following table—

Method of service	*Deemed day of service*
First class post (or other service which provides for delivery on the next business day)	The second day after it was posted, left with, delivered to or collected by the relevant service provider, provided that day is a business day; or, if not, the next business day after that day.
Document exchange	The second day after it was left with, delivered to or collected by the relevant service provider, provided that day is a business day; or, if not, the next business day after that day.
Delivering the document to or leaving it at a permitted address.	If it is delivered to or left at the permitted address on a business day before 4.30p.m., on that day; or in any other case, on the next business day after that day.
Fax.	If the transmission of the fax is completed on a business day before 4.30p.m., on that day; or, in any other case, the next business day after the day on which it was transmitted.

The Family Procedure Rules 2010

Method of service	Deemed day of service
Other electronic method.	If the e-mail or other electronic transmission is sent on a business day before 4.30p.m., on that day; or in any other case, on the next business day after the day on which it was sent.
Personal service	If the document is served personally before 4.30p.m. on a business day, on that day; or, in any other case, on the next business day after that day.

(Practice Direction 6A contains examples of how the date of deemed service is calculated.)

6.35. Service by an alternative method or at an alternative place
Rule 6.19 applies to any document in proceedings as it applies to an application for a matrimonial or civil partnership order and reference to the respondent in that rule is modified accordingly.

6.36. Power to dispense with service
The court may dispense with the service of any document which is to be served in proceedings.

6.37.— Certificate of service
(1) Where a rule, practice direction or court order requires a certificate of service, the certificate must state the details set out in the following table—

Method of service	Details to be certified
Personal service.	Date and time of personal service and method of identifying the person served.
First class post, document exchange or other service which provides for delivery on the next business day.	Date of posting, leaving with, delivering to or collection by the relevant service provider.
Delivery of document to or leaving it at a permitted place.	Date and time when the document was delivered to or left at the permitted place.
Fax.	Date and time of completion of transmission.
Other electronic method	Date and time of sending the email or other electronic transmission.
Alternative method or place permitted by court	As required by the court.

(2) An applicant who is required to file a certificate of service of an application form must do so at or before the earlier of—
    (a)   the first directions appointment in; or
    (b)   the hearing of,
the proceedings unless a rule or practice direction provides otherwise.
(Rule 17.2 requires a certificate of service to contain a statement of truth.)

6.38. Notification of outcome of service by the court
Where—
    (a)   a document to be served by a court officer is served by post or other service which provides for delivery on the next working day; and
    (b)   the document is returned to the court,
the court officer will send notification to the party who requested service that the document has been returned.

6.39. Notification of non-service by bailiff
Where—
    (a)   the bailiff is to serve a document; and
    (b)   the bailiff is unable to serve it,
the court officer must send notification to the party who requested service.

CHAPTER 4

SERVICE OUT OF THE JURISDICTION

6.40.— Scope and interpretation
    (1)   This Chapter contains rules about—
        (a)   service of application forms and other documents out of the jurisdiction; and
        (b)   the procedure for service.
("Jurisdiction" is defined in rule 2.3.)
    (2)   In this Chapter—
"application form" includes an application notice;
"Commonwealth State" means a State listed in Schedule 3 to the British Nationality Act 1981; and
"the Hague Convention" means the Convention on the service abroad of judicial and extrajudicial documents in civil or commercial matters signed at the Hague on November 15, 1965.

6.41. Permission to serve not required
Any document to be served for the purposes of these rules may be served out of the jurisdiction without the permission of the court.

6.42.— Period for acknowledging service or responding to application where application is served out of the jurisdiction
    (1)   This rule applies where, under these rules, a party is required to file—
        (a)   an acknowledgment of service; or
        (b)   an answer to an application,
and sets out the time period for doing so where the application is served out of the jurisdiction.
    (2)   Where the applicant serves an application on a respondent in—
        (a)   Scotland or Northern Ireland; or
        (b)   a Member State or Hague Convention country within Europe,
the period for filing an acknowledgment of service or an answer to an application is 21 days after service of the application.
    (3)   Where the applicant serves an application on a respondent in a Hague Convention country outside Europe, the period for filing an acknowledgment of service or an answer to an application is 31 days after service of the application.
    (4)   Where the applicant serves an application on a respondent in a country not referred to in paragraphs (2) and (3), the period for filing an acknowledgment of service or an answer to an application is set out in Practice Direction 6B.

6.43.— Method of service – general provisions
    (1)   This rule contains general provisions about the method of service of an application for a matrimonial or civil partnership order, or other document, on a party out of the jurisdiction.
Where service is to be effected on a party in Scotland or Northern Ireland
    (2)   Where a party serves an application form or other document on a party in Scotland or Northern Ireland, it must be served by a method permitted by Chapter 2 (and references to "jurisdiction" in that Chapter are modified accordingly) or Chapter 3 of this Part and rule 6.26(5) applies.
Where service is to be effected on a respondent out of the United Kingdom

The Family Procedure Rules 2010

(3) Where the applicant wishes to serve an application form, or other document, on a respondent out of the United Kingdom, it may be served by any method—
- (a) provided for by—
    - (i) rule 6.44 (service in accordance with the Service Regulation);
    - (ii) rule 6.45 (service through foreign governments, judicial authorities and British Consular authorities); or
- (b) permitted by the law of the country in which it is to be served.

(4) Nothing in paragraph (3) or in any court order authorises or requires any person to do anything which is contrary to the law of the country where the application form, or other document, is to be served.

6.44.— Service in accordance with the Service Regulation

(1) This rule applies where the applicant wishes to serve the application form, or other document, in accordance with the Service Regulation.

(2) The applicant must file—
- (a) the application form or other document;
- (b) any translation; and
- (c) any other documents required by the Service Regulation.

(3) When the applicant files the documents referred to in paragraph (2), the court officer will—
- (a) seal$^{(GL)}$, or otherwise authenticate with the stamp of the court, the copy of the application form; and
- (b) forward the documents to the Senior Master of the Queen's Bench Division.

(The Service Regulation is annexed to Practice Direction 6B.)
(Article 20(1) of the Service Regulation provides that the Regulation prevails over other provisions contained in any other agreement or arrangement concluded by Member States.)

6.45.— Service through foreign governments, judicial authorities and British Consular authorities

(1) Where the applicant wishes to serve an application form, or other document, on a respondent in any country which is a party to the Hague Convention, it may be served—
- (a) through the authority designated under the Hague Convention in respect of that country; or
- (b) if the law of that country permits—
    - (i) through the judicial authorities of that country; or
    - (ii) through a British Consular authority in that country.

(2) Where the applicant wishes to serve an application form, or other document, on a respondent in any country which is not a party to the Hague Convention, it may be served, if the law of that country so permits—
- (a) through the government of that country, where that government is willing to serve it; or
- (b) through a British Consular authority in that country.

(3) Where the applicant wishes to serve an application form, or other document, in—
- (a) any Commonwealth State which is not a party to the Hague Convention;
- (b) the Isle of Man or the Channel Islands; or
- (c) any British Overseas Territory,

the methods of service permitted by paragraphs (1)(b) and (2) are not available and the applicant or the applicant's agent must effect service on a respondent in accordance with rule 6.43 unless Practice Direction 6B provides otherwise.

(4) This rule does not apply where service is to be effected in accordance with the Service Regulation.
(A list of British overseas territories is reproduced in Practice Direction 6B.)

6.46.— Procedure where service is to be through foreign governments, judicial authorities and British Consular authorities

(1) This rule applies where the applicant wishes to serve an application form, or other document, under rule 6.45(1) or (2).

(2) Where this rule applies, the applicant must file—
 (a) a request for service of the application form, or other document, by specifying one or more of the methods in rule 6.45(1) or (2);
 (b) a copy of the application form or other document;
 (c) any other documents or copies of documents required by Practice Direction 6B; and
 (d) any translation required under rule 6.47.
(3) When the applicant files the documents specified in paragraph (2), the court officer will—
 (a) seal$^{(GL)}$, or otherwise authenticate with the stamp of the court, the copy of the application form or other document; and
 (b) forward the documents to the Senior Master of the Queen's Bench Division.
(4) The Senior Master will send documents forwarded under this rule—
 (a) where the application form, or other document, is being served through the authority designated under the Hague Convention, to that authority; or
 (b) in any other case, to the Foreign and Commonwealth Office with a request that it arranges for the application form or other document to be served.
(5) An official certificate which—
 (a) states that the method requested under paragraph (2)(a) has been performed and the date of such performance;
 (b) states, where more than one method is requested under paragraph (2)(a), which method was used; and
 (c) is made by—
  (i) a British Consular authority in the country where the method requested under paragraph (2)(a) was performed;
  (ii) the government or judicial authorities in that country; or
  (iii) the authority designated in respect of that country under the Hague Convention,
is evidence of the facts stated in the certificate.
(6) A document purporting to be an official certificate under paragraph (5) is to be treated as such a certificate, unless it is proved not to be.

6.47.— Translation of application form or other document
(1) Except where paragraphs (4) and (5) apply, every copy of the application form, or other document, filed under rule 6.45 (service through foreign governments, judicial authorities and British Consular authorities) must be accompanied by a translation of the application form or other document.
(2) The translation must be—
 (a) in the official language of the country in which it is to be served; or
 (b) if there is more than one official language of that country, in any official language which is appropriate to the place in the country where the application form or other document is to be served.
(3) Every translation filed under this rule must be accompanied by a statement by the person making it that it is a correct translation, and the statement must include that person's name, address and qualifications for making the translation.
(4) The applicant is not required to file a translation of the application form, or other document, filed under rule 6.45 where it is to be served in a country of which English is an official language.
(5) The applicant is not required to file a translation of the application form or other document filed under rule 6.45 where—
 (a) the person on whom the document is to be served is able to read and understand English; and
 (b) service of the document is to be effected directly on that person.
(This rule does not apply to service in accordance with the Service Regulation which contains its own provisions about the translation of documents.)

The Family Procedure Rules 2010

6.48. Undertaking to be responsible for expenses of the Foreign and Commonwealth Office

Every request for service filed under rule 6.46 (procedure where service is to be through foreign governments, judicial authorities etc.) must contain an undertaking by the person making the request—

(a) to be responsible for all expenses incurred by the Foreign and Commonwealth Office or foreign judicial authority; and

(b) to pay those expenses to the Foreign and Commonwealth Office or foreign judicial authority on being informed of the amount.

PART 6 COMMENTARY

Part 6 is supplemented by three practice directions: 6A – Service within the Jurisdiction, 6B – Service out of the Jurisdiction, and 6C – Disclosure of Address by Government Departments. (PD6C is in fact a pre-existing practice direction, remaining in force by the *Practice Direction – Practice Directions Relating to Family Proceedings in Force before 6th April 2011 which support the Family Procedure Rules 2010.* It is the Practice Direction (Disclosure of Addresses by Government Departments) (amending Practice Direction of 13 February 1989) of 20 July 1995. (It is noted that this practice direction does not apply to requests from the HMRC and related agencies which are covered by 'Disclosure Orders against the Inland Revenue – Guidance from the President's Office (November 2003)'.)

Part 6 contains the principal rules relating to the service of proceedings and applications. Chapter 2 contains provisions for service of an application for a matrimonial or civil partnership order in the Jurisdiction. The methods and proof of service are largely unchanged.

Chapter 3 contains provisions for other proceedings. These are broadly modeled on CPR Part 6. It should be noted that here there is provision in r 6.23(d) for service by fax or other electronic means in accordance with PD6A. The provisions in PD6A are at paragraph 4 thereof. Rules 6.28 to 6.33 deal with service on children or protected parties.

Chapter 4 contains provision for service out of the jurisdiction. As before permission is not required for service of any document out of the jurisdiction (r 6.41), but there are specific requirements to be observed where service is to be effected under the Service Regulation (Regulation (EC) No 1393/2007) or the 1965 Hague Convention on service abroad and in contrast with the old rules service abroad can now only be effected by service in accordance with the service regulation, service through foreign government, judicial authorities, and British Consular authorities and service permitted by the law of the country in which it is to be served.

PD6A supplements chapters 2 and 3. It contains at paragraph 5.1 and as an annex the provisions that apply for service on members of the Regular Forces and United Sates Air Force.

PD6B supplements chapter 4. It provides further information in relation to service in other EU states (para 2), documents to be filed when serving through foreign governments, judicial authorities and British Consular Authorities (para 3) and service in a Commonwealth State or British Overseas Territory which is not party to the Hague Convention (para 4.1). At para 5 and in the attached table the extended time period for filing an acknowledgment of service or an answer to an application when serving overseas is set out.

FPR 2010, Practice Direction 6A

The forms applicable to Part 6 are: C9 – Statement of Service, D5 – Notice to be indorsed on documents served in accordance with r 6.14 (service on children and protected parties), D89 – Request for personal service by a court bailiff (see r 6.9), FL415 – Statement of Service, FP6 - Certificate of Service (see r 6.37).

PRACTICE DIRECTION 6A – SERVICE WITHIN THE JURISDICTION

This Practice Direction Supplements FPR Part 6, Chapters 2 and 3

Contents of this Practice Direction

General provisions

Scope of this Practice Direction	Paragraph 1
When service may be by document exchange	Paragraph 2
How service is effected by post, an alternative service provider or DX	Paragraph 3
Service by fax or other electronic means	Paragraph 4
Service on members of the Regular Forces and United States Air Force	Paragraph 5
Application for an order for service by an alternative method or at an alternative place	Paragraph 6
Application for an order to dispense with service	Paragraph 7
Deemed service of a document other than an application for a matrimonial or civil partnership order	Paragraph 8
Service of application on children and protected parties	Paragraph 9

Provisions relating to applications for matrimonial and civil partnership orders

Acknowledgment of service	Paragraph 10
Personal service of application by bailiff	Paragraph 11
Proof of personal service by bailiff	Paragraph 12
Service by bailiff in proceedings in the Principal Registry	Paragraph 13
Service of application on children and protected parties	Paragraph 14

GENERAL PROVISIONS

Scope of this Practice Direction

1.1 This Practice Direction supplements the following provisions of Part 6—

(a) Chapter 2 (service of the application for a matrimonial order or civil partnership order in the jurisdiction);

(b) Chapter 3 (service of documents other than an application for a matrimonial order or civil partnership order in the United Kingdom); and

The Family Procedure Rules 2010

(c) rule 6.43(2) in relation to the method of service on a party in Scotland or Northern Ireland.

(Practice Direction B supplementing Part 6 contains provisions relevant to service on a party in Scotland or Northern Ireland, including provisions about the period for responding to an application notice.)

When service may be by document exchange

2.1 Subject to the provisions of rule 6.4 (which provides when an application for a matrimonial or civil partnership order may be served by document exchange) service by document exchange (DX) may take place only where—

(a) the address at which the party is to be served includes a numbered box at a DX; or
(b) the writing paper of the party who is to be served or of the solicitor acting for that party sets out a DX box number; and
(c) the party or the solicitor acting for that party has not indicated in writing that they are unwilling to accept service by DX.

How service is effected by post, an alternative service provider or DX

3.1 Service by post, DX or other service which provides for delivery on the next business day is effected by—

(a) placing the document in a post box;
(b) leaving the document with or delivering the document to the relevant service provider; or
(c) having the document collected by the relevant service provider.

Service by fax or other electronic means

4.1 This paragraph applies to the service of a document other than an application for a matrimonial or civil partnership order and documents in adoption proceedings and parental order proceedings.

4.2 Subject to the provisions of rule 6.26(6) and (7), where a document is to be served by fax or other electronic means—

(a) the party who is to be served or the solicitor acting for that party must previously have indicated in writing to the party serving—
  (i) that the party to be served or the solicitor is willing to accept service by fax or other electronic means; and
  (ii) the fax number, e-mail address or other electronic identification to which it must be sent; and
(b) the following are to be taken as sufficient written indications for the purposes of paragraph 4.2(a)—
  (i) a fax number set out on the writing paper of the solicitor acting for the party to be served;
  (ii) an e-mail address set out on the writing paper of the solicitor acting for the party to be served but only where it is stated that the e-mail address may be used for service; or
  (iii) a fax number, e-mail address or electronic identification set out on a statement of case or an answer to a claim filed with the court.

4.3 Where a party intends to serve a document by electronic means (other than by fax) that party must first ask the party who is to be served whether there are any limitations to the recipient's agreement to accept service by such means (for example, the format in which documents are to be sent and the maximum size of attachments that may be received).

4.4 Where a document is served by electronic means, the party serving the document need not in addition send or deliver a hard copy.

Service on members of the Regular Forces and United States Air Force

5.1 The provisions that apply to service on members of the regular forces (within the meaning of the Armed Forces Act 2006) and members of the United States Air Force are annexed to this practice direction.

Application for an order for service by an alternative method or at an alternative place

6.1 An application in the High Court or a county court for an order under rule 6.19 may be made without notice.

6.2 Where an application for an order under rule 6.19 is made before the document is served, the application must be supported by evidence stating—

(a) the reason why an order is sought;
(b) what alternative method or place is proposed; and
(c) why the applicant believes that the document is likely to reach the person to be served by the method or at the place proposed.

6.3 Where the application for an order is made after the applicant has taken steps to bring the document to the attention of the person to be served by an alternative method or at an alternative place, the application must be supported by evidence stating—

(a) the reason why the order is sought;
(b) what alternative method or alternative place was used;
(c) when the alternative method or place was used; and
(d) why the applicant believes that the document is likely to have reached the person to be served by the alternative method or at the alternative place.

6.4 Examples—

(a) an application to serve by posting or delivering to an address of a person who knows the other party must be supported by evidence that if posted or delivered to that address, the document is likely to be brought to the attention of the other party;
(b) an application to serve by sending a SMS text message or leaving a voicemail message at a particular telephone number saying where the document is must be accompanied by evidence that the person serving the document has taken, or will take, appropriate steps to ensure that the party being served is using that telephone number and is likely to receive the message.

Applications for an order to dispense with service

7.1 An application in the High Court or a county court for an order under rule 6.36 (power to dispense with service) may be made without notice.

Deemed service of a document other than an application for a matrimonial or civil partnership order

8.1 Rule 6.34 contains provisions about deemed service of a document other than an application for a matrimonial or civil partnership order. Examples of how deemed service is calculated are set out below.

Example 1

8.2 Where the document is posted (by first class post) on a Monday (a business day), the day of deemed service is the following Wednesday (a business day).

Example 2

8.3 Where the document is left in a numbered box at the DX on a Friday (a business day), the day of deemed service is the following Monday (a business day).

The Family Procedure Rules 2010

Example 3

8.4 Where the document is sent by fax on a Saturday and the transmission of that fax is completed by 4.30p.m. on that day, the day of deemed service is the following Monday (a business day).

Example 4

8.5 Where the document is served personally before 4.30p.m. on a Sunday, the day of deemed service is the next day (Monday, a business day).

Example 5

8.6 Where the document is delivered to a permitted address after 4.30p.m. on the Thursday (a business day) before Good Friday, the day of deemed service is the following Tuesday (a business day) as the Monday is a bank holiday.

Example 6

8.7 Where the document is posted (by first class post) on a bank holiday Monday, the day of deemed service is the following Wednesday (a business day).

Service of application on children and protected parties

9.1 Rule 16.14(1) and (2) are applied to service of an application form (other than an application for a matrimonial or civil partnership order) commencing proceedings on children and protected parties by rule 6.28. Rule 6.14(7) makes provision as to how an application form must be served where the respondent is a child or protected party. A document served in accordance with rule 6.14(7) must be endorsed with the following notice which is set out in Form D5-

Important Notice

The contents or purport of this document are to be communicated to the Respondent

[or as the case may be], [full name of Respondent]

if s/he is over 16 [add if the person to be served lacks capacity within the meaning of the Mental Capacity Act 2005 to conduct the proceedings] unless you are satisfied [after consultation with the responsible medical officer within the meaning of the Mental Health Act 1983 or, if s/he is not liable to be detained or subject to guardianship under that Act, his/her medical attendant]* that communication will be detrimental to his/her mental condition].

PROVISIONS RELATING TO APPLICATIONS FOR MATRIMONIAL AND CIVIL PARTNERSHIP ORDERS

Acknowledgment of service to be sent to applicant

10.1 Where the court office receives an acknowledgment of service the court officer must send a photographic copy of it to the applicant.

Personal service of application by bailiff

11.1 The court will only consider a request for personal service of the application by a bailiff if the address for service is in England and Wales.

11.2 In normal circumstances, a request should only be made if postal service has been attempted. In this case, if-

(a) a signed acknowledgment of service is not returned to the court within 14 days after posting; and
(b) the applicant reasonably believes the respondent is still living at the stated address,

the applicant may make a request to the court for personal service by a bailiff.

11.3 A request for personal service by a bailiff should be made in writing to the court officer on the prescribed form and accompanied by the relevant fee. The request should also be accompanied by-

(a) evidence that postal service has been attempted and failed; or
(b) if postal service has not been attempted, an explanation as to why postal service is not considered appropriate in the circumstances of the case.

11.4 A request will rarely be granted where the applicant is legally represented and it will be necessary for the representative to show why service by bailiff is required rather than by a process server.

Proof of personal service by bailiff

12.1 Once service of the application has been effected or attempted by the bailiff he must file a certificate of service in the issuing court.

12.2 If the respondent fails to sign and return an acknowledgment of service to the court office and-

(a) the certificate contains a signature of receipt of the application by the respondent; or
(b) the identity of the respondent is to be proved by a photograph supplied by the applicant,

the applicant must prove the signature or photograph in the affidavit filed by the applicant under rule 7.19(4).

Service by bailiff in proceedings in the Principal Registry

13.1 This paragraph applies where proceedings which are pending in the Principal Registry of the Family Division are treated as pending in a divorce county court.

13.2 Where a document is to be served by a bailiff it must be sent for service to the Principal Registry for onward transmission to the court officer of the county court in whose district the document is to be served.

Service of application on children and protected parties

14.1 A document served in accordance with rule 6.14(7) must be endorsed with the notice contained in paragraph 9.1.

ANNEX

Service on Members of the Regular Forces

1. The following information is for litigants and legal representatives who wish to serve legal documents in civil proceedings in the courts of England and Wales on parties to the proceedings who are (or who, at the material time, were) members of the regular forces (as defined in the Armed Forces Act 2006).

2. The proceedings may take place in the county court or the High Court, and the documents to be served may be claim forms, interim application notices and pre-action application notices. Proceedings for divorce or maintenance and proceedings in the Family Courts generally are subject to special rules as to service which are explained in

The Family Procedure Rules 2010

a practice direction issued by the Senior District Judge of the Principal Registry on 26 June 1979.

(now see *Practice Direction 1 Maintenance Orders: Service Personnel: 2 Disclosure of Addresses* [1995] 2 FLR 813.)

3. In this Annex, the person wishing to effect service is referred to as the 'claimant' and the member of the regular forces to be served is referred to as 'the member'; the expression 'overseas' means outside the United Kingdom.

Enquiries as to address

4. As a first step, the claimant's legal representative will need to find out where the member is serving, if this is not already known. For this purpose the claimant's legal representative should write to the appropriate officer of the Ministry of Defence as specified in paragraph 10 below.

5. The letter of enquiry should in every case show that the writer is a legal representative and that the enquiry is made solely with a view to the service of legal documents in civil proceedings.

6. In all cases the letter must give the full name, service number, rank or rate, and Ship, Arm or Trade, Regiment or Corps and Unit or as much of this information as is available. Failure to quote the service number and the rank or rate may result either in failure to identify the member or in considerable delay.

7. The letter must contain an undertaking by the legal representative that, if the address is given, it will be used solely for the purpose of issuing and serving documents in the proceedings and that so far as is possible the legal representative will disclose the address only to the court and not to the claimant or to any other person or body. A legal representative in the service of a public authority or private company must undertake that the address will be used solely for the purpose of issuing and serving documents in the proceedings and that the address will not be disclosed so far as is possible to any other part of the legal representative's employing organisation or to any other person but only to the court. Normally on receipt of the required information and undertaking the appropriate office will give the service address.

8. If the legal representative does not give the undertaking, the only information that will be given is whether the member is at that time serving in England or Wales, Scotland, Northern Ireland or overseas.

9. It should be noted that a member's address which ends with a British Forces Post Office address and reference (BFPO) will nearly always indicate that the member is serving overseas.

10. The letter of enquiry should be addressed as follows –

(a) Royal Navy and Royal Marine Officers, Ratings and Other Ranks
Director Naval Personnel
Fleet Headquarters
MP 3.1
Leach Building
Whale Island
Portsmouth
Hampshire PO2 8BY

Army Officers and other Ranks –
Army Personnel Centre
Disclosures 1
MP 520
Kentigern House
65 Brown Street
Glasgow G2 8EX

FPR 2010, Practice Direction 6A

Royal Air Force Officers and Other Ranks –
Manning 22E
RAF Disclosures
Room 221B
Trenchard Hall
RAF Cranwell
Sleaford
Lincolnshire NG34 8HB

Assistance in serving documents on members

11. Once the claimant's legal representative has ascertained the member's address, the legal representative may use that address as the address for service by post, in cases where this method of service is allowed by the Civil Procedure Rules. There are, however, some situations in which service of the proceedings, whether in the High Court or in the county court, must be effected personally; in these cases an appointment will have to be sought, through the Commanding Officer of the Unit, Establishment or Ship concerned, for the purpose of effecting service. The procedure for obtaining an appointment is described below, and it applies whether personal service is to be effected by the claimant's legal representative or the legal representative's agent or by a court bailiff, or, in the case of proceedings served overseas (with the leave of the court) through the British Consul or the foreign judicial authority.

12. The procedure for obtaining an appointment to effect personal service is by application to the Commanding Officer of the Unit, Establishment or Ship in which the member is serving. The Commanding Officer may grant permission for the document server to enter the Unit, Establishment or Ship but if this is not appropriate the Commanding Officer may offer arrangements for the member to attend at a place in the vicinity of the Unit, Establishment or Ship in order that the member may be served. If suitable arrangements cannot be made the legal representative will have evidence that personal service is impracticable, which may be useful in an application for service by an alternative method or at an alternative place.

General

13. Subject to the procedure outlined in paragraphs 11 and 12, there are no special arrangements to assist in the service of legal documents when a member is outside the United Kingdom. The appropriate office will, however, give an approximate date when the member is likely to return to the United Kingdom.

14. It sometimes happens that a member has left the regular forces by the time an enquiry as to address is made. If the claimant's legal representative confirms that the proceedings result from an occurrence when the member was in the regular forces and the legal representative gives the undertaking referred to in paragraph 7, the last known private address after discharge will normally be provided. In no other case, however, will the Ministry of Defence disclose the private address of a member of the regular forces.

Service on Members of United States Air Force

15. In addition to the information contained in the memorandum of 26 July 1979, and after some doubts having been expressed as to the correct procedure to be followed by persons having civil claims against members of the United States Air Force in England and Wales, the Lord Chancellor's Office (as it was then) issued the following notes for guidance with the approval of the appropriate United States authorities.

16. Instructions have been issued by the United States authorities to the commanding officers of all their units in England and Wales that every facility is to be given for the service of documents in civil proceedings on members of the United States Air Force. The proper course to be followed by a creditor or other person having a claim against a member of the United States Air Force is for that person to communicate with the commanding officer or, where the unit concerned has a legal officer, with the legal

The Family Procedure Rules 2010

officer of the defendant's unit requesting the provision of facilities for the service of documents on the defendant. It is not possible for the United States authorities to act as arbitrators when a civil claim is made against a member of their forces. It is, therefore, essential that the claim should either be admitted by the defendant or judgment should be obtained on it, whether in the High Court or a county court. If a claim has been admitted or judgment has been obtained and the claimant has failed to obtain satisfaction within a reasonable period, the claimant's proper course is then to write to: Office of the Staff Judge Advocate, Headquarters, Third Air Force, R.A.F. Mildenhall, Suffolk, enclosing a copy of the defendant's written admission of the claim or, as the case may be, a copy of the judgment. Steps will then be taken by the Staff Judge Advocate to ensure that the matter is brought to the defendant's attention with a view to prompt satisfaction of the claim.

PRACTICE DIRECTION 6B – SERVICE OUT OF THE JURISDICTION

This Practice Direction Supplements FPR Part 6, Chapter 4

Contents of this Practice Direction

Scope of this Practice Direction	Paragraph 1
Service in other Member States of the European Union	Paragraph 2
Documents to be filed under rule 6.46(2)(c)	Paragraph 3
Service in a Commonwealth State or British Overseas Territory	Paragraph 4
Period for responding to an application form	Paragraph 5
Service of application notices and orders	Paragraph 6
Period for responding to an application notice	Paragraph 7
Further information	Paragraph 8

SCOPE OF THIS PRACTICE DIRECTION

1.1 This Practice Direction supplements Chapter 4 (service out of the jurisdiction) of Part 6.

(Practice Direction 6A contains relevant provisions supplementing rule 6.43(2) in relation to the method of service on a party in Scotland or Northern Ireland.)

SERVICE IN OTHER MEMBER STATES OF THE EUROPEAN UNION

2.1 Where service is to be effected in another Member of State of the European Union, the Service Regulation applies.

2.2 The Service Regulation is Regulation (EC) No. 1393/2007 of the European Parliament and of the Council of 13 November 2007 on the service in the Member States of judicial and extrajudicial documents in civil or commercial matters (service of documents), and repealing Council Regulation (EC) no. 1348/2000, as amended from time to time and as applied by the Agreement made on 19 October 2005 between the European Community and the Kingdom of Denmark on the service of judicial and extrajudicial documents in civil and commercial matters.

2.3 The Service Regulation is annexed to this Practice Direction.

(Article 20(1) of the Service Regulation provides that the Regulation prevails over other provisions contained in bilateral or multilateral agreements or arrangements concluded

FPR 2010, Practice Direction 6B

by the Member of States and in particular Article IV of the protocol to the Brussels Convention of 1968 and the Hague Convention of 15 November 1965)

DOCUMENTS TO BE FILED UNDER RULE 6.46(2)

3.1 A duplicate of –

(a) the application form or other document to be served under rule 6.45(1) or (2);
(b) any documents accompanying the application or other document referred to in paragraph (a); and
(c) any translation required by rule 6.47;

must be provided for each party to be served out of the jurisdiction, together with forms for responding to the application.

3.2 Some countries require legalisation of the document to be served and some require a formal letter of request which must be signed by the Senior Master. Any queries on this should be addressed to the Foreign Process Section (Room E02) at the Royal Courts of Justice.

SERVICE IN A COMMONWEALTH STATE OR BRITISH OVERSEAS TERRITORY

4.1 The judicial authorities of certain Commonwealth States which are not a party to the Hague Convention require service to be in accordance with rule 6.45(1)(b)(i) and not 6.45(3). A list of such countries can be obtained from the Foreign Process Section (Room E02) at the Royal Courts of Justice.

4.2 The list of British overseas territories is contained in Schedule 6 to the British Nationality Act 1981. For ease of reference these are—

(a) Anguilla;
(b) Bermuda;
(c) British Antarctic Territory;
(d) British Indian Ocean Territory;
(e) Cayman Islands;
(f) Falkland Islands;
(g) Gibraltar;
(h) Montserrat;
(i) Pitcairn, Henderson, Ducie and Oeno Islands;
(j) St. Helena, Ascension and Tristan da Cunha;
(k) South Georgia and the South Sandwich Islands;
(l) Sovereign Base Areas of Akrotiri and Dhekelia;
(m) Turks and Caicos Islands;
(n) Virgin Islands.

PERIOD FOR RESPONDING TO AN APPLICATION FORM

5.1 Where rule 6.42 applies, the period within which the respondent must file an acknowledgment of service or an answer to the application is the number of days listed in the Table after service of the application.

5.2 Where an application is served out of the jurisdiction any statement as to the period for responding to the claim contained in any of the forms required by the Family Procedure Rules to accompany the application must specify the period prescribed under rule 6.42.

SERVICE OF APPLICATION NOTICES AND ORDERS

6.1 The provisions of Chapter 4 of Part 6 (special provisions about service out of the jurisdiction) also apply to service out of the jurisdiction of an application notice or order.

6.2 Where an application notice is to be served out of the jurisdiction in accordance

The Family Procedure Rules 2010

with Chapter 4 of Part 6 the court must have regard to the country in which the application notice is to be served in setting the date for the hearing of the application and giving any direction about service of the respondent's evidence.

PERIOD FOR RESPONDING TO AN APPLICATION NOTICE

7.1 Where an application notice or order is served out of the jurisdiction, the period for responding is 7 days less than the number of days listed in the Table.

FURTHER INFORMATION

8.1 Further information concerning service out of the jurisdiction can be obtained from the Foreign Process Section, Room E02, Royal Courts of Justice, Strand, London WC2A 2LL (telephone 020 7947 6691).

Table

Place or country	Number of days
Afghanistan	23
Albania	25
Algeria	22
Andorra	21
Angola	22
Anguilla	31
Antigua and Barbuda	23
Antilles (Netherlands)	31
Argentina	22
Armenia	21
Ascension Island	31
Australia	25
Austria	21
Azerbaijan	22
Azores	23
Bahamas	22
Bahrain	22
Balearic Islands	21
Bangladesh	23
Barbados	23
Belarus	21
Belgium	21
Belize	23
Benin	25
Bermuda	31
Bhutan	28
Bolivia	23
Bosnia and Herzegovina	21
Botswana	23
Brazil	22
British Virgin Islands	31
Brunei	25

FPR 2010, Practice Direction 6B

Place or country	Number of days
Bulgaria	23
Burkina Faso	23
Burma	23
Burundi	22
Cambodia	28
Cameroon	22
Canada	22
Canary Islands	22
Cape Verde	25
Caroline Islands	31
Cayman Islands	31
Central African Republic	25
Chad	25
Chile	22
China	24
China (Hong Kong)	31
China (Macau)	31
China (Taiwan)	23
China (Tibet)	34
Christmas Island	27
Cocos (Keeling) Islands	41
Colombia	22
Comoros	23
Congo (formerly Congo Brazzaville or French Congo)	25
Congo (Democratic Republic)	25
Corsica	21
Costa Rica	23
Croatia	21
Cuba	24
Cyprus	31
Czech Republic	21
Denmark	21
Djibouti	22
Dominica	23
Dominican Republic	23
East Timor	25
Ecuador	22
Egypt	22
El Salvador	25
Equatorial Guinea	23
Eritrea	22
Estonia	21
Ethiopia	22
Falkland Islands and Dependencies	31
Faroe Islands	31

The Family Procedure Rules 2010

Place or country	Number of days
Fiji	23
Finland	24
France	21
French Guyana	31
French Polynesia	31
French West Indies	31
Gabon	25
Gambia	22
Georgia	21
Germany	21
Ghana	22
Gibraltar	31
Greece	21
Greenland	31
Grenada	24
Guatemala	24
Guernsey	21
Guinea	22
Guinea-Bissau	22
Guyana	22
Haiti	23
Holland (Netherlands)	21
Honduras	24
Hungary	22
Iceland	22
India	23
Indonesia	22
Iran	22
Iraq	22
Ireland (Republic of)	21
Ireland (Northern)	21
Isle of Man	21
Israel	22
Italy	21
Ivory Coast	22
Jamaica	22
Japan	23
Jersey	21
Jordan	23
Kazakhstan	21
Kenya	22
Kiribati	23
Korea (North)	28
Korea (South)	24
Kosovo	21

FPR 2010, Practice Direction 6B

Place or country	Number of days
Kuwait	22
Kyrgyzstan	21
Laos	30
Latvia	21
Lebanon	22
Lesotho	23
Liberia	22
Libya	21
Liechtenstein	21
Lithuania	21
Luxembourg	21
Macedonia	21
Madagascar	23
Madeira	31
Malawi	23
Malaysia	24
Maldives	26
Mali	25
Malta	21
Mariana Islands	26
Marshall Islands	32
Mauritania	23
Mauritius	22
Mexico	23
Micronesia	23
Moldova	21
Monaco	21
Mongolia	24
Montenegro	21
Montserrat	31
Morocco	22
Mozambique	23
Namibia	23
Nauru	36
Nepal	23
Netherlands	21
Nevis	24
New Caledonia	31
New Zealand	26
New Zealand Island Territories	50
Nicaragua	24
Niger (Republic of)	25
Nigeria	22
Norfolk Island	31
Norway	21

The Family Procedure Rules 2010

Place or country	Number of days
Oman (Sultanate of)	22
Pakistan	23
Palau	23
Panama	26
Papua New Guinea	26
Paraguay	22
Peru	22
Philippines	23
Pitcairn, Henderson, Ducie and Oeno Islands	31
Poland	21
Portugal	21
Portuguese Timor	31
Puerto Rico	23
Qatar	23
Reunion	31
Romania	22
Russia	21
Rwanda	23
Sabah	23
St. Helena	31
St. Kitts and Nevis	24
St. Lucia	24
St. Pierre and Miquelon	31
St. Vincent and the Grenadines	24
Samoa (U.S.A. Territory) (See also Western Samoa)	30
San Marino	21
Sao Tome and Principe	25
Sarawak	28
Saudi Arabia	24
Scotland	21
Senegal	22
Serbia	21
Seychelles	22
Sierra Leone	22
Singapore	22
Slovakia	21
Slovenia	21
Society Islands (French Polynesia)	31
Solomon Islands	29
Somalia	22
South Africa	22
South Georgia (Falkland Island Dependencies)	31
South Orkneys	21
South Shetlands	21
Spain	21

FPR 2010, Practice Direction 6B

Place or country	Number of days
Spanish Territories of North Africa	31
Sri Lanka	23
Sudan	22
Surinam	22
Swaziland	22
Sweden	21
Switzerland	21
Syria	23
Tajikistan	21
Tanzania	22
Thailand	23
Togo	22
Tonga	30
Trinidad and Tobago	23
Tristan Da Cunha	31
Tunisia	22
Turkey	21
Turkmenistan	21
Turks & Caicos Islands	31
Tuvalu	23
Uganda	22
Ukraine	21
United Arab Emirates	22
United States of America	22
Uruguay	22
Uzbekistan	21
Vanuatu	29
Vatican City State	21
Venezuela	22
Vietnam	28
Virgin Islands - U.S.A	24
Wake Island	25
Western Samoa	34
Yemen (Republic of)	30
Zaire	25
Zambia	23
Zimbabwe	22

ANNEX – SERVICE REGULATION (RULE 6.44)

www.justice.gov.uk/civil/procrules_fin/contents/form_section_images/practice_directions/pd6b_pdf_eps/pd6b_ecreg2007.pdf

The Family Procedure Rules 2010

PRACTICE DIRECTION 6C – PRACTICE DIRECTION (DISCLOSURE OF ADDRESSES BY GOVERNMENT DEPARTMENTS)

[As amended by Practice Direction [1995] 2 FLR 813.]

The arrangements set out in the Registrar's Direction (Disclosure of Addresses) of April 26, 1988, [1988] 2 All ER 573, [1988] 1 WLR 648, whereby the court may request the disclosure of addresses by Government Departments have been further extended. These arrangements will now cover:

(a) tracing the address of a person in proceedings against whom another person is seeking to obtain or enforce an order for financial provision either for himself or herself or for the children of the former marriage; and,
(b) tracing the whereabouts of a child, or the person with whom the child is said to be, in proceedings under the Child Abduction and Custody Act 1985 or in which a [Part I] order is being sought or enforced.

Requests for such information will be made officially by the [District Judge]. The request, in addition to giving the information mentioned below, should certify:

(A) In financial provision applications

either (a) that a financial provision order is in existence, but can-not be enforced because the person against whom the order has been made cannot be traced; or (b) that the applicant has filed or issued a notice, petition or originating summons containing an application for financial provision which cannot be served because the respondent can-not be traced.

[A 'financial provision order' means any of the orders mentioned in s 21 of the Matrimonial Causes Act 1973 except an order under s 27(6) of that Act].

(B) In wardship proceedings

that the child is the subject of wardship proceedings and cannot be traced and is believed to be with the person whose address is sought. The following notes set out the information required by those departments which are likely to be of the greatest assistance to an applicant.

(1) DEPARTMENT OF SOCIAL SECURITY

The department most likely to be able to assist is the Department of Social Security, whose records are the most comprehensive and complete. The possibility of identifying one person amongst so many will depend on the particulars given. An address will not be supplied by the department unless it is satisfied from the particulars given that the record of the person has been reliably identified.

The applicant or his solicitor should therefore be asked to supply as much as possible of the following information about the person sought:

(i)   National Insurance number;
(ii)   surname;
(iii) forenames in full;
(iv)   date of birth (or, if not known, approximate age);
(v)   last known address, with date when living there;
(vi)   any other known address(es) with dates;
(vii) if the person sought is a war pensioner, his war pension and service particulars (if known);

and in applications for financial provision:

FPR 2010, Practice Direction 6C

(C) the exact date of the marriage and the wife's forenames.

Enquiries should be sent by the [District Judge] to:

Contribution Agency

Special Section A, Room 101B

Longbenton

Newcastle-upon-Tyne NE98 1YX

The department will be prepared to search if given full particulars of the person's name and date of birth, but the chances of accurate identification are increased by the provision of more identifying information.

Second requests for records to be searched, provided that a reasonable interval has elapsed, will be met by the Department of Social Security.

Supplementary Benefit/Income Support

Where, in the case of applications for financial provision, the wife is or has been in receipt of supplementary benefit/income support, it would be advisable in the first instance to make enquiries of the manager of the local Social Security office for the area in which she resides in order to avoid possible duplication of enquiries.

(2) OFFICE OF POPULATION CENSUSES AND SURVEYS; NATIONAL HEALTH SERVICE CENTRAL REGISTER

The Office of Population Censuses and Surveys administers the National Health Service Central Register for the Department of Health. The records held in the Central Register include individual's names, with dates of birth and National Health Service number, against a record of the Family Practitioner Committee area where the patient is currently registered with a National Health Service doctor. The Central Register does not hold individual patients' addresses, but can advise courts of the last Family Practitioner Committee area registration. Courts can then apply for information about addresses to the appropriate Family Practitioner Committee for independent action.

When application is made for the disclosure of Family Practitioner Committee area registrations from these records the applicant or his solicitor should supply as much as possible of the following information about the person sought:

(i) National Health Service number;
(ii) surname;
(iii) forenames in full;
(iv) date of birth (or, if not known, approximate age);
(v) last known address;
(vi) mother's maiden name.

Enquiries should be sent by the [District Judge] to:

Office of Population Censuses and Surveys

National Health Service Central Register

Smedley Hydro

Trafalgar Road

Southport

Merseyside PR8 2HH

(3) PASSPORT OFFICE

If all reasonable enquiries including the aforesaid methods have failed to re-veal an address, or if there are strong grounds for believing that the person sought may have

The Family Procedure Rules 2010

made a recent application for a passport, enquiries may be made to the Passport Office. The applicant or his solicitor should provide as much of the following information about the person as possible.

(i) surname;
(ii) forenames in full;
(iii) date of birth (or, if not known, approximate age);
(iv) place of birth;
(v) occupation;
(vi) whether known to have travelled abroad, and, if so, the destination and dates;
(vii) last known address, with date living there;
(viii) any other known address(es), with dates.

The applicant or his solicitor must also undertake in writing that information given in response to the enquiry will be used solely for the purpose for which it was requested, i e to assist in tracing the husband in connection with the making or enforcement of a financial provision order or in tracing a child in connection with [Part I] or wardship proceedings, as the case may be.

Enquiries should be sent to:

The Chief Passport Officer

UK Passport Agency

Home Office

Clive House

Petty France

London

SW1H 9HD

(4) MINISTRY OF DEFENCE

In cases where the person sought is known to be serving or to have recently served in any branch of HM Forces, the solicitor representing the applicant may obtain the address for service of financial provision or [Part I] and wardship proceedings direct from the appropriate Service Department. In the case of Army servicemen the solicitor can obtain a list of regiments and of the various manning and record offices from the Officer in Charge, Central Manning Support Office, Higher Barracks, Exeter, EX4 4ND.

The solicitor's request should be accompanied by a written undertaking that the address will be used for the purpose of service of process in those proceedings and that so far as is possible the solicitor will disclose the address only to the court and not to the applicant or any other person, except in the normal course of the proceedings.

Alternatively if the solicitor wishes to serve process on the person's commanding officer under the provisions contained in s 101 of the Naval Act 1957, s 153 of the Army Act 1955 and s 153 of the Air Force Act 1955 (all of which as amended by s 62 of the Armed Forces Act 1971) he may obtain the officer's address in the same way.

Where the applicant is acting in person the appropriate service department is prepared to disclose the address of the person sought, or that of his commanding officer, to a [District Judge] on receipt of an assurance that the applicant has given an undertaking that the information will be used solely for the purpose of serving process in the proceedings.

In all cases the request should include details of the person's full name, service number,

FPR 2010, Practice Direction 6C

rank or rating, and his ship, arm or trade, corps, regiment or unit or as much of this information as is available. The request should also include details of his date of birth, or, if not known, his age, his date of entry into the service and, if no longer serving, the date of discharge, and any other information, such as his last known address.

Enquiries should be addressed as follows:

(a) Officers of Royal Navy And Women's Royal Naval Service
The Naval Secretary
Room 161
Victory Building
HM Naval Base
Portsmouth
Hants PO1 3LS

Ratings in the Royal Navy WRNS Ratings QARNS Ratings
Captain
Naval Drafting
Centurion Building
Grange Road
Gosport
Hants PO13 9XA

RN Medical and Dental Officers
The Medical Director
General (Naval)
Room 114
Victory Building
HM Naval Base
Portsmouth
Hants PO1 3LS

Officers of Queen Alexandra's Royal Naval Nursing Service
QARNNS
Room 129
Victory Building
HM Naval Base
Portsmouth
Hants PO1 3LS

Naval Chaplains
Director General
Naval Chaplaincy Service
Room 201
Victory Building
HM Naval Base
Portsmouth
Hants PO1 3LS

(b) Royal Marine Officers
The Naval Secretary
Room 161
Victory Building
HM Naval Base
Portsmouth
Hants PO1 3LS

The Family Procedure Rules 2010

Royal Marine Ranks
HQRM (DROM)
West Battery
Whale Island
Portsmouth
Hants PO2 8DX

(c) Army Officers (Including WRAC and QARANC)
Army Officer
Documentation Office
Index Department
Room F7
Government Buildings
Stanmore
Middlesex

Other Ranks, Army
The Manning & Record Office which is appropriate to the Regiment or Corps

(d) Royal Air Force Officers and Other Ranks Women's Royal Air Force Officers and Other Ranks (Including PMRA FNS)
Ministry of Defence
RAF (Personnel Management 2b1(a) (RAF)
Building 248
RAF Innsworth
Gloucester GL3 1 EZ

General Notes

Records held by other departments are less likely to be of use, either because of their limited scope or because individual records cannot readily be identified. If, however, the circumstances suggest that the address may be known to another department, application may be made to it by the [District Judge], all relevant particulars available being given.

When any department is able to supply the address of the person sought to the [District Judge], it will be passed on by him to the applicant's solicitor (or, in proper cases, direct to the applicant if acting in person) on an understanding to use it only for the purpose of the proceedings.

Nothing in this practice direction affects the service in matrimonial causes of petitions which do not contain any application for financial provision, etc. The existing arrangements whereby the Department of Social Security will at the request of the solicitor forward a letter by ordinary post to a party's last known address remain in force in such cases.

The Registrar's Direction (Disclosure of Addresses) of 26 April 1988, is hereby revoked.

Issued with the concurrence of the Lord Chancellor

PART 7

PROCEDURE FOR APPLICATIONS IN MATRIMONIAL AND CIVIL PARTNERSHIP PROCEEDINGS

CHAPTER 1

APPLICATION AND INTERPRETATION

7.1.— Application and interpretation
(1) The rules in this Part apply to matrimonial and civil partnership proceedings.
(2) The rules in this Part do not apply to magistrates' courts.
(3) In this Part—
"defended case" means matrimonial proceedings or civil partnership proceedings in which—
- (a) an answer has been filed opposing the grant of a matrimonial or civil partnership order on the application, and has not been struck out; or
- (b) the respondent has filed an application for a matrimonial or civil partnership order in accordance with rule 7.14 and neither party's application has been disposed of; or
- (c) rule 7.12(11) applies, notice has been given of intention to rebut and that notice has not been withdrawn,

and in which no matrimonial or civil partnership order has been made; and
"undefended case" means matrimonial proceedings or civil partnership proceedings other than a defended case.

(4) In this Part—
- (a) a reference to a conditional order is a reference to a civil partnership order (other than a separation order) which has not been made final; and
- (b) a reference to a final order is a reference to a conditional order which has been made final.

7.2. District Registries
A reference in this Part to a registry for a place at which sittings of the High Court in matrimonial or civil partnership proceedings are authorised is a reference—
- (a) to the district registry for that place;
- (b) where the place has no district registry, such district registry as the Lord Chancellor may designate for the purpose; or
- (c) if the place is not situated within the district of any district registry, the principal registry.

7.3.— Principal Registry
(1) A provision of this Part which refers to—
- (a) proceedings being started or heard in a divorce county court or a civil partnership proceedings county court; or
- (b) the transfer of proceedings to or from such a court,

includes a reference to the principal registry when treated as such a court.
(2) Proceedings to which this Part applies which were started in the principal registry or have been transferred to it as if it were a county court are treated as pending—
- (a) if the proceedings are matrimonial proceedings, in a divorce county court; and
- (b) if the proceedings are civil partnership proceedings, in a civil partnership proceedings county court.

7.4.— References to respondents
(1) Where a respondent makes an application for a matrimonial order or a civil partnership order, unless the context otherwise requires, the rules in this Part shall apply

with necessary modifications as if the reference to a respondent is a reference to the applicant in the other party's application for a matrimonial order or a civil partnership order.

(2) Where a respondent makes an application for a matrimonial order, unless the context otherwise requires, the rules in this Part shall apply with necessary modifications as if the reference to a correspondent is a reference to a party cited in the respondent's application for a matrimonial order.

CHAPTER 2

Rules about starting and responding to proceedings

7.5.— Starting proceedings

(1) Matrimonial proceedings may be started in any divorce county court.

(2) Civil partnership proceedings may be started in any civil partnership proceedings county court.

7.6. Statement of reconciliation

Where the applicant is legally represented, the legal representative must, unless the court directs otherwise, complete and file with the application a statement in the form for this purpose referred to in Practice Direction 5A, certifying whether the legal representative has discussed with the applicant the possibility of a reconciliation and given the applicant the names and addresses of persons qualified to help effect a reconciliation.

7.7.— Limitation on applications in respect of same marriage or civil partnership

(1) Subject to paragraph (2), a person may not make more than one application for a matrimonial or civil partnership order in respect of the same marriage or civil partnership unless—

    (a)   the first application has been dismissed or finally determined; or

    (b)   the court gives permission.

(2) Where a person—

    (a)   has, within one year of the date of the marriage or civil partnership, made an application for, as the case may be, a decree of judicial separation or an order for separation; and

    (b)   then, after that one-year period has passed, wishes to apply for a decree of divorce or a dissolution order on the same facts as those mentioned in the first application,

that person does not need the court's permission to make the application referred to in subparagraph (b).

7.8.— Service of application

(1) After an application for a matrimonial or civil partnership order has been issued by the court, a copy of it must be served on the respondent and on any co-respondent.

(Rule 6.5 provides for who may serve an application for a matrimonial or civil partnership order.)

(2) When the application is served on a respondent it must be accompanied by—

    (a)   a form for acknowledging service;

    (b)   a notice of proceedings; and

    (c)   where applicable, a copy of the statement of arrangements for children.

7.9. Withdrawal of application before service

An application for a matrimonial or civil partnership order may be withdrawn at any time before it has been served by giving notice in writing to the court where the proceedings were started.

7.10.— Who the parties are

(1) The parties to matrimonial proceedings or civil partnership proceedings are—

    (a)   the parties to the marriage or civil partnership concerned; and

(b) any other person who is to be a party in accordance with a provision of the rules in this Part.

(2) Subject to paragraph (3), where an application for a matrimonial order or an answer to such an application alleges that the other party to the marriage has committed adultery with a named person, that named person is to be the co-respondent.

(3) The named person referred to in paragraph (2) is not to be a co-respondent where—
- (a) the court so directs;
- (b) that person has died; or
- (c) unless the court directs otherwise—
  - (i) that person is under 16 years of age; or
  - (ii) the other party to the marriage is alleged in the application or answer to have committed rape on the named person.

(4) Where an application for a matrimonial or civil partnership order or an answer alleges that the other party to the marriage or civil partnership has had an improper association with a named person, the court may direct that the named person is to be a party to the application, unless the named person has died.

(5) An application for directions under paragraph (3)(a) or (c) may be made without notice if the acknowledgment of service indicates that no party intends to defend the case.

7.11.— Nullity: Interim and full gender recognition certificates

(1) Where the application is for—
- (a) nullity of marriage under section 12(g) of, or paragraph 11(1)(e) of Schedule 1 to, the 1973 Act; or
- (b) an order of nullity of civil partnership under section 50(1)(d) of the 2004 Act,

the court officer must send to the Secretary of State a notice in writing that the application has been made.

(2) Where a copy of an interim gender recognition certificate has been filed with the application, that certificate must be attached to the notice.

(3) Where no copy of an interim gender recognition certificate has been filed the notice must also state—
- (a) in matrimonial proceedings—
  - (i) the names of the parties to the marriage and the date and place of the marriage, and
  - (ii) the last address at which the parties to the marriage lived together as husband and wife;
- (b) in civil partnership proceedings—
  - (i) the names of the parties to the civil partnership and the date on, and the place at which, the civil partnership was formed, and
  - (ii) the last address at which the parties to the civil partnership lived together as civil partners of each other; and
- (c) in either case, such further particulars as the court officer considers appropriate.

(4) Where—
- (a) the application is for a decree of nullity of marriage under section 12(h) of the 1973 Act or for an order of nullity of civil partnership under section 50(1)(e) of the 2004 Act; and
- (b) a full gender recognition certificate has been issued to the respondent,

the applicant must file a copy of that full certificate with the application unless the court, on an application made without notice, directs otherwise.

7.12.— What the respondent and co-respondent should do on receiving the application

(1) The respondent, and any co-respondent, must file an acknowledgment of service within 7 days beginning with the date on which the application for a matrimonial or civil partnership order was served.

(2) This rule is subject to rule 6.42 (which specifies how the period for filing an acknowledgment of service is calculated where the application is served out of the jurisdiction).
 (3) The acknowledgment of service must—
  (a) subject to paragraph (4), be signed by the respondent or the respondent's legal representative or, as the case may be, the co respondent or the co respondent's legal representative;
  (b) include the respondent's or, as the case may be, the co respondent's address for service; and
  (c) where it is filed by the respondent, indicate whether or not the respondent intends to defend the case.
 (4) Where paragraph (5) or (6) applies, the respondent must sign the acknowledgment of service personally.
 (5) This paragraph applies where—
  (a) the application for a matrimonial order alleges that the respondent has committed adultery; and
  (b) the respondent admits the adultery.
 (6) This paragraph applies where—
  (a) the application for a matrimonial or civil partnership order alleges that the parties to the marriage or civil partnership concerned have been separated for more than 2 years; and
  (b) the respondent consents to the making of the matrimonial or civil partnership order.
 (7) Where the respondent does not agree with the proposals set out in the applicant's statement of arrangements for children, the respondent may file a statement of arrangements for children under section 41(1) of the 1973 Act or section 63(1) of the 2004 Act.
 (8) A respondent who wishes to defend the case must file and serve an answer within 21 days beginning with the date by which the acknowledgment of service is required to be filed.
 (9) An answer is not required where the respondent does not object to the making of the matrimonial or civil partnership order but objects to paying the costs of the application or to the applicant's statement of arrangements for children.
 (10) A respondent may file an answer even if the intention to do so was not indicated in the acknowledgment of service.
 (11) Where the application is for nullity of marriage under section 12(d) of the 1973 Act or for nullity of civil partnership under section 50(1)(b) of the 2004 Act and the respondent files an answer containing no more than a simple denial of the facts stated in the application, the respondent must, if intending to rebut the matters stated in the application, give notice to the court of that intention when filing the answer.
 (12) A respondent to an application for a matrimonial or civil partnership order alleging 2 years' separation and the respondent's consent may—
  (a) indicate consent to the making of the matrimonial or civil partnership order in writing at any time after service of the application, whether in the acknowledgment of service or otherwise;
  (b) indicate lack of consent to the making of that order, or withdraw any such consent already given, by giving notice to the court.
 (13) Where a respondent gives a notice under paragraph (12)(b) and no other relevant fact is alleged, the proceedings must be stayed$^{(GL)}$, and notice of the stay$^{(GL)}$ given to the parties by the court officer.
 (14) In this rule, a "relevant fact" is—
  (a) in matrimonial proceedings, one of the facts mentioned in section (1)(2) of the 1973 Act; and
  (b) in civil partnership proceedings, one of the facts mentioned in section 44(5) of the 2004 Act.
(The form of the answer is referred to in Practice Direction 5A.)

7.13.— Amendments to the application and the answer
(1) Unless paragraph (2) applies—
- (a) a party making an application for a matrimonial or civil partnership order may amend the application at any time before an answer to it has been filed;
- (b) a party who has filed an answer may amend the answer.

(2) No amendment to an application for a matrimonial or civil partnership order or to an answer may be made under paragraph (1) if an application under rule 7.19(1) has been made in relation to the marriage or civil partnership concerned.

(3) Where an amendment is made under paragraph (1)—
- (a) if the document amended is the application—
  - (i) it must be served in accordance with rule 7.8 (service of application); and
  - (ii) rule 7.12 (what the respondent and co respondent should do) applies;
- (b) rule 7.10 (parties) applies; and
- (c) any person who becomes a co-respondent to the proceedings in accordance with rule 7.10 as a consequence of such an amendment must be served with the documents required to be served on a co-respondent with an application for a matrimonial or civil partnership order.

(4) Paragraphs (1) and (2) do not apply if the amendment is made—
- (a) with the written consent of all the other parties; or
- (b) with the permission of the court.

(5) Where the court gives permission for a party to amend that party's application for a matrimonial or civil partnership order or answer it may give directions as to—
- (a) the service of the amended application or answer and any accompanying documents;
- (b) the joining of any additional parties in accordance with rule 7.10; and
- (c) the extent to which rule 7.12 must be complied with in respect of any amended application.

(6) The court may direct that any person cease to be a party if, in consequence of any amendment made under this rule, that person—
- (a) no longer falls within rule 7.10(2) or (4); or
- (b) falls within rule 7.10(4) but it is no longer desirable for that person to be a party to the proceedings.

7.14.— How the respondent can make an application
(1) A respondent who wishes to make an application for a matrimonial or civil partnership order must make the application for that order within 21 days beginning with the date by which the respondent's acknowledgment of service is required to be filed, unless the court gives permission to make the application after that time has passed.

(2) Where the respondent makes an application under this rule, that application is to be treated as an application in the same proceedings for the purposes of this Part.

7.15.— Further information about the contents of the application and the answer
(1) The court may at any time order a party—
- (a) to clarify any matter which is in dispute in the proceedings; or
- (b) to give additional information in relation to any such matter,

whether or not the matter is contained or referred to in the application for a matrimonial or civil partnership order or in the answer.

(2) Paragraph (1) is subject to any rule of law to the contrary.

(3) Where the court makes an order under paragraph (1), the party against whom it is made must—
- (a) file the reply to the order made under paragraph (1); and
- (b) serve a copy of it on each of the other parties,

within the time specified by the court.

The Family Procedure Rules 2010

(4) The court may direct that information provided by a party to another party (whether given voluntarily or following an order made under paragraph (1)) must not be used for any purpose except for the proceedings in which it is given.

CHAPTER 3

HOW THE COURT DETERMINES MATRIMONIAL AND CIVIL PARTNERSHIP PROCEEDINGS

7.16.— General rule – hearing to be in public
(1) The general rule is that a hearing to which this Part applies is to be in public.
(2) The requirement for a hearing to be in public does not require the court to make special arrangements for accommodating members of the public.
(3) A hearing, or any part of it, may be in private if—
    (a) publicity would defeat the object of the hearing;
    (b) it involves matters relating to national security;
    (c) it involves confidential information (including information relating to personal financial matters) and publicity would damage that confidentiality;
    (d) a private hearing is necessary to protect the interests of any child or protected party;
    (e) it is a hearing of an application made without notice and it would be unjust to any respondent for there to be a public hearing; or
    (f) the court considers this to be necessary, in the interests of justice.
(4) A hearing of an application for rescission of an order by consent under rule 7.28 is, unless the court directs otherwise, to be in private.
(5) The court may order that the identity of any party or witness must not be disclosed if it considers non-disclosure necessary in order to protect the interests of that party or witness.

7.17. Exercise of jurisdiction in cases heard at place other than the court in which the case is proceeding
Where a defended case is to be heard at a place other than the court in which it is proceeding, a judge of that other court may exercise all the powers that would be exercisable by a judge of the court in which the case is proceeding.

7.18. Notice of hearing
The court officer will give notice to the parties—
    (a) of the date, time and place of every hearing which is to take place in a case to which they are a party; and
    (b) in the case of a hearing following a direction under rule 7.20(2)(a), of the fact that, unless the person wishes or the court requires, the person need not attend.

7.19.— Applications for a decree nisi or a conditional order
(1) An application may be made to the court for it to consider the making of a decree nisi, a conditional order, a decree of judicial separation or a separation order in the proceedings—
    (a) at any time after the time for filing the acknowledgment of service has expired, provided that no party has filed an acknowledgment of service indicating an intention to defend the case; and
    (b) in any other case, at any time after the time for filing an answer to every application for a matrimonial or civil partnership order made in the proceedings has expired.
(2) An application under paragraph (1) may be made—
    (a) in a case within paragraph (1)(a), by the applicant; and
    (b) in any other case, by either party to the marriage or civil partnership in question.

(3) An application under this rule must, if the information which was required to be provided by the application form is no longer correct, be accompanied by a statement setting out particulars of the change.

(4) If neither party has filed an answer opposing the making of a decree nisi, a conditional order, a decree of judicial separation or a separation order on the other's application, then an application under this rule must be accompanied by an affidavit—

- (a) stating whether there have been any changes in the information given in the application or in any statement of arrangements for children;
- (b) confirming that, subject to any changes stated, the contents of the application and any statement of arrangements for children are true; and
- (c) where the acknowledgment of service has been signed by the other party, confirming that party's signature on the acknowledgment of service.

7.20.— What the court will do on an application for a decree nisi, a conditional order, a decree of judicial separation or a separation order

(1) This rule applies where an application is made under rule 7.19.

(2) If at the relevant time the case is an undefended case, the court must—
- (a) if satisfied that the applicant is entitled to—
    - (i) in matrimonial proceedings, a decree nisi or a decree of judicial separation (as the case may be); or
    - (ii) in civil partnership proceedings, a conditional order or a separation order (as the case may be),

so certify and direct that the application be listed before a district judge for the making of the decree or order at the next available date;

- (b) if not so satisfied, direct—
    - (i) that any party to the proceedings provide such further information, or take such other steps, as the court may specify; or
    - (ii) that the case be listed for a case management hearing.

(3) If the applicant has applied for costs, the court may, on making a direction under paragraph (2)(a)—
- (a) if satisfied that the applicant is entitled to an order for costs, so certify; or
- (b) if not so satisfied, make no direction about costs.

(4) If at the relevant time the case is a defended case, the court must direct that the case be listed for a case management hearing.

(5) The court may, when giving a direction under paragraph (2)(b), direct that the further information provided be verified by an affidavit.

(6) The court must not give directions under this rule unless at the relevant time it is satisfied—
- (a) that a copy of each application for a matrimonial or civil partnership order or answer (including any amended application or answer) has been properly served on each party on whom it is required to be served; and
- (b) that —
    - (i) in matrimonial proceedings, the application for a decree nisi or a decree of judicial separation; or
    - (ii) in civil partnership proceedings, the application for a conditional order or separation order,

    was made at a time permitted by rule 7.19(1).

(7) In this rule, "the relevant time" means the time at which the court is considering an application made under rule 7.19(1).

7.21.— Further provisions about costs

(1) Subject to paragraph (2), any party to matrimonial or civil partnership proceedings may be heard on any question as to costs at the hearing of the proceedings.

(2) In the case of a hearing following a direction under rule 7.20(2)(a), a party will not be heard unless that party has, not less than 2 days before the hearing, served on every other

party written notice of that party's intention to attend the hearing and apply for, or oppose the making of, an order for costs.

7.22.— What the court must do for the case management hearing

(1) This rule applies to a case in which the court has directed a case management hearing under rule 7.20.

(2) Where a hearing has been directed under rule 7.20(4) the court must—
   (a) decide where the hearing in the case should take place;
   (b) set a timetable for the filing and service of evidence;
   (c) make such order for the disclosure and inspection of documents as it considers appropriate; and
   (d) give directions as to the conduct of the final hearing and the attendance of witnesses.

(Rule 21.1 explains what is meant by disclosure and inspection.)

(3) Where a hearing has been directed under rule 7.20(2)(b)(ii), the court must—
   (a) consider what further evidence is required properly to dispose of the proceedings and give directions about the filing and service of such evidence;
   (b) consider whether any further information is required about the arrangements for the children of the family and give directions about the filing and service of such information;
   (c) give directions for the further conduct of the proceedings, including—
      (i) giving a direction that on compliance with any directions under sub-paragraph (a) or (b) a further application may be made under rule 7.19(1) for the proceedings to be dealt with under rule 7.20(2)(a); or
      (ii) giving a direction that the case is not suitable for determination under that rule.

(4) Where the court gives a direction under paragraph (3)(c)(ii), it may also give directions under paragraph (2) or direct that the case be listed for a further hearing at which such directions will be given.

(5) Any party to proceedings which are not being dealt with under rule 7.20(2)(a) may apply to the court for further directions at any time.

(Part 3 sets out the court's powers to encourage the parties to use alternative dispute resolution and Part 4 sets out the court's general case management powers.)

7.23. Where proceedings under this Part may be heard

A case, other than one dealt with under rule 7.20(2)(a), may be heard, where it is proceeding in the court set out in column 1 of the following table—
   (a) in matrimonial proceedings, at the place referred to in column 2;
   (b) in civil partnership proceedings, at the place referred to in column 3.

	Matrimonial Proceedings	Civil Partnership Proceedings
A county court.	Any divorce county court designated as a court of trial.	Any civil partnership proceedings county court designated as a court of trial.
The principal registry when proceedings are treated as pending in a county court.	The Royal Courts of Justice.	The Royal Courts of Justice.

	Matrimonial Proceedings	*Civil Partnership Proceedings*
The High Court (including the principal registry other than when proceedings are treated as pending in a county court.).	a) The Royal Courts of Justice. b) Any court at which sittings of the High Court in matrimonial proceedings are authorised.	a) The Royal Courts of Justice. b) Any court at which sittings of the High Court in civil partnership proceedings are authorised.

7.24.— The circumstances in which proceedings may be transferred between courts

(1) A court may transfer the hearing of a case which is due to be heard in one court to another court of the same type at which hearings of those proceedings are permitted under rule 7.23.

(2) A court in which matrimonial or civil partnership proceedings are pending may order them, or an application made in the course of them—

- (a) if the proceedings are pending in the High Court, to be transferred from the registry in which they are pending to another district registry;
- (b) if the proceedings are matrimonial proceedings pending in a divorce county court, to be transferred from that county court to another divorce county court; and
- (c) if the proceedings are civil partnership proceedings pending in a civil partnership proceedings county court, to be transferred from that county court to another civil partnership proceedings county court.

(3) An order transferring the hearing of an application must not be made under paragraph (2) unless it would be more convenient than transferring the proceedings themselves.

(4) No transfer may be made under this rule or under section 38 or 39 of the 1984 Act (transfers between High Court and a county court) unless—

- (a) the parties consent to the transfer;
- (b) the court has held a hearing to determine whether a transfer should be ordered; or
- (c) the court has transferred a case without a hearing where neither party has, within 14 days of being notified in writing of the court's intention to make such an order, requested a hearing to determine whether a transfer should be ordered.

(5) Proceedings—

- (a) which are transferred from the High Court to a divorce county court or a civil partnership proceedings county court and are to continue after the transfer in the principal registry are to be treated as pending in a divorce or civil partnership proceedings county court (as the case may be); and
- (b) which are transferred from a divorce county court or a civil partnership proceedings county court to the High Court and are to continue after the transfer in the principal registry are no longer to be treated as pending in a divorce or civil partnership proceedings county court (as the case may be).

(6) Proceedings transferred from a divorce county court or a civil partnership proceedings county court to the High Court are to proceed in the registry nearest to the court from which they were transferred unless—

- (a) the order transferring the proceedings directs otherwise; or
- (b) the court subsequently orders.

7.25.— The procedure for complying with section 41 of 1973 Act or section 63 of 2004 Act

(1) Before the court—

- (a) gives a direction under rule 7.20(2)(a); or
- (b) makes—

The Family Procedure Rules 2010

    (i) in matrimonial proceedings, a decree nisi or decree of judicial separation; or
    (ii) in civil partnership proceedings, a conditional order or a separation order,
it must consider the matters set out in paragraph (2).
  (2) The matters referred to in paragraph (1) are—
   (a) whether there are any children of the family to whom section 41(1) of the 1973 Act or section 63(1) of the 2004 Act (as the case may be) applies; and
   (b) if there are such children, and no application is pending in relation to them under Part 1 or 2 of the 1989 Act, the matters set out in section 41(1)(b) of the 1973 Act or in section 63(1)(b) of the 2004 Act (as the case may be).
  (3) Where the court is satisfied that—
   (a) there are no children of the family to whom—
    (i) in matrimonial proceedings, section 41 of the 1973 Act applies; and
    (ii) in civil partnership proceedings, section 63 of the 2004 Act applies; or
   (b) there are such children but the court need not exercise its powers under the 1989 Act or its power to give a relevant direction with respect to any of them,
it must give a certificate to that effect.
  (4) Where the court does not issue a certificate under paragraph (3) it may direct that—
   (a) the parties, or any of them, must file further evidence relating to the arrangements for the children and may direct what specific matters must be dealt with in that evidence;
   (b) a welfare report on the children, or any of them, be prepared;
   (c) the parties, or any of them, attend a hearing for the court to consider the matter.
  (5) Where the court makes a direction under paragraph (4) or a relevant direction, it must state in writing—
   (a) its reasons for doing so; and
   (b) in the case of a relevant direction, the exceptional circumstances which make it desirable in the interests of the child that the court should make such a direction.
  (6) Nothing in this rule affects the court's power to make an order under the 1989 Act or a relevant direction.
  (7) The court officer must send the parties—
   (a) a copy of any certificate given under paragraph (3);
   (b) a copy of any direction made under paragraph (4);
   (c) a copy of any relevant direction; and
   (d) a copy of any statement under paragraph (5).
  (8) In this rule—
"parties" means a party to the marriage or civil partnership concerned and any person who appears to the court to have the care of any child of the family; and
"relevant direction" means—
   (a) in matrimonial proceedings, a direction under section 41(2) of the 1973 Act;
   (b) in civil partnership proceedings, a direction under section 63(2) of the 2004 Act.

7.26.— Medical examinations in proceedings for nullity of marriage

  (1) Where the application is for a decree of nullity of marriage on the ground of incapacity to consummate or wilful refusal to do so, the court must determine whether medical examiners should be appointed to examine the parties or either of them.
  (2) The court must only appoint medical examiners under paragraph (1) where it considers that it is necessary for the proper disposal of the case.
  (3) The person to be examined must, in the presence of the medical examiner, sign a statement identifying that person as the party to whom the order for examination applies.

(4) The medical examiner must certify on the same statement that it was signed in his or her presence by the person who has been examined.

(5) The person who carries out the examination must prepare a report and file it with the court by the date directed by the court.

(6) Either party is entitled to see a copy of a report filed under paragraph (5).

7.27.— Stay of proceedings

(1) Where—

(a) the court is considering an application in accordance with rule 7.20 or gives directions under rule 7.22;

(b) it appears to the court that there are proceedings continuing in any country outside England and Wales which are in respect of the marriage or civil partnership in question or which are capable of affecting its validity or subsistence; and

(c) the court considers that the question whether the proceedings should be stayed$^{(GL)}$ under paragraph 9 of Schedule 1 to the Domicile and Matrimonial Proceedings Act 1973 or, for civil partnership proceedings, under rules made under sections 75 and 76 of the Courts Act 2003,

the court must give directions for the hearing of that question.

(2) Where at any time after the making of an application under this Part it appears to the court in matrimonial proceedings that, under Articles 16 to 19 of the Council Regulation, the court does not have jurisdiction to hear the application and is or may be required to stay$^{(GL)}$ the proceedings, the court will—

(a) stay$^{(GL)}$ the proceedings; and

(b) fix a date for a hearing to determine the questions of jurisdiction and whether there should be a further stay$^{(GL)}$ or other order.

(3) The court must give reasons for its decision under Articles 16 to 19 of the Council Regulation and, where it makes a finding of fact, state such finding of fact.

(4) An order under Article 17 of the Council Regulation that the court has no jurisdiction over the proceedings will be recorded by the court or the court officer in writing.

(5) The court may, if all parties agree, deal with any question about the jurisdiction of the court without a hearing.

CHAPTER 4

COURT ORDERS

7.28.— The circumstances in which an order may be set aside (rescission)

(1) The court must not hear an application by a respondent for—

(a) the rescission of a decree of divorce under section 10(1) of the 1973 Act;

(b) the rescission of a dissolution order under section 48(1) of the 2004 Act,

less than 14 days after service of the application.

(2) Either party to the marriage concerned may apply—

(a) after the decree nisi has been made but before it has been made absolute; or

(b) after a decree of judicial separation has been made

for the rescission of the decree on the grounds that the parties are reconciled and both consent to the rescission.

(3) Either party to the civil partnership concerned may apply—

(a) after a conditional order has been made but before it has been made final; or

(b) after a separation order has been made,

for the rescission of the order on the grounds that the parties are reconciled and both consent to the rescission.

7.29. Applications under section 10(2) of 1973 Act or section 48(2) of 2004 Act

Where the court makes—

(a) in the case of divorce, a decree absolute following an application under section 10(2) of the 1973 Act; or

The Family Procedure Rules 2010

  (b) in the case of dissolution, a final order following an application under section 48(2) of the 2004 Act,

it must make a written record of the reasons for deciding to make that decree absolute or final order.

7.30.— Orders under section 10A(2) of the 1973 Act

(1) Where the court has made an order under section 10A(2) of the 1973 Act, the declaration referred to in that section must—

  (a) be made and signed by both parties to the marriage concerned;
  (b) give particulars of the proceedings in which the order was obtained;
  (c) confirm that the steps required to dissolve the marriage in accordance with the religious usages appropriate to the parties have been taken;
  (d) be accompanied by—
    (i) a certificate from a relevant religious authority that all such steps have been taken; or
    (ii) such other documents showing the relevant steps have been taken as the court may direct; and
    (iii) be filed at the court either before or together with an application to make the decree nisi absolute,

under rule 7.32 or 7.33.

(2) Where the certificate referred to in paragraph (1)(d)(i) is not in English it must be accompanied by a translation of that certificate into English, certified by a notary public or authenticated by statement of truth.

(3) The court may direct that the declaration need not be accompanied by the material mentioned in paragraph (1)(d).

(4) In this rule a religious authority is "relevant" if the party who made the application for the order under section 10A(2) of the 1973 Act considers that authority competent to confirm that the steps referred to in paragraph (1)(c) have been taken.

7.31.— Applications to prevent decrees nisi being made absolute or conditional orders being made final

(1) This rule applies to an application under section 8 or 9 of the 1973 Act or under section 39 or 40 of the 2004 Act to prevent —

  (a) in the case of divorce or nullity of marriage, a decree nisi being made absolute; or
  (b) in the case of dissolution or nullity of civil partnership, a conditional order being made final.

(2) An application to which this rule applies must be made using the Part 18 procedure, subject to paragraphs (3) to (6) of this rule.

(3) The person making an application to which this rule applies must within 28 days of filing the application apply to the court to give directions for the hearing of the application.

(4) Where the person making an application to which this rule applies does not apply for directions under paragraph (3), then the person in whose favour the decree nisi or conditional order (as the case may be) was made may do so.

(5) Rule 7.22(2) applies to an application to which this rule applies as it applies to an application for a matrimonial or civil partnership order.

(6) Where an application to which this rule applies is made by the Queen's Proctor—

  (a) the Queen's Proctor may give written notice, to the court and to the party in whose favour the decree nisi or conditional order (as the case may be) was made, of the Queen's Proctor's intention to make an application to prevent the decree nisi being made absolute or the conditional order being made final; and
  (b) where the Queen's Proctor does so the application under paragraph (1) must be made within 21 days beginning with the date on which the notice is given.

7.32.— **Making decrees nisi absolute or conditional orders final by giving notice**

(1) Unless rule 7.33 applies—
- (a) in matrimonial proceedings, a spouse in whose favour a decree nisi has been made may give notice to the court that he or she wishes the decree nisi to be made absolute; or
- (b) in civil partnership proceedings, a civil partner in whose favour a conditional order has been made may give notice to the court that he or she wishes the conditional order to be made final.

(2) Subject to paragraphs (3) and (4), where the court receives a notice under paragraph (1) it will make the decree nisi absolute or the conditional order final (as the case may be) if it is satisfied that—
- (a) no application for rescission of the decree nisi or the conditional order is pending;
- (b) no appeal against the making of the decree nisi or the conditional order is pending;
- (c) no order has been made by the court extending the time for bringing an appeal of the kind mentioned in sub-paragraph (b), or if such an order has been made, that the time so extended has expired;
- (d) no application for an order of the kind mentioned in sub-paragraph (c) is pending;
- (e) no application to prevent the decree nisi being made absolute or the conditional order being made final is pending;
- (f) the court has complied with section 41(1) of the 1973 Act or section 63(1) of the 2004 Act, as the case may be, and has not given any direction under subsection (2) of either of those sections;
- (g) the provisions of section 10(2) to (4) of the 1973 Act or section 48(2) to (4) of the 2004 Act do not apply or have been complied with;
- (h) any order under section 10A(2) of the 1973 Act has been complied with; and
- (i) where the decree nisi was made on the ground in section 12(g) of, or paragraph 11(1)(e) of Schedule 1 to, the 1973 Act, or the conditional order was made under section 50(1)(d) of the 2004 Act—
  - (i) there is not pending a reference under section 8(5) of the Gender Recognition Act 2004 in respect of the application on which the interim gender recognition certificate to which the application relates was granted;
  - (ii) that interim certificate has not been revoked under section 8(6)(b) of that Act; and
  - (iii) no appeal is pending against an order under section 8(6)(a) of that Act.

(3) Where the notice is received more than 12 months after the making of the decree nisi or the conditional order, it must be accompanied by an explanation in writing stating—
- (a) why the application has not been made earlier;
- (b) whether the applicant and respondent have lived together since the decree nisi or the conditional order was made, and, if so, between what dates;
- (c) if the applicant is female, whether she has given birth to a child since the decree nisi or the conditional order was made and whether it is alleged that the child is or may be a child of the family;
- (d) if the respondent is female, whether the applicant has reason to believe that she has given birth to a child since the decree nisi or the conditional order was made and whether it is alleged that the child is or may be a child of the family.

(4) Where paragraph (3) applies, the court may—
- (a) require the applicant to file an affidavit verifying the explanation; and
- (b) make such order on the application as it thinks fit, but where it orders the decree nisi to be made absolute or the conditional order to be made final

that order is not to take effect until the court is satisfied that none of the matters mentioned in paragraph (2)(a) to (i) applies.

7.33.— Applications to make decrees nisi absolute or conditional orders final
(1) An application must be made—
    (a) in matrimonial proceedings, for the decree nisi to be made absolute; or
    (b) in civil partnership proceedings, for the conditional order to be made final,
where the conditions set out in paragraph (2) apply.
(2) The conditions referred to in paragraph (1) are—
    (a) the Queen's Proctor gives notice to the court under rule 7.31(6)(a) and has not withdrawn that notice;
    (b) there are other circumstances which ought to be brought to the attention of the court before the application is granted; or
    (c) the application is made—
        (i) in matrimonial proceedings, by the spouse against whom the decree nisi was made; or
        (ii) in civil partnership proceedings, by the civil partner against whom the conditional order was made.
(3) An application under this rule to which paragraph (2)(a) applies must be—
    (a) made to a judge, but not a district judge; and
    (b) served on the Queen's Proctor.
(4) Where the court orders—
    (a) in matrimonial proceedings, a decree to be made absolute under this rule; or
    (b) in civil partnership proceedings, a conditional order to be made final under this rule,
that order is not to take effect until the court is satisfied about the matters mentioned in rule 7.32(2)(a) to (i).

7.34. What the court officer must do when a decree nisi is made absolute
In matrimonial proceedings, where a decree nisi is made absolute the court officer must—
    (a) endorse that fact on the decree nisi together with the precise time at which the decree was made absolute; and
    (b) send a certificate that a decree nisi has been made absolute to the applicant, the respondent, any co-respondent and any other party.

7.35. What the court officer must do when a conditional order is made final
Where a conditional order is made final the court officer must—
    (a) endorse that fact on the conditional order together with the precise time at which the order was made final; and
    (b) send the final order to the applicant, the respondent and any other party.

7.36.— Records of decrees absolute and final orders
(1) A central index of decrees absolute and final orders must be kept under the control of the principal registry.
(2) Any person, on payment of the prescribed fee, may require a search to be made of that index and to be provided with a certificate showing the results of that search.
(3) Any person who requests it must, on payment of the prescribed fee, be issued with a copy of the decree absolute or final order.

PART 7 COMMENTARY

Part 7 is supplemented by four practice directions: 7A – Procedure for Applications in Matrimonial and Civil Partnership Proceedings, 7B – Medical Examinations on Applications for Annulment of a Marriage, and 7C: Polygamous Marriages, 7D – Gender Recognition Act 2004. PD7D is in fact a pre-existing practice direction, remaining in force by the *Practice Direction –*

Practice Directions Relating to Family Proceedings in Force before 6th April 2011 which support the Family Procedure Rules 2010. It was issued on the 5 April 2005.

Part 7 deals with the procedural rules for applications in matrimonial and civil partnership proceedings.

Chapter 1 sets out that these rules do not apply to magistrates' courts and defines terms.

Chapter 2 contains the rules for starting and responding to proceedings. There are restrictions at r 7.10(3)(c) on naming a co–respondent to an adultery petition where the person has died, is alleged to have been raped by the respondent (as under the old rules) and where the person is under 16 years of age. There is further discouragement as to the naming of co-respondents in PD7A, para 2.1, where it is set out that the 'other person' should not be named unless it is believed that there is likely to be an objection by the respondent to the making of an order. At r 7.14 it is provided that a respondent who wishes to make an application for a matrimonial or civil partnership order must do so by making an application, as distinct from an answer to the application. The respondent's application is then to be treated as an application in the same proceedings.

Chapter 3 provides the rules for the determination of matrimonial and civil partnership proceedings. Rule 7.16 sets out that in general these hearings will be in public, there is then a list at r 7.16 (3) of matters that might require the hearing to be in private. The old 'special procedure' has become the standard procedure and now includes nullity petitions, with undefended cases being certified as fit for a decree nisi and defended cases being listed for a case management hearing r 7.20 (2). Provision for the case management hearing is made at r 7.22. If a costs application is made the certifying district judge may certify that the applicant is entitled to their costs, or make no direction about costs (r 7.20(3)). If no direction as to costs has been made then any party may be heard on the subsequent hearing, if a certificate on costs has been given then a party may not be heard on the issue of costs unless two days notice has been given of the parties intention to attend the hearing to apply for or oppose a costs order (r 7.21). Rule 7.25 sets out the procedure for complying with s 41 of the 1973 Act or s 63 of the 2004 Act. Rule 7.26 as supplemented by PD7B deals with medical examinations in proceedings for nullity of marriage. Rule 7.27 provides for the hearing of questions arising from proceedings outside the jurisdiction which are capable of affecting the validity or substance of a marriage or civil partnership, and for the staying of proceedings where it appears to the court that it does not have jurisdiction and may be required to stay the proceedings under Articles 16–19 of the Council Regulation.

Chapter 4 sets out the procedure after decree nisi, or a conditional order, as to rescission (r 7.28), in the case of applications under s 10A (religious marriage) of the 1973 Act (r 7.30) and in order to make the decree nisi absolute, or the conditional order final and the duties then on the court (rr 7.33–7.36).

Forms relevant to Part 7 are C60 (certificate referred to in Article 39 of Council Regulation (EC) No 2201/2203 concerning judgments on parental responsibility and matrimonial matters) and various D forms (broadly the non-financial ones).

The Family Procedure Rules 2010

PRACTICE DIRECTION 7A – PROCEDURE FOR APPLICATIONS IN MATRIMONIAL AND CIVIL PARTNERSHIP PROCEEDINGS

This Practice Direction supplements FPR Part 7

APPLICATIONS FOR MATRIMONIAL AND CIVIL PARTNERSHIP ORDERS: GENERAL

1.1 An application for a matrimonial or civil partnership order must be made in the form referred to in Practice Direction 5A. The application form sets out the documents which must accompany the application.

1.2 The application for a matrimonial order or a civil partnership order must be completed according to the detailed notes which accompany the form. It is especially important that the particulars provide evidence to show why the applicant is entitled to-

(a) in matrimonial proceedings, a dissolution or annulment of the marriage or a decree of judicial separation;
(b) in civil partnership proceedings, a dissolution or annulment of the civil partnership or a separation order.

The particulars should, however, be as concise as possible consistent with providing the necessary evidence.

RESPONDENTS: RESTRICTIONS

2.1 Where the application refers to adultery or to an improper association with another person, that other person should not be named in the application unless the applicant believes the other party to the marriage or civil partnership in question is likely to object to the making of a matrimonial or civil partnership order on the application. Furthermore, such a person should not be a respondent if under the age of 16 or alleged to have been the victim of rape committed by the other party to the marriage or civil partnership, unless the court gives permission.

PROOF OF MARRIAGE OR CIVIL PARTNERSHIP TO ACCOMPANY THE APPLICATION

3.1 The application form for a matrimonial order or a civil partnership order sets out the documents which must accompany the application. Where the existence and validity of a marriage or civil partnership is not disputed, its validity will be proved by the application being accompanied by—

(a) one of the following—
    (i) a certificate of the marriage or civil partnership to which the application relates;
    (ii) a similar document issued under the law in force in the country where the marriage or civil partnership registration took place; or
    (iii) a certified copy of such a certificate or document obtained from the appropriate register office; and
(b) where the certificate, document or certified copy is not in English (or, where the court is in Wales, in Welsh), a translation of that document certified by a notary public or authenticated by a statement of truth.

Filing without accompanying proof of marriage or civil partnership

3.2 If—

(a) the applicant cannot produce—
    (i) the certificate, similar document or a certified copy; and
    (ii) (where necessary) an authenticated translation;
at the time of filing the application; and
(b) it is urgent that the application be filed,

the applicant may apply to the court without notice for permission to file the application without the certificate, document, certified copy or authenticated translation.

3.3 The applicant or the applicant's solicitor must in such a case file with the application a statement explaining why—

(a) the required document is not available; and
(b) the application is urgent.

3.4 The court may give permission to file the application without the required document if the applicant gives an undertaking to file that document at the very earliest opportunity and within any time limit set by the court.

Other methods of proof of the marriage or civil partnership

3.5 The requirements of this Practice Direction do not prevent the existence and validity of a marriage, or of an overseas relationship which is not a marriage, being proved in accordance with—

(a) the Evidence (Foreign, Dominion and Colonial Documents) Act 1933; or
(b) any other method authorised in any other Practice Direction, rule or Act.

INFORMATION REQUIRED WHERE EVIDENCE OF A CONVICTION OR FINDING IS TO BE RELIED ON

4.1 An applicant for a matrimonial or civil partnership order who wishes to rely on evidence—

(a) under section 11 of the Civil Evidence Act 1968 of a conviction of an offence; or
(b) under section 12 of that Act of a finding or adjudication of adultery or paternity,

must include in the application form a statement to that effect and give the following details—

(i) the type of conviction, finding or adjudication and its date;
(ii) the court or Court-Martial which made the conviction, finding or adjudication; and
(iii) the issue in the proceedings to which it relates.

AMENDMENTS TO APPLICATIONS AND ANSWERS

5.1 An application for permission to amend an application for a matrimonial or civil partnership order or answer may be dealt with at a hearing.

5.2 When making an application for permission to amend an application for a matrimonial or civil partnership order or to amend an answer the applicant should file at court—

(a) the notice of application for permission; and
(b) a copy of the application for a matrimonial or civil partnership order or the answer showing the proposed amendments.

5.3 Where permission to amend has been given, the party applying to make the amendment should within 14 days of the date of the order, or within such other period as the court directs, file with the court the amended application for a matrimonial or civil partnership order or the amended answer.

REQUESTS FOR FURTHER INFORMATION UNDER RULE 7.15 (FURTHER INFORMATION)

6.1 Before making an application under rule 7.15, the party seeking clarification or information ("the requesting party") should first serve a written request for it on the party from whom the clarification or information is sought, giving a date by which a reply should be served. The date should be such as to allow the requested party a reasonable time to respond.

6.2 A request should be made by letter or in a separate document, should contain no other subject matter, and should make clear that it is made under rule 7.15. It must be concise and confined to matters which are reasonably necessary and proportionate to enable the requesting party to prepare his or her own case or understand the case of the party to whom the request is directed.

6.3 The reply to the request must be in writing, dated and signed by the requested party or that party's legal representative.

6.4 The reply may be made by letter or in a separate document, should contain no other subject matter, and should make clear that it is a reply to the request concerned. It should repeat each request together with the reply to it. It must be served on every party to the proceedings.

6.5 A party who objects to replying to all or part of a request under rule 7.15, or who is unable to do so, must inform the requesting party promptly, and in any event within the time within which a reply has been requested, and give reasons for objecting or being unable to reply (as the case may be).

DISCLOSURE AND INSPECTION

7.1 Where an application for a matrimonial or civil partnership order is not being dealt with as an undefended case the court may make an order for the disclosure of documents under rule 7.22(2)(c).

7.2 When an order for disclosure is made, the disclosing party must, in order to comply, make a reasonable search for the documents required to be disclosed. The extent of the search will depend upon the circumstances of the case and parties should bear in mind the overriding principle of proportionality.

7.3 Documents should be disclosed in a list which should normally list the documents in date order, numbering them consecutively and giving each a concise description. Where there are a large number of documents falling into a particular category they may be grouped together (e.g. 50 bank statements relating to x account from y date to z date).

7.4 The obligations imposed by a disclosure order continue until the proceedings come to an end. If, after the list of documents has been prepared and served, the existence of further documents to which the order applies comes to the attention of the disclosing party, that party must prepare and serve a supplemental list.

7.5 A list of documents must contain the following statement:

> I, [insert name] state that I have carried out a reasonable and proportionate search to locate all the documents which I am required to disclose under the disclosure order made by the court on [insert date]. [I did not search for [insert here any limitations on search by reference to date, location, nature of documents etc]]. I understand the duty of disclosure and to the best of my knowledge I have carried out that duty. I certify that the list above is a complete list of all the documents which are or have been in my control and which I am obliged under the order to disclose.

7.6 If the disclosing party wishes to claim a right or duty to withhold inspection of a document or part of a document, that party must indicate in writing in the disclosure statement that such a right or duty is claimed, and the grounds on which it is claimed.

DECREES ABSOLUTE AND FINAL ORDERS: NEED FOR EXPEDITION

8.1 Where a party in an application for a matrimonial order has grounds for expediting the making of the decree absolute, that party should ordinarily seek directions with a view to an early hearing of the case. Where such an application has not been possible, an application should be made to the district judge making the decree nisi for the time between the decree nisi and the making absolute of that decree to be shortened.

8.2 Where the need for expedition only becomes obvious after the making of the decree nisi, or where (exceptionally) it arises in an undefended case to which the summary procedure applies, an application, on notice to the other parties to the proceedings, should be made using the procedure in Part 18 for an order shortening the time before which the decree nisi may be made absolute.

8.3 Where a party in an application for a civil partnership order has grounds for expediting the making of the final order, that party should ordinarily seek directions with a view to an early hearing of the case. Where such an application has not been possible, an application should be made to the district judge making the conditional order for the time between the conditional and final order to be shortened.

8.4 Where the need for expedition only becomes obvious after the making of the conditional order, or where (exceptionally) it arises in an undefended case to which the summary procedure applies, an application, on notice to the other parties to the proceedings, should be made using the procedure in Part 18 for an order shortening the time before which the final order may be made.

PRACTICE DIRECTION 7B – MEDICAL EXAMINATIONS ON APPLICATIONS FOR ANNULMENT OF A MARRIAGE

This Practice Direction supplements FPR Part 7, rule 7.26 (Medical examinations in proceedings for nullity of marriage)

1.1 Where an application is made for the annulment of a marriage based on the incapacity of one of the parties to consummate, it will not usually be necessary to appoint a medical inspector where the application is undefended. Where the application is defended the court should not appoint a medical inspector unless it appears necessary to do so for the proper disposal of the case.

1.2 A medical examination ordered under rule 7.26 must, if the party to be examined so requests, be conducted by a doctor of the same gender as the person to be examined. Unless both parties are to be examined, each by a doctor of their own gender, it should not normally be necessary to appoint more than one medical inspector.

1.3 The costs of any medical examination ordered under rule 7.26 will be borne, in the first instance, by the party on whose application the medical inspector is appointed. Such costs form part of the costs of the proceedings.

1.4 It is the responsibility of the party on whose application the medical inspector is appointed to address, at the case management hearing, the question of whether any medical inspector is required to attend the final hearing of the proceedings. A medical inspector who is to give evidence at the proceedings is to be treated as an expert witness and the relevant rules in Part 25 (Experts and Assessors) will apply. The relevant rules in Part 25 will also apply to the medical inspector's report.

1.5 Nothing in this Practice Direction or in rule 7.26 affects the parties' right to adduce other evidence relevant to the proper disposal of the case. Such evidence must be verified by a statement of truth.

PRACTICE DIRECTION 7C – POLYGAMOUS MARRIAGES

This Practice Direction supplements FPR Part 7 (procedure for applications in matrimonial and civil partnership proceedings), Part 9 (applications for a financial remedy) and Part 18 (procedure for other applications in proceedings)

SCOPE OF THIS PRACTICE DIRECTION

1.1 This practice direction applies where an application is made for—

(a) a matrimonial order;
(b) an order under section 27 of the 1973 Act;
(c) an order under section 35 of the 1973 Act;

(d) an order under the 1973 Act which is made in connection with, or with proceedings for any of the above orders; or
(e) an order under Part 3 of the 1984 Act,

and either party to the marriage is, or has during the course of the marriage, been married to more than one person (a polygamous marriage).

POLYGAMOUS MARRIAGES

2.1 Where this practice direction applies the application must state—

(a) that the marriage is polygamous;
(b) whether, as far as the party to the marriage is aware, any other spouse (that is, a spouse other than the spouse to whom the application relates) of that party is still living (the "additional spouse"); and
(c) if there is such an additional spouse—
   (i) the additional spouse's name and address;
   (ii) the date and place of the marriage to the additional spouse.

2.2 A respondent who believes that the marriage is polygamous must include the details referred to in paragraph 2.1 above in the acknowledgment of service if they are not included in the application.

2.3 The applicant in any proceedings to which this practice direction applies must apply to the court for directions as soon as possible after the filing of the application or the receipt of an acknowledgment of service mentioning an additional spouse.

2.4 On such an application or of its own initiative the court may—

(a) give the additional spouse notice of any of the proceedings to which this practice direction applies; and
(b) make the additional spouse a party to such proceedings.

2.5 In any case where the application or acknowledgment of service states that the marriage is polygamous (whether or not there is an additional spouse) a court officer must clearly mark the file with the words "Polygamous Marriage". The court officer must also check whether an application under paragraph 2.4 has been made in the case and, where no application has been made, refer the file to the court for consideration.

REFERENCES IN DECREES TO SECTION 47 OF THE 1973 ACT

3.1 Every decree nisi and decree absolute which is made in respect of a polygamous marriage must refer to the fact that the order is made with reference to section 47 of the 1973 Act.

PRACTICE DIRECTION 7D – GENDER RECOGNITION ACT 2004

1. Introduction

The Gender Recognition Act 2004 ("the Act") provides transsexual people with the opportunity to obtain legal recognition in their acquired gender. Legal recognition follows from the issue of a full gender recognition certificate by a Gender Recognition Panel. Section 4 of the Act requires that where a Panel has granted an application to a married applicant, the gender recognition certificate that it must issue shall be an interim gender recognition certificate. The interim certificate may then be used by either party to the marriage as evidence in support of an application to annul the marriage under Section 12(g) of, or paragraph 11(1)(e) of Schedule 1 to, the Matrimonial Causes Act 1973 ('*that an interim gender recognition certificate has, after the time of the marriage, been issued to either party to the marriage*').

2. Application

2.1 This Practice Direction applies to proceedings for divorce, judicial separation and annulment of marriage commenced on or after **4**.

2.2 Where proceedings for divorce, judicial separation or annulment of marriage have been commenced prior to this date, paragraphs 3.2 to 3.5 below shall also apply to those proceedings if, but only if, the court acquires protected information (as defined by Section 22 of the Act) in respect of a party to those proceedings.

3. Title of the Cause

3.1 When a party to a matrimonial cause has changed his or her name since marriage, by deed poll or otherwise, the name currently being used by the party should appear first on any petition, answer and statement of arrangements followed by "formerly known as . . . . (married name)".

3.2 Subject to paragraph 3.3, when describing the parties in any Decree, Order, Notice or other document issued by the court, the parties should be described by their full current names only.

3.3 When giving details of the parties in any court list (including a special procedure cause list) they should be described by the initials and surname of their current names only. (For example, A B Jones –v- C D Jones).

3.4 For the sake of clarity, in any document or court list mentioned in paragraphs 3.2 and 3.3 above party titles (i.e. Mr, Mrs, Miss, etc.) should be omitted.

3.5 The Practice Note of 2nd May 1940 (Title of Cause) shall cease to have effect.

4. Evidence at trial of cause

4.1 This part of the Practice Direction applies where the following conditions are met:

(a) proceedings for annulment of marriage are brought under Section 12(g) of, or paragraph 11(1)(e) of Schedule 1 to, the Matrimonial Causes Act 1973 and under no other ground under Sections 11 or 12 of, or paragraph 11 of Schedule 1 to, that Act; and
(b) the cause is an undefended cause.

4.2 Any party requesting directions for trial may, in addition to the requirements of FPR rule 2.25(2), state in their request that they would wish to give their evidence at the trial of the cause in accordance with the provisions of this Practice Direction; and in that event, the request must be accompanied by an affidavit setting out the information required by the appendix to this Practice Direction.

4.3 Where directions for trial are given in accordance with FPR rule 2.24(5) in respect of a request to which paragraph 4.2 applies, a direction may also be given under Rule 2.28(3) that the affidavit lodged with the request for directions shall be treated as the evidence of that party at the trial of the cause (unless otherwise directed).

4.4 In the case of an undefended cause proceeding on the respondent's answer, this part of the Practice Direction and the contents of the appendix shall apply with appropriate modifications.

4.5 The appendix sets out a form of affidavit that may be used for the purposes of paragraph 4.2.

5. (Issued by the President with the approval and concurrence of the Lord Chancellor, 5 April 2005.)

APPENDIX

A form of affidavit for the purposes of paragraph 4.2

Affidavit by Petitioner in support of petition for annulment under Section 12(g) of the Matrimonial Causes Act 1973

No. of matter:

IN THE

The Family Procedure Rules 2010

Between	(Petitioner)
And	(Respondent)
And	(Co-Respondent)

QUESTION	ANSWER
About the Petition	
1. Have you read the petition in this case?	
2. Do you wish to alter or to add to any statement in the petition? If so, state the alterations or additions.	
3. Subject to these alterations or additions (if any) is everything stated **in your petition** true? If any statement is not within your own knowledge, indicate this and say whether it is true to the best of your information and belief.	
About the interim gender recognition certificate	
4. State the date on which the interim gender recognition certificate was issued:	
State the serial number of the interim certificate:	
State the name of the person to whom the certificate has been issued:	
State the date on which you commenced proceedings to annul your marriage:	
You must attach a copy of the interim gender recognition certificate to this form.	
About other proceedings	
5. To the best of your knowledge and belief has there been or is there continuing any of the following proceedings;	
• an application to amend an error in the interim certificate;	
• an appeal against a decision to amend (or not to amend) an error in the interim certificate;	
• a reference under section 8(5) of the Gender Recognition Act 2004; or	
• an appeal against a decision made following a reference under section 8(5)?	

FPR 2010, Practice Direction 7D

	If so, please give details of those proceedings and any order made. (You should also attach copies of any orders made).	
About the children of the family		
6.	Has a Statement of Arrangements been filed in this case? If so, answer questions 7, 8 and 9.	
7.	Have you read the Statement of Arrangements filed in this case?	
8.	Do you wish to alter anything in the Statement of Arrangements or add to it? If so, state the alterations or additions.	
9.	Subject to these alterations and additions (if any) is everything stated in the **Statement of Arrangements** true? If any statement is not within your own knowledge, indicate this and say whether it is true and correct to the best of your information and belief.	

I,   (full name)

of   (full residential address)

        (occupation)

make oath and say as follows:—

1. I am the petitioner in this cause.
2. The answers to Questions 1 to 9 above are true.
3.[1] I identify the signature . . [2] appearing in the copy acknowledgement of service now produced to me and marked "A" as the signature of my husband / wife, the respondent in this cause.
4. I exhibit marked "B" a copy of the interim gender recognition certificate issued to myself / the respondent in this cause.
5. [3]
6. I identify the signature [2] appearing at Part IV of the Statement of Arrangements dated . now produced to me and marked "C" as the signature of the respondent.
7. I ask the court to grant a decree annulling my marriage with the respondent on the ground stated in my petition [and to order the respondent / co-respondent to pay the costs of this suit].[4]

Sworn at

In the County of

this   day of   20

Before me, ...

A Commissioner for Oaths[5]

Officer of the Court appointed by the Judge to take Affidavits

---

[1] Delete if the acknowledgement is signed by a solicitor.

[2] Insert name of the respondent exactly as it appears on the acknowledgement signed by him or her.

(3) If you have answered "Yes" to question 5, exhibit any document on which you wish to reply.
(4) Amend or delete as appropriate
(5) Delete as the case may be.

PART 8

PROCEDURE FOR MISCELLANEOUS APPLICATIONS

CHAPTER 1

PROCEDURE

8.1. Procedure
Subject to rules 8.13 and 8.24, applications to which this Part applies must be made in accordance with the Part 19 procedure.

CHAPTER 2

APPLICATION FOR CORRECTED GENDER RECOGNITION CERTIFICATE

8.2. Scope of this Chapter
The rules in this Chapter apply to an application under section 6(1) of the Gender Recognition Act 2004 for the correction of a full gender recognition certificate issued under section 5(1) or 5A(1) of that Act.

8.3. Where to start proceedings
The application must be made to the court which issued the original certificate unless the court directs otherwise.

8.4. Who the parties are
Where the applicant is—
 (a) the person to whom the original certificate was issued, the Secretary of State must be a respondent;
 (b) the Secretary of State, the person to whom the original certificate was issued must be a respondent.

8.5. Delivery of copy certificate to Secretary of State
Where the court issues a corrected full gender recognition certificate, a court officer must send a copy of the corrected certificate to the Secretary of State.

CHAPTER 3

APPLICATION FOR ALTERATION OF MAINTENANCE AGREEMENT AFTER DEATH OF ONE PARTY

8.6. Scope of this Chapter
The rules in this Chapter apply to an application under section 36 of the 1973 Act or paragraph 73 of Schedule 5 to the 2004 Act to alter a maintenance agreement after the death of one of the parties.

8.7.— Where to start proceedings
(1) The application may be made in the High Court or a county court.
(2) Where the application is made in a county court it must be made in the divorce county court or civil partnership proceedings county court for the district in which—
 (a) the deceased resided at the time of death; or
 (b) if the deceased did not reside in England and Wales at the time of death—
  (i) the respondent or one of the respondents resides or carries on business; or

(ii) where the respondent is the personal representative of the deceased, the deceased's estate is situated; or
(c) if neither (a) nor (b) applies—
(i) the applicant resides or carries on business; or
(ii) where the applicant is the personal representative of the deceased, the deceased's estate is situated.

8.8.— Who the parties are
(1) Where the applicant is—
(a) the surviving party to the agreement, the personal representative of the deceased must be a respondent;
(b) the personal representative of the deceased, the surviving party to the agreement must be a respondent.
(2) The court may at any time direct that—
(a) any person be made a party to proceedings; or
(b) a party be removed.

8.9.— Representative parties
(1) The court may, before or after the application has been filed at court, make an order appointing a person to represent any other person or persons in the application where the person or persons to be represented—
(a) are unborn;
(b) cannot be found;
(c) cannot easily be ascertained; or
(d) are a class of persons who have the same interest in an application and—
(i) one or more members of that class are within sub-paragraphs (a), (b) or (c); or
(ii) to appoint a representative would further the overriding objective.
(2) An application for an order under paragraph (1) may be made by—
(a) any person who seeks to be appointed under the order; or
(b) any party to the application.
(3) An application for an order under paragraph (1) must be served on—
(a) all parties to the application to alter the maintenance agreement, if that application has been filed at court;
(b) the person sought to be appointed, if that person is not the applicant or a party to the application; and
(c) any other person as directed by the court.
(4) The court's approval is required to settle proceedings in which a party is acting as a representative.
(5) The court may approve a settlement where it is satisfied that the settlement is for the benefit of all the represented persons.
(6) Unless the court directs otherwise, any order made on an application in which a party is acting as a representative—
(a) is binding on all persons represented in the proceedings; and
(b) may only be enforced by or against a person who is not a party with the permission of the court.
(7) An application may be brought by or against trustees, executors or administrators without adding as parties any persons who have a beneficial interest in the trust or estate and any order made on the application is binding on the beneficiaries unless the court orders otherwise.

8.10.— Acknowledgment of service
(1) A respondent who is a personal representative of the deceased must file with the acknowledgment of service a statement setting out—
(a) full particulars of the value of the deceased's estate for probate after providing for the discharge of the funeral, testamentary and administration expenses, debts and liabilities (including inheritance tax and interest); and

(b) the people (including names, addresses and details of any persons under disability) or classes of people beneficially interested in the estate and the value of their interests so far as ascertained.

(2) The respondent must file the acknowledgment of service and any statement required under this rule within 28 days beginning with the date on which the application is served.

8.11. Hearings may be in private
The court may decide to hear any application to which this Chapter applies in private.

CHAPTER 4

APPLICATION FOR QUESTION AS TO PROPERTY TO BE DECIDED IN SUMMARY WAY

8.12. Scope of this Chapter
The rules in this Chapter apply to an application under section 17 of the Married Women's Property Act 1882 or section 66 of the 2004 Act.

8.13. Procedure
Where an application for an order under section 17 of the Married Women's Property Act 1882 or section 66 of the 2004 Act is made in any proceedings for a financial order, the application must be made in accordance with the Part 18 procedure.

8.14.— Where to start proceedings
(1) The application may be made in the High Court or a county court.
(2) Where the application is made in a county court it must be made in the court—
 (a) in which any matrimonial proceedings or civil partnership proceedings have been started or are intended to be started by the applicant or the respondent; or
 (b) in the absence of any such proceedings, for the district in which the applicant or respondent resides.
(3) The application may be made to the principal registry as if it were a county court if—
 (a) any matrimonial proceedings or civil partnership proceedings have been started there or are intended to be started there by the applicant or the respondent; and
 (b) those proceedings are or will be treated as pending in a divorce county court or civil partnership proceedings county court.

8.15.— Mortgagees as parties
(1) Where particulars of a mortgage are provided with the application—
 (a) the applicant must serve a copy of the application on the mortgagee; and
 (b) the mortgagee may, within 14 days beginning with the date on which the application was received, file an acknowledgment of service and be heard on the application.

(2) The court must direct that a mortgagee be made a party to the proceedings where the mortgagee requests to be one.

8.16.— Injunctions
(1) The court may grant an injunction$^{(GL)}$ only if the injunction$^{(GL)}$ is ancillary or incidental to the assistance sought by the applicant.

(2) Applications for injunctive relief must be made in accordance with the procedure in rule 20.4 (how to apply for an interim remedy) and the provisions of rule 20.5 (interim injunction$^{(GL)}$ to cease if application is stayed$^{(GL)}$) apply.

8.17. Application of other rules
Rule 9.24 applies where the court has made an order for sale under section 17 of the Married Women's Property Act 1882 or section 66 of the 2004 Act.

FPR 2010

CHAPTER 5

DECLARATIONS

8.18. Scope of this Chapter
The rules in this Chapter apply to applications made in accordance with—
- (a) section 55 of the 1986 Act (declarations as to marital status) and section 58 of the 2004 Act (declarations as to civil partnership status);
- (b) section 55A of the 1986 Act (declarations of parentage);
- (c) section 56(1)(b) and (2) of the 1986 Act (declarations of legitimacy or legitimation); and
- (d) section 57 of the 1986 Act (declarations as to adoptions effected overseas).

8.19. Where to start proceedings
The application may be made in the High Court or a county court and applications under section 55A of the 1986 Act may also be made in a magistrates' court.

8.20.— Who the parties are
(1) In relation to the proceedings set out in column 1 of the following table, column 2 sets out who the respondents to those proceedings will be.

Proceedings	Respondent
Applications for declarations as to marital or civil partnership status.	The other party to the marriage or civil partnership in question or, where the applicant is a third party, both parties to the marriage or civil partnership.
Applications for declarations of parentage.	The person whose parentage is in issue or any person who is or is alleged to be the parent of the person whose parentage is in issue.
Applications for declarations of legitimacy or legitimation.	The applicant's father and mother or the survivor of them.
Applications for declarations as to adoption effected overseas.	The person(s) whom the applicant is claiming are or are not the applicant's adoptive parents.

(2) The applicant must include in his application particulars of every person whose interest may be affected by the proceedings and his relationship to the applicant.

(3) The acknowledgment of service filed under rule 19.5 must give details of any other persons the respondent considers should be made a party to the application or be given notice of the application.

(4) Upon receipt of the acknowledgment of service, the court must give directions as to any other persons who should be made a respondent to the application or be given notice of the proceedings.

(5) A person given notice of proceedings under paragraph (4) may, within 21 days beginning with the date on which the notice was served, apply to be joined as a party.

(6) No directions may be given as to the future management of the case under rule 19.9 until the expiry of the notice period in paragraph (5).

8.21.— The role of the Attorney General
(1) The applicant must, except in the case of an application for a declaration of parentage, send a copy of the application and all accompanying documents to the Attorney General at least one month before making the application.

(2) The Attorney General may, when deciding whether to intervene in the proceedings, inspect any document filed at court relating to any family proceedings mentioned in the declaration proceedings.

The Family Procedure Rules 2010

(3) If the court is notified that the Attorney General wishes to intervene in the proceedings, a court officer must send the Attorney General a copy of any subsequent documents filed at court.

(4) The court must, when giving directions under rule 8.20(4), consider whether to ask the Attorney General to argue any question relating to the proceedings.

(5) If the court makes a request to the Attorney General under paragraph (4) and the Attorney General agrees to that request, the Attorney General must serve a summary of the argument on all parties to the proceedings.

8.22.— Declarations of parentage

(1) If the applicant or the person whose parentage or parenthood is in issue, is known by a name other than that which appears in that person's birth certificate, that other name must also be stated in any order and declaration of parentage.

(2) A court officer must send a copy of a declaration of parentage and the application to the Registrar General within 21 days beginning with the date on which the declaration was made.

CHAPTER 6

APPLICATION FOR PERMISSION TO APPLY FOR A FINANCIAL REMEDY AFTER OVERSEAS PROCEEDINGS

8.23. Scope of this Chapter

Subject to rule 9.26(6), the rules in this Chapter apply to an application for permission to apply for a financial remedy under section 13 of the 1984 Act and paragraph 4 of Schedule 7 to the 2004 Act.

(Rule 9.26(6) enables the application for permission to apply for a financial remedy under section 13 of the 1984 Act or paragraph 4 of Schedule 7 to the 2004 Act to be heard at the same time as the application for a financial remedy under Part 3 of the 1984 Act or Schedule 7 to the 2004 Act where that application is an application for a consent order.)

8.24.— Where and how to start proceedings

(1) Subject to paragraph (2), the application must be made in the principal registry.

(2) Where rule 9.26(6) applies, the application must be made in the court hearing the application for a financial remedy.

(Rule 9.5(2) specifies the court where the application for the consent order should be filed.)

(3) The application must be made in accordance with the Part 18 procedure.

8.25.— Application to be made without notice

(1) The court may grant an application made without notice if it appears to the court that there are good reasons for not giving notice.

(2) If the applicant makes an application without giving notice, the applicant must state the reasons why notice has not been given.

8.26. Notification of hearing date

The court officer must—

  (a) fix a date, time and place for the hearing of the application by a judge, but not a district judge; and
  (b) give notice of the date of the hearing to the applicant.

8.27. Hearings to be in private unless the court directs otherwise

An application under this Chapter must be heard in private unless the court directs otherwise.

8.28. Direction that application be dealt with by a district judge of the principal registry

If the application is granted, the judge may direct that the application for a financial remedy under Part 3 of the 1984 Act or Schedule 7 to the 2004 Act may be heard by a district judge of the principal registry.

CHAPTER 7

APPLICATION FOR THE TRANSFER OF A TENANCY UNDER SECTION 53 OF, AND SCHEDULE 7 TO, THE 1996 ACT

8.29. Scope of this Chapter
This Chapter applies to an application for the transfer of a tenancy under section 53 of, and Schedule 7 to, the 1996 Act.

8.30.— Where to start proceedings
(1) Subject to paragraph (2), the application may be made in the High Court or a county court.

(2) The application must be made to the court in which any divorce, judicial separation, nullity or civil partnership proceedings are pending between the parties.

8.31.— Service of the application
(1) The court will serve a copy of the application on—
   (a) the respondent; and
   (b) the landlord (as defined by paragraph 1 of Schedule 7 to the 1996 Act), unless the court directs that the applicant must do so.

(2) Where service is effected by the applicant, the applicant must file a certificate of service.

8.32. Who the parties are
The court will direct that a landlord be made a party to the proceedings where the landlord requests to be one.

8.33. Orders for disclosure
Any party may apply to the court under rule 21.2 for an order that any person must attend an appointment before the court and produce any documents that are specified or described in the order.

8.34.— Injunctions
(1) The court may grant an injunction$^{(GL)}$ only if the injunction$^{(GL)}$ is ancillary or incidental to the assistance sought by the applicant.

(2) Applications for injunctive relief must be made in accordance with the procedure in rule 20.4 (how to apply for an interim remedy) and the provisions of rule 20.5 (interim injunction$^{(GL)}$ to cease if application is stayed$^{(GL)}$) apply accordingly.

CHAPTER 8

APPLICATIONS FOR ORDERS PREVENTING AVOIDANCE UNDER SECTION 32L OF THE CHILD SUPPORT ACT 1991

8.35. Scope of this Chapter
Subject to rule 8.40, the rules in this Chapter apply to applications made under section 32L (1) and (2) of the 1991 Act.

8.36. Interpretation
In this Chapter—
"child support maintenance" has the meaning assigned to it in section 3(6) of the 1991 Act;
"reviewable disposition" has the meaning assigned to it in section 32L(5) of the 1991 Act.

8.37.— Where to start proceedings
(1) The application must be made to the High Court and be filed in—
   (a) the principal registry; or
   (b) any district registry.
(2) The application may be heard by a judge but not a district judge except —
   (a) a district judge of the principal registry of the Family Division; or

The Family Procedure Rules 2010

    (b)   a district judge in a district registry who is directed by a judge to hear the application.

(Section 32L(10)(a) of the 1991 Act defines "court" for the purposes of section 32L as being the High Court only.)

8.38.— Who the parties are

(1) The applicant to the proceedings is the Commission and the respondent is the person who has failed to pay child support maintenance.

(2) The court may at any time direct that —
    (a)   any person be made a party to proceedings; or
    (b)   a party be removed from the proceedings.

8.39.— Service of the application

(1) The applicant must serve the application and a copy of the applicant's written evidence on—
    (a)   any respondent;
    (b)   the person in whose favour the reviewable disposition is alleged to have been made; and
    (c)   such other persons as the court directs.

(2) Where an application includes an application relating to land, the applicant must serve a copy of the application on any —
    (a)   mortgagee;
    (b)   trustee of a trust of land or settlement; and
    (c)   other person who has an interest in the land,
of whom particulars are given in the application.

(3) Any person served under paragraph (2) may make a request to the court in writing, within 14 days beginning with the date of service of the application, for a copy of the applicant's written evidence.

(4) Any person who —
    (a)   is served with copies of the application and the applicant's written evidence under paragraph (1); or
    (b)   receives a copy of the applicant's written evidence following a request under paragraph (3),
may, within 14 days beginning with the date of service or receipt, file a statement in answer.

(5) A statement in answer filed under paragraph (4) must be verified by a statement of truth.

8.40.— Applications without notice

(1) This rule applies to an application under section 32L(1) of the 1991 Act.

(2) The court may grant an application made without notice if it appears to the court that there are good reasons for not giving notice.

(3) If the applicant makes an application without giving notice, the evidence in support of the application must state the reasons why notice has not been given.

(4) If the court grants an application under paragraph (2)—
    (a)   the order must include a provision allowing any respondent to apply to the court for an order to be reconsidered as soon as just and convenient at a full hearing; and
    (b)   the applicant must, as soon as reasonably practicable, serve upon each respondent a copy of the order and a copy of the written evidence in support of the application.

CHAPTER 9

APPLICATION FOR CONSENT TO MARRIAGE OF A CHILD OR TO REGISTRATION OF CIVIL PARTNERSHIP OF A CHILD

8.41. Scope of this Chapter

The rules in this Chapter apply to an application under—
- (a) section 3 of the Marriage Act 1949; or
- (b) paragraph 3, 4 or 10 of Schedule 2 to the 2004 Act.

8.42. Child acting without a children's guardian

The child may bring an application without a children's guardian, unless the court directs otherwise.

8.43. Who the respondents are

Where an application follows a refusal to give consent to—
- (a) the marriage of a child; or
- (b) a child registering as the civil partner of another person,

every person who has refused consent will be a respondent to the application.

PART 8 COMMENTARY

Part 8 is not supplemented by a practice direction.

Part 8 details the procedure for a number of different types of application.

Chapter 1 sets out that the procedure set out in Part 19 is to apply to these applications, save those dealt with under Chapter 4 (Married Woman's Property Act applications) and Chapter 6 (financial remedy after overseas proceedings).

Chapter 2 deals with applications for a correction of a gender recognition certificate under s 6(1) of the Gender Recognition Act 2004.

Chapter 3 deals with applications for the alteration of a maintenance agreement after death of one party under s 36 of the 1973 Act , or para 73 of Sch 5, or the 2004 Act.

Chapter 4 deals with applications under s 17 of the Married Women's Property Act 1882, or s 66 of the 2004 Act.

Chapter 5 deals with declarations under the Family Law Act 1986 as to marital status (s 55), parentage (s 55A), legitimacy (s 56) and overseas adoption (s 57).

Chapter 6 deals with applications for permission to apply for a financial remedy after overseas proceedings under Matrimonial and Family Proceedings Act 1984, s 13 or Sch 7, para 4 of the 2004 Act. Rule 8.25 is headed 'Application to be made without notice', however what follows provides only that the court 'may' grant an application made without notice if it appears to the court that there are good reasons for not giving notice and that if the applicant makes an application without giving notice the applicant must state the reason why no notice has been given. The practitioner will need to consider the guidance of Lord Collins in *Agbaje v Agbaje* [2010] UKSC 13, and the Court of Appeal in *Tarversa v Freddi* [2011] EWCA Civ 81, where these rules were considered and Munby LJ held that 'The application for leave should be listed ex parte for a hearing which can be appropriately brief, as can the judgment either giving or refusing leave.' Where permission is granted, the substantive application will proceed as a financial remedy in accordance with

The Family Procedure Rules 2010

Part 9. The permission application must (except in the case of a consent order) be heard by a judge of the High Court (r 8.26), but on granting permission the judge may direct that the substantive application be heard by a district judge of the PRFD: r 8.28; but see also r 9.26 in relation to consent orders.

Chapter 7 deals with applications for the transfer of tenancy under the Family Law Act 1996, s 53 and Sch 7.

Chapter 8 deals with applications for orders preventing the avoidance of disposition under the Child Support Act 1991, s 32L.

Chapter 9 deals with applications for consent to marriage or civil partnership of a child.

Forms relevant to Part 8 are D50–D50K.

PART 9

APPLICATIONS FOR A FINANCIAL REMEDY

CHAPTER 1

Application and interpretation

9.1. Application
The rules in this Part apply to an application for a financial remedy.
("Financial remedy" and "financial order" are defined in rule 2.3)

9.2. Application of Magistrates' Courts Rules 1981
Unless the context otherwise requires, and subject to the rules in this Part, the following rules of the Magistrates' Courts Rules 1981 apply to proceedings in a magistrates' court which are family proceedings under section 65 of the Magistrates' Courts Act 1980—

- (a) rule 39(6) (method of making periodical payments);
- (b) rule 41 (revocation etc. of orders for periodical payments);
- (c) rule 43 (service of copy of order);
- (d) rule 44 (remission of sums due under order);
- (e) rule 45 (duty of designated officer to notify subsequent marriage or formation of civil partnership of person entitled to payments under a maintenance order);
- (f) rule 48 (to whom payments are to be made);
- (g) rule 49 (duty of designated officer to give receipt);
- (h) rule 51 (application for further time);
- (i) rule 62 (particulars relating to payment of lump sum under a magistrates' courts maintenance order etc. to be entered in register);
- (j) rule 66 (register of convictions, etc.);
- (k) rule 67 (proof of service, handwriting, etc.);
- (l) rule 68 (proof of proceedings); and
- (m) rule 69 (proof that magistrates' court maintenance orders, etc, have not been revoked, etc.).

9.3.— Interpretation
(1) In this Part—
"avoidance of disposition order" means—
- (a) in proceedings under the 1973 Act, an order under section 37(2)(b) or (c) of that Act;
- (b) in proceedings under the 1984 Act, an order under section 23(2)(b) or 23(3) of that Act;

(c) in proceedings under Schedule 5 to the 2004 Act, an order under paragraph 74(3) or (4); or
(d) in proceedings under Schedule 7 to the 2004 Act, an order under paragraph 15(3) or (4);

"the Board" means the Board of the Pension Protection Fund;

"FDR appointment" means a Financial Dispute Resolution appointment in accordance with rule 9.17;

"order preventing a disposition" means—
(a) in proceedings under the 1973 Act, an order under section 37(2)(a) of that Act;
(b) in proceedings under the 1984 Act, an order under section 23(2)(a) of that Act;
(c) in proceedings under Schedule 5 to the 2004 Act, an order under paragraph 74(2); or
(d) in proceedings under Schedule 7 to the 2004 Act, an order under paragraph 15(2);

"pension arrangement" means—
(a) an occupational pension scheme;
(b) a personal pension scheme;
(c) shareable state scheme rights;
(d) a retirement annuity contract;
(e) an annuity or insurance policy purchased, or transferred, for the purpose of giving effect to rights under an occupational pension scheme or a personal pension scheme; and
(f) an annuity purchased, or entered into, for the purpose of discharging liability in respect of a pension credit under section 29(1)(b) of the Welfare Reform and Pensions Act 1999 or under corresponding Northern Ireland legislation;

"pension attachment order" means—
(a) in proceedings under the 1973 Act, an order making provision under section 25B or 25C of that Act;
(b) in proceedings under the 1984 Act, an order under section 17(1)(a)(i) of that Act making provision equivalent to an order referred to in paragraph (a);
(c) in proceedings under Schedule 5 to the 2004 Act, an order making provision under paragraph 25 or paragraph 26; or
(d) in proceedings under Schedule 7 to the 2004 Act, an order under paragraph 9(2) or (3) making provision equivalent to an order referred to in paragraph (c);

"pension compensation attachment order" means—
(a) in proceedings under the 1973 Act, an order making provision under section 25F of that Act;
(b) in proceedings under the 1984 Act, an order under section 17(1)(a)(i) of that Act making provision equivalent to an order referred in to paragraph (a);
(c) in proceedings under Schedule 5 to the 2004 Act, an order under paragraph 34A; and
(d) in proceedings under Schedule 7 to the 2004 Act, an order under paragraph 9(2) or (3) making provision equivalent to an order referred to in paragraph (c);

"pension compensation sharing order" means—
(a) in proceedings under the 1973 Act, an order under section 24E of that Act;
(b) in proceedings under the 1984 Act, an order under section 17(1)(c) of that Act;
(c) in proceedings under Schedule 5 to the 2004 Act, an order under paragraph 19A; and

The Family Procedure Rules 2010

(d) in proceedings under Schedule 7 to the 2004 Act, an order under paragraph 9(2) or (3) making provision equivalent to an order referred to in paragraph (c);

"pension sharing order" means—
- (a) in proceedings under the 1973 Act, an order making provision under section 24B of that Act;
- (b) in proceedings under the 1984 Act, an order under section 17(1)(b) of that Act;
- (c) in proceedings under Schedule 5 to the 2004 Act, an order under paragraph 15; or
- (d) in proceedings under Schedule 7 to the 2004 Act, an order under paragraph 9(2) or (3) making provision equivalent to an order referred to in paragraph (c);

"pension scheme" means, unless the context otherwise requires, a scheme for which the Board has assumed responsibility in accordance with Chapter 3 of Part 2 of the Pensions Act 2004 (pension protection) or any provision in force in Northern Ireland corresponding to that Chapter;

"PPF compensation" has the meaning given to it—
- (a) in proceedings under the 1973 Act, by section 21C of the 1973 Act;
- (b) in proceedings under the 1984 Act, by section 18(7) of the 1984 Act; and
- (c) in proceedings under the 2004 Act, by paragraph 19F of Schedule 5 to the 2004 Act;

"relevant valuation" means a valuation of pension rights or benefits as at a date not more than 12 months earlier than the date fixed for the first appointment which has been furnished or requested for the purposes of any of the following provisions—
- (a) the Pensions on Divorce etc (Provision of Information) Regulations 2000;
- (b) regulation 5 of and Schedule 2 to the Occupational Pension Schemes (Disclosure of Information) Regulations 1996 and regulation 11 of and Schedule 1 to the Occupational Pension Schemes (Transfer Value) Regulations 1996;
- (c) section 93A or 94(1)(a) or (aa) of the Pension Schemes Act 1993;
- (d) section 94(1)(b) of the Pension Schemes Act 1993 or paragraph 2(a) (or, where applicable, 2(b)) of Schedule 2 to the Personal Pension Schemes (Disclosure of Information) Regulations 1987;
- (e) the Dissolution etc. (Pensions) Regulations 2005;

"variation order" means—
- (a) in proceedings under the 1973 Act, an order under section 31 of that Act; or
- (b) in proceedings under the 2004 Act, an order under Part 11 of Schedule 5 to that Act.

(2) References in this Part to a county court are to be construed, in relation to proceedings for a financial order, as references to a divorce county court or a civil partnership proceedings county court, as the case may be.

CHAPTER 2

Procedure for applications

9.4. When an Application for a financial order may be made

An application for a financial order may be made—
- (a) in an application for a matrimonial or civil partnership order; or
- (b) at any time after an application for a matrimonial or civil partnership order has been made.

9.5.— Where to start proceedings

(1) An application for a financial remedy must be filed—
- (a) if there are proceedings for a matrimonial order or a civil partnership order which are proceeding in a designated county court, in that court; or

(b) if there are proceedings for a matrimonial order or a civil partnership order which are proceeding in the High Court, in the registry in which those proceedings are taking place.

(2) In any other case, in relation to the application set out in column 1 of the following table, column 2 sets out where the application must be filed.

Provision under which application is made	*Court where application must be filed*
Section 27 of the 1973 Act.	Divorce county court.
Part 9 of Schedule 5 to the 2004 Act.	Civil partnership proceedings county court.
Part 3 of the 1984 Act.	Principal Registry or, in relation to an application for a consent order, a divorce county court.
Schedule 7 to the 2004 Act.	Principal Registry or, in relation to an application for a consent order, a civil partnership proceedings county court.
Section 35 of the 1973 Act.	High Court, a divorce county court or a magistrates' court.
Paragraph 69 of Schedule 5 to the 2004 Act.	High Court, a civil partnership proceedings county court or a magistrates' court.
Schedule 1 to the 1989 Act.	High Court, designated county court or a magistrates' court.
Part 1 of the 1978 Act.	magistrates' court.
Schedule 6 to the 2004 Act.	magistrates' court.

(3) An application for a financial remedy under Part 3 of the 1984 Act or Schedule 7 to the 2004 Act which is proceeding in the High Court must be heard by a judge, but not a district judge, of that court unless a direction has been made that the application may be heard by a district judge of the principal registry.

(Rule 8.28 enables a judge to direct that an application for a financial remedy under Part 3 of the 1984 Act or Schedule 7 to the 2004 Act may be heard by a district judge of the principal registry.)

9.6.— Application for an order preventing a disposition

(1) The Part 18 procedure applies to an application for an order preventing a disposition.

(2) An application for an order preventing a disposition may be made without notice to the respondent.

("Order preventing a disposition" is defined in rule 9.3.)

9.7.— Application for interim orders

(1) A party may apply at any stage of the proceedings for—
   (a) an order for maintenance pending suit;
   (b) an order for maintenance pending outcome of proceedings;
   (c) an order for interim periodical payments;
   (d) an interim variation order; or
   (e) any other form of interim order.

(2) The Part 18 procedure applies to an application for an interim order.

(3) Where a party makes an application before filing a financial statement, the written evidence in support must—
   (a) explain why the order is necessary; and
   (b) give up to date information about that party's financial circumstances.

The Family Procedure Rules 2010

(4) Unless the respondent has filed a financial statement, the respondent must, at least 7 days before the court is to deal with the application, file a statement of his means and serve a copy on the applicant.

(5) An application for an order mentioned in paragraph (1)(e) may be made without notice.

9.8.— Application for periodical payments order at same rate as an order for maintenance pending suit

(1) This rule applies where there are matrimonial proceedings and—
    (a) a decree nisi of divorce or nullity of marriage has been made;
    (b) at or after the date of the decree nisi an order for maintenance pending suit is in force; and
    (c) the spouse in whose favour the decree nisi was made has made an application for an order for periodical payments.

(2) The spouse in whose favour the decree nisi was made may apply, using the Part 18 procedure, for an order providing for payments at the same rate as those provided for by the order for maintenance pending suit.

9.9.— Application for periodical payments order at same rate as an order for maintenance pending outcome of proceedings

(1) This rule applies where there are civil partnership proceedings and—
    (a) a conditional order of dissolution or nullity of civil partnership has been made;
    (b) at or after the date of the conditional order an order for maintenance pending outcome of proceedings is in force;
    (c) the civil partner in whose favour the conditional order was made has made an application for an order for periodical payments.

(2) The civil partner in whose favour the conditional order was made may apply, using the Part 18 procedure, for an order providing for payments at the same rate as those provided for by, the order for maintenance pending the outcome of proceedings.

CHAPTER 3

APPLICATIONS FOR FINANCIAL REMEDIES FOR CHILDREN

9.10.— Application by parent, guardian etc for financial remedy in respect of children

(1) The following people may apply for a financial remedy in respect of a child—
    (a) a parent, guardian or special guardian of any child of the family;
    (b) any person in whose favour a residence order has been made with respect to a child of the family, and any applicant for such an order;
    (c) any other person who is entitled to apply for a residence order with respect to a child;
    (d) a local authority, where an order has been made under section 31(1)(a) of the 1989 Act placing a child in its care;
    (e) the Official Solicitor, if appointed the children's guardian of a child of the family under rule 16.24; and
    (f) a child of the family who has been given permission to apply for a financial remedy.

(2) In this rule "residence order" has the meaning given to it by section 8(1) of the 1989 Act.

9.11.— Children to be separately represented on certain applications

(1) Where an application for a financial remedy includes an application for an order for a variation of settlement, the court must, unless it is satisfied that the proposed variation does not adversely affect the rights or interests of any child concerned, direct that the child be separately represented on the application.

(2) On any other application for a financial remedy the court may direct that the child be separately represented on the application.

(3) Where a direction is made under paragraph (1) or (2), the court may if the person to be appointed so consents, appoint—
  (a) a person other than the Official Solicitor; or
  (b) the Official Solicitor,
to be a children's guardian and rule 16.24(5) and (6) and rules 16.25 to 16.28 apply as appropriate to such an appointment.

CHAPTER 4

PROCEDURE IN THE HIGH COURT AND COUNTY COURT AFTER FILING AN APPLICATION

9.12.— Duties of the court and the applicant upon issuing an application

(1) When an application under this Part is issued in the High Court or in a county court—
  (a) the court will fix a first appointment not less than 12 weeks and not more than 16 weeks after the date of the filing of the application; and
  (b) subject to paragraph (2), within 4 days beginning with the date on which the application was filed, a court officer will—
    (i) serve a copy of the application on the respondent; and
    (ii) give notice of the date of the first appointment to the applicant and the respondent.
(2) Where the applicant wishes to serve a copy of the application on the respondent and on filing the application so notifies the court—
  (a) paragraph (1)(b) does not apply;
  (b) a court officer will return to the applicant the copy of the application and the notice of the date of the first appointment; and
  (c) the applicant must,—
    (i) within 4 days beginning with the date on which the copy of the application is received from the court, serve the copy of the application and notice of the date of the first appointment on the respondent; and
    (ii) file a certificate of service at or before the first appointment.
(Rule 6.37 sets out what must be included in a certificate of service.)
(3) The date fixed under paragraph (1), or for any subsequent appointment, must not be cancelled except with the court's permission and, if cancelled, the court must immediately fix a new date.

9.13.— Service of application on mortgagees, trustees etc

(1) Where an application for a financial remedy includes an application for an order for a variation of settlement, the applicant must serve copies of the application on—
  (a) the trustees of the settlement;
  (b) the settlor if living; and
  (c) such other persons as the court directs.
(2) In the case of an application for an avoidance of disposition order, the applicant must serve copies of the application on the person in whose favour the disposition is alleged to have been made.
(3) Where an application for a financial remedy includes an application relating to land, the applicant must serve a copy of the application on any mortgagee of whom particulars are given in the application.
(4) Any person served under paragraphs (1), (2) or (3) may make a request to the court in writing, within 14 days beginning with the date of service of the application, for a copy of the applicant's financial statement or any relevant part of that statement.
(5) Any person who—
  (a) is served with copies of the application in accordance with paragraphs (1), (2) or (3); or
  (b) receives a copy of a financial statement, or a relevant part of that statement, following an application made under paragraph (4),
may within 14 days beginning with the date of service or receipt file a statement in answer.

The Family Procedure Rules 2010

(6) Where a copy of an application is served under paragraphs (1), (2) or (3), the applicant must file a certificate of service at or before the first appointment.

(7) A statement in answer filed under paragraph (5) must be verified by a statement of truth.

9.14.— Procedure before the first appointment

(1) Not less than 35 days before the first appointment both parties must simultaneously exchange with each other and file with the court a financial statement in the form referred to in Practice Direction 5A.

(2) The financial statement must—
    (a) be verified by an affidavit; and
    (b) accompanied by the following documents only—
        (i) any documents required by the financial statement;
        (ii) any other documents necessary to explain or clarify any of the information contained in the financial statement; and
        (iii) any documents provided to the party producing the financial statement by a person responsible for a pension arrangement, either following a request under rule 9.30 or as part of a relevant valuation; and
        (iv) any notification or other document referred to in rule 9.37(2), (4) or (5) which has been received by the party producing the financial statement.

(3) Where a party was unavoidably prevented from sending any document required by the financial statement, that party must at the earliest opportunity—
    (a) serve a copy of that document on the other party; and
    (b) file a copy of that document with the court, together with a written explanation of the failure to send it with the financial statement.

(4) No disclosure or inspection of documents may be requested or given between the filing of the application for a financial remedy and the first appointment, except—
    (a) copies sent with the financial statement, or in accordance with paragraph (3); or
    (b) in accordance with paragraphs (5) and (6).

(Rule 21.1 explains what is meant by disclosure and inspection.)

(5) Not less than 14 days before the hearing of the first appointment, each party must file with the court and serve on the other party—
    (a) a concise statement of the issues between the parties;
    (b) a chronology;
    (c) a questionnaire setting out by reference to the concise statement of issues any further information and documents requested from the other party or a statement that no information and documents are required; and
    (d) a notice stating whether that party will be in a position at the first appointment to proceed on that occasion to a FDR appointment.

(6) Not less than 14 days before the hearing of the first appointment, the applicant must file with the court and serve on the respondent confirmation—
    (a) of the names of all persons served in accordance with rule 9.13(1) to (3); and
    (b) that there are no other persons who must be served in accordance with those paragraphs.

9.15.— Duties of the court at the first appointment

(1) The first appointment must be conducted with the objective of defining the issues and saving costs.

(2) At the first appointment the court must determine—
    (a) the extent to which any questions seeking information under rule 9.14(5)(c) must be answered; and
    (b) what documents requested under rule 9.14(5)(c) must be produced,
and give directions for the production of such further documents as may be necessary.

(3) The court must give directions where appropriate about—

    (a)   the valuation of assets (including the joint instruction of joint experts);
    (b)   obtaining and exchanging expert evidence, if required;
    (c)   the evidence to be adduced by each party; and
    (d)   further chronologies or schedules to be filed by each party.

(4) If the court decides that a referral to a FDR appointment is appropriate it must direct that the case be referred to a FDR appointment.

(5) If the court decides that a referral to a FDR appointment is not appropriate it must direct one or more of the following—
    (a)   that a further directions appointment be fixed;
    (b)   that an appointment be fixed for the making of an interim order;
    (c)   that the case be fixed for a final hearing and, where that direction is given, the court must determine the judicial level at which the case should be heard.

(By rule 3.3 the court may also direct that the case be adjourned if it considers that alternative dispute resolution is appropriate.)

(6) In considering whether to make a costs order under rule 28.3(5), the court must have particular regard to the extent to which each party has complied with the requirement to send documents with the financial statement and the explanation given for any failure to comply.

(7) The court may—
    (a)   where an application for an interim order has been listed for consideration at the first appointment, make an interim order;
    (b)   having regard to the contents of the notice filed by the parties under rule 9.14(5)(d), treat the appointment (or part of it) as a FDR appointment to which rule 9.17 applies;
    (c)   in a case where a pension sharing order or a pension attachment order is requested, direct any party with pension rights to file and serve a Pension Inquiry Form, completed in full or in part as the court may direct; and
    (d)   in a case where a pension compensation sharing order or a pension compensation attachment order is requested, direct any party with PPF compensation rights to file and serve a Pension Protection Fund Inquiry Form, completed in full or in part as the court may direct.

(8) Both parties must personally attend the first appointment unless the court directs otherwise.

9.16.— After the first appointment

(1) Between the first appointment and the FDR appointment, a party is not entitled to the production of any further documents except—
    (a)   in accordance with directions given under rule 9.15(2); or
    (b)   with the permission of the court.

(2) At any stage—
    (a)   a party may apply for further directions or a FDR appointment;
    (b)   the court may give further directions or direct that parties attend a FDR appointment.

9.17.— The FDR appointment

(1) The FDR appointment must be treated as a meeting held for the purposes of discussion and negotiation.

(2) The judge hearing the FDR appointment must have no further involvement with the application, other than to conduct any further FDR appointment or to make a consent order or a further directions order.

(3) Not less than 7 days before the FDR appointment, the applicant must file with the court details of all offers and proposals, and responses to them.

(4) Paragraph (3) includes any offers, proposals or responses made wholly or partly without prejudice[GL], but paragraph (3) does not make any material admissible as evidence if, but for that paragraph, it would not be admissible.

The Family Procedure Rules 2010

(5) At the conclusion of the FDR appointment, any documents filed under paragraph (3), and any filed documents referring to them, must, at the request of the party who filed them, be returned to that party and not retained on the court file.

(6) Parties attending the FDR appointment must use their best endeavours to reach agreement on matters in issue between them.

(7) The FDR appointment may be adjourned from time to time.

(8) At the conclusion of the FDR appointment, the court may make an appropriate consent order.

(9) If the court does not make an appropriate consent order as mentioned in paragraph (8), the court must give directions for the future course of the proceedings including, where appropriate—
- (a) the filing of evidence, including up to date information; and
- (b) fixing a final hearing date.

(10) Both parties must personally attend the FDR appointment unless the court directs otherwise.

CHAPTER 5

Procedure in the magistrates' court after filing an application

9.18.— Duties of the court and the applicant upon filing an application

(1) When an application for an order under this Part is issued in a magistrates' court—
- (a) the court will fix a first hearing date not less than 4 weeks and not more than 8 weeks after the date of the filing of the application; and
- (b) subject to paragraph (2), within 4 days beginning with the date on which the application was filed, a court officer will—
  - (i) serve a copy of the application on the respondent;
  - (ii) give notice of the date of the first hearing to the applicant and the respondent; and
  - (iii) send a blank financial statement to both the applicant and the respondent.

(2) Where the applicant wishes to serve a copy of the application on the respondent and, on filing the application, so notifies the court—
- (a) paragraph (1)(b) does not apply;
- (b) a court officer will return to the applicant the copy of the application and the notice of the date of the first hearing; and
- (c) the applicant must—
  - (i) within 4 days beginning with the date on which the copy of the application is received from the court, serve the copy of the application and notice of the date of the first hearing on the respondent;
  - (ii) send a blank financial statement to the respondent; and
  - (iii) file a certificate of service at or before the first hearing.

(3) The date fixed under paragraph (1), or for any other subsequent hearing or appointment must not be cancelled except with the court's permission and, if cancelled, the court must immediately fix a new date.

9.19.— Procedure before the first hearing

(1) Not more than 14 days after the date of the issue of the application both parties must simultaneously exchange with each other and file with the court a financial statement referred to in Practice Direction 5A.

(2) The financial statement must—
- (a) be verified by an affidavit; and
- (b) contain the following documents only—
  - (i) any documents required by the financial statement; and
  - (ii) any other documents necessary to explain or clarify any of the information contained in the financial statement.

(3) Where a party was unavoidably prevented from sending any document required by the financial statement, that party must at the earliest opportunity—
   (a) serve a copy of that document on the other party; and
   (b) file a copy of that document with the court, together with a statement explaining the failure to send it with the financial statement.

(4) No disclosure or inspection of documents may be requested or given between the filing of the application for a financial remedy and the first hearing except copies sent with the financial statement or in accordance with paragraph (3).

(Rule 21.1 explains what is meant by disclosure and inspection.)

9.20. Power of the court to direct filing of evidence and set dates for further hearings

Unless the court is able to determine the application at the first hearing the court may direct that further evidence be filed and set a date for a directions hearing or appointment or final hearing.

9.21. Who the respondent is on an application under section 20 or section 20A of the 1978 Act or Part 6 of Schedule 6 to the 2004 Act

In relation to proceedings set out in column 1 of the following table, column 2 sets out who the respondents to those proceedings will be.

Proceedings	*Respondent*
Application under section 20 of the 1978 Act, except an application for variation of an order.	The other party to the marriage; and where the order to which the application relates requires periodical payments to be made to, or in respect of, a child who is 16 years of age or over, that child.
Application under paragraphs 30 to 34 of Schedule 6 to the 2004 Act, except an application for variation of an order.	The other party to the civil partnership; and where the order to which the application relates requires periodical payments to be made to, or in respect of, a child who is 16 years of age or over, that child.
Application for the revival of an order under section 20A of the 1978 Act or paragraph 40 of Schedule 6 to the 2004 Act.	The parties to the proceedings leading to the order which it is sought to have revived.

9.22.— Proceedings by or against a person outside England and Wales for orders under section 20 of the 1978 Act or paragraphs 30 to 34 of Schedule 6 to the 2004 Act other than proceedings for variation of orders

(1) Subject to the provisions of this rule, the jurisdiction conferred on a court by virtue of section 20 of the 1978 Act or paragraphs 30 to 34 of Schedule 6 to the 2004 Act is exercisable when proceedings are brought by or against a person residing outside England and Wales.

(2) Subject to paragraph (3), where the court is satisfied that the respondent has been outside England and Wales for the whole of the period beginning one month before the making of the application and ending with the date of the hearing, it may proceed with the application provided that—
   (a) the applicant provided the court with an address for service of the application and written notice of the hearing on the respondent; or
   (b) the court is satisfied that the respondent has been made aware of the application and of the time and place appointed for the hearing otherwise than by service of the application upon the respondent by the court; and
   (c) it is reasonable in all the circumstances to proceed in the absence of the respondent.

(3) The court must not make the order for which the application is made unless it is satisfied that—

The Family Procedure Rules 2010

(a) during the period of 6 months immediately preceding the making of the application the respondent was continuously outside England and Wales, or was not in England and Wales on more than 30 days; and

(b) having regard to any communication to the court in writing purporting to be from the respondent, it is reasonable in all the circumstances to do so.

(4) This rule does not apply in relation to proceedings to vary an order for periodical payments.

(Rules made under section 144 of the Magistrates' Courts Act 1980 make provision in respect of proceedings by or against a person outside England and Wales for variation of orders under section 20 of the 1978 Act or paragraphs 30 to 34 of Schedule 6 to the 2004 Act.)

9.23.— Duty to make entries in the court's register

(1) Where the designated officer for the court receives notice of any direction made in the High Court or a county court under section 28 of the 1978 Act by virtue of which an order made by the court under that Act or the 2004 Act ceases to have effect, particulars of the direction must be entered in the court's register.

(2) Where—

(a) in proceedings under the 1978 Act, the hearing of an application under section 2 of that Act is adjourned after the court has decided that it is satisfied of any ground mentioned in section 1; or

(b) in proceedings under the 2004 Act, the hearing of an application under Part 1 of Schedule 6 to that Act is adjourned after the court has decided that it is satisfied of any ground mentioned in paragraph 1,

and the parties to the proceedings agree to the resumption of the hearing in accordance with section 31 of the 1978 Act by a court which includes justices who were not sitting when the hearing began, particulars of the agreement must be entered into the court's register.

CHAPTER 6

General procedure

9.24.— Power to order delivery up of possession etc.

(1) This rule applies where the court has made an order under—
 (a) section 24A of the 1973 Act;
 (b) section 17(2) of the 1984 Act;
 (c) Part 3 of Schedule 5 to the 2004 Act; or
 (d) paragraph 9(4) of Schedule 7 to the 2004 Act.

(2) When the court makes an order mentioned in paragraph (1), it may order any party to deliver up to the purchaser or any other person—
 (a) possession of the land, including any interest in, or right over, land;
 (b) receipt of rents or profits relating to it; or
 (c) both.

9.25.— Where proceedings may be heard

(1) Paragraph (2) applies to an application—
 (a) for a financial order;
 (b) under Part 3 of the 1984 Act; or
 (c) under Schedule 7 to the 2004 Act.

(2) An application mentioned in paragraph (1) must be heard—
 (a) where the case is proceeding in the county court, at any court of trial; and
 (b) where the case is proceeding in the High Court—
  (i) at the Royal Courts of Justice; or
  (ii) in matrimonial or civil partnership proceedings, any court at which sittings of the High Court are authorised.

(3) An application for an order under—
 (a) section 27 of the 1973 Act; or

(b) Part 9 of Schedule 5 to the 2004 Act,

must be heard in a court of trial or in the High Court.

(4) A court may transfer a case to another court exercising the same jurisdiction, either of its own initiative or on the application of one of the parties, if—
- (a) the parties consent to the transfer;
- (b) the court has held a hearing to determine whether a transfer should be ordered; or
- (c) paragraph (5) applies.

(5) A court may transfer a case without a hearing if—
- (a) the court has notified the parties in writing that it intends to order a transfer; and
- (b) neither party has, within 14 days of the notification being sent, requested a hearing to determine whether a transfer should be ordered.

9.26.— Applications for consent orders for financial remedy

(1) Subject to paragraph (5) and to rule 35.2, in relation to an application for a consent order—
- (a) the applicant must file two copies of a draft of the order in the terms sought, one of which must be endorsed with a statement signed by the respondent to the application signifying agreement; and
- (b) each party must file with the court and serve on the other party, a statement of information in the form referred to in Practice Direction 5A.

(2) Where each party's statement of information is contained in one form, it must be signed by both the applicant and respondent to certify that they have read the contents of the other party's statement.

(3) Where each party's statement of information is in a separate form, the form of each party must be signed by the other party to certify that they have read the contents of the statement contained in that form.

(4) Unless the court directs otherwise, the applicant and the respondent need not attend the hearing of an application for a consent order.

(5) Where all or any of the parties attend the hearing of an application for a financial remedy the court may—
- (a) dispense with the filing of a statement of information; and
- (b) give directions for the information which would otherwise be required to be given in such a statement in such a manner as it thinks fit.

(6) In relation to an application for a consent order under Part 3 of the 1984 Act or Schedule 7 to the 2004 Act, the application for permission to make the application may be heard at the same time as the application for a financial remedy if evidence of the respondent's consent to the order is filed with the application.

(The following rules contain provision in relation to applications for consent orders — rule 9.32 (pension sharing order), rule 9.34 (pension attachment order), rule 9.41 (pension compensation sharing orders) and rule 9.43 (pension compensation attachment orders.)

CHAPTER 7

Estimates of costs

9.27.— Estimates of Costs

(1) Subject to paragraph (2), at every hearing or appointment each party must produce to the court an estimate of the costs incurred by that party up to the date of that hearing or appointment.

(2) Not less than 14 days before the date fixed for the final hearing of an application for a financial remedy, each party ("the filing party") must (unless the court directs otherwise) file with the court and serve on each other party a statement giving full particulars of all costs in respect of the proceedings which the filing party has incurred or expects to incur, to enable the court to take account of the parties' liabilities for costs when deciding what order (if any) to make for a financial remedy.

(3) This rule does not apply to magistrates' courts.
(Rule 28.3 makes provision for orders for costs in financial remedy proceedings.)

9.28.— Duty to make open proposals

(1) Not less than 14 days before the date fixed for the final hearing of an application for a financial remedy, the applicant must (unless the court directs otherwise) file with the court and serve on the respondent an open statement which sets out concise details, including the amounts involved, of the orders which the applicant proposes to ask the court to make.

(2) Not more than 7 days after service of a statement under paragraph (1), the respondent must file with the court and serve on the applicant an open statement which sets out concise details, including the amounts involved, of the orders which the respondent proposes to ask the court to make.

CHAPTER 8

PENSIONS

9.29.— Application and interpretation of this Chapter

(1) This Chapter applies
  (a) where an application for a financial remedy has been made; and
  (b) the applicant or respondent is the party with pension rights.
(2) In this Chapter—
  (a) in proceedings under the 1973 Act and the 1984 Act, all words and phrases defined in sections 25D(3) and (4) of the 1973 Act have the meaning assigned by those subsections;
  (b) in proceedings under the 2004 Act—
    (i) all words and phrases defined in paragraphs 16(4) to (5) and 29 of Schedule 5 to that Act have the meanings assigned by those paragraphs; and
    (ii) "the party with pension rights" has the meaning given to "civil partner with pension rights" by paragraph 29 of Schedule 5 to the 2004 Act;
  (c) all words and phrases defined in section 46 of the Welfare Reform and Pensions Act 1999 have the meanings assigned by that section.

9.30.— What the party with pension rights must do when the court fixes a first appointment

(1) Where the court fixes a first appointment as required by rule 9.12(1)(a) the party with pension rights must request the person responsible for each pension arrangement under which the party has or is likely to have benefits to provide the information referred to in regulation 2(2) of the Pensions on Divorce etc (Provision of Information) Regulations 2000.
(The information referred to in regulation 2 of the Pensions on Divorce etc (Provision of Information) Regulations 2000 relates to the valuation of pension rights or benefits.)

(2) The party with pension rights must comply with paragraph (1) within 7 days beginning with the date on which that party receives notification of the date of the first appointment.

(3) Within 7 days beginning with the date on which the party with pension rights receives the information under paragraph (1) that party must send a copy of it to the other party, together with the name and address of the person responsible for each pension arrangement.

(4) A request under paragraph (1) need not be made where the party with pension rights is in possession of, or has requested, a relevant valuation of the pension rights or benefits accrued under the pension arrangement in question.

9.31. Applications for pension sharing orders

Where an application for a financial remedy includes an application for a pension sharing order, or where a request for such an order is added to an existing application for a financial

FPR 2010

remedy, the applicant must serve a copy of the application on the person responsible for the pension arrangement concerned.

9.32.— Applications for consent orders for pension sharing

(1) This rule applies where—
 (a) the parties have agreed on the terms of an order and the agreement includes a pension sharing order;
 (b) service has not been effected under rule 9.31; and
 (c) the information referred to in paragraph (2) has not otherwise been provided.

(2) The party with pension rights must—
 (a) request the person responsible for the pension arrangement concerned to provide the information set out in Section C of the Pension Inquiry Form; and
 (b) on receipt, send a copy of the information referred to in sub-paragraph (a) to the other party.

9.33.— Applications for pension attachment orders

(1) Where an application for a financial remedy includes an application for a pension attachment order, or where a request for such an order is added to an existing application for a financial remedy, the applicant must serve a copy of the application on the person responsible for the pension arrangement concerned and must at the same time send—
 (a) an address to which any notice which the person responsible is required to serve on the applicant is to be sent;
 (b) an address to which any payment which the person responsible is required to make to the applicant is to be sent; and
 (c) where the address in sub-paragraph (b) is that of a bank, a building society or the Department of National Savings, sufficient details to enable the payment to be made into the account of the applicant.

(2) A person responsible for a pension arrangement who receives a copy of the application under paragraph (1) may, within 21 days beginning with the date of service of the application, request the party with the pension rights to provide that person with the information disclosed in the financial statement relating to the party's pension rights or benefits under that arrangement.

(3) If the person responsible for a pension arrangement makes a request under paragraph (2), the party with the pension rights must provide that person with a copy of the section of that party's financial statement that relates to that party's pension rights or benefits under that arrangement.

(4) The party with the pension rights must comply with paragraph (3)—
 (a) within the time limited for filing the financial statement by rule 9.14(1); or
 (b) within 21 days beginning with the date on which the person responsible for the pension arrangement makes the request,
whichever is the later.

(5) A person responsible for a pension arrangement who receives a copy of the section of a financial statement as required pursuant to paragraph (4) may, within 21 days beginning with the date on which that person receives it, send to the court, the applicant and the respondent a statement in answer.

(6) A person responsible for a pension arrangement who files a statement in answer pursuant to paragraph (5) will be entitled to be represented at the first appointment, or such other hearing as the court may direct, and the court must within 4 days, beginning with the date on which that person files the statement in answer, give the person notice of the date of the first appointment or other hearing as the case may be.

9.34.— Applications for consent orders for pension attachment

(1) This rule applies where service has not been effected under rule 9.33(1).

(2) Where the parties have agreed on the terms of an order and the agreement includes a pension attachment order, then they must serve on the person responsible for the pension arrangement concerned—

The Family Procedure Rules 2010

- (a) a copy of the application for a consent order;
- (b) a draft of the proposed order, complying with rule 9.35; and
- (c) the particulars set out in rule 9.33(1).

(3) No consent order that includes a pension attachment order must be made unless either—

- (a) the person responsible for the pension arrangement has not made any objection within 21 days beginning with the date on which the application for a consent order was served on that person; or
- (b) the court has considered any such objection, and for the purpose of considering any objection the court may make such direction as it sees fit for the person responsible to attend before it or to furnish written details of the objection.

9.35. Pension sharing orders or pension attachment orders

An order for a financial remedy, whether by consent or not, which includes a pension sharing order or a pension attachment order, must—

- (a) in the body of the order, state that there is to be provision by way of pension sharing or pension attachment in accordance with the annex or annexes to the order; and
- (b) be accompanied by a pension sharing annex or a pension attachment annex as the case may require, and if provision is made in relation to more than one pension arrangement there must be one annex for each pension arrangement.

9.36.— Duty of the court upon making a pension sharing order or a pension attachment order

(1) A court which varies or discharges a pension sharing order or a pension attachment order, must send, or direct one of the parties to send—

- (a) to the person responsible for the pension arrangement concerned; or
- (b) where the Board has assumed responsibility for the pension scheme or part of it, the Board;

the documents referred to in paragraph (4).

(2) A court which makes a pension sharing order or pension attachment order, must send, or direct one of the parties to send to the person responsible for the pension arrangement concerned, the documents referred to in paragraph (4).

(3) Where the Board has assumed responsibility for the pension scheme or part of it after the making of a pension sharing order or attachment order but before the documents have been sent to the person responsible for the pension arrangement in accordance with paragraph (2), the court which makes the pension sharing order or the pension attachment order, must send, or direct one of the parties to send to the Board the documents referred to in paragraph (4).

(4) The documents to be sent in accordance with paragraph (1) to (3) are—

- (a) in the case of—
  - (i) proceedings under the 1973 Act, a copy of the decree of judicial separation;
  - (ii) proceedings under Schedule 5 to the 2004 Act, a copy of the separation order;
  - (iii) proceedings under Part 3 of the 1984 Act, a copy of the document of divorce, annulment or legal separation;
  - (iv) proceedings under Schedule 7 to the 2004 Act, a copy of the document of dissolution, annulment or legal separation;
- (b) in the case of divorce or nullity of marriage, a copy of the decree absolute under rule 7.31or 7.32; or
- (c) in the case of dissolution or nullity of civil partnership, a copy of the order making the conditional order final under rule 7.31 or 7.32; and

(d) a copy of the pension sharing order or the pension attachment order, or as the case may be of the order varying or discharging that order, including any annex to that order relating to that pension arrangement but no other annex to that order.

(5) The documents referred to in paragraph (1) must be sent—
- (a) in proceedings under the 1973 Act and the 1984 Act, within 7 days beginning with the date on which—
  - (i) the relevant pension sharing or pension attachment order is made; or
  - (ii) the decree absolute of divorce or nullity or decree of judicial separation is made,

  whichever is the later; and
- (b) in proceedings under the 2004 Act, within 7 days beginning with the date on which—
  - (i) the relevant pension sharing or pension attachment order is made; or
  - (ii) the final order of dissolution or nullity or separation order is made,

  whichever is the later.

9.37.— Procedure where Pension Protection Fund becomes involved with the pension scheme

(1) This rule applies where—
- (a) rules 9.30 to 9.34 or 9.36 apply; and
- (b) the party with the pension rights ("the member") receives or has received notification in compliance with the Pension Protection Fund (Provision of Information) Regulations 2005 ("the 2005 Regulations")—
  - (i) from the trustees or managers of a pension scheme, that there is an assessment period in relation to that scheme; or
  - (ii) from the Board that it has assumed responsibility for the pension scheme or part of it.

(2) If the trustees or managers of the pension scheme notify or have notified the member that there is an assessment period in relation to that scheme, the member must send to the other party, all the information which the Board is required from time to time to provide to the member under the 2005 Regulations including—
- (a) a copy of the notification; and
- (b) a copy of the valuation summary, in accordance with paragraph (3).

(3) The member must send the information or any part of it referred to in paragraph (2)—
- (a) if available, when the member sends the information received under rule 9.30(1); or
- (b) otherwise, within 7 days of receipt.

(4) If the Board notifies the member that it has assumed responsibility for the pension scheme, or part of it, the member must—
- (a) send a copy of the notification to the other party within 7 days of receipt; and
- (b) comply with paragraph (5).

(5) Where paragraph (4) applies, the member must—
- (a) within 7 days of receipt of the notification, request the Board in writing to provide a forecast of the member's compensation entitlement as described in the 2005 Regulations; and
- (b) send a copy of the forecast of the member's compensation entitlement to the other party within 7 days of receipt.

(6) In this rule—
- (a) "assessment period" means an assessment period within the meaning of Part 2 of the Pensions Act 2004; and
- (b) "valuation summary" has the meaning assigned to it by the 2005 Regulations.

The Family Procedure Rules 2010

CHAPTER 9

Pension protection fund compensation

9.38.— Application and interpretation of this Chapter
(1) This Chapter applies—
    (a) where an application for a financial remedy has been made; and
    (b) the applicant or respondent is, the party with compensation rights.
(2) In this Chapter "party with compensation rights" —
    (a) in proceedings under the 1973 Act and the 1984 Act, has the meaning given to it by section 25G(5) of the 1973 Act;
    (b) in proceedings under the 2004 Act, has the meaning given to "civil partner with compensation rights" by paragraph 37(1) of Schedule 5 to the 2004 Act.

9.39.— What the party with compensation rights must do when the court fixes a first appointment
(1) Where the court fixes a first appointment as required by rule 9.12(1)(a) the party with compensation rights must request the Board to provide the information about the valuation of entitlement to PPF compensation referred to in regulations made by the Secretary of State under section 118 of the Pensions Act 2008.
(2) The party with compensation rights must comply with paragraph (1) within 7 days beginning with the date on which that party receives notification of the date of the first appointment.
(3) Within 7 days beginning with the date on which the party with compensation rights receives the information under paragraph (1) that party must send a copy of it to the other party, together with the name and address of the trustees or managers responsible for each pension scheme.
(4) Where the rights to PPF Compensation are derived from rights under more than one pension scheme, the party with compensation rights must comply with this rule in relation to each entitlement.

9.40. Applications for pension compensation sharing orders
Where an application for a financial remedy includes an application for a pension compensation sharing order or where a request for such an order is added to an existing application for a financial remedy, the applicant must serve a copy of the application on the Board.

9.41.— Applications for consent orders for pension compensation sharing
(1) This rule applies where—
    (a) the parties have agreed on the terms of an order and the agreement includes a pension compensation sharing order;
    (b) service has not been effected under rule 9.40; and
    (c) the information referred to in paragraph (2) has not otherwise been provided.
(2) The party with compensation rights must—
    (a) request the Board to provide the information set out in Section C of the Pension Protection Fund Inquiry Form; and
    (b) on receipt, send a copy of the information referred to in sub-paragraph (a) to the other party.

9.42. Applications for pension compensation attachment orders
Where an application for a financial remedy includes an application for a pension compensation attachment order or where a request for such an order is added to an existing application for a financial remedy, the applicant must serve a copy of the application on the Board and must at the same time send—
    (a) an address to which any notice which the Board is required to serve on the applicant is to be sent;

(b) an address to which any payment which the Board is required to make to the applicant is to be sent; and

(c) where the address in sub-paragraph (b) is that of a bank, a building society or the Department of National Savings, sufficient details to enable the payment to be made into the account of the applicant.

9.43.— Applications for consent orders for pension compensation attachment

(1) This rule applies where service has not been effected under rule 9.42.

(2) Where the parties have agreed on the terms of an order and the agreement includes a pension compensation attachment order, then they must serve on the Board—

(a) a copy of the application for a consent order;

(b) a draft of the proposed order, complying with rule 9.44; and

(c) the particulars set out in rule 9.42.

9.44. Pension compensation sharing orders or pension compensation attachment orders

An order for a financial remedy, whether by consent or not, which includes a pension compensation sharing order or a pension compensation attachment order, must—

(a) in the body of the order, state that there is to be provision by way of pension compensation sharing or pension compensation attachment in accordance with the annex or annexes to the order; and

(b) be accompanied by a pension compensation sharing annex or a pension compensation attachment annex as the case may require, and if provision is made in relation to entitlement to PPF compensation that derives from rights under more than one pension scheme there must be one annex for each such entitlement.

9.45.— Duty of the court upon making a pension compensation sharing order or a pension compensation attachment order

(1) A court which makes, varies or discharges a pension compensation sharing order or a pension compensation attachment order, must send, or direct one of the parties to send, to the Board—

(a) in the case of—
 (i) proceedings under Part 3 of the 1984 Act, a copy of the document of divorce, annulment or legal separation;
 (ii) proceedings under Schedule 7 to the 2004 Act, a copy of the document of dissolution, annulment or legal separation;

(b) in the case of —
 (i) divorce or nullity of marriage, a copy of the decree absolute under rule 7.32 or 7.33;
 (ii) dissolution or nullity of civil partnership, a copy of the order making the conditional order final under rule 7.32 or 7.33;

(c) in the case of separation—
 (i) in the matrimonial proceedings, a copy of the decree of judicial separation;
 (ii) in civil partnership proceedings, a copy of the separation order; and

(d) a copy of the pension compensation sharing order or the pension compensation attachment order, or as the case may be of the order varying or discharging that order, including any annex to that order relating to that PPF compensation but no other annex to that order.

(2) The documents referred to in paragraph (1) must be sent—

(a) in proceedings under the 1973 Act and the 1984 Act, within 7 days beginning with the date on which—
 (i) the relevant pension compensation sharing or pension compensation attachment order is made; or
 (ii) the decree absolute of divorce or nullity or the decree of judicial separation is made,
 whichever is the later; and

The Family Procedure Rules 2010

(b) in proceedings under the 2004 Act, within 7 days beginning with the date on which—
(i) the relevant pension compensation sharing or pension compensation attachment order is made; or
(ii) the final order of dissolution or nullity or separation order is made, whichever is the later.

PART 9 COMMENTARY

Part 9 is supplemented by PD9A – Application for a Financial Remedy which is partly drawn from the President's Practice Direction of 25 May 2000, including the pre-application protocol, but also includes new elements. In particular, para 5.1 draws attention to the requirements of PD22A in relation to the preparation of financial statements and exhibits (and allows bulky exhibits to be returned to the parties) and para 5.2 requires replies to questionnaire, served in accordance with a court direction, to be verified by statement of truth.

Part 9 sets out the procedure for all applications for financial remedies, a term defined at r 2.3(1). It applies in general terms the old ancillary relief procedure to the following financial proceedings:

(a) a financial order (broadly, orders within the definition of ancillary relief under the FPR 1991);
(b) an order under the Children Act 1989, s 15 & Sch 1;
(c) an order under the MFPA 1984, Part 3 or the CPA 2004, Sch 7;
(d) an order under the MCA 1973, s 27 or the CPA 2004, Sch 5, Part 9 (failure to maintain);
(e) an order under the MCA 1973, s 35 or CPA 2004, Sch 5, para 69 (alteration of a maintenance agreement during lifetime);
(f) an order under the DPMCA 1978, Part 1 or the CPA 2004, Sch 6 (magistrates' court only);
(g) an order under the MCA 1973, s 10(2) or the CPA 2004, s 48(2) (financial protection in separation cases).

Chapter 1 provides for some limited application of the Magistrates' Courts Rules 1981 in proceedings in the magistrates' court (r 9.2), and provides relevant definitions (r 9.3).

Chapter 2 provides that where there are proceedings for a matrimonial or civil partnership order, the financial application must be made in the court or registry in which those proceedings are taking place (r 9.5(1)), otherwise, the court in which any particular type of application is to be made is specified in r 9.5(2). Rules 9.6, 9.7, 9.8 and 9.9 apply the Part 18 procedure to applications for orders preventing dispositions, interim orders, periodical payments at the same rate as maintenance pending suit, or pending the outcome of proceedings.

Chapter 3 deals with who may apply for financial remedies for children and contains provision at r 9.11 for the separate representation of children.

Chapter 4 sets out the procedure after filing an application: fixing and giving notice of a first appointment (r 9.12), service of mortgagees and trustees etc (r 9.13), Form E and first appointment documents (r 9.14), the duties of the court at the first appointment (r 9.15), and the FDR appointment (r 9.17).

Chapter 5 sets out the procedure in the magistrates' court. There is no provision in the magistrates' court for an FDR.

Chapter 6 deals with a number of points of general procedure: at r 9.24 the power to order delivery up of possession of land, and rent, at r 9.25 where proceedings are to be heard, and at r 9.26 in relation to consent orders for financial remedy – which now contains provision recording that each party has read the other's statement of information (r 9.26 (2) and (3)).

Chapter 7 sets out the requirement to provide costs estimates (r 9.27) and the duty to make open proposals (r 9.28).

Chapter 8 deals with pensions and makes provision at r 9.37 as to the procedure where the Pension Protection Fund becomes involved.

Chapter 9 deals with the procedure in relation to pension protection fund compensation and the attachment and sharing of compensation rights.

Forms relevant to Part 9 are Form A – Form F (note there are three different Forms E now), and Form I to Form PPF2

PRACTICE DIRECTION 9A – APPLICATION FOR A FINANCIAL REMEDY

This Practice Direction supplements FPR Part 9

INTRODUCTION

1.1 Part 9 of the Family Procedure Rules sets out the procedure applicable to the financial proceedings that are included in the definition of a "financial remedy".

1.2 The procedure is applicable to a limited extent to applications for financial remedies that are heard in magistrates' courts (namely, those under section 35 of the Matrimonial Causes Act 1973, paragraph 69 of Schedule 5 to the Civil Partnership Act 2004, Part I of the Domestic Proceedings and Magistrates' Courts Act 1978, Schedule 1 to the Children Act 1989 and Schedule 6 to the Civil Partnership Act 2004). However, unless the context otherwise requires, this Practice Direction does not apply to proceedings in a magistrates' court.

1.3 Where an application for a financial remedy includes an application relating to land, details of any mortgagee must be included in the application.

PRE-APPLICATION PROTOCOL

2.1 The "pre-application protocol" annexed to this Direction outlines the steps parties should take to seek and provide information from and to each other prior to the commencement of any application for a financial remedy. The court will expect the parties to comply with the terms of the protocol.

COSTS

3.1 Rule 9.27 applies in the High Court and county court. The rule requires each party to produce to the court, at every hearing or appointment, an estimate of the costs incurred by the party up to the date of that hearing or appointment.

3.2 The purpose of this rule is to enable the court to take account of the impact of each party's costs liability on their financial situations. Parties should ensure that the information contained in the estimate is as full and accurate as possible and that any sums already paid in respect of a party's financial remedy costs are clearly set out. Where relevant, any liability arising from the costs of other proceedings between the parties should continue to be referred to in the appropriate section of a party's financial statement; any such costs should not be included in the estimates under rule 9.27.

3.3   Rule 28.3 provides that the general rule in financial remedy proceedings is that the court will not make an order requiring one party to pay the costs of another party. However the court may make such an order at any stage of the proceedings where it considers it appropriate to do so because of the conduct of a party in relation to the proceedings.

3.4   Any breach of this practice direction or the pre-application protocol annexed to it will be taken into account by the court when deciding whether to depart from the general rule as to costs.

PROCEDURE BEFORE THE FIRST APPOINTMENT

4.1   In addition to the matters listed at rule 9.14(5), the parties should, if possible, with a view to identifying and narrowing any issues between the parties, exchange and file with the court—

(a)   a summary of the case agreed between the parties;
(b)   a schedule of assets agreed between the parties; and
(c)   details of any directions that they seek, including, where appropriate, the name of any expert they wish to be appointed.

4.2   Where a party is prevented from sending the details referred to in (c) above, the party should make that information available at the first appointment.

FINANCIAL STATEMENTS AND OTHER DOCUMENTS

5.1   Practice Direction 22A (Written Evidence) applies to any financial statement filed in accordance with rules 9.14 or 9.19 and to any exhibits to a financial statement. In preparing a bundle of documents to be exhibited to or attached to a financial statement, regard must be had in particular to paragraphs 11.1 to 11.3 and 13.1 to 13.4 of that Direction. Where on account of their bulk, it is impracticable for the exhibits to a financial statement to be retained on the court file after the First Appointment, the court may give directions as to their custody pending further hearings.

5.2   Where the court directs a party to provide information or documents by way of reply to a questionnaire or request by another party, the reply must be verified by a statement of truth. Unless otherwise directed, a reply to a questionnaire or request for information and documents shall not be filed with the court.

(Part 17 and Practice Direction 17A make further provision about statements of truth)

FINANCIAL DISPUTE RESOLUTION (FDR) APPOINTMENT

6.1   A key element in the procedure is the Financial Dispute Resolution (FDR) appointment. Rule 9.17 provides that the FDR appointment is to be treated as a meeting held for the purposes of discussion and negotiation. Such meetings have been developed as a means of reducing the tension which inevitably arises in family disputes and facilitating settlement of those disputes.

6.2   In order for the FDR to be effective, parties must approach the occasion openly and without reserve. Non-disclosure of the content of such meetings is vital and is an essential prerequisite for fruitful discussion directed to the settlement of the dispute between the parties. The FDR appointment is an important part of the settlement process. As a consequence of *Re D (Minors) (Conciliation: Disclosure of Information)* [1993] Fam 231, evidence of anything said or of any admission made in the course of an FDR appointment will not be admissible in evidence, except at the trial of a person for an offence committed at the appointment or in the very exceptional circumstances indicated in *Re D*.

6.3   Courts will therefore expect—

(a)   parties to make offers and proposals;
(b)   recipients of offers and proposals to give them proper consideration; and

(c) (subject to paragraph 6.4), that parties, whether separately or together, will not seek to exclude from consideration at the appointment any such offer or proposal.

6.4 Paragraph 6.3(c) does not apply to an offer or proposal made during alternative dispute resolution.

6.5 In order to make the most effective use of the first appointment and the FDR appointment, the legal representatives attending those appointments will be expected to have full knowledge of the case.

6.6 The rules do not provide for FDR appointments to take place during proceedings in magistrates' courts.

(Provision relating to experts in financial remedy proceedings is contained in the Practice Direction supplementing Part 25 of the FPR relating to Experts and Assessors in Family Proceedings)

CONSENT ORDERS

7.1 Rule 9.26 (1)(a) requires an application for a consent order to be accompanied by two copies of the draft order in the terms sought, one of which must be endorsed with a statement signed by the respondent to the application signifying the respondent's agreement. The rule is considered to have been properly complied with if the endorsed statement is signed by solicitors on record as acting for the respondent; but where the consent order applied for contains undertakings, it should be signed by the party giving the undertakings as well as by that party's solicitor.

(Provision relating to the enforcement of undertakings is contained in the Practice Direction 33A supplementing Part 33 of the FPR)

7.2 Rule 9.26(1)(b) requires each party to file with the court and serve on the other party a statement of information. Where this is contained in one form, both parties must sign the statement to certify that each has read the contents of the other's statement.

7.3 Rule 35.2 deals with applications for a consent order in respect of a financial remedy where the parties wish to have the content of a written mediation agreement to which the Mediation Directive applies made the subject of a consent order.

SECTION 10(2) OF THE MATRIMONIAL CAUSES ACT 1973 AND SECTION 48(2) OF THE CIVIL PARTNERSHIP ACT 2004

8.1 Where a respondent who has applied under section 10(2) of the Matrimonial Causes Act 1973, or section 48(2) of the Civil Partnership Act 2004, for the court to consider his or her financial position after a divorce or dissolution elects not to proceed with the application, a notice of withdrawal of the application signed by the respondent or by the respondent's solicitor may be filed without leave of the court. In this event a formal order dismissing or striking out the application is unnecessary. Notice of withdrawal should also be given to the applicant's solicitor.

8.2 An application under section 10(2) or section 48(2) which has been withdrawn is not a bar to making in matrimonial proceedings, the decree absolute and in civil partnership proceedings, the final order.

MAINTENANCE ORDERS – REGISTRATION IN MAGISTRATES' COURTS

9.1 Where periodical payments are required to be made to a child under an order registered in a magistrates' court, section 62 of the Magistrates' Courts Act 1980 permits the payments to be made instead to the person with whom the child has his home. That person may proceed in his own name for variation, revival or revocation of the order and may enforce payment either in his own name or by requesting the designated officer of the court to do so.

9.2 The registration in a magistrates' court of an order made direct to a child entails

The Family Procedure Rules 2010

a considerable amount of work. Accordingly, when the court is considering the form of an order where there are children, care should be taken not to make orders for payment direct where such orders would be of no benefit to the parties.

PENSIONS

10.1 The phrase "party with pension rights" is used in FPR Part 9, Chapter 8. For matrimonial proceedings, this phrase has the meaning given to it by section 25D(3) of the Matrimonial Causes Act 1973 and means "the party to the marriage who has or is likely to have benefits under a pension arrangement". There is a definition of "civil partner with pension rights" in paragraph 29 of Schedule 5 to the Civil Partnership Act 2004 which mirrors the definition of "party with pension rights" in section 25D(3) of the 1973 Act. The phrase "is likely to have benefits" in these definitions refers to accrued rights to pension benefits which are not yet in payment.

PPF COMPENSATION

11.1 The phrase "party with compensation rights" is used in FPR Part 9, Chapter 9. For matrimonial proceedings, the phrase has the meaning given to it by section 25G(5) of the Matrimonial Causes Act 1973 and means the party to the marriage who is or is likely to be entitled to PPF compensation. There is a definition of "civil partner with compensation rights" in paragraph 37(1) of Schedule 5 to the Civil Partnership Act 2004 which mirrors the definition of "party with compensation rights" in section 25G(5). The phrase "is likely to be entitled to PPF Compensation" in those definitions refers to statutory entitlement to PPF Compensation which is not yet in payment.

ANNEX
PRE-APPLICATION PROTOCOL

Notes of guidance

Scope of the Protocol

1 This protocol is intended to apply to all applications for a financial remedy as defined by rule 2.3. It is designed to cover all classes of case, ranging from a simple application for periodical payments to an application for a substantial lump sum and property adjustment order. The protocol is designed to facilitate the operation of the procedure for financial remedy applications.

2 In considering the options of pre-application disclosure and negotiation, solicitors should bear in mind the advantage of having a court timetable and court managed process. There is sometimes an advantage in preparing disclosure before proceedings are commenced. However, solicitors should bear in mind the objective of controlling costs and in particular the costs of discovery and that the option of pre-application disclosure and negotiation has risks of excessive and uncontrolled expenditure and delay. This option should only be encouraged where both parties agree to follow this route and disclosure is not likely to be an issue or has been adequately dealt with in mediation or otherwise.

3 Solicitors should consider at an early stage and keep under review whether it would be appropriate to suggest mediation and/or collaborative law to the clients as an alternative to solicitor negotiation or court based litigation.

4 Making an application to the court should not be regarded as a hostile step or a last resort, rather as a way of starting the court timetable, controlling disclosure and endeavouring to avoid the costly final hearing and the preparation for it.

First letter

5 The circumstances of parties to an application for a financial remedy are so various that it would be difficult to prepare a specimen first letter. The request for information

will be different in every case. However, the tone of the initial letter is important and the guidelines in paragraphs 14 and 15 should be followed. It should be approved in advance by the client. Solicitors writing to an unrepresented party should always recommend that he seeks independent legal advice and enclose a second copy of the letter to be passed to any solicitor instructed. A reasonable time limit for an answer may be 14 days.

Negotiation and Settlement

6   In the event of pre-application disclosure and negotiation, as envisaged in paragraph 12 an application should not be issued when a settlement is a reasonable prospect.

Disclosure

7   The protocol underlines the obligation of parties to make full and frank disclosure of all material facts, documents and other information relevant to the issues. Solicitors owe their clients a duty to tell them in clear terms of this duty and of the possible consequences of breach of the duty, which may include criminal sanctions under the Fraud Act 2006. This duty of disclosure is an ongoing obligation and includes the duty to disclose any material changes after initial disclosure has been given. Solicitors are referred to the Good Practice Guide for Disclosure produced by Resolution (obtainable from the Administrative Director, 366A Crofton Road, Orpington, Kent BR2 8NN) and can also contact the Law Society's Practice Advice Service on 0870 606 2522.

The Protocol

General principles

8   All parties must always bear in mind the overriding objective set out at rules 1.1 to 1.4 and try to ensure that applications should be resolved and a just outcome achieved as speedily as possible without costs being unreasonably incurred. The needs of any children should be addressed and safeguarded. The procedures which it is appropriate to follow should be conducted with minimum distress to the parties and in a manner designed to promote as good a continuing relationship between the parties and any children affected as is possible in the circumstances.

9   The principle of proportionality must be borne in mind at all times. It is unacceptable for the costs of any case to be disproportionate to the financial value of the subject matter of the dispute.

10   Parties should be informed that where a court is considering whether to make an order requiring one party to pay the costs of another party, it will take into account pre-application offers to settle and conduct of disclosure.

Identifying the issues

11   Parties must seek to clarify their claims and identify the issues between them as soon as possible. So that this can be achieved, they must provide full, frank and clear disclosure of facts, information and documents, which are material and sufficiently accurate to enable proper negotiations to take place to settle their differences. Openness in all dealings is essential.

Disclosure

12   If parties carry out voluntary disclosure before the issue of proceedings the parties should exchange schedules of assets, income, liabilities and other material facts, using the financial statement as a guide to the format of the disclosure. Documents should only be disclosed to the extent that they are required by the financial statement. Excessive or disproportionate costs should not be incurred.

The Family Procedure Rules 2010

Correspondence

13 Any first letter and subsequent correspondence must focus on the clarification of claims and identification of issues and their resolution. Protracted and unnecessary correspondence and "trial by correspondence" must be avoided.

14 The impact of any correspondence upon the reader and in particular the parties must always be considered. Any correspondence which raises irrelevant issues or which might cause the other party to adopt an entrenched, polarised or hostile position is to be discouraged.

Summary

15 The aim of all pre-application proceedings steps must be to assist the parties to resolve their differences speedily and fairly or at least narrow the issues and, should that not be possible, to assist the court to do so.

PART 10

APPLICATIONS UNDER PART 4 OF THE FAMILY LAW ACT 1996

10.1. Scope and interpretation of this Part
The rules in this Part apply to proceedings under Part 4 of the 1996 Act.

10.2.— Applications for an occupation order or a non-molestation order
(1) An application for an occupation order or a non-molestation order must be supported by a witness statement.

(2) Subject to paragraph (3), an application for an occupation order or a non-molestation order may be made without notice.

(3) An application for an occupation order or a non-molestation order may, in a magistrates' court, be made with the permission of the court without notice in which case the applicant must file the application at the time when the application is made or as directed by the court.

(4) Where an application is made without notice, the witness statement in support of the application must state the reasons why notice has not been given.

(Section 45 of the 1996 Act sets out the criteria for making an order without notice.)

10.3.— Service of the application
(1) In an application made on notice, the applicant must serve—
  (a) a copy of the application together with any statement in support; and
  (b) notice of any hearing or directions appointment set by the court,
on the respondent personally—
    (i) not less than 2 days before the hearing; or
    (ii) within such period as the court may direct.

(2) Where the applicant is acting in person, the applicant may request the court officer to serve the application on the respondent.

(3) In an application for an occupation order under section 33, 35 or 36 of the 1996 Act, the applicant must serve on the mortgagee and any landlord of the dwelling-house in question—
  (a) a copy of the application; and
  (b) notice of the right to make representations in writing or orally at any hearing.

(4) The applicant must file a certificate of service after serving the application.

(Rule 6.23 makes provision for the different methods of serving a document and rule 6.35 provides for the court to authorise service by an alternative method.)

FPR 2010

10.4. Transfer of pending proceedings to another court
Subject to any enactment, where an application for an occupation order or a non-molestation order is pending, the court may transfer the proceedings to another court of its own initiative or on the application of either party.

10.5. Privacy
In the High Court and a county court, any hearing relating to an application for an occupation order or a non-molestation order will be in private unless the court directs otherwise.

10.6.— Service of an order
(1) The applicant must, as soon as reasonably practicable, serve on the respondent personally—
- (a) a copy of the order; and
- (b) where the order is made without notice—
  - (i) a copy of the application together with any statement supporting it; and
  - (ii) in a magistrates' court, a copy of the record of the reasons for a decision.

(Rule 27.2(8) makes provision for the court officer to supply a copy of the reasons for the court's decision to the persons referred to in rule 27.2(9).)

(2) The court must serve the documents listed in paragraph (1) if—
- (a) an applicant, acting in person, so requests; or
- (b) the court made the order of its own initiative.

(3) In an application for an occupation order under section 33, 35 or 36 of the 1996 Act, the applicant must serve a copy of any order made on the mortgagee and any landlord of the dwellinghouse in question.

10.7. Representations made by a mortgagee or landlord
The court may direct that a hearing be held in order to consider any representations made by a mortgagee or a landlord.

10.8. Applications to vary, extend or discharge an order
Rules 10.5 to 10.7 apply to applications to vary, extend or discharge an order.

10.9. Orders containing provisions to which a power of arrest is attached
Where the court makes an occupation order containing one or more provisions to which a power of arrest is attached ("relevant provisions")—
- (a) each relevant provision must be set out in a separate paragraph in the order; and
- (b) a paragraph containing a relevant provision must not include a provision of the order to which the power of arrest is not attached.

10.10.— Service of an order on the officer for the time being in charge of a police station
(1) Where the court makes—
- (a) an occupation order to which a power of arrest is attached; or
- (b) a non-molestation order,

a copy of the order must be delivered to the officer for the time being in charge of—
  - (i) the police station for the applicant's address; or
  - (ii) such other police station as the court may specify.

(2) A copy of the order delivered under paragraph (1) must be accompanied by a statement showing that the respondent has been served with the order or informed of its terms (whether by being present when the order was made or by telephone or otherwise).

(3) The documentation referred to in paragraphs (1) and (2) must be delivered by—
- (a) the applicant; or
- (b) the court officer, where the order was served following a request under rule 10.6(2).

(4) Paragraph (5) applies where an order is made varying or discharging—

(a) a provision of an occupation order to which a power of arrest is attached; or
(b) a provision of a non-molestation order.
(5) The court officer must—
(a) immediately inform—
(i) the officer who received a copy of the order under paragraph (1); and
(ii) if the applicant's address has changed, the officer for the time being in charge of the police station for the new address; and
(b) deliver a copy of the order referred to in paragraph (4)(a) or (b) and the order referred to in paragraph (1) to any officer so informed.

10.11.— Proceedings following arrest in a county court or the High Court
(1) This rule applies where a person is arrested pursuant to—
(a) a power of arrest attached to a provision of an occupation order; or
(b) a warrant of arrest issued on an application under section 47(8) of the 1996 Act.
(2) The court before which a person is brought following arrest may—
(a) determine whether the facts, and the circumstances which led to the arrest, amounted to disobedience of the order; or
(b) adjourn the proceedings.
(3) Where the proceedings are adjourned and the arrested person is released—
(a) unless the court directs otherwise, the matter must be dealt with within 14 days beginning with the date of arrest; and
(b) the arrested person must be given not less than 2 days' notice of the hearing.
(4) An application notice seeking the committal for contempt of court of the arrested person may be issued if the arrested person is not dealt with within the period mentioned in paragraph (3)(a).
(The powers of a county court and the High Court to remand in custody or on bail are contained in section 47 of and Schedule 5 to the Family Law Act 1996.)
(For proceedings following arrest in a magistrates' court see rules made under section 144 of the Magistrates' Courts Act 1980.)

10.12. Enforcement of an order in a county court
Rule 1 of Order 29 of the CCR (enforcement of judgment to do or abstain from doing any act) has effect as if, for paragraph (3), there were substituted the following—
"(3) At the time when the order is drawn up, the court officer will—
(a) where the order made is (or includes) a non-molestation order; or
(b) where the order made is an occupation order and the court so directs,
issue a copy of the order, indorsed with or incorporating a notice as to the consequences of disobedience, for service in accordance with paragraph (2).".
(For enforcement of an order generally in a county court or the High Court see Part 33. For enforcement of an order in a magistrates' court see rules made under section 144 of the Magistrates' Courts Act 1980.)

10.13.— Enforcement of an undertaking in a county court
(1) This rule applies to applications for the enforcement of undertakings by committal order in a county court.
(2) Rule 1A of Order 29 of the CCR (undertaking given by party) applies with the necessary modifications, where an application is made in a county court to commit a person for breach of an undertaking.
(For enforcement of an undertaking in a magistrates' court see rules made under section 144 of the Magistrates' Courts Act 1980.)

10.14. Power to adjourn the hearing for consideration of the penalty
The High Court or a county court may adjourn the hearing for consideration of the penalty to be imposed for any contempt of court found proved and such a hearing may be restored if the respondent does not comply with any conditions specified by the court.

(Rules made under section 144 of the Magistrates' Courts Act 1980 contain an equivalent power for magistrates' courts.)

10.15.— Hospital orders or guardianship orders under the Mental Health Act 1983

(1) Where the High Court or a county court makes a hospital order under the Mental Health Act 1983 the court officer must—

(a) send to the hospital any information which will be of assistance in dealing with the patient; and

(b) inform the applicant when the respondent is being transferred to hospital.

(2) Where the High Court or a county court makes a guardianship order under the Mental Health Act 1983, the court officer must send any information which will be of assistance in dealing with the patient to—

(a) the patient's guardian; and

(b) where the guardian is a person other than the local services authority, the local services authority.

(Section 51 of the 1996 Act provides a magistrates' court with a power to make a hospital order or a guardianship order under the Mental Health Act 1983 and attention is drawn to rules made under section 144 of the Magistrates' Courts Act 1980.)

10.16.— Transfer directions under section 48 of the Mental Health Act 1983

(1) Where a transfer direction given by the Secretary of State under section 48 of the Mental Health Act 1983 is in force in respect of a person remanded in custody by the High Court or a county court, the court officer must notify—

(a) the governor of the prison to which that person was remanded; and

(b) the hospital where that person is detained,

of any committal hearing which that person is required to attend.

(2) The court officer must also give notice in writing of any further remand to the hospital where that person is detained.

(Rules made under section 144 of the Magistrates' Courts Act 1980 make provision for magistrates' courts.)

10.17.— Recognizances

(1) Where, in accordance with paragraph 2(1)(b)(ii) of Schedule 5 to the 1996 Act, the High Court or a county court fixes the amount of any recognizance with a view to it being taken subsequently, the recognizance may be taken by—

(a) a district judge;

(b) a police officer of the rank of inspector or above or in charge of a police station; or

(c) the governor or keeper of a prison where the arrested person is in custody.

(2) The person having custody of an applicant for bail must release that applicant if satisfied that the required recognizances have been taken.

(A magistrates' court has a similar power to require a recognizance under Part 6 of the Magistrates' Courts Act 1980. Section 119 of that Act provides a magistrates' court with a power to postpone the taking of a recognizance and rules made under section 144 of the Magistrates' Courts Act 1980 set out the people who may subsequently take the recognizance.)

PART 10 COMMENTARY

Part 10 is supplemented by PD10A – Part 4 of the Family Law Act 1996.

Part 10 makes provision for procedure in applications under Part 4 of the Family Law Act 1996 – domestic violence.

Rule 10.5 sets out that any hearing relating to an application for an occupation or non-molestation order will be in private unless the court directs otherwise. PD10A supplements this by directing that where a power of arrest is attached and the person to whom it was addressed was not present at the hearing then

The Family Procedure Rules 2010

the terms of the order and to whom it is addressed shall be announced in open court at the earliest opportunity. Further when someone has been arrested under a power of arrest and is brought before the relevant judicial authority the press and the public should be permitted to be present, as the liberty of the subject is involved, unless security needs make this impracticable.

Rules 10.12 and 10.13 deal with the enforcement of orders and undertakings in a county court. They provide that with modification Rules 1 and 1A of the CCR have effect.

PD10A, provides at para 2.1 that an application by a child under the age of 16 years for permission to apply for a non-molestation order or occupation order under s 43 of the 1996 Act is made by application notice in accordance with Part 18 of these rules

Forms relevant to Part 10 are FL401, FL403, FL407, FL415.

PRACTICE DIRECTION 10A – PART 4 OF THE FAMILY LAW ACT 1996

This Practice Direction supplements FPR Part 10

SCOPE OF THIS PRACTICE DIRECTION

1.1 Paragraphs 4.1 to 7.1 of this Practice Direction do not apply to proceedings heard in a magistrates' court. Attention is drawn to rules made under section 144 of the Magistrates' Courts Act 1980.

APPLICATIONS FOR AN OCCUPATION ORDER OR NON-MOLESTATION ORDER MADE BY A CHILD UNDER THE AGE OF SIXTEEN

2.1 If an application for an occupation order or non-molestation order is made by a child under the age of sixteen attention is drawn to section 43 of the 1996 Act. This provides that leave of the court is required for an application made by a child under the age of sixteen. Article 6(b) of the Allocation and Transfer of Proceedings Order 2008 (S.I 2008/2836) provides that such an application must be started in a county court. The application should be made in accordance with Part 18.

PRIVACY

3.1 If at a hearing which has been held in private—

(a) a non-molestation order is made or an occupation order is made to which a power of arrest is attached; and
(b) the person to whom it is addressed was not given notice of the hearing and was not present at the hearing,

the terms of the order and the name of the person to whom it is addressed shall be announced in open court at the earliest opportunity.

3.2 This announcement may be either on the same day when the court proceeds to hear cases in open court or where there is no further business in open court on that day at the next listed sitting of the court.

3.3 When a person arrested under a power of arrest attached to an occupation order cannot conveniently be brought before the relevant judicial authority sitting in a place normally used as a courtroom within 24 hours after the arrest, that person may be brought before the relevant judicial authority at any convenient place. As the liberty of the subject is involved, the press and public should be permitted to be present, unless security needs make this impracticable.

WARRANT OF ARREST ON AN APPLICATION UNDER SECTION 47(8) OF THE 1996 ACT

4.1 In accordance with section 47(9) of the 1996 Act, a warrant of arrest on an application under section 47(8) shall not be issued unless—

(a) the application is substantiated on oath; and
(b) the court has reasonable grounds for believing that the respondent has failed to comply with the order.

ATTENDANCE OF ARRESTING OFFICER

5.1 Attention is drawn to section 47(7) of the 1996 Act. This provides that a person arrested under a power of arrest attached to an occupation order must be brought before a judge within the period of 24 hours beginning at the time of arrest.

5.2 When the arrested person is brought before the judge the attendance of the arresting officer will not be necessary, unless the arrest itself is in issue. A written statement from the arresting officer as to the circumstances of the arrest should normally be sufficient.

5.3 In those cases where the arresting officer was also a witness to the events leading to the arrest and his or her evidence regarding those events is required, arrangements should be made for the arresting officer to attend at a subsequent hearing to give evidence.

APPLICATION FOR BAIL

6.1 An application for bail by a person arrested under—

(a) a power of arrest attached to an occupation order under section 47(2) or (3) of the 1996 Act; or
(b) a warrant of arrest issued on an application under section 47(8) or the 1996 Act,

may be made orally or in writing.

6.2 The court will require the following information, which an application in writing should therefore contain—

(a) the full name of the person making the application;
(b) the address of the place where the person making the application is detained at the time when the application is made;
(c) the address where the person making the application would reside if granted bail;
(d) the amount of the recognizance in which the person making the application would agree to be bound; and
(e) the grounds on which the application is made and, where a previous application has been refused, full particulars of any change in circumstances which has occurred since that refusal.

6.3 An application made in writing must be signed—

(a) by the person making the application or by a person duly authorised by that person in that behalf; or
(b) where the person making the application is a child or is for any reason incapable of acting, by a children's guardian or litigation friend acting on that person's behalf.

6.4 A copy of the application must be served on the person who obtained the injunction.

6.5 A copy of the bail notice must be given to a respondent who is remanded on bail.

REMAND FOR MEDICAL EXAMINATION AND REPORT

7.1 Section 48(4) of the 1996 Act provides that the judge has power to make an order under section 35 of the Mental Health Act 1983 (remand to hospital for report

The Family Procedure Rules 2010

on accused's mental condition) in certain circumstances. If the judge does so attention is drawn to section 35(8) of that Act, which provides that a person remanded to hospital under that section may obtain at his or her own expense an independent report on his or her mental condition from a registered medical practitioner or approved clinician of his or her choice and apply to the court on the basis of it for the remand to be terminated under section 35(7).

PART 11

APPLICATIONS UNDER PART 4A OF THE FAMILY LAW ACT 1996

11.1.— Scope and interpretation

(1) The rules in this Part apply to proceedings in the High Court or a county court under Part 4A of the 1996 Act.

(2) In this Part—

"a forced marriage protection order" means an order under section 63A of the 1996 Act; and

"the person who is the subject of the proceedings" means the person who will be protected by the forced marriage protection order applied for or being considered by the court of its own initiative, if that order is made, or who is being protected by such an order.

11.2.— Applications

(1) An application for a forced marriage protection order may be made without notice.

(2) Where an application is made without notice, it must be supported by a sworn statement explaining why notice has not been given.

(3) An application for a forced marriage protection order made by an organisation must state—

    (a)   the name and address of the person submitting the application; and

    (b)   the position which that person holds in the organisation.

11.3.— Permission to apply

(1) Where the permission of the court is required to apply for a forced marriage protection order, the person seeking permission must file—

    (a)   a Part 18 application notice setting out—

        (i)   the reasons for the application, for the making of which permission is sought ("the proposed application");

        (ii)   the applicant's connection with the person to be protected;

        (iii)   the applicant's knowledge of the circumstances of the person to be protected; and

        (iv)   the applicant's knowledge of the wishes and feelings of the person to be protected; and

    (b)   a draft of the proposed application, together with sufficient copies for one to be served on each respondent and (if different) the person to be protected.

(2) As soon as practicable after receiving an application under paragraph (1), the court must—

    (a)   grant the application; or

    (b)   direct that a date be fixed for the hearing of the application and fix the date.

(3) The court officer must inform the following persons of the court's action under paragraph (2)—

    (a)   the applicant;

    (b)   the respondent;

    (c)   (if different) the person to be protected; and

    (d)   any other person directed by the court.

(4) Where permission is granted to apply for a forced marriage protection order, the application must proceed in accordance with rule 11.2.

11.4.— Service of applications on notice

(1) Subject to paragraphs (3) and (4A), where an application is made on notice, the applicant must serve a copy of the application, together with the notice of proceedings, personally on—
- (a) the respondent;
- (b) the person who is the subject of the proceedings (if that person is neither the applicant nor a respondent); and
- (c) any other person directed by the court,

not less than 2 days before the date on which the application will be heard.

(2) The court may abridge the period specified in paragraph (1).

(3) Service of the application must be effected by the court if the applicant so requests (this does not affect the court's power to order substituted service).

(4) Where the application is served on the person who is the subject of the proceedings, it must be accompanied by a notice informing that person—
- (a) how to apply to become a party to the proceedings; and
- (b) of that person's right to make representations in writing or orally at any hearing.

(5) Where the person who is the subject of proceedings is not the applicant and is—
- (a) a child;
- (b) a person, not being a party, who lacks or may lack capacity within the meaning of the 2005 Act; or
- (c) a protected party,

the court will give the directions about the persons who are to be served with the application.

(6) Where an application is served by the applicant, the applicant must file a certificate of service stating the date and time of personal service.

11.5. Transfer of proceedings

Subject to any enactment, where proceedings to which this Part applies are pending, the court may transfer the proceedings to another court of its own initiative or on the application of a party or (if not a party) the person who is the subject of the proceedings.

11.6.— Parties

(1) In proceedings under this Part, a person may file a Part 18 application notice for that person or another person to—
- (a) be joined as a party; or
- (b) cease to be a party.

(2) As soon as practicable after receiving an application under paragraph (1), the court must do one of the following—
- (a) in the case only of an application under paragraph (1)(a), grant the application;
- (b) order that the application be considered at a hearing, and fix a date for the hearing; or
- (c) invite written representations as to whether the application should be granted, to be filed within a specified period, and upon expiry of that period act under sub-paragraph (a) or (b) as it sees fit.

(3) The court officer must inform the following persons of the court's action under paragraph (2)—
- (a) the applicant under paragraph (1);
- (b) (if different) the applicant for the forced marriage protection order and the respondent to that application;
- (c) (if different) the person who is the subject of the proceedings; and
- (d) any other person directed by the court.

(4) The court may at any time direct—
- (a) that a person who would not otherwise be a respondent under these rules be joined as a party to the proceedings; or

The Family Procedure Rules 2010

(b) that a party to the proceedings cease to be a party,

and such a direction may be made by the court of its own initiative as well as upon an application under paragraph (1).

(5) Where the court directs the addition or removal of a party, it may give consequential directions about—

(a) service on a new party of a copy of the application for the forced marriage protection order and other relevant documents; and

(b) the management of the proceedings.

11.7.— Hearings and service of orders

(1) Any hearing relating to an application for a forced marriage protection order must be in private unless the court otherwise directs.

(2) The court may direct the withholding of any submissions made, or any evidence adduced, for or at any hearing in proceedings to which this Part applies—

(a) in order to protect the person who is the subject of the proceedings or any other person; or

(b) for any other good reason.

(3) The applicant must, as soon as reasonably practical, serve personally—

(a) a copy of the order;

(b) a copy of the record of the hearing; and

(c) where the order is made without notice, a copy of the application together with any statement supporting it,

on the respondent, the person who is the subject of the proceedings (if neither the applicant nor a respondent), and any other person named in the order.

(4) The court must serve the documents listed in paragraph (3) if—

(a) an applicant, acting in person, so requests; or

(b) the court made the order of its own initiative.

11.8.— Orders made by the court of its own initiative

(1) Where the court makes a forced marriage protection order of its own initiative under section 63C of the 1996 Act, it must set out in the order—

(a) a summary of its reasons for making the order; and

(b) the names of the persons who are to be served with the order.

(2) The court may order service of the order on—

(a) any of the parties to the current proceedings;

(b) (if different) the person who is the subject of the proceedings; and

(c) any other person whom the court considers should be served.

(3) The court must give directions as to how the order is to be served.

11.9. Representations in respect of orders

Where the court makes an order (whether under rule 11.7 or 11.8), it may direct that a hearing (or further hearing) be held in order to consider any representations made by any of the persons named in, or directed to be served with, the order.

11.10 Applications to vary, extend or discharge an order

Rules 11.7 and 11.9 apply to applications to vary, extend or discharge a forced marriage protection order.

11.11. Orders containing provisions to which a power of arrest is attached

Where the court makes a forced marriage protection order containing one or more provisions to which a power of arrest is attached ("relevant provision")—

(a) each relevant provision must be set out in a separate paragraph in the order; and

(b) a paragraph containing a relevant provision must not include a provision of the order to which the power of arrest is not attached.

11.12.— Service where order contains a power of arrest

(1) This rule applies where the court makes a forced marriage protection order consisting of or including a relevant provision (which has the meaning given in rule 11.11).

(2) The following documents must be delivered to the officer for the time being in charge of any police station for the address of the person being protected by the order or of such other police station as the court may specify—

    (a) the power of arrest form; and

    (b) a statement showing that the respondents and any persons directed by the court to be served with the order have been so served or informed of its terms (whether by being present when the order was made or by telephone or otherwise).

(3) The documents referred to in paragraph (2) must be delivered by—

    (a) the applicant, if the applicant is responsible for serving the order in accordance with rule 11.7(3); or

    (b) the court officer, if the court is responsible for serving the order in accordance with rule 11.7(4) or a direction given under rule 11.8(3).

(4) Where an order is made varying, extending or discharging any of the relevant provisions, the court officer must—

    (a) immediately inform the officer who received a copy of the power of arrest form under paragraph (2) and, if the address of the person who is the subject of the proceedings has changed, the officer for the time being in charge of the police station for the new address; and

    (b) deliver a copy of the order, together with a copy of the order referred to in paragraph (1), to any officer so informed.

11.13.— Application for issue of warrant for arrest

(1) An application under section 63J(2) of the 1996 Act for the issue of a warrant for the arrest of a person must be supported by a sworn statement.

(2) An application for the issue of a warrant for arrest made by a person who is neither the person who is the subject of the proceedings nor (if different) the person who applied for the order, shall be treated, in the first instance, as an application for permission to apply for the warrant to be issued, and the court shall either—

    (a) grant the application; or

    (b) direct that a date be fixed for the hearing of the application and fix a date.

(3) The court officer must inform the following persons of the court's action under paragraph (2)—

    (a) the person applying for the issue of the warrant;

    (b) the person being protected by the order; and

    (c) any other person directed by the court.

11.14.— Proceedings following arrest

(1) This rule applies where a person is arrested pursuant to—

    (a) a power of arrest attached to a provision of a forced marriage protection order; or

    (b) a warrant of arrest issued on an application under section 63J(2) of the 1996 Act.

(2) The court before whom a person is brought following his arrest may—

    (a) determine whether the facts and the circumstances which led to the arrest amounted to disobedience of the order; or

    (b) adjourn the proceedings.

(3) Where the proceedings are adjourned, the arrested person may be released and—

    (a) unless the court directs otherwise, be dealt with within 14 days of the day on which the person was arrested; and

    (b) be given not less than 2 days' notice of the adjourned hearing.

The Family Procedure Rules 2010

(4) An application notice seeking the committal for contempt of court of the arrested person may be issued if the arrested person is not dealt with within the period mentioned in paragraph (3)(a).

(The powers of a county court and the High Court to remand in custody or on bail are contained in section 47 of and Schedule 5 to the 1996 Act.)

11.15.— Enforcement of orders

(1) The following provisions apply, with the necessary modifications, to the enforcement of orders made under this Part—

 (a) RSC Order 52, rule 7 (power to suspend execution of committal order);

 (b) in a case where an application for an order of committal is made to the High Court, RSC Order 52, rule 2 (application to Divisional Court);

 (c) CCR Order 29, rule 1 (enforcement of judgment to do or abstain from doing any act);

 (d) CCR Order 29, rule 1A (undertaking given by party);

 (e) CCR Order 29, rule 3 (discharge of person in custody).

(2) Rule 1 of Order 29 of the CCR (enforcement of judgment to do or abstain from doing any act) has effect as if, for paragraph (3), there were substituted the following—

 "(3) At the time when the order is drawn up, the court officer will, where the order made is (or includes) a forced marriage protection order, issue a copy of the order, indorsed with or incorporating a notice as to the consequences of disobedience, for service in accordance with paragraph (2)."

(For enforcement of an order generally in a county court or the High Court see Part 33.)

11.16. Power to adjourn the hearing for consideration of the penalty

The court may adjourn the hearing for consideration of the penalty to be imposed for any contempt of court found proved and such hearing may be restored if the contemnor does not comply with any conditions specified by the court.

11.17.— Hospital orders or guardianship orders under the Mental Health Act 1983

(1) Where the court makes a hospital order under the Mental Health Act 1983, the court officer must—

 (a) send to the hospital any information which will be of assistance in dealing with the patient; and

 (b) inform the persons directed by the court to be informed about when the patient is being transferred to hospital.

(2) Where the court makes a guardianship order under the Mental Health Act 1983, the court officer must send any information which will be of assistance in dealing with the patient to—

 (a) the patient's guardian; and

 (b) where the guardian is a person other than the local services authority, the local services authority.

11.18.— Transfer directions under section 48 of the Mental Health Act 1983

(1) Where a transfer direction given by the Secretary of State under section 48 of the Mental Health Act 1983 is in force in respect of a person remanded in custody by the court, the court officer must notify—

 (a) the governor of the prison to which that person was remanded; and

 (b) the hospital where that person is detained,

of any committal hearing which that person is required to attend.

(2) The court officer must also give notice in writing of any further remand to the hospital where that person is detained.

11.19.— Recognizances

(1) Where, in accordance with paragraph 2(1)(b)(ii) of Schedule 5 to the 1996 Act, the court fixes the amount of any recognizance with a view to it being taken subsequently, the recognizance may be taken by—

 (a) a district judge;

(b) a police officer of the rank of inspector or above or in charge of a police station; or
(c) the governor or keeper of a prison where the arrested person is in the custody of that governor or keeper.

(2) The person having custody of an applicant for bail must release him if satisfied that the required recognizances have been taken.

PART 11 COMMENTARY

Part 11 is not supplemented by a practice direction.

Part 11 makes provision for procedure in applications under Part 4A of the Family Law Act 1996 – forced marriage protection orders.

Rule 11.3 provides that where permission of the court is required to apply for a forced marriage protection order then a Part 18 application is required.

Rule 11.7(1) sets out that any hearing relating to an application for a forced marriage protection order will be in private unless the court directs otherwise.

Rule 11.15 deals with the enforcement of orders by applying, with the necessary modifications, RSC Order 52, r 7 and r 2, and CCR Order 29, r 1, 1A, and 3 (with express modification).

Forms relevant to Part 11 are FL401A, FL403A, FL407A, FL430, FL431.

PART 12

PROCEEDINGS RELATING TO CHILDREN EXCEPT PARENTAL ORDER PROCEEDINGS AND PROCEEDINGS FOR APPLICATIONS IN ADOPTION, PLACEMENT AND RELATED PROCEEDINGS

CHAPTER 1

INTERPRETATION AND APPLICATION OF THIS PART

12.1.— Application of this Part

(1) The rules in this Part apply to—
 (a) emergency proceedings;
 (b) private law proceedings;
 (c) public law proceedings;
 (d) proceedings relating to the exercise of the court's inherent jurisdiction (other than applications for the court's permission to start such proceedings);
 (e) proceedings relating to child abduction and the recognition and enforcement of decisions relating to custody under the European Convention;
 (f) proceedings relating to the Council Regulation or the 1996 Hague Convention in respect of children; and
 (g) any other proceedings which may be referred to in a practice direction.

(Part 18 sets out the procedure for making an application for permission to bring proceedings.)

(Part 31 sets out the procedure for making applications for recognition and enforcement of judgments under the Council Regulation or the 1996 Hague Convention.)

(2) The rules in Chapter 7 of this Part also apply to family proceedings which are not within paragraph (1) but which otherwise relate wholly or mainly to the maintenance or upbringing of a minor.

The Family Procedure Rules 2010

12.2. Interpretation

In this Part—

"the 2006 Act" means the Childcare Act 2006;

"advocate" means a person exercising a right of audience as a representative of, or on behalf of, a party;

"care proceedings" means proceedings for a care order under section 31(1)(a) of the 1989 Act;

"Case Management Order" means an order in the form referred to in Practice Direction 12A which may contain such of the provisions listed in that practice direction as may be appropriate to the proceedings;

"child assessment order" has the meaning assigned to it by section 43(2) of the 1989 Act;

"contact activity condition" has the meaning assigned to it by section 11C(2) of the 1989 Act;

"contact activity direction" has the meaning assigned to it by section 11A(3) of the 1989 Act;

"contribution order" has the meaning assigned to it by paragraph 23(2) of Schedule 2 to the 1989 Act;

"education supervision order" has the meaning assigned to it by section 36(2) of the 1989 Act;

"emergency proceedings" means proceedings for—

(a) the disclosure of information as to the whereabouts of a child under section 33 of the 1986 Act;

(b) an order authorising the taking charge of and delivery of a child under section 34 of the 1986 Act;

(c) an emergency protection order;

(d) an order under section 44(9)(b) of the 1989 Act varying a direction in an emergency protection order given under section 44(6) of that Act;

(e) an order under section 45(5) of the 1989 Act extending the period during which an emergency protection order is to have effect;

(f) an order under section 45(8) of the 1989 Act discharging an emergency protection order;

(g) an order under section 45(8A) of the 1989 Act varying or discharging an emergency protection order in so far as it imposes an exclusion requirement on a person who is not entitled to apply for the order to be discharged;

(h) an order under section 45(8B) of the 1989 Act varying or discharging an emergency protection order in so far as it confers a power of arrest attached to an exclusion requirement;

(i) warrants under sections 48(9) and 102(1) of the 1989 Act and under section 79 of the 2006 Act; or

(j) a recovery order under section 50 of the 1989 Act;

"emergency protection order" means an order under section 44 of the 1989 Act;

"enforcement order" has the meaning assigned to it by section 11J(2) of the 1989 Act;

"financial compensation order" means an order made under section 11O(2) of the 1989 Act;

"interim order" means an interim care order or an interim supervision order referred to in section 38(1) of the 1989 Act;

"private law proceedings" means proceedings for—

(a) a section 8 order except a residence order under section 8 of the 1989 Act relating to a child who is the subject of a care order;

(b) a parental responsibility order under sections 4(1)(c), 4ZA(1)(c) or 4A(1)(b) of the 1989 Act or an order terminating parental responsibility under sections 4(2A), 4ZA(5) or 4A(3) of that Act;

(c) an order appointing a child's guardian under section 5(1) of the 1989 Act or an order terminating the appointment under section 6(7) of that Act;

(d) an order giving permission to change a child's surname or remove a child from the United Kingdom under sections 13(1) or 14C(3) of the 1989 Act;

(e) a special guardianship order except where that order relates to a child who is subject of a care order;
(f) an order varying or discharging such an order under section 14D of the 1989 Act;
(g) an enforcement order;
(h) a financial compensation order;
(i) an order under paragraph 9 of Schedule A1 to the 1989 Act following a breach of an enforcement order;
(j) an order under Part 2 of Schedule A1 to the 1989 Act revoking or amending an enforcement order; or
(k) an order that a warning notice be attached to a contact order;

"public law proceedings" means proceedings for—
(a) a residence order under section 8 of the 1989 Act relating to a child who is the subject of a care order;
(b) a special guardianship order relating to a child who is the subject of a care order;
(c) a secure accommodation order under section 25 of the 1989 Act;
(d) a care order, or the discharge of such an order under section 39(1) of the 1989 Act;
(e) an order giving permission to change a child's surname or remove a child from the United Kingdom under section 33(7) of the 1989 Act;
(f) a supervision order under section 31(1)(b) of the 1989 Act, the discharge or variation of such an order under section 39(2) of that Act, or the extension or further extension of such an order under paragraph 6(3) of Schedule 3 to that Act;
(g) an order making provision regarding contact under section 34(2) to (4) of the 1989 Act or an order varying or discharging such an order under section 34(9) of that Act;
(h) an education supervision order, the extension of an education supervision order under paragraph 15(2) of Schedule 3 to the 1989 Act, or the discharge of such an order under paragraph 17(1) of Schedule 3 to that Act;
(i) an order varying directions made with an interim care order or interim supervision order under section 38(8)(b) of the 1989 Act;
(j) an order under section 39(3) of the 1989 Act varying a supervision order in so far as it affects a person with whom the child is living but who is not entitled to apply for the order to be discharged;
(k) an order under section 39(3A) of the 1989 Act varying or discharging an interim care order in so far as it imposes an exclusion requirement on a person who is not entitled to apply for the order to be discharged;
(l) an order under section 39(3B) of the 1989 Act varying or discharging an interim care order in so far as it confers a power of arrest attached to an exclusion requirement;
(m) the substitution of a supervision order for a care order under section 39(4) of the 1989 Act;
(n) a child assessment order, or the variation or discharge of such an order under section 43(12) of the 1989 Act;
(o) an order permitting the local authority to arrange for any child in its care to live outside England and Wales under paragraph 19(1) of Schedule 2 to the 1989 Act;
(p) a contribution order, or revocation of such an order under paragraph 23(8) of Schedule 2 to the 1989 Act;
(q) an appeal under paragraph 8(1) of Schedule 8 to the 1989 Act;

"special guardianship order" has the meaning assigned to it by section 14A(1) of the 1989 Act;
"supervision order" has the meaning assigned to it by section 31(11) of the 1989 Act;

The Family Procedure Rules 2010

"supervision proceedings" means proceedings for a supervision order under section 31(1)(b) of the 1989 Act;

"warning notice" means a notice attached to an order pursuant to section 8(2) of the Children and Adoption Act 2006.

(The 1980 Hague Convention, the 1996 Hague Convention, the Council Regulation, and the European Convention are defined in rule 2.3.)

CHAPTER 2

General rules

12.3.— Who the parties are

(1) In relation to the proceedings set out in column 1 of the following table, column 2 sets out who may make the application and column 3 sets out who the respondents to those proceedings will be.

Proceedings for	Applicants	Respondents
A parental responsibility order (section 4(1)(c), 4ZA(1)(c), or section 4A(1)(b) of the 1989 Act).	The child's father;	Every person whom the applicant believes to have parental responsibility for the child;
	the step parent; or	where the child is the subject of a care order, every person whom the applicant believes to have had parental responsibility immediately prior to the making of the care order;
	the child's parent (being a woman who is a parent by virtue of section 43 of the Human Fertilisation and Embryology Act 2008 and who is not a person to whom section 1(3) of the Family Law Reform Act 1987 applies) (sections 4(1)(c), 4ZA(1)(c) and 4A(1)(b) of the 1989 Act).	in the case of an application to extend, vary or discharge an order, the parties to the proceedings leading to the order which it is sought to have extended, varied or discharged; in the case of specified proceedings, the child.
An order terminating a parental responsibility order or agreement (section 4(2A), 4ZA(5) or section 4A(3) of the 1989 Act.	Any person who has parental responsibility for the child; or with the court's permission, the child (section 4(3), 4ZA(6) and section 4A(3) of the 1989 Act).	As above.
An order appointing a guardian (section 5(1) of the 1989 Act.	An individual who wishes to be appointed as guardian (section 5(1) of the 1989 Act).	As above.
An order terminating the appointment of a guardian (section 6(7) of the 1989 Act).	Any person who has parental responsibility for the child; or with the court's permission, the child (section 6(7) of the 1989 Act).	As above.

FPR 2010

Proceedings for	Applicants	Respondents
A section 8 order.	Any person who is entitled to apply for a section 8 order with respect to the child (section 10(4) to (7) of the 1989 Act); or with the court's permission, any person (section 10(2)(b) of the 1989 Act).	As above.
An enforcement order (section	A person who is, for the purposes of the contact order, a person with	The person the applicant alleges has failed to comply with the contact order.

Proceedings for	Applicants	Respondents
11J of the 1989 Act).	whom the child concerned lives or is to live; any person whose contact with the child concerned is provided for in the contact order; any individual subject to a condition under section 11(7)(b) of the 1989 Act or a contact activity condition imposed by a contact order; or with the court's permission, the child (section 11J(5) of the 1989 Act).	
A financial compensation order (section 11O of the 1989 Act).	Any person who is, for the purposes of the contact order, a person with whom the child concerned lives or is to live; any person whose contact with the child concerned is provided for in the contact order; any individual subject to a condition under section 11(7)(b) of the 1989 Act or a contact activity condition imposed by a contact order; or with the court's permission, the child (section 11O(6) of the 1989 Act).	The person the applicant alleges has failed to comply with the contact order.
An order permitting the child's name to be changed or the removal of the child from the United Kingdom (section 13(1), 14C(3) or 33(7) of the 1989 Act).	Any person (section 13(1), 14C(3), 33(7) of the 1989 Act).	As for a parental responsibility order.

351

The Family Procedure Rules 2010

Proceedings for	Applicants	Respondents
A special guardianship order (section 14A of the 1989 Act).	Any guardian of the child; any individual in whose favour a residence order is in force with respect to the child; any individual listed in subsection (5)(b) or (c) of section 10 (as read with subsection (10) of that section) of the 1989 Act; a local authority foster parent with whom the child has lived for a period of at least one year immediately preceding the application; or any person with the court's permission (section 14A(3) of the 1989 Act) (more than one such individual can apply jointly (section 14A(3) and (5) of that Act)).	As above, and if a care order is in force with respect to the child, the child.
Variation or discharge of a special guardianship order (section 14D of the 1989 Act).	The special guardian (or any of them, if there is more than one); any individual in whose favour a residence order is in force with respect to the child; the local authority designated in a care order with respect to the child; any individual within section 14D(1)(d) of the 1989 Act who has parental responsibility for the child; the child, any parent or guardian of the child and any step-parent of the child who has acquired, and has not lost, parental responsibility by virtue of section 4A of that Act with the court's permission; or any individual within section 14D(1)(d) of that Act who immediately before the making of the special guardianship order had, but no longer has, parental responsibility for the child with the court's permission.	As above.

Proceedings for	Applicants	Respondents
A secure accommodation order (section 25 section of the 1989 Act).	The local authority which is looking after the child; or the Health Authority, Primary Care Trust, National Health Service Trust established under section 25 of the National Health Service Act 2006 or section 18(1) of the National Health Service (Wales) Act 2006, National Health Service Foundation Trust or any local authority providing accommodation for the child (unless the child is looked after by a local authority).	As above.
A care or supervision order (section 31 of the 1989 Act).	Any local authority; the National Society for the Prevention of Cruelty to Children and any of its officers (section 31(1) of the 1989 Act); or any authorised person.	As above.
An order varying directions made with an interim care or interim supervision order (section 38(8)(b) of the 1989 Act).	The parties to proceedings in which directions are given under section 38(6) of the 1989 Act; or any person named in such a direction.	As above.
An order discharging a care order (section 39(1) of the 1989 Act).	Any person who has parental responsibility for the child; the child; or the local authority designated by the order (section 39(1) of the 1989 Act).	As above.
An order varying or discharging an interim care order in so far as it imposes an exclusion requirement (section 39(3A) of the 1989 Act).	A person to whom the exclusion requirement in the interim care order applies who is not entitled to apply for the order to be discharged (section 39(3A) of the 1989 Act).	As above.

Proceedings for	Applicants	Respondents
An order varying or discharging an interim care order in so far as it confers a power of arrest attached to an exclusion requirement (section 39(3B) of the 1989 Act).	Any person entitled to apply for the discharge of the interim care order in so far as it imposes the exclusion requirement (section 39(3B) of the 1989 Act).	As above.

The Family Procedure Rules 2010

Proceedings for	Applicants	Respondents
An order substituting a supervision order for a care order (section 39(4) of the 1989 Act).	Any person entitled to apply for a care order to be discharged under section 39(1) (section 39(4) of the 1989 Act).	As above.
A child assessment order (section 43(1) of the 1989 Act).	Any local authority; the National Society for the Prevention of Cruelty to Children and any of its officers; or any person authorised by order of the Secretary of State to bring the proceedings and any officer of a body who is so authorised (section 43(1) and (13) of the 1989 Act).	As above.
An order varying or discharging a child assessment order (section 43(12) of the 1989 Act).	The applicant for an order that has been made under section 43(1) of the 1989 Act; or the persons referred to in section 43(11) of the 1989 Act (section 43(12) of that Act).	As above.
An emergency protection order (section 44(1) of the 1989 Act).	Any person (section 44(1) of the 1989 Act).	As for a parental responsibility order.
An order extending the period during which an emergency protection order is to have effect (section 45(4) of the 1989 Act).	Any person who— has parental responsibility for a child as the result of an emergency protection order; and is entitled to apply for a care order with respect to the child (section 45(4) of the 1989 Act).	As above.
An order discharging an emergency protection order (section 45(8) of the 1989 Act).	The child; a parent of the child; any person who is not a parent of the child but who has parental responsibility for the child; or any person with whom the child was living before the making of the emergency protection order (section 45(8) of the 1989 Act).	As above.
An order varying or discharging an emergency protection order in so far as it imposes the exclusion requirement (section 45(8A) of the 1989 Act).	A person to whom the exclusion requirement in the emergency protection order applies who is not entitled to apply for the emergency protection order to be discharged (section 45(8A) of the 1989 Act).	As above.

Proceedings for	Applicants	Respondents
An order varying or discharging an emergency protection order in so far as it confers a power of arrest attached to an exclusion requirement (section 45(8B) of the 1989 Act).	Any person entitled to apply for the discharge of the emergency protection order in so far as it imposes the exclusion requirement (section 45(8B) of the 1989 Act).	As above.
An emergency protection order by the police (section 46(7) of the 1989 Act).	The officer designated for the purposes of section 46(3)(e) of the 1989 Act (section 46(7) of the 1989 Act).	As above.
A warrant authorising a constable to assist in exercise of certain powers to search for children and inspect premises (section 48 of the 1989 Act).	Any person attempting to exercise powers under an emergency protection order who has been or is likely to be prevented from doing so by being refused entry to the premises concerned or refused access to the child concerned (section 48(9) of the 1989 Act).	As above.
A warrant authorising a constable to assist in exercise of certain powers to search for children and inspect premises (section 102 of the 1989 Act).	Any person attempting to exercise powers under the enactments mentioned in section 102(6) of the 1989 Act who has been or is likely to be prevented from doing so by being refused entry to the premises concerned or refused access to the child concerned (section 102(1) of that Act).	As above.
An order revoking an enforcement order (paragraph 4 of Schedule A1 to the 1989 Act).	The person subject to the enforcement order.	The person who was the applicant for the enforcement order; and, where the child was a party to the proceedings in which the enforcement order was made, the child.
An order amending an enforcement order (paragraphs 5 to 7 of Schedule A1 to the 1989 Act).	The person subject to the enforcement order.	The person who was the applicant for the enforcement order. (Rule 12.33 makes provision about applications under paragraph 5 of Schedule A1 to the 1989 Act.)
An order following breach of an enforcement order (paragraph 9 of Schedule A1 to the 1989 Act).	Any person who is, for the purposes of the contact order, the person with whom the child lives or is to live; any person whose contact with the child concerned is provided for in the contact order;	The person the applicant alleges has failed to comply with the unpaid work requirement imposed by an enforcement order; and where the child was a party to the proceedings in which the enforcement order was made, the child.

The Family Procedure Rules 2010

Proceedings for	Applicants	Respondents
	any individual subject to a condition under section 11(7)(b) of the 1989 Act or a contact activity condition imposed by a contact order; or	
	with the court's permission, the child (paragraph 9 of Schedule A1 to the 1989 Act).	
An order permitting the local authority to arrange for any child in its care to live outside England and Wales (Schedule 2, paragraph 19(1), to the 1989 Act).	The local authority (Schedule 2, paragraph 19(1), to the 1989 Act).	As for a parental responsibility order.
A contribution order (Schedule 2, paragraph 23(1), to the 1989 Act).	The local authority (Schedule 2, paragraph 23(1), to the 1989 Act).	As above and the contributor.
An order revoking a contribution order (Schedule 2, paragraph 23(8), to the 1989 Act).	The contributor; or the local authority.	As above.
An order relating to contact with the child in care and any named person (section 34(2) of the 1989 Act) or permitting the local authority to refuse contact (section 34(4) of that Act).	The local authority; or the child (section 34(2) or 34(4) of the 1989 Act).	As above; and the person whose contact with the child is the subject of the application.
An order relating to contact with the child in care (section 34(3) of the 1989 Act).	The child's parents; any guardian or special guardian of the child; any person who by virtue of section 4A of the 1989 Act has parental responsibility for the child; a person in whose favour there was a residence order in force with respect to the child immediately before the care order was made; a person who by virtue of an order made in the exercise of the High Court's inherent jurisdiction with respect to children had care of the child immediately before the care order was made (section 34(3)(a) of the 1989 Act); or	As above; and the person whose contact with the child is the subject of the application.

FPR 2010

Proceedings for	Applicants	Respondents
	with the court's permission, any person (section 34(3) (b) of that Act).	
An order varying or discharging an order for contact with a child in care under section 34 (section 34(9) of the 1989 Act).	The local authority; the child; or any person named in the order (section 34(9) of the 1989 Act).	As above; and the person whose contact with the child is the subject of the application.
An education supervision order (section 36 of the 1989 Act).	Any local authority (section 36(1) of the 1989 Act).	As above; and the child.
An order varying or discharging a supervision order (section 39(2) of the 1989 Act).	Any person who has parental responsibility for the child; the child; or the supervisor (section 39(2) of the 1989 Act).	As above; and the supervisor.
An order varying a supervision order in so far as it affects the person with whom the child is living (section 39(3) of the 1989 Act).	The person with whom the child is living who is not entitled to apply for the order to be discharged (section 39(3) of the 1989 Act).	As above; and the supervisor.
An order varying a direction under section 44(6) of the 1989 Act in an emergency protection order (section 44(9)(b) of that Act).	The parties to the application for the emergency protection order in respect of which it is sought to vary the directions; the children's guardian; the local authority in whose area the child is ordinarily resident; or any person who is named in the directions.	As above, and the parties to the application for the order in respect of which it is sought to vary the directions; any person who was caring for the child prior to the making of the order; and any person whose contact with the child is affected by the direction which it is sought to have varied.
A recovery order (section 50 of the 1989 Act).	Any person who has parental responsibility for the child by virtue of a care order or an emergency protection order; or where the child is in police protection the officer designated for the purposes of section 46(3)(e) of the 1989 Act (section 50(4) of the 1989 Act).	As above; and the person whom the applicant alleges to have effected or to have been or to be responsible for the taking or keeping of the child.

The Family Procedure Rules 2010

Proceedings for	Applicants	Respondents
An order discharging an education supervision order (Schedule 3, paragraph 17(1), to the 1989 Act).	The child concerned; a parent of the child; or the local authority concerned (Schedule 3, paragraph 17(1), to the 1989 Act).	As above; and the local authority concerned; and the child.
An order extending an education supervision order (Schedule 3, paragraph, 15(2), to the 1989 Act).	The local authority in whose favour the education supervision order was made (Schedule 3, paragraph 15(2), to the 1989 Act).	As above; and the child.
An appeal under paragraph (8) of Schedule 8 to the 1989 Act.	A person aggrieved by the matters listed in paragraph 8(1) of Schedule 8 to the 1989 Act.	The appropriate local authority.
An order for the disclosure of information as to the whereabouts of a child under section 33 of the 1986 Act.	Any person with a legitimate interest in proceedings for an order under Part 1 of the 1986 Act; or a person who has registered an order made elsewhere in the United Kingdom or a specified dependent territory.	Any person alleged to have information as to the whereabouts of the child.
An order authorising the taking charge of and delivery of a child under section 34 of the 1986 Act.	The person to whom the child is to be given up under section 34(1) of the 1986 Act.	As above; and the person who is required to give up the child in accordance with section 34(1) of the 1986 Act.
An order relating to the exercise of the court's inherent jurisdiction (including wardship proceedings).	A local authority (with the court's permission); any person with a genuine interest in or relation to the child; or the child (wardship proceedings only).	The parent or guardian of the child; any other person who has an interest in or relationship to the child; and the child (wardship proceedings only and with the court's permission as described at rule 12.37).
A warrant under section 79 of the 2006 Act authorising any constable to assist Her Majesty's Chief Inspector for Education, Children's Services and Skills in the exercise of powers conferred on him by section 77 of the 2006 Act.	Her Majesty's Chief Inspector for Education, Children's Services and Skills.	Any person preventing or likely to prevent Her Majesty's Chief Inspector for Education, Children's Services and Skills from exercising powers conferred on him by section 77 of the 2006 Act.

Proceedings for	Applicants	Respondents
An order in respect of a child under the 1980 Hague Convention.	Any person, institution or body who claims that a child has been removed or retained in breach of rights of custody or claims that there has been a breach of rights of access in relation to the child.	The person alleged to have brought the child into the United Kingdom; the person with whom the child is alleged to be; any parent or guardian of the child who is within the United Kingdom and is not otherwise a party; any person in whose favour a decision relating to custody has been made if that person is not otherwise a party; and any other person who appears to the court to have sufficient interest in the welfare of the child.
An order concerning the recognition and enforcement of decisions relating to custody under the European Convention.	Any person who has a court order giving that person rights of custody in relation to the child.	As above.
An application for the High Court to request transfer of jurisdiction under Article 15 of the Council Regulation or Article 9 of the 1996 Hague Convention (rule 12.65).	Any person with sufficient interest in the welfare of the child and who would be entitled to make a proposed application in relation to that child, or who intends to seek the permission of the court to make such application if the transfer is agreed.	As directed by the court in accordance with rule 12.65.
An application under rule 12.71 for a declaration as to the existence, or extent, of parental responsibility under Article 16 of the 1996 Convention.	Any interested person including a person who holds, or claims to hold, parental responsibility for the child under the law of another State which subsists in accordance with Article 16 of the 1996 Hague Convention following the child becoming habitually resident in a territorial unit of the United Kingdom.	Every person whom the applicant believes to have parental responsibility for the child; any person whom the applicant believes to hold parental responsibility for the child under the law of another State which subsists in accordance with Article 16 of the 1996 Hague Convention following the child becoming habitually resident in a territorial unit of the United Kingdom; and

The Family Procedure Rules 2010

Proceedings for	Applicants	Respondents
		where the child is the subject of a care order, every person whom the applicant believes to have had parental responsibility immediately prior to the making of the care order.
A warning notice.	The person who is, for the purposes of the contact order, the person with whom the child concerned lives or is to live; the person whose contact with the child concerned is provided for in the contact order; any individual subject to a condition under section 11(7)(b) of the 1989 Act or a contact activity condition imposed by the contact order; or with the court's permission, the child.	Any person who was a party to the proceedings in which the contact order was made. (Rule 12.33 makes provision about applications for warning notices).

(2) The court will direct that a person with parental responsibility be made a party to proceedings where that person requests to be one.

(3) Subject to rule 16.2, the court may at any time direct that—

    (a) any person or body be made a party to proceedings; or

    (b) a party be removed.

(4) If the court makes a direction for the addition or removal of a party under this rule, it may give consequential directions about—

    (a) the service of a copy of the application form or other relevant documents on the new party;

    (b) the management of the proceedings.

(5) In this rule—

"a local authority foster parent" has the meaning assigned to it by section 23(3) of the 1989 Act; and

"care home", "independent hospital", "local authority" and "Primary Care Trust" have the meanings assigned to them by section 105 of the 1989 Act.

(Part 16 contains the rules relating to the representation of children.)

12.4.— Notice of proceedings to person with foreign parental responsibility

(1) This rule applies where a child is subject to proceedings to which this Part applies and —

    (a) a person holds or is believed to hold parental responsibility for the child under the law of another State which subsists in accordance with Article 16 of the 1996 Hague Convention following the child becoming habitually resident in a territorial unit of the United Kingdom; and

    (b) that person is not otherwise required to be joined as a respondent under rule 12.3.

(2) The applicant shall give notice of the proceedings to any person to whom the applicant believes paragraph (1) applies in any case in which a person whom the applicant believed to have parental responsibility under the 1989 Act would be a respondent to those proceedings in accordance with rule 12.3.

(3) The applicant and every respondent to the proceedings shall provide such details as they possess as to the identity and whereabouts of any person they believe to hold parental responsibility for the child in accordance with paragraph (1) to the court officer, upon making, or responding to the application as appropriate.

(4) Where the existence of a person who is believed to have parental responsibility for the child in accordance with paragraph (1) only becomes apparent to a party at a later date during the proceedings, that party must notify the court officer of those details at the earliest opportunity.

(5) Where a person to whom paragraph (1) applies receives notice of proceedings, that person may apply to the court to be joined as a party using the Part 18 procedure.

12.5. What the court will do when the application has been issued

When the proceedings have been issued the court will consider—
- (a) setting a date for—
  - (i) a directions appointment;
  - (ii) in private law proceedings, a First Hearing Dispute Resolution Appointment;
  - (iii) in care and supervision proceedings and in so far as practicable other public law proceedings, the First Appointment; or
  - (iv) the hearing of the application or an application for an interim order, and if the court sets a date it will do so in accordance with rule 12.13 and Practice Directions 12A and 12B;
- (b) giving any of the directions listed in rule 12.12 or, where Chapter 6, section 1 applies, rule 12.48; and
- (c) doing anything else which is set out in Practice Directions 12A or 12B or any other practice direction.

(Practice Directions 12A and 12B supplementing this Part set out details relating to the First Hearing Dispute Resolution Appointment and the First Appointment.)

12.6. Children's guardian, solicitor and reports under section 7 of the 1989 Act

As soon as practicable after the issue of proceedings or the transfer of the proceedings to the court, the court will—
- (a) in specified proceedings, appoint a children's guardian under rule 16.3(1) unless—
  - (i) such an appointment has already been made by the court which made the transfer and is subsisting; or
  - (ii) the court considers that such an appointment is not necessary to safeguard the interests of the child;
- (b) where section 41(3) of the 1989 Act applies, consider whether a solicitor should be appointed to represent the child, and if so, appoint a solicitor accordingly;
- (c) consider whether to ask an officer of the service or a Welsh family proceedings officer for advice relating to the welfare of the child;
- (d) consider whether a report relating to the welfare of the child is required, and if so, request such a report in accordance with section 7 of the 1989 Act.

(Part 16 sets out the rules relating to representation of children.)

12.7.— What a court officer will do

(1) As soon as practicable after the issue of proceedings the court officer will return to the applicant the copies of the application together with the forms referred to in Practice Direction 5A.

(2) As soon as practicable after the issue of proceedings or the transfer of proceedings to the court or at any other stage in the proceedings the court officer will—
- (a) give notice of any hearing set by the court to the applicant; and
- (b) do anything else set out in Practice Directions 12A or 12B or any other practice direction.

12.8. Service of the application

The applicant will serve—

(a) the application together with the documents referred to in Practice Direction 12C on the persons referred to and within the time specified in that Practice Direction; and

(b) notice of any hearing set by the court on the persons referred to in Practice Direction 12C at the same time as serving the application.

12.9.— Request for transfer from magistrates' court to county court or to another magistrates' court

(1) In accordance with the Allocation Order, a magistrates' court may order proceedings before the court (or any part of them) to be transferred to another magistrates' court or to a county court.

(2) Where any request to transfer proceedings to another magistrates' court or to a county court is refused, the court officer will send a copy of the written record of the reasons for refusing the transfer to the parties.

12.10.— Procedure following refusal of magistrates' court to order transfer

(1) Where a request under rule 12.9 to transfer proceedings to a county court in accordance with the provisions of the Allocation Order is refused, a party to the proceedings may apply to a county court for an order transferring proceedings from the magistrates' court.

(2) Such an application must be made in accordance with Part 18 and the Allocation Order.

12.11. Transfer of proceedings from one court to another court

Where proceedings are transferred from one court to another court in accordance with the provisions of the Allocation Order, the court officer from the transferring court will notify the parties of any order transferring the proceedings.

12.12.— Directions

(1) This rule does not apply to proceedings under Chapter 6 of this Part.

(2) At any stage in the proceedings, the court may give directions about the conduct of the proceedings including—

(a) the management of the case;
(b) the timetable for steps to be taken between the giving of directions and the final hearing;
(c) the joining of a child or other person as a party to the proceedings in accordance with rules 12.3(2) and (3);
(d) the attendance of the child;
(e) the appointment of a children's guardian or of a solicitor under section 41(3) of the 1989 Act;
(f) the appointment of a litigation friend;
(g) the service of documents;
(h) the filing of evidence including experts' reports; and
(i) the exercise by an officer of the Service, Welsh family proceedings officer or local authority officer of any duty referred to in rule 16.38(1)

(3) Paragraph (4) applies where—

(a) an officer of the Service or a Welsh family proceedings officer has filed a report or a risk assessment as a result of exercising a duty referred to in rule 16.38(1)(a); or
(b) a local authority officer has filed a report as a result of exercising a duty referred to in rule 16.38(1)(b).

(4) The court may—

(a) give directions setting a date for a hearing at which that report or risk assessment will be considered; and
(b) direct that the officer who prepared the report or risk assessment attend any such hearing.

(5) The court may exercise the powers in paragraphs (2) and (4) on an application or of its own initiative.

(6) Where the court proposes to exercise its powers of its own initiative the procedure set out in rule 4.3(2) to (6) applies.

(7) Directions of a court which are still in force immediately prior to the transfer of proceedings to another court will continue to apply following the transfer subject to—
- (a) any changes of terminology which are required to apply those directions to the court to which the proceedings are transferred; and
- (b) any variation or revocation of the direction.

(8) The court or court officer will—
- (a) take a note of the giving, variation or revocation of a direction under this rule; and
- (b) as soon as practicable serve a copy of the note on every party.

(Rule 12.48 provides for directions in proceedings under the 1980 Hague Convention and the European Convention.)

12.13.— Setting dates for hearings and setting or confirming the timetable and date for the final hearing

(1) At the—
- (a) transfer to a court of proceedings;
- (b) postponement or adjournment of any hearing; or
- (c) conclusion of any hearing at which the proceedings are not finally determined,

the court will set a date for the proceedings to come before the court again for the purposes of giving directions or for such other purposes as the court directs.

(2) At any hearing the court may—
- (a) confirm a date for the final hearing or the week within which the final hearing is to begin (where a date or period for the final hearing has already been set);
- (b) set a timetable for the final hearing unless a timetable has already been fixed, or the court considers that it would be inappropriate to do so; or
- (c) set a date for the final hearing or a period within which the final hearing of the application is to take place.

(3) The court officer will notify the parties of—
- (a) the date of a hearing fixed in accordance with paragraph (1);
- (b) the timetable for the final hearing; and
- (c) the date of the final hearing or the period in which it will take place.

(4) Where the date referred to in paragraph (1) is set at the transfer of proceedings, the date will be as soon as possible after the transfer.

(5) The requirement in paragraph (1) to set a date for the proceedings to come before the court again is satisfied by the court setting or confirming a date for the final hearing.

12.14.— Attendance at hearings

(1) This rule does not apply to proceedings under Chapter 6 of this Part except for proceedings for a declaration under rule 12.71.

(2) Unless the court directs otherwise and subject to paragraph (3), the persons who must attend a hearing are—
- (a) any party to the proceedings;
- (b) any litigation friend for any party or legal representative instructed to act on that party's behalf; and
- (c) any other person directed by the court or required by Practice Directions 12A or 12B or any other practice direction to attend.

(3) Proceedings or any part of them will take place in the absence of a child who is a party to the proceedings if—
- (a) the court considers it in the interests of the child, having regard to the matters to be discussed or the evidence likely to be given; and
- (b) the child is represented by a children's guardian or solicitor.

The Family Procedure Rules 2010

(4) When considering the interests of the child under paragraph (3) the court will give—
    (a) the children's guardian;
    (b) the solicitor for the child; and
    (c) the child, if of sufficient understanding,
an opportunity to make representations.

(5) Subject to paragraph (6), where at the time and place appointed for a hearing, the applicant appears but one or more of the respondents do not, the court may proceed with the hearing.

(6) The court will not begin to hear an application in the absence of a respondent unless the court is satisfied that—
    (a) the respondent received reasonable notice of the date of the hearing; or
    (b) the circumstances of the case justify proceeding with the hearing.

(7) Where, at the time and place appointed for a hearing one or more of the respondents appear but the applicant does not, the court may—
    (a) refuse the application; or
    (b) if sufficient evidence has previously been received, proceed in the absence of the applicant.

(8) Where at the time and place appointed for a hearing neither the applicant nor any respondent appears, the court may refuse the application.

(9) Paragraphs (5) to (8) do not apply to a hearing where the court—
    (a) is considering—
        (i) whether to make a contact activity direction or to attach a contact activity condition to a contact order; or
        (ii) an application for a financial compensation order, an enforcement order or an order under paragraph 9 of Schedule A1 to the 1989 Act following a breach of an enforcement order; and
    (b) has yet to obtain sufficient evidence from, or in relation to, the person who may be the subject of the direction, condition or order to enable it to determine the matter.

(10) Nothing in this rule affects the provisions of Article 18 of the Council Regulation in cases to which that provision applies.

(The Council Regulation makes provision in Article 18 for the court to stay proceedings where the respondent is habitually resident in another Member State of the European Union and has not been adequately served with the proceedings as required by that provision.)

12.15. Steps taken by the parties

If—
    (a) the parties or any children's guardian agree proposals for the management of the proceedings (including a proposed date for the final hearing or a period within which the final hearing is to take place); and
    (b) the court considers that the proposals are suitable,
it may approve them without a hearing and give directions in the terms proposed.

12.16.— Applications without notice

(1) This rule applies to—
    (a) proceedings for a section 8 order;
    (b) emergency proceedings; and
    (c) proceedings relating to the exercise of the court's inherent jurisdiction (other than an application for the court's permission to start such proceedings and proceedings for collection, location and passport orders where Chapter 6 applies).

(2) An application in proceedings referred to in paragraph (1) may, in the High Court or a county court, be made without notice in which case the applicant must file the application—

(a) where the application is made by telephone, the next business day after the making of the application; or
(b) in any other case, at the time when the application is made.

(3) An application in proceedings referred to in paragraph (1)(a) or (b) may, in a magistrates' court, be made with the permission of the court, without notice, in which case the applicant must file the application at the time when the application is made or as directed by the court.

(4) Where—
(a) a section 8 order;
(b) an emergency protection order;
(c) an order for the disclosure of information as to the whereabouts of a child under section 33 of the 1986 Act; or
(d) an order authorising the taking charge of and delivery of a child under section 34 of the 1986 Act,

is made without notice, the applicant must serve a copy of the application on each respondent within 48 hours after the order is made.

(5) Within 48 hours after the making of an order without notice, the applicant must serve a copy of the order on—
(a) the parties, unless the court directs otherwise;
(b) any person who has actual care of the child or who had such care immediately prior to the making of the order; and
(c) in the case of an emergency protection order and a recovery order, the local authority in whose area the child lives or is found.

(6) Where the court refuses to make an order on an application without notice it may direct that the application is made on notice in which case the application will proceed in accordance with rules 12.3 to 12.15.

(7) Where the hearing takes place outside the hours during which the court office is normally open, the court or court officer will take a note of the proceedings.

(Practice Direction 12E (Urgent Business) provides further details of the procedure for out of hours applications. See also Practice Direction 12D (Inherent Jurisdiction (including Wardship Proceedings)).)

(Rule 12.47 provides for without-notice applications in proceedings under Chapter 6, section 1 of this Part, (proceedings under the 1980 Hague Convention and the European Convention).)

12.17.— Investigation under section 37 of the 1989 Act

(1) This rule applies where a direction is given to an appropriate authority by the court under section 37(1) of the 1989 Act.
(2) On giving the direction the court may adjourn the proceedings.
(3) As soon as practicable after the direction is given the court will record the direction.
(4) As soon as practicable after the direction is given the court officer will—
(a) serve the direction on—
 (i) the parties to the proceedings in which the direction is given; and
 (ii) the appropriate authority where it is not a party;
(b) serve any documentary evidence directed by the court on the appropriate authority.

(5) Where a local authority informs the court of any of the matters set out in section 37(3)(a) to (c) of the 1989 Act it will do so in writing.

(6) Unless the court directs otherwise, the court officer will serve a copy of any report to the court under section 37 of the 1989 Act on the parties.

(Section 37 of the 1989 Act refers to the appropriate authority and section 37(5) of that Act sets out which authority should be named in a particular case.)

12.18.— Disclosure of a report under section 14A(8) or (9) of the 1989 Act

(1) In proceedings for a special guardianship order, the local authority must file the report under section 14A(8) or (9) of the 1989 Act[a] within the timetable fixed by the court.

The Family Procedure Rules 2010

(2) The court will consider whether to give a direction that the report under section 14A(8) or (9) of the 1989 Act be disclosed to each party to the proceedings.

(3) Before giving a direction for the report to be disclosed, the court must consider whether any information should be deleted from the report.

(4) The court may direct that the report must not be disclosed to a party.

(5) The court officer must serve a copy of the report in accordance with any direction under paragraph (2).

(6) In paragraph (3), information includes information which a party has declined to reveal under rule 29.1(1).

12.19.— Additional evidence

(1) This rule applies to proceedings for a section 8 order or a special guardianship order.

(2) Unless the court directs otherwise, a party must not—
- (a) file or serve any document other than in accordance with these rules or any practice direction;
- (b) in completing a form prescribed by these rules or any practice direction, give information or make a statement which is not required or authorised by that form; or
- (c) file or serve at a hearing—
  - (i) any witness statement of the substance of the oral evidence which the party intends to adduce; or
  - (ii) any copy of any document (including any experts' report) which the party intends to rely on.

(3) Where a party fails to comply with the requirements of this rule in relation to any witness statement or other document, the party cannot seek to rely on that statement or other document unless the court directs otherwise.

12.20.— Expert evidence-examination of child

(1) No person may cause the child to be medically or psychiatrically examined, or otherwise assessed, for the purpose of preparation of expert evidence for use in the proceedings without the court's permission.

(2) Where the court's permission has not been given under paragraph (1), no evidence arising out of an examination or assessment referred to in that paragraph may be adduced without the court's permission.

12.21.— Hearings

(1) The court may give directions about the order of speeches and the evidence at a hearing.

(2) Subject to any directions given under paragraph (1), the parties and the children's guardian must adduce their evidence at a hearing in the following order—
- (a) the applicant;
- (b) any party with parental responsibility for the child;
- (c) other respondents;
- (d) the children's guardian;
- (e) the child, if the child is a party to proceedings and there is no children's guardian.

CHAPTER 3

SPECIAL PROVISIONS ABOUT PUBLIC LAW PROCEEDINGS

12.22. Application of rules 12.23 to 12.26

Rules 12.23 to 12.26 apply to care and supervision proceedings and in so far as practicable other public law proceedings.

12.23.— Timetable for the Child
(1) The court will set the timetable for the proceedings in accordance with the Timetable for the Child.
(2) The "Timetable for the Child" means the timetable set by the court in accordance with its duties under section 1 and 32 of the 1989 Act and will—
- (a) take into account dates of the significant steps in the life of the child who is the subject of the proceedings; and
- (b) be appropriate for that child.

12.24. Directions
The court will direct the parties to—
- (a) monitor compliance with the court's directions; and
- (b) tell the court or court officer about—
  - (i) any failure to comply with a direction of the court; and
  - (ii) any other delay in the proceedings.

12.25.— First Appointment, Case Management Conference and Issues Resolution Hearing
(1) The court may set the date for the First Appointment, Case Management Conference and Issues Resolution Hearing at the times and in the circumstances referred to in Practice Direction 12A.
(2) The matters which the court will consider at the hearings referred to in paragraph (1) are set out in Practice Direction 12A.

12.26.— Discussion between advocates
(1) When setting a date for a Case Management Conference or an Issues Resolution Hearing the court will direct a discussion between the parties' advocates to—
- (a) discuss the provisions of a draft of the Case Management Order; and
- (b) consider any other matter set out in Practice Direction 12A.

(2) Where there is a litigant in person the court will give directions about how that person may take part in the discussions between the parties' advocates.
(3) The court will direct that following a discussion between advocates they must prepare or amend a draft of the Case Management Order for the court to consider.
(4) Where it is not possible for the advocates to agree the terms of a draft of the Case Management Order, the advocates should specify on a draft of the Case Management Order or on a separate document if more practicable—
- (a) those provisions on which they agree; and
- (b) those provisions on which they disagree.

(5) Unless the court directs otherwise—
- (a) any discussion between advocates must take place no later than 2 days; and
- (b) a draft of the Case Management Order must be filed with the court no later than 1 day,

before the Case Management Conference or the Issues Resolution Hearing whichever may be appropriate.
(6) For the purposes of this rule "advocate" includes a litigant in person.

12.27.— Matters prescribed for the purposes of the Act
(1) Proceedings for an order under any of the following provisions of the 1989 Act—
- (a) a secure accommodation order under section 25;
- (b) an order giving permission to change a child's surname or remove a child from the United Kingdom under section 33(7);
- (c) an order permitting the local authority to arrange for any child in its care to live outside England and Wales under paragraph 19(1) of Schedule 2;
- (d) the extension or further extension of a supervision order under paragraph 6(3) of Schedule 3;
- (e) appeals against the determination of proceedings of a kind set out in sub-paragraphs (a) to (d);

The Family Procedure Rules 2010

are specified for the purposes of section 41 of that Act in accordance with section 41(6)(i) of that Act.

(2) The persons listed as applicants in the table set out in rule 12.3 to proceedings for the variation of directions made with interim care or interim supervision orders under section 38(8) of the 1989 Act are the prescribed class of persons for the purposes of that section.

(3) The persons listed as applicants in the table set out in rule 12.3 to proceedings for the variation of a direction made under section 44(6) of the 1989 Act in an emergency protection order are the prescribed class of persons for the purposes of section 44(9) of that Act.

12.28.— Exclusion requirements: interim care orders and emergency protection orders

(1) This rule applies where the court includes an exclusion requirement in an interim care order or an emergency protection order.

(2) The applicant for an interim care order or emergency protection order must—
- (a) prepare a separate statement of the evidence in support of the application for an exclusion requirement;
- (b) serve the statement personally on the relevant person with a copy of the order containing the exclusion requirement (and of any power of arrest which is attached to it);
- (c) inform the relevant person of that person's right to apply to vary or discharge the exclusion requirement.

(3) Where a power of arrest is attached to an exclusion requirement in an interim care order or an emergency protection order, the applicant will deliver—
- (a) a copy of the order; and
- (b) a statement showing that the relevant person has been served with the order or informed of its terms (whether by being present when the order was made or by telephone or otherwise),

to the officer for the time being in charge of the police station for the area in which the dwellinghouse in which the child lives is situated (or such other police station as the court may specify).

(4) Rules 10.6(2) and 10.10 to 10.17 will apply, with the necessary modifications, for the service, variation, discharge and enforcement of any exclusion requirement to which a power of arrest is attached as they apply to an order made on an application under Part 4 of the 1996 Act.

(5) The relevant person must serve the parties to the proceedings with any application which that person makes for the variation or discharge of the exclusion requirement.

(6) Where an exclusion requirement ceases to have effect whether—
- (a) as a result of the removal of a child under section 38A(10) or 44A(10) of the 1989 Act;
- (b) because of the discharge of the interim care order or emergency protection order; or
- (c) otherwise,

the applicant must inform—
- (i) the relevant person;
- (ii) the parties to the proceedings;
- (iii) any officer to whom a copy of the order was delivered under paragraph (3); and
- (iv) (where necessary) the court.

(7) Where the court includes an exclusion requirement in an interim care order or an emergency protection order of its own motion, paragraph (2) will apply with the omission of any reference to the statement of the evidence.

(8) In this rule, "the relevant person" has the meaning assigned to it by sections 38A(2) and 44A(2) of the 1989 Act.

12.29.— Notification of consent

(1) Consent for the purposes of the following provisions of the 1989 Act—

(a) section 16(3);
(b) section 38A(2)(b)(ii) or 44A(2)(b)(ii); or
(c) paragraph 19(3)(c) or (d) of Schedule 2,

must be given either—
    (i) orally to the court; or
    (ii) in writing to the court signed by the person giving consent.

(2) Any written consent for the purposes of section 38A(2) or 44A(2) of the 1989 Act must include a statement that the person giving consent—
(a) is able and willing to give to the child the care which it would be reasonable to expect a parent to give; and
(b) understands that the giving of consent could lead to the exclusion of the relevant person from the dwelling-house in which the child lives.

12.30. Proceedings for secure accommodation orders: copies of reports

In proceedings under section 25 of the 1989 Act, the court will, if practicable, arrange for copies of all written reports filed in the case to be made available before the hearing to—
(a) the applicant;
(b) the parent or guardian of the child to whom the application relates;
(c) any legal representative of the child;
(d) the children's guardian; and
(e) the child, unless the court directs otherwise,

and copies of the reports may, if the court considers it desirable, be shown to any person who is entitled to notice of any hearing in accordance with Practice Direction 12C.

CHAPTER 4

SPECIAL PROVISIONS ABOUT PRIVATE LAW PROCEEDINGS

12.31.— The First Hearing Dispute Resolution Appointment

(1) The court may set a date for the First Hearing Dispute Resolution Appointment after the proceedings have been issued.

(2) The court officer will give notice of any of the dates so fixed to the parties.

(Provisions relating to the timing of and issues to be considered at the First Hearing Dispute Resolution Appointment are contained in Practice Direction 12B.)

12.32. Answer

A respondent must file and serve on the parties an answer to the application for an order in private law proceedings within 14 days beginning with the date on which the application is served.

12.33.— Applications for warning notices or applications to amend enforcement orders by reason of change of residence

(1) This rule applies in relation to an application to the High Court or a county court for—
(a) a warning notice to be attached to a contact order; or
(b) an order under paragraph 5 of Schedule A1 to the 1989 Act to amend an enforcement order by reason of change of residence.

(2) The application must be made without notice.

(3) The court may deal with the application without a hearing.

(4) If the court decides to deal with the application at a hearing, rules 12.5, 12.7 and 12.8 will apply.

12.34.— Service of a risk assessment

(1) Where an officer of the Service or a Welsh family proceedings officer has filed a risk assessment with the court, subject to paragraph (2), the court officer will as soon as practicable serve copies of the risk assessment on each party.

(2) Before serving the risk assessment, the court must consider whether, in order to prevent a risk of harm to the child, it is necessary for—
- (a) information to be deleted from a copy of the risk assessment before that copy is served on a party; or
- (b) service of a copy of the risk assessment (whether with information deleted from it or not) on a party to be delayed for a specified period,

and may make directions accordingly.

12.35.— Service of enforcement orders or orders amending or revoking enforcement orders

(1) Paragraphs (2) and (3) apply where the High Court or a county court makes—
- (a) an enforcement order; or
- (b) an order under paragraph 9(2) of Schedule A1 to the 1989 Act (enforcement order made following a breach of an enforcement order).

(2) As soon as practicable after an order has been made, a copy of it must be served by the court officer on—
- (a) the parties, except the person against whom the order is made;
- (b) the officer of the Service or the Welsh family proceedings officer who is to comply with a request under section 11M of the 1989 Act to monitor compliance with the order; and
- (c) the responsible officer.

(3) Unless the court directs otherwise, the applicant must serve a copy of the order personally on the person against whom the order is made.

(4) The court officer must send a copy of an order made under paragraph 4, 5, 6 or 7 of Schedule A1 to the 1989 Act (revocation or amendment of an enforcement order) to—
- (a) the parties;
- (b) the officer of the Service or the Welsh family proceedings officer who is to comply with a request under section 11M of the 1989 Act to monitor compliance with the order;
- (c) the responsible officer; and
- (d) in the case of an order under paragraph 5 of Schedule A1 to the 1989 Act (amendment of enforcement order by reason of change of residence), the responsible officer in the former local justice area.

(5) In this rule, "responsible officer" has the meaning given in paragraph 8(8) of Schedule A1 to the 1989 Act.

CHAPTER 5

Special provisions about inherent jurisdiction proceedings

12.36.— Where to start proceedings

(1) An application for proceedings under the Inherent Jurisdiction of the court must be started in the High Court.

(2) Wardship proceedings, except applications for an order that a child be made or cease to be a ward of court, may be transferred to the county court unless the issues of fact or law make them more suitable for hearing in the High Court.

(The question of suitability for hearing in the High Court is explained in Practice Direction 12D (Inherent Jurisdiction (including Wardship Proceedings)).)

12.37.— Child as respondent to wardship proceedings

(1) A child who is the subject of wardship proceedings must not be made a respondent to those proceedings unless the court gives permission following an application under paragraph (2).

(2) Where nobody other than the child would be a suitable respondent to wardship proceedings, the applicant may apply without notice for permission to make the wardship application—
- (a) without notice; or

(b) with the child as the respondent.

12.38. Registration requirements
The court officer will send a copy of every application for a child to be made a ward of court to the principal registry for recording in the register of wards.

12.39.— Notice of child's whereabouts
(1) Every respondent, other than a child, must file with the acknowledgment of service a notice stating—
    (a) the respondent's address; and
    (b) either—
        (i) the whereabouts of the child; or
        (ii) that the respondent is unaware of the child's whereabouts if that is the case.

(2) Unless the court directs otherwise, the respondent must serve a copy of that notice on the applicant.

(3) Every respondent other than a child must immediately notify the court in writing of—
    (a) any subsequent changes of address; or
    (b) any change in the child's whereabouts,
and, unless the court directs otherwise, serve a copy of that notice on the applicant.

(4) In this rule a reference to the whereabouts of a child is a reference to—
    (a) the address at which the child is living;
    (b) the person with whom the child is living; and
    (c) any other information relevant to where the child may be found.

12.40. Enforcement of orders in wardship proceedings
The High Court may secure compliance with any direction relating to a ward of court by an order addressed to the tipstaff.
(The role of the tipstaff is explained in Practice Direction 12D (Inherent Jurisdiction (including Wardship Proceedings)).)

12.41.— Child ceasing to be ward of court
(1) A child who, by virtue of section 41(2) of the Senior Courts Act 1981, automatically becomes a ward of court on the making of a wardship application will cease to be a ward on the determination of the application unless the court orders that the child be made a ward of court.

(2) Nothing in paragraph (1) affects the power of the court under section 41(3) of the Senior Courts Act 1981 to order that any child cease to be a ward of court.

12.42. Adoption of a child who is a ward of court
An application for permission—
    (a) to start proceedings to adopt a child who is a ward of court;
    (b) to place such a child for adoption with parental consent; or
    (c) to start proceedings for a placement order in relation to such a child,
may be made without notice in accordance with Part 18.

CHAPTER 6

PROCEEDINGS UNDER THE 1980 HAGUE CONVENTION, THE EUROPEAN CONVENTION, THE COUNCIL REGULATION, AND THE 1996 HAGUE CONVENTION

12.43. Scope
This Chapter applies to —
    (a) proceedings relating to children under the 1980 Hague Convention or the European Convention; and
    (b) applications relating to the Council Regulation or the 1996 Hague Convention in respect of children.

The Family Procedure Rules 2010

SECTION 1

PROCEEDINGS UNDER THE 1980 HAGUE CONVENTION OR THE EUROPEAN CONVENTION

12.44. Interpretation

In this section—
"the 1985 Act" means the Child Abduction and Custody Act 1985;
"Central Authority" means, in relation to England and Wales, the Lord Chancellor;
"Contracting State" has the meaning given in—
- (a) section 2 of the 1985 Act in relation to the 1980 Hague Convention; and
- (b) section 13 of the 1985 Act in relation to the European Convention; and

"decision relating to custody" has the same meaning as in the European Convention. ("the 1980 Hague Convention" and the "the European Convention" are defined in rule 2.3)

12.45. Where to start proceedings

Every application under the 1980 Hague Convention or the European Convention must be—
- (a) made in the High Court and issued in the principal registry; and
- (b) heard by a Judge of the High Court unless the application is;
  - (i) to join a respondent; or
  - (ii) to dispense with service or extend the time for acknowledging service.

12.46. Evidence in support of application

Where the party making an application under this section does not produce the documents referred to in Practice Direction 12F, the court may—
- (a) fix a time within which the documents are to be produced;
- (b) accept equivalent documents; or
- (c) dispense with production of the documents if the court considers it has sufficient information.

12.47.— Without-notice applications

(1) This rule applies to applications—
- (a) commencing or in proceedings under this section;
- (b) for interim directions under section 5 or 19 of the 1985 Act;
- (c) for the disclosure of information about the child and for safeguarding the child's welfare, under rule 12.57;
- (d) for the disclosure of relevant information as to where the child is, under section 24A of the 1985 Act; or
- (e) for a collection order, location order or passport order.

(2) Applications under this rule may be made without notice, in which case the applicant must file the application—
- (a) where the application is made by telephone, the next business day after the making of the application; or
- (b) in any other case, at the time when the application is made.

(3) Where an order is made without notice, the applicant must serve a copy of the order on the other parties as soon as practicable after the making of the order, unless the court otherwise directs.

(4) Where the court refuses to make an order on an application without notice, it may direct that the application is made on notice.

(5) Where any hearing takes place outside the hours during which the court office is usually open—
- (a) if the hearing takes place by telephone, the applicant's solicitors will, if practicable, arrange for the hearing to be recorded; and
- (b) in all other cases, the court or court officer will take a note of the proceedings.

(Practice Direction 12E (Urgent Business) provides further details of the procedure for out of hours applications. See also Practice Direction 12D (Inherent Jurisdiction (including Wardship Proceedings)).)

12.48.— Directions

(1) As soon as practicable after an application to which this section applies has been made, the court may give directions as to the following matters, among others—

- (a) whether service of the application may be dispensed with;
- (b) whether the proceedings should be transferred to another court under rule 12.54;
- (c) expedition of the proceedings or any part of the proceedings (and any direction for expedition may specify a date by which the court must issue its final judgment in the proceedings or a specified part of the proceedings);
- (d) the steps to be taken in the proceedings and the time by which each step is to be taken;
- (e) whether the child or any other person should be made a party to the proceedings;
- (f) if the child is not made a party to the proceedings, the manner in which the child's wishes and feelings are to be ascertained, having regard to the child's age and maturity and in particular whether an officer of the Service or a Welsh family proceedings officer should report to the court for that purpose;
- (g) where the child is made a party to the proceedings, the appointment of a children's guardian for that child unless a children's guardian has already been appointed;
- (h) the attendance of the child or any other person before the court;
- (i) the appointment of a litigation friend for a child or for any protected party, unless a litigation friend has already been appointed;
- (j) the service of documents;
- (k) the filing of evidence including expert evidence; and
- (l) whether the parties and their representatives should meet at any stage of the proceedings and the purpose of such a meeting.

(Rule 16.2 provides for when the court may make the child a party to the proceedings and rule 16.4 for the appointment of a children's guardian for the child who is made a party. Rule 16.5 (without prejudice to rule 16.6) requires a child who is a party to the proceedings but not the subject of those proceedings to have a litigation friend.)

(2) Directions of a court which are in force immediately prior to the transfer of proceedings to another court under rule 12.54 will continue to apply following the transfer subject to—

- (a) any changes of terminology which are required to apply those directions to the court to which the proceedings are transferred; and
- (b) any variation or revocation of the directions.

(3) The court or court officer will—

- (a) take a note of the giving, variation or revocation of directions under this rule; and
- (b) as soon as practicable serve a copy of the directions order on every party.

12.49.— Answer

(1) Subject to paragraph (2) and to any directions given under rule 12.48, a respondent must file and serve on the parties an answer to the application within 7 days beginning with the date on which the application is served.

(2) The court may direct a longer period for service where the respondent has been made a party solely on one of the following grounds—

- (a) a decision relating to custody has been made in the respondent's favour; or
- (b) the respondent appears to the court to have sufficient interest in the welfare of the child.

The Family Procedure Rules 2010

12.50.— Filing and serving written evidence

(1) The respondent to an application to which this section applies may file and serve with the answer a statement verified by a statement of truth, together with any further evidence on which the respondent intends to rely.

(2) The applicant may, within 7 days beginning with the date on which the respondent's evidence was served under paragraph (1), file and serve a statement in reply verified by a statement of truth, together with any further evidence on which the applicant intends to rely.

12.51. Adjournment

The court will not adjourn the hearing of an application to which this section applies for more than 21 days at at any one time.

12.52.— Stay of proceedings upon notification of wrongful removal etc.

(1) In this rule and in rule 12.53—
- (a) "relevant authority" means —
  - (i) the High Court;
  - (ii) a county court;
  - (iii) a magistrates' court;
  - (iv) the Court of Session;
  - (v) a sheriff court;
  - (vi) a children's hearing within the meaning of section 93 of the Children (Scotland) Act 1995;
  - (vii) the High Court in Northern Ireland;
  - (viii) a county court in Northern Ireland;
  - (ix) a court of summary jurisdiction in Northern Ireland;
  - (x) the Royal Court of Jersey;
  - (xi) a court of summary jurisdiction in Jersey;
  - (xii) the High Court of Justice of the Isle of Man;
  - (xiii) a court of summary jurisdiction in the Isle of Man; or
  - (xiv) the Secretary of State; and
- (b) "rights of custody" has the same meaning as in the 1980 Hague Convention.

(2) Where a party to proceedings under the 1980 Hague Convention knows that an application relating to the merits of rights of custody is pending in or before a relevant authority, that party must file within the proceedings under the 1980 Hague Convention a concise statement of the nature of that application, including the relevant authority in or before which it is pending.

(3) On receipt of a statement filed in accordance with paragraph (2) above, a court officer will notify the relegant authority in or before which the application is pending and will subsequently notify the relevant authority of the result of the proceedings.

(4) On receipt by the relevant authority of a notification under paragraph (3) from the High Court or equivalent notification from the Court of Session, the High Court in Northern Ireland or the High Court of Justice of the Isle of Man—
- (a) all further proceedings in the action will be stayed[GL] unless and until the proceedings under the 1980 Hague Convention in the High Court, Court of Session, the High Court in Northern Ireland or the High Court of Justice of the Isle of Man are dismissed; and
- (b) the parties to the action will be notified by the court officer of the stay[GL] and dismissal.

12.53.— Stay of proceedings where application made under s.16 of the 1985 Act (registration of decisions under the European Convention)

(1) A person who—
- (a) is a party to—
  - (i) proceedings under section 16 of the 1985 Act; or
  - (ii) proceedings as a result of which a decision relating to custody has been registered under section 16 of the 1985 Act; and

(b) knows that an application is pending under—
  (i) section 20(2) of the 1985 Act;
  (ii) Article 21(2) of the Child Abduction and Custody (Jersey) Law 2005; or
  (iii) section 42(2) of the Child Custody Act 1987 (an Act of Tynwald),
  must file within the proceedings under section 16 of the 1985 Act a concise statement of the nature of the pending application.

(2) On receipt of a statement filed in accordance with paragraph (1) above, a court officer will notify the relevant authority in or before which the application is pending and will subsequently notify the relevant authority of the result of the proceedings.

(3) On receipt by the relevant authority of a notification under paragraph (2) from the High Court or equivalent notification from the Court of Session, the High Court in Northern Ireland or the High Court of Justice of the Isle of Man, the court officer will notify the parties to the action.

12.54.— Transfer of proceedings

(1) At any stage in proceedings under the 1985 Act the court may-
  (a) of its own initiative; or
  (b) on the application of a party with a minimum of two days' notice;
order that the proceedings be transferred to a court listed in paragraph (4).

(2) Where the court makes an order for transfer under paragraph (1)—
  (a) the court will state its reasons on the face of the order;
  (b) a court officer will send a copy of the order, the application and the accompanying documents (if any) and any evidence to the court to which the proceedings are transferred; and
  (c) the costs of the proceedings both before and after the transfer will be at the discretion of the court to which the proceedings are transferred.

(3) Where proceedings are transferred to the High Court from a court listed in paragraph (4), a court officer will notify the parties of the transfer and the proceedings will continue as if they had been commenced in the High Court.

(4) The listed courts are the Court of Session, the High Court in Northern Ireland, the Royal Court of Jersey or the High Court of Justice of the Isle of Man.

12.55.— Revocation and variation of registered decisions

(1) This rule applies to decisions which—
  (a) have been registered under section 16 of the 1985 Act; and
  (b) are subsequently varied or revoked by an authority in the Contracting State in which they were made.

(2) The court will, on cancelling the registration of a decision which has been revoked, notify—
  (a) the person appearing to the court to have care of the child;
  (b) the person on whose behalf the application for registration of the decision was made; and
  (c) any other party to the application.

(3) The court will, on being informed of the variation of a decision, notify—
  (a) the party appearing to the court to have care of the child; and
  (b) any party to the application for registration of the decision;
and any such person may apply to make representations to the court before the registration is varied.

(4) Any person appearing to the court to have an interest in the proceedings may apply for the registration of a decision for the cancellation or variation of the decision referred to in paragraph (1).

12.56. The central index of decisions registered under the 1985 Act

A central index of decisions registered under section 16 of the 1985 Act, together with any variation of those decisions made under section 17 of that Act, will be kept by the principal registry.

The Family Procedure Rules 2010

12.57. Disclosure of information in proceedings under the European Convention
At any stage in proceedings under the European Convention the court may, if it has reason to believe that any person may have relevant information about the child who is the subject of those proceedings, order that person to disclose such information and may for that purpose order that the person attend before it or file affidavit[GL] evidence.

SECTION 2

APPLICATIONS RELATING TO THE COUNCIL REGULATION AND THE 1996 HAGUE CONVENTION

12.58.— Interpretation
(1) In this section —
"Central Authority" means, in relation to England and Wales, the Lord Chancellor;
"Contracting State" means a State party to the 1996 Hague Convention;
"judgment" has the meaning given in Article 2(4) of the Council Regulation;
"Member State" means a Member State bound by the Council Regulation or a country which has subsequently adopted the Council Regulation;
"parental responsibility" has the meaning given in —
  (a) Article 2(7) of the Council Regulation in relation to proceedings under that Regulation; and
  (b) Article 1(2) of the 1996 Hague Convention in relation to proceedings under that Convention; and
"seised" has the meaning given in Article 16 of the Council Regulation.

(2) In rules 12.59 to 12.70, references to the court of another member State or Contracting State include authorities within the meaning of "court" in Article 2(1) of the Council Regulation, and authorities of Contracting States which have jurisdiction to take measures directed to the protection of the person or property of the child within the meaning of the 1996 Hague Convention.

12.59.— Procedure under Article 11(6) of the Council Regulation where the court makes a nonreturn order under Article 13 of the 1980 Hague Convention

(1) Where the court makes an order for the non-return of a child under Article 13 of the 1980 Hague Convention, it must immediately transmit the documents referred to in Article 11(6) of the Council Regulation —
  (a) directly to the court with jurisdiction or the central authority in the Member State where the child was habitually resident immediately before the wrongful removal to, or wrongful retention in, England and Wales; or
  (b) to the Central Authority for England and Wales for onward transmission to the court with jurisdiction or the central authority in the other Member State mentioned in subparagraph (a).

(2) The documents required by paragraph (1) must be transmitted by a method which, in the case of direct transmission to the court with jurisdiction in the other Member State, ensures and, in any other case, will not prevent, their receipt by that court within one month of the date of the non-return order.

12.60.— Procedure under Article 11(7) of the Council Regulation where the court receives a nonreturn order made under Article 13 of the 1980 Hague Convention by a court in another Member State

(1) This rule applies where the court receives an order made by a court in another Member State for the non-return of a child.

(2) In this rule, the order for non-return of the child and the papers transmitted with that order from the court in the other Member State are referred to as "the non-return order".

(3) Where, at the time of receipt of the non-return order, the court is already seised of a question of parental responsibility in relation to the child, —
  (a) the court officer shall immediately —

(i) serve copies of the non-return order on each party to the proceedings in which a question of parental responsibility in relation to the child is at issue; and

(ii) where the non-return order was received directly from the court or the central authority in the other Member State, transmit to the Central Authority for England and Wales a copy of the non-return order.

(b) the court shall immediately invite the parties to the 1980 Hague Convention proceedings to file written submissions in respect of the question of custody by a specified date, or to attend a hearing to consider the future conduct of the proceedings in the light of the nonreturn order.

(4) Where, at the time of receipt of the non-return order, the court is not already seised of the question of parental responsibility in relation to the child, it shall immediately—

(a) open a court file in respect of the child and assign a court reference to the file;

(b) serve a copy of the non-return order on each party to the proceedings before the court in the Member State which made that order;

(c) invite each party to file, within 3 months of notification to that party of receipt of the non-return order, submissions in the form of—

(i) an application for an order under—
(aa) the 1989 Act; or
(bb) (in the High Court only) an application under the inherent jurisdiction in respect of the child; or

(ii) where permission is required to make an application for the order in question, an application for that permission;

(d) where the non-return order was received directly from the court or central authority in the other Member State, transmit to the Central Authority for England and Wales a copy of the non-return order.

(5) In a case to which paragraph (4) applies where no application is filed within the 3 month period provided for by paragraph (4)(c) the court must close its file in respect of the child.

(Enforcement of a subsequent judgment requiring the return of the child, made under Article 11(8) by a court examining custody of the child under Article 11(7), is dealt with in Part 31 below.)

12.61.— Transfer of proceedings under Article 15 of the Council Regulation or under Article 8 of the 1996 Hague Convention

(1) Where the court is considering the transfer of proceedings to the court of another Member State or Contracting State under rules 12.62 to 12.64 it will—

(a) fix a date for a hearing for the court to consider the question of transfer; and

(b) give directions as to the manner in which the parties may make representations.

(2) The court may, with the consent of all parties, deal with the question of transfer without a hearing.

(3) Directions which are in force immediately prior to the transfer of proceedings to a court in another Member State or Contracting State under rules 12.62 to 12.64 will continue to apply until the court in that other State accepts jurisdiction in accordance with the provisions of the Council Regulation or the 1996 Hague Convention (as appropriate), subject to any variation or revocation of the directions.

(4) The court or court officer will—

(a) take a note of the giving, variation or revocation of directions under this rule; and

(b) as soon as practicable serve a copy of the directions order on every party.

(5) A register of all applications and requests for transfer of jurisdiction to or from another Member State or Contracting State will be kept by the principal registry.

12.62.— Application by a party for transfer of the proceedings

(1) A party may apply to the court under Article 15(1) of the Council Regulation or under Article 8(1) of the 1996 Hague Convention —
  (a) to stay^(GL) the proceedings or a specified part of the proceedings and to invite the parties to introduce a request before a court of another Member State or Contracting State; or
  (b) to make a request to a court of another Member State or another Contracting State to assume jurisdiction for the proceedings, or a specified part of the proceedings.
(2) An application under paragraph (1) must be made—
  (a) to the court in which the relevant parental responsibility proceedings are pending; and
  (b) using the Part 18 procedure.
(3) The applicant must file the application notice and serve it on the respondents—
  (a) here the application is also made under Article 11 of the Council Regulation, not less than 5 days, and
  (b) n any other case, not less than 42 days,
before the hearing of the application.

12.63.— Application by a court of another Member State or another Contracting State for transfer of the proceedings

(1) This rule applies where a court of another Member State or another Contracting State makes an application under Article 15(2)(c) of the Council Regulation or under Article 9 of the 1996 Hague Convention that the court having jurisdiction in relation to the proceedings transfer the proceedings or a specific part of the proceedings to the applicant court.
(2) When the court receives the application, the court officer will—
  (a) as soon as practicable, notify the Central Authority for England and Wales of the application; and
  (b) serve the application, and notice of the hearing on all other parties in England and Wales not less than 5 days before the hearing of the application.

12.64.— Exercise by the court of its own initiative of powers to seek to transfer the proceedings

(1) The court having jurisdiction in relation to the proceedings may exercise its powers of its own initiative under Article 15 of the Council Regulation or Article 8 of the 1996 Hague Convention in relation to the proceedings or a specified part of the proceedings.
(2) Where the court proposes to exercise its powers, the court officer will give the parties not less than 5 days' notice of the hearing.

12.65.— Application to High Court to make request under Article 15 of the Council Regulation or Article 9 of the 1996 Hague Convention to request transfer of jurisdiction

(1) An application for the court to request transfer of jurisdiction in a matter concerning a child from another Member State or another Contracting State under Article 15 of the Council Regulation, or Article 9 of the 1996 Hague Convention (as the case may be) must be made to the principal registry and heard in the High Court.
(2) An application must be made without notice to any other person and the court may give directions about joining any other party to the application.
(3) Where there is agreement between the court and the court or competent authority to which the request under paragraph (1) is made to transfer the matter to the courts of England and Wales, the court will consider with that other court or competent authority the specific timing and conditions for the transfer.
(4) Upon receipt of agreement to transfer jurisdiction from the court or other competent authority in the Member State, or Contracting State to which the request has been made, the court officer will serve on the applicant a notice that jurisdiction has been accepted by the courts of England and Wales.

(5) The applicant must attach the notice referred to in paragraph (3) to any subsequent application in relation to the child.

(6) Nothing in this rule requires an application with respect to a child commenced following a transfer of jurisdiction to be made to or heard in the High Court.

(7) Upon allocation, the court to which the proceedings are allocated must immediately fix a directions hearing to consider the future conduct of the case.

12.66.— Procedure where the court receives a request from the authorities of another Member State or Contracting State to assume jurisdiction in a matter concerning a child

(1) Where any court other than the High Court receives a request to assume jurisdiction in a matter concerning a child from a court or other authority which has jurisdiction in another Member State or Contracting State, that court must immediately refer the request to a Judge of the High Court for a decision regarding acceptance of jurisdiction to be made.

(2) Upon the High Court agreeing to the request under paragraph (1), the court officer will notify the parties to the proceedings before the other Member State or Contracting State of that decision, and the case must be allocated as if the application had been made in England and Wales.

(3) Upon allocation, the court to which the proceedings are allocated must immediately fix a directions hearing to consider the future conduct of the case.

(4) The court officer will serve notice of the directions hearing on all parties to the proceedings in the other Member State or Contracting State no later than 5 days before the date of that hearing.

12.67. Service of the court's order or request relating to transfer of jurisdiction under the Council Regulation or the 1996 Hague Convention

The court officer will serve an order or request relating to transfer of jurisdiction on all parties, the Central Authority of the other Member State or Contracting State, and the Central Authority for England and Wales.

12.68.— Questions as to the court's jurisdiction or whether the proceedings should be stayed

(1) If at any time after issue of the application it appears to the court that under any of Articles 16 to 18 of the Council Regulation it does not or may not have jurisdiction to hear an application, or that under Article 19 of the Council Regulation or Article 13 of the 1996 Hague Convention it is or may be required to stay$^{(GL)}$ the proceedings or to decline jurisdiction, the court must—
  (a) stay$^{(GL)}$ the proceedings; and
  (b) fix a date for a hearing to determine jurisdiction or whether there should be a stay$^{(GL)}$ or other order.

(2) The court officer will serve notice of the hearing referred to at paragraph (1)(b) on the parties to the proceedings.

(3) The court must, in writing—
  (a) give reasons for its decision under paragraph (1); and
  (b) where it makes a finding of fact, state such finding.

(4) The court may with the consent of all the parties deal with any question as to the jurisdiction of the court, or as to whether the proceedings should be stayed$^{(GL)}$, without a hearing.

12.69.— Request for consultation as to contemplated placement of child in England and Wales

(1) This rule applies to a request made —
  (a) under Article 56 of the Council Regulation, by a court in another Member State; or
  (b) under Article 33 of the 1996 Hague Convention by a court in another Contracting State

for consultation on or consent to the contemplated placement of a child in England and Wales.

The Family Procedure Rules 2010

(2) Where the court receives a request directly from a court in another Member State or Contracting State, the court shall, as soon as practicable after receipt of the request, notify the Central Authority for England and Wales of the request and take the appropriate action under paragraph (4).

(3) Where it appears to the court officer that no proceedings relating to the child are pending before a court in England and Wales, the court officer must inform the Central Authority for England and Wales of that fact and forward to the Central Authority all documents relating to the request sent by the court in the other Member State or Contracting State.

(4) Where the court receives a request forwarded by the Central Authority for England and Wales, the court must, as soon as practicable after receipt of the request, either—
- (a) where proceedings relating to the child are pending before the court, fix a directions hearing; or
- (b) where proceedings relating to the child are pending before another court in England and Wales, send a copy of the request to that court.

12.70.— Request made by court in England and Wales for consultation as to contemplated placement of child in another Member State or Contracting State

(1) This rule applies where the court is contemplating the placement of a child in another Member State under Article 56 of the Council Regulation or another Contracting State under Article 33 of the 1996 Hague Convention, and proposes to send a request for consultation with or for the consent of the central authority or other authority having jurisdiction in the other State in relation to the contemplated placement.

(2) In this rule, a reference to "the request" includes a reference to a report prepared for purposes of Article 33 of the 1996 Hague Convention where the request is made under that Convention.

(3) Where the court sends the request directly to the central authority or other authority having jurisdiction in the other State, it shall at the same time send a copy of the request to the Central Authority for England and Wales.

(4) The court may send the request to the Central Authority for England and Wales for onward transmission to the central authority or other authority having jurisdiction in the other Member State.

(5) The court should give consideration to the documents which should accompany the request. (See Chapters 1 to 3 of this Part generally, for the procedure governing applications for an order under paragraph 19(1) of Schedule 2 to the 1989 Act permitting a local authority to arrange for any child in its care to live outside England and Wales.)

(Part 14 sets out the procedure governing applications for an order under section 84 (giving parental responsibility prior to adoption abroad) of the Adoption and Children Act 2002.)

12.71.— Application for a declaration as to the extent, or existence, of parental responsibility in relation to a child under Article 16 of the 1996 Hague Convention

(1) Any interested person may apply for a declaration —
- (a) that a person has, or does not have, parental responsibility for a child; or
- (b) as to the extent of a person's parental responsibility for a child,

where the question arises by virtue of the application of Article 16 of the 1996 Hague Convention.

(2) An application for a declaration as to the extent, or existence of a person's parental responsibility for a child by virtue of Article 16 of the 1996 Hague Convention must be made in the principal registry and heard in the High Court.

(3) An application for a declaration referred to in paragraph (1) may not be made where the question raised is otherwise capable of resolution in any other family proceedings in respect of the child.

CHAPTER 7

COMMUNICATION OF INFORMATION: PROCEEDINGS RELATING TO CHILDREN

12.72.— Interpretation

(1) In this Chapter "independent reviewing officer" means a person appointed in respect of a child in accordance with regulation 2A of the Review of Children's Cases Regulations 1991, or regulation 3 of the Review of Children's Cases (Wales) Regulations 2007.

12.73.— Communication of information: general

(1) For the purposes of the law relating to contempt of court, information relating to proceedings held in private (whether or not contained in a document filed with the court) may be communicated—
- (a) where the communication is to—
  - (i) a party;
  - (ii) the legal representative of a party;
  - (iii) a professional legal adviser;
  - (iv) an officer of the service or a Welsh family proceedings officer;
  - (v) the welfare officer;
  - (vi) the Legal Services Commission;
  - (vii) an expert whose instruction by a party has been authorised by the court for the purposes of the proceedings;
  - (viii) a professional acting in furtherance of the protection of children;
  - (ix) an independent reviewing officer appointed in respect of a child who is, or has been, subject to proceedings to which this rule applies;
- (b) where the court gives permission; or
- (c) subject to any direction of the court, in accordance with rule 12.75 and Practice Direction 12G.

(2) Nothing in this Chapter permits the communication to the public at large, or any section of the public, of any information relating to the proceedings.

(3) Nothing in rule 12.75 and Practice Direction 12G permits the disclosure of an unapproved draft judgment handed down by any court.

12.74.— Instruction of experts

(1) No party may instruct an expert for any purpose relating to proceedings, including to give evidence in those proceedings, without the permission of the court.

(2) Where the permission of the court has not been given under paragraph (1), no evidence arising out of an unauthorised instruction may be introduced without permission of the court.

12.75.— Communication of information for purposes connected with the proceedings

(1) A party or the legal representative of a party, on behalf of and upon the instructions of that party, may communicate information relating to the proceedings to any person where necessary to enable that party—
- (a) by confidential discussion, to obtain support, advice or assistance in the conduct of the proceedings;
- (b) to engage in mediation or other forms of alternative dispute resolution;
- (c) to make and pursue a complaint against a person or body concerned in the proceedings; or
- (d) to make and pursue a complaint regarding the law, policy or procedure relating to a category of proceedings to which this Part applies.

(2) Where information is communicated to any person in accordance with paragraph (1)(a) of this rule, no further communication by that person is permitted.

(3) When information relating to the proceedings is communicated to any person in accordance with paragraphs (1)(b),(c) or (d) of this rule—

(a) the recipient may communicate that information to a further recipient, provided that—
  (i) the party who initially communicated the information consents to that further communication; and
  (ii) the further communication is made only for the purpose or purposes for which the party made the initial communication; and
(b) the information may be successively communicated to and by further recipients on as many occasions as may be necessary to fulfil the purpose for which the information was initially communicated, provided that on each such occasion the conditions in subparagraph (a) are met.

PART 12 COMMENTARY

Part 12 is supplemented by 16 practice directions: 12A to 12P. By virtue of the *Practice Direction – Practice Directions Relating to Family Proceedings in Force before 6th April 2011 which support the Family Procedure Rules 2010* many of these are in fact pre-existing practice directions. The various directions are set out below, together with the original date for those that pre-existed:

12A Public Law Proceedings Guide to Case Management (April 2010)

12B The Revised Private Law Programme (April 2010)

12C Service of Proceedings

12D Inherent Jurisdiction (including Wardship) Proceedings

12E Urgent Business

12F International Child Abduction

12G Communication of Information - Tables

12H Contribution Orders

12I Applications for Reporting Restriction Orders (18 March 2005)

12J Residence & Contact Orders: Domestic Violence & Harm (14 January 2009). This is amended at paragraph 10 by updating the reference there to 'rule 12.34 of the Family Procedure Rules 2010'

12K President's Direction (Children Act 1989: Exclusion Requirement) (17 December 1997)

12L Children Act 1989: Risk Assessments under section 16A (3 September 2007)

12M Family Assistance Orders: consultation (3 September 2007)

12N Enforcement of Children Act 1989: Contact Orders: Disclosure of Information to Officers of the National Probation Service (High Court and county court) (6 November 2008)

12O Practice Direction (Arrival of Child in England by Air (18 January 1980)

12P Registrar's direction (Removal from Jurisdiction: Issue of Passports (15 May 1987)

Part 12 applies to:

- Emergency proceedings (as defined in r 12.2 the interpretation section) (and see PD12E Urgent Business).

- Public law proceedings (Chapter 3 and PD12A).
- Private law proceedings (Chapter 4 and PD12B).
- Proceedings relating to the exercise of the court's inherent jurisdiction (Chapter 5 and PD12D).
- Proceedings relating to child abduction (Chapter 6, section 1 and PD12F).
- Proceedings relating to the Council Regulation (EC) No 2201/2003 and the 1996 Hague Convention in respect of children (Chapter 6, section 2).

There is no significant change in the procedures for public law proceedings (Chapter 3) and the Public Law Outline (April 2010) is reproduced in PD12A. At r 12.23 it is provided that the court will set the timetable for the proceedings in accordance with the 'Timetable for the Child', which is defined at r 12.23 (2) as a timetable set by the court in accordance with its duties under ss 1 and 32 of the 1989 Act and will take into account dates of significant steps in the child's life and be appropriate for the child. There is provision at r 12.24 for the court to direct the parties to monitor compliance with court directions and there is provision at r 12.25 for the court to set dates for the First Appointment, Case Management Conference and Issues Resolution Hearing and at r 12.26 for the court to direct discussions between advocates, all in accordance with PD12A.

Similarly, for private law proceedings (Chapter 4), the revised Private Law Programme (April 2010) has been incorporated as PD12B. There is provision for the court to set a date for the First Hearing Dispute Resolution Appointment in r 12.31, in accordance with PD12B. There is a requirement at r 12.32 for a respondent to answer an application for an order in private law proceedings within 14 days beginning with the date on which the application was issued.

Chapter 5, supplemented by PD12D, sets out the rules for applications in proceedings under the Inherent Jurisdiction, including Wardship.

Chapter 6, supplemented by PD12F, deals with Hague convention and child abduction proceedings. This contains new provisions. Section 1 gives directions for proceedings under the 1980 Hague Convention or the European Convention (1980). Section 2 gives directions for applications relating to the Council Regulation (EC) No 2201/2001 and the 1996 Hague Convention.

Chapter 7 supplemented by PD12G, deals with the communication of information in children proceedings (these were previously in Part X1 of the FPR 1991).

Forms relevant to Part 12 are a large number of C forms, and PLO1 through to PLO9 and PLP 10.

PRACTICE DIRECTION 12A – PUBLIC LAW PROCEEDINGS GUIDE TO CASE MANAGEMENT

The Family Procedure Rules 2010

SCOPE

1.1 This Practice Direction applies to care and supervision proceedings. In so far as practicable, it is to be applied to all other Public Law Proceedings.

1.2 This Practice Direction replaces Practice Direction Guide to Case Management dated April 2008.

1.3 This Practice Direction will come into effect on 6th April 2010. The new form of application for a care or supervision order (Form C110) only applies to proceedings commenced on or after 6th April 2010. Subject to this it is intended that this Practice Direction should apply in so far as practicable to applications made and not disposed of before 6th April 2010. In relation to these applications–

(1) the Practice Direction Guide to Case Management in Public Law Proceedings dated April 2008 applies where it is not practicable to apply this Practice Direction; and
(2) the court may give directions relating to the application of this Practice Direction or the April 2008 Practice Direction.

This is subject to the overriding objective below and to the proviso that such a direction will neither cause further delay nor involve repetition of steps already taken or decisions already made in the case.

1.4 This Practice Direction is to be read with the Rules and is subject to them.

1.5 A Glossary of terms is at paragraph 26.

THE OVERRIDING OBJECTIVE

2.1 This Practice Direction has the overriding objective of enabling the court to deal with cases justly, having regard to the welfare issues involved.

Dealing with a case justly includes, so far as is practicable–

(1) ensuring that it is dealt with expeditiously and fairly;
(2) dealing with the case in ways which are proportionate to the nature, importance and complexity of the issues;
(3) ensuring that the parties are on an equal footing;
(4) saving expense; and
(5) allotting to it an appropriate share of the court's resources, while taking into account the need to allot resources to other cases.

Application by the court of the overriding objective

2.2 The court must seek to give effect to the overriding objective when it–

(1) exercises the case management powers referred to in this Practice Direction; or
(2) interprets any provision of this Practice Direction.

Duty of the parties

2.3 The parties are required to help the court further the overriding objective.

COURT CASE MANAGEMENT

The main principles

3.1 The main principles underlying court case management and the means of the court furthering the overriding objective in Public Law Proceedings are–

(1) **Timetable for the Child**: each case will have a timetable for the proceedings set by the court in accordance with the Timetable for the Child:

(2) **judicial continuity**: each case will be allocated to one or not more than two case management judges (in the case of magistrates' courts, case managers), who will be responsible for every case management stage in the proceedings through to the Final Hearing and, in relation to the High Court or county court, one of whom may be – and where possible should be – the judge who will conduct the Final Hearing;
(3) **main case management tools**: each case will be managed by the court by using the appropriate main case management tools;
(4) **active case management**: each case will be actively case managed by the court with a view at all times to furthering the overriding objective;
(5) **consistency**: each case will, so far as compatible with the overriding objective, be managed in a consistent way and using the standardised steps provided for in this Direction.

The main case management tools

The Timetable for the Child

3.2 The "Timetable for the Child" is defined by the rules as the timetable se t by the court in accordance with its duties under section 1 and 32 of the 1989 Act and shall–

(1) take into account dates of the significant steps in the life of the child who is the subject of the proceedings; and
(2) be appropriate for that child.

The court will set the timetable for the proceedings in accordance with the Timetable for the Child and review this Timetable regularly. Where adjustments are made to the Timetable for the Child, the timetable for the proceedings will have to be reviewed. The timetable for the Child is to be considered at every stage of the proceedings and whenever the court is asked to make directions whether at a hearing or otherwise.

3.3 The steps in the child's life which are to be taken account by the court when setting the Timetable for the Child include not only legal steps but also social, care, health and education steps.

3.4 Examples of the dates the court will record and take into account when setting the Timetable for the Child are the dates of–

(1) any formal review by the Local Authority of the case of a looked after child (within the meaning of section 22(1) of the 1989 Act);
(2) the child taking up a place at a new school;
(3) any review by the Local Authority of any statement of the child's special educational needs;
(4) an assessment by a paediatrician or other specialist;
(5) the outcome of any review of Local Authority plans for the child, for example, any plans for permanence through adoption, Special Guardianship or placement with parents or relatives;
(6) a change or proposed change of the child's placement.

3.5. Due regard should be paid to the Timetable for the Child to ensure that the court remains child-focussed throughout the progress of Public Law Proceedings and that any procedural steps proposed under the Public Law Outline are considered in the context of significant events in the child's life.

3.6. The applicant is required to provide the information needed about the significant steps in the child's life in the Application Form and to update this information regularly taking into account information received from others involved in the child's life such as other parties, members of the child's family, the person who is caring for the child, the children's guardian and the child's key social worker.

3.7. Before setting the timetable for the proceedings the factors which the court will consider will include the need to give effect to the overriding objective and the timescales in the Public Law Outline by which the steps on the Outline are to be taken. Where possible, the timetable for the proceedings should be in line with those

The Family Procedure Rules 2010

timescales. However, there will be cases where the significant steps in the child's life demand that the steps in the proceedings be taken at times which are outside the timescales set out in the Outline. In these cases the timetable for the proceedings may not adhere to one or more of the timescales set out in the Outline.

3.8. Where more than one child is the subject of the proceedings, the court should consider and may set a Timetable for the Child for each child. The children may not all have the same Timetable, and the court will consider the appropriate progress of the proceedings in relation to each child.

3.9. Where there are parallel care proceedings and criminal proceedings against a person connected with the child for a serious offence against the child, linked directions headings should where practicable take place as the case progresses. The timing of the proceedings in a linked care and criminal case should appear in the Timetable for the Child.

Case Management Documentation

3.10 The case management documents includes the–

(1) Application Form and Annex Documents;
(2) Case Analysis and Recommendations provided by Cafcass or CAFCASS CYMRU;
(3) Local Authority Case Summary;
(4) Other Parties' Case Summaries;

3.11 The court will encourage the use of the Case Management Documentation which is not prescribed by the rules.

The Case Management Record

3.12 The court 's filing system for the case will be known as the Case Management Record and will include the following main documents–

(1) the Case Management Documentation;
(2) Standard Directions on Issue and on First Appointment;
(3) Case Management Orders approved by the court.

3.13 Parties or their legal representatives will be expected to retain their own record containing copies of the documents on the court's Case Management Record.

The First Appointment

3.14 The purpose of the First Appointment is to confirm allocation of the case and give initial case management directions.

The Case Management Order

3.15 The Case Management Order is an order which will be made by the court at the conclusion of the Case Management Conference, the Issues Resolution Hearing and any other case management hearing. It is designed to achieve active case management as defined in paragraph 3.20 below. The parties are required to prepare and submit to the court a draft of this order in accordance with paragraph 5.8 to 5.10 below. The order will include such of the provisions referred to in the Glossary at paragraph 26(12) as are appropriate to the proceedings.

Advocates' Meeting/discussion

3.16 The court will consider directing advocates to have discussions before the Case Management Conference and the Issues Resolution Hearing. Advocates may well find that the best way to have these discussions is to meet. Such discussion is intended to facilitate agreement and to narrow the issues for the court to consider. Advocates and litigants in person may take part in the Advocates' Meeting or discussions.

The Case Management Conference

3.17 In each case there will be a Case Management Conference to enable the case management judge or case manager, with the co-operation of the parties, actively to manage the case and, at the earliest practicable opportunity to–

(1) identify the relevant and key issues; and
(2) give full case management directions including confirming the Timetable for the Child.

The Issues Resolution Hearing

3.18 In each case there will be an Issues Resolution Hearing before the Final Hearing to-

(1) identify any remaining key issues; and
(2) as far as possible, resolve or narrow those issues.

Active case management

3.19 The court must further the overriding objective by actively managing cases.

3.20 Active case management includes–

(1) identifying the Timetable for the Child;
(2) identifying the appropriate court to conduct the proceedings and transferring the proceedings as early as possible to that court;
(3) encouraging the parties to co-operate with each other in the conduct of the proceedings;
(4) retaining the Case Management Record;
(5) identifying all facts and matters that are in issue at the earliest stage in the proceedings and at each hearing;
(6) deciding promptly which issues need full investigation and hearing and which do not and whether a fact finding hearing is required;
(7) deciding the order in which issues are to be resolved;
(8) identifying at an early stage who should be a party to the proceedings;
(9) considering whether the likely benefits of taking a particular step justify any delay which will result and the cost of taking it;
(10) directing discussion between advocates and litigants in person before the Case Management Conference and Issues Resolution Hearing;
(11) requiring the use of the Case Management Order and directing advocates and litigants in person to prepare or adjust the draft of this Order where appropriate;
(12) standardising, simplifying and regulating–
    (a) the use of Case Management Documentation and forms;
    (b) the court's orders and directions;
(13) controlling–
    (a) the use and cost of experts;
    (b) the nature and extent of the documents which are to be disclosed to the parties and presented to the court;
    (c) whether and, if so, in what manner the documents disclosed are to be presented to the court;
    (d) the progress of the case;
(14) where it is demonstrated to be in the interests of the child, encouraging the parties to use an alternative dispute resolution procedure if the court considers such a procedure to be appropriate and facilitating the use of such procedure;
(15) helping the parties to reach agreement in relation to the whole or part of the case;
(16) fixing the dates for all appointments and hearings;
(17) dealing with as many aspects of the case as it can on the same occasion;
(18) where possible dealing with additional issues which may arise from time to time in the case without requiring the parties to attend at court;
(19) making use of technology; and
(20) giving directions to ensure that the case proceeds quickly and efficiently.

The Family Procedure Rules 2010

THE EXPECTATIONS

4.1 The expectations are that proceedings should be—

(1) conducted using the Case Management Tools and Case Management Documentation referred to in this Practice Direction in accordance with the Public Law Outline;
(2) finally determined within the timetable fixed by the court in accordance with the Timetable for the Child – the timescales in the Public Law Outline being adhered to and being taken as the maximum permissible time for the taking of the step referred to in the Outline unless the Timetable for the Child demands otherwise.

4.2 However, there may be cases where the court considers that the child's welfare requires a different approach from the one contained in the Public Law Outline. In those cases, the court will–

(1) determine the appropriate case management directions and timetable; and
(2) record on the face of the order the reasons for departing from the approach in the Public Law Outline.

HOW THE PARTIES SHOULD HELP COURT CASE MANAGEMENT

Main methods of helping

Good case preparation

5.1 The applicant should prepare the case before proceedings are issued. In care and supervision proceedings the Local Authority should use the Pre-proceedings checklist.

The Timetable for the Child

5.2 the applicant must state in the Application Form all information concerning significant steps in the child's life that are likely to take place during the proceedings. The applicant is to be responsible for updating this information regularly and giving it to the court. The applicant will need to obtain information about these significant steps and any variations and additions to them from others involved in the child's life such as other parties, members of the child's family, the person who is caring for the child, the children's guardian and the child's key social worker. When the other persons involved in the child's life become aware of a significant step in the child's life or a variation of an existing one, that information should be given to the applicant as soon as possible.

5.3 The information about the significant steps in the child's life will enable the court to set the Timetable for the Child and to review that Timetable in the light of new information. The Timetable for the Child will be included or referred to in the draft of a Case Management Order, the Case Management Order, Standard Directions on Issue and on First Appointment and the directions given at the Case Management Conference and Issues Resolution Hearing.

Case Management Documentation

5.4 The parties must use the Case Management Documentation.

Co-operation

5.5 The parties and their representatives should co-operate with the court in case management, including the fixing of timetables to avoid unacceptable delay, and in the crystallisation and resolution of the issues on which the case turns.

Directions

5.6 The parties will–

(1) monitor compliance with the court's directions; and

(2) tell the court or court officer about any failure to comply with a direction of the court or any other delay in the proceedings.

The Case Management Record

5.7 The parties are expected to retain a record containing copies of the documents on the court's Case Management Record.

Drafting the Case Management Order

5.8 Parties should start to consider the content of the draft of the Case Management Order at the earliest opportunity either before or in the course of completing applications to the court or the response to the application. They should in any event consider the drafting of a Case Management Order after the First Appointment.

5.9 Only one draft of the Case Management Order should be filed with the court for each of the Case Management Conference and the Issues Resolution Hearing. it is the responsibility of the advocate for the applicant, which in care and supervision proceedings will ordinarily be the Local Authority, to prepare those drafts and be responsible for obtaining comments from the advocates and the parties.

5.10 There should be ongoing consideration of the Case Management Orders throughout the proceedings. The Case Management Orders should serve as an *aide memoire* to everyone involved in the proceedings of–

(1) the Timetable for the Child;
(2) the case management decisions;
(3) the identified issues.

5.11 In paragraphs 5.4, 5.6 to 5.9 "parties" includes parties' legal representatives.

FINDINGS OF FACT HEARINGS

6 In a case where the court decides that a fact finding hearing is necessary, the starting point is that the proceedings leading to that hearing are to be managed in accordance with the case management steps in this Practice Direction.

ETHNICITY, LANGUAGE, RELIGION AND CULTURE

7 At each case management stage of the proceedings, particularly at the First Appointment and Case Management Conference, the court will consider giving directions regarding the obtaining of evidence about the ethnicity, language, religion and culture of the child and other significant persons involved in the proceedings. The court will subsequently consider the implications of this evidence for the child in the context of the issues in the case.

ADULTS WHO MAY BE PROTECTED PARTIES

8.1 The applicant must give details in the Application Form of any referral to or assessment by the local authority's Adult Learning Disability team (or its equivalent). The Local Authority should tell the court about other referrals or assessments if known such as a referral to Community Mental Health.

8.2 The court will investigate as soon as possible any issue as to whether an adult party or intended party to the proceedings lacks capacity (within the meaning of the Mental Capacity Act 2005) to conduct the proceedings. A representative (a litigation friend, next friend or guardian ad litem) is needed to conduct the proceedings on behalf of an adult who lacks capacity to do so (a "protected party"). The expectation of the Official Solicitor is that the Official Solicitor will only be invited to act for a protected party as guardian ad litem or litigation friend if there is no other person suitable and willing to act.

8.3 Any issue as to the capacity of an adult to conduct the proceedings must be determined before the court gives any directions relevant to that adult's role within the proceedings.

8.4 Where the adult is a protected party, that party's representative should be

The Family Procedure Rules 2010

involved in any instruction of an expert, including the instruction of an expert to assess whether the adult, although a protected party, is competent to give evidence. The instruction of an expert is a significant step in the proceedings. The representative will wish to consider (and ask the expert to consider), if the protected party is competent to give evidence, their best interests in this regard. The representative may wish to seek advice about 'special measures'. The representative may put forward an argument on behalf of the protected party that the protected party should not give evidence.

8.5 If at any time during the proceedings, there is reason to believe that a party may lack capacity to conduct the proceedings, then the court must be notified and directions sought to ensure that this issue is investigated without delay.

CHILD LIKELY TO LACK CAPACITY TO CONDUCT THE PROCEEDINGS WHEN AGED 18

9 Where it appears that a child is–

(1) a party to the proceedings and not the subject of them;
(2) nearing 18; and
(3) considered likely to lack capacity to conduct the proceedings when 18,

the court will consider giving directions relating to the investigation of a child's capacity in this respect.

OUTLINE OF THE PROCESS AND HOW TO USE THE MAIN CASE MANAGEMENT TOOLS

10.1 The Public Law Outline set out in the Table below contains an outline of–

(1) the order of the different stages of the process;
(2) the purposes of the main case management hearings and matters to be considered at them;
(3) the latest timescales within which the main stages of the process should take place.

10.2 In the Public Law Outline–

(1) "CMC" means the Case Management Conference;
(2) "FA" means the First Appointment;
(3) "IRH" means the Issues Resolution Hearing;
(4) "LA" means the Local Authority which is applying for a care or supervision order;
(5) "OS" means the Official Solicitor.

PUBLIC LAW OUTLINE

PRE-PROCEEDINGS
PRE-PROCEEDINGS CHECKLIST

Annex Documents (the documents specified in the Annex to the Application Form to be attached to that from where available)	Other Checklist Documents which already exist on LA's files which are to be disclosed in th event of proceedings normally before the day of the FA:
• Social Work Chronology	• Previous court orders & judgments/reasons
• Initial Social Work Statement	• Any relevant assessment materials
• Initial and Core Assessments	• Section 7 & 37 reports

FPR 2010, Practice Direction 12A

PRE-PROCEEDINGS
PRE-PROCEEDINGS CHECKLIST

- Letters Before Proceedings
- Schedule of proposed Findings
- Care Plan
- Relatives & friends materials (e.g., a genogram)
- Other relevant reports & records
- Single, joint or inter-agency materials (e.g., health & education/Home office & Immigration documents
- Records of discussions with the family
- Key LA minutes & records for the child (including Strategy Discussion Record)

STAGE 1 – ISSUE AND THE FIRST APPOINTMENT

ISSUE	FIRST APPOINTMENT
On DAY 1 and by DAY 3	**By DAY 6**
Objectives: To ensure compliance with pre-proceedings checklist; to allocate proceedings; to obtain the information necessary for initial case management at the FA	**Objectives:** To confirm allocation; to give initial case management directions
On Day 1:	• LA normally serves other Checklist Documents on the parties
• The LA files the Application Form and Annex Documents where available	
• Court officer issues application	• Parties notify LA & court of need for a contested hearing
• Court nominates case manager(s)	• Court makes arrangements for a contested hearing
	• Initial case management by court including:
• Court gives Standard Directions on Issue including:	– Confirm Timetable for the Child
– Pre-proceedings checklist compliance including preparation and service of any missing Annex Documents	– Confirm allocation or transfer
– Allocate and/or transfer	– Identify additional parties & representation (including allocation of children's guardian)
– Appoint children's guardian	
– Appoint solicitor for the child	– Identify "Early Final Hearing" cases
– Case Analysis for FA	– Scrutinise Care Plan

The Family Procedure Rules 2010

- Appoint a guardian ad litem or litigation friend for a protected party or any non subject child who is a party, including the OS where appropriate
- List FA by Day 6
- Make arrangements for contested hearing (if necessary)

By Day 3

• Cafcass/CAFCASS CYMRU expected to allocate case to children's guardian

• LA serves the Application Form and Annex Documents, on parties

• Court gives Standard Directions on FA including:

- Case Analysis and Recommendations for Stages 2 & 3
- Preparation and service of any missing Annex Documents
- What Other Checklist Documents are to be filed
- LA Case Summary
- Other Parties' Case Summaries
- Parties' initial witness statements
- For the Advocates' meeting
- List CMC or (if appropriate) an Early Final Hearing
- Upon transfer

STAGE 2 – CASE MANAGEMENT CONFERENCE

ADVOCATES' MEETING	CMC
No later than 2 days before CMC	No later than day 45
Objectives: To prepare a draft of the Case Management Order; to identify experts and draft questions for them	Objectives: To identify issues(s); to give full case management directions
• Consider information on the Application Form, all Other Parties' Case Summaries and Case Analysis and Recommendations	• Detailed case management by the court-
• Identify proposed experts and draft questions in accordance with Experts Practice Direction	– Scrutinise compliance with directions
• Draft Case Management Order	– Review and confirm Timetable for the Child
• Notify court of need for a contested hearing	– Identify key issue(s)
File Draft Case Management Order with the case manager/case management judge by 11am one working day before the CMC	– Confirm allocation or transfer
	– Consider case management directions in the draft of the Case Management Order
	– Scrutinise Care Plan

FPR 2010, Practice Direction 12A

– Check compliance with Experts Practice Direction

• Court issues Case Management Order

• Court lists IRH and, where necessary, a warned period for Final Hearing

STAGE 3 – ISSUES RESOLUTION HEARING

ADVOCATES' MEETING	IRH
Between 2 and 7 days before the IRH	Between 16 & 25 weeks
Objective: To prepare or update the Draft Case Management Order	Objectives: To resolve and narrow issue(s); to identify any remaining key issues
• Consider all Other Parties' Case Summaries and Case Analysis and Recommendations	• Identification by the court of the key issue(s) (if any) to be determined
• Draft Case Management Order	
• Notify court of need for a contested hearing/time for oral evidence to be given	
• File draft of the Case Management order with the case manager/case management judge by 11am one working day before the IRH	
	• Final case management by the court:
	– Scrutinise compliance with directions
	– Review and confirm the Timetable for the Child
	– Consider case management directions in the draft case Management Order
	– Scrutinise Care Plan
	– Give directions for Hearing documents:
	– Threshold agreement or facts/issues remaining to be determined
	– Final Evidence & Care Plan
	– Case Analysis and Recommendations
	– Witness templates
	– Skeleton arguments
	– Judicial reading lists/reading time/judgment writing time
	– Time estimate
	– Bundles Practice Direction compliance
	– List or confirm Hearing
	• Court issues Case Management Order

STAGE 4 – HEARING

Hearing set in accordance with the Timetable for the Child
Objective: To determine remaining issues

• All file & serve updated Case Management Documentation & bundle	• Judgment/Reasons

The Family Procedure Rules 2010

- Draft final order(s) in approved form
- Disclose documents as required after hearing

STARTING THE PROCEEDINGS

Pre-proceedings Checklist

11.1 The pre-proceedings Checklist is to be used by the applicant to help prepare for the start of the proceedings.

11.2 The Pre-proceedings Checklist contains the documents which are specified in the annex to the Application Form. The rules require those documents which are known as the "Annex Documents" to be filed with the Application Form where available. The Annex Documents are-

(1) Social work Chronology;
(2) Initial Social Work Statement;
(3) Initial and Core Assessments;
(4) Letters before proceedings;
(5) Schedule of Proposed Findings; and
(6) Care Plan.

11.3 In addition, the Pre-proceedings Checklist contains examples of documents other than the Annex Documents which will normally be on the Local Authority file at the start of the proceedings so that they can be served on parties in accordance with the Public Law Outline. These documents are known as the "Other Checklist Documents" and are not to be filed with the court at the start of the proceedings but are to be disclosed to the parties normally before the day of the First Appointment or in accordance with the court's directions and to be filed with the court only as directed by the court.

Compliance with Pre-proceedings Checklist

11.4 It is recognised that in some cases the circumstances are such that the safety and welfare of the child may be jeopardised if the start of proceedings is delayed until all of the documents appropriate to the case and referred to in the Pre-proceedings Checklist are available. The safety and welfare of the child should never be put in jeopardy because of lack of documentation. (Nothing in this Practice Direction affects an application for an emergency protection order under section 44 of the 1989 Act).

11.5 The court recognises that the preparation may need to be varied to suit the circumstances of the case. In cases where any of the Annex Documents required to be attached to the Application Form are not available at the time of issue of the application, the court will consider making directions on issue about when any missing documentation is to be filed. The expectation is that there will be a good reason why one or more of the documents are not available. Further directions relating to any missing documentation are likely to be made at the First Appointment. The court also recognises that some documents on the Pre-proceedings Checklist may not exist and may never exist, for example, the Section 37 report, and that in urgent proceedings no Letter Before proceedings may have been sent.

WHAT THE COURT WILL DO AT THE ISSUE OF PROCEEDINGS

Objectives

12.1 The objectives at this stage are for the court–

(1) to identify the Timetable for the Child;
(2) in care and supervision proceedings, to ensure compliance with the Pre-proceedings Checklist;
(3) to allocate proceedings;

(4) to obtain the information necessary to enable initial case management at the First Appointment.

12.2 The steps which the court will take once proceedings have been issued include those set out in paragraphs 12.3 to 12.5 below.

Allocation

12.3 By reference to the Allocation Order, the court will consider allocation of the case and transfer to the appropriate level of court those cases which are obviously suitable for immediate transfer.

OTHER STEPS TO BE TAKEN BY THE COURT

Directions

12.4 The court will–

(1) consider giving directions–
 (a) appropriate to the case including Standard Directions On Issue;
 (b) in care and supervision proceedings, relating to the preparation, filing and service of any missing Annex Documents and what Other Checklist Documents are to be filed and by when;
 (c) relating to representation of any protected party or any child who is a party to, but is not the subject of, the proceedings by a guardian ad litem or litigation friend, including the Official Solicitor where appropriate;
(2) appoint a children's guardian in specified proceedings (in relation to care and supervision proceedings the court will expect that Cafcass or CAFCASS CYMRU will have received notice from the Local Authority that proceedings were going to be started);
(3) appoint a solicitor for the child under section 41(3) of the 1989 Act where appropriate;
(4) request the children's guardian or if appropriate another officer of the service or Welsh family proceedings officer to prepare a Case Analysis and Recommendations for the First Appointment;
(5) make arrangements for a contested hearing, if necessary.

(A suggested form for the drafting of Standard Directions on Issue is Form PLO 8 which is available from HMCS).

Setting a date for the First Appointment

12.5 The court will record the Timetable for the Child and set a date for the First Appointment normally no later than 6 days from the date of issue of the proceedings and in any event in line with the Timetable for the Child.

Case managers in the magistrates' courts

12.6 In the magistrates' courts, the justices' clerk may nominate one but not more than two case managers.

THE FIRST APPOINTMENT

Objectives

13.1 The First Appointment is the first hearing in the proceedings. The main objectives of the First Appointment are to–

(1) confirm allocation; and
(2) give initial case management directions having regard to the Public Law Outline.

13.2 The steps which the court will take at the First Appointment include those set out in paragraphs 13.3 to 13.6 below.

The Family Procedure Rules 2010

Steps to be taken by the court

13.3 The court will—

(1) confirm the Timetable for the Child;
(2) make arrangements for any contested interim hearing such as an application for an interim care order;
(3) confirm the allocation of the case or, if appropriate, transfer the case;
(4) request the children's guardian or if appropriate another officer of the service or Welsh family proceedings officer to prepare a Case Analysis and Recommendations for the Case Management Conference or Issues Resolution Hearing;
(5) scrutinise the Care Plan;
(6) consider giving directions relating to–
  (a) those matters in the Public Law Outline which remain to be considered including preparation, filing and service of any missing Annex Documents and what Other Checklist documents are to be filed and by when;
  (b) the joining of a person who would not otherwise be a respondent under the Rules as a party to the proceedings;
  (c) where any person to be joined as a party may be a protected party, an investigation of that person's capacity to conduct the proceedings and the representation of that person by a guardian ad litem or litigation friend, including the Official Solicitor where appropriate;
  (d) the identification of family and friends as proposed carers and any overseas, immigration, jurisdiction and paternity issues;
  (e) any other documents to be filed with the court;
  (f) evidence to be obtained as to whether a parent who is a protected party is competent to make a statement.

(A suggested form for the drafting of Standard Directions on First Appointment is Form PLO9 which is available from HMCS)

Early Final Hearing

13.4 Cases which are suitable for an early Final Hearing are those cases where all the evidence necessary to determine issues of fact and welfare is immediately or shortly available to be filed. Those cases are likely to include cases where the child has no parents, guardians, relatives who want to care for the child, or other carers. The court will–

(1) identify at the First Appointment whether the case is one which is suitable for an early Final Hearing; and
(2) set a date for that Final Hearing.

Setting a date for the Case Management Conference

13.5 The court will set a date for the Case Management Conference normally no later than 45 days from the date of issue of the proceedings and in any event in line with the Timetable for the Child.

Advocates' Meeting/discussion and the drafting of the Case Management Order

13.6 The court will consider directing a discussion between the parties' advocates and any litigant in person and the preparation of a draft of the Case Management Order as outlined below.

Experts

13.7 A party who wishes to instruct an expert should comply with the Experts Practice Direction. Where the parties are agreed on any matter relating to experts or expert evidence, the draft agreement must be submitted for the court's approval as early as possible in the proceedings.

Advocates' Meeting/discussion and the drafting of the Case Management Order

14.1 The main objective of the Advocates' Meeting or discussion is to prepare a draft of the Case Management Order for approval by the court.

14.2 Where there is a litigant in person the court will consider the most effective way in which that person can be involved in the advocates discussions and give directions as appropriate including directions relating to the part to be played by any McKenzie Friend.

14.3 Timing of the discussions is of the utmost importance. Discussions of matters "outside the court room door", which could have been discussed at an earlier time, are to be avoided. Discussions are to take place no later than 2 days before the Case Management Hearing or the Issues Resolution Hearing whichever is appropriate. The discussions may take place earlier than 2 days before those hearings, for example, up to 7 days before them.

14.4 Following discussion the advocates should prepare or adjust the draft of the Case Management Order. In practice the intention is that the advocate for the applicant, which in care and supervision proceedings will ordinarily be the Local Authority, should take the lead in preparing and adjusting the draft of the Case Management Order following discussion with the other advocates. The aim is for the advocates to agree a draft of the Case Management Order which is to be submitted for the approval of the court.

14.5 Where it is not possible for the advocates to agree the terms of the draft of the Case Management Order, the advocates should specify on the draft, or on a separate document if more practicable–

(1) those provisions on which they agree; and
(2) those provisions on which they disagree.

14.6 Unless the court directs otherwise, the draft of the Case Management Order must be filed with the court no later than 11 am on the day before the Case Management Conference or the Issues Resolution Hearing whichever may be appropriate.

14.7 At the Advocates' Meeting or discussion before the Case Management Conference, the advocates should also try to agree the questions to be put to any proposed expert (whether jointly instructed or not) if not previously agreed. Under the Experts Practice Direction the questions on which the proposed expert is to give an opinion are a crucial component of the expert directions which the court is required to consider at the Case Management Conference.

CASE MANAGEMENT CONFERENCE

Objectives

15.1 The Case Management Conference is the main hearing at which the court manages the case. The main objectives of the Conference are to–

(1) identify key issues; and
(2) give full case management directions.

15.2 The steps which the court will take at the Case Management Conference include those steps set out in paragraphs 15.3 to 15.5 below.

Steps to be taken by the court

15.3 The court will–

(1) review and confirm the Timetable for the Child;
(2) confirm the allocation or the transfer of the case;
(3) scrutinise the Care Plan;
(4) identify the key issues;

The Family Procedure Rules 2010

(5) identify the remaining case management issues;
(6) resolve remaining case management issues set out in the draft of the Case Management Order;
(7) identify any special measures such as the need for access for the disabled or provision for vulnerable witnesses;
(8) scrutinise the Case Management Record to check whether directions have been complied with and if not, consider making further directions as appropriate;
(9) where expert evidence is required, check whether the parties have complied with the Experts Practice Direction, in particular the section on preparation for the relevant hearing and consider giving directions as appropriate.

Case Management Order

15.4 The court will issue the approved Case Management Order. Parties or their legal representatives will be expected to submit in electronic form the final approved draft of the Case Management Order on the conclusion of, and the same day as, the Case Management Conference.

Setting a date for the Issues Resolution Hearing/Final Hearing

15.5 The court will set—

(1) a date for the Issues Resolution Hearing normally at any time between 16 and 25 weeks from the date of issue of the proceedings and in any event in line with the Timetable for the Child; and
(2) if necessary, specify a period within which the Final Hearing of the application is to take place unless a date has already been set.

THE ISSUES RESOLUTION HEARING

Objectives

16.1 The objectives of this hearing are to–

(1) resolve and narrow issues;
(2) identify key remaining issues requiring resolution.

16.2 The Issues Resolution Hearing is likely to be the hearing before the Final Hearing. Final case management directions and other preparations for the Final Hearing will be made at this hearing.

Steps to be taken by the Court

16.3 The court will—

(1) identify the key issues (if any) to be determined;
(2) review and confirm the Timetable for the Child;
(3) consider giving case management directions relating to–
   (a) any outstanding matter contained in the draft of the Case Management Order;
   (b) the preparation and filing of final evidence including the filing of witness templates;
   (c) skeleton arguments;
   (d) preparation and filing of bundles in accordance with the Bundles Practice Direction;
   (e) any agreement relating to the satisfaction of the threshold criteria under section 31 of the 1989 Act or facts and issues remaining to be determined in relation to it or to any welfare question which arises;
   (f) time estimates;
   (g) the judicial reading list and likely reading time and judgment writing time;
(4) issue the Case Management Order.

16.4 For the avoidance of doubt the purpose of an Issues Resolution Hearing is to–

(1) identify key issues which are not agreed;
(2) examine if those key issues can be agreed; and
(3) where those issues cannot be agreed, examine the most proportionate method of resolving those issues.

16.5 The expectation is that the method of resolving the key issues which cannot be agreed will be at a hearing (ordinarily the Final hearing) where there is an opportunity for the relevant oral evidence to be heard and challenged.

ATTENDANCE AT THE CASE MANAGEMENT CONFERENCE AND THE ISSUES RESOLUTION HEARING

17 An advocate who has conduct of the Final Hearing should ordinarily attend the Case Management Conference and the Issues Resolution Hearing. Where the attendance of this advocate is not possible, then an advocate who is familiar with the issues in the proceedings should attend.

FLEXIBLE POWERS OF THE COURT

18.1 Attention is drawn to the flexible powers of the court either following the issue of the application in that court, the transfer of the case to that court or at any other stage in the proceedings.

18.2 The court may give directions without a hearing including setting a date for the Final Hearing or a period within which the Final Hearing will take place. The steps, which the court will ordinarily take at the various stages of the proceedings provided for in the Public Law Outline, may be taken by the court at another stage in the proceedings if the circumstances of the case merit this approach.

18.3 The flexible powers of the court include the ability for the court to cancel or repeat a particular hearing. For example, if the issue on which the case turns can with reasonable practicability be crystallised and resolved by having an early Final Hearing, then in the fulfilment of the overriding objective, such a flexible approach must be taken to secure compliance with section 1(2) of the 1989 Act.

ALTERNATIVE DISPUTE RESOLUTION

19.1 The court will encourage the parties to use an alternative dispute resolution procedure and facilitate the use of such a procedure where it is–

(1) readily available;
(2) demonstrated to be in the interests of the child; and
(3) reasonably practicable and safe.

19.2 At any stage in the proceedings, the parties can ask the court for advice about alternative dispute resolution.

19.3 At any stage in the proceedings the court itself will consider whether alternative dispute resolution is appropriate. If so, the court may direct that a hearing or proceedings be adjourned for such specified period as it considers appropriate–

(1) to enable the parties to obtain information and advice about alternative dispute resolution; and
(2) where the parties agree, to enable alternative dispute resolution to take place.

CO-OPERATION

20.1 Throughout the proceedings the parties and their representatives should co-operate wherever reasonably practicable to help towards securing the welfare of the child as the paramount consideration.

20.2 At each court appearance the court will ask the parties and their legal representatives–

(1) what steps they have taken to achieve co-operation and the extent to which they have been successful;

The Family Procedure Rules 2010

(2) if appropriate the reason why co-operation could not be achieved; and
(3) the steps needed to resolve any issues necessary to achieve co-operation.

AGREED DIRECTIONS

21.1 The parties, their advisers and the children's guardian, are encouraged to try to agree directions for the management of the proceedings.

21.2 To obtain the court's approval the agreed directions must–

(1) set out a Timetable for the Child by reference to calendar dates for the taking of steps for the preparation of the case;
(2) include a date when it is proposed that the next hearing will take place.

VARIATION OF CASE MANAGEMENT TIMETABLE

22 It is emphasised that a party or the children's guardian must apply to the court at the earliest opportunity if they wish to vary by extending the dates set by the court for–

(1) a directions appointment;
(2) a First Appointment;
(3) a Case Management Conference;
(4) an Issues Resolution Hearing;
(5) the Final Hearing;
(6) the period within which the Final Hearing of the application is to take place; or
(7) any Meeting/discussion between advocates or for the filing of the draft of the Case Management Orders.

WHO PERFORMS THE FUNCTIONS OF THE COURT

23.1 Where this Practice Direction provides for the Court to perform case management functions, then except where any rule, practice direction, any other enactment or the Family Proceedings (Allocation to Judiciary) Directions ((2009) 2 FLR 51) provides otherwise, the functions may be performed–

(1) in relation to proceedings in the High Court or in a district registry, by any judge or district judge of that Court including a district judge of the principal registry;
(2) in relation to proceedings in the county court, by any judge or district judge including a district judge of the principal registry when the principal registry is treated as if it were a county court; and
(3) in relation to proceedings in a magistrates' court by–
  (a) any family proceedings court constituted in accordance with sections 66 and 67 of the 1980 Act;
  (b) a single justice; or
  (c) a justices' clerk.

23.2 The case management functions to be exercised by a justices' clerk may be exercised by an assistant justices' clerk provided that person has been specifically authorised by a justices' clerk to exercise case management functions. Any reference in this Practice Direction to a justices' clerk is to be taken to include an assistant justices' clerk so authorised. The justices' clerk may in particular appoint one but not more than two assistant justices' clerks as case managers for each case.

23.3 In proceedings in a magistrates' court, where a party considers that there are likely to be issues arising at a hearing (including the First Appointment, Case Management Conference and Issues Resolution Hearing) which need to be decided by a family proceedings court, rather than a justices' clerk, then that party should give the court written notice of that need at least 2 days before the hearing.

23.4 Family proceedings courts may consider making arrangements to ensure a court constituted in accordance with s 66 of the 1980 Act is available at the same time as Issues Resolution Hearings are being heard by a justices' clerk. Any delay as a result of the justices' clerk considering for whatever reason that it is inappropriate for a justices' clerk to perform a case management function on a particular matter and the justices' clerk's referring of that matter to the court should then be minimal.

TECHNOLOGY

24 Where the facilities are available to the court and the parties, the court will consider making full use of technology including electronic information exchange and video or telephone conferencing.

OTHER PRACTICE DIRECTIONS

25.1 This Practice Direction must be read with the Bundles Practice Direction.

25.2 The Bundles Practice Direction is applied to Public Law Proceedings in the High Court and county court with the following adjustments–

(1) add "except the-First Appointment; Case Management Conference, and Issues Resolution Hearing referred to in the Practice Direction: Guide to Case Management: April 2010 where there are no contested applications being heard at those hearings" to paragraph 2.2;
(2) the reference to—
 (a) the "Protocol for Judicial Case Management in Public law Children Act Cases (2003) 2 FLR 719" in paragraph 6.1;
 (b) the "Practice Direction: Care Cases: Judicial Continuity and Judicial Case Management" in paragraph 15; and
 (c) "the Public Law Protocol" in paragraph 15.

shall be read as if it were a reference to this Practice Direction.

25.3 Paragraph 1.9 of the Practice Direction: Experts in Family proceedings relating to Children dated April 2008 should be read as if "Practice Direction: Guide to Case Management in Public law Proceedings, paragraphs 13.7, 14.3 and 25(29)" were a reference to "Practice Direction Public Law Proceedings Guide to Case Management: April 2010, paragraphs 14.7, 15.3 and 26(33)".

GLOSSARY

26 In this Practice Direction–

(1) "the 1989 Act" means the Children Act 1989;
(2) "the 1980 Act" means the Magistrates' Courts Act 1980;
(3) "advocate" means a person exercising a right of audience as a representative of, or on behalf of, a party;
(4) "Allocation Order" means any order made by the Lord Chancellor under Part 1 of Schedule 11 to the 1989 Act;
(5) "alternative dispute resolution" means the methods of resolving a dispute other than through the normal court process;
(6) "Annex Documents" means the documents specified in the Annex to the Application Form;
(7) "Application Form" means Form C110 and Annex Documents;
(8) "assistant justices' clerk" has the meaning assigned to it by section 27(5) of the Courts Act 2003;
(9) "the Bundles Practice Direction" means the Practice Direction Family Proceedings: Court Bundles (Universal Practice to be Applied in all Courts other than Family Proceedings Court) of 27 July 2006;
(10) "Case Analysis and Recommendations" means a written or oral outline of the case from the child's perspective prepared by the children's guardian or other officer of the service or Welsh family proceedings officer at different stages of the proceedings requested by the court, to provide–
 (a) an analysis of the issues that need to be resolved in the case including–
  (i) any harm or risk of harm;
  (ii) the child's own views;
  (iii) the family context including advice relating to ethnicity, language, religion and culture of the child and other significant persons;
  (iv) the Local Authority work and proposed care plan;
  (v) advice about the court process including the Timetable for the Child; and

The Family Procedure Rules 2010

        (vi)   identification of work that remains to be done for the child in the short and longer term; and
    (b)   recommendations for outcomes, in order to safeguard and promote the best interests of the child in the proceedings;

(11) "Case Management Documentation" includes the documents referred to in paragraph 3.10;

(12) "Case Management Order" means an order made by the court which identifies the Timetable for the Child, any delay in the proceedings and the reason for such delay and the key issues in the proceedings and includes such of the following provisions as are appropriate to the proceedings–
    (a)   preliminary information:
        (i)   the names and dates of birth of the children who are the subject of the proceedings;
        (ii)   the names and legal representatives of the parties, and whether they attended the hearing;
        (iii)   any interim orders made in respect of the children and any provisions made for the renewal of those orders;
    (b)   any recitals that the court considers should be recorded in the order, including those relating to:
        (i)   any findings made by the court or agreed between the parties;
        (ii)   any other agreements or undertakings made by the parties;
    (c)   orders made at the hearing by way of case management relating to:
        (i)   the joinder of parties;
        (ii)   the determination of parentage of the children;
        (iii)   the appointment of a guardian ad litem or litigation friend (including the Official Solicitor where appropriate);
        (iv)   the transfer of the proceedings to a different court;
        (v)   the allocation of the proceedings to a case management judge;
        (vi)   the filing and service of threshold criteria documents;
        (vii)   the preparation and filing of assessments, including Core Assessments and parenting assessments;
        (viii)   in accordance with the Experts' Practice Direction, the preparation and filing of other expert evidence, and experts' meetings;
        (ix)   care planning and directions in any application for placement for adoption;
        (x)   the filing and service of evidence/further evidence on behalf of the local authority;
        (xi)   the filing and serving of evidence/further evidence on behalf of the other parties;
        (xii)   the filing and service of the Case Analysis and Recommendations;
        (xiii)   the disclosure of documents into the proceedings held by third parties, including medical records, police records and Home Office information;
        (xiv)   the disclosure of documents and information relating to the proceedings to non-parties;
        (xv)   the listing of further hearings, and case management documentation to be prepared for those hearings;
        (xvi)   advocates' Meetings;
        (xvii)   the filing of bundles and other preparatory material for future hearings;
        (xviii)   technology/special measures;
        (xix)   media attendance and reporting;
        (xx)   linked or other proceedings;
        (xxi)   non-compliance with any court orders;
        (xxii)   such further or other directions as may be necessary for the purposes of case management;
        (xxiii)   attendance at court (including child/children's guardian);

(13) "Case Management Record" means the court's filing system for the case which includes the documents referred to at paragraph 3.12;

(14) "Case manager" means the justices' clerk or assistant justices' clerk who manages the case in the magistrates' courts;

FPR 2010, Practice Direction 12A

(15) "Care Plan" means a "section 31A plan" referred to in section 31A of the 1989 Act;
(16) "Core Assessment" means the assessment undertaken by the Local Authority in accordance with The Framework for the Assessment of Children in Need and their Families (Department of Health *et al*, 2000);
(17) "court" means the High Court, county court or the magistrates' court;
(18) "court officer" means–
 (a) in the High Court or a county court, a member of court staff; and
 (b) in a magistrates' court, the designated officer;
(19) "Experts Practice Direction" means the Practice Direction on Experts in Family Proceedings relating to Children;
(20) "genogram" means a family tree, setting out in diagrammatic form the family's background;
(21) "hearing" includes a directions appointment;
(22) "Initial Assessment" means the assessment undertaken by the Local Authority in accordance with The Framework for the Assessment of Children in Need and their Families (Department of Health et al, 2000);
(23) "Initial Social Work Statement" means a statement prepared by the Local Authority strictly limited to the following evidence–
 (a) the precipitating incident(s) and background circumstances relevant to the grounds and reasons for making the application including a brief description of any referral and assessment processes that have already occurred;
 (b) any facts and matters that are within the social worker's personal knowledge limited to the findings sought by the Local Authority;
 (c) any emergency steps and previous court orders that are relevant to the application;
 (d) any decisions made by the Local Authority that are relevant to the application;
 (e) information relevant to the ethnicity, language, religion, culture, gender and vulnerability of the child and other significant persons in the form of a 'family profile' together with a narrative description and details of the social care and other services that are relevant to the same;
 (f) where the Local Authority is applying for an interim order: the Local Authority's initial proposals for the child (which are also to be set out in the Care Plan) including placement, contact with parents and other significant persons and the social care services that are proposed;
 (g) the Local Authority's initial proposals for the further assessment of the parties during the proceedings including twin track /concurrent planning (where more than one permanence option for the child is being explored by the Local Authority);
(24) "legal representative" means a–
 (a) a barrister,
 (b) solicitor,
 (c) solicitor's employee,
 (d) manager of a body recognised under section 9 of the Administration of Justice Act 1985, or
 (e) person who, for the purposes of the Legal Services Act 2007, is an authorised person in relation to an activity which constitutes the conduct of litigation (within the meaning of that Act);
who has been instructed to act for a party in relation to the proceedings;
(25) "Letter Before Proceedings" means any letter from the Local Authority containing written notification to the parents and others with parental responsibility for the child of the Local Authority's plan to apply to court for a care or supervision order and any related subsequent correspondence confirming the Local Authority's position;
(26) "Local Authority Case Summary" means a document prepared by the Local Authority advocate for all case management hearings including–
 (a) a recommended reading list and suggested reading time;
 (b) the key issues in the case;
 (c) any additional information relevant to the Timetable for the Child or for the conduct of the hearing or the proceedings;

(d) a summary of updating information;
(e) the issues and directions which the court will need to consider at the hearing in question, including any interim orders sought;
(f) any steps which have not been taken or directions not complied with, an explanation of the reasons and the effect, if any, on the Timetable for the Child;
(g) any relevant information relevant to ethnicity, cultural or gender issues;
(27) "justices' clerk" has the meaning assigned to it by section 27(1) of the Courts Act 2003;
(28) "McKenzie Friend" means any person permitted by the court to sit beside an unrepresented litigant in court to assist the litigant by prompting, taking notes and giving advice to the litigant;
(29) "Other Checklist Documents" means the documents listed in the Pre-proceedings Checklist which will normally be on the local authority file prior to the start of proceedings but which are not-
(a) to be filed with the court on issue; or
(b) Annex Documents.
(30) "Other Parties' Case Summaries" means summaries by parties other than the Local Authority containing–
(a) the party's proposals for the long term future of the child (to include placement and contact);
(b) the party's reply to the Local Authority's Schedule of Proposed Findings;
(c) any proposal for assessment / expert evidence; and
(d) the names, addresses and contact details of any family or friends who it is suggested be approached in relation to long term care / contact or respite;
(31) "Pre-proceedings Checklist" means the Annex Documents and the Other Checklist Documents set out in the Public Law Outline;
(32) "Public Law Outline" means the Table contained in paragraph 10;
(33) "Public Law Proceedings" means proceedings for–
(a) a residence order under section 8 of the 1989 Act with respect to a child who is subject of a care order;
(b) a special guardianship order relating to a child who is the subject of a care order;
(c) a secure accommodation order under section 25 of the 1989 Act;
(d) a care order under section 31(1)(a) of the 1989 Act or the discharge of such an order under section 39(1) of the 1989 Act;
(e) an order giving permission to change a child's surname or remove a child from the United Kingdom under section 33(7) of the 1989 Act;
(f) a supervision order under section 31(1)(b) of the 1989 Act, the discharge or variation of such an order under section 39(2) of that Act, or the extension or further extension of such an order under paragraph 6(3) of Schedule 3 to that Act;
(g) an order making provision for contact under section 34(2) to (4) of the 1989 Act or an order varying or discharging such an order under section 34(9) of that Act;
(h) an education supervision order, the extension of an education supervision order under paragraph 15(2) of Schedule 3 to the 1989 Act, or the discharge of such an order under paragraph 17(1) of Schedule 3 to that Act;
(i) an order varying directions made with an interim care order or interim supervision order under section 38(8)(b) of the 1989 Act;
(j) an order under section 39(3) of the 1989 Act varying a supervision order in so far as it affects a person with whom the child is living but who is not entitled to apply for the order to be discharged;
(k) an order under section 39(3A) of the 1989 Act varying or discharging an interim care order in so far as it imposes an exclusion requirement on a person who is not entitled to apply for the order to be discharged;
(l) an order under section 39(3B) of the 1989 Act varying or discharging an interim care order in so far as it confers a power of arrest attached to an exclusion requirement;

(m) the substitution of a supervision order for a care order under section 39(4) of the 1989 Act;
(n) a child assessment order or the variation or discharge of such an order under section 43(12) of the 1989 Act;
(o) an order permitting the Local Authority to arrange for any child in its care to live outside England and Wales under paragraph 19(1) of Schedule 2 to the 1989 Act;
(p) a contribution order, or the variation or revocation of such an order under paragraph 23(8), of Schedule 2 to the 1989 Act;
(q) an appeal under paragraph 8(1) of Schedule 8 to the 1989 Act.

(34) "rules" means rules of court governing the practice and procedure to be followed in Public Law Proceedings;
(35) "Schedule of Proposed Findings" means the schedule of findings of fact prepared by the Local Authority sufficient to satisfy the threshold criteria under section 31 (2) of the 1989 Act and to inform the Care Plan;
(36) Section 7 report" means any report under section 7 of the 1989 Act;
(37) "Section 37 report" means any report by the Local Authority to the court as a result of a direction under section 37 of the 1989 Act;
(38) "Social Work Chronology" means a schedule containing–
 (a) a succinct summary of the significant dates and events in the child's life in chronological order- a running record to be updated during the proceedings;
 (b) information under the following headings–
  (i) serial number;
  (ii) date;
  (iii) event-detail;
  (iv) witness or document reference (where applicable);
(39) "Specified proceedings" has the meaning assigned to it by section 41(6) of the 1989 Act;
(40) "Standard Directions on Issue" mean directions made by the court which will include such of the directions set out in the Public Law Outline, Stage 1, column 1 as are appropriate to the proceedings;
(41) "Standard Directions on First Appointment" means directions made by the court which will include such of the directions set out in the Public Law Outline, Stage 1, column 2 and directions relating to the following as are appropriate to the proceedings–
 (a) the Timetable for the Child;
 (b) the joining of a party of the proceedings;
 (c) the appointment of a guardian ad litem or litigation friend including the Official Solicitor where appropriate for a protected party or non subject child;
 (d) allocation of the case to a case manager or case management judge;
 (e) experts in accordance with the Experts Practice Direction;
 (f) the interim care plan setting out details as to proposed placement and contact;
 (g) any other evidence (such as evidence relating to vulnerability, ethnicity, culture, language, religion or gender) and disclosure of evidence between the parties;
 (h) filing and service of the draft of the Case Management Order before the Case Management Conference;
 (i) listing the Issues Resolution hearing and Final Hearing;
 (j) media attendance and reporting;
(42) "Strategy Discussion Record" means a note of the strategy discussion within the meaning of "Working Together to Safeguard Children" (2006);
(43) "Timetable for the Child" has the meaning assigned to it by the rules. (See paragraph 3.2 of this Practice Direction.)

The Family Procedure Rules 2010

PRACTICE DIRECTION 12B – THE REVISED PRIVATE LAW PROGRAMME

1 Introduction

Effective from 1st April 2010

1.1 The Private Law Programme has achieved marked success in enabling the resolution of the majority of cases by consent at the First Hearing Dispute Resolution Appointment ("FHDRA"). It has been revised to build on the successes of the initial programme and to take account of recent developments in the law and practice associated with private family law.

1.2 In particular, there have been several legislative changes affecting private family law. The Allocation and Transfer of Proceedings Order 2008 (the "Allocation Order"), requires the transfer of cases from the County Court to the Family Proceedings Court (FPC). Sections 1 to 5 and Schedule 1 of the Children and Adoption Act 2006 which came into force on 8th December 2008, amends the Children Act 1989 by introducing Contact Activity Directions, Contact Activity Conditions, Contact Monitoring Requirements, Financial Compensation Orders and Enforcement Orders.

1.3 There has been growing recognition of the impact of domestic violence and abuse, drug and alcohol misuse and mental illness, on the proper consideration of the issues in private family law; this includes the acceptance that Court orders, even those made by consent, must be scrutinised to ensure that they are safe and take account of any risk factors. Coupled with this is the need to take account of the duty on Cafcass, pursuant to s 16A Children Act 1989, to undertake risk assessments where an officer of the Service ("Cafcass Officer") suspects that a child is at risk of harm. (References to Cafcass include CAFCASS CYMRU and references to the Cafcass Officer include the Welsh family proceedings officer in Wales).

1.4 There is awareness of the importance of involving children where appropriate in the decision making process.

1.5 The Revised Programme incorporates these developments. It also retains the essential feature of the FHDRA as the forum for the parties to be helped to reach agreement as to, and understanding of, the issues that divide them. It recognises that having reached agreement parties may need assistance in putting it into effect in a co-operative way.

1.6 The Revised Programme is designed to provide a framework for the consistent national approach to the resolution of the issues in private family law whilst enabling local practices and initiatives to be operated in addition and within the framework.

1.7 The Revised Programme is designed to assist parties to reach safe agreements where possible, to provide a forum in which to find the best way to resolve issues in each individual case and to promote outcomes that are sustainable, that are in the best interests of children and that take account of their perspectives.

2 Principles

2.1 Where an application is made to a court under Part II of the Children Act 1989, the child's welfare is the court's paramount concern. The court will apply the principle of the "Overriding Objective" to enable it to deal with a case justly, having regard to the welfare principles involved. So far as practicable the Court will –

(a) Deal expeditiously and fairly with every case;
(b) Deal with a case in ways which are proportionate to the nature, importance and complexity of the issues;
(c) Ensure that the parties are on an equal footing;
(d) Save unnecessary expense;
(e) Allot to each case an appropriate share of the court's resources, while taking account of the need to allot resources to other cases.

2.2 The court will give effect to the overriding objective when applying this programme and when exercising its powers to manage cases.

FPR 2010, Practice Direction 12B

The parties are required to help the court further the overriding objective and promote the welfare of the child by the application of the welfare principle, pursuant to s 1(1) of the Children Act 1989.

This Programme provides that consideration and discussion of all issues will not take place until the FHDRA when parties are on an equal footing and can hear what is said to and by each other. This excludes the safety checks and enquiries carried out by Cafcass before the first hearing that are required for that hearing and deal only with safety issues.

At the **FHDRA** the Court shall consider in particular –

(a) Whether and the extent to which the parties can safely resolve some or all of the issues with the assistance of the Cafcass Officer and any available mediator.
(b) Risk identification followed by active case management including risk assessment, and compliance with the Practice Direction 14th January 2009: "Residence and Contact Orders: Domestic Violence and Harm".
(c) Further dispute resolution.
(d) The avoidance of delay through the early identification of issues and timetabling, subject to the Allocation Order.
(e) Judicial scrutiny of the appropriateness of consent orders
(f) Judicial consideration of the way to involve the child.
(g) Judicial continuity

3 Practical Arrangements Before the FHDRA

3.1 Applications shall be issued on the day of receipt in accordance with the appropriate Rules of Procedure. It is important that the form C100 is fully completed, especially on pages 1, 2, 3, 10 and 11 otherwise delay may be caused by requests for information.

3.2 If possible at the time of issue, and in any event by no later than 24 hours after issue, or in courts where applications are first considered on paper, by no later than 48 hours after issue, the court shall
(i)   send or hand to the Applicant
(ii) send to Cafcass
    the following:
    (a) a copy of the Application Form C100, (together with Supplemental Information Form C1A)(if provided) (references to form C1A are to be read as form C100A following the introduction of this replacement form)
    (b) the Notice of Hearing,
    (c) the Acknowledgment Form C7,
    (d) a blank Form C1A
    (e) the Certificate of Service Form C9.
    (f) information leaflets for the parties.

3.3 Save in urgent cases that require an earlier listing, the fully effective operation of this Practice Direction requires the FHDRA to take place within **4** weeks of the application. Where practicable, the first hearing must be listed to be heard in this period and in any event no later than within **6** weeks of the application. Where, at the time of introduction of this Programme, the Designated Family Judge/ Justices' Clerk determines that it is not practicable to list the first hearing within 4 weeks, they should, in consultation with HMCS and Cafcass, formulate a timetable for revisiting the position and managing to list the FHDRA within 4 weeks.

3.4 Copies of each Application Form C100 and Notice of Hearing shall be sent by the court to Cafcass in accordance with 3.2 above.

The Respondent shall have at least 14 days notice of the hearing where practicable, but the court may abridge this time.

3.6 The Respondent should file a response on the Forms C7/C1A no later than 14 days before the hearing.

The Family Procedure Rules 2010

3.7 A copy of Forms C7/C1A shall be sent by the court to Cafcass on the day of receipt.

3.8 **NOTE:** This provision relates to cases that are placed in the FHDRA list for hearing other than by direct application in accordance with the procedure referred to in paragraph 3.1. Such listing may follow an application under the Family Law Act 1996, or a direction by the Court in other proceedings. In all such cases, or where the Court adjourns proceedings to a 'dispute resolution hearing' (sometimes called 'conciliation'), this will be treated as an adjournment to a FHDRA, and the documents referred to in para 3.2 must be filed and copied to parties and Cafcass for safety checks and enquiries, in the same way.

3.9 Before the FHDRA Cafcass shall identify any safety issues by the steps outlined below. Such steps shall be confined to matters of safety. Neither Cafcass nor a Cafcass Officer shall discuss with either party before the FHDRA any matter other than relates to safety. The Parties will not be invited to talk about other issues, for example relating to the substance of applications or replies or about issues concerning matters of welfare or the prospects of resolution. If such issues are raised by either party they will be advised that such matters will be deferred to the FHDRA when there is equality between the parties and full discussion can take place which will also be a time when any safety issues that have been identified also can be taken into account.

(a) In order to inform the court of possible risks of harm to the child in accordance with its safeguarding framework Cafcass will carry out safeguarding enquiries, including checks of local authorities and police, and telephone risk identification interviews with parties.

(b) If risks of harm are identified, Cafcass may invite parties to meet separately with the Cafcass Officer before the FHDRA to clarify any safety issue.

(c) Cafcass shall record and outline any safety issues for the court.

(d) The Cafcass Officer will not initiate contact with the child prior to the FHDRA. If contacted by a child, discussions relating to the issues in the case will be postponed to the day of the hearing or after when the Cafcass officer will have more knowledge of the issues.

(e) At least 3 days before the hearing the Cafcass Officer shall report the outcome of risk identification work to the court by completing the Form at Schedule 2.

4 The First Hearing Dispute Resolution Appointment

4.1 The parties and Cafcass Officer shall attend this hearing. A mediator may attend where available.

4.2 At the hearing, which is not privileged, the court should have the following documents:

(a) C100 application, and C1A if any
(b) Notice of Hearing
(c) C7 response and C1A if any
(d) Schedule 2 safeguarding information

4.3 The detailed arrangements for the participation of mediators will be arranged locally. These will include:

(a) Arrangements for the mediator to ask the parties in a particular case to consent to the mediator seeing the papers in the case where it seems appropriate to do so.

(b) Arrangements for the mediator to ask the parties to waive privilege for the purpose of the first hearing where it seems to the mediator appropriate to do so in order to assist the work of the mediator and the outcome of the first hearing.

(c) In all cases it is important that such arrangements are put in place in a way that avoids any pressure being brought to bear in this connection on the parties that is inconsistent with general good mediation practice.

FPR 2010, Practice Direction 12B

4.4 At the FHDRA the Court, in collaboration with the Cafcass Officer, and with the assistance of any mediator present, will seek to assist the parties in conciliation and in resolution of all or any of the issues between them. Any remaining issues will be identified, the Cafcass Officer will advise the court of any recommended means of resolving such issues and directions will be given for the future resolution of such issues. At all times the decisions of the Court and the work of the Cafcass Officer will take account of any risk or safeguarding issues that have been identified.

4.5 The Cafcass Officer shall, where practicable, speak separately to each party at court and before the hearing.

4.6 In the County Court, the Court shall have available a telephone contact to the Family Proceedings Court listing manager, diary dates for the appropriate Family Proceedings Court, or other means by which the County Court, at the time of the hearing, will be able to list subsequent hearings in the Family Proceedings Court.

5 Conduct of the Hearing

The following matters shall be considered

5.1 Safeguarding:

(a) The court shall inform the parties of the content of any screening report or other information which has been provided by Cafcass, unless it considers that to do so would create a risk of harm to a party or the child. The court may need to consider whether and how any information contained in the checks should be disclosed to the parties if Cafcass have not disclosed it.
(b) Whether a risk assessment is required and when.
(c) Whether a fact finding hearing is needed to determine allegations whose resolution is likely to affect the decision of the court.

5.2 Dispute Resolution:

(a) There will be at every FHDRA a period in which the Cafcass Officer, with the assistance of any Mediator and in collaboration with the Court, will seek to conciliate and explore with the parties the resolution of all or some of the issues between them. The procedure to be followed in this connection at the hearing will be determined by local arrangements between the Cafcass manager, or equivalent in Wales, and the Designated Family Judge or the Justices' Clerk where appropriate.
(b) What is the result of any such meeting at Court?
(c) What other options there are for resolution e.g. may the case be suitable for further intervention by Cafcass; mediation by an external provider; collaborative law or use of a parenting plan?
(d) Would the parties be assisted by attendance at Parenting Information Programmes or other activities, whether by formal statutory provision under section 11 Children Act 1989 as amended by Children and Adoption Act 2006 or otherwise?

5.3 Consent Orders:

Where agreement is reached at any hearing or submitted in writing to the court, no order will be made without scrutiny by the court. Where safeguarding checks or risk assessment work remain outstanding, the making of a final order may be deferred for such work. In such circumstances the court shall adjourn the case for no longer than 28 days to a fixed date. A written notification of this work is to be provided by Cafcass in accordance with the timescale specified by the court. If satisfactory information is then available, the order may be made at the adjourned hearing in the agreed terms without the need for attendance by the parties. If satisfactory information is not available, the order will not be made, and the case will be adjourned for further consideration with an opportunity for the parties to make further representations.

5.4 Reports:

(a) Are there welfare issues or other specific considerations which should be addressed in a report by Cafcass or the Local Authority? Before a report is

The Family Procedure Rules 2010

ordered, the court should consider alternative ways of working with the parties such as are referred to in paragraph 5.2 above. If a report is ordered in accordance with Section 7 of the Children Act 1989, it should be directed specifically towards and limited to those issues. General requests should be avoided and the Court should state in the Order the specific factual and other issues that are to be addressed in a focused report. In determining whether a request for a report should be directed to the relevant local authority or to Cafcass, the court should consider such information as Cafcass has provided about the extent and nature of the local authority's current or recent involvement with the subject of the application and the parties, and any relevant protocol between Cafcass and the Association of Directors of Children's Services.

(b) Is there a need for an investigation under S.37 Children Act 1989?
(c) A copy of the Order requesting the report and any relevant court documents are to be sent to Cafcass or, in the case of the Local Authority, to the Legal Adviser to the Director of the Local Authority Children's Services and, where known, to the allocated social worker by the court forthwith.
(d) Is any expert evidence required in compliance with the Experts' Practice Direction?

5.5 **Wishes and feelings of the child:**

(a) Is the child aware of the proceedings? How are the wishes and feelings of the child to be ascertained (if at all)?
(b) How is the child to be involved in the proceedings, if at all, and whether at or after the FHDRA?
(c) If consideration is given to the joining of the child as a party to the application, the court should consider the current Guidance from the President of the Family Division. Where the court is considering the appointment of a guardian ad litem, it should first seek to ensure that the appropriate Cafcass manager has been spoken to so as to consider any advice in connection with the prospective appointment and the timescale involved. In considering whether to make such an appointment the Court shall take account of the demands on the resources of Cafcass that such appointment would make.
(d) Who will inform the child of the outcome of the case where appropriate?

5.6 **Case Management:**

(a) What, if any, issues are agreed and what are the key issues to be determined?
(b) Are there any interim orders which can usefully be made (e.g. indirect, supported or supervised contact) pending final hearing?
(c) What directions are required to ensure the application is ready for final hearing – statements, reports etc?
(d) List for final hearing, consider the need for judicial continuity (especially if there has been or is to be a fact finding hearing or a contested interim hearing).

5.7 **Transfer to FPC:**

The case should be transferred to the FPC, pursuant to the Allocation and Transfer of Proceedings Order 2008 unless one of the specified exceptions applies. The date should be fixed at court and entered on the order.

6 The Order

6.1 The Order shall set out in particular:

(a) The issues about which the parties are agreed
(b) The issues that remain to be resolved
(c) The steps that are planned to resolve the issues
(d) Any interim arrangements pending such resolution, including arrangements for the involvement of children.
(e) The timetable for such steps and, where this involves further hearings, the date of such hearings.
(f) A statement as to any facts relating to risk or safety; in so far as they are resolved the result will be stated and, in so far as not resolved, the steps to be taken to resolve them will be stated.

FPR 2010, Practice Direction 12C

(g) If it be the case, the fact of the transfer of the case to the Family Proceedings Court with the date and purpose of the next hearing

(h) If it be the case, the fact that the case cannot be transferred to the Family Proceedings Court and the reason for the decision.

(i) Whether in the event of an order, by consent or otherwise, or pending such an order, the parties are to be assisted by participation in mediation, Parenting Information Programmes, or other types of parenting intervention, and to detail any contact activity directions or conditions imposed by the court.
A suggested template order is available as set out in Schedule 1 below.

7 Commencement and implementation

7.1 This Practice Direction will come into effect on April 1st 2010. So that procedural changes can be made by all agencies, the requirement for full implementation of the provisions is postponed, but in any event it should be effected by no later than October 4th 2010.

Schedule 1

The suggested form of Order which courts may wish to use is PLP10 which is available from Her Majesty's Court Service.

Schedule 2

Report Form on outcome of safeguarding enquiries. See version for Cafcass in England and for CAFCASS CYMRU in Wales.

Sir Mark Potter

President of the Family Division

PRACTICE DIRECTION 12C – SERVICE OF APPLICATION IN CERTAIN PROCEEDINGS RELATING TO CHILDREN

This Practice Direction supplements FPR Part 12 (Procedure Relating to Children except Parental Order Proceedings and Proceedings For Applications In Adoption, Placement and Related Proceedings), rule 12.8 (Service of the application)

PERSONS WHO RECEIVE COPY OF APPLICATION FORM

1.1 In relation to the proceedings in column 1 of the following table, column 2 sets out the documentation which persons listed in column 3 are to receive—

Proceedings	Documentation	Who receives a copy of the documentation
1. Private law proceedings; public law proceedings; emergency proceedings (except those proceedings referred to in entries 2 and 3 of the Table below);	Application form (including any supplementary forms); Form C6 (Notice of proceedings); and in private law proceedings, the form of answer.	All the respondents to the application.

The Family Procedure Rules 2010

Proceedings	Documentation	Who receives a copy of the documentation
proceedings for a declaration under rule 12.71 as to the existence, or extent, of parental responsibility under Article 16 of the 1996 Hague Convention; an order relating to the exercise of the court's inherent jurisdiction (including wardship proceedings).		
2. An enforcement order (section 11J of the 1989 Act); a financial compensation order (section 11O of the 1989 Act).	As above	All the respondents to the application; and where the child was a party to the proceedings in which the contact order was made— (a) the person who was the children's guardian or litigation friend in those proceedings; or (b) where there was no children's guardian or litigation friend, the person who was the legal representative of the child in those proceedings.
3. A care or a supervision order (section 31 of the 1989 Act).	As above and such of the documents specified in the Annex to Form C110 as are available.	All the respondents to the application; and Cafcass or CAFCASS CYMRU.
4 Proceedings for an order for the return of a child under the 1980 Hague Convention or registration of an order under the European Convention.	As above and the documents referred to in part 2 of the Practice Direction 12F (International Child Abduction).	All the respondents to the application.

(Rule 12.3 sets out who the parties to the proceedings are.)

1.2 When filing the documents referred to in column 2 of the Table in paragraph 1.1, the applicant must also file sufficient copies for one to be served on each respondent and Cafcass or CAFCASS CYMRU.

1.3 Where the application for an order in proceedings referred to in column 1 of the Table in paragraph 1.1 is made in respect of more than one child all the children must be included in the same application form.

1.4 The applicant will serve Form C6A (notice to non parties) on the persons referred to in the Table in paragraph 3.1 at the same time as serving the documents in column 2 of the Table in paragraph 1.1.

412

FPR 2010, Practice Direction 12C

TIME FOR SERVING APPLICATION

2.1 In relation to the proceedings in column 1 of the following table, column 2 sets out the time period within which the application and accompanying documents must be served on each respondent—

Proceedings	Minimum number of days prior to hearing or directions appointment for service
1. Private law proceedings; and proceedings for— an order permitting the child's name to be changed or the removal of the child from the United Kingdom (33(7) of the 1989 Act); an order permitting the local authority to arrange for any child in its care to live outside England and Wales (Schedule 2, paragraph 19(1) of the 1989 Act); a contribution order (Schedule 2, paragraph 23(1) of the 1989 Act); an order revoking a contribution order (Schedule 2, paragraph 23(8) of the 1989 Act); an appeal under paragraph 8(1) of Schedule 8 to the 1989 Act; an order relating to the exercise of the court's inherent jurisdiction (including wardship proceedings); a declaration under rule 12.71 as to the existence, or extent, of parental responsibility under Article 16 of the 1996 Hague Convention.	14 days.
2. Proceedings for— a residence order under section 8 of the 1989 Act relating to a child who is the subject of a care order; a special guardianship order relating to a child who is the subject of a care order (section 14A of the 1989 Act); an education supervision order (section 36 of the 1989 Act); an order discharging a care order (section 39(1) of the 1989 Act); an order varying or discharging a supervision order (section 39(2) of the 1989 Act) or extending or further extending a supervision order under paragraph 6(3) of Schedule 3 to the 1989 Act; an order varying a supervision order in so far as it affects the person with whom the child is living (section 39(3) of the 1989 Act); an application to substitute a supervision order for a care order (section 39(4) of the 1989 Act);	7 days.

413

The Family Procedure Rules 2010

Proceedings	Minimum number of days prior to hearing or directions appointment for service
an order extending an education supervision order (Schedule 3, paragraph 15(2) to the 1989 Act); an order discharging an education supervision order (Schedule 3, paragraph 17(1) to the 1989 Act).	
3. Proceedings for— a care or supervision order (section 31 of the 1989 Act); an order making provision for contact under section 34(2) to (4) of the 1989 Act or an order varying or discharging such an order under section 34(9) of the 1989 Act; an order varying directions made with an interim care order or interim supervision order under section 38(8)(b) of the 1989 Act; an order under section 39(3A) of the 1989 Act varying or discharging an interim care order in so far as it imposes an exclusion requirement on a person who is not entitled to apply for the order to be discharged; an order under section 39(3B) of the 1989 Act varying or discharging an interim care order in so far as it confers a power of arrest attached to an exclusion requirement. a child assessment order (section 43(1) of the 1989 Act).	3 days.
4. Proceedings for an order for the return of a child under the 1980 Hague Convention or registration of an order under the European Convention.	4 days
5. An order varying or discharging a child assessment order (section 43(12) of the 1989 Act).	2 days
6. Emergency proceedings; and proceedings for a secure accommodation order (section 25 of the 1989 Act);	1 day

2.2 The court may extend or shorten the time period referred to in column 2 of the table in paragraph 2.1 (see rule 4.1(3)(a)).

2.3 Where the application is to be served on a child, rule 6.33 provides that, in addition to the persons to be served in accordance with rules 6.28 and 6.32, the application must also be served on the persons or bodies listed in rule 6.33(3) unless the court orders otherwise.

PERSONS WHO RECEIVE A COPY OF FORM C6A (NOTICE TO NON-PARTIES)

3.1 In relation to each type of proceedings in column 1 of the following table, the persons listed in column 2 are to receive a copy of Form C6A (Notice of

Proceedings/Hearing/Directions Appointment to Non-Parties)—

Proceedings	Persons to whom notice is to be given
1. All applications.	Subject to separate entries below:
	local authority providing accommodation for the child;
	persons who are caring for the child at the time when the proceedings are commenced; and
	in the case of proceedings brought in respect of a child who is alleged to be staying in a refuge which is certified under section 51(1) or (2) of the 1989 Act, the person who is providing the refuge.
2. An order appointing a guardian (section 5(1) of the 1989 Act).	As for all applications; and
	the father or parent (being a woman who is a parent by virtue of section 43 of the Human Fertilisation and Embryology Act 2008) of the child if that person does not have parental responsibility.
3. A section 8 order (section 8 of the 1989 Act).	As for all applications; and,
	every person whom the applicant believes—
	(i) to be named in a court order with respect to the same child, which has not ceased to have effect;
	(ii) to be party to pending proceedings in respect of the same child; or
	(iii) to be a person with whom the child has lived for at least 3 years prior to the application,
	unless, in a case to which (i) or (ii) applies, the applicant believes that the court order or pending proceedings are not relevant to the application.
4. A special guardianship order (section 14A of the 1989 Act); variation or discharge of a special guardianship order (section 14D of the 1989 Act).	As for all applications; and
	every person whom the applicant believes—
	(i) to be named in a court order with respect to the same child, which has not ceased to have effect;
	(ii) to be party to pending proceedings in respect of the same child; or
	(iii) to be a person with whom the child has lived for at least 3 years prior to the application,
	unless, in a case to which (i) or (ii) applies, the applicant believes that the court order or pending proceedings are not relevant to the application;

Proceedings	Persons to whom notice is to be given
	if the child is not being accommodated by the local authority, the local authority in whose area the applicant is ordinarily resident; and
	in the case of an application under section 14D of the 1989 Act, the local authority that prepared the report under section 14A(8) or (9) in the proceedings leading to the order which it is sought to have varied or discharged, if different from any local authority that will otherwise be notified.
5. An order permitting the local authority to arrange for any child in its care to live outside England and Wales (Schedule 2, paragraph 19(1) of the 1989 Act).	As for all applications; and
	the parties to the proceedings leading to the care order.
6. A care or supervision order (section 31 of the 1989 Act).	As for all applications; and
	every person whom the applicant believes to be a party to pending relevant proceedings in respect of the same child; and
	every person whom the applicant believes to be a parent without parental responsibility for the child.
7. A child assessment order (section 43(1) of the 1989 Act).	As for all applications; and
	every person whom the applicant believes to be a parent of the child;
	every person whom the applicant believes to be caring for the child;
	every person in whose favour a contact order is in force with respect to the child; and
	every person who is allowed to have contact with the child by virtue of an order under section 34 of the 1989 Act.
8. An order varying or discharging a child assessment order (section 43(12) of the 1989 Act).	The persons referred to in section 43(11)(a) to (e) of the 1989 Act who were not party to the application for the order which it is sought to have varied or discharged.
9. An emergency protection order (section 44(1) of the 1989 Act).	As for all applications above; and
	every person whom the applicant believes to be a parent of the child.
10. An order varying a direction under section 44(6) in an emergency protection order (section 44(9)(b) of the 1989 Act).	As for all applications; and
	the local authority in whose area the child is living; and
	any person whom the applicant believes to be affected by the direction which it is sought to have varied.

Proceedings	Persons to whom notice is to be given
11. A warrant authorising a constable to assist in the exercise of certain powers to search for children and inspect premises (section 102 of the 1989 Act).	The person referred to in section 102(1) of the 1989 Act; and any person preventing or likely to prevent such a person from exercising powers under enactments mentioned in subsection (6) of that section.
12. An enforcement order (section 11J of the 1989 Act); a financial compensation order (section 11O of the 1989 Act).	Any officer of the Service or Welsh family proceedings officer who is monitoring compliance with a contact order (in accordance with section 11H(2) of the 1989 Act).
13. An order revoking or amending an enforcement order (Schedule A1, paragraphs 4 to 7 of the 1989 Act) (rule 12.33 makes provision regarding applications under Schedule A1, paragraph 5 of the 1989 Act); an order following a breach of an enforcement order (Schedule A1, paragraph 9 of the 1989 Act).	Any officer of the Service or Welsh family proceedings officer who is monitoring compliance with the enforcement order (in accordance with section 11M(1) of the 1989 Act); the responsible officer (as defined in section 197 of the Criminal Justice Act 2003, as modified by Schedule A1 to the 1989 Act).
14. A declaration under rule 12.71 as to the existence, or extent, of parental responsibility under Article 16 of the 1996 Hague Convention.	A person who the applicant believes is a parent of the child.

PRACTICE DIRECTION 12D – INHERENT JURISDICTION (INCLUDING WARDSHIP) PROCEEDINGS

This Practice Direction supplements FPR Part 12, Chapter 5

THE NATURE OF INHERENT JURISDICTION PROCEEDINGS

1.1 It is the duty of the court under its inherent jurisdiction to ensure that a child who is the subject of proceedings is protected and properly taken care of. The court may in exercising its inherent jurisdiction make any order or determine any issue in respect of a child unless limited by case law or statute. Such proceedings should not be commenced unless it is clear that the issues concerning the child cannot be resolved under the Children Act 1989.

1.2 The court may under its inherent jurisdiction, in addition to all of the orders which can be made in family proceedings, make a wide range of injunctions for the child's protection of which the following are the most common—

(a) orders to restrain publicity;
(b) orders to prevent an undesirable association;
(c) orders relating to medical treatment;
(d) orders to protect abducted children, or children where the case has another substantial foreign element; and
(e) orders for the return of children to and from another state.

1.3 The court's wardship jurisdiction is part of and not separate from the court's inherent jurisdiction. The distinguishing characteristics of wardship are that—

(a) custody of a child who is a ward is vested in the court; and
(b) although day to day care and control of the ward is given to an individual or to a local authority, no important step can be taken in the child's life without the court's consent.

TRANSFER OF PROCEEDINGS TO COUNTY COURT

2.1 Whilst county courts do not have jurisdiction to deal with applications that a child be made or cease to be a ward of court, consideration should be given to transferring the case in whole or in part to a county court where a direction has been given confirming the wardship and directing that the child remain a ward of court during his minority or until further order.

2.2 The county court must transfer the case back to the High Court if a decision is required as to whether the child should remain a ward of court.

2.3 The following proceedings in relation to a ward of court will be dealt with in the High Court unless the nature of the issues of fact or law makes them more suitable for hearing in the county court—

(a) those in which an officer of the Cafcass High Court Team or the Official Solicitor is or becomes the litigation friend or children's guardian of the ward or a party to the proceedings;
(b) those in which a local authority is or becomes a party;
(c) those in which an application for paternity testing is made;
(d) those in which there is a dispute about medical treatment;
(e) those in which an application is opposed on the grounds of lack of jurisdiction;
(f) those in which there is a substantial foreign element;
(g) those in which there is an opposed application for leave to take the child permanently out of the jurisdiction or where there is an application for temporary removal of a child from the jurisdiction and it is opposed on the ground that the child may not be duly returned.

PARTIES

3.1 Where the child has formed or is seeking to form an association, considered to be undesirable, with another person, that other person should not be made a party to the application. Such a person should be made a respondent only to an application within the proceedings for an injunction or committal. Such a person should not be added to the title of the proceedings nor allowed to see any documents other than those relating directly to the proceedings for the injunction or committal. He or she should be allowed time to obtain representation and any injunction should in the first instance extend over a few days only.

REMOVAL FROM JURISDICTION

4.1 A child who is a ward of court may not be removed from England and Wales without the court's permission. Practice Direction 12F (International Child Abduction) deals in detail with locating and protecting children at risk of unlawful removal.

CRIMINAL PROCEEDINGS

5.1 Where a child has been interviewed by the police in connection with contemplated criminal proceedings and the child subsequently becomes a ward of court, the permission of the court deciding the wardship proceedings ("the wardship court") is not required for the child to be called as a witness in the criminal proceedings.

5.2 Where the police need to interview a child who is already a ward of court, an application must be made for permission for the police to do so. Where permission is given the order should, unless there is some special reason to the contrary, give permission for any number of interviews which may be required by the prosecution or the police. If a need arises to conduct any interview beyond the permission contained in the order, a further application must be made.

5.3 The above applications must be made with notice to all parties.

5.4 Where a person may become the subject of a criminal investigation and it is considered necessary for the child who is a ward of court to be interviewed without that person knowing that the police are making inquiries, the application for permission to interview the child may be made without notice to that party. Notice should, however, where practicable be given to the children's guardian.

5.5 There will be other occasions where the police need to deal with complaints, or alleged offences, concerning children who are wards of court where it is appropriate, if not essential, for action to be taken straight away without the prior permission of the wardship court, for example—

(a) serious offences against the child such as rape, where a medical examination and the collection of forensic evidence ought to be carried out promptly;
(b) where the child is suspected by the police of having committed a criminal act and the police wish to interview the child in respect of that matter;
(c) where the police wish to interview the child as a potential witness.

5.6 In such instances, the police should notify the parent or foster parent with whom the child is living or another 'appropriate adult' (within the Police and Criminal Evidence Act 1984 – Code of Practice C for the Detention, Treatment and Questioning of Persons by Police Officers) so that that adult has the opportunity of being present when the police interview the child. Additionally, if practicable the child's guardian (if one has been appointed) should be notified and invited to attend the police interview or to nominate a third party to attend on the guardian's behalf. A record of the interview or a copy of any statement made by the child should be supplied to the children's guardian. Where the child has been interviewed without the guardian's knowledge, the guardian should be informed at the earliest opportunity of this fact and (if it be the case) that the police wish to conduct further interviews. The wardship court should be informed of the situation at the earliest possible opportunity thereafter by the children's guardian, parent, foster parent (through the local authority) or other responsible adult.

APPLICATIONS TO THE CRIMINAL INJURIES COMPENSATION AUTHORITY

6.1 Where a child who is a ward of court has a right to make a claim for compensation to the Criminal Injuries Compensation Authority ("CICA"), an application must be made by the child's guardian, or, if no guardian has been appointed, the person with care and control of the child, for permission to apply to CICA and disclose such documents on the wardship proceedings file as are considered necessary to establish whether or not the child is eligible for an award plus, as appropriate, the amount of the award.

6.2 Any order giving permission should state that any award made by CICA should normally be paid into court immediately upon receipt and, once that payment has been made, application should made to the court as to its management and administration. If it is proposed to invest the award in any other way, the court's prior approval must be sought

THE ROLE OF THE TIPSTAFF

7.1 The tipstaff is the enforcement officer for all orders made in the High Court. The tipstaff's jurisdiction extends throughout England and Wales. Every applicable order made in the High Court is addressed to the tipstaff in children and family matters (eg "The Court hereby directs the Tipstaff of the High Court of Justice, whether acting by himself or his assistants or a police officer as follows . . . ").

7.2 The tipstaff may effect an arrest and then inform the police. Sometimes the local bailiff or police will detain a person in custody until the tipstaff arrives to collect that person or give further directions as to the disposal of the matter. The tipstaff may also make a forced entry although there will generally be a uniformed police officer standing by to make sure there is no breach of the peace.

7.3 There is only one tipstaff (with two assistants) but the tipstaff can also call on any constable or bailiff to assist in carrying out the tipstaff's duties.

7.4 The majority of the tipstaff's work involves locating children and taking them into

The Family Procedure Rules 2010

protective custody, including cases of child abduction abroad.

PRACTICE DIRECTION 12E — URGENT BUSINESS

This Practice Direction is made by the President of the Family Division under the powers delegated to him by the Lord Chief Justice under Schedule 2, Part 1, paragraph 2(2) of the Constitutional Reform Act 2005, and is approved by the Parliamentary Under Secretary of State, by authority of the Lord Chancellor and comes into force on 6th April 2011.

This Practice Direction supplements FPR Part 12

INTRODUCTION

1.1 This Practice Direction describes the procedure to be followed in respect of urgent and out of hours cases in the Family Division of the High Court. For the avoidance of doubt, it does not relate to cases in respect of adults.

1.2 Urgent or out of hours applications, particularly those which have become urgent because they have not been pursued sufficiently promptly, should be avoided. A judge who has concerns that the urgent or out of hours facilities may have been abused may require a representative of the applicant to attend at a subsequent directions hearing to provide an explanation.

1.3 Urgent applications should whenever possible be made within court hours. The earliest possible liaison is required with the Clerk of the Rules who will attempt to accommodate genuinely urgent applications (at least for initial directions) in the Family Division applications court, from which the matter may be referred to another judge.

1.4 When it is not possible to apply within court hours, contact should be made with the security office at the Royal Courts of Justice (020 7947 6000 or 020 7947 6260) who will refer the matter to the urgent business officer. The urgent business officer can contact the duty judge. The judge may agree to hold a hearing, either convened at court or elsewhere, or by telephone.

1.5 When the hearing is to take place by telephone it should, unless not practicable, be by tape-recorded conference call arranged (and paid for in the first instance) by the applicant's solicitors. Solicitors acting for potential applicants should consider having standing arrangements with their telephone service providers under which such conference calls can be arranged. All parties (especially the judge) should be informed that the call is being recorded by the service provider. The applicant's solicitors should order a transcript of the hearing from the service provider. Otherwise the applicant's legal representative should prepare a note for approval by the judge.

GENERAL ISSUES

2.1 Parents, carers or other necessary respondents should whenever possible be given the opportunity to have independent legal advice or at least to have access to support or counselling.

2.2 In suitable cases, application may be made for directions providing for anonymity of the parties and others involved in the matter in any order or subsequent listing of the case. Exceptionally, a reporting restriction order may be sought.

2.3 Either the Official Solicitor or Cafcass, or CAFCASS CYMRU, as the case may be, may be invited by the court to be appointed as advocate to the court.

MEDICAL TREATMENT AND PRESS INJUNCTION CASES

3.1 It may be desirable for a child who is the subject of such proceedings to be made a party and represented through a children's guardian (usually an officer of Cafcass or a Welsh Family Proceedings Officer). Cafcass and CAFCASS CYMRU stand ready to arrange for an officer to accept appointment as a children's guardian. They should be contacted at the earliest opportunity where an urgent application is envisaged. For urgent out of hours applications, the urgent business officer will contact a representative of Cafcass. CAFCASS CYMRU is not able to deal with cases that arise out of office hours and those cases should be referred to Cafcass who will deal with the matter on behalf of CAFCASS CYMRU until the next working day. A child of sufficient understanding to instruct his or her own solicitor should be made a party and given notice of any application.

3.2 Interim declarations/orders under the wardship jurisdiction or Children Act 1989 may be made on application either by an NHS trust, a local authority, an interested adult (where necessary with the leave of the court) or by the child if he or she has sufficient understanding to make the application.

CONSULTATION WITH CAFCASS, CAFCASS CYMRU AND OFFICIAL SOLICITOR

4.1 Cafcass, CAFCASS CYMRU and members of the Official Solicitor's legal staff are prepared to discuss cases before proceedings are issued. In all cases in which the urgent and out of hours procedures are to be used it would be helpful if the Official Solicitor, Cafcass or CAFCASS CYMRU have had some advance notice of the application and its circumstances.

4.2 Enquiries about children cases should be directed to the duty lawyer at Cafcass National Office, 6th Floor, Sanctuary Buildings, Great Smith Street, London SW1P 3BT, telephone: 0844 353 3350, fax number: 0844 353 3351. Enquiries should be marked "F.A.O High Court Team or F.A.O. HCT".

4.3 Enquiries about children cases in Wales should be directed to the Social Care Team, Legal Services, Welsh Assembly Government, Cathays Park, Cardiff CF10 3NQ, telephone: 02920 823913, fax no. 02920 826727.

4.4 Medical and welfare cases relating to an adult lacking capacity in relation to their medical treatment or welfare are brought in the Court of Protection. Enquiries about adult medical and welfare cases should be addressed to a Court of Protection healthcare and welfare lawyer at the office of the Official Solicitor, 81 Chancery Lane, London WC2A 1DD, telephone 0207 911 7127, fax number: 0207 911 7105, e-mail: enquiries@offsol.gsi.gov.uk. Reference should also be made to Practice Direction E, accompanying Part 9 of the Court of Protection Rules 2007, and to Practice Direction B accompanying Part 10 of those Rules. Information for parties and practitioners is available on the website of the Ministry of Justice www.justice.gov.uk and general information for members of the public is available on www.direct.gov.uk

---

The Right Honourable

Sir Nicholas Wall

The President of the Family Division

Signed by authority of the Lord Chancellor:

Parliamentary Under Secretary of State

Ministry of Justice

PRACTICE DIRECTION 12F – INTERNATIONAL CHILD ABDUCTION

This Practice Direction is made by the President of the Family Division under the powers delegated to him by the Lord Chief Justice under Schedule 2, Part 1,

The Family Procedure Rules 2010

paragraph 2(2) of the Constitutional Reform Act 2005, and is approved by the Parliamentary Under Secretary of State, by authority of the Lord Chancellor and comes into force on 6th April 2011

This Practice Direction supplements FPR Part 12, Chapters 5 and 6

PART I - INTRODUCTION

1.1 This Practice Direction explains what to do if a child has been brought to, or kept in, England and Wales without the permission of anyone who has rights of custody in respect of the child in the country where the child was habitually resident immediately before the removal or retention. It also explains what to do if a child has been taken out of, or kept out of, England and Wales[a] without the permission of a parent or someone who has rights of custody in respect of the child. These cases are called "international child abduction cases" and are dealt with in the High Court. This Practice Direction also explains what to do if you receive legal papers claiming that you have abducted a child. You can find the legal cases which are mentioned in this Practice Direction, and other legal material, on the website http://www.bailii.org/ (British and Irish Legal Information Institute).

[a] The child must be taken or kept out of the United Kingdom without the permission of a parent or someone who has rights of custody for it to be an international child abduction. This practice direction relates to the law as it applies in England and Wales. If the child has been taken or kept out of the United Kingdom when the child was habitually resident in Scotland, you should contact the Central Authority for Scotland, Scottish Government Justice Directorate, Civil Law Division, St Andrew's House, Regent Road, Edinburgh EH1 3DG Tel: +44 (0) 131 244 4827/4832 Fax:: +44 (0) 131 244 4848 Website: http://www.scotland.gov.uk/Topics/Justice/law/17867/fm-children-root/18533.

If the child has been taken or kept out of the United Kingdom when the child was habitually resident in Northern Ireland, you should contact the Central Authority for Northern Ireland, Northern Ireland Courts and Tribunals Service, Civil Policy and Tribunal Reform Division, 3rd Floor Laganside House, 23-27 Oxford Street, Belfast BT1 3LA Tel: +44 (0) 2890 328 594; fax + 44 (0)2890 728 944.

Website: http://www.nics.gov.uk/ or
http://www.courtsni.gov.uk/en-GB/Services/ChildAbduction/

1.2. If you have rights of custody in respect of a child and the child has been brought to England or Wales without your permission, or has been brought here with your permission but the person your child is staying with is refusing to return the child, then you can apply to the High Court of Justice, which covers all of England and Wales, for an order for the return of the child.

1.3 How you make an application to the High Court, what evidence you need to provide and what orders you should ask the court to make are all explained in this Practice Direction.

1.4 If your child is under 16 years of age and has been brought to England or Wales from a country which is a party (a "State party") to the 1980 Hague Convention on the Civil Aspects of International Child Abduction ("the 1980 Hague Convention") then you can make an application to the High Court for an order under that Convention for the return of your child to the State in which he or she was habitually resident immediately before being removed or being kept away. This is explained in Part 2 below.

1.5 If your child is over 16 years of age and under 18, or has been brought to England or Wales from a country which is not a State party to the 1980 Hague Convention, then you can make an application for the return of your child under the inherent jurisdiction of the High Court with respect to children. In exercising this jurisdiction over children, the High Court will make your child's welfare its paramount consideration. How to make an application under the inherent jurisdiction of the High Court with respect to children is explained in Part 3 below.

1.6 It might be necessary for you to make an urgent application to the court if you are not sure where your child is, or you think that there is a risk that the person who is keeping your child away from you might take the child out of the United Kingdom or hide them away. Part 4 below explains how to make an urgent application to the High Court for orders to protect your child until a final decision can be made about returning the child and also how to ask for help from the police and government agencies if you think your child might be taken out of the country.

Rights of Access

1.7 Rights of access to children (also called contact or visitation) may be enforced in England and Wales. Access orders made in other Member States of the European Union can be enforced under EU law, and the 1980 Hague Convention expects State parties to comply with orders and agreements concerning access as well as rights of custody. If you have an access order and you want to enforce it in England or Wales, you should read Part 5 below.

PART 2 – HAGUE CONVENTION CASES

2.1 States which are party to the 1980 Hague Convention have agreed to return children who have been either wrongfully removed from, or wrongfully retained away from, the State where they were habitually resident immediately before the wrongful removal or retention. There are very limited exceptions to this obligation.

2.2 "Wrongfully removed" or "wrongfully retained" means removed or retained in breach of rights of custody in respect of the child attributed to a person or a body or an institution. "Rights of custody" are interpreted very widely (see paragraph 2.16 below).

2.3 The text of the 1980 Hague Convention and a list of Contracting States (that is, State parties) can be found on the website of the Hague Conference on Private International Law at http://www.hcch.net. All Member States of the European Union are State parties to the 1980 Hague Convention, and all but Denmark are bound by an EU Regulation which supplements the operation of the 1980 Hague Convention between the Member States of the EU (Council Regulation (EC) No 2201/2003, see paragraph 2.6).

2.4 In each State party there is a body called the Central Authority whose duty is to help people use the 1980 Hague Convention.

2.5 If you think that your child has been brought to, or kept in, England or Wales, and your State is a State party to the 1980 Hague Convention, then you should get in touch with your own Central Authority who will help you to send an application for the return of your child to the Central Authority for England and Wales. However, you are not obliged to contact your own Central Authority. You may contact the Central Authority for England and Wales directly, or you may simply instruct lawyers in England or Wales to make an application for you. The advantage of making your application through the Central Authority for England and Wales if you are applying from outside the United Kingdom is that you will get public funding ("legal aid") to make your application, regardless of your financial resources.

The Central Authority for England and Wales

2.6 The Child Abduction and Custody Act 1985 brings the 1980 Hague Convention into the law of England and Wales and identifies the Lord Chancellor as the Central Authority. His duties as the Central Authority are carried out by the International Child Abduction and Contact Unit (ICACU). ICACU also carries out the duties of the Central Authority for two other international instruments. These are the European Convention on Recognition and Enforcement of Decisions concerning Custody of Children signed at Luxembourg on 20 May 1980 (called "the European Convention" in this Practice Direction but sometimes also referred to as "the Luxembourg Convention") and the European Union Council Regulation (EC) No 2201/2003 of 27 November 2003 on jurisdiction and the recognition and enforcement of judgments in matrimonial matters and in matters of parental responsibility ("the Council Regulation[(b)]"). The Council Regulation has direct effect in the law of England and Wales.

The Family Procedure Rules 2010

(b) The Council Regulation (EC) No 2201/2003 of 27 November 2003 concerning jurisdiction and the recognition and enforcement of judgments in matrimonial matters and the matters of parental responsibility, repealing Regulation (EC) No 1347/2000 is also known as Brussels IIa, or Brussels II Revised, or Brussels II bis.

2.7 ICACU is open Mondays to Fridays from 9.00 a.m. to 5.00 p.m. It is located in the Office of the Official Solicitor and Public Trustee and its contact details are as follows:

International Child Abduction and Contact Unit
81 Chancery Lane
London WC2A 1DD
DX 0012 London Chancery Lane
Tel: + 44 (0)20 7911 7045 / 7047
Fax: + 44 (0)20 7911 7248
Email: enquiries@offsol.gsi.gov.uk

In an emergency (including out of normal working hours) contact should be made with the Royal Courts of Justice on one of the following telephone numbers:

+ 44 (0)20 7947 6000, or

+ 44 (0) 20 7947 6260.

In addition, in an emergency or outside normal working hours advice on international child abduction can be sought from **reunite International Child Abduction Centre** on + 44 (0)1162 556 234. Outside office hours you will be directed to the 24hour emergency service. You can also see information on **reunite's** website http://www.reunite.org/.

What ICACU Will Do

2.8 When ICACU receives your application for the return of your child, unless you already have a legal representative in England and Wales whom you want to act for you, it will send your application to a solicitor whom it knows to be experienced in international child abduction cases and ask them to take the case for you. You will then be the solicitor's client and the solicitor will make an application for public funding to meet your legal costs. The solicitor will then apply to the High Court for an order for the return of your child.

2.9 You can find out more about ICACU and about the 1980 Hague Convention and the other international instruments mentioned at paragraph 2.6 on two websites: Information for parties and practitioners is available on http://www.justice.gov.uk and general information for members of the public is available on http://www.direct.gov.uk.

Applying to the High Court – the Form and Content of Application

2.10 An application to the High Court for an order under the 1980 Hague Convention must be made in the Principal Registry of the Family Division in Form C67. If the Council Regulation applies, then the application must be headed both "in the matter of the Child Abduction and Custody Act 1985" and "in the matter of Council Regulation (EC) 2201/2003". This is to ensure that the application is handled quickly (see paragraph. 2.14 below) and to draw the court's attention to its obligations under the Council Regulation.

2.11 The application must include—

(a) the names and dates of birth of the children;
(b) the names of the children's parents or guardians;
(c) the whereabouts or suspected whereabouts of the children;
(d) the interest of the applicant in the matter (e.g. mother, father, or person with whom the child lives and details of any order placing the child with that person);
(e) the reasons for the application;

(f) details of any proceedings (including proceedings not in England or Wales, and including any legal proceedings which have finished) relating to the children;
(g) where the application is for the return of a child, the identity of the person alleged to have removed or retained the child and, if different, the identity of the person with whom the child is thought to be;
(h) in an application to which the Council Regulation also applies, any details of measures of which you are aware that have been taken by courts or authorities to ensure the protection of the child after its return to the Member State of habitual residence.

2.12 The application should be accompanied by all relevant documents including (but not limited to)—

(a) an authenticated copy of any relevant decision or agreement;
(b) a certificate or an affidavit from a Central Authority, or other competent authority of the State of the child's habitual residence, or from a qualified person, concerning the relevant law of that State.

2.13 As the applicant you may also file a statement in support of the application, although usually your solicitor will make and file a statement for you on your instructions. The statement must contain and be verified by a statement of truth in the following terms:

"I make this statement knowing that it will be placed before the court, and I confirm that to the best of my knowledge and belief its contents are true."

(Further provisions about statements of truth are contained in Part 17 of these Rules and in Practice Direction 17A.).

The Timetable for the Case

2.14 Proceedings to which the Council Regulation applies must be completed in 6 weeks "except where exceptional circumstances make this impossible". The following procedural steps are intended to ensure that applications under the 1980 Hague Convention and the Council Regulation are handled quickly—

(a) the application must be headed both "in the matter of the Child Abduction and Custody Act 1985" and "in the matter of Council Regulation (EC) 2201/2003";
(b) the court file will be marked to—
  (i) draw attention to the nature of the application; and
  (ii) state the date on which the 6 week period will expire (the "hear-by date");
(c) listing priority will, where necessary, be given to such applications;
(d) the trial judge will expedite the transcript of the judgment and its approval and ensure that it is sent to the Central Authority without delay.

[The above is taken from the judgment of the Court of Appeal, Civil Division in Vigreux v Michel & anor [2006] EWCA Civ 630, [2006] 2 FLR 1180.]

Applications for Declarations

2.15 If a child has been taken from England and Wales to another State party, the judicial or administrative authorities of that State may ask for a declaration that the removal or retention of the child was wrongful. Or it might be thought that a declaration from the High Court that a child has been wrongfully removed or retained away from the United Kingdom would be helpful in securing his return. The High Court can make such declarations under section 8 of the Child Abduction and Custody Act 1985. An application for a declaration is made in the same way as an application for a return order, the only difference being that the details of relevant legal proceedings in respect of which the declaration is sought (if any), including a copy of any order made relating to the application, should be included in the documentation.

Rights of Custody

2.16 "Rights of custody" includes rights relating to the care of the person of the child and, in particular, the right to determine the child's place of residence. Rights of custody

The Family Procedure Rules 2010

may arise by operation of law (that is, they are conferred on someone automatically by the legal system in which they are living) or by a judicial or administrative decision or as a result of an agreement having legal effect. The rights of a person, an institution or any other body are a matter for the law of the State of the child's habitual residence, but it is for the State which is being asked to return the child to decide: if those rights amount to rights of custody for the purposes of the 1980 Hague Convention; whether at the time of the removal or retention those rights were actually being exercised; and whether there has been a breach of those rights.

2.17 In England and Wales a father who is not married to the mother of their child does not necessarily have "rights of custody" in respect of the child. An unmarried father in England and Wales who has parental responsibility for a child has rights of custody in respect of that child. In the case of an unmarried father without parental responsibility, the concept of rights of custody may include more than strictly legal rights and where immediately before the removal or retention of the child he was exercising parental functions over a substantial period of time as the only or main carer for the child he may have rights of custody. An unmarried father can ask ICACU or his legal representative for advice on this. It is important to remember that it will be for the State which is being asked to return the child to decide if the father's circumstances meet that State's requirements for the establishment of rights of custody.

2.18 Sometimes, court orders impose restrictions on the removal of children from the country in which they are living. These can be orders under the Children Act 1989 ("section 8" orders) or orders under the inherent jurisdiction of the High Court (sometimes called "injunctions"). Any removal of a child in breach of an order imposing such a restriction would be wrongful under the 1980 Hague Convention.

2.19 The fact that court proceedings are in progress about a child does not of itself give rise to a prohibition on the removal of the child by a mother with sole parental responsibility from the country in which the proceedings are taking place unless:

(a) the proceedings are Wardship proceedings in England and Wales (in which case removal would breach the rights of custody attributed to the High Court and fathers with no custody rights could rely on that breach); or
(b) the court is actually considering the custody of the child, because then the court itself would have rights of custody.

Particular provisions for European Convention applications

2.20 The European Convention provides for the mutual recognition and enforcement of decisions relating to custody and access, so if a child has been brought here or retained here in breach of a custody order, then that order can be enforced. The European Convention has now been superseded to a very great extent by the Council Regulation. If however you want to make an application under the European Convention, then you make it in the same way as is described in paragraphs 2.10 and 2.11 above, but in addition you must include a copy of the decision relating to custody (or rights of access – see paragraph 5.1 below) which you are seeking to register or enforce, or about which you are seeking a declaration by the court.

Defending Abduction Proceedings

2.21 If you are served with an application - whether it is under the 1980 Hague or the European Convention or the inherent jurisdiction of the High Court - you must not delay. You must obey any directions given in any order with which you have been served, and you should seek legal advice at the earliest possible opportunity, although neither you nor the child concerned will automatically be entitled to legal aid.

2.22 It is particularly important that you tell the court where the child is, because the child will not be permitted to live anywhere else without the permission of the court, or to leave England and Wales, until the proceedings are finished.

2.23 It is also particularly important that you present to the court any defence to the application which you or the child might want to make at the earliest possible opportunity, although the orders with which you will have been served are likely to tell you the time by which you will have to do this.

2.24 If the child concerned objects to any order sought in relation to them, and if the child is of an age and understanding at which the court will take account of their views, the court is likely to direct that the child is seen by an officer of the Children and Family Court Advisory and Support Service (Cafcass) or in Wales CAFCASS CYMRU. You should cooperate in this process. Children are not usually made parties to abduction cases, but in certain exceptional circumstances the court can make them parties so that they have their own separate legal representation. These are all matters about which you should seek legal advice.

(Provisions about the power of the court to join parties are contained in rule 12.3 and provisions about the joining and representation of children are contained in Part 16 of these Rules and the Practice Direction 16A (Representation of Children.).

PART 3 – NON-CONVENTION CASES

3.1 Applications for the return of children wrongfully removed or retained away from States which are not parties to the 1980 Hague Convention or in respect of children to whom that Convention does not apply, can be made to the High Court under its inherent jurisdiction with respect to children. Such proceedings are referred to as "non-Convention" cases. In proceedings under the inherent jurisdiction of the High Court with respect to children, the child's welfare is the court's paramount consideration. The extent of the court's enquiry into the child's welfare will depend on the circumstances of the case; in some cases the child's welfare will be best served by a summary hearing and, if necessary, a prompt return to the State from which the child has been removed or retained. In other cases a more detailed enquiry may be necessary (see Re J *(Child Returned Abroad: Convention Rights)* [2005] UKHL 40; [2005] 2 FLR 802).

3.2 Every application for the return of a child under the inherent jurisdiction must be made in the Principal Registry of the Family Division and heard in the High Court.

Provision about the inherent jurisdiction is made at Chapter 5 of Part 12 of the Rules and in Practice Direction 12D (Inherent Jurisdiction (including Wardship) Proceedings).

The Form and content of the application

3.3 An application for the return of a child under the inherent jurisdiction must be made in Form C66 and must include the information in paragraph 2.11 above.

3.4 You must file a statement in support of your application, which must exhibit all the relevant documents. The statement must contain and be verified by a statement of truth in the following terms:

> "*I make this statement knowing that it will be placed before the court, and I confirm that to the best of my knowledge and belief its contents are true.*"

(Further provisions about statements of truth are contained in Part 17 of these Rules and Practice Direction 17A.).

Timetable for Non-Convention Cases

3.5 While the 6 week deadline referred to in paragraph 2.14 is set out in the 1980 Hague Convention and in the Council Regulation, non-Convention child abduction cases must similarly be completed in 6 weeks except where exceptional circumstances make this impossible. Paragraph 2.14 applies to these cases as appropriate for a non-Convention case.

PART 4 – GENERAL PROVISIONS

Urgent applications, or applications out of business hours

4.1 Guidance about urgent and out of hours applications is in Practice Direction 12E (Urgent Business).

The Family Procedure Rules 2010

Police assistance to prevent removal from England and Wales

4.2 The Child Abduction Act 1984 sets out the circumstances in which the removal of a child from this jurisdiction is a criminal offence. The police provide the following 24 hour service to prevent the unlawful removal of a child:

(a) they inform ports directly when there is a real and imminent threat that a child is about to be removed unlawfully from the country; and
(b) they liaise with Immigration Officers at the ports in an attempt to identify children at risk of removal.

4.3 Where the child is under 16, it is not necessary to obtain a court order before seeking police assistance. The police do not need an order to act to protect the child. If an order has already been obtained it should however be produced to the police. Where the child is between 16 and 18, an order must be obtained restricting or restraining removal before seeking police assistance.

4.4 Where the child is a ward of court (*see Practice Direction 12D (Inherent Jurisdiction (including Wardship) Proceedings*) the court's permission is needed to remove that child from the jurisdiction. When the court has not given that permission and police assistance is sought to prevent the removal of the ward, the applicant must produce evidence that the child is a ward such as:

(a) an order confirming wardship;
(b) an injunction; or
(c) where the matter is urgent and no order has been made, a certified copy of the wardship application.

4.5 The application for police assistance must be made by the applicant or his legal representative to the applicant's local police station except that applications may be made to any police station:

(a) in urgent cases;
(b) where the wardship application has just been issued; or
(c) where the court has just made the order relied on.

4.6 The police will, if they consider it appropriate, institute the "port alert" system (otherwise known as "an all ports warning") to try to prevent removal from the jurisdiction where the danger of removal is:

(a) real (i.e., not being sought merely by way of insurance); and
(b) imminent (i.e. within 24 to 48 hours).

4.7 The request for police assistance must be accompanied by as much of the following information as possible:

(a) *the child*: the name, sex, date of birth, physical description, nationality and passport number; if the child has more than one nationality or passport, provide details;
(b) *the person likely to remove*: the name, age, physical description, nationality, passport number, relationship to the child, and whether the child is likely to assist him or her; if the person has more than one nationality or passport, provide details;
(c) *person applying for a port alert*: the name, relationship to the child, nationality, telephone number and (if appropriate) solicitor's or other legal representative's name and contact details; if the person has more than one nationality, provide details;
(d) likely destination;
(e) likely time of travel and port of embarkation and, if known, details of travel arrangements;
(f) grounds for port alert (as appropriate)—
  (i) suspected offence under section 1 or section 2 of the Child Abduction Act 1984;
  (ii) the child is subject to a court order.
(g) details of person to whom the child should be returned if intercepted.

4.8 If the police decide that the case is one in which the port-alert system should be used, the child's name will remain on the stop list for **four weeks**. <u>After that time it will be removed automatically unless a further application is made.</u>

The Identity and Passport Service

4.9 Where the court makes an order prohibiting or otherwise restricting the removal of a child from the United Kingdom, or from any specified part of it, or from a specified dependent territory, the court may make an order under section 37 of the Family Law Act 1986 requiring any person to surrender any UK passport which has been issued to, or contains particulars of, the child.

4.10 The Identity and Passport Service ("IPS") will take action to prevent a United Kingdom passport or replacement passport being issued only where the IPS has been served with a court order expressly requiring a United Kingdom passport to be surrendered, or expressly prohibiting the issue of any further United Kingdom passport facilities to the child without the consent of the court, or the holder of such an order. Accordingly, in every case in which such an order has been made, the IPS must be served the same day if possible, or at the latest the following day, with a copy of the order. It is the responsibility of the applicant to do this. The specimen form of letter set out below should be used and a copy of the court order must be attached to the letter. Delay in sending the letter to the IPS must be kept to an absolute minimum.

"The Caveat Officer
Fraud and Intelligence Unit
Identity and Passport Service
Globe House
89 Eccleston Square
London SW1V 1PN
Dear Sir/Madam
. . . . v. . . . .
Case no: . . . .
This is to inform you that the court has today made an order
*prohibiting the issue of a passport/passports to [name(s)] [date of birth (if known)] of [address] without the consent of the holder of the order.
*requiring [name(s)] [date of birth (if known)] of [address] to surrender the passport(s) issued to him/her/them/the following child[ren] / or which contain(s) particulars of the following child[ren]:
Name   Date of Birth
*and has granted an injunction/*made an order restraining the removal of the child[ren] from the jurisdiction.
(*Delete as appropriate)
Please add these names to your records to prevent the issue of further passport facilities for the child[ren]. I enclose a copy of the court order.
Yours faithfully
Applicant's name / Applicant's Solicitor's name"

4.11 Following service on the IPS of an order either expressly requiring a United Kingdom passport to be surrendered by, or expressly prohibiting the issue of any further United Kingdom passport facilities to the child, the IPS will maintain a prohibition on issuing a passport, or further passport facilities until the child's 16th birthday. The order should state that a passport must not be granted/applied for without the consent of the court or the holder of the order.

Note: These requests may also be sent to any of the regional Passport Offices.

4.12 Further information on communicating with the IPS where the court has made a request of, or an order against, the IPS, may be found in the Protocol: <u>Communicating with the Identity and Passport Service in Family Proceedings</u> of August 2003.

4.13 Information about other circumstances, in which the IPS will agree not to issue a passport to a child if the IPS receives an application, or an order in more general terms than set out at 4.11 above, from a person who claims to have parental responsibility for

The Family Procedure Rules 2010

the child, is available from the IPS or at www.direct.gov.uk.

The Home Office

4.14 Information about communicating with the Home Office, where a question of the immigration status of a party arises in family proceedings, may be found in the Protocol: Communicating with the Home Office in Family Proceedings (revised and re-issued October 2010).

Press Reporting

4.15 When a child has been abducted and a judge considers that publicity may help in tracing the child, the judge may adjourn the case for a short period to enable representatives of the Press to attend to give the case the widest possible publicity.

4.16. If a Child Rescue Alert has been used concerning a child, within the UK or abroad, it will give rise to media publicity. The court should be informed that this has happened. If there are already court proceedings concerning a child, it is advisable to obtain the agreement of the court before there is publicity to trace a missing child. If the court has not given its permission for a child who is the subject of children proceedings to be identified as the subject of proceedings, to do so would be contempt of court.

Other Assistance

4.17 The Missing Persons Bureau will be participating for the UK in the European Union wide 116 000 hotline for missing children. Parents and children can ring this number for assistance. (It is primarily intended to deal with criminal matters, for example stranger kidnapping.)

4.18 It may also be possible to trace a child by obtaining a court order under the inherent jurisdiction or the wardship jurisdiction of the High Court addressed to certain government departments, as set out in Practice Direction 6C.

PART 5 – APPLICATIONS ABOUT RIGHTS OF ACCESS

5.1 Access orders made in another Member State of the European Union (except Denmark) can be enforced in England or Wales under the Council Regulation.

5.2 Chapter III of the Council Regulation sets out provision for recognition and enforcement of parental responsibility orders, which include orders for custody and access (residence and contact) between Member States. Under Article 41 of the Council Regulation you can enforce an access order in your favour from another Member State directly, provided you produce the certificate given under Article 41(2) by the court which made the order. This is a quick procedure. The unsuccessful party is not allowed to oppose recognition of the order.

5.3 The rules on recognition and enforcement of parental responsibility orders are in Part 31. You should apply to the High Court using Form C69. Rule 31.8 covers applications for Article 41 of the Council Regulation. You can make the application without notice.

5.4 If the Council Regulation does not apply, and the access order was made by a State party to the European Convention, an application can be made to enforce the order under Article 11 of the European Convention. Paragraph 2.20 above gives further information about how to make the application.

5.5 Article 21 of the 1980 Hague Convention requires the States parties to respect rights of access. However, in the case of Re G (A Minor) (Hague Convention: Access) [1993] 1 FLR 669, the Court of Appeal took the view that Article 21 conferred no jurisdiction to determine matters relating to access, or to recognise or enforce foreign access orders (see Practice Note of 5 March 1993: Child Abduction Unit: Lord Chancellor's Department set out in the Annex to this Practice Direction). (The Child Abduction Unit is now called ICACU see paragraph 2.6.) An access order which does not fall within the Council Regulation or the (very limited) application of the European Convention may only be enforced by applying for a "contact order" under section 8 of the Children Act 1989.

5.6 This means that if, during the course of proceedings under the 1980 Hague Convention for a return order, the applicant decides to ask for access (contact) instead of the return of the child, but no agreement can be reached, a separate application for a contact order will have to be made, or the court invited to make a contact order without an application being made (Children Act 1989, s10(1)(b)).

PART 6 - CHILD ABDUCTION CASES BETWEEN THE UNITED KINGDOM AND PAKISTAN

6.1 A consensus was reached in January 2003 between the President of the Family Division and the Hon. Chief Justice of Pakistan as to the principles to be applied in resolving child abduction cases between the UK and Pakistan.

The Protocol setting out that consensus can be accessed at:

http://www.fco.gov.uk/resources/en/pdf/2855621/3069133

ANNEX

See paragraph 5.5

Practice Note

5 March 1993

Citations: [1993] 1 FLR 804

Child Abduction Unit: Lord Chancellor's Department

Duties of the Central Authority for England and Wales under Article 21 of the Hague Convention on the Civil Aspects of International Child Abduction

Child Abduction and Custody Act 1985

In the case of *Re G (A Minor) (Hague Convention: Access)* [1993] 1 FLR 669 the Court of Appeal considered the duties of the Central Authority for England and Wales on receiving an application in respect of rights of access under Art 21 of the Hague Convention.

The Court of Appeal took the view that Art 21 conferred no jurisdiction to determine matters relating to access, or to recognise or enforce foreign access orders. It provides, however, for executive co-operation in the enforcement of such recognition as national law allows.

Accordingly, the duty of the Central Authority is to make appropriate arrangements for the applicant by providing solicitors to act on his behalf in applying for legal aid and instituting proceedings in the High Court under s 8 of the Children Act 1989.

If, during the course of proceedings under Art 21 of the Convention, the applicant decides to seek access instead of the return of the child, but no agreement can be reached and the provisions of the European Convention on the Recognition and Enforcement of Decisions Concerning Custody of Children and on Restoration of Custody of Children are not available, a separate application under s 8 of the Children

The Family Procedure Rules 2010

Act 1989 will have to be made.

Central Authority for England and Wales

NOTE: The Child Abduction Unit is now called ICACU, see paragraph 2.6.

The Right Honourable

Sir Nicholas Wall

The President of the Family Division

Signed by authority of the Lord Chancellor:

Parliamentary Under Secretary of State

Ministry of Justice

PRACTICE DIRECTION 12G – COMMUNICATION OF INFORMATION

This Practice Direction supplements FPR Part 12, Chapter 7

1.1 Chapter 7 deals with the communication of information (whether or not contained in a document filed with the court) relating to proceedings which relate to children.

1.2 Subject to any direction of the court, information may be communicated for the purposes of the law relating to contempt in accordance with paragraphs 2.1, 3.1 or 4.1.

COMMUNICATION OF INFORMATION BY A PARTY ETC. FOR OTHER PURPOSES

2.1 A person specified in the first column of the following table may communicate to a person listed in the second column such information as is specified in the third column for the purpose or purposes specified in the fourth column—

A party	A lay adviser, a McKenzie Friend, or a person arranging or providing pro bono legal services	Any information relating to the proceedings	To enable the party to obtain advice or assistance in relation to the proceedings
A party	A health care professional or a person or body providing counselling services for children or families		To enable the party or any child of the party to obtain health care or counselling

A party	The Child Maintenance and Enforcement Commission, a McKenzie Friend, a lay adviser or the First-tier Tribunal dealing with an appeal made under section 20 of the Child Support Act 1991		For the purposes of making or responding to an appeal under section 20 of the Child Support Act 1991 or the determination of such an appeal
A party	An adoption panel		To enable the adoption panel to discharge its functions as appropriate
A party	The European Court of Human Rights		For the purpose of making an application to the European Court of Human Rights
A party or any person lawfully in receipt of information	The Children's Commissioner or the Children's Commissioner for Wales		To refer an issue affecting the interests of children to the Children's Commissioner or the Children's Commissioner for Wales
A party, any person lawfully in receipt of information or a proper officer	A person or body conducting an approved research project		For the purpose of an approved research project
A legal representative or a professional legal adviser	A person or body responsible for investigating or determining complaints in relation to legal representatives or professional legal advisers		For the purposes of the investigation or determination of a complaint in relation to a legal representative or a professional legal adviser
A legal representative or a professional legal adviser	A person or body assessing quality assurance systems		To enable the legal representative or professional legal adviser to obtain a quality assurance assessment
A legal representative or a professional legal adviser	An accreditation body	Any information relating to the proceedings providing that it does not, or is not likely to, identify any person involved in the proceedings	To enable the legal representative or professional legal adviser to obtain accreditation

The Family Procedure Rules 2010

A party	A police officer	The text or summary of the whole or part of a judgment given in the proceedings	For the purpose of a criminal investigation
A party or any person lawfully in receipt of information	A member of the Crown Prosecution Service		To enable the Crown Prosecution Service to discharge its functions under any enactment

COMMUNICATION FOR THE EFFECTIVE FUNCTIONING OF CAFCASS AND CAFCASS CYMRU

3.1 An officer of the Service or a Welsh family proceedings officer, as appropriate, may communicate to a person listed in the second column such information as is specified in the third column for the purpose or purposes specified in the fourth column—

A Welsh family proceedings officer	A person or body exercising statutory functions relating to inspection of CAFCASS CYMRU	Any information relating to the proceedings which is required by the person or body responsible for the inspection	For the purpose of an inspection of CAFCASS CYMRU by a body or person appointed by the Welsh Ministers
An officer of the Service or a Welsh family proceedings officer	The General Social Care Council or the Care Council for Wales	Any information relating to the proceedings providing that it does not, or is not likely to, identify any person involved in the proceedings	For the purpose of initial and continuing accreditation as a social worker of a person providing services to Cafcass or CAFCASS CYMRU in accordance with section 13(2) of the Criminal Justice and Courts Services Act 2000 or section 36 of the Children Act 2004 as the case may be
An officer of the Service or a Welsh family proceedings officer	A person or body providing services relating to professional development or training to Cafcass or CAFCASS CYMRU	Any information relating to the proceedings providing that it does not, or is not likely to, identify any person involved in the proceedings without that person's consent	To enable the person or body to provide the services, where the services cannot be effectively provided without such disclosure

An officer of the Service or a Welsh family proceedings officer	A person employed by or contracted to Cafcass or CAFCASS CYMRU for the purposes of carrying out the functions referred to in column 4 of this row	Any information relating to the proceedings	Engagement in processes internal to Cafcass or CAFCASS CYMRU which relate to the maintenance of necessary records concerning the proceedings, or to ensuring that Cafcass or CAFCASS CYMRU functions are carried out to a satisfactory standard

COMMUNICATION TO AND BY MINISTERS OF THE CROWN AND WELSH MINISTERS

4.1 A person specified in the first column of the following table may communicate to a person listed in the second column such information as is specified in the third column for the purpose or purposes specified in the fourth column—

A party or any person lawfully in receipt of information relating to the proceedings	A Minister of the Crown with responsibility for a government department engaged, or potentially engaged, in an application before the European Court of Human Rights relating to the proceedings	Any information relating to the proceedings of which he or she is in lawful possession	To provide the department with information relevant, or potentially relevant, to the proceedings before the European Court of Human Rights
A Minister of the Crown	The European Court of Human Rights		For the purpose of engagement in an application before the European Court of Human Rights relating to the proceedings
A Minister of the Crown	Lawyers advising or representing the United Kingdom in an application before the European Court of Human Rights relating to the proceedings		For the purpose of receiving advice or for effective representation in relation to the application before the European Court of Human Rights.

The Family Procedure Rules 2010

A Minister of the crown or a Welsh Minister	Another Minister, or Ministers, of the Crown or a Welsh Minister		For the purpose of notification, discussion and the giving or receiving of advice regarding issues raised by the information in which the relevant departments have, or may have, an interest

5.1 This paragraph applies to communications made in accordance with paragraphs 2.1, 3.1 and 4.1 and the reference in this paragraph to "the table" means the table in the relevant paragraph.

5.2 A person in the second column of the table may only communicate information relating to the proceedings received from a person in the first column for the purpose or purposes—

(a) for which he or she received that information; or
(b) of professional development or training, providing that any communication does not, or is not likely to, identify any person involved in the proceedings without that person's consent.

6.1 In this Practice Direction—

"accreditation body" means—

(a) The Law Society,
(b) Resolution, or
(c) The Legal Services Commission;

"adoption panel" means a panel established in accordance with regulation 3 of the Adoption Agencies Regulations 2005 or regulation 3 of the Adoption Agencies (Wales) Regulations 2005;

"approved research project" means a project of research—

(a) approved in writing by a Secretary of State after consultation with the President of the Family Division,
(b) approved in writing by the President of the Family Division, or
(c) conducted under section 83 of the Act of 1989 or section 13 of the Criminal Justice and Court Services Act 2000;

"body assessing quality assurance systems" includes—

(a) The Law Society,
(b) The Legal Services Commission, or
(c) The General Council of the Bar;

"body or person responsible for investigating or determining complaints in relation to legal representatives or professional legal advisers" means—

(a) The Law Society,
(b) The General Council of the Bar,
(c) The Institute of Legal Executives,
(d) The Legal Services Ombudsman; or
(e) The Office of Legal Complaints.

"Cafcass" has the meaning assigned to it by section 11 of the Criminal Justice and Courts Services Act 2000;

"CAFCASS CYMRU" means the part of the Welsh Assembly Government exercising

FPR 2010, Practice Direction 12I

the functions of Welsh Ministers under Part 4 of the Children Act 2004;

"criminal investigation" means an investigation conducted by police officers with a view to it being ascertained—

(a) whether a person should be charged with an offence, or
(b) whether a person charged with an offence is guilty of it;

"health care professional" means—

(a) a registered medical practitioner,
(b) a registered nurse or midwife,
(c) a clinical psychologist, or
(d) a child psychotherapist;

"lay adviser" means a non-professional person who gives lay advice on behalf of an organisation in the lay advice sector;

"McKenzie Friend" means any person permitted by the court to sit beside an unrepresented litigant in court to assist that litigant by prompting, taking notes and giving him advice; and

"social worker" has the meaning assigned to it by section 55 of the Care Standards Act 2000.

PRACTICE DIRECTION 12H – CONTRIBUTION ORDERS

This Practice Direction supplements FPR Part 12

1.1 Paragraph 23(6) of Schedule 2 to the 1989 Act provides that where-

(a) a contribution order is in force;
(b) the local authority serve another contribution notice; and
(c) the contributor and the local authority reach an agreement under paragraph 22(7) in respect of that other contribution notice,

the effect of the agreement shall be to discharge the order from the date on which it is agreed that the agreement shall take effect.

1.2 Where a local authority notifies the court of an agreement reached under paragraph 23(6) of Schedule 2 to the 1989 Act, the notification must be sent in writing to the designated officer of the court.

PRACTICE DIRECTION 12I – APPLICATIONS FOR REPORTING RESTRICTION ORDERS

1. This direction applies to any application in the Family Division founded on Convention rights for an order restricting publication of information about children or incapacitated adults.

2. Applications to be heard in the High Court

Orders can only be made in the High Court and are normally dealt with by a Judge of the Family Division. If the need for an order arises in existing proceedings in the county court, judges should either transfer the application to the High Court or consult their Family Division Liaison Judge. Where the matter is urgent, it can be heard by the Urgent Applications Judge of the Family Division (out of hours contact number 020 7947 6000).

3. Service of Application on the National News Media

Section 12(2) of the Human Rights Act 1998 means that an injunction restricting the exercise of the right to freedom of expression must not be granted where the person

437

The Family Procedure Rules 2010

against whom the application is made is neither present nor represented unless the court is satisfied (a) that the applicant has taken all practicable steps to notify the respondent, or (b) that there are compelling reasons why the respondent should not be notified.

Service of applications for reporting restriction orders on the national media can now be effected via the Press Association's CopyDirect service, to which national newspapers and broadcasters subscribe as a means of receiving notice of such applications.

The court will bear in mind that legal advisers to the media (i) are used to participating in hearings at very short notice where necessary; and (ii) are able to differentiate between information provided for legal purposes and information for editorial use. Service of applications via the CopyDirect service should henceforth be the norm.

The court retains the power to make without notice orders, but such cases will be exceptional, and an order will always give persons affected liberty to apply to vary or discharge it at short notice.

4. Further Guidance

The Practice Note "Applications for Reporting Restriction Orders" dated 18 March 2005 and issued jointly by the Official Solicitor and the Deputy Director of Legal Services, provides valuable guidance and should be followed.

5. (Issued by the President with the concurrence and approval of the Lord Chancellor, 18 March 2005)

PRACTICE DIRECTION 12J – RESIDENCE AND CONTACT ORDERS: DOMESTIC VIOLENCE AND HARM

14 January 2009

PRESIDENT OF THE FAMILY DIVISION

1. This Practice Direction applies to any family proceedings in the High Court, a county court or a magistrates' court in which an application is made for a residence order or a contact order in respect of a child under the Children Act 1989 ("the 1989 Act") or the Adoption and Children Act 2002 ("the 2002 Act") or in which any question arises about residence or about contact between a child and a parent or other family member.

2. The practice set out in this Direction is to be followed in any case in which it is alleged, or there is otherwise reason to suppose, that the subject child or a party has experienced domestic violence perpetrated by another party or that there is a risk of such violence. For the purpose of this Direction, the term 'domestic violence' includes physical violence, threatening or intimidating behaviour and any other form of abuse which, directly or indirectly, may have caused harm to the other party or to the child or which may give rise to the risk of harm.

('Harm' in relation to a child means ill-treatment or the impairment of health or development, including, for example, impairment suffered from seeing or hearing the ill-treatment of another: *Children Act 1989, ss 31(9),105(1)*)

GENERAL PRINCIPLES

3. The court must, at all stages of the proceedings, consider whether domestic violence is raised as an issue, either by the parties or otherwise, and if so must:

- identify at the earliest opportunity the factual and welfare issues involved;
- onsider the nature of any allegation or admission of domestic violence and the extent to which any domestic violence which is admitted, or which may be proved, would be relevant in deciding whether to make an order about residence or contact and, if so, in what terms;

- give directions to enable the relevant factual and welfare issues to be determined expeditiously and fairly.

4. In all cases it is for the court to decide whether an order for residence or contact accords with Section 1(1) of the 1989 Act or section 1(2) of the 2002 Act, as appropriate; any proposed residence or contact order, whether to be made by agreement between the parties or otherwise must be scrutinised by the court accordingly. The court shall not make a consent order for residence or contact or give permission for an application for a residence or contact order to be withdrawn, unless the parties are present in court, except where it is satisfied that there is no risk of harm to the child in so doing.

5. In considering, on an application for a consent order for residence or contact, whether there is any risk of harm to the child, the court shall consider all the evidence and information available. The court may direct a report under Section 7 of the 1989 Act either orally or in writing before it makes its determination; in such a case, the court may ask for information about any advice given by the officer preparing the report to the parties and whether they or the child have been referred to any other agency, including local authority children's services. If the report is not in writing, the court shall make a note of its substance on the court file.

ISSUE

6. Immediately on receipt of an application for a residence order or a contact order, or of the acknowledgement of the application, the court shall send a copy of it, together with any accompanying documents, to Cafcass or Cafcass Cymru, as appropriate, to enable Cafcass or Cafcass Cymru to undertake initial screening in accordance with their safeguarding policies.

LIAISON

7. The Designated Family Judge, or in the magistrates' court the Justices' Clerk, shall take steps to ensure that arrangements are in place for:

- the prompt delivery of documents to Cafcass or Cafcass Cymru in accordance with paragraph 6
- any information obtained by Cafcass or Cafcass Cymru as a result of initial screening or otherwise and any risk assessments prepared by Cafcass or Cafcass Cymru under section 16A of the 1989 Act to be placed before the appropriate court for consideration and directions
- a copy of any record of admissions or findings of fact made pursuant to paragraphs 12 & 21 below to be made available as soon as possible to any Officer of Cafcass or Welsh family proceedings officer or local authority officer preparing a report under section 7 of the 1989 Act.

RESPONSE OF THE COURT ON RECEIPT OF INFORMATION

8. Where any information provided to the court before the first hearing, whether as a result of initial screening by Cafcass or Cafcass Cymru or otherwise, indicates that there are issues of domestic violence which may be relevant to the court's determination, the court may give directions about the conduct of the hearing and for written evidence to be filed by the parties before the hearing.

9. If at any stage the court is advised by Cafcass or Cafcass Cymru or otherwise that there is a need for special arrangements to secure the safety of any party or child attending any hearing, the court shall ensure that appropriate arrangements are made for the hearing and for all subsequent hearings in the case, unless it considers that these are no longer necessary.

FIRST HEARING

10. At the first hearing, the court shall inform the parties of the content of any screening report or other information which has been provided by Cafcass or Cafcass Cymru, unless it considers that to do so would create a risk of harm to a party or the child.

(Specific provision about service of a risk assessment under section 16A of the 1989 Act

The Family Procedure Rules 2010

is made by the [rule 12.34 of the Family Procedure Rules 2010])

11. The court must ascertain at the earliest opportunity whether domestic violence is raised as an issue and must consider the likely impact of that issue on the conduct and outcome of the proceedings. In particular, the court should consider whether the nature and effect of the domestic violence alleged is such that, if proved, the decision of the court is likely to be affected.

ADMISSIONS

12. Where at any hearing an admission of domestic violence to another person or the child is made by a party, the admission should be recorded in writing and retained on the court file.

DIRECTIONS FOR A FACT-FINDING HEARING

13. The court should determine as soon as possible whether it is necessary to conduct a fact-finding hearing in relation to any disputed allegation of domestic violence before it can proceed to consider any final order(s) for residence or contact. Where the court determines that a finding of fact hearing is not necessary, the order shall record the reasons for that decision.

14. Where the court considers that a fact-finding hearing is necessary, it must give directions to ensure that the matters in issue are determined expeditiously and fairly and in particular it should consider:

- directing the parties to file written statements giving particulars of the allegations made and of any response in such a way as to identify clearly the issues for determination;
- whether material is required from third parties such as the police or health services and may give directions accordingly;
- whether any other evidence is required to enable the court to make findings of fact in relation to the allegations and may give directions accordingly.

15. Where the court fixes a fact-finding hearing, it must at the same time fix a further hearing for determination of the application. The hearings should be arranged in such a way that they are conducted by the same judge or, in the magistrates' court, by at least the same chairperson of the justices.

REPORTS UNDER SECTION 7

16. In any case where domestic violence is raised as an issue, the court should consider directing that a report on the question of contact, or any other matters relating to the welfare of the child, be prepared under section 7 of the 1989 Act by an Officer of Cafcass or a Welsh family proceedings officer (or local authority officer if appropriate), unless the court is satisfied that it is not necessary to do so in order to safeguard the child's interests. If the court so directs, it should consider the extent of any enquiries which can properly be made at this stage and whether it is appropriate to seek information on the wishes and feelings of the child before findings of fact have been made.

REPRESENTATION OF THE CHILD

17. Subject to the seriousness of the allegations made and the difficulty of the case, the court shall consider whether it is appropriate for the child who is the subject of the application to be made a party to the proceedings and be separately represented. If the case is proceeding in the magistrates' court and the court considers that it may be appropriate for the child to be made a party to the proceedings, it may transfer the case to the relevant county court for determination of that issue and following such transfer the county court shall give such directions for the further conduct of the case as it considers appropriate.

INTERIM ORDERS BEFORE DETERMINATION OF RELEVANT FACTS

18. Where the court gives directions for a fact-finding hearing, the court should consider whether an interim order for residence or contact is in the interests of the child;

FPR 2010, Practice Direction 12J

and in particular whether the safety of the child and the residential parent can be secured before, during and after any contact.

19. In deciding any question of interim residence or contact pending a full hearing the court should: -

(a) take into account the matters set out in section 1(3) of the 1989 Act or section 1(4) of the 2002 Act ("the welfare check-list"), as appropriate;
(b) give particular consideration to the likely effect on the child of any contact and any risk of harm, whether physical, emotional or psychological, which the child is likely to suffer as a consequence of making or declining to make an order;

20. Where the court is considering whether to make an order for interim contact, it should in addition consider

(a) the arrangements required to ensure, as far as possible, that any risk of harm to the child is minimised and that the safety of the child and the parties is secured; and in particular:
 (i) whether the contact should be supervised or supported, and if so, where and by whom; and
 (ii) the availability of appropriate facilities for that purpose
(b) if direct contact is not appropriate, whether it is in the best interests of the child to make an order for indirect contact.

THE FACT-FINDING HEARING

21 At the fact-finding hearing, the court should, wherever practicable, make findings of fact as to the nature and degree of any domestic violence which is established and its effect on the child, the child's parents and any other relevant person. The court shall record its findings in writing, and shall serve a copy on the parties. A copy of any record of findings of fact or of admissions must be sent to any officer preparing a report under Section 7 of the 1989 Act

22. At the conclusion of any fact-finding hearing, the court shall consider, notwithstanding any earlier direction for a section 7 report, whether it is in the best interests of the child for the court to give further directions about the preparation or scope of any report under section 7; where necessary, it may adjourn the proceedings for a brief period to enable the officer to make representations about the preparation or scope of any further enquiries.

The court should also consider whether it would be assisted by any social work, psychiatric, psychological or other assessment of any party or the child and if so (subject to any necessary consent) make directions for such assessment to be undertaken and for the filing of any consequent report.

23. Where the court has made findings of fact on disputed allegations, any subsequent hearing in the proceedings should be conducted by the same judge or, in the magistrates' court, by at least the same chairperson of the justices. Exceptions may be made only where observing this requirement would result in delay to the planned timetable and the judge or chairperson is satisfied, for reasons recorded in writing, that the detriment to the welfare of the child would outweigh the detriment to the fair trial of the proceedings

IN ALL CASES WHERE DOMESTIC VIOLENCE HAS OCCURRED

24. The court should take steps to obtain (or direct the parties or an Officer of CAFCASS or a Welsh family proceedings officer to obtain) information about the facilities available locally to assist any party or the child in cases where domestic violence has occurred.

25. Following any determination of the nature and extent of domestic violence, whether or not following a fact-finding hearing, the court should consider whether any party should seek advice or treatment as a precondition to an order for residence or contact being made or as a means of assisting the court in ascertaining the likely risk of harm to the child from that person, and may (with the consent of that party) give

FACTORS TO BE TAKEN INTO ACCOUNT WHEN DETERMINING WHETHER TO MAKE RESIDENCE OR CONTACT ORDERS IN ALL CASES WHERE DOMESTIC VIOLENCE HAS OCCURRED

26. When deciding the issue of residence or contact the court should, in the light of any findings of fact, apply the individual matters in the welfare checklist with reference to those findings; in particular, where relevant findings of domestic violence have been made, the court should in every case consider any harm which the child has suffered as a consequence of that violence and any harm which the child is at risk of suffering if an order for residence or contact is made and should only make an order for contact if it can be satisfied that the physical and emotional safety of the child and the parent with whom the child is living can, as far as possible, be secured before during and after contact.

27. In every case where a finding of domestic violence is made, the court should consider the conduct of both parents towards each other and towards the child; in particular, the court should consider;

(a) the effect of the domestic violence which has been established on the child and on the parent with whom the child is living;
(b) the extent to which the parent seeking residence or contact is motivated by a desire to promote the best interests of the child or may be doing so as a means of continuing a process of violence, intimidation or harassment against the other parent;
(c) the likely behaviour during contact of the parent seeking contact and its effect on the child;
(d) the capacity of the parent seeking residence or contact to appreciate the effect of past violence and the potential for future violence on the other parent and the child;
(e) the attitude of the parent seeking residence or contact to past violent conduct by that parent; and in particular whether that parent has the capacity to change and to behave appropriately.

DIRECTIONS AS TO HOW CONTACT IS TO PROCEED

28. Where the court has made findings of domestic violence but, having applied the welfare checklist, nonetheless considers that direct contact is in the best interests of the child, the court should consider what if any directions or conditions are required to enable the order to be carried into effect and in particular should consider:

(a) whether or not contact should be supervised, and if so, where and by whom;
(b) whether to impose any conditions to be complied with by the party in whose favour the order for contact has been made and if so, the nature of those conditions, for example by way of seeking advice or treatment (subject to any necessary consent);
(c) whether such contact should be for a specified period or should contain provisions which are to have effect for a specified period;
(d) whether or not the operation of the order needs to be reviewed; if so the court should set a date for the review and give directions to ensure that at the review the court has full information about the operation of the order.

29. Where the court does not consider direct contact to be appropriate, it shall consider whether it is in the best interests of the child to make an order for indirect contact.

THE REASONS OF THE COURT

30. In its judgment or reasons the court should always make clear how its findings on the issue of domestic violence have influenced its decision on the issue of residence or contact. In particular, where the court has found domestic violence proved but nonetheless makes an order, the court should always explain, whether by way of reference to the welfare check-list or otherwise, why it takes the view that the

order which it has made is in the best interests of the child.

31 This Practice Direction is issued by the President of the Family Division, as the nominee of the Lord Chief Justice, with the agreement of the Lord Chancellor.

The Right Honourable Sir Mark Potter

President of the Family Division and Head of Family Justice

PRACTICE DIRECTION 12K – PRACTICE DIRECTION (CHILDREN ACT 1989 EXCLUSION REQUIREMENT)

FAMILY DIVISION

17 December 1997

Procedure — Power of arrest attached to order in absence of party — Arrest made under such order —Order of committal made otherwise in public or open court — Children Act 1989, ss 38A(5), 44A(5)

Under s 38A(5) and s 44A(5) of the Children Act 1989 the court may attach a power of arrest to an exclusion requirement included in an interim care order or an emergency protection order. In cases where an order is made which includes an exclusion requirement, the following shall apply.

(1) If a power of arrest is attached to the order then unless the person to whom the exclusion requirement refers was given notice of the hearing and attended the hearing, the name of that person and that an order has been made including an exclusion requirement to which a power of arrest has been attached shall be announced in open court at the earliest opportunity. This may be either on the same day when the court proceeds to hear cases in open court or where there is no further business in open court on that day at the next listed sitting of the court

(2) When a person arrested under a power of arrest cannot conveniently be brought before the relevant judicial authority sitting in a place normally used as a courtroom within 24 hours after the arrest, he may be brought before the relevant judicial authority at any convenient place but, as the liberty of the subject is involved, the press and the public should be permitted to be present, unless security needs make this impracticable.

(3) Any order of committal made otherwise than in public or in a courtroom open to the public, shall be announced in open court at the earliest opportunity. This may be either on the same day when the court proceeds to hear cases in open court or where there is no further business in open court on that day at the next listed sitting of the court. The announcement shall state (a) the name of the person committed, (b) in general terms the nature of the contempt of the court in respect of which the order of committal has been made and (c) the length of the period of committal.

Issued by the President with the concurrence of the Lord Chancellor.

PRACTICE DIRECTION 12L – CHILDREN ACT 1989: RISK ASSESSMENTS UNDER SECTION 16A

1 This Practice Direction applies to any family proceedings in the High Court, a county court or a magistrates' court in which a risk assessment is made under section 16A of the Children Act 1989 ("the 1989 Act"). It has effect from 1st October 2007.

2 Section 16A(2) of the 1989 Act provides that, if in carrying out any function to which the section applies (as set out in section 16A(1)), an officer of the Service or a

Welsh family proceedings officer is given cause to suspect that the child concerned is at risk of harm, the officer must make a risk assessment in relation to the child and provide the risk assessment to the court.

3 The duty to provide the risk assessment to the court arises irrespective of the outcome of the assessment. Where an officer is given cause to suspect that the child concerned is at risk of harm and makes a risk assessment in accordance with section 16A(2), the officer must provide the assessment to the court, even if he or she reaches the conclusion that there is no risk of harm to the child.

4 The fact that a risk assessment has been carried out is a material fact that should be placed before the court, whatever the outcome of the assessment. In reporting the outcome to the court, the officer should make clear the factor or factors that triggered the decision to carry out the assessment.

5 (Issued by the President of the Family Division, as the nominee of the Lord Chief Justice, with the agreement of the Lord Chancellor, 3 September 2007).

PRACTICE DIRECTION 12M – FAMILY ASSISTANCE ORDERS: CONSULTATION

1. This Practice Direction applies to any family proceedings in the High Court, a county court or a magistrates' court in which the court is considering whether to make a family assistance order under section 16 of the Children Act 1989, as amended ("the 1989 Act"). It has effect from 1st October 2007.

2. Before making a family assistance order the court must have obtained the opinion of the appropriate officer about whether it would be in the best interests of the child in question for a family assistance order to be made and, if so, how the family assistance order could operate and for what period.

3. The appropriate officer will be an officer of the Service, a Welsh family proceedings officer or an officer of a local authority, depending on the category of officer the court proposes to require to be made available under the family assistance order.

4. The opinion of the appropriate officer may be given orally or in writing (for example, it may form part of a report under section 7 of the 1989 Act).

5. Before making a family assistance order the court must give any person whom it proposes be named in the order an opportunity to comment upon any opinion given by the appropriate officer.

6. (Issued by the President of the Family Division, as the nominee of the Lord Chief Justice, with the agreement of the Lord Chancellor, 3 September 2007).

PRACTICE DIRECTION 12N – ENFORCEMENT OF CHILDREN ACT 1989 CONTACT ORDERS: DISCLOSURE OF INFORMATION TO THE OFFICERS OF THE NATIONAL PROBATION SERVICE (HIGH COURT AND COUNTY COURT)

This Practice Direction is issued by the President of the Family Division with the agreement of the Lord Chancellor.

1. This Practice Direction applies to proceedings in the High Court or a county court where:

(a) the court is considering an application for an enforcement order[1] or for an order following an alleged breach of an enforcement order[2] and asks an officer of the Service or a Welsh family proceedings officer to provide information to the court in accordance with section 11L(5) of the Children Act 1989; or

(b) the court makes an enforcement order or an order following an alleged breach of an enforcement order and asks an officer of the Service or a Welsh family proceedings officer to monitor compliance with that order and to report to the court in accordance with section 11M of the Children Act 1989.

2. In all cases in which paragraph 1 applies, the officer of the Service or Welsh family proceedings officer will need to discuss aspects of the court case with an officer of the National Probation Service.

3. In order to ensure that the officer of the Service or Welsh family proceedings officer will not potentially be in contempt of court by virtue of such discussions, the court should, when making a request under section 11L(5) or section 11M of the Children Act 1989, give leave to that officer to disclose to the National Probation Service such information (whether or not contained in a document filed with the court) in relation to the proceedings as is necessary.

4. This Practice Direction comes into force on 8th December 2008.

NOTES

[1] under section 11J of the Children Act 1989.

[2] under paragraph 9 of Schedule A1 to the Children Act 1989.

PRACTICE DIRECTION 12O – ARRIVAL OF CHILD IN ENGLAND BY AIR

FAMILY DIVISION

18 January 1980

Child — Practice — Order for return of child — Arrival of child in England by air — Direction that airline and immigration officer supply information relating to arrival.

Where a person seeks an order for the return to him of children about to arrive in England by air and desires to have information to enable him to meet the aeroplane, the judge should be asked to include in his order a direction that the airline operating the flight, and, if he has the information, the immigration officer at the appropriate airport, should supply such information to that person.

To obtain such information in such circumstances in a case where a person already has an order for the return to him of children, that person should apply to a judge ex parte for such a direction.

Issued with the concurrence of the Lord Chancellor.

PRACTICE DIRECTION 12P – REGISTRAR'S DIRECTION (REMOVAL FROM JURISDICTION: ISSUE OF PASSPORTS)

FAMILY DIVISION

15 May 1987

1 REMOVAL FROM JURISDICTION

The President has directed that on application for leave to remove from the jurisdiction for holiday periods a ward of court who has been placed by a local authority with foster parents whose identity the Court considers should remain confidential, for example because they are prospective adopters, it is important that such foster parents should not be identified in the Court's order. In such cases the order should be expressed as giving leave to the local authority to arrange for the child to be removed from England and Wales for the purposes of holidays.

It is also considered permissible, where care and control has been given to a local

The Family Procedure Rules 2010

authority, or to an individual, for the Court to give general leave to make such arrangements in suitable cases, thereby obviating the need to make application for leave each time it is desired to remove the child from the jurisdiction.

2 ISSUE OF PASSPORTS

It is the practice of the Passport Department of the Home Office to issue passports for wards in accordance with the Court's direction. This frequently results in passports being restricted to the holiday period specified in the order giving leave. It is the President's opinion that it is more convenient for wards' passports to be issued without such restriction.

The Passport Department has agreed to issue passports on this basis unless the Court otherwise directs. It will of course still be necessary for the leave of the Court to be obtained for the child's removal.

PART 13

PROCEEDINGS UNDER SECTION 54 OF THE HUMAN FERTILISATION AND EMBRYOLOGY ACT 2008

13.1.— Interpretation and application
  (1) A reference in this Part to the 2002 Act is a reference to that Act as applied with modifications by the Human Fertilisation and Embryology (Parental Order) Regulations 2010.
  (2) In this Part—
    "the other parent" means any person who is a parent of the child but is not one of the applicants or the woman who carried the child (including any man who is the father by virtue of section 35 or 36 of the 2008 Act or any woman who is a parent by virtue of section 42 or 43 of that Act);
    "parental order" means an order under section 54 of the 2008 Act;
    "parental order proceedings" means proceedings for the making of a parental order under the 2008 Act or an order under any provision of the 2002 Act;
    "parental order reporter" means an officer of the service or a Welsh family proceedings officer appointed to act on behalf of a child who is the subject of parental order proceedings;
    "provision for contact" means a contact order under section 8 or 34 of the 1989 Act.
  (3) Except where the contrary intention appears, the rules in this Part apply to parental order proceedings.

13.2. Application of Part 12
Rules 12.9 to 12.11, 12.19 and 12.21 apply as appropriate, with any necessary modifications, to parental order proceedings.

13.3.— Who the parties are
  (1) An application for a parental order may be made by such of the following who satisfy the conditions set out in section 54(1) of the 2008 Act—
    (a) a husband and wife;
    (b) civil partners of each other; or
    (c) two persons who are living as partners in an enduring family relationship and are not within the prohibited degrees of relationship in relation to each other.
  (2) The respondents to an application for a parental order are—
    (a) the woman who carried the child;
    (b) the other parent (if any);
    (c) any person in whose favour there is provision for contact; and

(d) any other person or body with parental responsibility for the child at the date of the application.

(3) The court will direct that a person with parental responsibility for the child be made a party to proceedings where that person requests to be one.

(4) The court may at any time direct that—
- (a) any other person or body be made a respondent to the proceedings; or
- (b) a respondent be removed from the proceedings.

(5) If the court makes a direction for the addition or removal of a party, it may give consequential directions about—
- (a) serving a copy of the application form on any new respondent;
- (b) serving relevant documents on the new party; and
- (c) the management of the proceedings.

13.4.— Notice of proceedings to person with foreign parental responsibility

(1) This rule applies where a child is subject to proceedings to which this Part applies and at the date of the application –
- (a) a person holds or is believed to hold parental responsibility for the child under the law of another State which subsists in accordance with Article 16 of the 1996 Hague Convention following the child becoming habitually resident in a territorial unit of the United Kingdom; and
- (b) that person is not otherwise required to be joined as a respondent under rule 13.3.

(2) The applicant shall give notice of the proceedings to any person to whom the applicant believes paragraph (1) applies.

(3) The applicant and every respondent to the proceedings shall provide such details as they possess as to the identity and whereabouts of any person they believe to hold parental responsibility for the child in accordance with paragraph (1) to the court officer, upon making, or responding to the application as appropriate.

(4) Where the existence of such a person only becomes apparent to a party at a later date during the proceedings, that party must notify the court officer of those details at the earliest opportunity.

(5) Where a person to whom paragraph (1) applies receives notice of proceedings, that person may apply to the court to be joined as a party using the Part 18 procedure.

13.5.— What the court or a court officer will do when the application has been issued

(1) As soon as practicable after the issue of proceedings—
- (a) the court will—
  - (i) if section 48(1) of the 2002 Act applies (restrictions on making parental orders), consider whether it is proper to hear the application;
  - (ii) subject to paragraph (2), set a date for the first directions hearing;
  - (iii) appoint a parental order reporter; and
  - (iv) set a date for the hearing of the application; and
- (b) a court officer will—
  - (i) return to the applicants the copies of the application together with any other documents the applicant is required to serve; and
  - (ii) send a certified copy of the entry in the register of live births to the parental order reporter.

(2) Where it considers it appropriate the court may, instead of setting a date for a first directions appointment, give the directions provided for in rule 13.9.

13.6.— Service of the application and other documents

(1) The applicants must, within 14 days before the hearing or first directions hearing, serve on the respondents —
- (a) the application;
- (b) a form for acknowledging service; and
- (c) a notice of proceedings.

The Family Procedure Rules 2010

(2) The applicants must serve a notice of proceedings on any local authority or voluntary organisation that has at any time provided accommodation for the child.

13.7. Acknowledgement
Within 7 days of the service of an application for a parental order, each respondent must file an acknowledgment of service and serve it on all the other parties.

13.8. Date for first directions hearing
Unless the court directs otherwise, the first directions hearing must be within 4 weeks beginning with the date on which the application is issued.

13.9.— The first directions hearing
(1) At the first directions hearing in the proceedings the court will—
- (a) fix a timetable for the filing of—
  - (i) any report from a parental order reporter;
  - (ii) if a statement of facts has been filed, any amended statement of facts; and
  - (iii) any other evidence;
- (b) give directions relating to the report of the parental order reporter and other evidence;
- (c) consider whether any other person should be a party to the proceedings and, if so, give directions in accordance with rule 13.3(3) or (4) joining that person as a party;
- (d) give directions relating to the appointment of a litigation friend for any protected party unless a litigation friend has already been appointed;
- (e) consider whether the case needs to be transferred to another court and, if so, give directions to transfer the proceedings to another court in accordance with the Allocation Order;
- (f) give directions about—
  - (i) tracing the other parent or the woman who carried the child;
  - (ii) service of documents;
  - (iii) subject to paragraph (2), disclosure as soon as possible of information and evidence to the parties; and
  - (iv) the final hearing.

(2) Rule 13.12 (reports of the parental order reporter and disclosure to parties) applies to any direction given under paragraph (1)(f)(iii) as it applies to a direction given under rule 13.12(1).

(3) The parties or their legal representatives must attend the first directions hearing unless the court directs otherwise.

(4) Directions may also be given at any stage in the proceedings—
- (a) of the court's own initiative; or
- (b) on the application of a party or the parental order reporter.

(5) Where the court proposes to exercise its powers in paragraph (1) of its own initiative the procedure set out in rule 4.3(2) to (7) applies.

(6) For the purposes of giving directions or for such purposes as the court directs—
- (a) the court may set a date for a further directions hearing or other hearing; and
- (b) the court officer will give notice of any date so fixed to the parties and to the parental order reporter.

(7) Directions of a court which are still in force immediately prior to the transfer of proceedings to another court shall continue to apply following the transfer subject to—
- (a) any changes of terminology which are required to apply those directions to the court to which the proceedings are transferred; and
- (b) any variation or revocation of the direction.

(8) The court or court officer will—
- (a) take a note of the giving, variation or revocation of a direction under this rule; and

(b) as soon as practicable serve a copy of the note on every party.

(9) After the first directions hearing the court will monitor compliance by the parties with the court's timetable and directions.

13.10.— **Where the agreement of the other parent or the woman who carried the child is not required**

(1) This rule applies where the agreement of the other parent or the woman who carried the child to the making of the parental order is not required as the person in question cannot be found or is incapable of giving agreement.

(2) The applicants must—
- (a) state that the agreement is not required in the application form, or at any later stage by filing a written note with the court;
- (b) file a statement of facts setting out a summary of the history of the case and any other facts to satisfy the court that the other parent or the woman who carried the child cannot be found or is incapable of giving agreement.

(3) On receipt of the application form or written note—
- (a) a court officer will—
  - (i) unless the other parent or the woman who carried the child cannot be found, inform the other parent or the woman who carried the child that their agreement is not required;
  - (ii) send a copy of the statement of facts filed in accordance with paragraph (2)(b) to—
    - (aa) the other parent unless the other parent cannot be found;
    - (bb) the woman who carried the child unless the woman cannot be found; and
    - (cc) the parental order reporter; and
- (b) if the applicants consider that the other parent or the woman who carried the child is incapable of giving agreement the court will consider whether to—
  - (i) appoint a litigation friend for the other parent or the woman who carried the child under rule 15.6(1) or
  - (ii) give directions for an application to be made under rule 15.6(3), unless a litigation friend is already appointed for the other parent or the woman who carried the child.

13.11.— **Agreement**

(1) Unless the court directs otherwise, the agreement of the other parent or the woman who carried the child to the making of the parental order may be given in the form referred to in Practice Direction 5A or a form to the like effect.

(2) Any form of agreement executed in Scotland must be witnessed by a Justice of the Peace or a Sheriff.

(3) Any form of agreement executed in Northern Ireland must be witnessed by a Justice of the Peace.

(4) Any form of agreement executed outside the United Kingdom must be witnessed by—
- (a) any person for the time being authorised by law in the place where the document is executed to administer an oath for any judicial or other legal purpose;
- (b) a British Consular officer;
- (c) a notary public; or
- (d) if the person executing the document is serving in any of the regular armed forces of the Crown, an officer holding a commission in any of those forces.

13.12.— **Reports of the parental order reporter and disclosure to the parties**

(1) The court will consider whether to give a direction that a confidential report of the parental order reporter be disclosed to each party to the proceedings.

(2) Before giving such a direction the court will consider whether any information should be deleted including information which discloses the particulars referred to in rule 29.1(1) where a party has given notice under rule 29.1(2) (disclosure of personal details).

(3) The court may direct that the report shall not be disclosed to a party.

13.13. Notice of final hearing

A court officer will give notice to the parties and to the parental order reporter—
- (a) of the date and place where the application will be heard; and (b) of the fact that, unless the person wishes or the court requires, the person need not attend.

13.14.— The final hearing

(1) Any person who has been given notice in accordance with rule 13.13 may attend the final hearing and be heard on the question of whether an order should be made.

(2) The court may direct that any person must attend a final hearing.

13.15.— Proof of identity of the child

(1) Unless the contrary is shown, the child referred to in the application will be deemed to be the child referred to in the form of agreement to the making of the parental order where the conditions in paragraph (2) apply.

(2) The conditions are—
- (a) the application identifies the child by reference to a full certified copy of an entry in the registers of live-births;
- (b) the form of agreement identifies the child by reference to a full certified copy of an entry in the registers of live-births attached to the form; and
- (c) the copy of the entry in the registers of live-births referred to in sub-paragraph (a) is the same or relates to the same entry in the registers of live-births as the copy of the entry in the registers of live-births attached to the form of agreement.

(3) Where the precise date of the child's birth is not proved to the satisfaction of the court, the court will determine the probable date of birth.

(4) The probable date of the child's birth may be specified in the parental order as the date of the child's birth.

(5) Where the child's place of birth cannot be proved to the satisfaction of the court—
- (a) the child may be treated as having been born in the registration district of the court where it is probable that the child may have been born in—
  - (i) the United Kingdom;
  - (ii) the Channel Islands; or
  - (iii) the Isle of Man; or
- (b) in any other case, the particulars of the country of birth may be omitted from the parental order.

13.16.— Disclosing information to an adult who was subject to a parental order

(1) Subject to paragraph (2), the person who is subject to the parental order has the right to receive from the court which made the parental order a copy of the following—
- (a) the application form for a parental order (but not the documents attached to that form);
- (b) the parental order and any other orders relating to the parental order proceedings;
- (c) a transcript of the court's decision; and
- (d) a report made to the court by the parental order reporter.

(2) The court will not provide a copy of a document or order referred to in paragraph (1) unless the person making the request has completed the certificate relating to counselling in the form for that purpose referred to in Practice Direction 5A.

(3) This rule does not apply to a person under the age of 18 years.

13.17.— Application for recovery orders

(1) An application for any of the orders referred to in section 41(2) of the 2002 Act (recovery orders) may—

- (a) in the High Court or a county court, be made without notice in which case the applicant must file the application—
  - (i) where the application is made by telephone, the next business day after the making of the application; or
  - (ii) in any other case, at the time when the application is made; and
- (b) in a magistrates' court, be made, with the permission of the court, without notice in which case the applicant must file the application at the time when the application is made or as directed by the court.

(2) Where the court refuses to make an order on an application without notice it may direct that the application is made on notice in which case the application shall proceed in accordance with rules 13.1 to 13.14.

(3) The respondents to an application under this rule are—

- (a) in a case where parental order proceedings are pending, all parties to those proceedings;
- (b) any person having parental responsibility for the child;
- (c) any person in whose favour there is provision for contact;
- (d) any person who was caring for the child immediately prior to the making of the application; and
- (e) any person whom the applicant alleges to have effected, or to have been or to be responsible for, the taking or keeping of the child.

13.18.— Keeping of registers, custody, inspection and disclosure of documents and information

(1) Such part of the register kept in a family proceedings court in pursuance of rules made under the Magistrates' Courts Act 1980 as relates to parental order proceedings, must be kept in a separate book and the book must not contain particulars of any other proceedings.

(2) All documents relating to parental order proceedings and related proceedings under the 2002 Act including, in a family proceedings court, the book kept in accordance with paragraph (1), must, while they are in the custody of the court, be kept in a place of special security.

(3) Any person who obtains any information in the course of, or relating to, parental order proceedings must treat that information as confidential and must only disclose it if—

- (a) the disclosure is necessary for the proper exercise of that person's duties; or
- (b) the information is requested by—
  - (i) a court or public authority (whether in Great Britain or not) having power to determine parental order proceedings and related matters, for the purpose of that court or authority discharging its duties relating to those proceedings and matters; or
  - (ii) a person who is authorised in writing by the Secretary of State to obtain the information for the purposes of research.

13.19. Documents held by the court not to be inspected or copied without the court's permission

Subject to the provisions of these rules, any practice direction or any direction given by the court—

- (a) no document or order held by the court in parental order proceedings and related proceedings under the 2002 Act will be open to inspection by any person; and
- (b) no copy of any such document or order, or of an extract from any such document or order, shall be taken by or given to any person.

13.20.— Orders

(1) A parental order takes effect from the date when it is made, or such later date as the court may specify.

(2) In proceedings in Wales a party may request that an order be drawn up in Welsh as well as English.

13.21.— Copies of orders

(1) Within 7 days beginning with the date on which the final order was made in proceedings, or such shorter time as the court may direct, a court officer will send—
- (a) a copy of the order to the applicant;
- (b) a copy, which is sealed[GL], authenticated with the stamp of the court or certified as a true copy of a parental order, to the Registrar General;
- (c) a notice of the making or refusal of—
  - (i) the final order; or
  - (ii) an order quashing or revoking a parental order or allowing an appeal against an order in proceedings,

to every respondent and, with the permission of the court, any other person.

(2) The court officer will also send notice of the making of a parental order to—
- (a) any court in Great Britain which appears to the court officer to have made any such order as is referred to in section 46(2) of the 2002 Act (order relating to parental responsibility for, and maintenance of, the child); and
- (b) the principal registry, if it appears to the court officer that a parental responsibility agreement has been recorded at the principal registry.

(3) A copy of any final order may be sent to any other person with the permission of the court.

(4) The court officer will send a copy of any order made during the course of the proceedings to all the parties to those proceedings unless the court directs otherwise.

(5) If an order has been drawn up in Welsh as well as in English in accordance with rule 13.20(2), any reference in this rule to sending an order is to be taken as a reference to sending both the Welsh and English orders.

13.22.— Amendment and revocation of orders

(1) This rule applies to an application under paragraph 4 of Schedule 1 to the 2002 Act (amendment of a parental order and revocation of direction).

(2) If the application is made in a family proceedings court it must be made to a family proceedings court for the same local justice area as the family proceedings court which made the parental order, by delivering it or sending it by post to the designated officer of the court.

(3) Subject to paragraph (4), an application may be made without serving a copy of the application notice.

(4) The court may direct that an application notice be served on such persons as it thinks fit.

(5) Where the court makes an order granting the application, a proper officer shall send the Registrar General a notice—
- (a) specifying the amendments; or
- (b) informing the Registrar General of the revocation,

giving sufficient particulars of the order to enable the Registrar General to identify the case.

PART 13 COMMENTARY

Part 13 is not supplemented by any practice directions.

Part 13 applies to parental orders under s 54 of the Human Fertilisation and Embryology Act 2008. These rules incorporate the provision of Part IVA of the FPR 1991 without significant alteration.

Forms relevant to Part 13 are C51, C52, A64A and A101A.

PART 14

PROCEDURE FOR APPLICATIONS IN ADOPTION, PLACEMENT AND RELATED PROCEEDINGS

14.1.— Application of this Part and interpretation

(1) The rules in this Part apply to the following proceedings—
- (a) adoption proceedings;
- (b) placement proceedings; and
- (c) proceedings for—
  - (i) the making of a contact order under section 26 of the 2002 Act;
  - (ii) the variation or revocation of a contact order under section 27 of the 2002 Act;
  - (iii) an order giving permission to change a child's surname or remove a child from the United Kingdom under section 28(2) and (3) of the 2002 Act;
  - (iv) a section 84 order;
  - (v) a section 88 direction;
  - (vi) a section 89 order; or
  - (vii) any other order that may be referred to in a practice direction.

(2) In this Part—

"Central Authority" means—
- (a) in relation to England, the Secretary of State; and
- (b) in relation to Wales, the Welsh Ministers;

"Convention adoption order" means an adoption order under the 2002 Act which, by virtue of regulations under section 1 of the Adoption (Intercountry Aspects) Act 1999 (regulations giving effect to the Convention on Protection of Children and Co-operation in Respect of Intercountry Adoption, concluded at the Hague on 29th May 1993), is made as a Convention adoption order;

"guardian" means—
- (a) a guardian (other than the guardian of the estate of a child) appointed in accordance with section 5 of the 1989 Act; and
- (b) a special guardian within the meaning of section 14A of the 1989 Act;

"provision for contact" means a contact order under section 8 or 34 of the 1989 Act or a contact order under section 26 of the 2002 Act;

"section 88 direction" means a direction given by the High Court under section 88 of the 2002 Act that section 67(3) of that Act (status conferred by adoption) does not apply or does not apply to any extent specified in the direction.

14.2.— Application for a serial number

(1) This rule applies to any application in proceedings by a person who intends to adopt the child.

(2) If, before the proceedings have started, the applicant requests a court officer to assign a serial number to identify the applicant in connection with the proceedings in order for the applicant's identity to be kept confidential in those proceedings, a serial number will be so assigned.

(3) The court may at any time direct that a serial number identifying the applicant in the proceedings referred to in paragraph (2) must be removed.

(4) If a serial number has been assigned to a person under paragraph (2)—
- (a) the court officer will ensure that any application form or application notice sent in accordance with these rules does not contain information which discloses, or is likely to disclose, the identity of that person to any other party to that application who is not already aware of that person's identity; and

The Family Procedure Rules 2010

(b) the proceedings on the application will be conducted with a view to securing that the applicant is not seen by or made known to any party who is not already aware of the applicant's identity except with the applicant's consent.

14.3.— Who the parties are

(1) In relation to the proceedings set out in column 1 of the following table, column 2 sets out who the application may be made by and column 3 sets out who the respondents to those proceedings will be.

Proceedings for	*Applicants*	*Respondents*
An adoption order (section 46 of the 2002 Act).	The prospective adopters (sections 50 and 51 of the 2002 Act).	Each parent who has parental responsibility for the child unless that parent has given notice under section 20(4)(a) of the 2002 Act (statement of wish not to be informed of any application for an adoption order) which has effect; any guardian of the child unless that guardian has given notice under section 20(4)(a) of the 2002 Act (statement of wish not to be informed of any application for an adoption order) which has effect; any person in whose favour there is provision for contact; any adoption agency having parental responsibility for the child under section 25 of the 2002 Act; any adoption agency which has taken part at any stage in the arrangements for adoption of the child; any local authority to whom notice under section 44 of the 2002 Act (notice of intention to adopt or apply for a section 84 order) has been given; any local authority or voluntary organisation which has parental responsibility for, is looking after or is caring for, the child; and the child where— — permission has been granted to a parent or guardian to oppose the making of the adoption order (section 47(3) or 47(5) of the 2002 Act); — the child opposes the making of an adoption order; — a children and family reporter recommends that it is in the best interests of the child to be a party to the proceedings and that recommendation is accepted by the court;

Proceedings for	Applicants	Respondents
		— the child is already an adopted child;
		— any party to the proceedings or the child is opposed to the arrangements for allowing any person contact with the child, or a person not being allowed contact with the child after the making of the adoption order;
		— the application is for a Convention adoption order or a section 84 order;
		— the child has been brought into the United Kingdom in the circumstances where section 83(1) of the 2002 Act applies (restriction on bringing children in);
		— the application is for an adoption order other than a Convention adoption order and the prospective adopters intend the child to live in a country or territory outside the British Islands after the making of the adoption order; or
		— the prospective adopters are relatives of the child.
A section 84 order.	The prospective adopters asking for parental responsibility prior to adoption abroad.	As for an adoption order.
A placement order (section 21 of the 2002 Act).	A local authority (section 22 of the 2002 Act).	Each parent who has parental responsibility for the child: any guardian of the child;
		any person in whose favour an order under the 1989 Act is in force in relation to the child;
		any adoption agency or voluntary organisation which has parental responsibility for, is looking after, or is caring for, the child;
		the child; and
		the parties or any persons who are or have been parties to proceedings for a care order in respect of the child where those proceedings have led to the application for the placement order.
An order varying a placement order (section 23 of the 2002 Act).	The joint application of the local authority authorised by the placement order to place the child for adoption and the local authority which is to be substituted for that authority (section 23 of the 2002 Act).	The parties to the proceedings leading to the placement order which it is sought to have varied except the child who was the subject of those proceedings; and any person in whose favour there is provision for contact.

The Family Procedure Rules 2010

Proceedings for	Applicants	Respondents
An order revoking a placement order (section 24 of the 2002 Act).	The child; the local authority authorised to place the child for adoption; or where the child is not placed for adoption by the authority, any other person who has the permission of the court to apply (section 24 of the 2002 Act).	The parties to the proceedings leading to the placement order which it is sought to have revoked; and any person in whose favour there is provision for contact.
A contact order (section 26 of the 2002 Act).	The child; the adoption agency; any parent, guardian or relative; any person in whose favour there was provision for contact under the 1989 Act which ceased to have effect on an adoption agency being authorised to place a child for adoption, or placing a child for adoption who is less than six weeks old (section 26(1) of the 2002 Act); a person in whose favour there was a residence order in force immediately before the adoption agency was authorised to place the child for adoption or placed the child for adoption at a time when the child was less than six weeks old; a person who by virtue of an order made in the exercise of the High Court's inherent jurisdiction with respect to children had care of the child immediately before that time; or any person who has the permission of the court to make the application (section 26 of the 2002 Act).	The adoption agency authorised to place the child for adoption or which has placed the child for adoption; the person with whom the child lives or is to live; each parent with parental responsibility for the child; any guardian of the child; and the child where— — the adoption agency authorised to place the child for adoption or which has placed the child for adoption or a parent with parental responsibility for the child opposes the making of the contact order under section 26 of the 2002 Act; — the child opposes the making of the contact order under section 26 of the 2002 Act; — existing provision for contact is to be revoked; — relatives of the child do not agree to the arrangements for allowing any person contact with the child, or a person not being allowed contact with the child; or — the child is suffering or is at risk of suffering harm within the meaning of the 1989 Act.

Proceedings for	*Applicants*	*Respondents*
An order varying or revoking a contact order (section 27 of the 2002 Act).	The child; the adoption agency; or any person named in the contact order (section 27(1) of the 2002 Act).	The parties to the proceedings leading to the contact order which it is sought to have varied or revoked; and any person named in the contact order.
An order permitting the child's name to be changed or the removal of the child from the United Kingdom (section 28(2) and (3) of the 2002 Act).	Any person including the adoption agency or the local authority authorised to place, or which has placed, the child for adoption (section 28(2) of the 2002 Act).	The parties to proceedings leading to any placement order; the adoption agency authorised to place the child for adoption or which has placed the child for adoption; any prospective adopters with whom the child is living; each parent with parental responsibility for the child; and any guardian of the child.
A section 88 direction.	The adopted child; the adopters; any parent; or any other person.	The adopters; the parents; the adoption agency; the local authority to whom notice under section 44 of the 2002 Act (notice of intention to apply for a section 84 order) has been given; and the Attorney-General.
A section 89 order.	The adopters; the adopted person; any parent; the relevant Central Authority; the adoption agency; the local authority to whom notice under section 44 of the 2002 Act (notice of intention to adopt or apply for a section 84 order) has been given; the Secretary of State for the Home Department; or any other person.	The adopters; the parents; the adoption agency; and the local authority to whom notice under section 44 of the 2002 Act (notice of intention to adopt or apply for a section 84 order) has been given.

(2) The court may at any time direct that a child, who is not already a respondent to proceedings, be made a respondent to proceedings where—

    (a)   the child—

(i) wishes to make an application; or
(ii) has evidence to give to the court or a legal submission to make which has not been given or made by any other party; or
    (b) there are other special circumstances.
(3) The court may at any time direct that—
    (a) any other person or body be made a respondent to proceedings; or
    (b) a party be removed.
(4) If the court makes a direction for the addition or removal of a party, it may give consequential directions about—
    (a) serving a copy of the application form on any new respondent;
    (b) serving relevant documents on the new party; and
    (c) the management of the proceedings.

14.4.— Notice of proceedings to person with foreign parental responsibility
(1) This rule applies where a child is subject to proceedings to which this Part applies and –
    (a) a parent of the child holds or is believed to hold parental responsibility for the child under the law of another State which subsists in accordance with Article 16 of the 1996 Hague Convention following the child becoming habitually resident in a territorial unit of the United Kingdom; and
    (b) that parent is not otherwise required to be joined as a respondent under rule 14.3.
(2) The applicant shall give notice of the proceedings to any parent to whom the applicant believes paragraph (1) applies in any case in which a person who was a parent with parental responsibility under the 1989 Act would be a respondent to the proceedings in accordance with rule 14.3.
(3) The applicant and every respondent to the proceedings shall provide such details as they possess as to the identity and whereabouts of any parent they believe to hold parental responsibility for the child in accordance with paragraph (1) to the court officer, upon making, or responding to the application as appropriate.
(4) Where the existence of such a parent only becomes apparent to a party at a later date during the proceedings, that party must notify the court officer of those details at the earliest opportunity.
(5) Where a parent to whom paragraph (1) applies receives notice of proceedings, that parent may apply to the court to be joined as a party using the Part 18 procedure.

14.5.— Who is to serve
(1) The general rules about service in Part 6 are subject to this rule.
(2) In proceedings to which this Part applies, a document which has been issued or prepared by a court officer will be served by the court officer except where—
    (a) a practice direction provides otherwise; or
    (b) the court directs otherwise.
(3) Where a court officer is to serve a document, it is for the court to decide which of the methods of service specified in rule 6.23 is to be used.

14.6.— What the court or a court officer will do when the application has been issued
(1) As soon as practicable after the application has been issued in proceedings—
    (a) the court will—
        (i) if section 48(1) of the 2002 Act (restrictions on making adoption orders) applies, consider whether it is proper to hear the application;
        (ii) subject to paragraph (4), set a date for the first directions hearing;
        (iii) appoint a children's guardian in accordance with rule 16.3(1);
        (iv) appoint a reporting officer in accordance with rule 16.30;
        (v) consider whether a report relating to the welfare of the child is required, and if so, request such a report in accordance with rule 16.33;
        (vi) set a date for the hearing of the application; and

(vii) do anything else that may be set out in a practice direction; and
(b) a court officer will—
(i) subject to receiving confirmation in accordance with paragraph (2)(b)(ii), give notice of any directions hearing set by the court to the parties and to any children's guardian, reporting officer or children and family reporter;
(ii) serve a copy of the application form (but, subject to sub-paragraphs (iii) and (iv), not the documents attached to it) on the persons referred to in Practice Direction 14A;
(iii) send a copy of the certified copy of the entry in the register of live-births or Adopted Children Register and any health report attached to an application for an adoption order to—
(aa) any children's guardian, reporting officer or children and family reporter; and
(bb) the local authority to whom notice under section 44 of the 2002 Act (notice of intention to adopt or apply for a section 84 order) has been given;
(iv) if notice under rule 14.9(2) has been given (request to dispense with consent of parent or guardian), in accordance with that rule inform the parent or guardian of the request and send a copy of the statement of facts to—
(aa) the parent or guardian;
(bb) any children's guardian, reporting officer or children and family reporter;
(cc) any local authority to whom notice under section 44 of the 2002 Act (notice of intention to adopt or apply for a section 84 order) has been given; and
(dd) any adoption agency which has placed the child for adoption; and
(v) do anything else that may be set out in a practice direction.

(2) In addition to the matters referred to in paragraph (1), as soon as practicable after an application for an adoption order or a section 84 order has been issued the court or the court officer will—
(a) where the child is not placed for adoption by an adoption agency—
(i) ask either the Service or the Assembly to file any relevant form of consent to an adoption order or a section 84 order; and
(ii) ask the local authority to prepare a report on the suitability of the prospective adopters if one has not already been prepared; and
(b) where the child is placed for adoption by an adoption agency, ask the adoption agency to—
(i) file any relevant form of consent to—
(aa) the child being placed for adoption;
(bb) an adoption order;
(cc) a future adoption order under section 20 of the 2002 Act; or
(dd) a section 84 order;
(ii) confirm whether a statement has been made under section 20(4)(a) of the 2002 Act (statement of wish not to be informed of any application for an adoption order) and if so, to file that statement;
(iii) file any statement made under section 20(4)(b) of the 2002 Act (withdrawal of wish not to be informed of any application for an adoption order) as soon as it is received by the adoption agency; and
(iv) prepare a report on the suitability of the prospective adopters if one has not already been prepared.

(3) In addition to the matters referred to in paragraph (1), as soon as practicable after an application for a placement order has been issued—

The Family Procedure Rules 2010

    (a)   the court will consider whether a report giving the local authority's reasons for placing the child for adoption is required, and if so, will direct the local authority to prepare such a report; and

    (b)   the court or the court officer will ask either the Service or the Assembly to file any form of consent to the child being placed for adoption.

(4) Where it considers it appropriate the court may, instead of setting a date for a first directions hearing, give the directions provided for by rule 14.8.

14.7. Date for first directions hearing

Unless the court directs otherwise, the first directions hearing must be within 4 weeks beginning with the date on which the application is issued.

14.8.— The first directions hearing

(1) At the first directions hearing in the proceedings the court will—
    (a)   fix a timetable for the filing of—
        (i)   any report relating to the suitability of the applicants to adopt a child;
        (ii)   any report from the local authority;
        (iii)   any report from a children's guardian, reporting officer or children and family reporter;
        (iv)   if a statement of facts has been filed, any amended statement of facts;
        (v)   any other evidence, and
        (vi)   give directions relating to the reports and other evidence;
    (b)   consider whether the child or any other person should be a party to the proceedings and, if so, give directions in accordance with rule 14.3(2) or (3) joining that child or person as a party;
    (c)   give directions relating to the appointment of a litigation friend for any protected party or child who is a party to, but not the subject of, proceedings unless a litigation friend has already been appointed;
    (d)   consider whether the case needs to be transferred to another court and, if so, give directions to transfer the proceedings to another court in accordance with any order made by the Lord Chancellor under Part 1 of Schedule 11 to the 1989 Act;
    (e)   give directions about—
        (i)   tracing parents or any other person the court considers to be relevant to the proceedings;
        (ii)   service of documents;
        (iii)   subject to paragraph (2), disclosure as soon as possible of information and evidence to the parties; and
        (iv)   the final hearing.

(By rule 3.3 the court may also direct that the case be adjourned if it considers that alternative dispute resolution is appropriate.)

(2) Rule 14.13(2) applies to any direction given under paragraph (1)(e)(iii) as it applies to a direction given under rule 14.13(1).

(3) In addition to the matters referred to in paragraph (1), the court will give any of the directions listed in Practice Direction 14B in proceedings for—
    (a)   a Convention adoption order;
    (b)   a section 84 order;
    (c)   a section 88 direction;
    (d)   a section 89 order; or
    (e)   an adoption order where section 83(1) of the 2002 Act applies (restriction on bringing children in).

(4) The parties or their legal representatives must attend the first directions hearing unless the court directs otherwise.

(5) Directions may also be given at any stage in the proceedings—
    (a)   of the court's own initiative; or

(b) on the application of a party or any children's guardian or, where the direction concerns a report by a reporting officer or children and family reporter, the reporting officer or children and family reporter.

(6) For the purposes of giving directions or for such purposes as the court directs—
(a) the court may set a date for a further directions hearing or other hearing; and
(b) the court officer will give notice of any date so fixed to the parties and to any children's guardian, reporting officer or children and family reporter.

(7) After the first directions hearing the court will monitor compliance by the parties with the court's timetable and directions.

14.9.— Requesting the court to dispense with the consent of any parent or guardian

(1) This rule applies where the applicant wants to ask the court to dispense with the consent of any parent or guardian of a child to—
(a) the child being placed for adoption;
(b) the making of an adoption order except a Convention adoption order; or
(c) the making of a section 84 order.

(2) The applicant requesting the court to dispense with the consent must—
(a) give notice of the request in the application form or at any later stage by filing a written request setting out the reasons for the request; and
(b) file a statement of facts setting out a summary of the history of the case and any other facts to satisfy the court that—
 (i) the parent or guardian cannot be found or is incapable of giving consent; or
 (ii) the welfare of the child requires the consent to be dispensed with.

(3) If a serial number has been assigned to the applicant under rule 14.2, the statement of facts supplied under paragraph (2)(b) must be framed so that it does not disclose the identity of the applicant.

(4) On receipt of the notice of the request—
(a) a court officer will—
 (i) inform the parent or guardian of the request unless the parent or guardian cannot be found; and
 (ii) send a copy of the statement of facts filed in accordance with paragraph (2)(b) to—
  (aa) the parent or guardian unless the parent or guardian cannot be found;
  (bb) any children's guardian, reporting officer or children and family reporter;
  (cc) any local authority to whom notice under section 44 of the 2002 Act (notice of intention to adopt or apply for a section 84 order) has been given; and
  (dd) any adoption agency which has placed the child for adoption; and
(b) if the applicant considers that the parent or guardian is incapable of giving consent, the court will consider whether to—
 (i) appoint a litigation friend for the parent or guardian under rule 15.6(1); or
 (ii) give directions for an application to be made under rule 15.6(3),
 (iii) unless a litigation friend is already appointed for that parent or guardian.

14.10.— Consent

(1) Consent of any parent or guardian of a child—
(a) under section 19 of the 2002 Act, to the child being placed for adoption; and

(b) under section 20 of the 2002 Act, to the making of a future adoption order, must be given in the form referred to in Practice Direction 5A or a form to the like effect.

(2) Subject to paragraph (3), consent—
- (a) to the making of an adoption order; or
- (b) to the making of a section 84 order, may be given in the form referred to in Practice Direction 5A or a form to the like effect or otherwise as the court directs.

(3) Any consent to a Convention adoption order must be in a form which complies with the internal law relating to adoption of the Convention country of which the child is habitually resident.

(4) Any form of consent executed in Scotland must be witnessed by a Justice of the Peace or a Sheriff.

(5) Any form of consent executed in Northern Ireland must be witnessed by a Justice of the Peace.

(6) Any form of consent executed outside the United Kingdom must be witnessed by—
- (a) any person for the time being authorised by law in the place where the document is executed to administer an oath for any judicial or other legal purpose;
- (b) a British Consular officer;
- (c) a notary public; or
- (d) if the person executing the document is serving in any of the regular armed forces of the Crown, an officer holding a commission in any of those forces.

14.11.— Reports by the adoption agency or local authority

(1) The adoption agency or local authority must file the report on the suitability of the applicant to adopt a child within the timetable fixed by the court.

(2) A local authority that is directed to prepare a report on the placement of the child for adoption must file that report within the timetable fixed by the court.

(3) The reports must cover the matters specified in Practice Direction 14C.

(4) The court may at any stage request a further report or ask the adoption agency or local authority to assist the court in any other manner.

(5) A court officer will send a copy of any report referred to in this rule to any children's guardian, reporting officer or children and family reporter.

(6) A report to the court under this rule is confidential.

14.12.— Health reports

(1) Reports by a registered medical practitioner ("health reports") made not more than 3 months earlier on the health of the child and of each applicant must be attached to an application for an adoption order or a section 84 order except where—
- (a) the child was placed for adoption with the applicant by an adoption agency;
- (b) the applicant or one of the applicants is a parent of the child; or
- (c) the applicant is the partner of a parent of the child.

(2) Health reports must contain the matters set out in Practice Direction 14D.

(3) A health report is confidential.

14.13.— Confidential reports to the court and disclosure to the parties

(1) The court will consider whether to give a direction that a confidential report be disclosed to each party to the proceedings.

(2) Before giving such a direction the court will consider whether any information should be deleted including information which—
- (a) discloses, or is likely to disclose, the identity of a person who has been assigned a serial number under rule 14.2(2); or
- (b) discloses the particulars referred to in rule 29.1(1) where a party has given notice under rule 29.1(2) (disclosure of personal details).

(3) The court may direct that the report will not be disclosed to a party.

14.14. Communication of information relating to proceedings

For the purposes of the law relating to contempt of court, information (whether or not it is recorded in any form) relating to proceedings held in private may be communicated—

- (a) where the court gives permission;
- (b) unless the court directs otherwise, in accordance with Practice Direction 14E; or
- (c) where the communication is to—
  - (i) a party;
  - (ii) the legal representative of a party;
  - (iii) a professional legal adviser;
  - (iv) an officer of the service or a Welsh family proceedings officer;
  - (v) a welfare officer;
  - (vi) the Legal Services Commission;
  - (vii) an expert whose instruction by a party has been authorised by the court for the purposes of the proceedings; or
  - (viii) a professional acting in furtherance of the protection of children.

14.15. Notice of final hearing

A court officer will give notice to the parties, any children's guardian, reporting officer or children and family reporter and to any other person to whom a practice direction may require such notice to be given—

- (a) of the date and place where the application will be heard; and
- (b) of the fact that, unless the person wishes or the court requires, the person need not attend.

14.16.— The final hearing

(1) Any person who has been given notice in accordance with rule 14.15 may attend the final hearing and, subject to paragraph (2), be heard on the question of whether an order should be made.

(2) A person whose application for the permission of the court to oppose the making of an adoption order under section 47(3) or (5) of the 2002 Act has been refused is not entitled to be heard on the question of whether an order should be made.

(3) Any member or employee of a party which is a local authority, adoption agency or other body may address the court at the final hearing if authorised to do so.

(4) The court may direct that any person must attend a final hearing.

(5) Paragraphs (6) and (7) apply to—
- (a) an adoption order;
- (b) a section 84 order; or
- (c) a section 89 order.

(6) Subject to paragraphs (7) and (8), the court cannot make an order unless the applicant and the child personally attend the final hearing.

(7) The court may direct that the applicant or the child need not attend the final hearing.

(8) In a case of adoption by a couple under section 50 of the 2002 Act, the court may make an adoption order after personal attendance of one only of the applicants if there are special circumstances.

(9) The court cannot make a placement order unless a legal representative of the applicant attends the final hearing.

14.17.— Proof of identity of the child

(1) Unless the contrary is shown, the child referred to in the application will be deemed to be the child referred to in the form of consent—

- (a) to the child being placed for adoption;
- (b) to the making of an adoption order; or
- (c) to the making of a section 84 order,

where the conditions in paragraph (2) apply.

(2) The conditions are—
- (a) the application identifies the child by reference to a full certified copy of an entry in the registers of live-births;
- (b) the form of consent identifies the child by reference to a full certified copy of an entry in the registers of live-births attached to the form; and
- (c) the copy of the entry in the registers of live-births referred to in sub-paragraph (a) is the same or relates to the same entry in the registers of live-births as the copy of the entry in the registers of live-births attached to the form of consent.

(3) Where the child is already an adopted child paragraph (2) will have effect as if for the references to the registers of live-births there were substituted references to the Adopted Children Register.

(4) Subject to paragraph (7), where the precise date of the child's birth is not proved to the satisfaction of the court, the court will determine the probable date of birth.

(5) The probable date of the child's birth may be specified in the placement order, adoption order or section 84 order as the date of the child's birth.

(6) Subject to paragraph (7), where the child's place of birth cannot be proved to the satisfaction of the court—
- (a) the child may be treated as having been born in the registration district of the court where it is probable that the child may have been born in—
  - (i) the United Kingdom;
  - (ii) the Channel Islands; or
  - (iii) the Isle of Man; or
- (b) in any other case, the particulars of the country of birth may be omitted from the placement order, adoption order or section 84 order.

(7) A placement order identifying the probable date and place of birth of the child will be sufficient proof of the date and place of birth of the child in adoption proceedings and proceedings for a section 84 order.

14.18.— Disclosing information to an adopted adult

(1) The adopted person has the right, on request, to receive from the court which made the adoption order a copy of the following—
- (a) the application form for an adoption order (but not the documents attached to that form);
- (b) the adoption order and any other orders relating to the adoption proceedings;
- (c) orders allowing any person contact with the child after the adoption order was made; and
- (d) any other document or order referred to in Practice Direction 14F.

(2) The court will remove any protected information from any copy of a document or order referred to in paragraph (1) before the copies are given to the adopted person.

(3) This rule does not apply to an adopted person under the age of 18 years.

(4) In this rule "protected information" means information which would be protected information under section 57(3) of the 2002 Act if the adoption agency gave the information and not the court.

14.19.— Translation of documents

(1) Where a translation of any document is required for the purposes of proceedings for a Convention adoption order the translation must—
- (a) unless the court directs otherwise, be provided by the applicant; and
- (b) be signed by the translator to certify that the translation is accurate.

(2) This rule does not apply where the document is to be served in accordance with the Service Regulation.

14.20.— Application for recovery orders

(1) An application for any of the orders referred to in section 41(2) of the 2002 Act (recovery orders) may—

(a) in the High Court or a county court, be made without notice in which case the applicant must file the application—
  (i) where the application is made by telephone, the next business day after the making of the application; or
  (ii) in any other case, at the time when the application is made; and
(b) in a magistrates' court, be made, with the permission of the court, without notice in which case the applicant must file the application at the time when the application is made or as directed by the court.

(2) Where the court refuses to make an order on an application without notice it may direct that the application is made on notice in which case the application will proceed in accordance with rules 14.1 to 14.17.

(3) The respondents to an application under this rule are—
(a) in a case where—
  (i) placement proceedings;
  (ii) adoption proceedings; or
  (iii) proceedings for a section 84 order, are pending, all parties to those proceedings;
(b) any adoption agency authorised to place the child for adoption or which has placed the child for adoption;
(c) any local authority to whom notice under section 44 of the 2002 Act (notice of intention to adopt or apply for a section 84 order) has been given;
(d) any person having parental responsibility for the child;
(e) any person in whose favour there is provision for contact;
(f) any person who was caring for the child immediately prior to the making of the application; and
(g) any person whom the applicant alleges to have effected, or to have been or to be responsible for, the taking or keeping of the child.

14.21. Inherent jurisdiction and fathers without parental responsibility
Where no proceedings have started an adoption agency or local authority may ask the High Court for directions on the need to give a father without parental responsibility notice of the intention to place a child for adoption.

14.22. Timing of applications for section 89 order
An application for a section 89 order must be made within 2 years beginning with the date on which—
(a) the Convention adoption or Convention adoption order; or
(b) the overseas adoption or determination under section 91 of the 2002 Act,
to which it relates was made.

14.23. Custody of documents
All documents relating to proceedings under the 2002 Act must, while they are in the custody of the court, be kept in a place of special security.

14.24. Documents held by the court not to be inspected or copied without the court's permission
Subject to the provisions of these rules, any practice direction or any direction given by the court—
(a) no document or order held by the court in proceedings under the 2002 Act will be open to inspection by any person; and
(b) no copy of any such document or order, or of an extract from any such document or order, will be taken by or given to any person.

14.25.— Orders
(1) An order takes effect from the date when it is made, or such later date as the court may specify.
(2) In proceedings in Wales a party may request that an order be drawn up in Welsh as well as English.

The Family Procedure Rules 2010

14.26.— Copies of orders

(1) Within 7 days beginning with the date on which the final order was made in proceedings, or such shorter time as the court may direct, a court officer will send—
- (a) a copy of the order to the applicant;
- (b) a copy, which is sealed$^{(GL)}$, authenticated with the stamp of the court or certified as a true copy, of—
  - (i) an adoption order;
  - (ii) a section 89 order; or
  - (iii) an order quashing or revoking an adoption order or allowing an appeal against an adoption order, to the Registrar General;
- (c) a copy of a Convention adoption order to the relevant Central Authority;
- (d) a copy of a section 89 order relating to a Convention adoption order or a Convention adoption to the—
  - (i) relevant Central Authority;
  - (ii) adopters;
  - (iii) adoption agency; and
  - (iv) local authority;
- (e) unless the court directs otherwise, a copy of a contact order under section 26 of the 2002 Act or a variation or revocation of a contact order under section 27 of the 2002 Act to the—
  - (i) person with whom the child is living;
  - (ii) adoption agency; and
  - (iii) local authority; and
- (f) a notice of the making or refusal of—
  - (i) the final order; or
  - (ii) an order quashing or revoking an adoption order or allowing an appeal against an order in proceedings, to every respondent and, with the permission of the court, any other person.

(2) The court officer will also send notice of the making of an adoption order or a section 84 order to—
- (a) any court in Great Britain which appears to the court officer to have made any such order as is referred to in section 46(2) of the 2002 Act (order relating to parental responsibility for, and maintenance of, the child); and
- (b) the principal registry, if it appears to the court officer that a parental responsibility agreement has been recorded at the principal registry.

(3) A copy of any final order may be sent to any other person with the permission of the court.

(4) The court officer will send a copy of any order made during the course of the proceedings to the following persons or bodies, unless the court directs otherwise—
- (a) all the parties to those proceedings;
- (b) any children and family reporter appointed in those proceedings;
- (c) any adoption agency or local authority which has prepared a report on the suitability of an applicant to adopt a child;
- (d) any local authority which has prepared a report on placement for adoption.

(5) If an order has been drawn up in Welsh as well as English in accordance with rule 14.25(2) any reference in this rule to sending an order is to be taken as a reference to sending both the Welsh and English orders.

14.27.— Amendment and revocation of orders

(1) Subject to paragraph (2), an application under—
- (a) section 55 of the 2002 Act (revocation of adoptions on legitimation); or
- (b) paragraph 4 of Schedule 1 to the 2002 Act (amendment of adoption order and revocation of direction),

may be made without serving a copy of the application notice.

(2) The court may direct that an application notice be served on such persons as it thinks fit.

(3) Where the court makes an order granting the application, a court officer will send the Registrar General a notice—
- (a) specifying the amendments; or
- (b) informing the Registrar General of the revocation, giving sufficient particulars of the order to enable the Registrar General to identify the case.

14.28.— Keeping registers in the family proceedings court

(1) A magistrates' court officer will keep a register in which there will be entered a minute or memorandum of every adjudication of the court in proceedings to which this Part applies.

(2) The register may be stored in electronic form on the court computer system and entries in the register will include, where relevant, the following particulars—
- (a) the name and address of the applicant;
- (b) the name of the child including, in adoption proceedings, the name of the child prior to, and after, adoption;
- (c) the age and sex of the child;
- (d) the nature of the application; and
- (e) the minute of adjudication.

(3) The part of the register relating to adoption proceedings will be kept separately to any other part of the register and will—
- (a) not contain particulars of any other proceedings; and
- (b) be kept by the court in a place of special security.

PART 14 COMMENTARY

Part 14 is supplemented by six practice directions 14A to 14F. These reproduce existing adoption practice directions which previously supplemented the Family Procedure (Adoption) Rules 2005. They are as follows:

14A Who receives copy of Application. This is amended in the heading by updating the reference there to 'Part 14, rule 14.6(1)(b)(ii) of the Family Procedure Rules 2010'.

14B First Directions Hearing – Foreign Element. This is amended in the heading by updating the reference there to 'Part 14, rule 14.8(3) of the Family Procedure Rules 2010', and in paragraph 2, for 'rule 26(1)' substitute 'rule 14.8(1)'.

14C Reports by Adoption Agency or Local Authority. This is amended in the heading by updating the reference there to 'Part 14, rule 14.11(3) of the Family Procedure Rules 2010'.

14D Report by a Registered Medical Practitioner (Health Reports). This is amended in the heading by updating the reference there to 'Part 14, rule 14.12(2) of the Family Procedure Rules 2010' and in paragraph 1.1, for 'rule 30 (1)' substitute 'rule 14.12(1)'.

14E Communication of Information relating to the Proceedings. This is amended in the heading by updating the reference there to 'Part 14, rule 14.14(b) of the Family Procedure Rules 2010' and in paragraph 1.1, for 'rule 78' substitute 'rule 14.14'.

14F Disclosing Information to Adopted Adult. This is amended in the heading by updating the reference there to 'Part 14, rule 14.18(1)(d) of the Family

The Family Procedure Rules 2010

Procedure Rules 2010' and in paragraph 1.1 and 1.2, for 'rule 84)' substitute 'rule 14.18'.

Part 14 applies to adoption, placement and related proceedings. The relevant Parts of the Family Procedure (Adoption) Rules 2005 have been incorporated without significant alteration.

A new provision in r 14.10(2) (formerly r 28(2) of the 2005 Rules) allows the court to give directions about the manner in which consent to the making of an adoption order or of a section 84 order may be given, if the form referred to in PD5A (or a form to like effect) is not used.

Forms relevant to Part 14 are the majority of the A forms.

PRACTICE DIRECTION 14A – WHO RECEIVES COPY OF THE APPLICATION FORM FOR ORDERS IN PROCEEDINGS

This Practice Direction supplements Part 5, rule 24(1)(b)(ii) of the Family Procedure (Adoption) Rules 2005 [Part 14, rule 14.6(1)(b)(ii) of the Family Procedure Rules 2010]

PERSONS WHO RECEIVE COPY OF APPLICATION FORM

1 In relation to each type of proceedings in column 1 of the following table, column 2 sets out which persons are to receive a copy of the application form—

Proceeding for	Who Receives a Copy of the Application Form
An adoption order (section 46 of the Act); or a section 84 order	Any appointed children's guardian, children and family reporter and reporting officer;
	the local authority to whom notice under section 44 (notice of intention to apply to adopt or apply for a section 84 order) has been given;
	the adoption agency which placed the child for adoption with the applicants;
	any other person directed by the court to receive a copy.
A placement order (section 21 of the Act); or an order varying a placement order (section 23 of the Act)	Each parent with parental responsibility for the child or guardian of the child;
	any appointed children's guardian, children and family reporter and reporting officer;
	any other person directed by the court to receive a copy.
An order revoking a placement order (section 24 of the Act)	Each parent with parental responsibility for the child or guardian of the child;
	any appointed children's guardian and children and family reporter;
	the local authority authorised by the placement order to place the child for adoption;
	any other person directed by the court to receive a copy.
A contact order (section 26 of the Act);	All the parties;

FPR 2010, Practice Direction 14B

Proceeding for	Who Receives a Copy of the Application Form
an order varying or revoking a contact order (section 27 of the Act);	any appointed children's guardian and children and family reporter;
an order permitting the child's name to be changed or the removal of the child from the United Kingdom (section 28(2) of the Act);	any other person directed by the court to receive a copy.
a recovery order (section 41(2) of the Act);	
a section 89 order;	
and a section 88 direction	

PRACTICE DIRECTION 14B – THE FIRST DIRECTIONS HEARING – ADOPTIONS WITH A FOREIGN ELEMENT

This Practice Direction supplements Part 5, rule 26(3) of the Family Procedure (Adoption) Rules 2005 [Part 14, rule 14.8(3) of the Family Procedure Rules 2010]

APPLICATION

1   This Practice Direction applies to proceedings for—

(a) a Convention adoption order;
(b) a section 84 order;
(c) a section 88 direction;
(d) a section 89 order; and
(e) an adoption order where the child has been brought into the United Kingdom in the circumstances where section 83(1) of the Act applies.

THE FIRST DIRECTIONS HEARING

2   At the first directions hearing the court will, in addition to any matters referred to in *rule 26(1* [rule 14.8(1)]),—

(a) consider whether the requirements of the Act and the Adoptions with a Foreign Element Regulations 2005 (S.I. 005/392) appear to have been complied with and, if not, consider whether or not it is appropriate to transfer the case to the High Court;
(b) consider whether all relevant documents are translated into English and, if not, fix a timetable for translating any outstanding documents;
(c) consider whether the applicant needs to file an affidavit setting out the full details of the circumstances in which the child was brought to the United Kingdom, of the attitude of the parents to the application and confirming compliance with the requirements of The Adoptions with A Foreign Element Regulations 2005;
(d) give directions about—
   (i) the production of the child's passport and visa;
   (ii) the need for the Official Solicitor and a representative of the Home Office to attend future hearings; and
   (iii) personal service on the parents (via the Central Authority in the case of an application for a Convention Adoption Order) including information

The Family Procedure Rules 2010

(e)   consider fixing a further directions appointment no later than 6 weeks after the date of the first directions appointment and timetable a date by which the Official Solicitor should file an interim report in advance of that further appointment.

about the role of the Official Solicitor and availability of legal aid to be represented within the proceedings; and

PRACTICE DIRECTION 14C – REPORTS BY THE ADOPTION AGENCY OR LOCAL AUTHORITY

This Practice Direction supplements Part 5, rule 29(3) of the Family Procedure (Adoption) Rules 2005 [Part 14, rule 14.11(3) of the Family Procedure Rules 2010]

MATTERS TO BE CONTAINED IN REPORTS

1.1 The matters to be covered in the report on the suitability of the applicant to adopt a child are set out in Annex A to this Practice Direction.

1.2 The matters to be covered in a report on the placement of the child for adoption are set out in Annex B to this Practice Direction.

1.3 Where a matter to be covered in the reports set out in Annex A and Annex B does not apply to the circumstances of a particular case, the reasons for not covering the matter should be given.

ANNEX A
REPORT TO THE COURT WHERE THERE HAS BEEN AN APPLICATION FOR AN ADOPTION ORDER OR AN APPLICATION FOR A SECTION 84 ORDER

Section A: The Report and Matters for the Proceedings

Part 1 The Report

For each of the principal author/s of the report:

(i)   name;
(ii)   role in relation to this case;
(iii) sections completed in this report;
(iv) qualifications and experience;
(v)   name and address of the adoption agency; and
(vi) adoption agency case reference number.

Part 2 Matters for the Proceedings

(a)   Whether the adoption agency considers that any other person should be made a respondent or a party to the proceedings, including the child.
(b)   Whether any of the respondents is under the age of 18.
(c)   Whether a respondent is a person who, by reason of mental disorder within the meaning of the Mental Health Act 1983, is incapable of managing and administering his or her property and affairs. If so, medical evidence should be provided with particular regard to the effect on that person's ability to make decisions in the proceedings.

Section B: The Child and the Birth Family

Part 1

(i) Information about the Child

(a) Name, sex, date and place of birth and address including local authority area.
(b) Photograph and physical description.
(c) Nationality.
(d) Racial origin and cultural and linguistic background.
(e) Religious persuasion (including details of baptism, confirmation or equivalent ceremonies).
(f) Details of any siblings, half-siblings and step-siblings, including dates of birth.
(g) Whether the child is looked after by a local authority.
(h) Whether the child has been placed for adoption with the prospective adopter by a UK adoption agency.
(i) Whether the child was being fostered by the prospective adopter.
(j) Whether the child was brought into the UK for adoption, including date of entry and whether an adoption order was made in the child's country of origin.
(k) Personality and social development, including emotional and behavioural development and any related needs.
(l) Details of interests, likes and dislikes.
(m) A summary, written by the agency's medical adviser, of the child's health history, his current state of health and any need for health care which is anticipated, and date of the most recent medical examination.
(n) Any known learning difficulties or known general medical or mental health factors which are likely to have, or may have, genetic implications.
(o) Names, addresses and types of nurseries or schools attended, with dates.
(p) Educational attainments.
(q) Any special needs in relation to the child (whether physical, learning, behavioural or any other) and his emotional and behavioural development.
(r) Whether the child is subject to a statement under the Education Act 1996.
(s) Previous orders concerning the child:
    (i) the name of the court;
    (ii) the order made; and
    (iii) the date of the order.
(t) Inheritance rights and any claim to damages under the Fatal Accidents Act 1976 the child stands to retain or lose if adopted.
(u) Any other relevant information which might assist the court.

(ii) Information about each Parent of the Child

(a) Name, date and place of birth and address (date on which last address was confirmed current) including local authority area.
(b) Photograph, if available, and physical description.
(c) Nationality.
(d) Racial origin and cultural and linguistic background.
(e) Whether the mother and father were married to each other at the time of the child's birth or have subsequently married.
(f) Where the parent has been previously married or entered into a civil partnership, dates of those marriages or civil partnerships.
(g) Where the mother and father are not married, whether the father has parental responsibility and, if so, how it was acquired.
(h) If the identity or whereabouts of the father are not known, the information about him that has been ascertained and from whom, and the steps that have been taken to establish paternity.
(i) Past and present relationship with the other parent.
(j) Other information about the parent, where available:

The Family Procedure Rules 2010

   (i) health, including any known learning difficulties or known general medical or mental health factors which are likely to have, or may have, genetic implications;
   (ii) religious persuasion;
   (iii) educational history;
   (iv) employment history; and
   (v) personality and interests.
(k) Any other relevant information which might assist the court.

Part 2 Relationships, contact arrangements and views

The Child

(a) If the child is in the care of a local authority or voluntary organisation, or has been, details (including dates) of any placements with foster parents, or other arrangements in respect of the care of the child, including particulars of the persons with whom the child has had his home and observations on the care provided.
(b) The child's wishes and feelings (if appropriate, having regard to the child's age and understanding) about adoption, the application and its consequences, including any wishes in respect of religious and cultural upbringing.
(c) The child's wishes and feelings in relation to contact (if appropriate, having regard to the child's age and understanding).
(d) The child's wishes and feelings recorded in any other proceedings.
(e) Date when the child's views were last ascertained.

The Child's Parents (or guardian) and relatives

(a) The parents' wishes and feelings before the placement, about the placement and about adoption, the application and its consequences, including any wishes in respect of the child's religious and cultural upbringing.
(b) Each parent's (or guardian's) wishes and feelings in relation to contact.
(c) Date/s when the views of each parent or guardian were last ascertained.
(d) Arrangements concerning any siblings, including half-siblings and step-siblings, and whether any are the subject of a parallel application or have been the subject of any orders. If so, for each case give:
   (i) the name of the court;
   (ii) the order made, or (if proceedings are pending) the order applied for; and
   (iii) the date of order, or date of next hearing if proceedings are pending.
(e) Extent of contact with the child's mother and father and, in each case, the nature of the relationship enjoyed.
(f) The relationship which the child has with relatives, and with any other person considered relevant, including:
   (i) the likelihood of any such relationship continuing and the value to the child of its doing so; and
   (ii) the ability and willingness of any of the child's relatives, or of any such person, to provide the child with a secure environment in which the child can develop, and otherwise to meet the child's needs.
(g) The wishes and feelings of any of the child's relatives, or of any such person, regarding the child.
(h) Whether the parents (or members of the child's family) have met or are likely to meet the prospective adopter and, if they have met, the effect on all involved of such meeting.
(i) Dates when the views of members of the child's wider family and any other relevant person were last ascertained.

Part 3 A summary of the actions of the adoption agency

(a) Brief account of the agency's actions in the case, with particulars and dates of all written information and notices given to the child and his parents and any person with parental responsibility.
(b) If consent has been given for the child to be placed for adoption, and also consent for the child to be adopted, the names of those who gave consent and the date such consents were given. If such consents were subsequently withdrawn, the dates of these withdrawals.
(c) If any statement has been made under section 20(4)(a) of the Adoption and Children Act 2002 (the "2002 Act") that a parent or guardian does not wish to be informed of any application for an adoption order, the names of those who have made such statements and the dates the statements were made. If such statements were subsequently withdrawn, the dates of these withdrawals.
(d) Whether an order has been made under section 21 of the 2002 Act, section 18 of the Adoption (Scotland) Act 1978 or Article 17(1) or 18(1) of the Northern Ireland Order 1987.
(e) Details of the support and advice given to the parents and any services offered or taken up.
(f) If the father does not have parental responsibility, details of the steps taken to inform him of the application for an adoption order.
(g) Brief details and dates of assessments of the child's needs, including expert opinions.
(h) Reasons for considering that adoption would be in the child's best interests (with date of relevant decision and reasons for any delay in implementing the decision).

Section C: The Prospective Adopter of the Child

Part 1 Information about the Prospective Adopter, including suitability to adopt

(a) Name, date and place of birth and address (date on which last address was confirmed current) including local authority area.
(b) Photograph and physical description.
(c) Whether the prospective adopter is domiciled or habitually resident in a part of the British Islands and, if habitually resident, for how long they have been habitually resident.
(d) Racial origin and cultural and linguistic background.
(e) Marital status or civil partnership status, date and place of most recent marriage (if any) or civil partnership (if any).
(f) Details of any previous marriage, civil partnership, or relationship where the prospective adopter lived with another person as a partner in an enduring family relationship.
(g) Relationship (if any) to the child.
(h) Where adopters wish to adopt as a couple, the status of the relationship and an assessment of the stability and permanence of their relationship.
(i) If a married person or a civil partner is applying alone, the reasons for this.
(j) Description of how the prospective adopter relates to adults and children.
(k) Previous experience of caring for children (including as a step-parent, foster parent, child-minder or prospective adopter) and assessment of ability in this respect, together where appropriate with assessment of ability in bringing up the prospective adopter's own children.
(l) A summary, written by the agency's medical adviser, of the prospective adopter's health history, current state of health and any need for health care which is anticipated, and date of most recent medical examination.

The Family Procedure Rules 2010

(m) Assessment of ability and suitability to bring up the child throughout his childhood.
(n) Details of income and comments on the living standards of the household with particulars of the home and living conditions (and particulars of any home where the prospective adopter proposes to live with the child, if different).
(o) Details of other members of the household, including any children of the prospective adopter even if not resident in the household.
(p) Details of the parents and any siblings of the prospective adopter, with their ages or ages at death.
(q) Other information about the prospective adopter:
    (i) religious persuasion;
    (ii) educational history;
    (iii) employment history; and
    (iv) personality and interests.
(r) Confirmation that the applicants have not been convicted of, or cautioned for, a specified offence within the meaning of regulation 23(3) of the Adoption Agencies Regulations 2005 (S.I. 2005/389).
(s) Confirmation that the prospective adopter is still approved.
(t) Confirmation that any referees have been interviewed, with a report of their views and opinion of the weight to be placed thereon and whether they are still valid.
(u) Details of any previous family court proceedings in which the prospective adopter has been involved (which have not been referred to elsewhere in this report.)

Part 2 Wishes, views and contact arrangements

Prospective Adopter

(a) Whether the prospective adopter is willing to follow any wishes of the child or his parents or guardian in respect of the child's religious and cultural upbringing.
(b) The views of other members of the prospective adopter's household and wider family in relation to the proposed adoption.
(c) Reasons for the prospective adopter wishing to adopt the child and extent of understanding of the nature and effect of adoption. Whether the prospective adopter has discussed adoption with the child.
(d) Any hope and expectations the prospective adopter has for the child's future.
(e) The prospective adopter's wishes and feelings in relation to contact.

Part 3 Actions of the adoption agency

(a) Brief account of the Agency's actions in the case, with particulars and dates of all written information and notices given to the prospective adopter.
(b) The Agency's proposals for contact, including options for facilitating or achieving any indirect contact or direct contact.
(c) The Agency's opinion on the likely effect on the prospective adopter and on the security of the placement of any proposed contact.
(d) Where the prospective adopter has been approved by an agency as suitable to be an adoptive parent, the agency's reasons for considering that the prospective adopter is suitable to be an adoptive parent for this child (with dates of relevant decision).

Section D: The Placement

(a) Where the child was placed for adoption by an adoption agency (section 18 of the 2002 Act), the date and circumstances of the child's placement with prospective adopter.

(b) Where the child is living with persons who have applied for the adoption order to be made (section 44 of the 2002 Act), the date when notice of intention to adopt was given.
(c) Where the placement is being provided with adoption support, this should be summarised and should include the plan and timescales for continuing the support beyond the making of the adoption order.
(d) Where the placement is not being provided with adoption support, the reasons why.
(e) A summary of the information obtained from the Agency's visits and reviews of the placement, including whether the child has been seen separately to the prospective adopter and whether there has been sufficient opportunity to see the family group and the child's interaction in the home environment.
(f) An assessment of the child's integration within the family of the prospective adopter and the likelihood of the child's full integration into the family and community.
(g) Any other relevant information that might assist the court.

Section E: Recommendations

(a) The relative merits of adoption and other orders with an assessment of whether the child's long term interests would be best met by an adoption order or by other orders (such as residence and special guardianship orders).
(b) Recommendations as to whether or not the order sought should be made (and, if not, alternative proposals).
(c) Recommendations as to whether there should be future contact arrangements (or not).

Section F: Further information for proceedings relating to Convention Adoption Orders, Convention adoptions, section 84 Orders or adoptions where section 83(1) of the 2002 Act applies

(a) The child's knowledge of their racial and cultural origin.
(b) The likelihood of the child's adaptation to living in the country he/she is to be placed.
(c) Where the UK is the State of origin, reasons for considering that, after possibilities for placement of the child within the UK have been given due consideration, intercountry adoption is in the child's best interests.
(d) Confirmation that the requirements of regulations made under sections 83(4), (5), (6) and (7) and 84(3) and (6) of the 2002 Act have been complied with.
(e) For a Convention adoption or a Convention Adoption Order where the United Kingdom is either the State of origin or the receiving State, confirmation that the Central Authorities of both States have agreed that the adoption may proceed.
(f) Where the State of origin is not the United Kingdom, the documents supplied by the Central Authority of the State of origin should be attached to the report, together with translation if necessary.
(g) Where a Convention adoption order is proposed, details of the arrangements which were made for the transfer of the child to the UK and that they were in accordance with the Adoptions with a Foreign Element Regulations 2005 (SI 2005/392).

The Family Procedure Rules 2010

ANNEX B
REPORT TO THE COURT WHERE THERE HAS BEEN AN APPLICATION FOR A PLACEMENT ORDER

Section A: The Report and Matters for the Proceedings

Part 1 The Report

For each of the principal author/s of the report:

(i) name;
(ii) role in relation to this case;
(iii) section completed in this report;
(iv) qualifications and experience;
(v) name and address of the adoption agency; and
(vi) adoption agency case reference number.

Part 2 Matters for the Proceedings

(a) Whether the adoption agency considers that any other person should be made a respondent or a party to the proceedings.
(b) Whether any of the respondents is under the age of 18.
(c) Whether a respondent is a person who, by reason of mental disorder within the meaning of the Mental Health Act 1983, is incapable of managing and administering his or her property and affairs. If so, medical evidence should be provided with particular regard to the effect on that person's ability to make decisions in the proceedings.

Section B: The Child and the Birth Family

Part 1

(i) Information about the Child

(a) Name, sex, date and place of birth and address including local authority area.
(b) Photograph and physical description.
(c) Nationality.
(d) Racial origin and cultural and linguistic background.
(e) Religious persuasion (including details of baptism, confirmation or equivalent ceremonies).
(f) Details of any siblings, half-siblings and step-siblings, including dates of birth.
(g) Whether the child is looked after by a local authority.
(h) Personality and social development, including emotional and behavioural development and any related needs.
(i) Details of interests, likes and dislikes.
(j) A summary, written by the agency's medical adviser, of the child's health history, his current state of health and any need for health care which is anticipated, and date of the most recent medical examination.
(k) Any known learning difficulties or known general medical or mental health factors which are likely to have, or may have, genetic implications.
(l) Names, addresses and types of nurseries or schools attended, with dates.
(m) Educational attainments.
(n) Any special needs in relation to the child (whether physical, learning, behavioural or any other) and his emotional and behavioural development.
(o) Whether the child is subject to a statement under the Education Act 1996.
(p) Previous orders concerning the child:
    (i) the name of the court;

(ii) the order made; and
(iii) the date of the order.
(q) Inheritance rights and any claim to damages under the Fatal Accidents Act 1976 the child stands to retain or lose if adopted.
(r) Any other relevant information which might assist the court.

(ii) Information about each Parent of the Child

(a) Name, date and place of birth and address (date on which last address was confirmed current) including local authority area.
(b) Photograph, if available, and physical description.
(c) Nationality.
(d) Racial origin and cultural and linguistic background.
(e) Whether the mother and father were married to each other at the time of the child's birth, or have subsequently married.
(f) Where the parent has been previously married or entered into a civil partnership, dates of those marriages or civil partnerships.
(g) Where the mother and father are not married, whether the father has parental responsibility and, if so, how it was acquired.
(h) If the identity or whereabouts of the father are not known, the information about him that has been ascertained and from whom, and the steps that have been taken to establish paternity.
(i) Past and present relationship with the other parent.
(j) Other information about the parent, where available:
   (i) health, including any known learning difficulties or known general medical or mental health factors which are likely to have, or may have, genetic implications;
   (ii) religious persuasion;
   (iii) educational history;
   (iv) employment history; and
   (v) personality and interests.
(k) Any other relevant information which might assist the court.

Part 2 Relationships, contact arrangements and views

The Child

(a) If the child is in the care of a local authority or voluntary organisation, or has been, details (including dates) of any placements with foster parents, or other arrangements in respect of the care of the child, including particulars of the persons with whom the child has had his home and observations on the care provided.
(b) The child's wishes and feelings (if appropriate, having regard to the child's age and understanding) about the application, its consequences, and adoption, including any wishes in respect of religious and cultural upbringing.
(c) The child's wishes and feelings in relation to contact (if appropriate, having regard to the child's age and understanding).
(d) The child's wishes and feelings recorded in any other proceedings.
(e) Date when the child's views were last ascertained.

The Child's Parents (or guardian) and relatives

(a) The parents' wishes and feelings about the application, its consequences, and adoption, including any wishes in respect of the child's religious and cultural upbringing.
(b) Each parent's (or guardian's) wishes and feelings in relation to contact.
(c) Date/s when the views of each parent or guardian were last ascertained.

(d) Arrangements concerning any siblings, including half-siblings and step-siblings, and whether any are the subject of a parallel application or have been the subject of any orders. If so, for each case give:
  (i) the name of the court;
  (ii) the order made, or (if proceedings are pending) the order applied for; and
  (iii) the date of order, or date of next hearing if proceedings are pending.
(e) Extent of contact with the child's mother and father and in each case the nature of the relationship enjoyed.
(f) The relationship which the child has with relatives, and with any other person considered relevant, including:
  (i) the likelihood of any such relationship continuing and the value to the child of its doing so; and
  (ii) the ability and willingness of any of the child's relatives, or of any such person, to provide the child with a secure environment in which the child can develop, and otherwise to meet the child's needs.
(g) The wishes and feelings of any of the child's relatives, or of any such person, regarding the child.
(h) Dates when the views of members of the child's wider family and any other relevant person were last ascertained.

Part 3 Summary of the actions of the adoption agency

(a) Brief account of the Agency's actions in the case, with particulars and dates of all written information and notices given to the child and his parents and any person with parental responsibility.
(b) If consent has been given for the child to be placed for adoption, and also consent for the child to be adopted, the names of those who gave consent and the date such consents were given. If such consents were subsequently withdrawn, the dates of these withdrawals.
(c) If any statement has been made under section 20(4)(a) of the 2002 Act that a parent or guardian does not wish to be informed of any application for an adoption order, the names of those who have made such statements and the dates the statements were made. If such statements were subsequently withdrawn, the dates of these withdrawals.
(d) Details of the support and advice given to the parents and any services offered or taken up.
(e) If the father does not have parental responsibility, details of the steps taken to inform him of the application for a placement order.
(f) Brief details and dates of assessments of the child's needs, including expert opinions.
(g) Reasons for considering that adoption would be in the child's best interests (with date of relevant decision and reasons for any delay in implementing the decision).

Section C: Recommendations

(a) The relative merits of a placement order and other orders (such as a residence or special guardianship order) with an assessment of why the child's long term interests are likely to be best met by a placement order rather than by any other order.
(b) Recommendations as to whether there should be future contact arrangements (or not), including whether a contact order under section 26 of the 2002 Act should be made.

FPR 2010, Practice Direction 14D

PRACTICE DIRECTION 14D – REPORTS BY A REGISTERED MEDICAL PRACTITIONER ("HEALTH REPORTS")

This Practice Direction supplements Part 5, rule 30(2) of the Family Procedure (Adoption) Rules 2005 [Part 14, rule 14.12(2) of the Family Procedure Rules 2010]

MATTERS TO BE CONTAINED IN HEALTH REPORTS

1.1 *Rule 30(1)* [Rule 14.12(1)] requires that health reports must be attached to an application for an adoption order or a section 84 order except where—

(a) the child was placed for adoption with the applicant by an adoption agency;
(b) the applicant or one of the applicants is a parent of the child; or
(c) the applicant is the partner of a parent of the child.

1.2 The matters to be contained in the health reports are set out in the Annex to this Practice Direction.

1.3 Where a matter to be contained in the health report does not apply to the circumstances of a particular case, the reasons for not covering the matter should be given.

ANNEX
CONTENTS OF HEALTH REPORTS

This information is required for reports on the health of children and their prospective adopter(s). Its purpose is to build up a full picture of each child's health history and current state of health, including strengths and weaknesses. This will enable local authorities' medical adviser to base their advice to the court on the fullest possible information when commenting on the health implications of the proposed adoption. The reports made by the examining doctor should cover, as far as practicable, the following matters.

1 The Child

Name, date of birth, sex, weight and height.

(A) A health history of each natural parent, so far as is possible, including:
  (i) name, date of birth, sex, weight and height;
  (ii) a family health history, covering the parents, the brothers and sisters and the other children of the natural parent, with details of any serious physical or mental illness and inherited and congenital disease;
  (iii) past health history, including details of any serious physical or mental illness, disability, accident, hospital admission or attendance at an out-patient department, and in each case any treatment given;
  (iv) a full obstetric history of the mother, including any problems in the ante-natal, labour and post-natal periods, with the results of any tests carried out during or immediately after pregnancy;
  (v) details of any present illness including treatment and prognosis;
  (vi) any other relevant information which might assist the medical adviser; and
  (vii) the name and address of any doctor(s) who might be able to provide further information about any of the above matters.
(B) A neo-natal report on the child, including:
  (i) details of the birth, and any complications;
  (ii) results of a physical examination and screening tests;
  (iii) details of any treatment given;
  (iv) details of any problem in management and feeding;
  (v) any other relevant information which might assist the medical adviser; and

The Family Procedure Rules 2010

- (vi) the name and address of any doctor(s) who might be able to provide further information about any of the above matters.
- (C) A full health history and examination of the child, including:
  - (i) details of any serious illness, disability, accident, hospital admission or attendance at an out-patient department, and in each case any treatment given;
  - (ii) details and dates of immunisations;
  - (iii) a physical and developmental assessment according to age, including an assessment of vision and hearing and of neurological, speech and language development and any evidence of emotional or conduct disorder;
  - (iv) details, if relevant, of the impact of any addiction or substance use on the part of the natural mother before, during or following the pregnancy, and its impact or likely future impact on the child;
  - (v) the impact, if any, on the child's development and likely future development of any past exposure to physical, emotional or sexual abuse or neglectful home conditions and/or any non-organic failure to thrive;
  - (vi) for a child of school age, the school health history (if available);
  - (vii) any other relevant information which might assist the medical adviser; and
  - (viii) the name and address of any doctor(s) who might be able to provide further information about any of the above matters.
- (D) The signature, name, address and qualifications of the registered medical practitioner who prepared the report, and the date of the report and of the examinations carried out.

2 The Applicant

(If there is more than one applicant, a report on each applicant should be supplied covering all the matters listed below.)

- (i) name, date of birth, sex, weight and height;
- (ii) a family health history, covering the parents, the brothers and sisters and the children of the applicant, with details of any serious physical or mental illness and inherited and congenital disease;
- (iii) marital history, including (if applicable) reasons for inability to have children, and any history of domestic violence;
- (iv) past health history, including details of any serious physical or mental illness, disability, accident, hospital admission or attendance at an out-patient department, and in each case any treatment given;
- (v) obstetric history (if applicable);
- (vi) details of any present illness, including treatment and prognosis;
- (vii) a full medical examination;
- (viii) details of any consumption of alcohol, tobacco and habit-forming drugs;
- (ix) any other relevant information which might assist the medical adviser; and
- (x) the name and address of any doctor(s) who might be able to provide further information about any of the above matters.
- (B) The signature, name, address and qualifications of the registered medical practitioner who prepared the report, and the date of the report and of the examinations carried out.

PRACTICE DIRECTION 14E – COMMUNICATION OF INFORMATION RELATING TO THE PROCEEDINGS

This Practice Direction supplements Part 8, rule 78(1)(b) of the Family Procedure (Adoption) Rules 2005 [Part 14, rule 14.14(b) of the Family Procedure Rules 2010]

COMMUNICATION OF INFORMATION RELATING TO PROCEEDINGS

1.1 *Rule 78* [Rule 14.14] deals with the communication of information (whether or not it is recorded in any form) relating to proceedings.

1.2 Subject to any direction of the court, information may be communicated for the purposes of the law relating to contempt in accordance with paragraphs 1.3 or 1.4.

1.3 A person specified in the first column of the following table may communicate to a person listed in the second column such information as is specified in the third column for the purpose or purposes specified in the fourth column.

Communication of information without permission of the court

Communicated by	To	Information	Purpose
A party	A lay adviser or a McKenzie Friend	Any information relating to the proceedings	To enable the party to obtain advice or assistance in relation to the proceedings.
A party	The party's spouse, civil partner, cohabitant or close family member		For the purpose of confidential discussions enabling the party to receive support from his spouse, civil partner, cohabitant or close family member.
A party	A health care professional or a person or body providing counselling services for children or families		To enable the party or any child of the party to obtain health care or counselling.
[A party	The Secretary of State, a McKenzie Friend, a lay adviser or an ppeal tribunal dealing with an appeal made under section 20 of the Child Support Act 1991		For the purposes of making or responding to an appeal under section 20 of the Child Support Act 1991 or the determnination of such an appeal.
A party	An adoption panel		To enable the adoption panel to discharge its functions as appropriate.]

The Family Procedure Rules 2010

Communicated by	To	Information	Purpose
A party or any person lawfully in receipt of information	The Children's Commissioner or the Children's Commissioner for Wales		To refer an issue affecting the interests of children to the Children's Commissioner or the Children's Commissioner for Wales.
A party or a legal representative	A mediator		For the purpose of mediation in relation to the proceedings.
A party, any person lawfully in receipt of information or a proper officer	A person or body conducting an approved research project		For the purpose of an approved research project.
A party, a legal representative or a professional legal adviser	A person or body responsible for investigating or determining complaints in relation to legal representatives or professional legal advisers		For the purposes of making a complaint or the investigation or determination of a complaint in relation to a legal representative or a professional legal adviser.
A legal representative or a professional legal adviser	A person or body assessing quality assurance systems		To enable the legal representative or professional legal adviser to obtain a quality assurance assessment.
A legal representative or a professional legal adviser	An accreditation body	Any information relating to the proceedings providing that it does not, or is not likely to, identify any person involved in the proceedings	To enable the legal representative or professional legal adviser to obtain accreditation.
A party	An elected representative or peer	The text or summary of the whole or part of a judgment given in the proceedings	To enable the elected representative or peer to give advice, investigate any complaint or raise any question of policy or procedure.
A party	The General Medical Council		For the purpose of making a complaint to the General Medical Council.
A party	A police officer		For the purpose of a criminal investigation.

Communicated by	To	Information	Purpose
A party or any person lawfully in receipt of information	A member of the Crown Prosecution Service		To enable the Crown Prosecution Service to discharge its functions under any enactment.

1.4 A person in the second column of the table in paragraph 1.3 may only communicate information relating to the proceedings received from a person in the first column for the purpose or purposes—

(a) for which he received that information, or
(b) of professional development or training, providing that any communication does not, or is not likely to, identify any person involved in the proceedings without that person's consent.

1.5 In this Practice Direction—
(1) 'accreditation body' means—

    (a) The Law Society,
    (b) Resolution, or
    (c) The Legal Services Commission;

[(1A) 'adoption panel' means a panel established in accordance with regulation 3 of the Adoption Agencies Regulations 2005 or reg 3 of the Adoption Agencies (Wales) Regulations;]
(2) 'approved research project' means a project of research—

    (a) approved in writing by a Secretary of State after consultation with the President of the Family Division,
    (b) approved in writing by the President of the Family Division, or
    (c) conducted under section 83 of the Act of 1989 or section 13 of the Criminal Justice and Court Services Act 2000;

(3) 'body assessing quality assurance systems' includes—

    (a) The Law Society,
    (b) The Legal Services Commission, or
    (c) The General Council of the Bar;

(4) 'body or person responsible for investigating or determining complaints in relation to legal representatives or professional legal advisers' means—

    (a) The Law Society,
    (b) The General Council of the Bar,
    (c) The Institute of Legal Executives, or
    (d) The Legal Services Ombudsman;

(5) 'cohabitant' means one of two persons who are neither married to each other nor civil partners of each other but are living together as husband and wife or as if they were civil partners;
(6) 'criminal investigation' means an investigation conducted by police officers with a view to it being ascertained—

    (a) whether a person should be charged with an offence, or
    (b) whether a person charged with an offence is guilty of it;

(7) 'elected representative' means—

    (a) a member of the House of Commons,
    (b) a member of the National Assembly for Wales, or
    (c) a member of the European Parliament elected in England and Wales;

(8) 'health care professional' means—

    (a) a registered medical practitioner,
    (b) a registered nurse or midwife,
    (c) a clinical psychologist, or
    (d) a child psychotherapist;

The Family Procedure Rules 2010

(9) 'lay adviser' means a non-professional person who gives lay advice on behalf of an organisation in the lay advice sector;
(10) 'McKenzie Friend' means any person permitted by the court to sit beside an unrepresented litigant in court to assist that litigant by prompting, taking notes and giving him advice;
(11) 'mediator' means a family mediator who is—

(a) undertaking, or has successfully completed, a family mediation training course approved by the United Kingdom College of Family Mediators, or
(b) a member of the Law Society's Family Mediation Panel;

(12) 'peer' means a member of the House of Lords as defined by the House of Lords Act 1999.

PRACTICE DIRECTION 14F – DISCLOSING INFORMATION TO AN ADOPTED ADULT

This Practice Direction supplements Part 8, rule 84(1)(d) of the Family Procedure (Adoption) Rules 2005 [Part 14, rule 14.18(1)(d) of the Family Procedure Rules 2010]

HOW TO REQUEST FOR INFORMATION

1.1 *Rule 84* [Rule 14.18] states that an adopted person who is over the age of 18 has the right to receive from the court which made the adoption order a copy of—

(a) the application form for an adoption order (but not the documents attached to that form);
(b) the adoption order and any other orders relating to the adoption proceedings; and
(c) orders allowing any person contact with the child after the adoption order was made.

1.2 An application under *rule 84* [rule 14.18] must be made in form A64 which is contained in the practice direction supplementing *rule 17* [rule 5] and must have attached to it a full certified copy of the entry in the Adopted Children Register relating to the applicant.

1.3 The completed application form must be taken to the court which made the adoption order along with evidence of the applicant's identity showing a photograph and signature, such as a passport or driving licence.

ADDITIONAL DOCUMENTS THAT THE ADOPTED PERSON IS ALSO ENTITLED TO RECEIVE FROM THE COURT

2 The adopted adult is also entitled to receive the following documents—

(a) any transcript or written reasons of the court's decision; and
(b) a report made to the court by—
  (i) a children's guardian, reporting officer or children and family reporter;
  (ii) a local authority; or
  (iii) an adoption agency.

BEFORE THE DOCUMENTS ARE SENT TO THE ADOPTED ADULT

3 The court will remove protected information from documents before they are sent to the adopted adult.

PART 15

REPRESENTATION OF PROTECTED PARTIES

15.1. Application of this Part
This Part contains special provisions which apply in proceedings involving protected parties.

15.2. Requirement for litigation friend in proceedings

A protected party must have a litigation friend to conduct proceedings on that party's behalf.

15.3.— Stage of proceedings at which a litigation friend becomes necessary

(1) A person may not without the permission of the court take any step in proceedings except—

    (a)   filing an application form; or

    (b)   applying for the appointment of a litigation friend under rule 15.6, until the protected party has a litigation friend.

(2) If during proceedings a party lacks capacity (within the meaning of the 2005 Act) to continue to conduct proceedings, no party may take any step in proceedings without the permission of the court until the protected party has a litigation friend.

(3) Any step taken before a protected party has a litigation friend has no effect unless the court orders otherwise.

15.4.— Who may be a litigation friend for a protected party without a court order

(1) This rule does not apply if the court has appointed a person to be a litigation friend.

(2) A person with authority as a deputy to conduct the proceedings in the name of a protected party or on that party's behalf is entitled to be the litigation friend of the protected party in any proceedings to which that person's authority extends.

(3) If there is no person with authority as a deputy to conduct the proceedings in the name of a protected party or on that party's behalf, a person may act as a litigation friend if that person—

    (a)   can fairly and competently conduct proceedings on behalf of the protected party;

    (b)   has no interest adverse to that of the protected party; and

    (c)   subject to paragraph (4), undertakes to pay any costs which the protected party may be ordered to pay in relation to the proceedings, subject to any right that person may have to be repaid from the assets of the protected party.

(4) Paragraph (3)(c) does not apply to the Official Solicitor.

("deputy" is defined in rule 2.3.)

15.5.— How a person becomes a litigation friend without a court order

(1) If the court has not appointed a litigation friend, a person who wishes to act as a litigation friend must follow the procedure set out in this rule.

(2) A person with authority as a deputy to conduct the proceedings in the name of a protected party or on that party's behalf must file an official copy$^{(GL)}$ of the order, declaration or other document which confers that person's authority to act.

(3) Any other person must file a certificate of suitability stating that that person satisfies the conditions specified in rule 15.4(3).

(4) A person who is to act as a litigation friend must file—

    (a)   the document conferring that person's authority to act; or

    (b)   the certificate of suitability,

at the time when that person first takes a step in the proceedings on behalf of the protected party.

(5) A court officer will send the certificate of suitability to every person on whom, in accordance with rule 6.28, the application form should be served.

(6) This rule does not apply to the Official Solicitor.

15.6.— How a person becomes a litigation friend by court order

(1) The court may, if the person to be appointed so consents, make an order appointing—

    (a)   a person other than the Official Solicitor; or

    (b)   the Official Solicitor,

as a litigation friend.

(2) An order appointing a litigation friend may be made by the court of its own initiative or on the application of—
  (a) a person who wishes to be a litigation friend; or
  (b) a party to the proceedings.
(3) The court may at any time direct that a party make an application for an order under paragraph (2).
(4) An application for an order appointing a litigation friend must be supported by evidence.
(5) Unless the court directs otherwise, a person appointed under this rule to be a litigation friend for a protected party will be treated as a party for the purpose of any provision in these rules requiring a document to be served on, or sent to, or notice to be given to, a party to the proceedings.
(6) Subject to rule 15.4(4), the court may not appoint a litigation friend under this rule unless it is satisfied that the person to be appointed complies with the conditions specified in rule 15.4(3).

15.7.— Court's power to change litigation friend and to prevent person acting as litigation friend
(1) The court may—
  (a) direct that a person may not act as a litigation friend;
  (b) terminate a litigation friend's appointment; or
  (c) appoint a new litigation friend in substitution for an existing one.
(2) An application for an order or direction under paragraph (1) must be supported by evidence.
(3) Subject to rule 15.4(4), the court may not appoint a litigation friend under this rule unless it is satisfied that the person to be appointed complies with the conditions specified in rule 15.4(3).

15.8.— Appointment of litigation friend by court order – supplementary
(1) A copy of the application for an order under rule 15.6 or 15.7 must be sent by a court officer to—
  (a) every person on whom, in accordance with rule 6.28, the application form should be served; and
  (b) unless the court directs otherwise, the protected party.
(2) A copy of an application for an order under rule 15.7 must also be sent to—
  (a) the person who is the litigation friend, or who is purporting to act as the litigation friend when the application is made; and
  (b) the person, if not the applicant, who it is proposed should be the litigation friend.

15.9.— Procedure where appointment of litigation friend comes to an end
(1) When a party ceases to be a protected party, the litigation friend's appointment continues until it is brought to an end by a court order.
(2) An application for an order under paragraph (1) may be made by—
  (a) the former protected party;
  (b) the litigation friend; or
  (c) a party.
(3) On the making of an order under paragraph (1), the court officer will send a notice to the other parties stating that the appointment of the protected party's litigation friend to act has ended.

PART 15 COMMENTARY

Part 15 is supplemented by PD15A.

Part 15 contains the rules relating to the representation of protected parties. A protected party is defined by r 2.3 as a party or an intended party who lacks capacity (within the meaning of the 2005 Act) to conduct proceedings. The former terms 'next friend' and 'guardian ad litem' are replaced by 'litigation friend'.

The form relevant to this section is FP9 – Certificate of suitability of litigation friend (see r 15.5).

PRACTICE DIRECTION 15A – PROTECTED PARTIES

This Practice Direction supplements FPR Part 15

GENERAL

1.1 A protected party must have a litigation friend to conduct proceedings on the protected party's behalf.

1.2 In the proceedings the protected party should be referred to in the title as "A.B. (by C.D. his/her litigation friend).

DUTIES OF THE LITIGATION FRIEND

2.1 It is the duty of a litigation friend fairly and competently to conduct proceedings on behalf of a protected party. The litigation friend must have no interest in the proceedings adverse to that of the protected party and all steps and decisions the litigation friend takes in the proceedings must be taken for the benefit of the protected party.

BECOMING A LITIGATION FRIEND WITHOUT A COURT ORDER

3.1 In order to become a litigation friend without a court order the person who wishes to act as litigation friend must—

(a) file an official copy of the order, declaration or other document which confers the litigation friend's authority as a deputy to conduct the proceedings in the name of a protected party or on his/her behalf; or
(b) file a certificate of suitability—
  (i) stating that the litigation friend consents to act;
  (ii) stating that the litigation friend knows or believes that the [applicant-][respondent] lacks capacity (within the meaning of the 2005 Act) to conduct proceedings;
  (iii) stating the grounds of that belief and if the belief is based upon medical opinion attaching any relevant document to the certificate;
  (iv) stating that the litigation friend can fairly and competently conduct proceedings on behalf of the protected party and has no interest adverse to that of the protected party;
  (v) undertaking to pay any costs which the protected party may be ordered to pay in relation to the proceedings, subject to any right the litigation friend may have to be repaid from the assets of the protected party; and
  (vi) which the litigation friend has verified by a statement of truth.

3.2 Paragraph 3.1 does not apply to the Official Solicitor.

3.3 The court officer will send the certificate of suitability to the person who is the attorney of a registered enduring power of attorney, donee of a lasting power of attorney or deputy or, if there is no such person, to the person with whom the protected party resides or in whose care the protected party is.

3.4 The court officer is not required to send the documents referred to in paragraph 3.1(b)(iii) when sending the certificate of suitability to the person to be served under paragraph 3.3.

3.5 The litigation friend must file either the certificate of suitability or the authority referred to in paragraph 3.1(a) at a time when the litigation friend first takes a step in the proceedings on behalf of the protected party.

APPLICATION FOR A COURT ORDER APPOINTING A LITIGATION FRIEND

4.1 An application for a court order appointing a litigation friend should be made in accordance with Part 18 and must be supported by evidence.

4.2 The court officer must serve the application notice—

(a) on the persons referred to in paragraph 3.3; and
(b) on the protected party unless the court directs otherwise.

4.3 The evidence in support must satisfy the court that the proposed litigation friend—

(a) consents to act;
(b) can fairly and competently conduct proceedings on behalf of the protected party;
(c) has no interest adverse to that of the protected party; and
(d) undertakes to pay any costs which the protected party may be ordered to pay in relation to the proceedings, subject to any right the litigation friend may have to be repaid from the assets of the protected party.

4.4 Paragraph 4.3(d) does not apply to the Official Solicitor.

4.5 The proposed litigation friend may be one of the persons referred to in paragraph 3.3 where appropriate, or otherwise may be the Official Solicitor. Where it is sought to appoint the Official Solicitor, provision must be made for payment of his charges.

CHANGE OF LITIGATION FRIEND AND PREVENTION OF PERSON ACTING AS LITIGATION FRIEND.

5.1 Where an application is made for an order under rule 15.7, the application must set out the reasons for seeking it and must be supported by evidence.

5.2 Subject to paragraph 4.4, if the order sought is substitution of a new litigation friend for an existing one, the evidence must satisfy the court of the matters set out in paragraph 4.3.

5.3 The court officer will serve the application notice on—

(a) the persons referred to in paragraph 3.3; and
(b) the litigation friend or person purporting to act as litigation friend.

PROCEDURE WHERE THE NEED FOR A LITIGATION FRIEND HAS COME TO AN END

6.1 Where a person who was a protected party regains or acquires capacity (within the meaning of the 2005 Act) to conduct the proceedings, an application under rule 15.9(2) must be made for an order under rule 15.9(1) that the litigation friend's appointment has ceased.

6.2 The application must be supported by the following evidence—

(a) a medical report or other suitably qualified expert's report indicating that the protected party has regained or acquired capacity (within the meaning of the 2005 Act) to conduct the proceedings; and
(b) a copy of any relevant order or declaration of the Court of Protection.

PART 16

REPRESENTATION OF CHILDREN AND REPORTS IN PROCEEDINGS INVOLVING CHILDREN

CHAPTER 1

APPLICATION OF THIS PART

16.1. Application of this Part
This Part—
- (a) sets out when the court will make a child a party in family proceedings; and
- (b) contains special provisions which apply in proceedings involving children.

CHAPTER 2

CHILD AS PARTY IN FAMILY PROCEEDINGS

16.2.— When the court may make a child a party to proceedings
(1) The court may make a child a party to proceedings if it considers it is in the best interests of the child to do so.
(2) This rule does not apply to a child who is the subject of proceedings—
- (a) which are specified proceedings; or
- (b) to which Part 14 applies.

(The Practice Direction 16A sets out the matters which the court will take into consideration before making a child a party under this rule.)

CHAPTER 3

WHEN A CHILDREN'S GUARDIAN OR LITIGATION FRIEND WILL BE APPOINTED

16.3.— Appointment of a children's guardian in specified proceedings or proceedings to which Part 14 applies
(1) Unless it is satisfied that it is not necessary to do so to safeguard the interests of the child, the court must appoint a children's guardian for a child who is—
- (a) the subject of; and
- (b) a party to,

proceedings—
- (i) which are specified proceedings; or
- (ii) to which Part 14 applies.

(Rules 12.6 and 14.6 set out the point in the proceedings when the court will appoint a children's guardian in specified proceedings and proceedings to which Part 14 applies respectively.)

(2) At any stage in the proceedings—
- (a) a party may apply, without notice to the other parties unless the court directs otherwise, for the appointment of a children's guardian; or
- (b) the court may of its own initiative appoint a children's guardian.

(3) Where the court refuses an application under paragraph (2)(a) it will give reasons for the refusal and the court or a court officer will—
- (a) record the refusal and the reasons for it; and
- (b) as soon as practicable, notify the parties and either the Service or the Assembly of a decision not to appoint a children's guardian.

(4) When appointing a children's guardian the court will consider the appointment of anyone who has previously acted as a children's guardian of the same child.

(5) Where the court appoints a children's guardian in accordance with this rule, the provisions of Chapter 6 of this Part apply.

The Family Procedure Rules 2010

16.4.— Appointment of a children's guardian in proceedings not being specified proceedings or proceedings to which Part 14 applies

(1) Without prejudice to rule 8.42 or 16.6, the court must appoint a children's guardian for a child who is the subject of proceedings, which are not proceedings of a type referred to in rule 16.3(1), if—
- (a) the child is an applicant in the proceedings;
- (b) a provision in these rules provides for the child to be a party to the proceedings; or
- (c) the court has made the child a party in accordance with rule 16.2.

(2) The provisions of Chapter 7 of this Part apply where the appointment of a children's guardian is required in accordance with paragraph (1).

("children's guardian" is defined in rule 2.3.)

16.5.— Requirement for a litigation friend

(1) Without prejudice to rule 16.6, where a child is—
- (a) a party to proceedings; but
- (b) not the subject of those proceedings,

the child must have a litigation friend to conduct proceedings on the child's behalf.

(2) The provisions of Chapter 5 of this Part apply where a litigation friend is required in accordance with paragraph (1).

CHAPTER 4

Where a children's guardian or litigation friend is not required

16.6.— Circumstances in which a child does not need a children's guardian or litigation friend

(1) Subject to paragraph (2), a child may conduct proceedings without a children's guardian or litigation friend where the proceedings are proceedings—
- (a) under the 1989 Act;
- (b) to which Part 11 (applications under Part 4A of the Family Law Act 1996) or Part 14 (applications in adoption, placement and related proceedings) of these rules apply; or
- (c) relating to the exercise of the court's inherent jurisdiction with respect to children, and one of the conditions set out in paragraph (3) is satisfied.

(2) Paragraph (1) does not apply where the child is the subject of and a party to proceedings—
- (a) which are specified proceedings; or
- (b) to which Part 14 applies.

(3) The conditions referred to in paragraph (1) are that either—
- (a) the child has obtained the court's permission; or
- (b) a solicitor—
  - (i) considers that the child is able, having regard to the child's understanding, to give instructions in relation to the proceedings; and
  - (ii) has accepted instructions from that child to act for that child in the proceedings and, if the proceedings have begun, the solicitor is already acting.

(4) An application for permission under paragraph (3)(a) may be made by the child without notice.

(5) Where a child—
- (a) has a litigation friend or children's guardian in proceedings to which this rule applies; and
- (b) wishes to conduct the remaining stages of the proceedings without the litigation friend or children's guardian,

the child may apply to the court, on notice to the litigation friend or children's guardian, for permission for that purpose and for the removal of the litigation friend or children's guardian.

(6) The court will grant an application under paragraph (3)(a) or (5) if it considers that the child has sufficient understanding to conduct the proceedings concerned or proposed without a litigation friend or children's guardian.

(7) In exercising its powers under paragraph (6) the court may require the litigation friend or children's guardian to take such part in the proceedings as the court directs.

(8) The court may revoke any permission granted under paragraph (3)(a) where it considers that the child does not have sufficient understanding to participate as a party in the proceedings concerned without a litigation friend or children's guardian.

(9) Where a solicitor is acting for a child in proceedings without a litigation friend or children's guardian by virtue of paragraph (3)(b) and either of the conditions specified in paragraph (3)(b)(i) or (ii) cease to be fulfilled, the solicitor must inform the court immediately.

(10) Where—
    (a) the court revokes any permission under paragraph (8); or
    (b) either of the conditions specified in paragraph (3)(b)(i) or (ii) is no longer fulfilled,

the court may, if it considers it necessary in order to protect the interests of the child concerned, appoint a person to be that child's litigation friend or children's guardian.

CHAPTER 5

Litigation friend

16.7. Application of this Chapter

This Chapter applies where a child must have a litigation friend to conduct proceedings on the child's behalf in accordance with rule 16.5.

16.8.— Stage of proceedings at which a litigation friend becomes necessary

(1) This rule does not apply in relation to a child who is conducting proceedings without a litigation friend in accordance with rule 16.6.

(2) A person may not without the permission of the court take any step in proceedings except—
    (a) filing an application form; or
    (b) applying for the appointment of a litigation friend under rule 16.11,
until the child has a litigation friend.

(3) Any step taken before a child has a litigation friend has no effect unless the court orders otherwise.

16.9.— Who may be a litigation friend for a child without a court order

(1) This rule does not apply if the court has appointed a person to be a litigation friend.

(2) A person may act as a litigation friend if that person—
    (a) can fairly and competently conduct proceedings on behalf of the child;
    (b) has no interest adverse to that of the child; and
    (c) subject to paragraph (3), undertakes to pay any costs which the child may be ordered to pay in relation to the proceedings, subject to any right that person may have to be repaid from the assets of the child.

(3) Paragraph (2)(c) does not apply to the Official Solicitor, an officer of the Service or a Welsh family proceedings officer.

16.10.— How a person becomes a litigation friend without a court order

(1) If the court has not appointed a litigation friend, a person who wishes to act as such must file a certificate of suitability stating that that person satisfies the conditions specified in rule 16.9(2).

(2) The certificate of suitability must be filed at the time when the person who wishes to act as litigation friend first takes a step in the proceedings on behalf of the child.

(3) A court officer will send the certificate of suitability to every person on whom, in accordance with rule 6.28, the application form should be served.

(4) This rule does not apply to the Official Solicitor, an officer of the Service or a Welsh family proceedings officer.

16.11.— Appointment of litigation friend by the court

(1) The court may, if the person to be appointed consents, make an order appointing as a litigation friend—
- (a) the Official Solicitor;
- (b) an officer of the Service or a Welsh family proceedings officer; or
- (c) some other person.

(2) An order appointing a litigation friend may be made by the court of its own initiative or on the application of—
- (a) a person who wishes to be a litigation friend; or
- (b) a party to the proceedings.

(3) The court may at any time direct that a party make an application for an order under paragraph (2).

(4) An application for an order appointing a litigation friend must be supported by evidence.

(5) Unless the court directs otherwise, a person appointed under this rule to be a litigation friend for a child will be treated as a party for the purpose of any provision in these rules requiring a document to be served on, or sent to, or notice to be given to, a party to the proceedings.

(6) Subject to rule 16.9(3), the court may not appoint a litigation friend under this rule unless it is satisfied that the person to be appointed complies with the conditions specified in rule 16.9(2).

(7) This rule is without prejudice to rule 16.6.

16.12.— Court's power to change litigation friend and to prevent person acting as litigation friend

(1) The court may—
- (a) direct that a person may not act as a litigation friend;
- (b) terminate a litigation friend's appointment; or
- (c) appoint a new litigation friend in substitution for an existing one.

(2) An application for an order or direction under paragraph (1) must be supported by evidence.

(3) Subject to rule 16.9(3), the court may not appoint a litigation friend under this rule unless it is satisfied that the person to be appointed complies with the conditions specified in rule 16.9(2).

16.13.— Appointment of litigation friend by court order – supplementary

(1) A copy of the application for an order under rule 16.11 or 16.12 must be sent by a court officer to every person on whom, in accordance with rule 6.28, the application form should be served.

(2) A copy of an application for an order under rule 16.12 must also be sent to—
- (a) the person who is the litigation friend, or who is purporting to act as the litigation friend when the application is made; and
- (b) the person, if not the applicant, who it is proposed should be the litigation friend.

16.14.— Powers and duties of litigation friend

(1) The litigation friend—
- (a) has the powers and duties set out in Practice Direction 16A; and
- (b) must exercise those powers and duties in accordance with Practice Direction 16A.

(2) Where the litigation friend is an officer of the Service or a Welsh family proceedings officer, rule 16.20 applies as it applies to a children's guardian appointed in accordance with Chapter 6.

16.15.— Procedure where appointment of litigation friend comes to an end
(1) When a child who is not a protected party reaches the age of 18, a litigation friend's appointment comes to an end.
(2) A court officer will send a notice to the other parties stating that the appointment of the child's litigation friend to act has ended.

CHAPTER 6

Children's guardian appointed under rule 16.3

16.16. Application of this Chapter
This Chapter applies where the court must appoint a children's guardian in accordance with rule 16.3.

16.17. Who may be a children's guardian
Where the court is appointing a children's guardian under rule 16.3 it will appoint an officer of the Service or a Welsh family proceedings officer.

16.18.— What the court or a court officer will do once the court has made a decision about appointing a children's guardian
(1) Where the court appoints a children's guardian under rule 16.3 a court officer will record the appointment and, as soon as practicable, will—
 (a) inform the parties and either the Service or the Assembly; and
 (b) unless it has already been sent, send the children's guardian a copy of the application and copies of any document filed with the court in the proceedings.
(2) A court officer has a continuing duty to send the children's guardian a copy of any other document filed with the court during the course of the proceedings.

16.19.— Termination of the appointment of the children's guardian
(1) The appointment of a children's guardian under rule 16.3 continues for such time as is specified in the appointment or until terminated by the court.
(2) When terminating an appointment in accordance with paragraph (1), the court will give reasons for doing so, a note of which will be taken by the court or a court officer.

16.20.— Powers and duties of the children's guardian
(1) The children's guardian is to act on behalf of the child upon the hearing of any application in proceedings to which this Chapter applies with the duty of safeguarding the interests of the child.
(2) The children's guardian must also provide the court with such other assistance as it may require.
(3) The children's guardian, when carrying out duties in relation to specified proceedings, other than placement proceedings, must have regard to the principle set out in section 1(2) and the matters set out in section 1(3)(a) to (f) of the 1989 Act as if for the word "court" in that section there were substituted the words "children's guardian".
(4) The children's guardian, when carrying out duties in relation to proceedings to which Part 14 applies, must have regard to the principle set out in section 1(3) and the matters set out in section 1(4)(a) to (f) of the 2002 Act as if for the word "court" in that section there were substituted the words "children's guardian".
(5) The children's guardian's duties must be exercised in accordance with Practice Direction 16A.
(6) A report to the court by the children's guardian is confidential.

The Family Procedure Rules 2010

16.21.— Where the child instructs a solicitor or conducts proceedings on the child's own behalf

(1) Where it appears to the children's guardian that the child—

    (a)   is instructing a solicitor direct; or

    (b)   intends to conduct and is capable of conducting the proceedings on that child's own behalf,

the children's guardian must inform the court of that fact.

(2) Where paragraph (1) applies the children's guardian—

    (a)   must perform such additional duties as the court may direct;

    (b)   must take such part in the proceedings as the court may direct; and

    (c)   may, with the permission of the court, have legal representation in the conduct of those duties.

CHAPTER 7

CHILDREN'S GUARDIAN APPOINTED UNDER RULE 16.4

16.22. Application of this Chapter

This Chapter applies where the court must appoint a children's guardian under rule 16.4.

16.23.— Stage of proceedings at which a children's guardian becomes necessary

(1) This rule does not apply in relation to a child who is conducting proceedings without a children's guardian in accordance with rule 16.6.

(2) A person may not without the permission of the court take any step in proceedings except—

    (a)   filing an application form; or

    (b)   applying for the appointment of a children's guardian under rule 16.24,

until the child has a children's guardian.

(3) Any step taken before a child has a children's guardian has no effect unless the court orders otherwise.

16.24.— Appointment of a children's guardian

(1) The court may make an order appointing as a children's guardian, an officer of the Service or a Welsh family proceedings officer or, if the person to be appointed consents —

    (a)   a person other than the Official Solicitor; or

    (b)   the Official Solicitor.

(2) An order appointing a children's guardian may be made by the court of its own initiative or on the application of—

    (a)   a person who wishes to be a children's guardian; or

    (b)   a party to the proceedings.

(3) The court may at any time direct that a party make an application for an order under paragraph (2).

(4) An application for an order appointing a children's guardian must be supported by evidence.

(5) The court may not appoint a children's guardian under this rule unless it is satisfied that that person—

    (a)   can fairly and competently conduct proceedings on behalf of the child;

    (b)   has no interest adverse to that of the child; and

    (c)   subject to paragraph (6), undertakes to pay any costs which the child may be ordered to pay in relation to the proceedings, subject to any right that person may have to be repaid from the assets of the child.

(6) Paragraph (5)(c) does not apply to the Official Solicitor, an officer of the Service or a Welsh family proceedings officer.

(7) This rule is without prejudice to rule 16.6 and rule 9.11. (Rule 9.11 provides for a child to be separately represented in certain applications for a financial remedy.)

16.25.— **Court's power to change children's guardian and to prevent person acting as children's guardian**

(1) The court may—
   (a) direct that a person may not act as a children's guardian;
   (b) terminate the appointment of a children's guardian; or
   (c) appoint a new children's guardian in substitution for an existing one.

(2) An application for an order or direction under paragraph (1) must be supported by evidence.

(3) Subject to rule 16.24(6), the court may not appoint a children's guardian under this rule unless it is satisfied that the person to be appointed complies with the conditions specified in rule 16.24(5).

16.26.— **Appointment of children's guardian by court order – supplementary**

(1) A copy of the application for an order under rule 16.24 or 16.25 must be sent by a court officer to every person on whom, in accordance with rule 6.28, the application form should be served.

(2) A copy of an application for an order under rule 16.25 must also be sent to—
   (a) the person who is the children's guardian, or who is purporting to act as the children's guardian when the application is made; and
   (b) the person, if not the applicant, who it is proposed should be the children's guardian.

16.27.— **Powers and duties of children's guardian**

(1) The children's guardian—
   (a) has the powers and duties set out in Practice Direction 16A; and
   (b) must exercise those powers and duties in accordance with Practice Direction 16A.

(2) Where the children's guardian is an officer of the Service or a Welsh family proceedings officer, rule 16.20 applies to a children's guardian appointed in accordance with this Chapter as it applies to a children's guardian appointed in accordance with Chapter 6.

16.28.— **Procedure where appointment of children's guardian comes to an end**

(1) When a child reaches the age of 18, the appointment of a children's guardian comes to an end.

(2) A court officer will send a notice to the other parties stating that the appointment of the child's children's guardian to act has ended.

CHAPTER 8

Duties of solicitor acting for the child

16.29.— **Solicitor for child**

(1) Subject to paragraphs (2) and (4), a solicitor appointed—
   (a) under section 41(3) of the 1989 Act; or
   (b) by the children's guardian in accordance with the Practice Direction 16A,

must represent the child in accordance with instructions received from the children's guardian.

(2) If a solicitor appointed as mentioned in paragraph (1) considers, having taken into account the matters referred to in paragraph (3), that the child—
   (a) wishes to give instructions which conflict with those of the children's guardian; and
   (b) is able, having regard to the child's understanding, to give such instructions on the child's own behalf,

the solicitor must conduct the proceedings in accordance with instructions received from the child.

(3) The matters the solicitor must take into account for the purposes of paragraph (2) are—
- (a) the views of the children's guardian; and
- (b) any direction given by the court to the children's guardian concerning the part to be taken by the children's guardian in the proceedings.

(4) Where—
- (a) no children's guardian has been appointed; and
- (b) the condition in section 41(4)(b) of the 1989 Act is satisfied,

a solicitor appointed under section 41(3) of the 1989 Act must represent the child in accordance with instructions received from the child.

(5) Where a solicitor appointed as mentioned in paragraph (1) receives no instructions under paragraphs (1), (2) or (4), the solicitor must represent the child in furtherance of the best interests of the child.

(6) A solicitor appointed under section 41(3) of the 1989 Act or by the children's guardian in accordance with Practice Direction 16A must serve documents, and accept service of documents, on behalf of the child in accordance with rule 6.31 and, where the child has not been served separately and has sufficient understanding, advise the child of the contents of any document so served.

(7) Where the child wishes an appointment of a solicitor—
- (a) under section 41(3) of the 1989 Act; or
- (b) by the children's guardian in accordance with the Practice Direction 16A,

to be terminated—
- (i) the child may apply to the court for an order terminating the appointment; and
- (ii) the solicitor and the children's guardian will be given an opportunity to make representations.

(8) Where the children's guardian wishes an appointment of a solicitor under section 41(3) of the 1989 Act to be terminated—
- (a) the children's guardian may apply to the court for an order terminating the appointment; and
- (b) the solicitor and, if of sufficient understanding, the child, will be given an opportunity to make representations.

(9) When terminating an appointment in accordance with paragraph (7) or (8), the court will give its reasons for so doing, a note of which will be taken by the court or a court officer.

(10) The court or a court officer will record the appointment under section 41(3) of the 1989 Act or the refusal to make the appointment.

CHAPTER 9

Reporting officer

16.30. When the court appoints a reporting officer

In proceedings to which Part 14 applies, the court will appoint a reporting officer where—
- (a) it appears that a parent or guardian of the child is willing to consent to the placing of the child for adoption, to the making of an adoption order or to a section 84 order; and
- (b) that parent or guardian is in England or Wales.

16.31. Appointment of the same reporting officer in respect of two or more parents or guardians

The same person may be appointed as the reporting officer for two or more parents or guardians of the child.

16.32.— The duties of the reporting officer

(1) The reporting officer must witness the signature by a parent or guardian on the document in which consent is given to—

(a) the placing of the child for adoption;
(b) the making of an adoption order; or
(c) the making of a section 84 order.

(2) The reporting officer must carry out such other duties as are set out in Practice Direction 16A.

(3) A report to the court by the reporting officer is confidential.

(4) The reporting officer's duties must be exercised in accordance with Practice Direction 16A.

CHAPTER 10

CHILDREN AND FAMILY REPORTER AND WELFARE OFFICER

16.33.— Request by court for a welfare report in respect of the child

(1) Where the court is considering an application for an order in proceedings, the court may ask—
(a) in proceedings to which Parts 12 and 14 apply, a children and family reporter; or
(b) in proceedings to which Part 12 applies, a welfare officer,

to prepare a report on matters relating to the welfare of the child, and, in this rule, the person preparing the report is called "the officer".

(2) It is the duty of the officer to—
(a) comply with any request for a report under this rule; and
(b) provide the court with such other assistance as it may require.

(3) A report to the court under this rule is confidential.

(4) The officer, when carrying out duties in relation to proceedings under the 1989 Act, must have regard to the principle set out in section 1(2) and the matters set out in section 1(3)(a) to (f) of that Act as if for the word "court" in that section there were substituted the words "children and family reporter" or "welfare officer" as the case may be.

(5) A party may question the officer about oral or written advice tendered by that officer to the court.

(6) The court officer will notify the officer of a direction given at a hearing at which—
(a) the officer is not present; and
(b) the welfare report is considered.

(7) The officer's duties must be exercised in accordance with Practice Direction 16A ("children and family reporter" and "welfare officer" are defined in rule 2.3)

CHAPTER 11

PARENTAL ORDER REPORTER

16.34. When the court appoints a parental order reporter

In proceedings to which Part 13 applies, the court will appoint a parental order reporter in accordance with rule 13.5.

16.35.— Powers and duties of the parental order reporter

(1) The parental order reporter is to act on behalf of the child upon the hearing of any application in proceedings to which Part 13 applies with the duty of safeguarding the interests of the child.

(2) The parental order reporter must—
(a) investigate the matters set out in sections 54(1) to (8) of the 2008 Act;
(b) so far as the parental order reporter considers necessary, investigate any matter contained in the application form or other matter which appears relevant to the making of the parental order; and
(c) advise the court on whether there is any reason under section 1 of the 2002 Act (as applied with modifications by the Human Fertilisation and

Embryology (Parental Orders) Regulations 2010) to refuse the parental order.

(3) The parental order reporter must also provide the court with such other assistance as it may require.

(4) The parental order reporter's duties must be exercised in accordance with Practice Direction 16A.

(5) A report to the court by the parental order reporter is confidential.

CHAPTER 12

SUPPLEMENTARY APPOINTMENT PROVISIONS

16.36.— **Persons who may not be appointed as children's guardian, reporting officer or children and family reporter**

(1) In adoption proceedings or proceedings for a section 84 order or a section 89 order, no person may be appointed as a children's guardian, reporting officer or children and family reporter who—

- (a) is a member, officer or servant of a local authority which is a party to the proceedings;
- (b) is, or has been, a member, officer or servant of a local authority or voluntary organisation who has been directly concerned in that capacity in arrangements relating to the care, accommodation or welfare of the child during the 5 years prior to the start of the proceedings; or
- (c) is a serving probation officer who has, in that capacity, been previously concerned with the child or the child's family.

(2) In placement proceedings, a person described in paragraph (1)(b) or (c) may not be appointed as a children's guardian, reporting officer or children and family reporter.

16.37. Appointment of the same person as children's guardian, reporting officer and children and family reporter

The same person may be appointed to act as one or more of the following—

- (a) the children's guardian;
- (b) the reporting officer; and
- (c) the children and family reporter.

CHAPTER 13

OFFICERS OF THE SERVICE, WELSH FAMILY PROCEEDINGS OFFICERS AND LOCAL AUTHORITY OFFICERS: FURTHER DUTIES

16.38.— **Officers of the Service, Welsh family proceedings officers and local authority officers acting under certain duties**

(1) This rule applies when—

- (a) an officer of the Service or a Welsh family proceedings officer is acting under a duty in accordance with—
    - (i) section 11E(7) of the 1989 Act (providing the court with information as to the making of a contact activity direction or a contact activity condition);
    - (ii) section 11G(2) of the 1989 Act (monitoring compliance with a contact activity direction or a contact activity condition);
    - (iii) section 11H(2) of the 1989 Act (monitoring compliance with a contact order);
    - (iv) section 11L(5) of the 1989 Act (providing the court with information as to the making of an enforcement order);
    - (v) section 11M(1) of the 1989 Act (monitoring compliance with an enforcement order);
    - (vi) section 16(6) of the 1989 Act (providing a report to the court in accordance with a direction in a family assistance order); and

(vii) section 16A of the 1989 Act (making a risk assessment); and (b) a local authority officer is acting under a duty in accordance with section 16(6) of the 1989 Act (providing a report to the court in accordance with a direction in a family assistance order).

(2) In this rule,—
   (a) "contact activity direction", "contact activity condition" and "enforcement order" have the meanings given in rule 12.2; and
   (b) references to "the officer" are to the officer of the Service, Welsh family proceedings officer or local authority officer referred to in paragraph (1).

(3) In exercising the duties referred to in paragraph (1), the officer must have regard to the principle set out in section 1(2) of the 1989 Act and the matters set out in section 1(3)(a) to (f) of the 1989 Act as if for the word "court" in that section there were substituted the words "officer of the Service, Welsh family proceedings officer or local authority officer".

(4) The officer's duties referred to in paragraph (1) must be exercised in accordance with Practice Direction 16A.

CHAPTER 14

ENFORCEMENT ORDERS AND FINANCIAL COMPENSATION ORDERS: PERSONS NOTIFIED

16.39.— Application for enforcement orders and financial compensation orders: duties of the person notified

(1) This rule applies where a person who was the child's children's guardian, litigation friend or legal representative in the proceedings in which a contact order was made has been notified of an application for an enforcement order or for a financial compensation order as required by Practice Direction 12C.

(2) The person who has been notified of the application must—
   (a) consider whether it is in the best interests of the child for the child to be made a party to the proceedings for an enforcement order or a financial compensation order (as applicable); and
   (b) before the date fixed for the first hearing in the case notify the court, orally or in writing, of the opinion reached on the question, together with the reasons for this opinion.

(3) In this rule, "enforcement order" and "financial compensation order" have the meanings given in rule 12.2.

PART 16 COMMENTARY

Part 16 is supplemented by PD16A which incorporates the President's Practice Direction on the Representation of Children of the 5 April 2004.

Part 16 contains provisions relating to the representation of children, and reports in children proceedings.

Chapter 2 sets out at r 16.2 when the court may make a child party to proceedings if it considers that it is in the best interests of the child to do so, save in relation to specified proceedings (see r 12.27) and where Part 14 applies (adoption proceedings). There is assistance as to the circumstances when a child should be made a party to proceedings in PD16A (para 7.1)

Chapter 3 provides for three different types of representation: a guardian under r 16.3 (generally public law and adoption), a guardian under r 16.4 (generally private law) and a litigation friend under r 16.5 (in circumstances where the child is party to the proceedings but not the subject of those proceedings). The old term, 'guardian ad litem' has not been retained.

Chapter 5 applies to litigation friends.

Chapter 6 applies to r 16.3 Guardians (generally public law and adoption).

The Family Procedure Rules 2010

Chapter 7 applies to r 16.4 Guardians (generally private law).

Chapter 8 sets out duties of the solicitor acting for the child.

Chapter 9 makes provisions for reporting officers in adoption proceedings.

Chapter 10 makes provision in relation to welfare reports.

Chapter 11 makes provision in relation to a parental order reporter.

The form relevant to this section is FP9 – Certificate of suitability of litigation friend (see r 16.10).

PRACTICE DIRECTION 16A – REPRESENTATION OF CHILDREN

This Practice Direction supplements FPR Part 16

PART 1 GENERAL

Reference in title of proceedings

1.1 Where a litigation friend represents a child in family proceedings in accordance with rule 16.5 and Chapter 5 of Part 16, the child should be referred to in the title of the proceedings as "A.B. (a child by C.D. his/her litigation friend).

1.2 Where a children's guardian represents a child in family proceedings in accordance with rule 16.4 and Chapter 7 of Part 16, the child should be referred to in the title as "A.B. (a child by C.D. his/her children's guardian).

1.3 A child who is conducting proceedings on that child's own behalf should be referred to in the title as "A.B. (a child)."

PART 2 LITIGATION FRIEND

Duties of the Litigation Friend

2.1 It is the duty of a litigation friend fairly and competently to conduct proceedings on behalf of the child. The litigation friend must have no interest in the proceedings adverse to that of the child and all steps and decisions the litigation friend takes in the proceedings must be taken for the benefit of the child.

2.2. A litigation friend who is an officer of the Service or a Welsh family proceedings officer has, in addition, the duties set out in Part 3 of this Practice Direction and must exercise those duties as set out in that Part.

Becoming a Litigation Friend without a court order

3.1 In order to become a litigation friend without a court order the person who wishes to act as litigation friend must file a certificate of suitability—

(a) stating that the litigation friend consents to act;
(b) stating that the litigation friend knows or believes that the [applicant][respondent] is a child to whom rule 16.5 and Chapter 5 of Part 16 apply;
(c) stating that the litigation friend can fairly and competently conduct proceedings on behalf of the child and has no interest adverse to that of the child;
(d) undertaking to pay any costs which the child may be ordered to pay in relation to the proceedings, subject to any right the litigation friend may have to be repaid from the assets of the child; and
(e) which the litigation friend has verified by a statement of truth.

3.2 Paragraph 3.1 does not apply to the Official Solicitor, an officer of the Service or a Welsh family proceedings officer.

3.3 The court officer will send the certificate of suitability to one of the child's parents or guardians or, if there is no parent or guardian, to the person with whom the child resides or in whose care the child is.

3.4 The litigation friend must file the certificate of suitability at a time when the litigation friend first takes a step in the proceedings on behalf of the child.

Application for a court order appointing a litigation friend

4.1 An application for a court order appointing a litigation friend should be made in accordance with Part 18 and must be supported by evidence.

4.2 The court officer must serve the application notice on the persons referred to in paragraph 3.3.

4.3 The evidence in support must satisfy the court that the proposed litigation friend—

(a) consents to act;
(b) can fairly and competently conduct proceedings on behalf of the child;
(c) has no interest adverse to that of the child; and
(d) undertakes to pay any costs which the child may be ordered to pay in relation to the proceedings, subject to any right the litigation friend may have to be repaid from the assets of the child.

4.4 Paragraph 4.3(d) does not apply to the Official Solicitor, an officer of the Service or a Welsh family proceedings officer.

4.5 The proposed litigation friend may be one of the persons referred to in paragraph 3.3 where appropriate, or otherwise may be the Official Solicitor, an officer of the Service or a Welsh family proceedings officer. Where it is sought to appoint the Official Solicitor, an officer of the Service or a Welsh family proceedings officer, provision should be made for payment of that person's charges.

Change of litigation friend and prevention of person acting as litigation friend.

5.1 Where an application is made for an order under rule 16.12, the application must set out the reasons for seeking it and the application must be supported by evidence.

5.2 Subject to paragraph 4.4, if the order sought is substitution of a new litigation friend for an existing one, the evidence must satisfy the court of the matters set out in paragraph 4.3.

5.3 The court officer will serve the application notice on—

(a) the persons referred to in paragraph 3.3; and
(b) the litigation friend or person purporting to act as litigation friend.

PART 3 CHILDREN'S GUARDIAN APPOINTED UNDER RULE 16.3

How the children's guardian exercises duties – investigations and appointment of solicitor

6.1 The children's guardian must make such investigations as are necessary to carry out the children's guardian's duties and must, in particular—

(a) contact or seek to interview such persons as the children's guardian thinks appropriate or as the court directs; and
(b) obtain such professional assistance as is available which the children's guardian thinks appropriate or which the court directs be obtained.

6.2 The children's guardian must—

(a) appoint a solicitor for the child unless a solicitor has already been appointed;
(b) give such advice to the child as is appropriate having regard to that child's understanding; and

The Family Procedure Rules 2010

(c) where appropriate instruct the solicitor representing the child on all matters relevant to the interests of the child arising in the course of proceedings, including possibilities for appeal.

6.3 Where the children's guardian is authorised in the terms mentioned by and in accordance with section 15(1) of the Criminal Justice and Court Services Act 2000 or section 37(1) of the Children Act 2004 (right of officer of the Service or Welsh family proceedings officer to conduct litigation or exercise a right of audience), paragraph 6.2(a) will not apply if the children's guardian intends to have conduct of the proceedings on behalf of the child unless—

(a) the child wishes to instruct a solicitor direct; and
(b) the children's guardian or the court considers that the child is of sufficient understanding to do so.

6.4 Where rule 16.21 (Where the child instructs a solicitor or conducts proceedings on the child's own behalf) applies, the duties set out in paragraph 6.2(a) and (c) do not apply.

How the children's guardian exercises duties – attendance at court, advice to the court and reports

6.5 The children's guardian or the solicitor appointed under section 41(3) of the 1989 Act or in accordance with paragraph 6.2(a) must attend all directions hearings unless the court directs otherwise.

6.6 The children's guardian must advise the court on the following matters—

(a) whether the child is of sufficient understanding for any purpose including the child's refusal to submit to a medical or psychiatric examination or other assessment that the court has the power to require, direct or order;
(b) the wishes of the child in respect of any matter relevant to the proceedings including that child's attendance at court;
(c) the appropriate forum for the proceedings;
(d) the appropriate timing of the proceedings or any part of them;
(e) the options available to it in respect of the child and the suitability of each such option including what order should be made in determining the application; and
(f) any other matter on which the court seeks advice or on which the children's guardian considers that the court should be informed.

6.7 The advice given under paragraph 6.6 may, subject to any direction of the court, be given orally or in writing. If the advice is given orally, a note of it must be taken by the court or the court officer.

6.8 The children's guardian must—

(a) unless the court directs otherwise, file a written report advising on the interests of the child in accordance with the timetable set by the court; and
(b) in proceedings to which Part 14 applies, where practicable, notify any person the joining of whom as a party to those proceedings would be likely, in the opinion of the children's guardian, to safeguard the interests of the child, of the court's power to join that person as a party under rule 14.3 and must inform the court—
   (i) of any notification;
   (ii) of anyone whom the children's guardian attempted to notify under this paragraph but was unable to contact; and
   (iii) of anyone whom the children's guardian believes may wish to be joined to the proceedings.

(Part 18 sets out the procedure for making an application to be joined as a party in proceedings.)

How the children's guardian exercises duties – service of documents and inspection of records

6.9 The children's guardian must serve and accept service of documents on behalf of the child in accordance with rule 6.31 and, where the child has not himself been served and has sufficient understanding, advise the child of the contents of any document so served.

6.10 Where the children's guardian inspects records of the kinds referred to in—

(a) section 42 of the 1989 Act (right to have access to local authority records); or
(b) section 103 of the 2002 Act (right to have access to adoption agency records)

the children's guardian must bring all records and documents which may, in the opinion of the children's guardian, assist in the proper determination of the proceedings to the attention of—

(i) the court; and
(ii) unless the court directs otherwise, the other parties to the proceedings.

How the children's guardian exercises duties – communication of a court's decision to the child

6.11 The children's guardian must ensure that, in relation to a decision made by the court in the proceedings—

(a) if the children's guardian considers it appropriate to the age and understanding of the child, the child is notified of that decision; and
(b) if the child is notified of the decision, it is explained to the child in a manner appropriate to that child's age and understanding.

PART 4 APPOINTMENT OF CHILDREN'S GUARDIAN UNDER RULE 16.4

Section 1 – When a child should be made a party to proceedings

7.1 Making the child a party to the proceedings is a step that will be taken only in cases which involve an issue of significant difficulty and consequently will occur in only a minority of cases. Before taking the decision to make the child a party, consideration should be given to whether an alternative route might be preferable, such as asking an officer of the Service or a Welsh family proceedings officer to carry out further work or by making a referral to social services or, possibly, by obtaining expert evidence.

7.2 The decision to make the child a party will always be exclusively that of the court, made in the light of the facts and circumstances of the particular case. The following are offered, solely by way of guidance, as circumstances which may justify the making of such an order—

(a) where an officer of the Service or Welsh family proceedings officer has notified the court that in the opinion of that officer the child should be made a party;
(b) where the child has a standpoint or interest which is inconsistent with or incapable of being represented by any of the adult parties;
(c) where there is an intractable dispute over residence or contact, including where all contact has ceased, or where there is irrational but implacable hostility to contact or where the child may be suffering harm associated with the contact dispute;
(d) where the views and wishes of the child cannot be adequately met by a report to the court;
(e) where an older child is opposing a proposed course of action;
(f) where there are complex medical or mental health issues to be determined or there are other unusually complex issues that necessitate separate representation of the child;
(g) where there are international complications outside child abduction, in particular where it may be necessary for there to be discussions with overseas authorities or a foreign court;
(h) where there are serious allegations of physical, sexual or other abuse in relation to the child or there are allegations of domestic violence not capable of being resolved with the help of an officer of the Service or Welsh family proceedings officer;

The Family Procedure Rules 2010

(i) where the proceedings concern more than one child and the welfare of the children is in conflict or one child is in a particularly disadvantaged position;
(j) where there is a contested issue about scientific testing.

7.3 It must be recognised that separate representation of the child may result in a delay in the resolution of the proceedings. When deciding whether to direct that a child be made a party, the court will take into account the risk of delay or other facts adverse to the welfare of the child. The court's primary consideration will be the best interests of the child.

7.4 When a child is made a party and a children's guardian is to be appointed—

(a) consideration should first be given to appointing an officer of the Service or Welsh family proceedings officer. Before appointing an officer, the court will cause preliminary enquiries to be made of Cafcass or CAFCASS CYMRU. For the relevant procedure, reference should be made to the practice note issued by Cafcass in June 2006 and any modifications of that practice note.
(b) If Cafcass or CAFCASS CYMRU is unable to provide a children's guardian without delay, or if for some other reason the appointment of an officer of the Service of Welsh family proceedings officer is not appropriate, rule 16.24 makes further provision for the appointment of a children's guardian.

7.5 The court may, at the same time as deciding whether to join a child as a party, consider whether the proceedings should be transferred to another court taking into account the provisions of Part 3 of the Allocation and Transfer of Proceedings Order 2008.

Section 2 – Children's guardian appointed under rule 16.4

Duties of the children's guardian

7.6 It is the duty of a children's guardian fairly and competently to conduct proceedings on behalf of the child. The children's guardian must have no interest in the proceedings adverse to that of the child and all steps and decisions the children's guardian takes in the proceedings must be taken for the benefit of the child.

7.7 A children's guardian who is an officer of the Service or a Welsh family proceedings officer has, in addition, the duties set out in Part 3 of this Practice Direction and must exercise those duties as set out in that Part.

Becoming a children's guardian without a court order

7.8 In order to become a children's guardian without a court order the person who wishes to act as children's guardian must file a certificate of suitability—

(a) stating that the children's guardian consents to act;
(b) stating that the children's guardian knows or believes that the [applicant][respondent] is a child to whom rule 16.4 and Chapter 7 of Part 16 apply;
(c) stating that the children's guardian can fairly and competently conduct proceedings on behalf of the child and has no interest adverse to that of the child;
(d) undertaking to pay any costs which the child may be ordered to pay in relation to the proceedings, subject to any right the children's guardian may have to be repaid from the assets of the child; and
(e) which the children's guardian has verified by a statement of truth.

7.9 Paragraph 7.8 does not apply to the Official Solicitor, an officer of the Service or a Welsh family proceedings officer.

7.10 The court officer will send the certificate of suitability to one of the child's parents or guardians or, if there is no parent or guardian, to the person with whom the child resides or in whose care the child is.

7.11 The children's guardian must file either the certificate of suitability at a time when the children's guardian first takes a step in the proceedings on behalf of the child.

Application for a court order appointing a children's guardian

7.12 An application for a court order appointing a children's guardian should be made in accordance with Part 18 and must be supported by evidence.

7.13 The court officer must serve the application notice on the persons referred to in paragraph 7.10.

7.14 The evidence in support must satisfy the court that the proposed children's guardian—

(a) consents to act;
(b) can fairly and competently conduct proceedings on behalf of the child;
(c) has no interest adverse to that of the child; and
(d) undertakes to pay any costs which the child may be ordered to pay in relation to the proceedings, subject to any right the children's guardian may have to be repaid from the assets of the child.

7.15 Paragraph 7.14 does not apply to the Official Solicitor, an officer of the Service or a Welsh family proceedings officer.

7.16 The proposed children's guardian may be one of the persons referred to in paragraph 7.10 where appropriate, or otherwise may be the Official Solicitor, an officer of the Service or a Welsh family proceedings officer. Where it is sought to appoint the Official Solicitor, an officer of the Service or a Welsh family proceedings officer, provision should be made for payment of that person's charges.

Change of children's guardian and prevention of person acting as children's guardian.

7.17 Where an application is made for an order under rule 16.25, the application must set out the reasons for seeking it and must be supported by evidence.

7.18 Subject to paragraph 7.15, if the order sought is substitution of a new children's guardian for an existing one, the evidence must satisfy the court of the matters set out in paragraph 7.14.

7.19 The court officer will serve the application notice on—

(a) the persons referred to in paragraph 7.10; and
(b) the children's guardian or person purporting to act as children's guardian.

PART 5 REPORTING OFFICER

How the reporting officer exercises duties

8.1 The reporting officer must—

(a) ensure so far as reasonably practicable that the parent or guardian is—
  (i) giving consent unconditionally to the placing of the child for adoption or to the making of an adoption order (as defined in section 46 of the Adoption and Children Act 2002) or a section 84 order; and
  (ii) with full understanding of what is involved;
(b) investigate all the circumstances relevant to a parent's or guardian's consent; and
(c) on completing the investigations the reporting officer must—
  (i) make a report in writing to the court in accordance with the timetable set by the court, drawing attention to any matters which, in the opinion of the reporting officer, may be of assistance to the court in considering the application; or
  (ii) make an interim report to the court if a parent or guardian of the child is unwilling to consent to the placing of the child for adoption or to the making of an adoption order or section 84 order.

8.2 On receipt of an interim report under paragraph 8.1(1)(c)(ii) a court officer must inform the applicant that a parent or guardian of the child is unwilling to consent to the placing of the child for adoption or to the making of an adoption order or section 84 order.

8.3 The reporting officer may at any time before the final hearing make an interim

The Family Procedure Rules 2010

report to the court if the reporting officer considers it necessary and ask the court for directions.

8.4 The reporting officer must attend hearings as directed by the court.

PART 6 CHILDREN AND FAMILY REPORTER AND WELFARE OFFICER

How the children and family reporter or welfare officer exercises powers and duties

9.1 In this Part, the person preparing the welfare report in accordance with rule 16.33 is called "the officer".

9.2 The officer must make such investigations as may be necessary to perform the officer's powers and duties and must, in particular—

(a) contact or seek to interview such persons as appear appropriate or as the court directs; and
(b) obtain such professional assistance as is available which the children and family reporter thinks appropriate or which the court directs be obtained.

9.3 The officer must—

(a) notify the child of such contents of the report (if any) as the officer considers appropriate to the age and understanding of the child, including any reference to the child's own views on the application and the recommendation; and
(b) if the child is notified of any contents of the report, explain them to the child in a manner appropriate to the child's age and understanding.

9.4 The officer must—

(a) attend hearings as directed by the court;
(b) advise the court of the child's wishes and feelings;
(c) advise the court if the officer considers that the joining of a person as a party to the proceedings would be likely to safeguard the interests of the child;
(d) consider whether it is in the best interests of the child for the child to be made a party to the proceedings, and if so, notify the court of that opinion together with the reasons for that opinion; and
(e) where the court has directed that a written report be made—
　(i) file the report; and
　(ii) serve a copy on the other parties and on any children's guardian,

in accordance with the timetable set by the court.

PART 7 PARENTAL ORDER REPORTER

How the parental order reporter exercises duties – investigations and reports

10.1 The parental order reporter must make such investigations as are necessary to carry out the parental order reporter's duties and must, in particular—

(a) contact or seek to interview such persons as the parental order reporter thinks appropriate or as the court directs; and
(b) obtain such professional assistance as is available which the parental order reporter thinks appropriate or which the court directs be obtained.

How the parental order reporter exercises duties – attendance at court, advice to the court and reports

10.2 The parental order reporter must attend all directions hearings unless the court directs otherwise.

10.3 The parental order reporter must advise the court on the following matters—

(a) the appropriate forum for the proceedings;

(b) the appropriate timing of the proceedings or any part of them;
(c) the options available to it in respect of the child and the suitability of each such option including what order should be made in determining the application; and
(d) any other matter on which the court seeks advice or on which the parental order reporter considers that the court should be informed.

10.4 The advice given under paragraph 10.3 may, subject to any direction of the court, be given orally or in writing. If the advice is given orally, a note of it must be taken by the court or the court officer.

10.5 The parental order reporter must—

(a) unless the court directs otherwise, file a written report advising on the interests of the child in accordance with the timetable set by the court; and
(b) where practicable, notify any person the joining of whom as a party to those proceedings would be likely, in the opinion of the parental order reporter, to safeguard the interests of the child, of the court's power to join that person as a party under rule 13.3 and must inform the court—
  (i) of any notification;
  (ii) of anyone whom the parental order reporter attempted to notify under this paragraph but was unable to contact; and
  (iii) of anyone whom the parental order reporter believes may wish to be joined to the proceedings.

(Part 18 sets out the procedure for making an application to be joined as a party in proceedings.)

PART 8 OFFICERS OF THE SERVICE, WELSH FAMILY PROCEEDINGS OFFICERS AND LOCAL AUTHORITY OFFICERS: FURTHER DUTIES

How officers of the Service, Welsh family proceedings officers and local authority officers exercise certain further duties

11.1 This Part applies when an officer of the Service, a Welsh family proceedings officer or a local authority officer is acting under a duty referred to in rule 16.38(1). In this Part, the person acting under a duty referred to in rule 16.38(1) is referred to as "the officer".

11.2 The officer must make such investigations as may be necessary to perform the officer's duties and must, in particular—

(a) contact or seek to interview such persons as the officer thinks appropriate or as the court directs; and
(b) obtain such professional assistance as the officer thinks appropriate or which the court directs.

11.3 The officer must—

(a) notify the child of such (if any) of the contents of any report or risk assessment as the officer considers appropriate to the age and understanding of the child;
(b) if the child is notified of any contents of a report or risk assessment, explain them to the child in a manner appropriate to the child's age and understanding;
(c) consider whether to recommend in any report or risk assessment that the court lists a hearing for the purposes of considering the report or risk assessment;
(d) consider whether it is in the best interests of the child for the child to be made a party to the proceedings, and, if so, notify the court of that opinion together with the reasons for that opinion.

11.4 When making a risk assessment, the officer must, if of the opinion that the court should exercise its discretion under rule 12.34(2), state in the risk assessment—

(a) the way in which the officer considers the court should exercise its discretion (including the officer's view on the length of any suggested delay in service); and
(b) the officer's reasons for that reaching that view.

11.5 The officer must file any report or risk assessment with the court —

The Family Procedure Rules 2010

(a) at or by the time directed by the court;
(b) in the absence of any direction, at least 14 days before a relevant hearing; or
(c) where there has been no direction from the court and there is no relevant hearing listed, as soon as possible following the completion of the report or risk assessment.

11.6 In paragraph 11.5, a hearing is relevant if the court officer has given the officer notice that a report prepared by the officer is to be considered at it.

11.7 A copy of any report prepared as a result of acting under a duty referred to in rule 16.38(1)(a)(i) to (vi) or (b) (but not any risk assessment) must, as soon as practicable, be served by the officer on the parties.

(Rule 12.34 makes provision for the service of risk assessments.)

PART 17

STATEMENTS OF TRUTH

17.1. Interpretation
In this Part "statement of case" has the meaning given to it in Part 4 except that a statement of case does not include an application for a matrimonial order or a civil partnership order or an answer to such an application.
(Rule 4.1 defines "statement of case" for the purposes of Part 4.)

17.2.— Documents to be verified by a statement of truth
(1) Subject to paragraph (9), the following documents must be verified by a statement of truth—
    (a) a statement of case;
    (b) a witness statement;
    (c) an acknowledgement of service in a claim begun by the Part 19 procedure;
    (d) a certificate of service;
    (e) a statement of arrangements for children;
    (f) a statement of information filed under rule 9.26(1)(b); and
    (g) any other document where a rule or practice direction requires it.

(2) Where a statement of case is amended, the amendments must be verified by a statement of truth unless the court orders otherwise.

(3) If an applicant wishes to rely on matters set out in the application form or application notice as evidence, the application form or notice must be verified by a statement of truth.

(4) Subject to paragraph (5), a statement of truth is a statement that—
    (a) the party putting forward the document;
    (b) in the case of a witness statement, the maker of the witness statement; or
    (c) in the case of a certificate of service, the person who signs the certificate,
believes the facts stated in the document are true.

(5) If a party is conducting proceedings with a litigation friend, the statement of truth in—
    (a) a statement of case; or
    (b) an application notice,
is a statement that the litigation friend believes the facts stated in the document being verified are true.

(6) The statement of truth must be signed by—
    (a) in the case of a statement of case—
        (i) the party or litigation friend; or
        (ii) the legal representative on behalf of the party or litigation friend; and
    (b) in the case of a witness statement or statement of arrangements for children, the maker of the statement.

(7) A statement of truth, which is not contained in the document which it verifies, must clearly identify that document.

(8) A statement of truth in a statement of case may be made by—
- (a) a person who is not a party; or
- (b) by two parties jointly,

where this is permitted by a practice direction.

(9) An application that does not contain a statement of facts need not be verified by a statement of truth.

(Practice Direction 17A sets out the form of statement of truth.)

17.3.— Failure to verify a statement of case

(1) If a party fails to verify that party's statement of case by a statement of truth—
- (a) the statement of case shall remain effective unless struck out; but
- (b) the party may not rely on the statement of case as evidence of any of the matters set out in it.

(2) The court may strike out(GL) a statement of case which is not verified by a statement of truth.

(3) Any party may apply for an order under paragraph (2).

17.4. Failure to verify a witness statement

If the maker of a witness statement fails to verify the witness statement by a statement of truth, the court may direct that it shall not be admissible as evidence.

17.5.— Power of the court to require a document to be verified

(1) The court may order a person who has failed to verify a document in accordance with rule 17.2 to verify the document.

(2) Any party may apply for an order under paragraph (1).

17.6.— False statements

(1) Proceedings for contempt of court may be brought against a person who makes, or causes to be made, a false statement in a document verified by a statement of truth without an honest belief in its truth.

(2) Proceedings under this rule may be brought only—
- (a) by the Attorney General; or
- (b) with the permission of the court.

(3) This rule does not apply to proceedings in a magistrates' court.

Part 17

Part 17 is supplemented by PD17A.

Part 17 introduces and makes provision for a new method of verifying documents, a statement of truth.

The following must be verified by a statement of truth (r 17.2(1)):

- A statement of case (the whole or part of an application form or answer, but not including an application for a matrimonial or civil partnership order or an answer to it: rr 4.1, 17.1).
- A witness statement.
- An acknowledgement of service in a claim begun by the Part 19 procedure.
- A certificate of service.
- A statement of arrangements for children.
- A statement of information filed under r 9.26(1)(b).
- Any other document where a rule or PD requires it (eg PD9A, para 5.2, as noted above).

The Family Procedure Rules 2010

The Practice Direction provides at para 1.6 that where the form to be used includes a *jurat* for the content to be verified by an affidavit, then a statement of truth is not required in addition.

The form of the statement of truth verifying a statement of case or application notice is set out in PD17A, para 2.1 and the form for a witness statement in para 2.2.

In the case of a statement of case, not a witness statement or statement of arrangements for children, the statement of truth may be signed by the legal representative (r 17.2(6)). The practice direction sets out that where a legal representative has signed a statement of truth that will be taken by the court as a statement that he or she has authority to sign, that he or she has explained to the client that he or she is confirming the client's belief that the facts stated are true, and that he or she has informed the client of the possible consequences if it should appear that the client did not have an honest belief in those facts.

Rule 17.6 provides that proceedings may be brought for contempt of court against a person who makes a false statement in a document verified by a statement of truth without an honest belief in its truth. Such proceedings may only be brought by the Attorney General, or with the permission of the court. The process of referring the matter to the Attorney General or deciding to give such permission is detailed in paragraph 6 of the Practice Direction.

PRACTICE DIRECTION 17A – STATEMENTS OF TRUTH

This Practice Direction supplements FPR Part 17

DOCUMENTS TO BE VERIFIED BY A STATEMENT OF TRUTH

1.1 Rule 17.2 sets out the documents which must be verified by a statement of truth.

1.2 If an applicant wishes to rely on matters set out in his application notice as evidence, the application notice must be verified by a statement of truth.

1.3 An expert's report should also be verified by a statement of truth. For the form of the statement of truth verifying an expert's report (which differs from that set out below), see the practice direction which supplements Part 25.

1.4 In addition, the following documents must be verified by a statement of truth—

(a) an application notice for—
    (i) a third party debt order (CPR Part 72 as modified by rule 33.24);
    (ii) a hardship payment order (CPR Part 72 as modified by rule 33.24); or
    (iii) a charging order (CPR Part 73 as modified by rule 33.25); and
(b) a notice of objections to an account being taken by the court, unless verified by an affidavit or witness statement.

1.5 The statement of truth may be contained in the document it verifies or it may be in a separate document served subsequently, in which case it must identify the document to which it relates.

1.6 Where the form to be used includes a jurat for the content to be verified by an affidavit, then a statement of truth is not required in addition.

1.7 In this Practice Direction, "statement of case" has the meaning given to it by rule 17.1.

FORM OF THE STATEMENT OF TRUTH

2.1 The form of the statement of truth verifying a statement of case or an application notice should be as follows:

"[I believe] [the *(applicant or as may be)* believes] that the facts stated in this *[name document being verified]* are true."

2.2 The form of the statement of truth verifying a witness statement should be as follows:

"I believe that the facts stated in this witness statement are true."

2.3 Where the statement of truth is contained in a separate document, the document containing the statement of truth must be headed with the title of and court reference for the proceedings. The document being verified should be identified in the statement of truth as follows—

(a) application form: "the application form issued on [*date*]";
(b) statement of case: "the (application or answer as may be) served on [*name of party*] on [*date*]";
(c) application notice: "the application notice issued on [*date*] for [*set out the remedy sought*]";
(d) witness statement: "the witness statement filed on [*date*] or served on [*party*] on [*date*]".

WHO MAY SIGN THE STATEMENT OF TRUTH

3.1 In a statement of case or an application notice, the statement of truth must be signed by—

(a) the party or his litigation friend; or
(b) the legal representative of the party or litigation friend.

3.2 A statement of truth verifying a witness statement must be signed by the witness.

3.3 A statement of truth verifying a notice of objections to an account must be signed by the objecting party or his or her legal representative.

3.4 Where a document is to be verified on behalf of a company or corporation, subject to paragraph 3.7 below, the statement of truth must be signed by a person holding a senior position in the company or corporation. That person must state the office or position he or she holds.

3.5 Each of the following persons is a person holding a senior position:

(a) in respect of a registered company or corporation, a director, the treasurer, secretary, chief executive, manager or other officer of the company or corporation; and
(b) in respect of a corporation which is not a registered company, in addition to those persons set out in (a), the major, chairman, president, chief executive of a local authority or town clerk or other similar officer of the corporation.

3.6 Where the document is to be verified on behalf of a partnership, those who may sign the statement of truth are—

(a) any of the partners; or
(b) a person having the management or control of the partnership business.

3.7 Where a party is legally represented, the legal representative may sign the statement of truth on his or her behalf. The statement signed by the legal representative will refer to the client's belief, not his or her own. In signing he or she must state the capacity in which he or she signs and the name of his or her firm where appropriate.

3.8 Where a legal representative has signed a statement of truth, his or her signature will be taken by the court as his or her statement—

(a) that the client on whose behalf he or she has signed had authorised him or her to do so;

(b) that before signing he or she had explained to the client that in signing the statement of truth he or she would be confirming the client's belief that the facts stated in the document were true; and
(c) that before signing he or she had informed the client of the possible consequences to the client if it should subsequently appear that the client did not have an honest belief in the truth of those facts (see rule 17.6).

3.9 A legal representative who signs a statement of truth must print his or her full name clearly beneath his or her signature.

3.10 The individual who signs a statement of truth must sign in his or her own name and not that of his or her firm or employer.

3.11 The following are examples of the possible application of this practice direction describing who may sign a statement of truth verifying statements in documents other than a witness statement. These are only examples and not an indication of how a court might apply the practice direction to a specific situation.

Managing Agent

An agent who manages property or investments for the party cannot sign a statement of truth. It must be signed by the party or by the legal representative of the party.

Trusts

Where some or all of the trustees comprise a single party one, some or all of the trustees comprising the party may sign a statement of truth. The legal representative of the trustees may sign it.

Companies

Paragraphs 3.4 and 3.5 apply. The word "manager" will be construed in the context of the phrase "a person holding a senior position" which it is used to define. The court will consider the size of the company and the importance and nature of the proceedings. It would expect the manager signing the statement of truth to to have personal knowledge of the content of the document or to be responsible for those who have that knowledge of the content. A small company may not have a manager, apart from the directors, who holds a senior position. A large company will have many such managers. In a large company with specialist claims, insurance or legal departments the statement may be signed by the manager of such a department if he or she is responsible for handling the claim or managing the staff handling it.

INABILITY OF PERSONS TO READ OR SIGN DOCUMENTS TO BE VERIFIED BY A STATEMENT OF TRUTH

4.1 Where a document containing a statement of truth is to be signed by a person who is unable to read or sign the document, it must contain a certificate made by an authorised person.

4.2 An authorised person is a person able to administer oaths and take affidavits but need not be independent of the parties or their representatives.

4.3 The authorised person must certify—

(a) that the document has been read to the person signing it;
(b) that the person appeared to understand it and approved its content as accurate;
(c) that the declaration of truth has been read to that person;
(d) that that person appeared to understand the declaration and the consequences of making a false declaration; and
(e) that that person signed or made his mark in the presence of the authorised person.

4.4 The form of the certificate is set out at the Annex to this Practice Direction.

CONSEQUENCES OF FAILURE TO VERIFY

5.1 If a statement of case is not verified by a statement of truth, the statement of case will remain effective unless it is struck out, but a party may not rely on the contents of a statement of case as evidence until it has been verified by a statement of truth.

5.2 Any party may apply to the court for an order that unless within such period as the court may specify the statement of case is verified by the service of a statement of truth, the statement of case will be struck out.

5.3 The usual order for the costs of an application referred to in paragraph 5.2 will be that the costs be paid by the party who had failed to verify, in any event and immediately.

PENALTY

6.1 Rule 17.6 sets out the consequences of verifying a statement of case containing a false statement without an honest belief in its truth. Where a party alleges that a statement of truth is false, the party shall refer that allegation to the court dealing with the proceedings in which the statement of truth has been made.

6.2 On a reference under paragraph 6.1 the court may—

(a) exercise any of its powers under the FPR;
(b) initiate steps to consider if there is a contempt of court and, where there is, to punish it;
(Order 52 of the Rules of the Supreme Court and Order 29 of the County Court Rules (Schedules 1 and 2 to the CPR) make provision where committal to prison is a possibility if contempt is proved.)
(c) direct the party making the allegation to refer the matter to the Attorney General with a request to him or her to consider whether he or she wishes to bring proceedings for contempt of court.

6.3 A request to the Attorney General must be made in writing and sent to the Attorney General's Office at 20 Victoria Street, London, SW1H 0NF. The request must be accompanied by a copy of the order directing that the matter be referred to the Attorney General and must—

(a) identify the statement said to be false; and
(b) explain—
    (i) why it is false; and
    (ii) why the maker knew it to be false at the time it was made; and
(c) explain why contempt proceedings would be appropriate in the light of the overriding objective in Part 1 of the FPR.

6.4 The practice of the Attorney General is to prefer an application that comes from the court, and so has received preliminary consideration by a judge or district judge, to one made direct to him or her by a party to the proceedings in which the alleged contempt occurred without prior consideration by the court. An application to the Attorney General is not a way of appealing against, or reviewing, the decision of the judge or district judge.

6.5 Where a party makes an application to the court for permission for that party to commence proceedings for contempt of court, it must be supported by written evidence containing the information specified in paragraph 6.3 and the result of the application to the Attorney General made by the applicant.

6.6 The FPR do not change the law of contempt or introduce new categories of contempt. A person applying to commence such proceedings should consider whether the incident complained of does amount to contempt of court and whether such proceedings would further the overriding objective in Part 1 of the FPR.

ANNEX

Certificate to be used where a person is unable to read or sign a document to be verified by a statement of truth

I certify that I [name and address of authorised person] have read the contents of this document and the declaration of truth to the person signing the document [if there are

The Family Procedure Rules 2010

exhibits, add "and explained the nature and effect of the exhibits referred to in it"] who appeared to understand (a) the document and approved its content as accurate and (b) the declaration of truth and the consequences of making a false declaration, and made his or her mark in my presence.

PART 18

PROCEDURE FOR OTHER APPLICATIONS IN PROCEEDINGS

18.1.— Types of application for which Part 18 procedure may be followed
(1) The Part 18 procedure is the procedure set out in this Part.
(2) An applicant may use the Part 18 procedure if the application is made—
   (a) in the course of existing proceedings;
   (b) to start proceedings except where some other Part of these rules prescribes the procedure to start proceedings; or
   (c) in connection with proceedings which have been concluded.
(3) Paragraph (2) does not apply—
   (a) to applications where any other rule in any other Part of these rules sets out the procedure for that type of application;
   (b) if a practice direction provides that the Part 18 procedure may not be used in relation to the type of application in question.

18.2. Applications for permission to start proceedings
An application for permission to start proceedings must be made to the court where the proceedings will be started if permission is granted.

18.3.— Respondents to applications under this Part
(1) The following persons are to be respondents to an application under this Part—
   (a) where there are existing proceedings or the proceedings have been concluded—
      (i) the parties to those proceedings; and
      (ii) if the proceedings are proceedings under Part 11, the person who is the subject of those proceedings;
   (b) where there are no existing proceedings—
      (i) if notice has been given under section 44 of the 2002 Act (notice of intention to adopt or apply for an order under section 84 of that Act), the local authority to whom notice has been given; and
      (ii) if an application is made for permission to apply for an order in proceedings, any person who will be a party to the proceedings brought if permission is granted; and
   (c) any other person as the court may direct.

18.4.— Application notice to be filed
(1) Subject to paragraph (2), the applicant must file an application notice.
(2) An applicant may make an application without filing an application notice if—
   (a) this is permitted by a rule or practice direction; or
   (b) the court dispenses with the requirement for an application notice.

18.5.— Notice of an application
(1) Subject to paragraph (2), a copy of the application notice must be served on—
   (a) each respondent;
   (b) in relation to proceedings under Part 11, the person who is, or, in the case of an application to start proceedings, it is intended will be, the subject of the proceedings; and
   (c) in relation to proceedings under Parts 12 and 14, the children's guardian (if any).

(2) An application may be made without serving a copy of the application notice if this is permitted by—
- (a) a rule;
- (b) a practice direction; or
- (c) the court.

(Rule 18.8 deals with service of a copy of the application notice.)

18.6. Time when an application is made

When an application must be made within a specified time, it is so made if the court receives the application notice within that time.

18.7.— What an application notice must include

(1) An application notice must state—
- (a) what order the applicant is seeking; and
- (b) briefly, why the applicant is seeking the order.

(2) A draft of the order sought must be attached to the application notice.

(Part 17 requires an application notice to be verified by a statement of truth if the applicant wishes to rely on matters set out in his application as evidence.)

18.8.— Service of a copy of an application notice

(1) Subject to rule 2.4, a copy of the application notice must be served in accordance with the provisions of Part 6—
- (a) as soon as practicable after it is filed; and
- (b) in any event—
  - (i) where the application is for an interim order under rule 9.7 at least 14 days; and
  - (ii) in any other case, at least 7 days; before the court is to deal with the application.

(2) The applicant must, when filing the application notice, file a copy of any written evidence in support.

(3) If a copy of an application notice is served by a court officer it must be accompanied by—
- (a) a notice of the date and place where the application will be heard;
- (b) a copy of any witness statement in support; and
- (c) a copy of the draft order which the applicant has attached to the application.

(4) If—
- (a) an application notice is served; but
- (b) the period of notice is shorter than the period required by these rules or a practice direction,

the court may direct that, in the circumstances of the case, sufficient notice has been given and hear the application.

(5) This rule does not require written evidence—
- (a) to be filed if it has already been filed; or
- (b) to be served on a party on whom it has already been served.

18.9.— Applications which may be dealt with without a hearing

(1) The court may deal with an application without a hearing if—
- (a) the court does not consider that a hearing would be appropriate; or
- (b) the parties agree as to the terms of the order sought or the parties agree that the court should dispose of the application without a hearing and the court does not consider that a hearing would be appropriate.

(2) Where—
- (a) an application is made for permission to make an application in proceedings under the 1989 Act; and
- (b) the court refuses the application without a hearing in accordance with paragraph (1)(a),

The Family Procedure Rules 2010

the court must, at the request of the applicant, re-list the application and fix a date for a hearing.

(3) Paragraph (2) does not apply to magistrates' courts.

18.10.— Service of application notice following court order where application made without notice

(1) This rule applies where the court has disposed of an application which it permitted to be made without service of a copy of the application notice.

(2) Where the court makes an order, whether granting or dismissing the application, a copy of the application notice and any evidence in support must unless the court orders otherwise, be served with the order on—
   (a) all the parties in proceedings; and
   (b) in relation to proceedings under Part 11, the person who is, or, in the case of an application to start proceedings, it is intended will be, the subject of the proceedings.

(3) The order must contain a statement of the right to make an application to set aside$^{(GL)}$ or vary the order under rule 18.11.

18.11.— Application to set aside or vary order made without notice

(1) A person who was not served with a copy of the application notice before an order was made under rule 18.10 may apply to have the order set aside$^{(GL)}$ or varied.

(2) An application under this rule must be made within 7 days beginning with the date on which the order was served on the person making the application.

18.12.— Power of the court to proceed in the absence of a party

(1) Where the applicant or any respondent fails to attend the hearing of an application, the court may proceed in the absence of that person.

(2) Where—
   (a) the applicant or any respondent fails to attend the hearing of an application; and
   (b) the court makes an order at the hearing,
the court may, on application or of its own initiative, re-list the application.

(3) Paragraph (2) does not apply to magistrates' courts.

18.13. Dismissal of totally without merit applications

If the High Court or a county court dismisses an application (including an application for permission to appeal) and it considers that the application is totally without merit—
   (a) the court's order must record that fact; and
   (b) the court must at the same time consider whether it is appropriate to make a civil restraint order.

PART 18 COMMENTARY

Part 18 is supplemented by PD18A.

Part 18 sets out the procedure where a party wishes to make an application in the course of proceedings or to start proceedings where no other procedure is prescribed or in connection with proceedings which have been concluded (r 18.1), or where permission to make an application is required (r 18.2). This procedure replaces the use of the summons as a means of making applications in the course of proceedings.

An application is generally to be made by application notice, save where an application without notice is permitted by the rules, or the court dispenses with the need for an application notice (r 18.4).

The application notice must state what order is being sought and why, and a draft of the order sought must be attached to the notice (r 18.7).

FPR 2010, Practice Direction 18A

Except where the application is made without notice, the application, together with any written evidence in support, must be served on the other party at least 7 days (or in the case of an interim order in financial remedy proceedings 14 days) before the hearing (r 18.8(1, 2)).

There is provision for the court to deal with an application without a hearing if the court does not consider that a hearing would be appropriate, or the parties agree the terms of the order and the parties agree that there should not be a hearing and the court does not consider that a hearing would be appropriate (r 18.9).

The practice direction provides at paragraph 8 for telephone hearings.

Where the court has disposed of an application without it having been served, provision is made for service of the application together with the order (r 18.10), and for a person who was not served with the application before the order was made, to apply within seven days to set the order aside (r 18.10).

Forms relevant to Part 18 are: C2 – Application for:

(a) permission to start proceedings; and
(b) an order or directions in existing proceedings, to be joined or cease to be joined in existing proceedings under the Children Act 1989, D11 – Application Notice, FP2 – Application notice Part 18 of the Family Procedure Rules 2010.

PRACTICE DIRECTION 18A – OTHER APPLICATIONS IN PROCEEDINGS

This Practice Direction supplements FPR Part 18

APPLICATION OF PART 18

1.1 Part 18 makes general provision for a procedure for making applications. All applications for the court's permission should be made under this Part, with the exception of applications for permission for which specific provision is made in other Parts of the FPR, in which case the application should be made under the specific provision. Examples of where specific provision has been made in another Part of the FPR for applications for permission are rule 11.3 (Permission to apply for a forced marriage protection order) and rule 30.3 (Permission to appeal).

REFERENCE TO A JUDGE

2.1 In the High Court or a county court a district judge may refer to a judge any matter which the district judge thinks should properly be decided by a judge, and the judge may either dispose of the matter or refer it back to the district judge.

ADDITIONAL REQUIREMENTS IN RELATION TO APPLICATION NOTICES

3.1 In addition to the requirements set out in rule 18.7, the following requirements apply to the applications to which the respective paragraph refers.

3.2 An application notice must be signed and include—

(a) the title of the case (if available);
(b) the reference number of the case (if available);
(c) the full name of the applicant;

(d) where the applicant is not already a party, the applicant's address for service, including a postcode. Postcode information may be obtained from www.royalmail.com or the Royal Mail Address Management Guide; and

(e) either a request for a hearing or a request that the application be dealt with without a hearing.

3.3 An application notice relating to an application under section 42(6) of the Adoption and Children Act 2002 (permission to apply for an adoption order) must include—

(a) the child's name, sex, date of birth and nationality;
(b) in relation to each of the child's parents or guardians, their name, address and nationality;
(c) the length of time that the child has had his or her home with the applicant;
(d) the reason why the child has had his or her home with the applicant;
(e) details of any local authority or adoption agency involved in placing the child in the applicant's home; and
(f) if there are or have been other court proceedings relating to the child, the nature of those proceedings, the name of the court in which they are being or have been dealt with, the date and type of any order made and, if the proceedings are still ongoing, the date of the next hearing.

3.4 An application notice relating to an application in the High Court by a local authority for permission under section 100(3) of the Children Act 1989 must include a draft of the application form.

3.5 Where permission is required to take any step under the Children Act 1989 (for example an application to be joined as a party to the proceedings) the application notice must include a draft of the application for the making of which permission is sought together with sufficient copies for one to be served on each respondent.

3.6 In an application for permission to bring proceedings under Schedule 1 of the Children Act 1989, the draft application for the making of which permission is sought must be accompanied by a statement setting out the financial details which the person seeking permission believes to be relevant to the request and contain a declaration that it is true to the maker's best knowledge and belief, together with sufficient copies for one to be served on each respondent.

3.7 The provisions in Schedule 1 which require an application for permission to bring proceedings are—

(a) paragraph 7(2) – permission is required to make an application for variation of a secured periodical payments order after the death of the parent liable to make the payments if a period of 6 months has passed from the date on which representation in regard to that parent's estate is first taken out; and
(b) paragraph 11(3) – permission is required to make an application to alter a maintenance agreement following the death of one of the parties if a period of 6 months has passed beginning with the day on which representation in regard to the estate of the deceased is first taken out.

OTHER PROVISIONS IN RELATION TO APPLICATION NOTICES.

4.1 On receipt of an application notice containing a request for a hearing, unless the court considers that the application is suitable for consideration without a hearing, the court officer will, if serving a copy of the application notice, notify the applicant of the time and date fixed for the hearing of the application.

4.2 On receipt of an application notice containing a request that the application be dealt with without a hearing, the court will decide whether the application is suitable for consideration without a hearing.

4.3 Where the court—

(a) considers that the application is suitable for consideration without a hearing; but
(b) is not satisfied that it has sufficient material to decide the application immediately,

it may give directions for the filing of evidence and will inform the applicant and the respondent(s) of its decision. (Rule 18.11 enables a party to apply for an order made without notice to be set aside or varied.)

4.4 Where the court does not consider that the application is suitable for consideration without a hearing—

(a) it may give directions as to the filing of evidence; and
(b) the court officer will notify the applicant and the respondent of the time, date and place for the hearing of the application and any directions given.

4.5 In the High Court or a county court if the application is intended to be made to a judge, the application notice should so state. In that case, paragraphs 4.2, 4.3 and 4.4 will apply as though references to the court were references to a judge.

4.6 Every application should be made as soon as it becomes apparent that it is necessary or desirable to make it.

4.7 Applications should, wherever possible, be made so that they are considered at any directions hearing or other hearing for which a date has been fixed or for which a date is about to be fixed.

4.8 The parties must anticipate that at any hearing (including any directions hearing) the court may wish to review the conduct of the case as a whole and give any necessary directions. They should be ready to assist the court in doing so and to answer questions the court may ask for this purpose.

4.9 Where a date for a hearing has been fixed, a party who wishes to make an application at that hearing but does not have sufficient time to file an application notice should as soon as possible inform the court (if possible in writing) and, if possible, the other parties of the nature of the application and the reason for it. That party should then make the application orally at the hearing.

APPLICATIONS WITHOUT SERVICE OF APPLICATION NOTICE

5.1 An application may be made without service of an application notice only—

(a) where there is exceptional urgency;
(b) where the overriding objective is best furthered by doing so;
(c) by consent of all parties;
(d) with the permission of the court;
(e) where paragraph 4.9 applies; or
(f) where a court order, rule or practice direction permits.

GIVING NOTICE OF AN APPLICATION

6.1 Unless the court otherwise directs or paragraph 5.1 of this practice direction applies, the application notice must be served as soon as practicable after it has been issued and, if there is to be a hearing, at least 7 days before the hearing date.

6.2 Where an application notice should be served but there is not sufficient time to do so, informal notification of the application should be given unless the circumstances of the application require no notice of the application to be given.

PRE-ACTION APPLICATIONS

7.1 All applications made before proceedings are commenced should be made under this Part.

TELEPHONE HEARINGS

8.1 The court may direct that an application be dealt with by a telephone hearing.

8.2 The applicant should, if seeking a direction under paragraph 8.1, indicate this on the application notice. Where the applicant has not indicated such an intention but nevertheless wishes to seek a direction the request should be made as early as possible.

8.3 A direction under paragraph 8.1 will not normally be made unless every party

The Family Procedure Rules 2010

entitled to be given notice of the application and to be heard at the hearing has consented to the direction.

8.4 No representative of a party to an application being heard by telephone may attend the court in person while the application is being heard unless the other party to the application has agreed that the representative may do so.

8.5 If an application is to be heard by telephone the following directions will apply, subject to any direction to the contrary—

(a) the applicant's legal representative is responsible for arranging the telephone conference for precisely the time fixed by the court. The telecommunications provider used must be one of the approved panel of service providers (see HMCS website at www.hmcourts-service.gov.uk);
(b) the applicant's legal representative must tell the operator the telephone numbers of all those participating in the conference call and the sequence in which they are to be called;
(c) it is the responsibility of the applicant's legal representative to ascertain from all the other parties whether they have instructed counsel and, if so the identity of counsel, and whether the legal representative and counsel will be on the same or different telephone numbers;
(d) the sequence in which those involved are to be called will be—
    (i) the applicant's legal representative and (if on a different number) his counsel;
    (ii) the legal representative (and counsel) for all other parties; and
    (iii) the judge or justices, as the case may be;
(e) each speaker is to remain on the line after being called by the operator setting up the conference call. The call may be 2 or 3 minutes before the time fixed for the application;
(f) when the judge has or justices have been connected the applicant's legal representative (or counsel) will introduce the parties in the usual way;
(g) if the use of a "speakerphone" by any party causes the court or any other party any difficulty in hearing what is said the judge or justices may require that party to use a hand held telephone;
(h) the telephone charges debited to the account of the party initiating the conference call will be treated as part of the costs of the application.

VIDEO CONFERENCING

9.1 Where the parties to a matter wish to use video conferencing facilities, and those facilities are available in the relevant court, the parties should apply to the court for directions. (Practice Direction 22A provides guidance on the use of video conferencing)

NOTE OF PROCEEDINGS

10.1 The court or court officer should keep, either by way of a note or a tape recording, brief details of all proceedings before the court, including the dates of the proceedings and a short statement of the decision taken at each hearing.

EVIDENCE

11.1 The requirement for evidence in certain types of applications is set out in some of the rules in the FPR and practice directions. Where there is no specific requirement to provide evidence it should be borne in mind that, as a practical matter, the court will often need to be satisfied by evidence of the facts that are relied on in support of or for opposing the application.

11.2 The court may give directions for the filing of evidence in support of or opposing a particular application. The court may also give directions for the filing of evidence in relation to any hearing that it fixes on its own initiative. The directions may specify the form that evidence is to take and when it is to be served.

11.3. Where it is intended to rely on evidence which is not contained in the application itself, the evidence, if it has not already been served, should be served with the application.

11.4 Where a respondent to an application wishes to rely on evidence, that evidence must be filed in accordance with any directions the court may have given and a court officer will serve the evidence on the other parties, unless the court directs otherwise.

11.5 If it is necessary for the applicant to serve any evidence in reply the court officer will serve it on the other parties unless the court directs otherwise.

11.6 Evidence must be filed with the court as well as served on the parties.

11.7 The contents of an application notice may be used as evidence provided the contents have been verified by a statement of truth.

CONSENT ORDERS

12.1 The parties to an application for a consent order must ensure that they provide the court with any material it needs to be satisfied that it is appropriate to make the order. Subject to any rule in the FPR or practice direction a letter will generally be acceptable for this purpose.

12.2 Where a judgment or order has been agreed in respect of an application where a hearing date has been fixed, the parties must inform the court immediately.

OTHER APPLICATIONS CONSIDERED WITHOUT A HEARING

13.1 Where rule 18.9(1)(b) applies the court will treat the application as if it were proposing to make an order on its own initiative.

13.2 Where the parties agree that the court should dispose of the application without a hearing they should so inform the court in writing and each should confirm that all evidence and other material on which he or she relies has been disclosed to the other parties to the application.

MISCELLANEOUS

14.1 If the case is proceeding in the High Court and the draft order is unusually long or complex it should also be supplied in electronic form on such storage medium as shall be agreed with the judge or court staff, for use by the court office.

14.2 Where rule 18.12 applies the power to re-list the application in rule 18.12(2) is in addition to any other powers of the court with regard to the order (for example to set aside, vary, discharge or suspend the order).

COSTS

15.1 Attention is drawn to the CPR costs practice direction and, in particular, to the court's power to make a summary assessment of costs.

15.2 Attention is also drawn to rule 44.13(1) of the CPR which provides that if an order makes no mention of costs, none are payable in respect of the proceedings to which it relates.

PART 19

ALTERNATIVE PROCEDURE FOR APPLICATIONS

19.1.— **Types of application for which Part 19 procedure may be followed**
(1) The Part 19 procedure is the procedure set out in this Part.
(2) An applicant may use the Part 19 procedure where the Part 18 procedure does not apply and—
    (a) there is no form prescribed by a rule or referred to in Practice Direction 5A in which to make the application;

(b) the applicant seeks the court's decision on a question which is unlikely to involve a substantial dispute of fact; or
(c) paragraph (5) applies.

(3) The court may at any stage direct that the application is to continue as if the applicant had not used the Part 19 procedure and, if it does so, the court may give any directions it considers appropriate.

(4) Paragraph (2) does not apply if a practice direction provides that the Part 19 procedure may not be used in relation to the type of application in question.

(5) A rule or practice direction may, in relation to a specified type of proceedings—
- (a) require or permit the use of the Part 19 procedure; and
- (b) disapply or modify any of the rules set out in this Part as they apply to those proceedings.

19.2.— Applications for which the Part 19 procedure must be followed

(1) The Part 19 procedure must be used in an application made in accordance with—
- (a) section 60(3) of the 2002 Act (order to prevent disclosure of information to an adopted person);
- (b) section 79(4) of the 2002 Act (order for Registrar General to give any information referred to in section 79(3) of the 2002 Act); and
- (c) rule 14.21 (directions of High Court regarding fathers without parental responsibility).

(2) The respondent to an application made in accordance with paragraph (1)(b) is the Registrar General.

19.3. Contents of the application

Where the applicant uses the Part 19 procedure, the application must state—
- (a) that this Part applies;
- (b) either—
  - (i) the question which the applicant wants the court to decide; or
  - (ii) the order which the applicant is seeking and the legal basis of the application for that order;
- (c) if the application is being made under an enactment, what that enactment is;
- (d) if the applicant is applying in a representative capacity, what that capacity is; and
- (e) if the respondent appears or is to appear in a representative capacity, what that capacity is.

(Part 17 requires a statement of case to be verified by a statement of truth.)

19.4.— Issue of application without naming respondents

(1) A practice direction may set out circumstances in which an application may be issued under this Part without naming a respondent.

(2) The practice direction may set out those cases in which an application for permission must be made by application notice before the application is issued.

(3) The application for permission—
- (a) need not be served on any other person; and
- (b) must be accompanied by a copy of the application which the applicant proposes to issue.

(4) Where the court gives permission, it will give directions about the future management of the application.

19.5.— Acknowledgment of service

(1) Subject to paragraph (2), each respondent must—
- (a) file an acknowledgment of service within 14 days beginning with the date on which the application is served; and
- (b) serve the acknowledgment of service on the applicant and any other party.

(2) If the application is to be served out of the jurisdiction, the respondent must file and serve an acknowledgment of service within the period set out in Practice Direction 6B.

(3) The acknowledgment of service must—
- (a) state whether the respondent contests the application;
- (b) state, if the respondent seeks a different order from that set out in the application, what that order is; and
- (c) be signed by the respondent or the respondent's legal representative.

19.6.— Consequence of not filing an acknowledgment of service

(1) This rule applies where—
- (a) the respondent has failed to file an acknowledgment of service; and
- (b) the time period for doing so has expired.

(2) The respondent may attend the hearing of the application but may not take part in the hearing unless the court gives permission.

19.7.— Filing and serving written evidence

(1) The applicant must, when filing the application, file the written evidence on which the applicant intends to rely.

(2) The applicant's evidence must be served on the respondent with the application.

(3) A respondent who wishes to rely on written evidence must file it when filing the acknowledgment of service.

(4) A respondent who files written evidence must also, at the same time, serve a copy of that evidence on the other parties.

(5) Within 14 days beginning with the date on which a respondent's evidence was served on the applicant, the applicant may file further written evidence in reply.

(6) An applicant who files further written evidence must also, within the same time limit, serve a copy of that evidence on the other parties.

19.8.— Evidence – general

(1) No written evidence may be relied on at the hearing of the application unless—
- (a) it has been served in accordance with rule 19.7; or
- (b) the court gives permission.

(2) The court may require or permit a party to give oral evidence at the hearing.

(3) The court may give directions requiring the attendance for cross-examination[GL] of a witness who has given written evidence.

(Rule 22.1 contains a general power for the court to control evidence.)

19.9.— Procedure where respondent objects to use of the Part 19 procedure

(1) A respondent who contends that the Part 19 procedure should not be used because—
- (a) there is a substantial dispute of fact; and
- (b) the use of the Part 19 procedure is not required or permitted by a rule or practice direction,

must state the reasons for that contention when filing the acknowledgment of service.

(2) When the court receives the acknowledgment of service and any written evidence, it will give directions as to the future management of the case.

(Rule 19.7 requires a respondent who wishes to rely on written evidence to file it when filing the acknowledgment of service.)

(Rule 19.1(3) allows the court to make an order that the application continue as if the applicant had not used the Part 19 procedure.)

PART 19 COMMENTARY

Part 19 is supplemented by PD19A.

Part 19, the Alternative Procedure, applies where part 18 does not apply, and, either there is no form prescribed by the rules or referred to in PD 5A, there is unlikely to be a substantial dispute of fact, or rules or practice directions

The Family Procedure Rules 2010

require or permit the use of Part 19 (r 19.1). Specified applications which must use Part 19 are listed in r 19.2.

There is provision at r 19.9 for a respondent to object to the use of Part 19 and by r 19.1 (3) the court may allow the case to continue as if the applicant had not used the Part 19 procedure.

The contents of the application are set out in r 19.3 they include:

- that Part 19 applies;
- either the question which the applicant wants the court to decide, or the order which is sought and the legal basis or the application for the order; and
- if the application is being made under an enactment, what that enactment is.

There is provision pursuant to r 19.4 at para 2.2 of the PD for certain applications to be issued without naming a respondent.

An Acknowledgment of Service is to be filed within 14 days of service (or such longer time as is provided by PD 16B when the application is served out of the jurisdiction). The acknowledgment of service must set out whether the application is contested, and, if it is, what other order is sought (r 19.5).

Written evidence is to be filed with the application, with the acknowledgment of service, and then within 14 days in reply (r 19.8).

Relevant forms for Part 19 are FP1 – Application under Part 19 of the Family Procedure Rules 2010, FP3 Application for injunction, and FP5 – Acknowledgment of service of Application under Part 19 of the Family Procedure Rules 2010.

PRACTICE DIRECTION 19A – ALTERNATIVE PROCEDURE FOR APPLICATIONS

This Practice Direction supplements FPR Part 19

TYPES OF APPLICATION IN WHICH PART 19 PROCEDURE MUST BE USED

1.1 An applicant must use the Part 19 procedure if the application is for an order under—

(a) section 60(3) of the 2002 Act, to prevent disclosure of information to an adopted person;
(b) section 79(4) of the 2002 Act, to require the Registrar General to provide information; or
(c) rule 14.21 (Inherent jurisdiction and fathers without parental responsibility) in Part 14, to request directions of the High Court regarding fathers without parental responsibility.

TYPES OF APPLICATION IN WHICH PART 19 PROCEDURE MAY BE USED

1.2 An applicant may use the Part 19 procedure if Part 18 does not apply and if—

(a) there is no prescribed form in which to make the application; or
(b) the applicant seeks the court's decision on a question which is unlikely to involve a substantial dispute of fact.

1.3 An applicant may also use the Part 19 procedure if a practice direction permits or requires its use for the type of proceedings concerned.

1.4 The practice directions referred to in paragraph 1.3 may in some respects modify or disapply the Part 19 procedure and, where that is so, it is those practice directions, rather than this one, which must be complied with.

1.5 The types of application for which the Part 19 procedure may be used include an application for an order or direction which is unopposed by each respondent before the commencement of the proceedings and the sole purpose of the application is to obtain the approval of the court to the agreement.

1.6 Where it appears to a court officer that an applicant is using the Part 19 procedure inappropriately, the officer may refer the application to the court for consideration of the point.

1.7 The court may at any stage order the application to continue as if the applicant had not used the Part 19 procedure and, if it does so, the court will give such directions as it considers appropriate (see rule 19.1(3)).

THE APPLICATION

2.1 Where an applicant uses the Part 19 procedure, the application form referred to in Practice Direction 5A should be used and must state the matters set out in rule 19.3 and, if paragraphs 1.3 and 1.4 apply, must comply with the requirements of the practice direction in question. In particular, the application form must state that Part 19 applies. A Part 19 application form means an application form which so states.

2.2 An application—

(a) in accordance with rule 19.4, to ask the High Court for directions on the need to give a father without parental responsibility notice of the intention to place a child for adoption; or
(b) under section 60(3) of the 2002 Act for an order to prevent disclosure of information to an adopted person,

may be issued without naming a respondent.

RESPONDING TO THE APPLICATION

3.1 Where a respondent who wishes to respond to a Part 19 application is required to file an acknowledgement of service, that acknowledgement of service should be in form FP5 which is referred to in Practice Direction 5A but can, alternatively be given in an informal document such as a letter.

3.2 Rule 19.5 sets out provisions relating to an acknowledgement of service of a Part 19 application.

3.3 Rule 19.6 sets out the consequence of failing to file an acknowledgement of service.

3.4 A respondent who believes that the Part 19 procedure should not be used because there is a substantial dispute of fact or, as the case may be, because its use is not authorised by any rule in the FPR or any practice direction, must state the reasons for that belief in writing when filing the acknowledgement of service (see rule 19.9). If the statement of reasons includes matters of evidence, it should be verified by a statement of truth.

MANAGING THE APPLICATION

4.1 The court may give directions immediately a Part 19 application is issued either on the application of a party or of its own initiative. The directions may include fixing a hearing date where—

(a) there is no dispute; or
(b) where there may be a dispute, but a hearing date could conveniently be given.

4.2 Where the court does not fix a hearing date when the application is issued, it will

The Family Procedure Rules 2010

give directions for the disposal of the application as soon as practicable after the respondent has acknowledged service of the application or, as the case may be, after the period for acknowledging service has expired.

4.3 Certain applications may not require a hearing.

4.4 The court may convene a directions hearing before giving directions.

EVIDENCE

5.1 An applicant wishing to rely on written evidence should file it when the Part 19 application form is issued.

5.2 Evidence will normally be in the form of a witness statement or an affidavit but an applicant may rely on the matters set out in the application form provided it has been verified by a statement of truth.

(For information about statements of truth see Part 17 and Practice Direction 17A, and about written evidence see Part 22 and Practice Direction 22A.)

5.3 A respondent wishing to rely on written evidence should file it with the acknowledgement of service (see rule 19.7(3)).

5.4 Rule 19.7 sets out the times and provisions for filing and serving written evidence.

5.5 A party may apply to the court for an extension of time to serve and file evidence under rule 19.7 or for permission to serve and file additional evidence under rule 19.8(1).

(For information about applications see Part 18 and Practice Direction 18A.)

5.6 The parties may, subject to paragraphs 5.7 and 5.8, agree in writing on an extension of time for serving and filing evidence under rule 19.7(3) or rule 19.7(5).

5.7 An agreement extending time for a respondent to file evidence in reply under rule 19.7(3)—

(a) must be filed by the respondent at the same time as the acknowledgement of service; and
(b) must not extend time by more than 17 days after the respondent files the acknowledgement of service.

5.8 An agreement extending time for an applicant to file evidence in reply under rule 19.7(5) must not extend time to more than 28 days after service of the respondent's evidence on the applicant.

HEARING

6.1 The court may on the hearing date—

(a) proceed to hear the case and dispose of the application;
(b) give case management directions.

PART 20

INTERIM REMEDIES AND SECURITY FOR COSTS

CHAPTER 1

Interim remedies

20.1. Scope of this Part
The rules in this Part do not apply to proceedings in a magistrates' court.

20.2.— Orders for interim remedies
(1) The court may grant the following interim remedies—

(a) an interim injunction$^{(GL)}$;
(b) an interim declaration;
(c) an order—
  (i) for the detention, custody or preservation of relevant property;
  (ii) for the inspection of relevant property;
  (iii) for the taking of a sample of relevant property;
  (iv) for the carrying out of an experiment on or with relevant property;
  (v) for the sale of relevant property which is of a perishable nature or which for any other good reason it is desirable to sell quickly; and
  (vi) for the payment of income from relevant property until an application is decided;
(d) an order authorising a person to enter any land or building in the possession of a party to the proceedings for the purposes of carrying out an order under sub-paragraph (c);
(e) an order under section 4 of the Torts (Interference with Goods) Act 1977 to deliver up goods;
(f) an order (referred to as a 'freezing injunction$^{(GL)}$')—
  (i) restraining a party from removing from the jurisdiction assets located there; or
  (ii) restraining a party from dealing with any assets whether located within the jurisdiction or not;
(g) an order directing a party to provide information about the location of relevant property or assets or to provide information about relevant property or assets which are or may be the subject of an application for a freezing injunction$^{(GL)}$;
(h) an order (referred to as a "search order") under section 7 of the Civil Procedure Act 1997 (order requiring a party to admit another party to premises for the purpose of preserving evidence etc.);
(i) an order under section 34 of the Senior Courts Act 1981 or section 53 of the County Courts Act 1984 (order in certain proceedings for disclosure of documents or inspection of property against a non-party);
(j) an order for a specified fund to be paid into court or otherwise secured, where there is a dispute over a party's right to the fund;
(k) an order permitting a party seeking to recover personal property to pay money into court pending the outcome of the proceedings and directing that, if money is paid into court, the property must be given up to that party;
(l) an order directing a party to prepare and file accounts relating to the dispute;
(m) an order directing any account to be taken or inquiry to be made by the court.

(2) In paragraph (1)(c) and (g), 'relevant property' means property (including land) which is the subject of an application or as to which any question may arise on an application.

(3) The fact that a particular kind of interim remedy is not listed in paragraph (1) does not affect any power that the court may have to grant that remedy.

20.3.— Time when an order for an interim remedy may be made

(1) An order for an interim remedy may be made at any time, including—
  (a) before proceedings are started; and
  (b) after judgment has been given.

(Rule 5.3 provides that proceedings are started when the court issues an application form.)

(2) However—
  (a) paragraph (1) is subject to any rule, practice direction or other enactment which provides otherwise; and
  (b) the court may grant an interim remedy before an application has been started only if—

The Family Procedure Rules 2010

(i) the matter is urgent; or
(ii) it is otherwise desirable to do so in the interests of justice.

(3) Where the court grants an interim remedy before an application has been started, it will give directions requiring an application to be started.

(4) The court need not direct that an application be started where the application is made under section 33 of the Senior Courts Act 1981 or section 52 of the County Courts Act 1984 (order for disclosure, inspection etc. before starting an application).

20.4.— How to apply for an interim remedy

(1) The court may grant an interim remedy on an application made without notice if it appears to the court that there are good reasons for not giving notice.

(2) An application for an interim remedy must be supported by evidence, unless the court orders otherwise.

(3) If the applicant makes an application without giving notice, the evidence in support of the application must state the reasons why notice has not been given.

(Part 4 lists general case-management powers of the court.)
(Part 18 contains general rules about making an application.)

20.5. Interim injunction to cease if application is stayed

If—

(a) the court has granted an interim injunction^(GL) other than a freezing injunction^(GL); and
(b) the application is stayed^(GL) other than by agreement between the parties,

the interim injunction^(GL) will be set aside^(GL) unless the court orders that it should continue to have effect even though the application is stayed^(GL).

CHAPTER 2

Security for costs

20.6.— Security for costs

(1) A respondent to any application may apply under this Chapter of this Part for security for costs of the proceedings.

(Part 4 provides for the court to order payment of sums into court in other circumstances.)

(2) An application for security for costs must be supported by written evidence.

(3) Where the court makes an order for security for costs, it will—
   (a) determine the amount of security; and
   (b) direct—
       (i) the manner in which; and
       (ii) the time within which,
       the security must be given.

20.7.— Conditions to be satisfied

(1) The court may make an order for security for costs under rule 20.6 if—
   (a) it is satisfied, having regard to all the circumstances of the case, that it is just to make such an order; and
   (b) either—
       (i) one or more of the conditions in paragraph (2) applies; or
       (ii) an enactment permits the court to require security for costs.

(2) The conditions are—
   (a) the applicant is—
       (i) resident out of the jurisdiction; but
       (ii) not resident in a Brussels Contracting State, a Lugano Contracting State or a Regulation State, as defined in section 1(3) of the Civil Jurisdiction and Judgments Act 1982 or a Member State bound by the Council Regulation;

(b) the applicant has changed address since the application was started with a view to evading the consequences of the litigation;
(c) the applicant failed to give an address in the application form, or gave an incorrect address in that form;
(d) the applicant has taken steps in relation to the applicant's assets that would make it difficult to enforce an order for costs against the applicant.

(3) The court may not make an order for security for costs under rule 20.6 in relation to the costs of proceedings under the 1980 Hague Convention.

(Rule 4.4 allows the court to strike out$^{(GL)}$ a statement of case.)

20.8. Security for costs of an appeal

The court may order security for costs of an appeal against—
(a) an appellant;
(b) a respondent who also appeals,
on the same grounds as it may order security for costs against an applicant under this Part.

PART 20 COMMENTARY

Part 20 is supplemented in relation to Interim Remedies by PD20A.

Part 20 deals with interim remedies and security for costs.

Chapter 1 deals with interim injunctions.

Rule 20.2 lists the interim remedies which the court may grant: the list is extensive.

Rule 20.4 provides for interim applications to be made without notice.

Rule 20.5 provides that interim injunctions will be set aside if the application is stayed unless the court orders that it should continue.

Chapter 2 deals with security for costs.

Rule 20.6 sets out that a respondent to any application may apply for security for costs.

Rule 20.7 provides that the court may make an order for security of costs if it is just to make such an order, and either an enactment permits the court to require security for costs or one of four specified conditions are met, save in relation to proceedings under the 1980 Hague Convention.

Rule 20.8 provides that the court may order security for costs of an appeal against an appellant, or a respondent who also appeals.

PRACTICE DIRECTION 20A – INTERIM REMEDIES

This Practice Direction supplements FPR Part 20

SCOPE AND JURISDICTION

1.1 This Practice Direction does not apply to an order under section 48 (Powers to assist in discovery of children who may be in need of emergency protection), section 50 (Recovery of abducted children, etc.) of the Children Act 1989 or section 33 (Power to order disclosure of child's whereabouts) or section 34 (Power to order recovery of child) of the Family Law Act 1986.

1.2 High Court Judges and any other judge duly authorised may grant 'search orders' and 'freezing injunctions' (see rules 20.2(1)(h) and 20.2(1)(f)).

1.3 In a case in the High Court, district judges have the power to grant injunctions—

The Family Procedure Rules 2010

(a) by consent;
(b) in connection with charging orders and appointments of receivers;
(c) in aid of execution of judgments.

1.4 In any other case any judge who has jurisdiction to conduct the hearing of the proceedings has the power to grant an injunction in those proceedings.

1.5. A district judge has the power to vary or discharge an injunction granted by any judge with the consent of all the parties.

MAKING AN APPLICATION

2.1 The application notice must state—

(a) the order sought; and
(b) the date, time and place of the hearing.

2.2 The application notice and evidence in support must be served as soon as practicable after issue and in any event not less than 7 days before the court is due to hear the application unless the court directs otherwise.

2.3 Where the court is to serve, sufficient copies of the application notice and evidence in support for the court and for each respondent should be filed for issue and service.

2.4 Whenever possible a draft of the order sought should be filed with the application notice and an electronic version of the draft should also be available to the court in a format compatible with the word processing software used by the court and on such storage medium as shall be agreed by the court. This will enable the court officer to arrange for any amendments to be incorporated and for the speedy preparation and sealing of the order.

EVIDENCE

3.1 Applications for search orders and freezing injunctions must be supported by affidavit evidence.

3.2 Applications for other interim injunctions must be supported by evidence set out in either—

(a) a witness statement; or
(b) the application notice provided that it is verified by a statement of truth,

unless the court, an Act, a rule in the FPR or a practice direction requires evidence by affidavit.

3.3 The evidence must set out the facts on which the applicant relies for the application being made against the respondent, including all material facts of which the court should be made aware.

3.4 Where an application is made without notice to the respondent, the evidence must also set out why notice was not given.

(See Part 22 and the practice direction that supplements it for information about evidence.)

URGENT APPLICATIONS AND APPLICATIONS WITHOUT NOTICE

4.1 These fall into two categories—

(a) applications where an application in proceedings has already been issued; and
(b) applications where an application in proceedings has not yet been issued,

and, in both cases, where notice of the application has not been given to the respondent.

4.2 These applications are normally dealt with at a court hearing but cases of extreme urgency may be dealt with by telephone.

4.3 In relation to applications dealt with at a court hearing after issue of an application form—

(a) the application notice, evidence in support and a draft order (as in paragraph 2.4) should be filed with the court two hours before the hearing wherever possible;
(b) if an application is made before the application notice has been issued, a draft order (as in paragraph 2.4) should be provided at the hearing, and the application notice and evidence in support must be filed with the court on the same or next working day or as ordered by the court; and
(c) except in cases where it is essential that the respondent must not be aware of the application, the applicant should take steps to notify the respondent informally of the application.

4.4 In relation to applications made before the issue of an application—

(a) in addition to the provisions set out at paragraph 4.3, unless the court orders otherwise, either the applicant must undertake to the court to issue an application notice immediately or the court will give directions for the commencement of the application (see rule 20.3(3));
(b) where possible the application should be served with the order for the injunction;
(c) an order made before the issue of an application should state in the title after the names of the applicant and respondent 'the Applicant and Respondent in Intended Proceedings'.

4.5 In relation to applications made outside normal working hours—

(a) the applicant should either—
 (i) telephone the Royal Courts of Justice on 020 7947 6000 to be put in contact with the clerk to the appropriate duty judge in the High Court (or the appropriate area Circuit Judge where known); or
 (ii) telephone the Urgent Court Business Officer of the appropriate Circuit who will contact the local duty judge;
(b) where the facility is available it is likely that the judge will require a draft order to be faxed to him;
(c) the application notice and evidence in support must be filed with the court on the same or next working day or as ordered, together with two copies of the order for sealing;
(d) injunctions will be heard by telephone only where the applicant is acting by counsel or solicitors.

ORDERS FOR INJUNCTIONS

5.1 Any order for an injunction, unless the court orders otherwise, must contain—

(a) an undertaking by the applicant to the court to pay any damages which the respondent sustains which the court considers the applicant should pay;
(b) if the order is made without notice to any other party, an undertaking by the applicant to the court to serve on the respondent the application notice, evidence in support and any order made as soon as practicable;
(c) if the order is made without notice to any other party, a return date for a further hearing at which the other party can be present;
(d) if the order is made before filing the application notice, an undertaking to file and pay the appropriate fee on the same or next working day; and
(e) if the order is made before issue of an application in proceedings—
 (i) an undertaking to issue and pay the appropriate fee on the same or next working day; or
 (ii) directions for the commencement of the application.

5.2 When the court makes an order for an injunction, it should consider whether to require an undertaking by the applicant to pay any damages sustained by a person other than the respondent, including another party to the proceedings or any other person who may suffer loss as a consequence of the order.

5.3 An order for an injunction made in the presence of all parties to be bound by it or made at a hearing of which they have had notice, may state that it is effective until final hearing or further order.

5.4 Any order for an injunction must set out clearly what the respondent must do or not do.

SEARCH ORDERS

Orders for the preservation of evidence and property

6.1 The following provisions apply to search orders in addition to those listed above.

The Supervising Solicitor

6.2 The Supervising Solicitor must be experienced in the operation of search orders. A Supervising Solicitor may be contacted either through the Law Society or, for the London area, through the London Solicitors Litigation Association.

Evidence

6.3

(1) The affidavit must state the name, firm and its address, and experience of the Supervising Solicitor, also the address of the premises and whether it is a private or business address.
(2) The affidavit must disclose very fully the reason the order is sought, including the probability that relevant material would disappear if the order were not made.

Service

6.4.

(1) The order must be served personally by the Supervising Solicitor, unless the court directs otherwise, and must be accompanied by the evidence in support and any documents capable of being copied.
(2) Confidential exhibits need not be served but they must be made available for inspection by the respondent in the presence of the applicant's solicitors while the order is carried out and afterwards be retained by the respondent's solicitors on their undertaking not to permit the respondent—
 (a) to see them or copies of them except in their presence; and
 (b) to make or take away any note or record of them.
(3) The Supervising Solicitor may be accompanied only by the persons mentioned in the order.
(4) The Supervising Solicitor must explain the terms and effect of the order to the respondent in everyday language and advise the respondent—
 (a) of the respondent's right to take legal advice, and to apply to vary or discharge the order; and
 (b) that the respondent may be entitled to avail himself of—
  (i) legal professional privilege; and
  (ii) the privilege against self-incrimination.
(5) Where the Supervising Solicitor is a man and the respondent is likely to be an unaccompanied woman, at least one other person named in the order must be a woman and must accompany the Supervising Solicitor.
(6) The order may only be served between 9.30 a.m. and 5.30 p.m. Monday to Friday unless the court directs otherwise.

Search and custody of materials

6.5

(1) No material shall be removed unless clearly covered by the terms of the order.

(2) The premises must not be searched and no items shall be removed from them except in the presence of the respondent or a person who appears to be a responsible employee of the respondent.
(3) Where copies of documents are sought, the documents should be retained for no more than 2 days before return to the owner.
(4) Where material in dispute is removed pending hearing, the applicant's solicitors should place it in the custody of the respondent's solicitors on their undertaking to retain it in safekeeping and to produce it to the court when required.
(5) In appropriate cases the applicant should insure the material retained in the respondent's solicitors' custody.
(6) The Supervising Solicitor must make a list of all material removed from the premises and supply a copy of the list to the respondent.
(7) No material shall be removed from the premises until the respondent has had reasonable time to check the list.
(8) If any of the listed items exists only in computer readable form, the respondent must immediately give the applicant's solicitors effective access to the computers, with all necessary passwords, to enable them to be searched, and cause the listed items to be printed out.
(9) The applicant must take all reasonable steps to ensure that no damage is done to any computer or data.
(10) The applicant and his representatives may not themselves search the respondent's computers unless they have sufficient expertise to do so without damaging the respondent's system;
(11) the Supervising Solicitor shall provide a report on the carrying out of the order to the applicant's solicitors.
(12) As soon as the report is received the applicant's solicitors shall—
 (a) serve a copy of it on the respondent; and
 (b) file a copy of it with the court.
(13) Where the Supervising Solicitor is satisfied that full compliance with paragraph 6.5(7) and (8) above is impracticable, that Solicitor may permit the search to proceed and items to be removed without compliance with the impracticable requirements.

General

6.6 The Supervising Solicitor must not be an employee or member of the applicant's firm of solicitors.

6.7 If the court orders that the order need not be served by the Supervising Solicitor, the reason for so ordering must be set out in the order.

6.8 The search order must not be carried out at the same time as a police search warrant.

6.9 There is no privilege against self incrimination in proceedings in which a court is hearing an application for an order under Part 4 or 5 of the Children Act 1989 (see section 98 of the Children Act 1989).

Delivery up orders

7.1 The following provision applies to orders, other than search orders, for delivery up or preservation of evidence or property where it is likely that such an order will be executed at the premises of the respondent or a third party.

7.2 In such cases the court will consider whether to include in the order for the benefit or protection of the parties similar provisions to those specified above in relation to injunctions and search orders.

Injunctions against third parties

8.1 The following provision applies to orders which will affect a person other than the applicant or respondent, who—

(a) did not attend the hearing at which the order was made; and

The Family Procedure Rules 2010

(b) is served with the order.

8.2 Where such a person served with the order requests—

(a) a copy of any materials read by the court, including material prepared after the hearing at the direction of the court or in compliance with the order; or
(b) a note of the hearing,

the applicant, or the applicant's legal representative, must comply promptly with the request, unless the court directs otherwise.

PART 21

MISCELLANEOUS RULES ABOUT DISCLOSURE AND INSPECTION OF DOCUMENTS

21.1.— Interpretation

(1) A party discloses a document by stating that the document exists or has existed.

(2) Inspection of a document occurs when a party is permitted to inspect a document disclosed by another person.

(3) For the purposes of disclosure and inspection—

(a) "document" means anything in which information of any description is recorded; and
(b) "copy" in relation to a document, means anything onto which information recorded in the document has been copied, by whatever means and whether directly or indirectly.

21.2.— Orders for disclosure against a person not a party

(1) This rule applies where an application is made to the court under any Act for disclosure by a person who is not a party to the proceedings.

(2) The application—

(a) may be made without notice; and
(b) must be supported by evidence.

(3) The court may make an order under this rule only where disclosure is necessary in order to dispose fairly of the proceedings or to save costs.

(4) An order under this rule must—

(a) specify the documents or the classes of documents which the respondent must disclose; and
(b) require the respondent, when making disclosure, to specify any of those documents—
    (i) which are no longer in the respondent's control; or
    (ii) in respect of which the respondent claims a right or duty to withhold inspection.

(5) Such an order may—

(a) require the respondent to indicate what has happened to any documents which are no longer in the respondent's control; and
(b) specify the time and place for disclosure and inspection.

(6) An order under this rule must not compel a person to produce any document which that person could not be compelled to produce at the final hearing.

(7) This rule does not limit any other power which the court may have to order disclosure against a person who is not a party to proceedings.

(Rule 35.3 contains provisions in relation to the disclosure and inspection of evidence arising out of mediation of cross-border disputes.)

21.3.— Claim to withhold inspection or disclosure of a document

(1) A person may apply, without notice, for an order permitting that person to withhold disclosure of a document on the ground that disclosure would damage the public interest.

(2) Unless the court otherwise orders, an order of the court under paragraph (1)—
   (a) must not be served on any other person; and
   (b) must not be open to inspection by any other person.
(3) A person who wishes to claim a right or a duty to withhold inspection of a document, or part of a document, must state in writing—
   (a) the right or duty claimed; and
   (b) the grounds on which that right or duty is claimed.
(4) The statement referred to in paragraph (3) must be made to the person wishing to inspect the document.
(5) A party may apply to the court to decide whether a claim made under paragraph (3) should be upheld.
(6) Where the court is deciding an application under paragraph (1) or (5) it may—
   (a) require the person seeking to withhold disclosure or inspection of a document to produce that document to the court; and
   (b) invite any person, whether or not a party, to make representations.
(7) An application under paragraph (1) or (5) must be supported by evidence.
(8) This Part does not affect any rule of law which permits or requires a document to be withheld from disclosure or inspection on the ground that its disclosure or inspection would damage the public interest.

PART 21 COMMENTARY

Part 21 is supplemented by PD21A.

Part 21 contains rules about the disclosure and inspection of documents. Rule 21.2 provides for disclosure and inspection of documents belonging to a person who is not a party to proceedings. This is similar to the 'inspection appointment' previously available only in financial proceedings under the FPR 1991, r 2.62.

PRACTICE DIRECTION 21A – DISCLOSURE AND INSPECTION

This Practice Direction supplements FPR Part 21

CHAPTER 1 ORDERS FOR DISCLOSURE AND INSPECTION OF DOCUMENTS

Interpretation

1.1 A party discloses a document by stating that the document exists or has existed. Inspection occurs when a party is permitted to inspect a document disclosed by another party.

1.2 For the purposes of disclosure and inspection in family proceedings—

"document" means anything in which information of any description is recorded and any copy of a document which contains a modification, obliteration or other marking or feature shall be treated as a separate document; and
"copy", in relation to a document, means anything on which information recorded in the document has been copied, by whatever means and whether directly or indirectly.

Types of order for disclosure in family proceedings

2.1 In family proceedings other than proceedings for a financial remedy, where the court orders disclosure, the normal order will be for disclosure by each party setting out, in a list or questionnaire, the documents material to the proceedings, of the existence of which that party is aware and which are or have been in that party's control. This process is known as "standard disclosure".

2.2 In proceedings for a financial remedy, the process of disclosure is staged. First, Form E (the financial statement referred to in rule 9.14(1)) is served together with the documents which are required to be attached to it. The second stage occurs by the parties requesting (further) disclosure of each other by a questionnaire served before the first appointment; the questionnaire can request both information and documents. With the court's permission, a further questionnaire can be served later in the proceedings.

2.3 In matrimonial and civil partnership proceedings, under rule 7.15, the court – either on its own initiative or on the application of the other party – may order a party to clarify any matter which is in dispute in the proceedings or give additional information in relation to any such matter, whether or not the matter is contained in or referred to in the application or in the answer.

2.4 In any family proceedings, the court may order "specific disclosure", which is an order that a party must—

(a) disclose documents or classes of documents specified in the order;
(b) carry out a search to the extent stated in the order; or
(c) disclose any documents located as a result of that search.

PART 22

EVIDENCE

CHAPTER 1

General rules

22.1.— Power of court to control evidence

(1) The court may control the evidence by giving directions as to—
    (a) the issues on which it requires evidence;
    (b) the nature of the evidence which it requires to decide those issues; and
    (c) the way in which the evidence is to be placed before the court.

(2) The court may use its power under this rule to exclude evidence that would otherwise be admissible.

(3) The court may permit a party to adduce evidence, or to seek to rely on a document, in respect of which that party has failed to comply with the requirements of this Part.

(4) The court may limit cross-examination$^{(GL)}$.

22.2.— Evidence of witnesses – general rule

(1) The general rule is that any fact which needs to be proved by the evidence of witnesses is to be proved—
    (a) at the final hearing, by their oral evidence; and
    (b) at any other hearing, by their evidence in writing.

(2) The general rule does not apply—
    (a) to proceedings under Part 12 for secure accommodation orders, interim care orders or interim supervision orders; or
    (b) where an enactment, any of these rules, a practice direction or a court order provides to the contrary.

(Section 45(7) of the Children Act 1989 (emergency protection orders) is an example of an enactment which makes provision relating to the evidence that a court may take into account when hearing an application.)

22.3. Evidence by video link or other means

The court may allow a witness to give evidence through a video link or by other means.

22.4.— Witness statements

(1) A witness statement is a written statement signed by a person which contains the evidence which that person would be allowed to give orally.

(2) A witness statement must comply with the requirements set out in the Practice Direction 22A.

(Part 17 requires a witness statement to be verified by a statement of truth.)

22.5.— Service of witness statements for use at the final hearing

(1) The court may give directions as to service on the other parties of any witness statement of the oral evidence on which a party intends to rely in relation to any issues of fact to be decided at the final hearing.

(2) The court may give directions as to—
- (a) the order in which witness statements are to be served; and
- (b) whether or not the witness statements are to be filed.

(3) Where the court directs that a court officer is to serve a witness statement on the other parties, any reference in this Chapter to a party serving a witness statement is to be read as including a reference to a court officer serving the statement.

22.6.— Use at the final hearing of witness statements which have been served

(1) If a party—
- (a) has served a witness statement; and
- (b) wishes to rely at the final hearing on the evidence of the witness who made the statement,

that party must call the witness to give oral evidence unless the court directs otherwise or the party puts the statement in as hearsay evidence.

(Part 23 (miscellaneous rules about evidence) contains provisions about hearsay evidence.)

(2) The witness statement of a witness called to give oral evidence under paragraph (1) is to stand as the evidence in chief$^{(GL)}$ of that witness unless the court directs otherwise.

(3) A witness giving oral evidence at the final hearing may with the permission of the court—
- (a) amplify his witness statement; and
- (b) give evidence in relation to new matters which have arisen since the witness statement was served on the other parties.

(4) The court will give permission under paragraph (3) only if it considers that there is good reason not to confine the evidence of the witness to the contents of the witness statement.

(5) If a party who has served a witness statement does not—
- (a) call the witness to give evidence at the final hearing; or
- (b) put the witness statement in as hearsay evidence,

any other party may put the witness statement in as hearsay evidence.

22.7.— Evidence at hearings other than the final hearing

(1) Subject to paragraph (2), the general rule is that evidence at hearings other than the final hearing is to be by witness statement unless the court, any other rule, a practice direction or any other enactment requires otherwise.

(2) At hearings other than the final hearing, a party may rely on the matters set out in that party's—
- (a) application form;
- (b) application notice; or
- (c) answer,

if the application form, application notice or answer, as the case may be, is verified by a statement of truth.

22.8.— Order for cross-examination

(1) Where, at a hearing other than the final hearing, evidence is given in writing, any party may apply to the court for permission to cross-examine$^{(GL)}$ the person giving the evidence.

The Family Procedure Rules 2010

(2) If the court gives permission under paragraph (1) but the person in question does not attend, that person's evidence may not be used unless the court directs otherwise.
(Rules 35.3 and 35.4 contain rules in relation to evidence arising out of mediation of cross-border disputes.)

22.9.— Witness summaries
(1) A party who—
   (a) is required to serve a witness statement for use at any hearing; but
   (b) is unable to obtain one,
may apply, without notice, for permission to serve a witness summary instead.
(2) A witness summary is a summary of—
   (a) the evidence, if known, which would otherwise be included in a witness statement; or
   (b) if the evidence is not known, the matters about which the party serving the witness summary proposes to question the witness.
(3) Unless the court directs otherwise, a witness summary must include the name and address of the intended witness.
(4) Unless the court directs otherwise, a witness summary must be served within the period in which a witness statement would have had to be served.
(5) Where a party serves a witness summary, so far as practicable rules 22.4(2) (form of witness statements), 22.5 (service of witness statements for use at the final hearing) and 22.6(3) (amplifying witness statements) apply to the summary.

22.10. Consequence of failure to serve witness statement
If a witness statement for use at the final hearing is not served in respect of an intended witness within the time specified by the court, then the witness may not be called to give oral evidence unless the court gives permission.

22.11. Cross-examination on a witness statement
A witness who is called to give evidence at the final hearing may be cross-examined[GL] on the witness statement, whether or not the statement or any part of it was referred to during the witness's evidence in chief[GL].

22.12.— Affidavit evidence
(1) Evidence must be given by affidavit[GL] instead of or in addition to a witness statement if this is required by the court, a provision contained in any other rule, a practice direction or any other enactment.
(2) In relation to proceedings which are pending or treated as pending in a divorce county court or civil partnership county court, section 58(1)(c) of the County Courts Act 1984, shall have effect as if after paragraph (c) there were inserted—
"or
   (d) a district judge of the principal registry; or
   (e) any officer of the principal registry authorised by the President under section 2 of the Commissioner for Oaths Act 1889; or
   (f) any clerk in the Central Office of the Royal Courts of Justice authorised to take affidavits[GL] for the purposes of proceedings in the Supreme Court.".
(Rule 7.3 sets out when proceedings are treated as pending in a divorce county court or civil partnership proceedings county court.)

22.13. Form of affidavit
An affidavit[GL] must comply with the requirements set out in the Practice Direction 22A.

22.14. Affidavit made outside the jurisdiction
A person may make an affidavit [GL] outside the jurisdiction in accordance with—
   (a) this Part; or
   (b) the law of the place where the affidavit[GL] is made.

22.15.— Notice to admit facts

(1) A party may serve notice on another party requiring the other party to admit the facts, or the part of the case of the serving party, specified in the notice.

(2) A notice to admit facts must be served no later than 21 days before the final hearing.

(3) Where the other party makes any admission in answer to the notice, the admission may be used against that party only—
- (a) in the proceedings in which the notice to admit is served; and
- (b) by the party who served the notice.

(4) The court may allow a party to amend or withdraw any admission made by that party on such terms as it thinks just.

22.16.— Notice to admit or produce documents

(1) A party to whom a document is disclosed is deemed to admit the authenticity of that document unless notice is served by that party that the party wishes the document to be proved at the final hearing.

(2) A notice to prove a document must be served—
- (a) by the latest date for serving witness statements; or
- (b) within 7 days beginning with the date of service of the document, whichever is later.

22.17. Notarial acts and instruments

A notarial act or instrument may be received in evidence without further proof as duly authenticated in accordance with the requirements of law unless the contrary is proved.

CHAPTER 2

Rules applying only to particular proceedings

22.18. Scope of this Chapter

This Chapter of this Part applies to affidavits(GL) and affirmations as it applies to witness statements.

22.19.— Availability of witness statements for inspection during the final hearing

(1) This rule applies to proceedings under Part 7 (matrimonial and civil partnership proceedings).

(2) A witness statement which stands as evidence in chief(GL) is open to inspection during the course of the final hearing unless the court directs otherwise.

(3) Any person may ask for a direction that a witness statement is not open to inspection.

(4) The court will not make a direction under paragraph (2) unless it is satisfied that a witness statement should not be open to inspection because of—
- (a) the interests of justice;
- (b) the public interest;
- (c) the nature of any expert medical evidence in the statement;
- (d) the nature of any confidential information (including information relating to personal financial matters) in the statement; or
- (e) the need to protect the interests of any child or protected party.

(5) The court may exclude from inspection words or passages in the witness statement.

22.20.— Use of witness statements for other purposes

(1) This rule applies to proceedings under Part 7 (matrimonial and civil partnership proceedings) or Part 9 (financial remedies).

(2) Except as provided by this rule, a witness statement may be used only for the purpose of the proceedings in which it is served.

(3) Paragraph (2) does not apply if and to the extent that—
- (a) the court gives permission for some other use; or

The Family Procedure Rules 2010

    (b)   the witness statement has been put in evidence at a hearing held in public.

PART 22 COMMENTARY

Part 22 is supplemented by PD22A.

Part 22 contains in Chapter 1 general rules of evidence, and in Chapter 2 rules applying to specific proceedings.

Rule 22.1 provides that the court controls the evidence and can exclude evidence that would otherwise be admissible and can limit cross examination.

Rule 22.2 sets out the general rule that any fact which needs to be proved at a final hearing is to be proved by oral evidence, but at any other hearing by evidence in writing. Exceptions to this are secure accommodation orders and interim care and supervision orders and where there is provision by enactment, rule, practice direction or court order to the contrary.

Rule 22.6 provides that if a party has filed a witness statement and wishes to rely on the evidence at the final hearing the witness must be called to give evidence, unless the court directs otherwise, or the party puts in the statement as hearsay evidence. The witness statement is to stand as the evidence in chief unless the court directs otherwise.

Rule 22.7 provides that at hearings other than a final hearing evidence is to be given by witness statement and application form or notice or answer, if the application form or notice or answer is verified by a statement of truth.

Rule 22.9 makes provision for witness summaries in lieu of witness statements.

Rule 22.12 deals with affidavit evidence.

PD22A deals with the form of witness statements and affidavits.

Rule 22.15 makes provision for a notice to admit facts, and r 22.16 notice to prove documents.

Chapter 2 provides in r 22.19 that witness statements and affidavits in matrimonial and civil partnership proceedings which stand as evidence in chief are open for inspection, save as directed by the court. In r 22.10 it is provided that witness statements and affidavits used in matrimonial and civil partnership proceedings and financial remedy proceedings may only be used for the purpose of those proceedings, save if the court gives permission for other use, or they are used at a hearing held in public.

Relevant to Part 22 is Form N285 – General Affidavit.

PRACTICE DIRECTION 22A – WRITTEN EVIDENCE

This Practice Direction supplements FPR Part 22

EVIDENCE IN GENERAL

1.1   Rule 22.2(1) sets out the general rule as to how evidence is to be given and facts are to be proved. This is that, at the final hearing, witnesses will normally give oral evidence and, at any hearing other than the final hearing, by evidence in writing (which under rule 22.7(1) will usually be by witness statement).

1.2   Rule 22.2(2) excludes the general rule—

(a) from proceedings under Part 12 (Children) for secure accommodation orders, interim care orders or interim supervision orders; or
(b) where an enactment, any rule in the FPR, a practice direction or a court order provides to the contrary.

1.3 Application forms, application notices and answers except an application for a matrimonial order or a civil partnership order or an answer to such an application may also be used as evidence provided that their contents have been verified by a statement of truth (see Part 17 for information about statements of truth).

(For information regarding evidence by deposition see Part 24 and the practice direction which supplements it.)

1.4 Affidavits must be used as evidence—

(a) where sworn evidence is required by an enactment, rule, order or practice direction; and
(b) in any application for an order against anyone for alleged contempt of court.

1.5 If a party believes that sworn evidence is required by a court in another jurisdiction for any purpose connected with the proceedings, he may apply to the court for a direction that evidence shall be given only by affidavit on any applications to be heard before the final hearing.

1.6 The court may give a direction under rule 22.12 that evidence shall be given by affidavit instead of or in addition to a witness statement—

(a) on its own initiative; or
(b) after any party has applied to the court for such a direction.

1.7 An affidavit, where referred to in the FPR or a practice direction, also means an affirmation unless the context requires otherwise.

AFFIDAVITS AND WITNESS STATEMENTS

Meaning of "deponent" and "witness"

2.1 For the purposes of the FPR—

a "deponent" is a person who gives evidence by affidavit, affirmation or deposition; and
a "witness" is a person who gives evidence by witness statement.

2.2 References in the following paragraphs to "the maker of", or "making", an affidavit, affirmation, deposition or witness statement are to be construed accordingly.

Heading and format

3.1 The affidavit/statement should be headed with the title of the proceedings where the proceedings are between several parties with the same status it is sufficient to identify the parties, subject to paragraph 4.2, as follows—

Number:
A.B. (and others)   Applicants
C.D. (and others)   Respondents

3.2 Subject to paragraph 4.2, at the top right-hand corner of the first page (and on the backsheet) there should be clearly written—

(a) the party on whose behalf it is made;
(b) the initials and surname of the maker;
(c) the number of the affidavit/statement in relation to its maker;
(d) the identifying initials and number of each exhibit referred to; and

The Family Procedure Rules 2010

(e) the date made.

3.3 The affidavit/statement should—

(a) be produced on durable quality A4 paper with a 3.5 cm margin;
(b) be fully legible and should normally be typed on one side of the paper only;
(c) where possible, should be bound securely in a manner which would not hamper filing or, where secure binding is not possible, each page should be endorsed with the case number and should bear the following initials—
   (i) in the case of an affidavit, of the maker and of the person before whom it is sworn; or
   (ii) in the case of a witness statement, of the maker and, where the maker is unable to read or sign the statement, of the authorised person (see paragraphs 7.3 and 7.4 below);
(d) have the pages numbered consecutively as a separate document (or as one of several documents contained in a file);
(e) be divided into numbered paragraphs;
(f) have all numbers, including dates, expressed in figures; and
(g) give the reference to any document or documents mentioned either in the margin or in bold text in the body of the affidavit/statement.

Body

4.1 Subject to paragraph 4.2 and rules 14.2 and 29.1, the affidavit/statement must, if practicable, be in the maker's own words, it should be expressed in the first person, and the maker should—

(a) commence-
   (i) in an affidavit, "I (full name) of (residential address) state on oath . . . . ";
   (ii) in a statement, by giving his or her full name and residential address;
(b) if giving evidence in a professional, business or other occupational capacity, give the address at which he or she works in (a) above, the position held and the name of the firm or employer;
(c) give his or her occupation or (if none) description; and
(d) if it be the case that the maker is a party to the proceedings or is employed by a party to the proceedings, state that fact.

4.2 If, in proceedings to which Part 14 (Adoption, placement and related proceedings) applies, a serial number has been assigned under rule 14.2, the affidavit/statement must be framed so that it does not disclose the identity of the applicant.

(Rule 29.1 provides that, unless the court directs otherwise, a party to family proceedings is not required to reveal the address of his or her private residence or other contact details.)

4.3 An affidavit/statement must indicate—

(a) which of the statements in it are made from the maker's own knowledge and which are matters of information and belief; and
(b) the source for any matters of information and belief.

4.4 It is usually convenient to follow the chronological sequence of events or matters dealt with. Each paragraph should as far as possible be confined to a distinct portion of the subject.

4.5 The maker should, when referring to an exhibit or exhibits, state "there is now shown to me marked" . . . "the (description of exhibit)".

Alterations to affidavits and witness statements

5.1 Any alteration to an affidavit must be initialled by both the maker and the person before whom the affidavit is sworn.

5.2 Any alteration to a witness statement must be initialled by the maker or by the

FPR 2010, Practice Direction 22A

authorised person where appropriate (see paragraphs 7.3 and 7.4 below).

5.3 An affidavit/statement which contains an alteration that has not been initialled in accordance with paragraphs 5.1 and 5.2 may be filed or used in evidence only with the permission of the court.

Swearing an affidavit or verifying a witness statement

6.1 An affidavit is the testimony of the person who swears it. A witness statement is the equivalent of the oral evidence which the maker would, if called, give in evidence.

6.2 The jurat of an affidavit is a statement set out at the end of the document which authenticates the affidavit. It must—

(a) be signed by all deponents;
(b) be completed and signed by the person before whom the affidavit was sworn whose name and qualification must be printed beneath his signature;
(c) contain the full address of the person before whom the affidavit was sworn; and
(d) follow immediately on from the text and not be put on a separate page.

6.3 An affidavit must be sworn before a person independent of the parties or their representatives. Only the following may administer oaths and take affidavits—

(a) a Commissioner for Oaths (Commissioners for Oaths Acts 1889 and 1891);
(b) other persons specified by statute (sections 12 and 18 of, and Schedules 2 and 4 to, the Legal Services Act 2007);
(c) certain officials of the Senior Courts (section 2 of the Commissioners for Oaths Act 1889);
(d) a circuit judge or district judge (section 58 of the County Courts Act 1984);
(e) any justice of the peace (section 58 of the County Courts Act 1984); and
(f) certain officials of any county court appointed by the judge of that court for the purpose (section 58 of the County Courts Act 1984).

6.4 A witness statement must include a statement of truth by the intended maker as follows:

"I believe that the facts stated in this witness statement are true."

(Attention is drawn to rule 17.6 which sets out the consequences of verifying a witness statement containing a false statement without an honest belief in its truth.)

(For information regarding statements of truth, see Part 17 (Statements of truth) and Practice Direction 17A.)

(Paragraphs 7.1 to 7.4 below set out the procedures to be followed where the intended maker of an affidavit or witness statement is unable to read or sign the affidavit/statement.)

6.5 If, in proceedings under Part 14 (Adoption, placement and related proceedings), a serial number has been assigned under rule 14.2 or the name of the maker of the affidavit/statement is not being revealed in accordance with rule 29.1, the signature of the maker will be edited from the affidavit/statement before it is served on the other party.

Inability of maker to read or sign affidavit/statement

7.1 Where an affidavit is sworn by a deponent who is unable to read or sign it, the person before whom the affidavit is sworn must certify in the jurat that—

(a) that person read the affidavit to the deponent;
(b) the deponent appeared to understand it; and
(c) the deponent signed, or made his mark, in that person's presence.

7.2 If that certificate is not included in the jurat, the affidavit may not be used in evidence unless the court is satisfied that it was read to the deponent and that the

The Family Procedure Rules 2010

deponent appeared to understand it. Annex 1 to this practice direction sets out forms of the jurat with the certificate for an affidavit and an affirmation respectively.

7.3 Where a witness statement is made by a person who is unable to read or sign the statement, it must contain a certificate made by an authorised person. An authorised person is a person able to administer oaths and take affidavits but need not be independent of the parties or their representatives.

7.4 The authorised person must certify—

(a) that the witness statement has been read to the witness;
(b) that the witness appeared to understand it and approved its content as accurate;
(c) that the statement of truth has been read to the witness;
(d) that the witness appeared to understand the statement of truth and the consequences of making a false witness statement; and
(e) that the witness signed or made his or her mark in the presence of the authorised person.

The form of the certificate is set out at Annex 2 to this practice direction.

Filing of affidavits and witness statements

8.1 If the court directs that an affidavit/statement is to be filed, it must be filed in the court or Division, or office or Registry of the court or Division, where the action in which it was or is to be used, is proceeding or will proceed.

8.2 Where the affidavit/statement is in a foreign language—

(a) the party wishing to rely on it must—
 (i) have it translated; and
 (ii) must file the foreign language affidavit/statement with the court; and
(b) the translator must sign the translation to certify that it is accurate.

EXHIBITS

Manner of Exhibiting Documents

9.1 A document used in conjunction with an affidavit/statement should be—

(a) shown to and verified by the maker, and remain separate from the affidavit/statement; and
(b) identified by a declaration of the person before whom the affidavit/statement was sworn.

9.2 The declaration should be headed with the name of the proceedings in the same way as the affidavit/statement is headed.

9.3 The first page of each exhibit should be marked—

(a) as in paragraph 3.2 above; and
(b) with the exhibit mark referred to in the affidavit/statement in accordance with paragraph 4.5 above.

9.4 Where the maker makes more than one affidavit/statement, to which there are exhibits, in the same proceedings, the numbering of the exhibits should run consecutively throughout and not start again with each affidavit/statement.

Letters

10.1 Copies of individual letters should be collected together and exhibited in a bundle or bundles. They should be arranged in chronological order with the earliest at the top, and firmly secured.

10.2 When a bundle of correspondence is exhibited, the exhibit should have a front page attached stating that the bundle consists of original letters and copies. They should be arranged and secured as above and numbered consecutively.

Other documents

11.1 Photocopies instead of original documents may be exhibited provided the originals are made available for inspection by the other parties before the hearing and by the court at the hearing.

11.2 Court documents must not be exhibited (official copies of such documents prove themselves).

11.3 Where an exhibit contains more than one document, a front page should be attached setting out a list of the documents contained in the exhibit. The list should contain the dates of the documents.

Exhibits other than documents

12.1 Items other than documents should be clearly marked with an exhibit number or letter in such a manner that the mark cannot become detached from the exhibit.

12.2 Small items may be placed in a container and the container appropriately marked.

General provisions

13.1 Where an exhibit contains more than one document—

(a) the bundle should not be stapled but should be securely fastened in a way that does not hinder the reading of the documents; and
(b) the pages should be numbered consecutively at bottom centre.

13.2 Every page of an exhibit should be clearly legible; typed copies of illegible documents should be included, paginated with "a" numbers.

13.3 Where affidavits/statements and exhibits have become numerous, they should be put into separate bundles and the pages numbered consecutively throughout.

13.4 Where on account of their bulk the service of exhibits or copies of exhibits on the other parties would be difficult or impracticable, the directions of the court should be sought as to arrangements for bringing the exhibits to the attention of the other parties and as to their custody pending trial.

MISCELLANEOUS

Defects in affidavits, witness statement and exhibits

14.1 Where—

(a) an affidavit;
(b) a witness statement; or
(c) an exhibit to either an affidavit or a witness statement,

does not comply with Part 22 or this practice direction in relation to its form, the court may refuse to admit it as evidence and may refuse to allow the costs arising from its preparation.

14.2 Permission to file a defective affidavit or witness statement or to use a defective exhibit may be obtained from the court where the case is proceeding.

Affirmations

15.1 All provisions in this or any other practice direction relating to affidavits apply to affirmations with the following exceptions—

The Family Procedure Rules 2010

(a) the deponent should commence "I (full name) of (residential address) do solemnly and sincerely affirm . . . ";and
(b) in the jurat the word "sworn" is replaced by the word "affirmed".

Certificate of court officer

16.1 In proceedings under Part 7 (Matrimonial and Civil Partnership Proceedings), where the court has ordered that a witness statement, affidavit, affirmation or deposition is not be open to inspection by the public (see rule 22.19(2) and (3)) or that words or passages in the statement etc are not to be open to inspection (see rule 22.19(5)), the court officer will so certify on the statement etc and make any deletions directed by the court under rule 22.19(3).

Video Conferencing

17.1 Guidance on the use of video conferencing in the family courts is set out at Annex 3 to this practice direction.

A list of the sites which are available for video conferencing can be found on Her Majesty's Court Service's website at www.hm-courts-service.gov.uk.

ANNEX 1

Certificate to be used where a deponent to an affidavit is unable to read or sign it

Sworn at . . . this . . . day of . . . Before me, I having first read over the contents of this affidavit to the deponent [if there are exhibits, add "and explained the nature and effect of the exhibits referred to in it"] who appeared to understand it and approved its content as accurate, and made his/her* mark on the affidavit in my presence. Or, (after "Before me") the witness to the mark of the deponent having been first sworn that the witness had read over etc. (as above) and that the witness saw the deponent make his/her* mark on the affidavit. (Witness must sign.)

* *delete as appropriate*

Certificate to be used where a deponent to an affirmation is unable to read or sign it

Affirmed at . . . this . . . day of . . . Before me, I having first read over the contents of this affirmation to the deponent [if there are exhibits, add "and explained the nature and effect of the exhibits referred to in it"] who appeared to understand it and approved its content as accurate, and made his/her* mark on the affirmation in my presence. Or, (after "Before me") the witness to the mark of the deponent having been first sworn that the witness had read over etc. (as above) and that the witness saw the deponent make his/her* mark on the affirmation. (Witness must sign.)

* *delete as appropriate*

ANNEX 2

Certificate to be used where a witness is unable to read or sign a witness statement

I certify that I [name and address of authorised person] have read over the contents of this witness statement and the statement of truth to the witness [if there are exhibits, add "and explained the nature and effect of the exhibits referred to in it"] who (a) appeared to understand the witness statement and approved its content as accurate and (b) appeared to understand the statement of truth and the consequences of making a false witness statement, and [signed the statement] [made his/her mark]* in my presence.

* *delete as appropriate.*

FPR 2010, Practice Direction 22A

ANNEX 3

Video Conferencing Guidance

1   This guidance is for the use of video conferencing (VCF) in proceedings to which the Family Procedure Rules apply. It is in part based, with permission, upon the protocol of the Federal Court of Australia. It is intended to provide a guide to all persons involved in the use of VCF, although it does not attempt to cover all the practical questions which might arise.

Any reference in this guide to a judge is to be taken as including a district judge or justices of the peace if the proceedings are before a magistrates' court.

Video conferencing generally

2   The guidance covers the use of VCF equipment both (a) in a courtroom, whether via equipment which is permanently placed there or via a mobile unit, and (b) in a separate studio or conference room. In either case, the location at which the judge sits is referred to as the 'local site'. The other site or sites to and from which transmission is made are referred to as 'the remote site' and in any particular case any such site may be another courtroom. The guidance applies to cases where VCF is used for the taking of evidence and also to its use for other parts of any legal proceedings

3   VCF may be a convenient way of dealing with any part of proceedings— it can involve considerable savings in time and cost. Its use for the taking of evidence from overseas witnesses will, in particular, be likely to achieve a material saving of costs, and such savings may also be achieved by its use for taking domestic evidence. It is, however, inevitably not as ideal as having the witness physically present in court. Its convenience should not therefore be allowed to dictate its use. A judgment must be made in every case in which the use of VCF is being considered not only as to whether it will achieve an overall cost saving but as to whether its use will be likely to be beneficial to the efficient, fair and economic disposal of the litigation. In particular, it needs to be recognised that the degree of control a court can exercise over a witness at the remote site is or may be more limited than it can exercise over a witness physically before it.

4   When used for the taking of evidence, the objective should be to make the VCF session as close as possible to the usual practice in court where evidence is taken in open court. To gain the maximum benefit, several differences have to be taken into account. Some matters, which are taken for granted when evidence is taken in the conventional way, take on a different dimension when it is taken by VCF— for example, the administration of the oath, ensuring that the witness understands who is at the local site and what their various roles are, the raising of any objections to the evidence and the use of documents.

5   It should not be presumed that all foreign governments are willing to allow their nationals or others within their jurisdiction to be examined before a court in England or Wales by means of VCF. If there is any doubt about this, enquiries should be directed to the Foreign and Commonwealth Office (International Legal Matters Unit, Consular Division) with a view to ensuring that the country from which the evidence is to be taken raises no objection to it at diplomatic level. The party who is directed to be responsible for arranging the VCF (see paragraph 8) will be required to make all necessary inquiries about this well in advance of the VCF and must be able to inform the court what those inquiries were and of their outcome.

6   Time zone differences need to be considered when a witness abroad is to be examined in England or Wales by VCF. The convenience of the witness, the parties, their representatives and the court must all be taken into account. The cost of the use of a commercial studio is usually greater outside normal business hours.

7   Those involved with VCF need to be aware that, even with the most advanced systems currently available, there are the briefest of delays between the receipt of the picture and that of the accompanying sound. If due allowance is not made for this, there

The Family Procedure Rules 2010

will be a tendency to 'speak over' the witness, whose voice will continue to be heard for a millisecond or so after he or she appears on the screen to have finished speaking.

8   With current technology, picture quality is good, but not as good as a television picture. The quality of the picture is enhanced if those appearing on VCF monitors keep their movements to a minimum.

Preliminary arrangements

9   The court's permission is required for any part of any proceedings to be dealt with by means of VCF. Before seeking a direction, the applicant should notify the listing officer, diary manager or other appropriate court officer of the intention to seek it, and should enquire as to the availability of court VCF equipment for the day or days of the proposed VCF. If all parties consent to a direction, permission can be sought by letter, fax or e-mail, although the court may still require an oral hearing. All parties are entitled to be heard on whether or not such a direction should be given and as to its terms. If a witness at a remote site is to give evidence by an interpreter, consideration should be given at this stage as to whether the interpreter should be at the local site or the remote site. If a VCF direction is given, arrangements for the transmission will then need to be made. The court will ordinarily direct that the party seeking permission to use VCF is to be responsible for this. That party is hereafter referred to as 'the VCF arranging party'.

10   Subject to any order to the contrary, all costs of the transmission, including the costs of hiring equipment and technical personnel to operate it, will initially be the responsibility of, and must be met by, the VCF arranging party. All reasonable efforts should be made to keep the transmission to a minimum and so keep the costs down. All such costs will be considered to be part of the costs of the proceedings and the court will determine at such subsequent time as is convenient or appropriate who, as between the parties, should be responsible for them and (if appropriate) in what proportions.

11   The local site will, if practicable, be a courtroom but it may instead be an appropriate studio or conference room. The VCF arranging party must contact the listing officer, diary manager or other appropriate officer of the court which made the VCF direction and make arrangements for the VCF transmission. Details of the remote site, and of the equipment to be used both at the local site (if not being supplied by the court) and the remote site (including the number of ISDN lines and connection speed), together with all necessary contact names and telephone numbers, will have to be provided to the listing officer, diary manager or other court officer. The court will need to be satisfied that any equipment provided by the parties for use at the local site and also that at the remote site is of sufficient quality for a satisfactory transmission. The VCF arranging party must ensure that an appropriate person will be present at the local site to supervise the operation of the VCF throughout the transmission in order to deal with any technical problems. That party must also arrange for a technical assistant to be similarly present at the remote site for like purposes.

12   It is recommended that the judge, practitioners and witness should arrive at their respective VCF sites about 20 minutes prior to the scheduled commencement of the transmission.

13   If the local site is not a courtroom, but a conference room or studio, the judge will need to determine who is to sit where. The VCF arranging party must take care to ensure that the number of microphones is adequate for the speakers and that the panning of the camera for the practitioners' table encompasses all legal representatives so that the viewer can see everyone seated there.

14   If the local site is to be a studio or conference room, the VCF arranging party must ensure that it provides sufficient accommodation to enable a reasonable number of members of the public to attend if appropriate.

15   In cases where the local site is a studio or conference room, the VCF arranging party should make arrangements, if practicable, for the royal coat of arms to be placed above the judge's seat.

16   In cases in which the VCF is to be used for the taking of evidence, the VCF

arranging party must arrange for recording equipment to be provided by the court which made the VCF direction so that the evidence can be recorded. An associate will normally be present to operate the recording equipment when the local site is a courtroom. The VCF arranging party should take steps to ensure that an associate is present to do likewise when it is a studio or conference room. The equipment should be set up and tested before the VCF transmission. It will often be a valuable safeguard for the VCF arranging party also to arrange for the provision of recording equipment at the remote site. This will provide a useful back-up if there is any reduction in sound quality during the transmission. A direction from the court for the making of such a back-up recording must, however, be obtained first. This is because the proceedings are court proceedings and, save as directed by the court, no other recording of them must be made. The court will direct what is to happen to the back-up recording.

17   Some countries may require that any oath or affirmation to be taken by a witness accord with local custom rather than the usual form of oath or affirmation used in England and Wales. The VCF arranging party must make all appropriate prior inquiries and put in place all arrangements necessary to enable the oath or affirmation to be taken in accordance with any local custom. That party must be in a position to inform the court what those inquiries were, what their outcome was and what arrangements have been made. If the oath or affirmation can be administered in the manner normal in England and Wales, the VCF arranging party must arrange in advance to have the appropriate holy book at the remote site. The associate will normally administer the oath.

18   Consideration will need to be given in advance to the documents to which the witness is likely to be referred. The parties should endeavour to agree on this. It will usually be most convenient for a bundle of the copy documents to be prepared in advance, which the VCF arranging party should then send to the remote site.

19   Additional documents are sometimes quite properly introduced during the course of a witness's evidence. To cater for this, the VCF arranging party should ensure that equipment is available to enable documents to be transmitted between sites during the course of the VCF transmission. Consideration should be given to whether to use a document camera. If it is decided to use one, arrangements for its use will need to be established in advance. The panel operator will need to know the number and size of documents or objects if their images are to be sent by document camera. In many cases, a simpler and sufficient alternative will be to ensure that there are fax transmission and reception facilities at the participating sites.

The hearing

20   The procedure for conducting the transmission will be determined by the judge. He will determine who is to control the cameras. In cases where the VCF is being used for an application in the course of the proceedings, the judge will ordinarily not enter the local site until both sites are on line. Similarly, at the conclusion of the hearing, he will ordinarily leave the local site while both sites are still on line. The following paragraphs apply primarily to cases where the VCF is being used for the taking of the evidence of a witness at a remote site.

21   At the beginning of the transmission, the judge will probably wish to introduce himself or herself and the advocates to the witness. He will probably want to know who is at the remote site and will invite the witness to introduce himself or herself and anyone else who is with the witness. The judge may wish to give directions as to the seating arrangements at the remote site so that those present are visible at the local site during the taking of the evidence and to explain to the witness the method of taking the oath or of affirming, the manner in which the evidence will be taken, and who will be conducting the examination and cross-examination. The judge will probably also wish to inform the witness of the matters referred to in paragraphs 7 and 8 (co-ordination of picture with sound, and picture quality).

22   The examination of the witness at the remote site should follow as closely as possible the practice adopted when a witness is in the courtroom. During examination, cross-examination and re-examination, the witness must be able to see the legal representative asking the question and also any other person (whether another legal

The Family Procedure Rules 2010

representative or the judge) making any statements in regard to the witness's evidence. It will in practice be most convenient if everyone remains seated throughout the transmission

PART 23

MISCELLANEOUS RULES ABOUT EVIDENCE

23.1. Scope and interpretation of this Part
Rules 23.2 to 23.6 apply to evidence to which the Children (Admissibility of Hearsay Evidence) Order 1993 does not apply.

23.2.— Notice of intention to rely on hearsay evidence
(1) Where a party intends to rely on hearsay evidence at the final hearing and either—
    (a) that evidence is to be given by a witness giving oral evidence; or
    (b) that evidence is contained in a witness statement of a person who is not being called to give oral evidence,
that party complies with section 2(1)(a) of the Civil Evidence Act 1995 by serving a witness statement on the other parties in accordance with the court's directions.

(2) Where paragraph (1)(b) applies, the party intending to rely on the hearsay evidence must, when serving the witness statement—
    (a) inform the other parties that the witness is not being called to give oral evidence; and
    (b) give the reason why the witness will not be called.

(3) In all other cases where a party intends to rely on hearsay evidence at the final hearing, that party complies with section 2(1)(a) of the Civil Evidence Act 1995 by serving a notice on the other parties which—
    (a) identifies the hearsay evidence;
    (b) states that the party serving the notice proposes to rely on the hearsay evidence at the final hearing; and
    (c) gives the reason why the witness will not be called.

(4) The party proposing to rely on the hearsay evidence must—
    (a) serve the notice no later than the latest date for serving witness statements; and
    (b) if the hearsay evidence is to be in a document, supply a copy to any party who requests it.

23.3. Circumstances in which notice of intention to rely on hearsay evidence is not required
Section 2(1) of the Civil Evidence Act 1995 (duty to give notice of intention to rely on hearsay evidence) does not apply—
    (a) to evidence at hearings other than final hearings;
    (b) to an affidavit[GL] or witness statement which is to be used at the final hearing but which does not contain hearsay evidence; or
    (c) where the requirement is excluded by a practice direction.

23.4.— Power to call witness for cross-examination on hearsay evidence
(1) Where a party—
    (a) proposes to rely on hearsay evidence; and
    (b) does not propose to call the person who made the original statement to give oral evidence,
the court may, on the application of any other party, permit that party to call the maker of the statement to be cross-examined[GL] on the contents of the statement.

(2) An application for permission to cross-examine[GL] under this rule must be made within 14 days beginning with the date on which a notice of intention to rely on the hearsay evidence was served on the applicant.

(Rules 35.3 and 35.4 contain rules in relation to evidence arising out of mediation of cross-border disputes.)

23.5.— Credibility

(1) Where a party proposes to rely on hearsay evidence, but—
  (a) does not propose to call the person who made the original statement to give oral evidence; and
  (b) another party wishes to call evidence to attack the credibility of the person who made the statement,

the party who so wishes must give notice of that intention to the party who proposes to give the hearsay statement in evidence.

(2) A party must give notice under paragraph (1) within 14 days after the date on which a hearsay notice relating to the hearsay evidence was served on that party.

23.6.— Use of plans, photographs and models etc as evidence

(1) This rule applies to—
  (a) evidence (such as a plan, photograph or model) which is not—
    (i) contained in a witness statement, affidavit$^{(GL)}$ or expert's report;
    (ii) to be given orally at the final hearing; or
    (iii) evidence of which prior notice must be given under rule 23.2; and
  (b) documents which may be received in evidence without further proof under section 9 of the Civil Evidence Act 1995.

(2) Except as provided below, section 2(1)(a) of the Civil Evidence Act 1995 (notice of proposal to adduce hearsay evidence) does not apply to evidence falling within paragraph (1).

(3) Such evidence is not receivable at the final hearing unless the party intending to rely on it (in this rule, "the party") has—
  (a) served it or, in the case of a model, a photograph of it with an invitation to inspect the original, on the other party in accordance with this rule; or
  (b) complied with such directions as the court may give for serving the evidence on, or for giving notice under section 2(1)(a) of the Civil Evidence Act 1995 in respect of the evidence to, the other party.

(4) Where the party intends to use the evidence as evidence of any fact then, except where paragraph (6) applies, the party must serve the evidence not later than the latest date for serving witness statements.

(5) The party must serve the evidence at least 21 days before the hearing at which the party proposes to rely on it if—
  (a) there are not to be witness statements; or
  (b) the party intends to put in the evidence solely in order to disprove an allegation made in a witness statement.

(6) Where the evidence forms part of expert evidence, the party must serve the evidence when the expert's report is served on the other party.

(7) Where the evidence is being produced to the court for any reason other than as part of factual or expert evidence, the party must serve the evidence at least 21 days before the hearing at which the party proposes to rely on it.

(8) Where the court directs a party to give notice that the party intends to put in the evidence, the court may direct that every other party be given an opportunity to inspect it and to agree to its admission without further proof.

23.7.— Evidence of finding on question of foreign law

(1) This rule sets out the procedure which must be followed by a party (in this rule, "the party") who intends to put in evidence a finding on a question of foreign law by virtue of section 4(2) of the Civil Evidence Act 1972.

(2) The party must give any other party notice of that intention.

(3) The party must give the notice—
  (a) if there are to be witness statements, not later than the latest date for serving them; or

(b) otherwise, not less than 21 days before the hearing at which the party proposes to put the finding in evidence.
(4) The notice must—
   (a) specify the question on which the finding was made; and
   (b) enclose a copy of a document where it is reported or recorded.

23.8. Evidence of consent of trustee to act
In proceedings to which Part 9 (financial remedies) applies, a document purporting to contain the written consent of a person to act as trustee and to bear that person's signature verified by some other person is evidence of such consent.

23.9. Note of oral evidence in magistrates' courts
In proceedings in a magistrates' court, the justices' clerk or the court shall keep a note of the substance of the oral evidence given at a directions appointment or at a hearing of any proceedings.

PART 23 COMMENTARY

No practice directions supplements Part 23.

Part 23 contains further rules of evidence. Rules 23.2 to 23.6 deal with hearsay evidence. Rule 23.7 deals with evidence of a finding of foreign law, r 23.8 deals with evidence of the consent of a person to act as trustee, and r 23.9 requires the court or justice's clerk to keep a note of oral evidence in the magistrates' court.

PART 24

WITNESSES, DEPOSITIONS GENERALLY AND TAKING OF EVIDENCE IN MEMBER STATES OF THE EUROPEAN UNION

CHAPTER 1

WITNESSES AND DEPOSITIONS

24.1.— Scope of this Chapter
(1) This Chapter provides—
   (a) for the circumstances in which a person may be required to attend court to give evidence or to produce a document; and
   (b) for a party to obtain evidence before a hearing to be used at the hearing.
(2) This Chapter, apart from rule 24.10(2) to (4), does not apply to proceedings in a magistrates' court.
(Rules 34.16 to 34.21 and 34.24 of the CPR apply to incoming requests for evidence.)

24.2.— Witness summonses
(1) A witness summons is a document issued by the court requiring a witness to—
   (a) attend court to give evidence; or
   (b) produce documents to the court.
(2) A witness summons must be in the form set out in Practice Direction 24A.
(3) There must be a separate witness summons for each witness.
(4) A witness summons may require a witness to produce documents to the court either—
   (a) on the date fixed for a hearing; or
   (b) on such date as the court may direct.
(5) The only documents that a summons under this rule can require a person to produce before a hearing are documents which that person could be required to produce at the hearing.

(Rules 35.3 and 35.4 contain rules in relation to evidence arising out of mediation of cross-border disputes.)

24.3.— Issue of a witness summons
(1) A witness summons is issued on the date entered on the summons by the court.
(2) A party must obtain permission from the court where that party wishes to—
- (a) have a summons issued less than 7 days before the date of the final hearing;
- (b) have a summons issued for a witness to attend court to give evidence or to produce documents on any date except the date fixed for the final hearing; or
- (c) have a summons issued for a witness to attend court to give evidence or to produce documents at any hearing except the final hearing.

(3) A witness summons must be issued by—
- (a) the court where the case is proceeding; or
- (b) the court where the hearing in question will be held.

(4) The court may set aside (GL.)or vary a witness summons issued under this rule.

24.4.— Time for serving a witness summons
(1) The general rule is that a witness summons is binding if it is served at least 7 days before the date on which the witness is required to attend before the court.

(2) The court may direct that a witness summons is binding although it is served less than 7 days before the date on which the witness is required to attend before the court.

(3) A witness summons which is—
- (a) served in accordance with this rule; and
- (b) requires the witness to attend court to give evidence,

is binding until the conclusion of the hearing at which the attendance of the witness is required.

(Rules 35.3 and 35.4 contain rules in relation to evidence arising out of mediation of cross-border disputes.)

24.5.— Who is to serve a witness summons
(1) Subject to paragraph (2), a witness summons is to be served by the party on whose behalf it is issued unless that party indicates in writing, when asking the court to issue the summons, that that party wishes the court to serve it instead.

(2) In proceedings to which Part 14 (procedure for applications in adoption, placement and related proceedings) applies, a witness summons is to be served by the court unless the court directs otherwise.

(3) Where the court is to serve the witness summons, the party on whose behalf it is issued must deposit, in the court office, the money to be paid or offered to the witness under rule 24.6.

24.6. Right of witness to travelling expenses and compensation for loss of time
At the time of service of a witness summons the witness must be offered or paid—
- (a) a sum reasonably sufficient to cover the expenses of the witness in travelling to and from the court; and
- (b) such sum by way of compensation for loss of time as may be specified in Practice Direction 24A.

24.7.— Evidence by deposition
(1) A party may apply for an order for a person to be examined before the hearing takes place.

(2) A person from whom evidence is to be obtained following an order under this rule is referred to as a 'deponent' and the evidence is referred to as a 'deposition'.

(3) An order under this rule is for a deponent to be examined on oath before—
- (a) a judge;
- (b) an examiner of the court; or
- (c) such other person as the court appoints.

The Family Procedure Rules 2010

(Rule 24.14 makes provision for the appointment of examiners of the court.)

(4) The order may require the production of any document which the court considers is necessary for the purposes of the examination.

(5) The order must state the date, time and place of the examination.

(6) At the time of service of the order the deponent must be offered or paid—
- (a) a sum reasonably sufficient to cover the expenses of the deponent in travelling to and from the place of examination; and
- (b) such sum by way of compensation for loss of time as may be specified in Practice Direction 24A.

(7) Where the court makes an order for a deposition to be taken, it may also order the party who obtained the order to serve a witness statement or witness summary in relation to the evidence to be given by the person to be examined.

(Part 22 (evidence) contains the general rules about witness statements and witness summaries.)

(Rules 35.3 and 35.4 contain rules in relation to evidence arising out of mediation of cross-border disputes.)

24.8.— Conduct of examination

(1) Subject to any directions contained in the order for examination, the examination must be conducted in the same way as if the witness were giving evidence at a final hearing.

(2) If all the parties are present, the examiner may conduct the examination of a person not named in the order for examination if all the parties and the person to be examined consent.

(3) In defended proceedings under Part 7 (matrimonial and civil partnership proceedings), the examiner may conduct the examination in private if of the view that it is appropriate to do so.

(4) Save in proceedings to which paragraph (3) applies, the examiner will conduct the examination in private unless of the view that it is not appropriate to do so.

(5) The examiner must ensure that the evidence given by the witness is recorded in full.

(6) The examiner must send a copy of the deposition—
- (a) to the person who obtained the order for the examination of the witness; and
- (b) to the court where the case is proceeding.

(7) The court will give directions as to service of the deposition on the other party.

24.9.— Enforcing attendance of witness

(1) If a person served with an order to attend before an examiner—
- (a) fails to attend; or
- (b) refuses to be sworn for the purpose of the examination or to answer any lawful question or produce any document at the examination,

a certificate of that person's failure or refusal, signed by the examiner, must be filed by the party requiring the deposition.

(2) On the certificate being filed, the party requiring the deposition may apply to the court for an order requiring that person to attend or to be sworn or to answer any question or produce any document, as the case may be.

(3) An application for an order under this rule may be made without notice.

(4) The court may order the person against whom an order is made under this rule to pay any costs resulting from that person's failure or refusal.

(Rules 35.3 and 35.4 contain rules in relation to evidence arising out of mediation of cross-border disputes. Rule 35.4(1)(d) relates specifically to this rule.)

24.10.— Use of deposition at a hearing

(1) A deposition ordered under rule 24.7 may be given in evidence at a hearing unless the court orders otherwise.

(2) A party intending to put in evidence a deposition at a hearing must file notice of intention to do so on the court and the court will give directions about serving the notice on every other party.

(3) The party must file the notice at least 21 days before the day fixed for the hearing.

(4) The court may require a deponent to attend the hearing and give evidence orally.

(5) Where a deposition is given in evidence at the final hearing, it is treated as if it were a witness statement for the purposes of rule 22.19 (availability of witness statements for inspection).

(Rules 35.3 and 35.4 contain rules in relation to evidence arising out of mediation of cross-border disputes. Rule 35.4(1)(e) relates specifically to this rule.)

24.11.— Restrictions on subsequent use of deposition taken for the purpose of any hearing except the final hearing

(1) This rule applies to proceedings under Part 7 (matrimonial and civil partnership proceedings) or Part 9 (financial remedies).

(2) Where the court orders a party to be examined about that party's or any other assets for the purpose of any hearing except the final hearing, the deposition may be used only for the purpose of the proceedings in which the order was made.

(3) However it may be used for some other purpose—
- (a) by the party who was examined;
- (b) if the party who was examined agrees; or
- (c) if the court gives permission.

24.12.— Where a person to be examined is out of the jurisdiction – letter of request

(1) This rule applies where a party wishes to take a deposition from a person who is—
- (a) out of the jurisdiction; and
- (b) not in a Regulation State within the meaning of Chapter 2 of this Part.

(2) The High Court may order the issue of a letter of request to the judicial authorities of the country in which the proposed deponent is.

(3) A letter of request is a request to a judicial authority to take the evidence of that person, or arrange for it to be taken.

(4) The High Court may make an order under this rule in relation to county court proceedings.

(5) If the government of a country allows a person appointed by the High Court to examine a person in that country, the High Court may make an order appointing a special examiner for that purpose.

(6) A person may be examined under this rule on oath or affirmation or in accordance with any procedure permitted in the country in which the examination is to take place.

(7) If the High Court makes an order for the issue of a letter of request, the party who sought the order must file—
- (a) the following documents and, except where paragraph (8) applies, a translation of them—
  - (i) a draft letter of request;
  - (ii) a statement of the issues relevant to the proceedings; and
  - (iii) a list of questions or the subject matter of questions to be put to the person to be examined; and
- (b) an undertaking to be responsible for the Secretary of State's expenses.

(8) There is no need to file a translation if—
- (a) English is one of the official languages of the country where the examination is to take place; or
- (b) a practice direction has specified that country as a country where no translation is necessary.

(Rules 35.3 and 35.4 contain rules in relation to evidence arising out of mediation of cross-border disputes. Rule 35.4(1)(f) relates specifically to this rule.)

24.13.— Fees and expenses of examiner of the court

(1) An examiner of the court may charge a fee for the examination.

(2) The examiner need not send the deposition to the court unless the fee is paid.

(3) The examiner's fees and expenses must be paid by the party who obtained the order for examination.

(4) If the fees and expenses due to an examiner are not paid within a reasonable time, the examiner may report that fact to the court.

(5) The court may order the party who obtained the order for examination to deposit in the court office a specified sum in respect of the examiner's fees and, where it does so, the examiner will not be asked to act until the sum has been deposited.

(6) An order under this rule does not affect any decision as to the party who is ultimately to bear the costs of the examination.

24.14.— Examiners of the court

(1) The Lord Chancellor will appoint persons to be examiners of the court.

(2) The persons appointed must be barristers or solicitor-advocates who have been practising for a period of not less than 3 years.

(3) The Lord Chancellor may revoke an appointment at any time.

CHAPTER 2

Taking of evidence – member states of the European Union

24.15. Interpretation

In this Chapter—

"designated court" has the meaning given in Practice Direction 24A;

"Regulation State" has the same meaning as 'Member State' in the Taking of Evidence Regulation, that is all Member States except Denmark;

"the Taking of Evidence Regulation" means Council Regulation (EC) No. 1206/2001 of 28 May 2001 on co-operation between the courts of the Member States in the taking of evidence in civil or commercial matters.

24.16.— Where a person to be examined is in another Regulation State

(1) This rule applies where a party wishes to take a deposition from a person who is—
    (a) outside the jurisdiction; and
    (b) in a Regulation State.

(2) The court may order the issue of a request to a designated court ('the requested court') in the Regulation State in which the proposed deponent is.

(3) If the court makes an order for the issue of a request, the party who sought the order must file—
    (a) a draft Form A as set out in the annex to the Taking of Evidence Regulation (request for the taking of evidence);
    (b) except where paragraph (4) applies, a translation of the form;
    (c) an undertaking to be responsible for costs sought by the requested court in relation to—
        (i) fees paid to experts and interpreters; and
        (ii) where requested by that party, the use of special procedures or communications technology; and
    (d) an undertaking to be responsible for the court's expenses.

(4) There is no need to file a translation if—
    (a) English is one of the official languages of the Regulation State where the examination is to take place; or
    (b) the Regulation State has indicated, in accordance with the Taking of Evidence Regulation, that English is a language which it will accept.

(5) Where article 17 of the Taking of Evidence Regulation (direct taking of evidence by the requested court) allows evidence to be taken directly in another Regulation State, the court may make an order for the submission of a request in accordance with that article.

(6) If the court makes an order for the submission of a request under paragraph (5), the party who sought the order must file—
    (a) a draft Form I as set out in the annex to the Taking of Evidence Regulation (request for direct taking of evidence);
    (b) except where paragraph (4) applies, a translation of the form; and

(c) an undertaking to be responsible for the court's expenses.

PART 24 COMMENTARY

Part 24 is supplemented by PD24A.

Part 24 deals with witnesses, depositions and taking evidence in member states of the European Union.

Chapter 1 deals with witness summons (rr 24.2 to 24.6) including provision for the production of documents (r 24.2(1)), and at r 24.3(2) to have a witness summons issued for a date or a hearing other than the final hearing (subject to obtaining permission of the court). It introduces and makes provision for evidence by deposition (rr 24.7 to 24.11). And it provides for letters of request (to non-Regulation states).

Chapter 2 deals with taking a deposition from a person in another Regulation state (that is all EU member states except Denmark).

The form relevant to Part 24 is Form FP 25 – Witness summons.

PRACTICE DIRECTION 24A – WITNESSES, DEPOSITIONS AND TAKING OF EVIDENCE IN MEMBER STATES OF THE EUROPEAN UNION

This Practice Direction supplements FPR Part 24

WITNESS SUMMONSES

Issue of witness summons

1.1 A witness summons may require a witness to—

(a) attend court to give evidence;
(b) produce documents to the court; or
(c) both,

on either a date fixed for the hearing or such date as the court may direct (see rule 24.2).

(In relation to cases to which the Mediation Directive applies, rules 35.3 and 35.4 contain rules in relation to mediation evidence)

1.2 Two copies of the witness summons should be filed with the court for sealing, one of which will be retained on the court file.

1.3 A mistake in the name or address of a person named in a witness summons may be corrected if the summons has not been served.

1.4 The corrected summons must be re-sealed by the court and marked "Amended and Re-Sealed'.

Magistrates' courts proceedings

2.1 An application for the issue of a summons or warrant under section 97 of the Magistrates' Courts Act 1980 may be made by the applicant in person or by his legal representative.

2.2 An application for the issue of such a summons may be made by delivering or sending the application in writing to the court officer for the magistrates' court.

The Family Procedure Rules 2010

Travelling expenses and compensation for loss of time

3.1 When a witness is served with a witness summons the witness must be offered a sum to cover travelling expenses to and from the court and compensation for loss of time (see rule 24.6).

3.2 If the witness summons is to be served by the court, the party issuing the summons must deposit with the court—

(a) a sum sufficient to pay for the witness's expenses in travelling to the court and in returning to his or her home or place of work; and
(b) a sum in respect of the period during which earnings or benefit are lost, or such lesser sum as it may be proved that the witness will lose as a result of attendance at court in answer to the witness summons.

3.3 The sum referred to in paragraph 3.2(b) is to be based on the sums payable to witnesses attending the Crown Court (fixed pursuant to the Prosecution of Offences Act 1985 and Costs in Criminal Cases (General) Regulations 1986).

Depositions to be taken in England and Wales for use as evidence in proceedings in courts in England and Wales

4.1 A party may apply for an order for a person to be examined on oath before—

(a) a judge;
(b) an examiner of the court; or
(c) such other person as the court may appoint (see rule 24.7(3)).

(This is subject to rules about mediation evidence in cases to which the Mediation Directive applies: see rules 35.3 and 35.4)

4.2 The party who obtains an order for the examination of a deponent (see rule 24.7(2)) before an examiner of the court must—

(a) apply to the Foreign Process Section of the Masters' Secretary's Department at the Royal Courts of Justice for the allocation of an examiner;
(b) when allocated, provide the examiner with copies of all documents in the proceedings necessary to inform the examiner of the issues; and
(c) pay the deponent a sum to cover travelling expenses to and from the examination and compensation for loss of time (see rule 24.7(6)).

4.3 In ensuring that the deponent's evidence is recorded in full, the court or the examiner may permit it to be recorded on audiotape or videotape, but the deposition (see rule 24.7(2)) must always be recorded in writing by the examiner or by a competent shorthand writer or stenographer.

4.4 If the deposition is not recorded word for word, it must contain, as nearly as may be, the statement of the deponent. The examiner may record word for word any particular questions and answers which appear to have special importance.

4.5 If a deponent objects to answering any question or where any objection is taken to any question, the examiner must—

(a) record in the deposition or a document attached to it—
    (i) the question;
    (ii) the nature of and grounds for the objection;
    (iii) any answer given; and
(b) give the examiner's opinion as to the validity of the objection and must record it in the deposition or a document attached to it.

The court will decide as to the validity of the objection and any question of costs arising from it.

4.6 Documents and exhibits must—

(a) have an identifying number or letter marked on them by the examiner; and

(b) be preserved by the party or legal representative (see rule 2.3) who obtained the order for the examination, or as the court or the examiner may direct.

4.7 The examiner may put any question to the deponent as to—

(a) the meaning of any of the deponent's answers; or
(b) any matter arising in the course of the examination.

4.8 Where a deponent—

(a) fails to attend the examination; or
(b) refuses to—
   (i) be sworn; or
   (ii) answer any lawful question; or
   (iii) produce any document,

the examiner will sign a certificate (see rule 24.9) of such failure or refusal and may include in the certificate any comment as to the conduct of the deponent or of any person attending the examination.

4.9 The party who obtained the order for the examination must file the certificate with the court and may apply for an order that the deponent attend for examination or produce any document, as the case may be (see rule 24.9(2) and (3)). The application may be made without notice.

4.10 The court will make such order on the application as it thinks fit including an order for the deponent to pay any costs resulting from the failure or refusal (see rule 24.9(4)).

4.11 A deponent who wilfully refuses to obey an order of the High Court or the county court made under Part 24 may be proceeded against for contempt of court. (Where a person fails to attend before a magistrates' court in answer to a summons issued under section 97 of the Magistrates' Court Act 1980, the court may, under certain circumstances, issue a warrant for that party's arrest and to bring that party before the court at a time and place specified in the warrant: see section 97(3) of the 1980 Act.)

4.12 A deposition must—

(a) be signed by the examiner;
(b) have any amendments to it initialled by the examiner and the deponent;
(c) be endorsed by the examiner with—
   (i) a statement of the time occupied by the examination; and
   (ii) a record of any refusal by the deponent to sign the deposition and of the deponent's reasons for not doing so; and
(d) be sent by the examiner to the court where the proceedings are taking place for filing on the court file.

4.13 Rule 24.13 deals with the fees and expenses of an examiner.

Depositions to be taken abroad for use as evidence in proceedings before courts in England and Wales (where the Taking of Evidence Regulation does not apply)

5.1 Where a party wishes to take a deposition from a person outside the jurisdiction, the High Court may order the issue of a letter of request to the judicial authorities of the country in which the proposed deponent is (see rule 24.12).

(Rule 35.4(1)(f) deals with letters of request where the Mediation Directive applies)

5.2 An application for an order referred to in paragraph 5.1 should be made by application notice in accordance with Part 18 (Procedure for other applications in proceedings).

5.3 The documents which a party applying for an order for the issue of a letter of request must file with the application notice are set out in rule 24.12(7). They are as follows—

The Family Procedure Rules 2010

(a) a draft letter of request in the form set out in Annex A to this practice direction;
(b) a statement of the issues relevant to the proceedings;
(c) a list of questions or the subject matter of questions to be put to the proposed deponent;
(d) a translation of the documents in (a), (b) and (c), unless the proposed deponent is in a country of which English is an official language; and
(e) an undertaking to be responsible for the expenses of the Secretary of State.

In addition to the documents listed above the party applying for the order must file a draft order.

5.4 The above documents should be filed with the Masters' Secretary in Room E214, Royal Courts of Justice, Strand, London WC2A 2LL.

5.5 The application will be dealt with by the Senior Master of the Queen's Bench Division of the Senior Courts who will, if appropriate, sign the letter of request.

5.6 Attention is drawn to the provisions of rule 18.11 (Application to set aside or vary order made without notice).

5.7 If parties are in doubt as to whether a translation under paragraph 5.3(d) is required, they should seek guidance from the Foreign Process Section of the Masters' Secretary's Department.

5.8 A special examiner appointed under rule 24.12(5) may be the British Consul or the Consul-General or his deputy in the country where the evidence is to be taken if—

(a) there is in respect of that country a Civil Procedure Convention providing for the taking of evidence in that country for the assistance of proceedings in the High Court or other court in this country; or
(b) the Secretary of State has consented.

5.9 The provisions of paragraphs 4.1 to 4.12 apply to the depositions referred to in this paragraph.

TAKING OF EVIDENCE BETWEEN EU MEMBER STATES

Taking of Evidence Regulation

6.1 Where evidence is to be taken from a person in another Member State of the European Union for use as evidence in proceedings before courts in England and Wales Council Regulation (EC) No 1206/2001 of 28 May 2001 on co-operation between the courts of the Member States in the taking of evidence in civil or commercial matters ('the Taking of Evidence Regulation') applies.

6.2 The Taking of Evidence Regulation is annexed to this practice direction as Annex B.

6.3 The Taking of Evidence Regulation does not apply to Denmark. In relation to Denmark, therefore, rule 24.12 will continue to apply.

(Article 21(1) of the Taking of Evidence Regulation provides that the Regulation prevails over other provisions contained in bilateral or multilateral agreements or arrangements concluded by the Member States.)

Originally published in the official languages of the European Community in the Official Journal of the European Communities by the Office for Official Publications of the European Communities.

Meaning of 'designated court'

7.1 In accordance with the Taking of Evidence Regulation, each Regulation State has prepared a list of courts competent to take evidence in accordance with the Regulation indicating the territorial and, where appropriate, special jurisdiction of those courts.

7.2 Where Chapter 2 of this Part refers to a 'designated court' in relation to another

Regulation State, the reference is to the court, referred to in the list of competent courts of that State, which is appropriate to the application in hand.

7.3 Where the reference is to the 'designated court' in England and Wales, the reference is to the appropriate competent court in the jurisdiction. The designated courts for England and Wales are listed in Annex C to this practice direction.

Central Body

8.1 The Taking of Evidence Regulation stipulates that each Regulation State must nominate a Central Body responsible for—

(a)   supplying information to courts;
(b)   seeking solutions to any difficulties which may arise in respect of a request; and
(c)   forwarding, in exceptional cases, at the request of a requesting court, a request to the competent court.

8.2 The United Kingdom has nominated the Senior Master of the Queen's Bench Division, to be the Central Body for England and Wales.

8.3 The Senior Master, as Central Body, has been designated responsible for taking decisions on requests pursuant to Article 17 of the Regulation. Article 17 allows a court to submit a request to the Central Body or a designated competent authority in another Regulation State to take evidence directly in that State.

Evidence to be taken in another Regulation State for use in England and Wales

9.1 Where a person wishes to take a deposition from a person in another Regulation State, the court where the proceedings are taking place may order the issue of a request to the designated court in the Regulation State (rule 24.16 (2)). The form of request is prescribed as Form A in the Taking of Evidence Regulation.

9.2 An application to the court for an order under rule 24.16(2) should be made by application notice in accordance with Part 18 (Procedure for other applications in proceedings).

9.3 Rule 24.16(3) provides that the party applying for the order must file a draft form of request in the prescribed form. Where completion of the form requires attachments or documents to accompany the form, these must also be filed.

9.4 If the court grants an order under rule 24.16(2), it will send the form of request directly to the designated court.

9.5 Where the taking of evidence requires the use of an expert, the designated court may require a deposit in advance towards the costs of that expert. The party who obtained the order is responsible for the payment of any such deposit which should be deposited with the court for onward transmission. Under the provisions of the Taking of Evidence Regulation, the designated court is not required to execute the request until such payment is received.

9.6 Article 17 permits the court where proceedings are taking place to take evidence directly from a deponent in another Regulation State if the conditions of the article are satisfied. Direct taking of evidence can only take place if evidence is given voluntarily without the need for coercive measures. Rule 24.16(5) provides for the court to make an order for the submission of a request to take evidence directly. The form of request is Form I annexed to the Taking of Evidence Regulation and rule 24.16(6) makes provision for a draft of this form to be filed by the party seeking the order. An application for an order under rule 24.16(5) should be by application notice in accordance with Part 18.

9.7 Attention is drawn to the provisions of rule 18.11 (Application to set aside or vary order made without notice).

The Family Procedure Rules 2010

ANNEX A

Draft Letter of Request (where the Taking of Evidence Regulation does not apply)
(see paragraph 5.3(a) above)

To the Competent Judicial Authority of   in the
of

[*name*] Senior Master of the Queen's Bench Division of the Senior Courts of England and Wales respectfully request the assistance of your court with regard to the following matters.

2   An application is now pending in the   Division of the High Court of Justice in England and Wales entitled as follows [*set out full title and case number*] in which [*name*] of [*address*] is the applicant and [*name*] of [*address*] is the respondent.

3   The names and addresses of the representatives or agents of [*set out names and addresses of representatives of the parties*].

4   The application by the applicant is for—

(a)   [set out the nature of the application]
(b)   [the order sought] and
(c)   [a summary of the facts.]

5   It is necessary for the purposes of justice between the parties that you cause the following witnesses, who are resident within your jurisdiction, to be examined. The names and addresses of the witnesses are as follows:

6   The witnesses should be examined on oath or if that is not possible within your laws or is impossible of performance by reason of the internal practice and procedure of your court or by reason of practical difficulties, they should be examined in accordance with whatever procedure your laws provide for in these matters.

7   Either/

The witnesses should be examined in accordance with the list of questions annexed hereto.

Or/

The witnesses should be examined regarding [set out full details of evidence sought]

N.B. Where the witness is required to produce documents, these should be clearly identified.

8   I would ask that you cause me, or the agents of the parties (if appointed), to be informed of the date and place where the examination is to take place.

9   Finally, I request that you will cause the evidence of the said witnesses to be reduced into writing and all documents produced on such examinations to be duly marked for identification and that you will further be pleased to authenticate such examinations by the seal of your court or in such other way as is in accordance with your procedure and return the written evidence and documents produced to me addressed as follows—

Senior Master of the Queen's Bench Division
Royal Courts of Justice
Strand
London WC2A 2LL
England

ANNEX B – TAKING OF EVIDENCE REGULATION

www.justice.gov.uk/civil/procrules_fin/contents/form_section_images/practice_directions/pd34_pdf_tif_gif/pd34_cr_1206_2001.pdf

ANNEX C

Designated courts in England and Wales under the Taking of Evidence Regulation
(see paragraph 7.3 above)

Area	Designated court
London and South Eastern Circuit	Royal Courts of Justice (Queen's Bench Division)
Midland Circuit	Birmingham Civil Justice Centre
Western Circuit	Bristol County Court
Wales and Chester Circuit	Cardiff Civil Justice Centre
Northern Circuit	Manchester County Court
North Eastern Circuit	Leeds County Court

PART 25

EXPERTS AND ASSESSORS

25.1. Duty to restrict expert evidence

Expert evidence will be restricted to that which is reasonably required to resolve the proceedings.

25.2.— Interpretation

(1) A reference to an "expert" in this Part—
  (a) is a reference to a person who has been instructed to give or prepare expert evidence for the purpose of family proceedings; and
  (b) does not include—
    (i) a person who is within a prescribed description for the purposes of section 94(1) of the 2002 Act (persons who may prepare a report for any person about the suitability of a child for adoption or of a person to adopt a child or about the adoption, or placement for adoption, of a child); or
    (ii) an officer of the Service or a Welsh family proceedings officer when acting in that capacity.

(Regulation 3 of the Restriction on the Preparation of Adoption Reports Regulations 2005 (S.I. 2005/1711) sets out which persons are within a prescribed description for the purposes of section 94(1) of the 2002 Act.)

(2) "Single joint expert" means an expert instructed to prepare a report for the court on behalf of two or more of the parties (including the applicant) to the proceedings.

25.3.— Experts- overriding duty to the court

(1) It is the duty of experts to help the court on matters within their expertise.
(2) This duty overrides any obligation to the person from whom experts have received instructions or by whom they are paid.

25.4.— Court's power to restrict expert evidence

(1) No party may call an expert or put in evidence an expert's report without the court's permission.
(2) When parties apply for permission they must identify—
  (a) the field in which the expert evidence is required; and
  (b) where practicable, the name of the proposed expert.
(3) If permission is granted it will be in relation only to the expert named or the field identified under paragraph (2).

(4) The court may limit the amount of a party's expert's fees and expenses that may be recovered from any other party.

25.5.— General requirement for expert evidence to be given in a written report

(1) Expert evidence is to be given in a written report unless the court directs otherwise.

(2) The court will not direct an expert to attend a hearing unless it is necessary to do so in the interests of justice.

25.6.— Written questions to experts

(1) A party may put written questions about an expert's report (which must be proportionate) to—
- (a) an expert instructed by another party; or
- (b) a single joint expert appointed under rule 25.7.

(2) Written questions under paragraph (1)—
- (a) may be put once only;
- (b) must be put within 10 days beginning with the date on which the expert's report was served; and
- (c) must be for the purpose only of clarification of the report,

unless in any case—
- (i) the court directs otherwise; or
- (ii) a practice direction provides otherwise.

(3) An expert's answers to questions put in accordance with paragraph (1) are treated as part of the expert's report.

(4) Where—
- (a) a party has put a written question to an expert instructed by another party; and
- (b) the expert does not answer that question,

the court may make use of one or both of the following orders in relation to the party who instructed the expert—
- (i) that the party may not rely on the evidence of that expert; or
- (ii) that the party may not recover the fees and expenses of that expert from any other party.

25.7.— Court's power to direct that evidence is to be given by a single joint expert

(1) Where two or more parties wish to submit expert evidence on a particular issue, the court may direct that the evidence on that issue is to be given by a single joint expert.

(2) Where the parties who wish to submit the evidence ("the relevant parties") cannot agree who should be the single joint expert, the court may—
- (a) select the expert from a list prepared or identified by the instructing parties; or
- (b) direct that the expert be selected in such other manner as the court may direct.

25.8.— Instructions to a single joint expert

(1) Where the court gives a direction under rule 25.7(1) for a single joint expert to be used, the instructions are to be contained in a jointly agreed letter unless the court directs otherwise.

(2) Where the instructions are to be contained in a jointly agreed letter, in default of agreement the instructions may be determined by the court on the written request of any relevant party copied to the other relevant parties.

(3) Where the court permits the relevant parties to give separate instructions to a single joint expert, each instructing party must, when giving instructions to the expert, at the same time send a copy of the instructions to the other relevant parties.

(4) The court may give directions about—
- (a) the payment of the expert's fees and expenses; and
- (b) any inspection, examination or assessments which the expert wishes to carry out.

(5) The court may, before an expert is instructed, limit the amount that can be paid by way of fees and expenses to the expert.

(6) Unless the court directs otherwise, the relevant parties are jointly and severally liable for the payment of the expert's fees and expenses.

25.9.— Power of court to direct a party to provide information

(1) Subject to paragraph (2), where a party has access to information which is not reasonably available to another party, the court may direct the party who has access to the information to prepare, file and serve a document recording the information. (2) In proceedings under Part 14 (procedure for applications in adoption, placement and related proceedings),—

(a) the court may direct the party with access to the information to prepare and file a document recording the information; and

(b) a court officer will send a copy of that document to the other party.

25.10.— Contents of report

(1) An expert's report must comply with the requirements set out in Practice Direction 25A.

(2) At the end of an expert's report there must be a statement that the expert understands and has complied with their duty to the court.

(3) The instructions to the expert are not privileged against disclosure.

(Rule 21.1 explains what is meant by disclosure.)

25.11. Use by one party of expert's report disclosed by another

Where a party has disclosed an expert's report, any party may use that expert's report as evidence at any relevant hearing.

25.12.— Discussions between experts

(1) The court may, at any stage, direct a discussion between experts for the purpose of requiring the experts to—

(a) identify and discuss the expert issues in the proceedings; and

(b) where possible, reach an agreed opinion on those issues.

(2) The court may specify the issues which the experts must discuss.

(3) The court may direct that following a discussion between the experts they must prepare a statement for the court setting out those issues on which—

(a) they agree; and

(b) they disagree,

with a summary of their reasons for disagreeing.

25.13.— Expert's right to ask court for directions

(1) Experts may file written requests for directions for the purpose of assisting them in carrying out their functions.

(2) Experts must, unless the court directs otherwise, provide copies of the proposed request for directions under paragraph (1)—

(a) to the party instructing them, at least 7 days before they file the requests; and

(b) to all other parties, at least 4 days before they file them.

(3) The court, when it gives directions, may also direct that a party be served with a copy of the directions.

25.14.— Assessors

(1) This rule applies where the court appoints one or more persons under section 70 of the Senior Courts Act 1981 or section 63 of the County Courts Act 1984 as an assessor

(2) An assessor will assist the court in dealing with a matter in which the assessor has skill and experience.

(3) The assessor will take such part in the proceedings as the court may direct and in particular the court may direct an assessor to—

(a) prepare a report for the court on any matter at issue in the proceedings; and

The Family Procedure Rules 2010

      (b)   attend the whole or any part of the hearing to advise the court on any such matter.

(4)   If the assessor prepares a report for the court before the hearing has begun—

      (a)   the court will send a copy to each of the parties; and

      (b)   the parties may use it at the hearing.

(5)   Unless the court directs otherwise, an assessor will be paid at the daily rate payable for the time being to a fee-paid deputy district judge of the principal registry and an assessor's fees will form part of the costs of the proceedings.

(6)   The court may order any party to deposit in the court office a specified sum in respect of an assessor's fees and, where it does so, the assessor will not be asked to act until the sum has been deposited.

(7)   Paragraphs (5) and (6) do not apply where the remuneration of the assessor is to be paid out of money provided by Parliament.

PART 25 COMMENTARY

Part 25 is supplemented by PD25A. This practice directions has its origins in CPR PD35 and the Practice Direction on Expert Evidence (issued alongside the Public Law Outline in 2008).

Part 25 contains the rules by which expert evidence is to be given in Family Proceedings, and provisions for Assessors (r 25.14). An expert's overriding duty is to the court (r 25.3). No party may call an expert or put in expert evidence without the court's permission (r 25.4). Expert evidence is usually to be given in a written report (r 25.5). Written questions for the purpose of clarifying the report of an expert may be put by a party within ten days of service of the report (r 25.6). There is power to direct that expert evidence be given by a single joint expert (r 25.7) and provision for a single joint expert's instruction (r 25.8). The court may direct discussion between experts (r 25.12).

PD25A at para 1.5 reminds the practitioner that although the general rule in family proceedings is that the court's permission is required to call an expert or to put in evidence an expert's report, in proceedings relating to children the court's permission is required to instruct an expert (r 12.74(1)).

PRACTICE DIRECTION 25A – EXPERTS AND ASSESSORS IN FAMILY PROCEEDINGS

This Practice Direction is made by the President of the Family Division under the powers delegated to him by the Lord Chief Justice under Schedule 2, Part 1, paragraph 2(2) of the Constitutional Reform Act 2005, and is approved by the Parliamentary Under Secretary of State, by authority of the Lord Chancellor and comes into force on 6th April 2011

This Practice Direction supplements FPR Part 25

INTRODUCTION

1.1.   Sections 1 to 9 of this Practice Direction deal with the use of expert evidence and the instruction of experts, and section 10 deals with the appointment of assessors, in all types of family proceedings. The guidance incorporates and supersedes the *Practice Direction on Experts in Family Proceedings relating to Children* (1 April 2008) and other relevant guidance with effect on and from 6 April 2011.

Where the guidance refers to "an expert" or "the expert", this includes a reference to an expert team.

1.2. For the purposes of this guidance, the phrase "proceedings relating to children" is a convenient description. It is not a legal term of art and has no statutory force. In this guidance it means—

(a) placement and adoption proceedings; or
(b) family proceedings which—
  (i) relate to the exercise of the inherent jurisdiction of the High Court with respect to children;
  (ii) are brought under the Children Act 1989 in any family court; or
  (iii) are brought in the High Court and county courts and "otherwise relate wholly or mainly to the maintenance or upbringing of a minor".

Aims of the guidance on experts and expert evidence

1.3. The aim of the guidance in sections 1 to 9 is to:

(a) provide the court with early information to determine whether expert evidence or assistance will help the court;
(b) help the court and the parties to identify and narrow the issues in the case and encourage agreement where possible;
(c) enable the court and the parties to obtain an expert opinion about a question that is not within the skill and experience of the court;
(d) encourage the early identification of questions that need to be answered by an expert; and
(e) encourage disclosure of full and frank information between the parties, the court and any expert instructed.

1.4. The guidance does not aim to cover all possible eventualities. Thus it should be complied with so far as consistent in all the circumstances with the just disposal of the matter in accordance with the rules and guidance applying to the procedure in question.

Permission to instruct an expert or to use expert evidence

1.5. The general rule in family proceedings is that the court's permission is required to call an expert or to put in evidence an expert's report: see rule 25.4(1). In addition, in proceedings relating to children, the court's permission is required to instruct an expert: see rule 12.74(1).

1.6. The court and the parties must have regard in particular to the following considerations:

(a) proceedings relating to children are confidential and, in the absence of the court's permission, disclosure of information and documents relating to such proceedings may amount to a contempt of court or contravene statutory provisions protecting this confidentiality.
(b) for the purposes of the law of contempt of court, information relating to such proceedings (whether or not contained in a document filed with the court or recorded in any form) may be communicated only to an expert whose instruction by a party has been permitted by the court (see rules 12.73 and 14.14).
(c) in proceedings to which Part 12 of the FPR applies, the court's permission is required to cause the child to be medically or psychiatrically examined or otherwise assessed for the purpose of the preparation of expert evidence for use in the proceedings; where the court's permission has not been given, no evidence arising out of such an examination or assessment may be adduced without the court's permission (see rule 12.20).

1.7. In practice, the need to have the court's permission to disclose information or documents to an expert, or to have the child examined or assessed, means that in proceedings relating to children the court strictly controls the number, fields of expertise and identity of the experts who may be first instructed and then called.

1.8. Before permission is obtained from the court to instruct an expert in proceedings

The Family Procedure Rules 2010

relating to children, it will be necessary for the party seeking permission to make enquiries of the expert in order to provide the court with information to enable it to decide whether to give permission. In practice, enquiries may need to be made of more than one expert for this purpose. This will in turn require each expert to be given sufficient information about the case to decide whether or not he or she is in a position to accept instructions. Such preliminary enquiries, and the disclosure of information about the case which is a necessary part of such enquiries, will not require the court's permission and will not amount to a contempt of court: see sections 4.1 and 4.2 (*Preliminary Enquiries of the Expert* and *Expert's Response to Preliminary Enquiries*).

1.9. Section 4 (*Proceedings relating to children*) gives guidance on applying for the court's permission to instruct an expert, and on instructing the expert, in proceedings relating to children. The court, when granting permission to instruct an expert, will also give directions about the preparation and filing of the expert's report and the attendance of the expert to give evidence: see section 4.4 (*Draft Order for the relevant hearing*).

1.10. In proceedings other than those relating to children, the court's permission is not required to instruct an expert. Section 5 (*Proceedings other than those relating to children*) gives guidance on instructing an expert, and on seeking the court's permission to use expert evidence, prior to and in such proceedings. Section 5 emphasises that the use of a single joint expert should be considered in all cases where expert evidence is required.

When should the court be asked for permission?

1.11. Any application (or proposed application) for permission to instruct an expert or to use expert evidence should be raised with the court – and, where appropriate, with the other parties – as soon as possible. This will normally mean—

(a) in public law proceedings under the Children Act 1989, by or at the Case Management Conference: see rule 12.25;
(b) in private law proceedings under the Children Act 1989, by or at the First Hearing Dispute Resolution Appointment: see rule 12.31;
(c) in placement and adoption proceedings, by or at the First Directions Hearing: see rule 14.8;
(d) in financial proceedings, by or at the First Appointment: see rule 9.15;
(e) in defended matrimonial and civil partnership proceedings, by or at the Case Management Hearing: see rules 7.20 and 7.22.

In this practice direction the "relevant hearing" means any hearing at which the court's permission is sought to instruct an expert or to use expert evidence.

GENERAL MATTERS

Scope of the Guidance

2.1. Sections 1 to 9 of this guidance apply to all experts who are or may be instructed to give or prepare evidence for the purpose of family proceedings in a court in England and Wales. The guidance also applies to those who instruct, or propose to instruct, an expert for such a purpose. Section 10 applies to the appointment of assessors in family proceedings in England and Wales.

2.2. This guidance does not apply to proceedings issued before 6 April 2011 but in any such proceedings the court may direct that this guidance will apply either wholly or partly. This is subject to the overriding objective for the type of proceedings, and to the proviso that such a direction will neither cause further delay nor involve repetition of steps already taken or of decisions already made in the case.

Pre-application instruction of experts

2.3. When experts' reports are commissioned before the commencement of proceedings, it should be made clear to the expert that he or she may in due course be reporting to the court and should therefore consider himself or herself bound by this guidance. A prospective party to family proceedings relating to children (for example, a local authority) should always write a letter of instruction when asking a potential witness for a report or an opinion, whether that request is within proceedings or pre-proceedings (for example, when commissioning specialist assessment materials, reports from a treating expert or other evidential materials); and the letter of instruction should conform to the principles set out in this guidance.

Emergency and urgent cases

2.4. In emergency or urgent cases – for example, where, before formal issue of proceedings, a without-notice application is made to the court during or out of business hours; or where, after proceedings have been issued, a previously unforeseen need for (further) expert evidence arises at short notice – a party may wish to call expert evidence without having complied with all or any part of this guidance. In such circumstances, the party wishing to call the expert evidence must apply forthwith to the court – where possible or appropriate, on notice to the other parties – for directions as to the future steps to be taken in respect of the expert evidence in question.

Orders

2.5. Where an order or direction requires an act to be done by an expert, or otherwise affects an expert, the party instructing that expert – or, in the case of a jointly instructed expert, the lead solicitor – must serve a copy of the order or direction on the expert forthwith upon receiving it.

Adults who may be protected parties

2.6. The court will investigate as soon as possible any issue as to whether an adult party or intended party to family proceedings lacks capacity (within the meaning of the Mental Capacity Act 2005) to conduct the proceedings. An adult who lacks capacity to act as a party to the proceedings is a protected party and must have a litigation friend to conduct the proceedings on their behalf. The expectation of the Official Solicitor is that the Official Solicitor will only be invited to act for the protected party as litigation friend if there is no other person suitable or willing to act.

2.7. Any issue as to the capacity of an adult to conduct the proceedings must be determined before the court gives any directions relevant to that adult's role in the proceedings.

2.8. Where the adult is a protected party, that party's representative should be involved in any instruction of an expert, including the instruction of an expert to assess whether the adult, although a protected party, is competent to give evidence. The instruction of an expert is a significant step in the proceedings. The representative will wish to consider (and ask the expert to consider), if the protected party is competent to give evidence, their best interests in this regard. The representative may wish to seek advice about "special measures". The representative may put forward an argument on behalf of the protected party that the protected party should not give evidence.

2.9. If at any time during the proceedings there is reason to believe that a party may lack capacity to conduct the proceedings, then the court must be notified and directions sought to ensure that this issue is investigated without delay.

Child likely to lack capacity to conduct the proceedings on when he or she reaches 18

2.10. Where it appears that a child is—

(a) a party to the proceedings and not the subject of them;
(b) nearing age 18; and
(c) considered likely to lack capacity to conduct the proceedings when 18,

the court will consider giving directions for the child's capacity in this respect to be investigated.

The Family Procedure Rules 2010

THE DUTIES OF EXPERTS

Overriding Duty

3.1. An expert in family proceedings has an overriding duty to the court that takes precedence over any obligation to the person from whom the expert has received instructions or by whom the expert is paid.

Particular Duties

3.2. An expert shall have regard to the following, among other, duties:

(a) to assist the court in accordance with the overriding duty;
(b) to provide advice to the court that conforms to the best practice of the expert's profession;
(c) to provide an opinion that is independent of the party or parties instructing the expert;
(d) to confine the opinion to matters material to the issues between the parties and in relation only to questions that are within the expert's expertise (skill and experience);
(e) where a question has been put which falls outside the expert's expertise, to state this at the earliest opportunity and to volunteer an opinion as to whether another expert is required to bring expertise not possessed by those already involved or, in the rare case, as to whether a second opinion is required on a key issue and, if possible, what questions should be asked of the second expert;
(f) in expressing an opinion, to take into consideration all of the material facts including any relevant factors arising from ethnic, cultural, religious or linguistic contexts at the time the opinion is expressed;
(g) to inform those instructing the expert without delay of any change in the opinion and of the reason for the change.

Content of the Expert's Report

3.3. The expert's report shall be addressed to the court and prepared and filed in accordance with the court's timetable and shall—

(a) give details of the expert's qualifications and experience;
(b) include a statement identifying the document(s) containing the material instructions and the substance of any oral instructions and, as far as necessary to explain any opinions or conclusions expressed in the report, summarising the facts and instructions which are material to the conclusions and opinions expressed;
(c) state who carried out any test, examination or interview which the expert has used for the report and whether or not the test, examination or interview has been carried out under the expert's supervision;
(d) give details of the qualifications of any person who carried out the test, examination or interview;
(e) in expressing an opinion to the court—
  (i) take into consideration all of the material facts including any relevant factors arising from ethnic, cultural, religious or linguistic contexts at the time the opinion is expressed, identifying the facts, literature and any other material including research material that the expert has relied upon in forming an opinion;
  (ii) describe their own professional risk assessment process and process of differential diagnosis, highlighting factual assumptions, deductions from the factual assumptions, and any unusual, contradictory or inconsistent features of the case;
  (iii) indicate whether any proposition in the report is an hypothesis (in particular a controversial hypothesis), or an opinion deduced in accordance with peer-reviewed and tested technique, research and experience accepted as a consensus in the scientific community;

FPR 2010: Practice Direction 25A

- (iv) indicate whether the opinion is provisional (or qualified, as the case may be), stating the qualification and the reason for it, and identifying what further information is required to give an opinion without qualification;
- (f) where there is a range of opinion on any question to be answered by the expert—
  - (i) summarise the range of opinion;
  - (ii) identify and explain, within the range of opinions, any "unknown cause", whether arising from the facts of the case (for example, because there is too little information to form a scientific opinion) or from limited experience or lack of research, peer review or support in the relevant field of expertise;
  - (iii) give reasons for any opinion expressed: the use of a balance sheet approach to the factors that support or undermine an opinion can be of great assistance to the court;
- (g) contain a summary of the expert's conclusions and opinions;
- (h) contain a statement that the expert—
  - (i) has no conflict of interest of any kind, other than any conflict disclosed in his or her report;
  - (ii) does not consider that any interest disclosed affects his or her suitability as an expert witness on any issue on which he or she has given evidence;
  - (iii) will advise the instructing party if, between the date of the expert's report and the final hearing, there is any change in circumstances which affects the expert's answers to (i) or (ii) above;
  - (iv) understands their duty to the court and has complied with that duty; and
  - (v) is aware of the requirements of Part 25 and this practice direction;
- (i) be verified by a statement of truth in the following form—

"I confirm that I have made clear which facts and matters referred to in this report are within my own knowledge and which are not. Those that are within my own knowledge I confirm to be true. The opinions I have expressed represent my true and complete professional opinions on the matters to which they refer."

(Part 17 deals with statements of truth. Rule 17.6 sets out the consequences of verifying a document containing a false statement without an honest belief in its truth.)

PROCEEDINGS RELATING TO CHILDREN

Preparation for the relevant hearing

Preliminary Enquiries of the Expert

4.1. In good time for the information requested to be available for the relevant hearing or for the advocates' meeting or discussion where one takes place before the relevant hearing, the solicitor for the party proposing to instruct the expert (or lead solicitor or solicitor for the child if the instruction proposed is joint) shall approach the expert with the following information—

- (a) the nature of the proceedings and the issues likely to require determination by the court;
- (b) the questions about which the expert is to be asked to give an opinion (including any ethnic, cultural, religious or linguistic contexts);
- (c) the date when the court is to be asked to give permission for the instruction (or if – unusually – permission has already been given, the date and details of that permission);
- (d) whether permission is to be asked of the court for the instruction of another expert in the same or any related field (that is, to give an opinion on the same or related questions);
- (e) the volume of reading which the expert will need to undertake;
- (f) whether or not permission has been applied for or given for the expert to examine the child;

The Family Procedure Rules 2010

(g) whether or not it will be necessary for the expert to conduct interviews – and, if so, with whom;
(h) the likely timetable of legal and social work steps;
(i) in care and supervision proceedings, any dates in the Timetable for the Child which would be relevant to the proposed timetable for the assessment;
(j) when the expert's report is likely to be required;
(k) whether and, if so, what date has been fixed by the court for any hearing at which the expert may be required to give evidence (in particular the Final Hearing); and whether it may be possible for the expert to give evidence by telephone conference or video link: see section 8 *(Arrangements for experts to give evidence)* below;
(l) the possibility of making, through their instructing solicitors, representations to the court about being named or otherwise identified in any public judgment given by the court.

It is essential that there should be proper co-ordination between the court and the expert when drawing up the case management timetable: the needs of the court should be balanced with the needs of the expert whose forensic work is undertaken as an adjunct to his or her main professional duties.

Expert's Response to Preliminary Enquiries

4.2. In good time for the relevant hearing or for the advocates' meeting or discussion where one takes place before the relevant hearing, the solicitors intending to instruct the expert shall obtain confirmation from the expert—

(a) that acceptance of the proposed instructions will not involve the expert in any conflict of interest;
(b) that the work required is within the expert's expertise;
(c) that the expert is available to do the relevant work within the suggested time scale;
(d) when the expert is available to give evidence, of the dates and times to avoid and, where a hearing date has not been fixed, of the amount of notice the expert will require to make arrangements to come to court (or to give evidence by telephone conference or video link) without undue disruption to his or her normal professional routines;
(e) of the cost, including hourly or other charging rates, and likely hours to be spent, attending experts' meetings, attending court and writing the report (to include any examinations and interviews);
(f) of any representations which the expert wishes to make to the court about being named or otherwise identified in any public judgment given by the court.

Where parties have not agreed on the appointment of a single joint expert before the relevant hearing, they should obtain the above confirmations in respect of all experts whom they intend to put to the court for the purposes of rule 25.7(2)(a) as candidates for the appointment.

The proposal to instruct an expert

4.3. Any party who proposes to ask the court for permission to instruct an expert shall, **by 11 a.m. on the business day before the relevant hearing**, file and serve a written proposal to instruct the expert, in the following detail—

(a) the name, discipline, qualifications and expertise of the expert (by way of C.V. where possible);
(b) the expert's availability to undertake the work;
(c) the relevance of the expert evidence sought to be adduced to the issues in the proceedings and the specific questions upon which it is proposed that the expert should give an opinion (including the relevance of any ethnic, cultural, religious or linguistic contexts);
(d) the timetable for the report;
(e) the responsibility for instruction;
(f) whether or not the expert evidence can properly be obtained by the joint instruction of the expert by two or more of the parties;

(g) whether the expert evidence can properly be obtained by only one party (for example, on behalf of the child);
(h) why the expert evidence proposed cannot be given by social services undertaking a core assessment or by the Children's Guardian in accordance with their respective statutory duties;
(i) the likely cost of the report on an hourly or other charging basis: where possible, the expert's terms of instruction should be made available to the court;
(j) the proposed apportionment (at least in the first instance) of any jointly instructed expert's fee; when it is to be paid; and, if applicable, whether public funding has been approved.

Draft Order for the relevant hearing

4.4. Any party proposing to instruct an expert shall, **by 11 a.m. on the business day before the relevant hearing**, submit to the court a draft order for directions dealing in particular with—

(a) the party who is to be responsible for drafting the letter of instruction and providing the documents to the expert;
(b) the issues identified by the court and the questions about which the expert is to give an opinion;
(c) the timetable within which the report is to be prepared, filed and served;
(d) the disclosure of the report to the parties and to any other expert;
(e) the organisation of, preparation for and conduct of an experts' discussion;
(f) the preparation of a statement of agreement and disagreement by the experts following an experts' discussion;
(g) making available to the court at an early opportunity the expert reports in electronic form;
(h) the attendance of the expert at court to give oral evidence (alternatively, the expert giving his or her evidence in writing or remotely by video link), whether at or for the Final Hearing or another hearing; unless agreement about the opinions given by the expert is reached at or before the Issues Resolution Hearing ("IRH") or, if no IRH is to be held, by a specified date prior to the hearing at which the expert is to give oral evidence ("the specified date").

Letter of Instruction

4.5. The solicitor or party instructing the expert shall, **within 5 business days after the relevant hearing**, prepare (in agreement with the other parties where appropriate), file and serve a letter of instruction to the expert which shall—

(a) set out the context in which the expert's opinion is sought (including any ethnic, cultural, religious or linguistic contexts);
(b) set out the specific questions which the expert is required to answer, ensuring that they—
  (i) are within the ambit of the expert's area of expertise;
  (ii) do not contain unnecessary or irrelevant detail;
  (iii) are kept to a manageable number and are clear, focused and direct; and
  (iv) reflect what the expert has been requested to do by the court.

(The Annex to this guidance sets out suggested questions in letters of instruction to (1) child mental health professionals or paediatricians, and (2) adult psychiatrists and applied psychologists, in Children Act 1989 proceedings.)

(c) list the documentation provided, or provide for the expert an indexed and paginated bundle which shall include—
  (i) a copy of the order (or those parts of the order) which gives permission for the instruction of the expert, immediately the order becomes available;
  (ii) an agreed list of essential reading; and
  (iii) a copy of this guidance;
(d) identify any materials provided to the expert which have not been produced either as original medical (or other professional) records or in response to an

The Family Procedure Rules 2010

instruction from a party, and state the source of that material (such materials may contain an assumption as to the standard of proof, the admissibility or otherwise of hearsay evidence, and other important procedural and substantive questions relating to the different purposes of other enquiries, for example, criminal or disciplinary proceedings);

(e) identify all requests to third parties for disclosure and their responses, to avoid partial disclosure, which tends only to prove a case rather than give full and frank information;

(f) identify the relevant people concerned with the proceedings (for example, the treating clinicians) and inform the expert of his or her right to talk to them provided that an accurate record is made of the discussions;

(g) identify any other expert instructed in the proceedings and advise the expert of their right to talk to the other experts provided that an accurate record is made of the discussions;

(h) subject to any public funding requirement for prior authority, define the contractual basis upon which the expert is retained and in particular the funding mechanism including how much the expert will be paid (an hourly rate and overall estimate should already have been obtained), when the expert will be paid, and what limitation there might be on the amount the expert can charge for the work which they will have to do. In cases where the parties are publicly funded, there should also be a brief explanation of the costs and expenses excluded from public funding by Funding Code criterion 1.3 and the detailed assessment process.

Asking the court to settle the letter of instruction to a single joint expert

4.6. Where possible, the written request for the court to consider the letter of instruction referred to in rule 25.8(2) should be set out in an e-mail to the court and copied by e-mail to the other instructing parties. The request should be sent to the relevant court or (by prior arrangement only) directly to the judge dealing with the proceedings; in the magistrates' court, the request should be sent to the legal adviser who will refer it to the appropriate judge or justices, if necessary. The court will settle the letter of instruction, usually without a hearing to avoid delay; and will send (where practicable, by e-mail) the settled letter to the lead solicitor for transmission forthwith to the expert, and copy it to the other instructing parties for information.

Keeping the expert up to date with new documents

4.7. As often as may be necessary, the expert should be provided promptly with a copy of any new document filed at court, together with an updated document list or bundle index.

PROCEEDINGS OTHER THAN THOSE RELATING TO CHILDREN

5.1. Wherever possible, expert evidence should be obtained from a single joint expert instructed by both or all the parties ("SJE"). To that end, a party wishing to instruct an expert should first give the other party or parties a list of the names of one or more experts in the relevant speciality whom they consider suitable to be instructed.

5.2. Within 10 days after receipt of the list of proposed experts, the other party or parties should indicate any objection to one or more of the named experts and, if so, supply the name(s) of one or more experts whom they consider suitable.

5.3. Each party should disclose whether they have already consulted any of the proposed experts about the issue(s) in question.

5.4. Where the parties cannot agree on the identity of the expert, each party should think carefully before instructing their own expert because of the costs implications. Disagreements about the use and identity of an expert may be better managed by the court in the context of an application for directions. (see paragraphs 5.8 and 5.9 below).

Agreement to instruct separate experts

5.5. If the parties agree to instruct separate experts,-

(a) they should agree in advance that the reports will be disclosed; and
(b) the instructions to each expert should comply, so far as appropriate, with paragraphs 4.5 to 4.7 above (*Letter of instruction*).

Agreement to instruct an SJE

5.6. If there is agreement to instruct an SJE, **before instructions are given** the parties should-

(a) so far as appropriate, comply with the guidance in paragraphs 4.1 (Preliminary inquiries of the expert) and 4.2 (Expert's confirmation in response to preliminary enquiries) above;
(b) have agreed in what proportion the SJE's fee is to be shared between them (at least in the first instance) and when it is to be paid; and
(c) if applicable, have obtained agreement for public funding.

5.7. The instructions to the SJE should comply, so far as appropriate, with paragraphs 4.5 to 4.7 above (*Letter of instruction*).

Seeking the court's directions for the use of an SJE

5.8. Where the parties seek the court's directions for the use of an SJE, they should comply, so far as appropriate, with paragraphs 4.1 to 4.4 (*Preparation for the relevant hearing*) above.

5.9. The instructions to the SJE should comply, so far as appropriate, with paragraphs 4.5 to 4.7 above (*Letter of instruction*).

THE COURT'S CONTROL OF EXPERT EVIDENCE: CONSEQUENTIAL ISSUES

Written Questions

6.1. Where—

(a) written questions are put to an expert in accordance with rule 25.6, the court will specify the timetable according to which the expert is to answer the written questions;
(b) a party sends a written question or questions under rule 25.6 direct to an expert, a copy of the questions must, at the same time, be sent to the other party or parties.

Experts' Discussion or Meeting: Purpose

6.2. In accordance with rule 25.12, the court may, at any stage, direct a discussion between experts for the purpose outlined in paragraph (1) of that rule. Rule 25.12(2) provides that the court may specify the issues which the experts must discuss. The expectation is that those issues will include-

(a) the reasons for disagreement on any expert question and what, if any, action needs to be taken to resolve any outstanding disagreement or question;
(b) explanation of existing evidence or additional evidence in order to assist the court to determine the issues.

One of the aims of specifing the issues for discussion is to limit, wherever possible, the need for the experts to attend court to give oral evidence.

Experts' Discussion or Meeting: Arrangements

6.3. Subject to the directions given by the court under rule 25.12, the solicitor or other professional who is given the responsibility by the court ("the nominated

The Family Procedure Rules 2010

professional") shall – **within 15 business days after the experts' reports have been filed and copied to the other parties** – make arrangements for the experts to meet or communicate. Subject to any specification by the court of the issues which experts must discuss under rule 25.12(2), the following matters should be considered as appropriate—

(a) where permission has been given for the instruction of experts from different disciplines, a global discussion may be held relating to those questions that concern all or most of them;

(b) separate discussions may have to be held among experts from the same or related disciplines, but care should be taken to ensure that the discussions complement each other so that related questions are discussed by all relevant experts;

(c) **5 business days prior to a discussion or meeting**, the nominated professional should formulate an agenda including a list of questions for consideration. The agenda should, subject always to the provisions of rule 25.12(1), focus on those questions which are intended to clarify areas of agreement or disagreement.

Questions which repeat questions asked in the letter of instruction or which seek to rehearse cross-examination in advance of the hearing should be rejected as likely to defeat the purpose of the meeting.

The agenda may usefully take the form of a list of questions to be circulated among the other parties in advance and should comprise all questions that each party wishes the experts to consider.

The agenda and list of questions should be sent to each of the experts **not later than 2 business days before the discussion;**

(d) the nominated professional may exercise his or her discretion to accept further questions after the agenda with list of questions has been circulated to the parties. **Only in exceptional circumstances should questions be added to the agenda within the 2-day period before the meeting. Under no circumstances should any question received on the day of or during the meeting be accepted.** This does not preclude questions arising during the meeting for the purposes of clarification. Strictness in this regard is vital, for adequate notice of the questions enables the parties to identify and isolate the expert issues in the case before the meeting so that the experts' discussion at the meeting can concentrate on those issues;

(e) the discussion should be chaired by the nominated professional. A minute must be taken of the questions answered by the experts. Where the court has given a direction under rule 25.12(3) and subject to that direction, a Statement of Agreement and Disagreement must be prepared which should be agreed and signed by each of the experts who participated in the discussion. In accordance with rule 25.12(3) the statement must contain a summary of the experts' reasons for disagreeing. The statement should be served and filed **not later than 5 business days after the discussion has taken place;**

(f) in each case, whether some or all of the experts participate by telephone conference or video link to ensure that minimum disruption is caused to professional schedules and that costs are minimised.

Meetings or conferences attended by a jointly instructed expert

6.4. Jointly instructed experts should not attend any meeting or conference which is not a joint one, unless all the parties have agreed in writing or the court has directed that such a meeting may be held, and it is agreed or directed who is to pay the expert's fees for the meeting or conference. Any meeting or conference attended by a jointly instructed expert should be proportionate to the case.

Court-directed meetings involving experts in public law Children Act cases

6.5. In public law Children Act proceedings, where the court gives a direction that a meeting shall take place between the local authority and any relevant named experts for the purpose of providing assistance to the local authority in the formulation of plans and proposals for the child, the meeting shall be arranged, chaired and minuted in accordance with the directions given by the court.

POSITIONS OF THE PARTIES

7.1. Where a party refuses to be bound by an agreement that has been reached at an experts' discussion or meeting, that party must inform the court and the other parties in writing, **within 10 business days after the discussion or meeting or, where an IRH is to be held, not less than 5 business days before the IRH**, of his or her reasons for refusing to accept the agreement.

ARRANGEMENTS FOR EXPERTS TO GIVE EVIDENCE

Preparation

8.1. Where the court has directed the attendance of an expert witness, the party who is responsible for the instruction of the expert shall, **by the specified date or, where an IRH is to be held, by the IRH**, ensure that—

(a) a date and time (if possible, convenient to the expert) are fixed for the court to hear the expert's evidence, substantially in advance of the hearing at which the expert is to give oral evidence and no later than a specified date prior to that hearing or, where an IRH is to be held, than the IRH;
(b) if the expert's oral evidence is not required, the expert is notified as soon as possible;
(c) the witness template accurately indicates how long the expert is likely to be giving evidence, in order to avoid the inconvenience of the expert being delayed at court;
(d) consideration is given in each case to whether some or all of the experts participate by telephone conference or video link, or submit their evidence in writing, to ensure that minimum disruption is caused to professional schedules and that costs are minimised.

Experts attending Court

8.2. Where expert witnesses are to be called, all parties shall, **by the specified date or, where an IRH is to be held, by the IRH**, ensure that—

(a) the parties' advocates have identified (whether at an advocates' meeting or by other means) the issues which the experts are to address;
(b) wherever possible, a logical sequence to the evidence is arranged, with experts of the same discipline giving evidence on the same day;
(c) the court is informed of any circumstance where all experts agree but a party nevertheless does not accept the agreed opinion, so that directions can be given for the proper consideration of the experts' evidence and opinion and of the party's reasons for not accepting the agreed opinion;
(d) in the exceptional case the court is informed of the need for a witness summons.

ACTION AFTER THE FINAL HEARING

9.1. **Within 10 business days after the Final Hearing**, the solicitor instructing the expert shall inform the expert in writing of the outcome of the case, and of the use made by the court of the expert's opinion.

9.2. Where the court directs preparation of a transcript, it may also direct that the solicitor instructing the expert shall send a copy to the **expert within 10 business days after receiving the transcript.**

9.3. After a Final Hearing in the Family Proceedings Court, the (lead) solicitor instructing the expert shall send the expert a copy of the court's written reasons for its decision **within 10 business days after receiving the written reasons.**

APPOINTMENT OF ASSESSORS IN FAMILY PROCEEDINGS

10.1. The power to appoint one or more assessors to assist the court is conferred on the High Court by section 70(1) of the Senior Courts Act 1981, and on a county court by section 63(1) of the County Courts Act 1984. In practice, these powers have been used in appeals from a district judge or costs judge in costs assessment proceedings – although, in principle, the statutory powers permit one or more assessors to be appointed in any family proceedings where the High Court or a county court sees fit.

10.2. **Not less than 21 days before making any such appointment**, the court will notify each party in writing of the name of the proposed assessor, of the matter in respect of which the assistance of the assessor will be sought and of the qualifications of the assessor to give that assistance.

10.3. Any party may object to the proposed appointment, either personally or in respect of the proposed assessor's qualifications.

10.4. Any such objection must be made in writing and filed and served **within 7 business days of receipt of the notification from the court of the proposed appointment**, and will be taken into account by the court in deciding whether or not to make the appointment.

ANNEX

(drafted by the Family Justice Council)

Suggested questions in letters of instruction to child mental health professional or paediatrician in Children Act 1989 proceedings

A. The Child(ren)

1. Please describe the child(ren)'s current health, development and functioning (according to your area of expertise), and identify the nature of any significant changes which have occurred

- Behavioural
- Emotional
- Attachment organisation
- Social/peer/sibling relationships
- Cognitive/educational
- Physical
    - Growth, eating, sleep
    - Non-organic physical problems (including wetting and soiling)
    - Injuries
    - Paediatric conditions

2. Please comment on the likely explanation for/aetiology of the child(ren)'s problems/difficulties/injuries

- History/experiences (including intrauterine influences, and abuse and neglect)
- Genetic/innate/developmental difficulties
- Paediatric/psychiatric disorders

3. Please provide a prognosis and risk if difficulties not addressed above.

4. Please describe the child(ren)'s needs in the light of the above

- Nature of care-giving
- Education
- Treatment

in the short and long term (subject, where appropriate, to further assessment later).

B. The parents/primary carers

5. Please describe the factors and mechanisms which would explain the parents' (or primary carers) harmful or neglectful interactions with the child(ren) (if relevant).

6. What interventions have been tried and what has been the result?

7. Please assess the ability of the parents or primary carers to fulfil the child(ren)'s identified needs now.

8. What other assessments of the parents or primary carers are indicated?

- Adult mental health assessment
- Forensic risk assessment
- Physical assessment
- Cognitive assessment

9. What, if anything, is needed to assist the parents or primary carers now, within the child(ren)'s time scales and what is the prognosis for change?

- Parenting work
- Support
- Treatment/therapy

C. Alternatives

10. Please consider the alternative possibilities for the fulfilment of the child(ren)'s needs

- What sort of placement
- Contact arrangements

Please consider the advantages, disadvantages and implications of each for the child(ren).

Suggested questions in letters of instruction to adult psychiatrists and applied psychologists in Children Act 1989 proceedings

1. Does the parent/adult have – whether in his/her history or presentation – a mental illness/disorder (including substance abuse) or other psychological/emotional difficulty and, if so, what is the diagnosis?

2. How do any/all of the above (and their current treatment if applicable) affect his/her functioning, including interpersonal relationships?

3. If the answer to Q1 is yes, are there any features of either the mental illness or psychological/emotional difficulty or personality disorder which could be associated with risk to others, based on the available evidence base (whether published studies or evidence from clinical experience)?

4. What are the experiences/antecedents/aetiology which would explain his/her difficulties, if any, (taking into account any available evidence base or other clinical experience)?

5. What treatment is indicated, what is its nature and the likely duration?

6. What is his/her capacity to engage in/partake of the treatment/therapy?

7. Are you able to indicate the prognosis for, time scales for achieving, and likely durability of, change?

8. What other factors might indicate positive change?

(It is assumed that this opinion will be based on collateral information as well as interviewing the adult).

The Right Honourable

Sir Nicholas Wall

The President of the Family Division

Signed by authority of the Lord Chancellor:

[]

Parliamentary Under Secretary of State

Ministry of Justice

The Family Procedure Rules 2010

PART 26

CHANGE OF SOLICITOR

26.1. Solicitor acting for a party
Where the address for service of a party is the business address of that party's solicitor, the solicitor will be considered to be acting for that party until the provisions of this Part have been complied with.
(Part 6 contains provisions about the address for service.)

26.2.— Change of solicitor – duty to give notice
   (1) This rule applies where—
      (a) a party for whom a solicitor is acting wants to change solicitor;
      (b) a party, after having conducted the application in person, appoints a solicitor to act for that party (except where the solicitor is appointed only to act as an advocate for a hearing); or
      (c) a party, after having conducted the application by a solicitor, intends to act in person.
   (2) Where this rule applies, the party or the party's solicitor (where one is acting) must—
      (a) serve notice of the change on—
         (i) every other party; and
         (ii) where paragraph (1)(a) or (c) applies, the former solicitor; and
      (b) file notice of the change.
   (3) Except where a serial number has been assigned under rule 14.2 or the name or address of a party is not being revealed in accordance with rule 29.1, the notice must state the party's new address for service.
   (4) The notice filed at court must state that notice has been served as required by paragraph (2)(a) or, where rule 2.4 applies, in accordance with the court's directions given under that rule.
   (5) Subject to paragraph (6), where a party has changed solicitor or intends to act in person, the former solicitor will be considered to be the party's solicitor unless and until—
      (a) notice is filed and served in accordance with paragraph (2)(a) or, where rule 2.4 applies, in accordance with the court's directions given under that rule; or
      (b) the court makes an order under rule 26.3 and the order is served as required by paragraph (3) of that rule.
   (6) Where the certificate of a LSC funded client or an assisted person (in this rule "C") is revoked or discharged –
      (a) the solicitor who acted for C will cease to be the solicitor acting in the case as soon as the retainer is determined under regulation 4 of the Community Legal Service (Costs) Regulations 2000; and
      (b) if C wishes to continue—
         (i) where C appoints a solicitor to act on C's behalf, paragraph (2) will apply as if C had previously conducted the application in person; and
         (ii) where C wants to act in person, C must give an address for service, in accordance with rule 6.26, unless the court directs otherwise.
   (7) In this rule—
"assisted person" means an assisted person within the statutory provisions relating to legal aid;
"certificate" means a certificate issued under the Funding Code (approved under section 9 of the Access to Justice Act 1999); and
"LSC funded client" means an individual who receives services funded by the Legal Services Commission as part of the Community Legal Service within the meaning of Part 1 of the Access to Justice Act 1999.

26.3.— Order that a solicitor has ceased to act

(1) A solicitor may apply for an order declaring that that solicitor has ceased to be the solicitor acting for—
- (a) a party; or
- (b) a children's guardian.

(2) Where an application is made under this rule—
- (a) notice of the application must be given to the party, or children's guardian, for whom the solicitor is acting, unless the court directs otherwise; and
- (b) the application must be supported by evidence.

(3) Where the court makes an order declaring that a solicitor has ceased to act, a court officer will serve a copy of the order on—
- (a) every party to the proceedings; and
- (b) where applicable, a children's guardian.

26.4.— Removal of solicitor who has ceased to act on application of another party

(1) Where—
- (a) a solicitor who has acted for a party—
  - (i) has died;
  - (ii) has become bankrupt;
  - (iii) has ceased to practise; or
  - (iv) cannot be found; and
- (b) the party has not given notice of a change of solicitor or notice of intention to act in person as required by rule 26.2(2),

any other party may apply for an order declaring that the solicitor has ceased to be the solicitor acting for the other party in the case.

(2) Where an application is made under this rule, notice of the application must be given to the party to whose solicitor the application relates unless the court directs otherwise.

(3) Where the court makes an order made under this rule, a court officer will serve a copy of the order on every other party to the proceedings.

PART 26 COMMENTARY

Part 26 is supplemented by PD26A.

Part 26 contains the rules by which a party changes solicitor, or changes from having a solicitor to acting in person, or the reverse. There is also provision at r 26.4 for the other party to apply for an order that a solicitor has ceased to act – having died, become bankrupt, ceased to practise, or if he or she cannot be found.

The form relevant to Part 26 is FP8 – Notice of Change of Solicitor.

PRACTICE DIRECTION 26A – CHANGE OF SOLICITOR

This Practice Direction supplements FPR Part 26

SOLICITOR ACTING FOR A PARTY

1.1 Rule 26.1 states that where the address for service of a party is the business address of his solicitor, the solicitor will be considered to be acting for that party until the provisions of Part 26 have been complied with.

1.2 Subject to rule 26.2(6) (where the certificate of a LSC funded client or assisted person is revoked or discharged), where a party has changed his solicitor or intends to act in person, the former solicitor will be considered to be the party's solicitor unless or until—

The Family Procedure Rules 2010

(a) a notice of the change is—
  (i) served on every other party (see rule 26.2(2)(a)); and
  (ii) filed with the court (see rule 26.2(2)(b)); or
(b) the court makes an order under rule 26.3 and the order is served on the former solicitor and every other party in accordance with directions of the court (see rule 26.2(5)).

1.3 A solicitor appointed to represent a party only as an advocate at a hearing will not be considered to be acting for that party within the meaning of Part 26.

NOTICE OF CHANGE OF SOLICITOR

2.1 Rule 26.2(1) sets out the circumstances following which a notice of the change must be filed and served.

2.2 A notice of the change giving the last known address of the former assisted person must also be filed and served on every party where, under rule 26.2(6)—

(a) the certificate of a LSC funded client or assisted person is revoked or discharged; and
(b) the LSC funded client or the assisted person wishes either to act in person or appoint another solicitor to act on his behalf.

2.3 Where a solicitor has given notice that he or she acts for a child directly, and an officer of the Service, a Welsh family proceedings officer or the Official Solicitor continues with the permission of the court to have legal representation, notice of that legal representation must be given to the court.

2.4 In addition, where a party or solicitor changes his address for service, a notice of that change should be filed and served on every party.

2.5 A party who, having conducted an application by a solicitor, intends to act in person must give in his notice an address for service that is within the United Kingdom (see rule 6.26).

2.6 The form giving notice of any change is referred to in Practice Direction 5A. The notice should be filed in the court office in which the application is proceeding.

APPLICATION FOR AN ORDER THAT A SOLICITOR HAS CEASED TO ACT

3.1 A solicitor may apply under rule 26.3 for an order declaring that he has ceased to be the solicitor acting for a party.

3.2 The application should be made in accordance with Part 18 and must be supported by evidence (see Part 18 and the Practice Direction 18A). Unless the court directs otherwise the application notice must be served on the party (see rule 26.3(2)).

3.3 An order made under rule 26.3 will be served on every party by the court officer and takes effect when it is served.

APPLICATION BY ANOTHER PARTY TO REMOVE A SOLICITOR

4.1 Rule 26.4 sets out circumstances in which any other party may apply for an order declaring that a solicitor has ceased to be the solicitor acting for another party in the proceedings.

4.2 The application should be made in accordance with Part 18 and must be supported by evidence. Unless the court directs otherwise the application notice must be served on the party to whose solicitor the application relates.

4.3 An order made under rule 26.4 will be served on every party by the court officer.

NEW ADDRESS FOR SERVICE WHERE ORDER MADE UNDER RULES 26.3 OR 26.4

5.1 Where the court has made an order under rule 26.3 that a solicitor has ceased to act or under rule 26.4 declaring that a solicitor has ceased to be the solicitor for a party,

FPR 2010

the party for whom the solicitor was acting must give a new address for service to comply with rule 6.26.

(Rule 6.26 provides that a party must give an address for service within the United Kingdom, or where a solicitor is acting for a party, an address for service either in the United Kingdom or any other EEA state, at which that party resides or carries on business. Where that party does not have such an address, an address within the United Kingdom must generally be given (see rule 6.26(3) and (4)).

(Until such time as a new address for service is given directions may be needed under rule 6.19.)

PART 27

HEARINGS AND DIRECTIONS APPOINTMENTS

27.1. Application of this Part

This Part is subject to any enactment, any provision in these rules or a practice direction. (Rule 27.4(7) makes additional provision in relation to requirements to stay proceedings where the respondent does not appear and a relevant European regulation or international convention applies)

27.2.— Reasons for a decision of the magistrates' courts

(1) This rule applies to proceedings in a magistrates' court.

(2) After a hearing, the court will make its decision as soon as is practicable.

(3) The court must give written reasons for its decision.

(4) Paragraphs (5) and (6) apply where the functions of the court are being performed by—
    (a) two or three lay justices; or
    (b) by a single lay justice in accordance with these rules and Practice Direction 2A.

(5) The justices' clerk must, before the court makes an order or refuses an application or request, make notes of—
    (a) the names of the justice or justices constituting the court by which the decision is made; and
    (b) in consultation with the justice or justices, the reasons for the court's decision.

(6) The justices' clerk must make a written record of the reasons for the court's decision.

(7) When making an order or refusing an application, the court, or one of the justices constituting the court by which the decision is made, will announce its decision and—
    (a) the reasons for that decision; or
    (b) a short explanation of that decision.

(8) Subject to any other rule or practice direction, the court officer will supply a copy of the order and the reasons for the court's decision to the persons referred to in paragraph (9)—
    (a) by close of business on the day when the court announces its decision; or
    (b) where that time is not practicable and the proceedings are on notice, no later than 72 hours from the time when the court announced its decision.

(9) The persons referred to in paragraph (8) are—
    (a) the parties (unless the court directs otherwise);
    (b) any person who has actual care of a child who is the subject of proceedings, or who had such care immediately prior to the making of the order;
    (c) in the case of an emergency protection order and a recovery order, the local authority in whose area the child lives or is found;
    (d) in proceedings to which Part 14 applies—

The Family Procedure Rules 2010

        (i)   an adoption agency or local authority which has prepared a report on the suitability of the applicant to adopt a child;
        (ii)   a local authority which has prepared a report on the placement of the child for adoption;
    (e)   any other person who has requested a copy if the court is satisfied that it is required in connection with an appeal or possible appeal.

(10) In this rule, "lay justice" means a justice of the peace who is not a District Judge (Magistrates' Courts).

(Rule 12.16(5) provides for the applicant to serve a section 8 order and an order in emergency proceedings made without notice within 48 hours after the making of the order. Rule 10.6(1) provides for the applicant to serve the order in proceedings under Part 4 of the 1996 Act. Rule 4.1(3)(a) permits the court to extend or shorten the time limit for compliance with any rule. Rule 6.33 provides for other persons to be supplied with copy documents under paragraph (8).)

27.3. Attendance at hearing or directions appointment

Unless the court directs otherwise, a party shall attend a hearing or directions appointment of which that party has been given notice.

27.4.— Proceedings in the absence of a party

(1) Proceedings or any part of them shall take place in the absence of any party, including a party who is a child, if—
    (a)   the court considers it in the interests of the party, having regard to the matters to be discussed or the evidence likely to be given; and
    (b)   the party is represented by a children's guardian or solicitor,
and when considering the interests of a child under sub-paragraph (a) the court shall give the children's guardian, the solicitor for the child and, if of sufficient understanding and the court thinks it appropriate, the child, an opportunity to make representations.

(2) Subject to paragraph (3), where at the time and place appointed for a hearing or directions appointment the applicant appears but one or more of the respondents do not, the court may proceed with the hearing or appointment.

(3) The court shall not begin to hear an application in the absence of a respondent unless—
    (a)   it is proved to the satisfaction of the court that the respondent received reasonable notice of the date of the hearing; or
    (b)   the court is satisfied that the circumstances of the case justify proceeding with the hearing.

(4) Where, at the time and place appointed for a hearing or directions appointment, one or more of the respondents appear but the applicant does not, the court may refuse the application or, if sufficient evidence has previously been received, proceed in the absence of the applicant.

(5) Where, at the time and place appointed for a hearing or directions appointment, neither the applicant nor any respondent appears, the court may refuse the application.

(6) Paragraphs (2) to (5) do not apply to a hearing to which paragraphs (5) to (8) of rule 12.14 do not apply by virtue of paragraph (9) of that rule.

(7) Nothing in this rule affects any provision of a European regulation or international convention by which the United Kingdom is bound which requires a court to stay proceedings where a respondent in another State has not been adequately served with proceedings in accordance with the requirements of that regulation or convention.

27.5.— Application to set aside judgment or order following failure to attend

(1) Where a party does not attend a hearing or directions appointment and the court gives judgment or makes an order against him, the party who failed to attend may apply for the judgment or order to be set aside[(GL.)].

(2) An application under paragraph (1) must be supported by evidence.

(3) Where an application is made under paragraph (1), the court may grant the application only if the applicant—

(a) acted promptly on finding out that the court had exercised its power to enter judgment or make an order against the applicant;
(b) had a good reason for not attending the hearing or directions appointment; and
(c) has a reasonable prospect of success at the hearing or directions appointment.

(4) This rule does not apply to magistrates' courts.

27.6.— Court bundles and place of filing of documents and bundles

(1) The provisions of Practice Direction 27A must be followed for the preparation of court bundles and for other related matters in respect of hearings and directions appointments.

(2) Paragraph (3) applies where the file of any family proceedings has been sent from one designated county court or registry to another for the purpose of a hearing or for some other purpose.

(3) A document needed for the purpose for which the proceedings have been sent to the other court or registry must be filed in that court or registry.

(Practice Direction 27A (Family Proceedings: Court Bundles (Universal Practice to be applied in All Courts other than the Family Proceedings Courts)) does not apply to magistrates' courts.)

27.7. Representation of companies or other corporations

A company or other corporation may be represented at a hearing or directions appointment by an employee if—

(a) the employee has been authorised by the company or corporation to appear at the hearing or directions appointment on its behalf; and
(b) the court gives permission.

27.8.— Impounded documents

(1) Documents impounded by order of the court must not be released from the custody of the court except in compliance with—

(a) a court order; or
(b) a written request made by a Law Officer or the Director of Public Prosecutions.

(2) A document released from the custody of the court under paragraph (1)(b) must be released into the custody of the person who requested it.

(3) Documents impounded by order of the court, while in the custody of the court, may not be inspected except by a person authorised to do so by a court order.

27.9.— Official shorthand note etc of proceedings

(1) Unless the judge directs otherwise, an official shorthand note will be taken at the hearing in open court of proceedings pending in the High Court.

(2) An official shorthand note may be taken of any other proceedings before a judge if directions for the taking of such a note are given by the Lord Chancellor.

(3) The shorthand writer will sign the note and certify it to be a correct shorthand note of the proceedings and will retain the note unless directed by the district judge to forward it to the court.

(4) On being so directed, the shorthand writer will furnish the court with a transcript of the whole or such part of the shorthand note as may be directed.

(5) Any party, any person who has intervened in the proceedings, the Queen's Proctor or, where a declaration of parentage has been made under section 55A of the 1986 Act, the Registrar General is entitled to require from the shorthand writer a transcript of the shorthand note, and the shorthand writer will, at the request of any person so entitled, supply that person with a transcript of the whole or any part of the note on payment of the shorthand writer's charges authorised by any scheme in force providing for the taking of official shorthand notes of legal proceedings.

The Family Procedure Rules 2010

(6) Save as permitted by this rule, the shorthand writer will not, without the permission of the court, furnish the shorthand note or a transcript of the whole or any part of it to anyone.

(7) In these rules, references to a shorthand note include references to a record of the proceedings made by mechanical means and in relation to such a record references to the shorthand writer include the person responsible for transcribing the record.

27.10.— Hearings in private
(1) Proceedings to which these rules apply will be held in private, except—
    (a) where these rules or any other enactment provide otherwise;
    (b) subject to any enactment, where the court directs otherwise.

(2) For the purposes of these rules, a reference to proceedings held "in private" means proceedings at which the general public have no right to be present.

27.11.— Attendance at private hearings
(1) This rule applies when proceedings are held in private, except in relation to —
    (a) hearings conducted for the purpose of judicially assisted conciliation or negotiation;
    (b) proceedings to which the following provisions apply—
        (i) Part 13 (proceedings under section 54 of the Human Fertilisation and Embryology Act 2008);
        (ii) Part 14 (procedure for applications in adoption, placement and related proceedings); and
        (iii) any proceedings identified in a practice direction as being excepted from this rule.

(2) When this rule applies, no person shall be present during any hearing other than—
    (a) an officer of the court;
    (b) a party to the proceedings;
    (c) a litigation friend for any party, or legal representative instructed to act on that party's behalf;
    (d) an officer of the service or Welsh family proceedings officer;
    (e) a witness;
    (f) duly accredited representatives of news gathering and reporting organisations; and
    (g) any other person whom the court permits to be present.

(3) At any stage of the proceedings the court may direct that persons within paragraph (2)(f) shall not attend the proceedings or any part of them, where satisfied that—
    (a) this is necessary—
        (i) in the interests of any child concerned in, or connected with, the proceedings;
        (ii) for the safety or protection of a party, a witness in the proceedings, or a person connected with such a party or witness; or
        (iii) for the orderly conduct of the proceedings; or
    (b) justice will otherwise be impeded or prejudiced.

(4) The court may exercise the power in paragraph (3) of its own initiative or pursuant to representations made by any of the persons listed in paragraph (5), and in either case having given to any person within paragraph (2)(f) who is in attendance an opportunity to make representations.

(5) At any stage of the proceedings, the following persons may make representations to the court regarding restricting the attendance of persons within paragraph (2)(f) in accordance with paragraph (3)—
    (a) a party to the proceedings;
    (b) any witness in the proceedings;
    (c) where appointed, any children's guardian;
    (d) where appointed, an officer of the service or Welsh family proceedings officer, on behalf of the child the subject of the proceedings;

(e) the child, if of sufficient age and understanding.

(6) This rule does not affect any power of the court to direct that witnesses shall be excluded until they are called for examination.

(7) In this rule "duly accredited" refers to accreditation in accordance with any administrative scheme for the time being approved for the purposes of this rule by the Lord Chancellor.

PART 27 COMMENTARY

Part 27 is supplemented by three practice directions 27A to 27C. By virtue of the *Practice Direction – Practice Directions Relating to Family Proceedings in Force before 6th April 2011 which support the Family Procedure Rules 2010* these are in fact pre-existing practice directions. The various directions are set out below, together with the date on which they were issued:

27A Family Proceedings Court Bundles (Universal Practice to be applied in all courts other than the Family Proceedings Court) (27 July 2006).

27B Attendance of Media Representatives at Hearings in Family Proceedings (High Court and County Court) (20 April 2009). (This practice direction, it is set out, should be read as if amended by *Re X (a child) (residence and contact: rights of media attendance* [2009] EWHC 1728 (Fam)). A series of updating references are provided in the *Practice Direction – Practice Directions Relating to Family Proceedings in Force before 6th April 2011 which support the Family Procedure Rules 2010*.

27C Attendance of Media Representatives at Hearings in Family Proceedings (Family Proceedings Court) (20 April 2009). (Again, this practice direction, it is set out, should be read as if amended by *Re X (a child) (residence and contact: rights of media attendance* [2009] EWHC 1728 (Fam)). A series of updating references are provided in the *Practice Direction – Practice Directions Relating to Family Proceedings in Force before 6th April 2011 which support the Family Procedure Rules 2010*.

Part 27 contains a variety of miscellaneous provisions in relation to hearings and directions appointments.

Rule 27.2 requires magistrates' courts to give written reasons for their decisions and sets out the manner in which they are to do so.

Rule 27.3 provides that unless the court otherwise directs a party shall attend a hearing or directions appointment of which they have been given notice.

Rule 27.4 makes provision at (1) for dealing with proceedings in the absence of a party who is a child, and at (2) to (7) proceeding with a hearing or directions appointment where the applicant or respondent does not attend.

Rule 27.5 gives a party who failed to attend a hearing the opportunity to apply to set aside the order.

Rule 27.6 requires the following of PD27A in relation to bundles.

Rule 27.7 allows a company or corporation to be represented by an employee in specified circumstances.

Rule 27.8 prohibits release of documents impounded by the court save in specified circumstances.

The Family Procedure Rules 2010

Rule 27.9 makes provision in relation to the noting (recording) and transcription of hearings.

Rule 27.10 provides that save for other provision family proceedings will be held in private.

Rule 27.11 provides who may attend at the private hearing, including at (2)(f) duly accredited representatives of the press, and making provision in rr 27.11 (3) – (5) as to restriction of the press's attendance.

PRACTICE DIRECTION 27A – FAMILY PROCEEDINGS: COURT BUNDLES (UNIVERSAL PRACTICE TO BE APPLIED IN ALL COURTS OTHER THAN THE FAMILY PROCEEDINGS COURT)

27th July 2006

1 The President of the Family Division has issued this practice direction to achieve consistency across the country in all family courts (other than the Family Proceedings Court) in the preparation of court bundles and in respect of other related matters.

APPLICATION OF THE PRACTICE DIRECTION

2.1 Except as specified in paragraph 2.4, and subject to specific directions given in any particular case, the following practice applies to:

(a) all hearings of whatever nature (including but not limited to hearings in family proceedings, CPR Part 7 and Part 8 claims and appeals) before a judge of the Family Division of the High Court wherever the court may be sitting;
(b) all hearings in family proceedings in the Royal Courts of Justice ("RCJ");
(c) all hearings in the Principal Registry of the Family Division ("PRFD") at First Avenue House; and
(d) all hearings in family proceedings in all other courts except for Family Proceedings Courts.

2.2 "Hearings" includes all appearances before a judge or district judge, whether with or without notice to other parties and whether for directions or for substantive relief.

2.3 This practice direction applies whether a bundle is being lodged for the first time or is being re-lodged for a further hearing (see paragraph 9.2).

2.4 This practice direction does not apply to:

(a) cases listed for one hour or less at a court referred to in paragraph 2.1(c) or 2.1(d); or
(b) the hearing of any urgent application if and to the extent that it is impossible to comply with it.

2.5 The Designated Family Judge responsible for any court referred to in paragraph 2.1(c) or 2.1(d) may, after such consultation as is appropriate (but in the case of hearings in the PRFD at First Avenue House only with the agreement of the Senior District Judge), direct that in that court this practice direction shall apply to all family proceedings irrespective of the length of hearing.

RESPONSIBILITY FOR THE PREPARATION OF THE BUNDLE

3.1 A bundle for the use of the court at the hearing shall be provided by the party in the position of applicant at the hearing (or, if there are cross-applications, by the party whose application was first in time) or, if that person is a litigant in person, by the first listed respondent who is not a litigant in person.

3.2 The party preparing the bundle shall paginate it. If possible the contents of the bundle shall be agreed by all parties.

FPR 2010, Practice Direction 27A

CONTENTS OF THE BUNDLE

4.1 The bundle shall contain copies of all documents relevant to the hearing, in chronological order from the front of the bundle, paginated and indexed, and divided into separate sections (each section being separately paginated) as follows:

(a) preliminary documents (see paragraph 4.2) and any other case management documents required by any other practice direction;
(b) applications and orders;
(c) statements and affidavits (which must be dated in the top right corner of the front page);
(d) care plans (where appropriate);
(e) experts' reports and other reports (including those of a guardian, children's guardian or litigation friend); and
(f) other documents, divided into further sections as may be appropriate.

Copies of notes of contact visits should normally not be included in the bundle unless directed by a judge.

4.2 At the commencement of the bundle there shall be inserted the following documents ("the preliminary documents"):

(i) an up to date summary of the background to the hearing confined to those matters which are relevant to the hearing and the management of the case and limited, if practicable, to one A4 page;
(ii) a statement of the issue or issues to be determined (1) at that hearing and (2) at the final hearing;
(iii) a position statement by each party including a summary of the order or directions sought by that party (1) at that hearing and (2) at the final hearing;
(iv) an up to date chronology, if it is a final hearing or if the summary under (i) is insufficient;
(v) skeleton arguments, if appropriate, with copies of all authorities relied on; and

a list of essential reading for that hearing.

4.3 Each of the preliminary documents shall state on the front page immediately below the heading the date when it was prepared and the date of the hearing for which it was prepared.

4.4 The summary of the background, statement of issues, chronology, position statement and any skeleton arguments shall be cross-referenced to the relevant pages of the bundle.

4.5 The summary of the background, statement of issues, chronology and reading list shall in the case of a final hearing, and shall so far as practicable in the case of any other hearing, each consist of a single document in a form agreed by all parties. Where the parties disagree as to the content the fact of their disagreement and their differing contentions shall be set out at the appropriate places in the document.

4.6 Where the nature of the hearing is such that a complete bundle of all documents is unnecessary, the bundle (which need not be repaginated) may comprise only those documents necessary for the hearing, but

(i) the summary (paragraph 4.2(i)) must commence with a statement that the bundle is limited or incomplete; and
(ii) the bundle shall if reasonably practicable be in a form agreed by all parties.

4.7 Where the bundle is re-lodged in accordance with paragraph 9.2, before it is re-lodged:

(a) the bundle shall be updated as appropriate; and
(b) all superseded documents (and in particular all outdated summaries, statements of issues, chronologies, skeleton arguments and similar documents) shall be removed from the bundle.

The Family Procedure Rules 2010

FORMAT OF THE BUNDLE

5.1 The bundle shall be contained in one or more A4 size ring binders or lever arch files (each lever arch file being limited to 350 pages).

5.2 All ring binders and lever arch files shall have clearly marked on the front and the spine:

(a) the title and number of the case;
(b) the court where the case has been listed;
(c) the hearing date and time;
(d) if known, the name of the judge hearing the case; and
(e) where there is more than one ring binder or lever arch file, a distinguishing letter (A, B, C etc).

TIMETABLE FOR PREPARING AND LODGING THE BUNDLE

6.1 The party preparing the bundle shall, whether or not the bundle has been agreed, provide a paginated index to all other parties not less than 4 working days before the hearing (in relation to a case management conference to which the provisions of the Public Law Protocol [2003] 2 FLR 719 apply, not less than 5 working days before the case management conference).

6.2 Where counsel is to be instructed at any hearing, a paginated bundle shall (if not already in counsel's possession) be delivered to counsel by the person instructing that counsel not less than 3 working days before the hearing.

6.3 The bundle (with the exception of the preliminary documents if and insofar as they are not then available) shall be lodged with the court not less than 2 working days before the hearing, or at such other time as may be specified by the judge.

6.4 The preliminary documents shall be lodged with the court no later than 11 am on the day before the hearing and, where the hearing is before a judge of the High Court and the name of the judge is known, shall at the same time be sent by e-mail to the judge's clerk.

LODGING THE BUNDLE

7.1 The bundle shall be lodged at the appropriate office. If the bundle is lodged in the wrong place the judge may:

(a) treat the bundle as having not been lodged; and
(b) take the steps referred to in paragraph 12.

7.2 Unless the judge has given some other direction as to where the bundle in any particular case is to be lodged (for example a direction that the bundle is to be lodged with the judge's clerk) the bundle shall be lodged:

(a) for hearings in the RCJ, in the office of the Clerk of the Rules, Room TM 9.09, Royal Courts of Justice, Strand, London WC2A 2LL (DX 44450 Strand);
(b) for hearings in the PRFD at First Avenue House, at the List Office counter, 3rd floor, First Avenue House, 42/49 High Holborn, London, WC1V 6NP (DX 396 Chancery Lane); and
(c) for hearings at any other court, at such place as may be designated by the Designated Family Judge or other judge at that court and in default of any such designation at the court office of the court where the hearing is to take place.

7.3 Any bundle sent to the court by post, DX or courier shall be clearly addressed to the appropriate office and shall show the date and place of the hearing on the outside of any packaging as well as on the bundle itself.

LODGING THE BUNDLE – ADDITIONAL REQUIREMENTS FOR CASES BEING HEARD AT FIRST AVENUE HOUSE OR AT THE RCJ

8.1 In the case of hearings at the RCJ or First Avenue House, parties shall:

(a) if the bundle or preliminary documents are delivered personally, ensure that they obtain a receipt from the clerk accepting it or them; and
(b) if the bundle or preliminary documents are sent by post or DX, ensure that they obtain proof of posting or despatch.

The receipt (or proof of posting or despatch, as the case may be) shall be brought to court on the day of the hearing and must be produced to the court if requested. If the receipt (or proof of posting or despatch) cannot be produced to the court the judge may (i) treat the bundle as having not been lodged and (ii) take the steps referred to in paragraph 12.

8.2 For hearings at the RCJ:

(a) bundles or preliminary documents delivered after 11 am on the day before the hearing will not be accepted by the Clerk of the Rules and shall be delivered:
  (i) in a case where the hearing is before a judge of the High Court, directly to the clerk of the judge hearing the case;
  (ii) in a case where the hearing is before a Circuit Judge, Deputy High Court Judge or Recorder, directly to the messenger at the Judge's entrance to the Queen's Building (with telephone notification to the personal assistant to the Designated Family Judge, 020 7947 7155, that this has been done).
(b) upon learning before which judge a hearing is to take place, the clerk to counsel, or other advocate, representing the party in the position of applicant shall no later than 3pm the day before the hearing:
(i) in a case where the hearing is before a judge of the High Court, telephone the clerk of the judge hearing the case;
(ii) in a case where the hearing is before a Circuit Judge, Deputy High Court Judge or Recorder, telephone the personal assistant to the Designated Family Judge;

to ascertain whether the judge has received the bundle (including the preliminary documents) and, if not, shall organise prompt delivery by the applicant's solicitor.

REMOVING AND RE-LODGING THE BUNDLE

9.1 Following completion of the hearing the party responsible for the bundle shall retrieve it from the court immediately or, if that is not practicable, shall collect it from the court within five working days. Bundles which are not collected in due time may be destroyed.

9.2 The bundle shall be re-lodged for the next and any further hearings in accordance with the provisions of this practice direction and in a form which complies with paragraph 4.7.

TIME ESTIMATES

10.1 In every case a time estimate (which shall be inserted at the front of the bundle) shall be prepared which shall so far as practicable be agreed by all parties and shall:

(a) specify separately (i) the time estimated to be required for judicial pre-reading and (ii) the time required for hearing all evidence and submissions and (iii) the time estimated to be required for preparing and delivering judgment; and
(b) be prepared on the basis that before they give evidence all witnesses will have read all relevant filed statements and reports.

10.2 Once a case has been listed, any change in time estimates shall be notified immediately by telephone (and then immediately confirmed in writing):

(a) in the case of hearings in the RCJ, to the Clerk of the Rules;
(b) in the case of hearings in the PRFD at First Avenue House, to the List Officer at First Avenue House; and
(c) in the case of hearings elsewhere, to the relevant listing officer.

TAKING CASES OUT OF THE LIST

11 As soon as it becomes known that a hearing will no longer be effective, whether as a result of the parties reaching agreement or for any other reason, the parties and

their representatives shall immediately notify the court by telephone and by letter. The letter, which shall wherever possible be a joint letter sent on behalf of all parties with their signatures applied or appended, shall include:

(a) a short background summary of the case;
(b) the written consent of each party who consents and, where a party does not consent, details of the steps which have been taken to obtain that party's consent and, where known, an explanation of why that consent has not been given;
(c) a draft of the order being sought; and
(d) enough information to enable the court to decide (i) whether to take the case out of the list and (ii) whether to make the proposed order.

PENALTIES FOR FAILURE TO COMPLY WITH THE PRACTICE DIRECTION

12 Failure to comply with any part of this practice direction may result in the judge removing the case from the list or putting the case further back in the list and may also result in a "wasted costs" order in accordance with CPR Part 48.7 or some other adverse costs order.

Commencement of the practice direction and application of other practice directions

13 This practice direction replaces President's Direction (Family Proceedings: Court Bundles) [2000] 1 FLR 536 and shall have effect from 2 October 2006.

14 Any reference in any other practice direction to President's Direction (Family Proceedings: Court Bundles) [2000] 1 FLR 536 shall be read as if substituted by a reference to this practice direction.

15 This practice direction should where appropriate be read in conjunction with *President's Direction (Human Rights Act 1998)* [2000] 2 FLR 429 and with Practice Direction (Care Cases: Judicial Continuity and Judicial Case Management) appended to the Public Law Protocol [2003] 2 FLR 719. In particular, nothing in this practice direction is to be read as removing or altering any obligation to comply with the requirements of the Public Law Protocol.

This Practice Direction is issued:

(i) in relation to family proceedings, by the President of the Family Division, as the nominee of the Lord Chief Justice, with the agreement of the Lord Chancellor; and
(ii) to the extent that it applies to proceedings to which section 5 of the Civil Procedure Act 1997 applies, by the Master of the Rolls as the nominee of the Lord Chief Justice, with the agreement of the Lord Chancellor.

PRACTICE DIRECTION 27B – ATTENDANCE OF MEDIA REPRESENTATIVES AT HEARINGS IN FAMILY PROCEEDINGS IN FAMILY PROCEEDINGS (HIGH COURT AND COUNTY COURTS)

This Practice Direction below is made by the President of the Family Division under the powers delegated to him by the Lord Chief Justice under Schedule 2, Part 1, paragraph 2(2) of the Constitutional Reform Act 2005, and is approved by Bridget Prentice, Parliamentary Under Secretary of State, by the authority of the Lord Chancellor.

1. INTRODUCTION

This Practice Direction supplements *rule 10.28 of the Family Proceedings Rules 1991 ("FPR 1991")* [rule 27.11 of the Family Proceedings Rules 2010] and deals with the right of representatives of news gathering and reporting organisations ("media representatives") to attend at hearings of family proceedings which take place in private subject to the discretion of the court to exclude such representatives from the whole or part of any hearing on specified grounds[1]. It takes effect on 27 April 2009.

[1] It does not, accordingly, apply where hearings are held in open court where the general public including media representatives may attend as of right, such as committal hearings or the hearing of matrimonial or civil partnership causes.

2. MATTERS UNCHANGED BY THE RULE

2.1 Rule 10.28(1) contains an express exception in respect of hearings which are conducted for the purpose of judicially assisted conciliation or negotiation and media representatives do not have a right to attend these hearings. Financial Dispute Resolution hearings will come within this exception. First Hearing Dispute Resolution appointments in private law Children Act cases will also come within this exception to the extent that the judge plays an active part in the conciliation process. Where the judge plays no part in the conciliation process or where the conciliation element of a hearing is complete and the judge is adjudicating upon the issues between the parties, media representatives should be permitted to attend, subject to the discretion of the court to exclude them on the specified grounds. Conciliation meetings or negotiation conducted between the parties with the assistance of an officer of the service or a Welsh Family Proceedings officer, and without the presence of the judge, are not "hearings" within the meaning of this rule and media representatives have no right to attend such appointments.

The exception in rule 10.28(1) does not operate to exclude media representatives from:

- Hearings to consider applications brought under Parts IV and V of the Children Act 1989, including Case Management Conferences and Issues Resolution Hearings
- Hearings relating to findings of fact
- Interim hearings
- Final hearings.

The rights of media representatives to attend such hearings are limited only by the powers of the court to exclude such attendance on the limited grounds and subject to the procedures set out in paragraphs (4)–(6) of rule 10.28.

2.2 During any hearing, courts should consider whether the exception in rule 10.28(1) becomes applicable so that media representatives should be directed to withdraw.

2.3 The provisions of the rules permitting the attendance of media representatives and the disclosure to third parties of information relating to the proceedings do not entitle a media representative to receive or peruse court documents referred to in the course of evidence, submissions or judgment without the permission of the court or otherwise in accordance with *Part 11 of the Family Proceedings Rules 1991* [Part 12, Chapter 7 of the Family Procedure Rules 2010 and Practice Direction 12G] (rules relating to disclosure to third parties). (This is in contrast to the position in civil proceedings, where the court sits in public and where members of the public are entitled to seek copies of certain documents[2])

2.4 The question of attendance of media representatives at hearings in family proceedings to which rule 10.28 and this guidance apply must be distinguished from statutory restrictions on publication and disclosure of information relating to proceedings, which continue to apply and are unaffected by the rule and this guidance.

2.5 The prohibition in section 97(2) of the Children Act 1989, on publishing material intended to or likely to identify a child as being involved in proceedings or the address or school of any such child, is limited to the duration of the proceedings[3]. However, the limitations imposed by section 12 of the Administration of Justice Act 1960 on publication of information relating to certain proceedings in private[4] apply during and after the proceedings. In addition, in proceedings to which s. 97(2) of the Children Act 1989 applies the court should continue to consider at the conclusion of the proceedings whether there are any outstanding welfare issues which require a continuation of the

The Family Procedure Rules 2010

protection afforded during the course of the proceedings by that provision.

[2] See *GIO Services Ltd v Liverpool and London Ltd* [1999] 1 WLR 984.

[3] See *Clayton v Clayton* [2006] EWCA Civ 878.

[4] In particular proceedings which

    (a)   relate to the exercise of the inherent jurisdiction of the High Court with respect to minors;

    (b)   are brought under the Children Act 1989; or

    (c)   otherwise relate wholly or mainly to the maintenance or upbringing of a minor.

3. AIMS OF THE GUIDANCE

3.1 This Practice Direction is intended to provide guidance regarding:

- the handling of applications to exclude media representatives from the whole or part of a hearing: and
- the exercise of the court's discretion to exclude media representatives whether upon the court's own motion or any such application

3.2 While the guidance does not aim to cover all possible eventualities, it should be complied with so far as consistent in all the circumstances with the just determination of the proceedings.

4. IDENTIFICATION OF MEDIA REPRESENTATIVES AS "ACCREDITED"

4.1 Media representatives will be expected to carry with them identification sufficient to enable court staff, or if necessary the court itself, to verify that they are "accredited" representatives of news gathering or reporting organisations within the meaning of the rule.

4.2 By virtue of *paragraph (8)* [paragraph (7)] of the rule, it is for the Lord Chancellor to approve a scheme which will provide for accreditation. The Lord Chancellor has decided that the scheme operated by the UK Press Card Authority provides sufficient accreditation; a card issued under that scheme will be the expected form of identification, and production of the Card will be both necessary and sufficient to demonstrate accreditation.

4.3 A media representative unable to demonstrate accreditation in accordance with the UK Press Card Authority scheme, so as to be able to attend by virtue of *paragraph (3)(f)* [paragraph 2(f)] of the rule, may nevertheless be permitted to attend at the court's discretion under *paragraph (3)(g)* [paragraph (2)(g)].

5. EXERCISE OF THE DISCRETION TO EXCLUDE MEDIA REPRESENTATIVES FROM ALL OR PART OF THE PROCEEDINGS

5.1 The rule anticipates and should be applied on the basis that media representatives have a right to attend family proceedings throughout save and to the extent that the court exercises its discretion to exclude them from the whole or part of any proceedings on one or more of the grounds set out in *paragraph (4)* [paragraph (3)] of the rule.

5.2 When considering the question of exclusion on any of the grounds set out in *paragraph (4)* [paragraph (3)] of the rule the court should —

- specifically identify whether the risk to which such ground is directed arises from the mere fact of media presence at the particular hearing or hearings the subject of the application or whether the risk identified can be adequately addressed by exclusion of media representatives from a part only of such hearing or hearings;
- consider whether the reporting or disclosure restrictions which apply by operation of law, or which the court otherwise has power to order will provide sufficient protection to the party on whose behalf the application is made or any of the persons referred to in *paragraph (4)(a)* [paragraph 3(a)] of the rule;

- consider the safety of the parties in cases in which the court considers there are particular physical or health risks against which reporting restrictions may be inadequate to afford protection;
- in the case of any vulnerable adult or child who is unrepresented before the court, consider the extent to which the court should of its own motion take steps to protect the welfare of that adult or child.

5.3 *Paragraph (4)(a)(iii)* [Paragraph 3(a)(iii)] of the rule permits exclusion where necessary "for the orderly conduct of proceedings". This enables the court to address practical problems presented by media attendance. In particular, it may be difficult or even impossible physically to accommodate all (or indeed any) media representatives who wish to attend a particular hearing on the grounds of the restricted size or layout of the court room in which it is being heard. Court staff will use their best efforts to identify more suitable accommodation in advance of any hearing which appears likely to attract particular media attention, and to move hearings to larger court rooms where possible. However, the court should not be required to adjourn a hearing in order for larger accommodation to be sought where this will involve significant disruption or delay in the proceedings.

5.4 *Paragraph (4)(b)* [Paragraph 3(b)] of the rule permits exclusion where, unless the media are excluded, justice will be impeded or prejudiced for some reason other than those set out in sub-paragraph (a). Reasons of administrative inconvenience are not sufficient. Examples of circumstances where the impact on justice of continued attendance might be sufficient to necessitate exclusion may include:

- a hearing relating to the parties' finances where the information being considered includes price sensitive information (such as confidential information which could affect the share price of a publicly quoted company); or
- any hearing at which a witness (other than a party) states for credible reasons that he or she will not give evidence in front of media representatives, or where there appears to the court to be a significant risk that a witness will not give full or frank evidence in the presence of media representatives.

5.5 In the event of a decision to exclude media representatives, the court should state brief reasons for the decision.

6. APPLICATIONS TO EXCLUDE MEDIA REPRESENTATIVES FROM ALL OR PART OF PROCEEDINGS

6.1 The court may exclude media representatives on the permitted grounds of its own motion or after hearing representations from the interested persons listed at *paragraph (6)* [paragraph (5)] of the rule. Where exclusion is proposed, any media representatives who are present are entitled to make representations about that proposal. There is, however, no requirement to adjourn proceedings to enable media representatives who are not present to attend in order to make such representations, and in such a case the court should not adjourn unless satisfied of the necessity to do so having regard to the additional cost and delay which would thereby be caused.

6.2 Applications to exclude media representatives should normally be dealt with as they arise and by way of oral representations, unless the court directs otherwise.

6.3 When media representatives are expected to attend a particular hearing (for example, where a party is encouraging media interest and attendance) and a party intends to apply to the court for the exclusion of the media, that party should, if practicable, give advance notice to the court, to the other parties and (where appointed) any children's guardian, officer of the service or Welsh Family Proceedings officer, NYAS or other representative of the child of any intention to seek the exclusion of media representatives from all or part of the proceedings. Equally, legal representatives and parties should ensure that witnesses are aware of the right of media representatives to attend and should notify the court at an early stage of the intention of any witness to request the exclusion of media representatives

6.4 Prior notification by the court of a pending application for exclusion will not be given to media interests unless the court so directs. However, where such an application has been made, the applicant must where possible, notify the relevant media organisations.

Sir Mark Potter

President of the Family Division

PRACTICE DIRECTION 27C – ATTENDANCE OF MEDIA REPRESENTATIVES IN FAMILY PROCEEDINGS (FAMILY PROCEEDINGS COURT)

1. INTRODUCTION

1.1 This Practice Direction supplements *rule 16A of the Family Proceedings Courts (Children Act 1989) Rules 1991 ("the Rules")* [rule 27.11 of the Family Procedure Rules 2010 ("FPR 2010")] and deals with the right of representatives of news gathering and reporting organisations ("media representatives") to attend at hearings of relevant proceedings[1] subject to the discretion of the court to exclude such representatives from the whole or part of any hearing on specified grounds[2]. It takes effect on 27th April 2009. References to a "hearing" within this Practice Direction include reference to a directions appointment, whether conducted by the justices, a district judge or a justices' clerk.

[1] "relevant proceedings" are defined in rule 1 of these Rules by reference to section 93(3) of the Children Act 1989.

[2] It does not, accordingly, apply where hearings are held in open court where the general public including media representatives attend as of right.

2. MATTERS UNCHANGED BY THE RULE

2.1 *Rule 16A(2)*[Rule 27.11(1)] contains an express exception in respect of hearings which are conducted for the purpose of judicially assisted conciliation or negotiation and media representatives do not have a right to attend these hearings. First Hearing Dispute Resolution appointments in private law Children Act cases will come within this exception to the extent that the justices, a district judge or a justices' clerk play an active part in the conciliation process. Where the justices, a district judge or a justices' clerk play no part in the conciliation process or where the conciliation element of a hearing is complete and the court is adjudicating upon the issues between the parties, media representatives should be permitted to attend subject to the discretion of the court to exclude them on the specified grounds. Conciliation meetings or negotiation conducted between the parties with the assistance of an officer of the service or a Welsh Family Proceedings officer, and without the presence of the justices, a district judge or a justices' clerk, are not "hearings" within the meaning of this rule and media representatives have no right to attend such appointments.

The exception in *rule 16A(2)* [rule 27.11(1)] does not operate to exclude media representatives from:

- Hearings to consider applications brought under Parts IV and V of the Children Act 1989, including Case Management Conferences and Issues Resolution Hearings
- Hearings relating to findings of fact
- Interim hearings
- Final hearings.

The rights of media representatives to attend such hearings are limited only by the powers of the court to exclude such attendance on the limited grounds and subject to the procedures set out in *paragraphs (3) to (5) of rule 16A* [paragraphs (3) to (5) of rule 27.11)].

2.2 During any hearing, the court should consider whether the exception in *rule 16A(2)*[rule 27.11(1)] becomes applicable so that media representatives should be directed to withdraw.

2.3 The provisions of the rules permitting the attendance of media representatives and the disclosure to third parties of information relating to the proceedings do not entitle a media representative to receive or peruse court documents referred to in the course of evidence, submissions or decisions of the court (in particular, written reasons) without the permission of the court or otherwise in accordance with *Part IIC (rules relating to disclosure to third parties)* [Part 12, Chapter 7 of the Family Procedure Rules 2010 and Practice Direction 12G].

2.4 The question of attendance of media representatives at hearings in family proceedings to which *rule 16A* [rule 27.11] and this guidance apply must be distinguished from statutory restrictions on publication and disclosure of information relating to proceedings, which continue to apply and are unaffected by the rule and this guidance.

2.5 The prohibition in section 97(2) of the Children Act 1989, on publishing material intended to or likely to identify a child as being involved in proceedings or the address or school of any such child, is limited to the duration of the proceedings[3]. However, the limitations imposed by section 12 of the Administration of Justice Act 1960 on publication of information relating to certain proceedings in private[4] apply during and after the proceedings. In addition, in the course of proceedings to which s.97(2) of the Children Act 1989 applies the court should consider whether at the conclusion of the proceedings there may be outstanding welfare issues which may require a continuation of the protection afforded during the course of the proceedings by s. 97 (2) of the Children Act 1989 and which are not fully met by a direction under section 39 Children and Young Persons Act 1933[5], so that any party seeking such protection has an opportunity to apply to the county court or High Court for the appropriate order before the proceedings are finally concluded.

[3] See *Clayton v Clayton* [2006] EWCA Civ 878
[4] In particular proceedings which

    (a)   relate to the exercise of the inherent jurisdiction of the High Court with respect to minors;
    (b)   are brought under the Children Act 1989; or
    (c)   otherwise relate wholly or mainly to the maintenance or upbringing of a minor

[5] Power of court to prohibit publication of certain matters in newspapers.

3. AIMS OF THE GUIDANCE

3.1 This Practice Direction is intended to provide guidance regarding:

- the handling of applications to exclude media representatives from the whole or part of a hearing: and
- the exercise of the court's discretion to exclude media representatives whether upon the court's own motion or any such application.

3.2 While the guidance does not aim to cover all possible eventualities, it should be complied with so far as consistent in all the circumstances with the just determination of the proceedings.

4. IDENTIFICATION OF MEDIA REPRESENTATIVES AS "ACCREDITED"

4.1 Media representatives will be expected to carry with them identification sufficient to enable court staff, or if necessary the court itself, to verify that they are "accredited" representatives of news gathering or reporting organisations within the meaning of the rule.

4.2 By virtue of paragraph (7) of the rule, it is for the Lord Chancellor to approve a scheme which will provide for accreditation. The Lord Chancellor has decided that the

The Family Procedure Rules 2010

scheme operated by the UK Press Card Authority provides sufficient accreditation: a card issued under that scheme will be the expected form of identification, and production of the Card will be both necessary and sufficient to demonstrate accreditation.

4.3 A media representative unable to demonstrate accreditation in accordance with the UK Press Card Authority scheme so as to be able to attend by virtue of *paragraph (1)(f)* [paragraph 2(f)] of the rule may nevertheless be permitted to attend at the court's discretion under *paragraph (1)(g)* [paragraph 2(g)].

5. EXERCISE OF THE DISCRETION TO EXCLUDE MEDIA REPRESENTATIVES FROM ALL OR PART OF THE PROCEEDINGS.

5.1 The rule anticipates and should be applied on the basis that media representatives have a right to attend family proceedings throughout save and to the extent that the court exercises its discretion to exclude them from the whole or part of any proceedings on one or more of the grounds set out in paragraph (3) of the rule.

5.2 When considering the question of exclusion on any of the grounds set out in paragraph (3) of the rule the court should -

- specifically identify whether the risk to which such ground is directed arises from the mere fact of media presence at the particular hearing or hearings the subject of the application or whether the risk identified can be adequately addressed by exclusion of media representatives from a part only of such hearing or hearings;
- consider whether the reporting or disclosure restrictions which apply by operation of law, or which the court otherwise has power to order will provide sufficient protection to the party on whose behalf the application is made or any of the persons referred to in paragraph (3)(a) of the rule;
- consider the safety of the parties in cases in which the court considers there are particular physical or health risks against which reporting restrictions may be inadequate to afford protection;
- in the case of any vulnerable adult or child who is unrepresented before the court, consider the extent to which the court should of its own motion take steps to protect the welfare of that adult or child.

5.3 Paragraph (3)(a)(iii) of the rule permits exclusion where necessary "for the orderly conduct of proceedings". This enables the court to address practical problems presented by media attendance. In particular, it may be difficult or even impossible physically to accommodate all (or indeed any) media representatives who wish to attend a particular hearing on the grounds of the restricted size or layout of the court room in which it is being heard. Court staff will use their best efforts to identify more suitable accommodation in advance of any hearing which appears likely to attract particular media attention, and to move hearings to larger court rooms where possible. However, the court should not be required to adjourn a hearing in order for larger accommodation to be sought where this will involve significant disruption or delay in the proceedings.

5.4 Paragraph (3)(b) of the rule permits exclusion where, unless the media are excluded, justice will be impeded or prejudiced for some reason other than those set out in sub-paragraph (a). Reasons of administrative inconvenience are not sufficient. An example of circumstances where the impact on justice of continued attendance might be sufficient to necessitate exclusion would be any hearing at which a witness (other than a party) states for credible reasons that he or she will not give evidence in front of media representatives, or where there appears to the court to be a significant risk that a witness will not give full or frank evidence in the presence of media representatives.

5.5 In the event of a decision to exclude media representatives, the court should state brief reasons for the decision.

6. APPLICATIONS TO EXCLUDE MEDIA REPRESENTATIVES FROM ALL OR PART OF PROCEEDINGS.

6.1 The court may exclude media representatives on the permitted grounds of its own motion or after hearing representations from the interested persons listed at paragraph (5) of the rule. Where exclusion is proposed, any media representatives who are present are entitled to make representations about that proposal. There is, however, no requirement to adjourn proceedings to enable media representatives who are not present to attend in order to make such representations, and in such a case the court should not adjourn unless satisfied of the necessity to do so having regard to the additional cost and delay which would thereby be caused.

6.2 Applications to exclude media representatives should normally be dealt with as they arise and by way of oral representations, unless the court directs otherwise.

6.3 When media representatives are expected to attend a particular hearing (for example, where a party is encouraging media interest and attendance) and a party intends to apply to the court for the exclusion of the media, such party should, if practicable, give advance notice to the court, to the other parties and (where appointed) any children's guardian, officer of the service or Welsh Family Proceedings officer, NYAS or other representative of the child of any intention to seek the exclusion of media representatives from all or part of the proceedings. Equally, legal representatives and parties should ensure that witnesses are aware of the right of media representatives to attend and should notify the court at an early stage of the intention of any witness to request the exclusion of media representatives.

6.4 Prior notification by the court of a pending application for exclusion will not be given to media interests unless the court so directs. However, where such an application has been made, the applicant must where possible, notify the relevant media organisations.

Sir Mark Potter

President of the Family Division

20 April 2009

[2009] 2 FCR 606, [2009] 2 FLR 157

PART 28

COSTS

28.1. Costs
The court may at any time make such order as to costs as it thinks just.

28.2.— Application of other rules
(1) Subject to rule 28.3 and to paragraph (2), Parts 43, 44 (except rules 44.3(2) and (3), 44.9 to 44.12C, 44.13(1A) and (1B) and 44.18 to 20), 47 and 48 and rule 45.6 of the CPR apply to costs in proceedings, with the following modifications—
    (a) in rule 43.2(1)(c)(ii), "district judge" includes a district judge of the principal registry;
    (b) in rule 48.7(1) after "section 51(6) of the Senior Courts Act 1981" insert "or section 145A of the Magistrates' Courts Act 1980";
    (c) in accordance with any provisions in Practice Direction 28A; and
    (d) any other necessary modifications.

(2) Part 47 and rules 44.3C and 45.6 of the CPR do not apply to proceedings in a magistrates' court.

28.3.— Costs in financial remedy proceedings
(1) This rule applies in relation to financial remedy proceedings.

(2) Rule 44.3(1), (4) and (5) of the CPR do not apply to financial remedy proceedings.

(3) Rule 44.3(6) to (9) of the CPR apply to an order made under this rule as they apply to an order made under rule 44.3 of the CPR.

(4) In this rule –
    (a) "costs" has the same meaning as in rule 43.2(1)(a) of the CPR; and

(b) "financial remedy proceedings" means proceedings for—
   (i) a financial order except an order for maintenance pending suit, an order for maintenance pending outcome of proceedings, an interim periodical payments order or any other form of interim order for the purposes of rule 9.7(1)(a), (b), (c) and (e);
   (ii) an order under Part 3 of the 1984 Act;
   (iii) an order under Schedule 7 to the 2004 Act;
   (iv) an order under section 10(2) of the 1973 Act;
   (v) an order under section 48(2) of the 2004 Act.

(5) Subject to paragraph (6), the general rule in financial remedy proceedings is that the court will not make an order requiring one party to pay the costs of another party.

(6) The court may make an order requiring one party to pay the costs of another party at any stage of the proceedings where it considers it appropriate to do so because of the conduct of a party in relation to the proceedings (whether before or during them).

(7) In deciding what order (if any) to make under paragraph (6), the court must have regard to—
   (a) any failure by a party to comply with these rules, any order of the court or any practice direction which the court considers relevant;
   (b) any open offer to settle made by a party;
   (c) whether it was reasonable for a party to raise, pursue or contest a particular allegation or issue;
   (d) the manner in which a party has pursued or responded to the application or a particular allegation or issue;
   (e) any other aspect of a party's conduct in relation to proceedings which the court considers relevant; and
   (f) the financial effect on the parties of any costs order.

(8) No offer to settle which is not an open offer to settle is admissible at any stage of the proceedings, except as provided by rule 9.17.

28.4. Wasted costs orders in the magistrates' court: appeals

A legal or other representative against whom a wasted costs order is made in the magistrates' court may appeal to the Crown Court.

PART 28 COMMENTARY

Part 28 is supplemented by PD28A. This applies and modifies the Practice Directions about costs which supplements Part 43 to 48 of the CPR. It sets out at paragraph 4.5 that parties who intend to seek a costs order against another party in proceedings to which r 28.3 apply (see below) should ordinarily make this plain in open correspondence or in skeleton arguments prior to the date of the hearing. And that in any case in which summary assessment is sought there is an obligation to file a statement of costs in CPR Form N260.

Part 28 deals with costs, there is a distinction drawn between financial remedy proceedings and other applications.

At r 28.2 the CPR costs rules are applied with modification, in particular the CPR provision that costs follow the event does not apply.

Rule 28.3 restates, with some changes, the costs rules applying to ancillary relief applications, extending the provisions to Part 3 of the 1984 Act. Rule 28.3 applies to costs in 'financial remedy proceedings', but that phrase is defined more narrowly here than in r 2.3: it extends to 'financial orders' (old style ancillary relief, similar orders under the 2004 Act (the Civil Partnership Act) and Part 3 of the 1984 Act (financial relief after overseas divorce), but not Sch 1 of the Children Act 1989 however specifically excluded are maintenance pending suit orders and outcome of proceedings orders, interim periodical payments orders and other specified interim orders. The general rule, stated at r 28.3 (5) is that when dealing with financial remedy proceedings (with this limited definition) the court will not make an order requiring one party to pay the costs of the other party, but may do so where it considers it appropriate to do so because of the conduct of a party in relation to the proceedings (r 28.3(5),(6)). By r 28.3 (8) it is provided that in relation to financial remedy proceedings (with this limited definition) no offer which is not an open offer to settle is admissible at any stage of the proceedings (save for the FDR). It therefore appears that it is now possible to rely on 'without prejudice save as to costs offers' in maintenance pending suit and the other specified interim applications.

Notice of change of Solicitor is by form FP8.

Forms Relevant to Part 28 are D252 –D259, Form H, Form H1 and N260.

PRACTICE DIRECTION 28A – COSTS

This Practice Direction is made by the President of the Family Division under the powers delegated to him by the Lord Chief Justice under Schedule 2, Part 1, paragraph 2(2) of the Constitutional Reform Act 2005, and is approved by the Parliamentary Under Secretary of State, by authority of the Lord Chancellor and comes into force on 6th April 2011

This Practice Direction supplements FPR Part 28

APPLICATION AND MODIFICATION OF THE CPR

1.1 Rule 28.2 provides that subject to rule 28.3 of the FPR and to paragraph (2) of rule 28.2, Parts 43, 44 (except rules 44.3(2) and (3),44.9 to 44.12C, 44.13(1A) and (1B) and 44.18 to 20),47 and 48 and rule 45.6 of the CPR apply to costs in family proceedings with the modifications listed in rule 28.2(1)(a) to (d). Rule 28.2(1)(c) refers to modifications in accordance with this Practice Direction.

1.2 In addition to the modifications to the CPR listed in rule 28.2(1), in rule 48.1(1)(b) after paragraph (ii) insert "(iii) section 68A of the Magistrates' Courts Act 1980.".

1.3 Rule 28.2(2) provides that Part 47 and rules 44.3C and 45.6 of the CPR do not apply to proceedings in a magistrates' court.

APPLICATION AND MODIFICATION OF THE PRACTICE DIRECTION SUPPLEMENTING CPR PARTS 43 TO 48

2.1 For the purpose of proceedings to which these Rules apply, the Practice Direction about costs which supplements Parts 43 to 48 of the CPR ("the costs practice direction") will apply, but with the exclusions and modifications explained below to reflect the exclusions and modifications to those Parts of the CPR as they are applied by Part 28 of these Rules.

2.2 Rule 28.2(1) applies, with modifications and certain exceptions, Parts 43 to 48 of the CPR to costs in family proceedings. Paragraph 1.2 of this Practice Direction modifies rule 48.1(1)(b) when it applies to family proceedings. Rule 28.2(2), by way of exception, disapplies Part 47, rules 44.3C and 45.6 of the CPR in the case of family proceedings in a magistrates' court. Rule 28.3, again by way of exception, additionally disapplies CPR rule 44.3(1), (4) and (5) in the case of financial remedy proceedings, regardless of court.

2.3 The costs practice direction does not, therefore, apply in its entirety but with the exclusion of certain sections reflecting the non-application of certain rules of the CPR which those sections supplement.

2.4 The costs practice direction applies as follows—

The Family Procedure Rules 2010

- to family proceedings generally, other than in magistrates' courts, with the exception of sections 6, 15, 16, 17 and 23A;
- to family proceedings generally, in magistrates' courts only, with the exception of sections 6, 15, 16, 17, 23A and sections 28-49A;
- to financial remedy proceedings, other than in magistrates' courts, with the exception of section 6, paragraphs 8.1 to 8.4 of section 8 and sections 15, 16,17 and 23A;
- to financial remedy proceedings in magistrates' courts only, with the exception of section 6, paragraphs 8.1 to 8.4 of section 8, sections 15, 16, 17, 23A and sections 28-49A.

2.5 All subsequent editions of the costs practice direction as and when they are published and come into effect shall in the same way extend to all family proceedings.

2.6 The costs practice direction includes provisions applicable to proceedings following changes in the manner in which legal services are funded pursuant to the Access to Justice Act 1999. It should be noted that although the cost of the premium in respect of legal costs insurance (section 29) or the cost of funding by a prescribed membership organisation (section 30) may be recoverable, family proceedings (within section 58A(2) of the Courts and Legal Services Act 1990) cannot be the subject of an enforceable conditional fee agreement.

2.7 Paragraph 1.4 of section 1 of the costs practice direction shall be modified as follows—in the definition of "counsel" for "High court or in the county courts" substitute "High Court, county courts or in a magistrates' court".

GENERAL INTERPRETATION OF REFERENCES IN CPR

3.1 References in the costs practice direction to "claimant" and "defendant" are to be read as references to equivalent terms used in proceedings to which these Rules apply and other terms and expressions used in the costs practice direction shall be similarly treated.

3.2 References in CPR Parts 43 to 48 to other rules or Parts of the CPR shall be read, where there is an equivalent rule or Part in these Rules, to that equivalent rule or Part.

COSTS IN FINANCIAL REMEDY PROCEEDINGS

4.1 Rule 28.3 relates to the court's power to make costs orders in financial remedy proceedings. For the purposes of rule 28.3, "financial remedy proceedings" are defined in accordance with rule 28.3(4)(b). That definition, which is more limited than the principal definition in rule 2.3(1), includes:

(a) an application for a financial order, except:
  (i) an order for maintenance pending suit or an order for maintenance pending outcome of proceedings;
  (ii) an interim periodical payments order or any other form of interim order for the purposes of rule 9.7(1)(a),(b),(c) and (e);
(b) an application for an order under Part 3 of the Matrimonial and Family Proceedings Act 1984 or Schedule 7 to the Civil Partnership Act 2004; and
(c) an application under section 10(2) of the Matrimonial Causes Act 1973 or section 48(2) of the Civil Partnership Act 2004.

4.2 Accordingly, it should be noted that:

(a) while most interim financial applications are excluded from rule 28.3, the rule does apply to an application for an interim variation order within rule 9.7(1)(d),
(b) rule 28.3 does not apply to an application for any of the following financial remedies:
  (i) an order under Schedule 1 to the Children Act 1989;
  (ii) an order under section 27 of the Matrimonial Causes Act 1973 or Part 9 of Schedule 5 to the Civil Partnership Act 2004;
  (iii) an order under section 35 of the Matrimonial Causes Act 1973 or paragraph 69 of Schedule 5 to the Civil Partnership Act 2004; or

(iv) an order under Part 1 of the Domestic Proceedings and Magistrates' Courts Act 1978 or Schedule 6 to the Civil Partnership Act 2004.

4.3 Under rule 28.3 the court only has the power to make a costs order in financial remedy proceedings when this is justified by the litigation conduct of one of the parties. When determining whether and how to exercise this power the court will be required to take into account the list of factors set out in that rule. The court will not be able to take into account any offers to settle expressed to be "without prejudice" or "without prejudice save as to costs" in deciding what, if any, costs orders to make.

4.4 In considering the conduct of the parties for the purposes of rule 28.3(6) and (7) (including any open offers to settle), the court will have regard to the obligation of the parties to help the court to further the overriding objective (see rules 1.1 and 1.3) and will take into account the nature, importance and complexity of the issues in the case. This may be of particular significance in applications for variation orders and interim variation orders or other cases where there is a risk of the costs becoming disproportionate to the amounts in dispute.

4.5 Parties who intend to seek a costs order against another party in proceedings to which rule 28.3 applies should ordinarily make this plain in open correspondence or in skeleton arguments before the date of the hearing. In any case where summary assessment of costs awarded under rule 28.3 would be appropriate parties are under an obligation to file a statement of costs in CPR Form N260.

4.6 An interim financial order which includes an element to allow a party to deal with legal fees (see *A v A (maintenance pending suit: provision for legal fees)* [2001] 1 WLR 605; *G v G (maintenance pending suit; costs)* [2002] EWHC 306 (Fam); *McFarlane v McFarlane, Parlour v Parlour* [2004] EWCA Civ 872; *Moses-Taiga v Taiga* [2005] EWCA Civ 1013; *C v C (Maintenance Pending Suit: Legal Costs)* [2006] Fam Law 739; *Currey v Currey (No 2)* [2006] EWCA Civ 1338) is an order made pursuant to section 22 of the Matrimonial Causes Act 1973 or an order under paragraph 38 of Schedule 5 of the 2004 Act, and is not a "costs order" within the meaning of rule 28.3.

4.7 By virtue of rule 28.2(1), where rule 28.3 does not apply, the exercise of the court's discretion as to costs is governed by the relevant provisions of the CPR and in particular rule 44.3 (excluding r 44.3(2) and (3)).

The Right Honourable

Sir Nicholas Wall

The President of the Family Division

Signed by authority of the Lord Chancellor:

[]

Parliamentary Under Secretary of State

Ministry of Justice

PART 29

MISCELLANEOUS

29.1.— Personal details
  (1) Unless the court directs otherwise, a party is not required to reveal—
    (a) the party's home address or other contact details;
    (b) the address or other contact details of any child;
    (c) the name of a person with whom the child is living, if that person is not the applicant; or

The Family Procedure Rules 2010

      (d)   in relation to an application under section 28(2) of the 2002 Act (application for permission to change the child's surname), the proposed new surname of the child.

(2) Where a party does not wish to reveal any of the particulars in paragraph (1), that party must give notice of those particulars to the court and the particulars will not be revealed to any person unless the court directs otherwise.

(3) Where a party changes home address during the course of proceedings, that party must give notice of the change to the court.

29.2. Disclosure of information under the 1991 Act

Where the Commission requires a person mentioned in regulation 3(1), 4(2) or 6(2)(a) of the Child Support Information Regulations 2008 to furnish information or evidence for a purpose mentioned in regulation 4(1) of those Regulations, nothing in these rules will—

      (a)   prevent that person from furnishing the information or evidence sought; or
      (b)   require that person to seek permission of the court before doing so.

29.3.— Method of giving notice

(1) Unless directed otherwise, a notice which is required by these rules to be given to a person must be given—

      (a)   in writing; and
      (b)   in a manner in which service may be effected in accordance with Part 6.

(2) Rule 6.33 applies to a notice which is required by these rules to be given to a child as it applies to a document which is to be served on a child.

29.4.— Withdrawal of applications in proceedings

(1) This rule applies to applications in proceedings—

      (a)   under Part 7;
      (b)   under Parts 10 to 14 or under any other Part where the application relates to the welfare or upbringing of a child or;
      (c)   where either of the parties is a protected party.

(2) Where this rule applies, an application may only be withdrawn with the permission of the court.

(3) Subject to paragraph (4), a person seeking permission to withdraw an application must file a written request for permission setting out the reasons for the request.

(4) The request under paragraph (3) may be made orally to the court if the parties are present.

(5) A court officer will notify the other parties of a written request.

(6) The court may deal with a written request under paragraph (3) without a hearing if the other parties, and any other persons directed by the court, have had an opportunity to make written representations to the court about the request.

29.5.— The Human Rights Act 1998

(1) In this rule—

"the 1998 Act" means the Human Rights Act 1998;

"Convention right" has the same meaning as in the 1998 Act; and

"declaration of incompatibility" means a declaration of incompatibility under section 4 of the 1998 Act.

(2) A party who seeks to rely on any provision of or right arising under the 1998 Act or seeks a remedy available under that Act must inform the court in that party's application or otherwise in writing specifying—

      (a)   the Convention right which it is alleged has been infringed and details of the alleged infringement; and
      (b)   the relief sought and whether this includes a declaration of incompatibility.

(3) The High Court may not make a declaration of incompatibility unless 21 days' notice, or such other period of notice as the court directs, has been given to the Crown.

(4) Where notice has been given to the Crown, a Minister, or other person permitted by the 1998 Act, will be joined as a party on giving notice to the court.

(5) Where a claim is made under section 7(1) of the 1998 Act (claim that public authority acted unlawfully) in respect of a judicial act—
- (a) that claim must be set out in the application form or the appeal notice; and
- (b) notice must be given to the Crown.

(6) Where paragraph (4) applies and the appropriate person (as defined in section 9(5) of the 1998 Act) has not applied within 21 days, or such other period as the court directs, beginning with the date on which the notice to be joined as a party was served, the court may join the appropriate person as a party.

(7) On any application concerning a committal order, if the court ordering the release of the person concludes that that person's Convention rights have been infringed by the making of the order to which the application or appeal relates, the judgment or order should so state, but if the court does not do so, that failure will not prevent another court from deciding the matter.

(8) Where by reason of a rule, practice direction or court order the Crown is permitted or required—
- (a) to make a witness statement;
- (b) to swear an affidavit(GL);
- (c) to verify a document by a statement of truth; or
- (d) to discharge any other procedural obligation,

that function will be performed by an appropriate officer acting on behalf of the Crown, and the court may if necessary nominate an appropriate officer.

(Practice Direction 29A (Human Rights – Joining the Crown) makes provision for the notices mentioned in this rule.)

29.6.— Documents in proceedings concerning gender recognition

(1) This rule applies to all documents in proceedings brought under—
- (a) section 12(g) or (h) of, or paragraph 11(1)(e) of Schedule 1 to, the 1973 Act; or
- (b) the Gender Recognition Act 2004.

(2) Documents to which this rule applies must, while they are in the custody of the court, be kept in a place of special security.

29.7.— Stamping or sealing court documents

(1) A court officer must, when issuing the following documents, seal(GL), or otherwise authenticate them with the stamp of the court—
- (a) the application form;
- (b) an order; and
- (c) any other document which a rule or practice direction requires the court officer to seal(GL) or stamp.

(2) The court officer may place the seal(GL) or the stamp on the document—
- (a) by hand; or
- (b) by printing a facsimile of the seal(GL) on the document whether electronically or otherwise.

(3) A document purporting to bear the court's seal(GL) or stamp will be admissible in evidence without further proof.

29.8.— Applications for relief which is precluded by the 1991 Act

(1) This rule applies where an application is made for an order which, in the opinion of the court, it would be prevented from making under section 8 or 9 of the 1991 Act and in this rule, "the matter" means the question of whether or not the court would be so prevented.

(2) The court will consider the matter without holding a hearing.

(3) Where the court officer receives the opinion of the court, as mentioned in paragraph (1), the court officer must send a notice to the applicant of that opinion.

(4) Paragraphs (5) to (11) apply where the court officer sends a notice under paragraph (3).

The Family Procedure Rules 2010

(5) Subject to paragraph (6), no requirement of these rules apply except the requirements—
- (a) of this rule;
- (b) as to service of the application by the court officer; and
- (c) as to any procedural step to be taken following the making of an application of the type in question.

(6) The court may direct that the requirements of these rules apply, or apply to such extent or with such modifications as are set out in the direction.

(7) If the applicant informs the court officer, within 14 days of the date of the notice, that the applicant wishes to persist with the application, the court will give appropriate directions for the matter to be heard and determined and may provide for the hearing to be without notice.

(8) Where directions are given in accordance with paragraph (7), the court officer must—
- (a) inform the applicant of the directions;
- (b) send a copy of the application to the other parties;
- (c) if the hearing is to be without notice, inform the other parties briefly—
  - (i) of the nature and effect of the notice given to the applicant under paragraph (3);
  - (ii) that the matter is being resolved without a hearing on notice; and
  - (iii) that they will be notified of the result; and
- (d) if the hearing is to be on notice, inform the other parties of—
  - (i) the circumstances which led to the directions being given; and
  - (ii) the directions.

(9) If the applicant does not inform the court officer as mentioned in paragraph (7), the application shall be treated as having been withdrawn.

(10) Where—
- (a) the matter is heard in accordance with directions given under paragraph (7); and
- (b) the court determines that it would be prevented, under section 8 or 9 of the 1991 Act, from making the order sought by the applicant,

the court will dismiss the application.

(11) Where the court dismisses the application—
- (a) the court must give its reasons in writing; and
- (b) the court officer must send a copy of the reasons to the parties.

29.9.— Modification of rule 29.8 where the application is not freestanding

(1) Where the court officer sends a notice under rule 29.8(3) in relation to an application which is contained in another document ("the document") which contains material extrinsic to the application—
- (a) subject to paragraph (2), the document will be treated as if it did not contain the application in respect of which the notice was served; and
- (b) the court officer, when sending copies of the documents to the respondents under any provision of these rules, must attach—
  - (i) a copy of the notice under rule 29.8(3); and
  - (ii) a notice informing the respondents of the effect of paragraph (1)(a).

(2) If the court determines that it is not prevented by section 8 or 9 of the 1991 Act from making the order sought by the application, the court—
- (a) must direct that the document shall be treated as if it contained the application; and
- (b) may give such directions as it considers appropriate for the subsequent conduct of the proceedings.

29.10.— Standard requirements

(1) Every judgment or order must state the name and judicial title of the person who made it.

(2) Every judgment or order must—
    (a) bear the date on which it is given or made; and
    (b) be sealed$^{(GL)}$ by the court.

29.11.— Drawing up and filing of judgments and orders
(1) Except as provided by a rule or a practice direction, every judgment or order will be drawn up by the court unless—
    (a) the court orders a party to draw it up;
    (b) a party, with the permission of the court, agrees to draw it up; or
    (c) the court dispenses with the need to draw it up.
(2) The court may direct that—
    (a) a judgment or an order drawn up by a party must be checked by the court before it is sealed$^{(GL)}$; or
    (b) before a judgment or an order is drawn up by the court, the parties must file an agreed statement of its terms.
(3) Where a judgment or an order is to be drawn up by a party—
    (a) that party must file it no later than 7 days after the date on which the court ordered or gave permission for the order to be drawn up so that it can be sealed by the court; and
    (b) if that party fails to file it within that period, any other party may draw it up and file it.

29.12. Copies of orders made in open court
A copy of an order made in open court will be issued to any person who requests it on payment of the prescribed fee.

29.13.— Service of judgments and orders
(1) The court officer must, unless the court directs otherwise, serve a copy of a judgment or an order made in family proceedings to every party affected by it.
(2) Where a judgment or an order has been drawn up by a party and is to be served by the court officer the party who drew it up must file a copy to be retained at court and sufficient copies for service on all the parties.
(3) A party in whose favour an order is made need not prove that a copy of the order has reached a party to whom it is required to be sent under this rule.
(4) This rule does not affect the operation of any rule or enactment which requires an order to be served in a particular way

29.14. Power to require judgment or order to be served on a party as well as the party's solicitor
Where the party on whom a judgment or order is served is acting by a solicitor, the court may order the judgment or order to be served on the party as well as on the party's solicitor.

29.15. When judgment or order takes effect
A judgment or order takes effect from the day when it is given or made, or such later date as the court may specify.

29.16.— Correction of errors in judgments and orders
(1) The court may at any time correct an accidental slip or omission in a judgment or order.
(2) A party may apply for a correction without notice.

Part 29

Part 29 r 5 is supplemented by PD29A – Human Rights, Joining the Crown, and PD29B. PD29B is in fact a Pre-existing Practice Direction, *Human Rights Act 1998* (24 July 2000) which has been retained by virtue of the *Practice Direction – Practice Directions Relating to Family Proceedings in Force before 6th April 2011 which support the Family Procedure Rules 2010.*

The Family Procedure Rules 2010

Part 29 contains various diverse provisions.

Rule 29.1 provides that a party is not required to reveal certain personal information including his or her home address, a child's address, and the name of the person with whom a child is living if not the applicant unless the court directs otherwise. The court however must be given those details.

Rule 29.2 provides that when the Child Support Commission requires specified information these rules do not prevent that information being supplied.

Rule 29.3 requires that notice when required by these rules, must be given in writing and in a manner in which service may be effected in accordance with Part 6.

Rule 29.4 requires the permission of the court for withdrawal of applications in specified proceedings.

Rule 29.5 deals with circumstances in which a party seeks to rely on a provision of the Human Right Act 1998.

Rule 29.6 requires security for documents in proceedings concerning gender recognition.

Rule 29.7 requires the court to seal or stamp application forms and orders.

Rules 29.8 and 9 allow the court to send out an opinion indicating that an application is precluded by the Child Support Act 1991 without holding a hearing, and makes provision for a party to indicate that they nevertheless wish to persist with the application.

Rule 29.11 sets out that save as otherwise provided the court will draw orders and judgments.

Rule 29.15 provides that a judgment or order will have effect from the day it is made, or such later date as the court might specify.

Rule 29.16 allows the court to correct accidental slips or omissions in a judgment or order at any time, and provides that a party may apply for a correction without notice.

PRACTICE DIRECTION 29A – HUMAN RIGHTS, JOINING THE CROWN

This Practice Direction supplements FPR Part 29, rule 29.5

(The Human Rights Act 1998)

SECTION 4 OF THE HUMAN RIGHTS ACT 1998

1.1 Where a party has informed the court about –

(a) a claim for a declaration of incompatibility in accordance with section 4 of the Human Rights Act 1998; or
(b) an issue for the court to decide which may lead to the court considering making a declaration,

then the court may at any time consider whether notice should be given to the Crown as required by that Act and give directions for the content and service of the notice. The rule allows a period of 21 days before the court will make the declaration but the court may vary this period of time.

1.2 The court will normally consider the issues and give the directions referred to in paragraph 1.1 at a directions hearing.

1.3 The notice must be served on the person named in the list published under section 17 of the Crown Proceedings Act 1947.

1.4 The notice will be in the form directed by the court and will normally include the directions given by the court. The notice will also be served on all the parties.

1.5 The court may require the parties to assist in the preparation of the notice.

1.6 Unless the court orders otherwise, the Minister or other person permitted by the Human Rights Act 1998 to be joined as a party must, if he or she wishes to be joined, give notice of his or her intention to be joined as a party to the court and every other party. Where the Minister has nominated a person to be joined as a party the notice must be accompanied by the written nomination.

(Section 5(2)(a) of the Human Rights Act 1998 permits a person nominated by a Minister of the Crown to be joined as a party. The nomination may be signed on behalf of the Minister.)

SECTION 9 OF THE HUMAN RIGHTS ACT 1998

2.1 The procedure in paragraphs 1.1 to 1.6 also applies where a claim is made under sections 7(1)(a) and 9(3) of the Human Rights Act 1998 for damages in respect of a judicial act.

2.2 Notice must be given to the Lord Chancellor and should be served on the Treasury Solicitor on his behalf.

2.3 The notice will also give details of the judicial act, which is the subject of the claim for damages, and of the court that made it.

(Section 9(4) of the Human Rights Act 1998 provides that no award of damages may be made against the Crown as provided for in section 9(3) unless the appropriate person is joined in the proceedings. The appropriate person is the Minister responsible for the court concerned or a person or department nominated by him or her (section 9(5) of the Act).)

PRACTICE DIRECTION 29B – HUMAN RIGHTS ACT 1998

THE PRINCIPAL REGISTRY OF THE FAMILY DIVISION

1 It is directed that the following practice shall apply as from the 2nd October 2000 in all family proceedings:

CITATION OF AUTHORITIES

2 When an authority referred to in section 2 of the Human Rights Act 1998 ('the Act') is to be cited at a hearing:

(a) the authority to be cited shall be an authorative and complete report;
(b) the court must be provided with a list of authorities it is intended to cite and copies of the reports:-
    (i) in cases to which he President's Direction (Court Bundles) dated 10th March 2000 applies, as part of the bundle;
    (ii) otherwise, not less than 2 clear days before the hearing; and
(c) copies of the complete original texts issued by the European Court and Commission, either paper based or from the Court's judgment database (HUDOC) which is available on the internet, may be used.

ALLOCATION TO JUDGES

(1) The hearing and determination of the following will be confined to a High Court Judge:
 (a) a claim for a declaration of incompatibility under section 4 of the Act; or
 (b) an issue which may lead to the court considering making such a declaration.

PART 30

APPEALS

30.1.— Scope and interpretation

(1) The rules in this Part apply to appeals to—
 (a) the High Court; and
 (b) a county court.

(2) This Part does not apply to an appeal in detailed assessment proceedings against a decision of an authorised court officer.

(Rules 47.20 to 47.23 of the CPR deal with appeals against a decision of an authorised court officer in detailed assessment proceedings.)

(3) In this Part—

"appeal court" means the court to which an appeal is made;

"appeal notice" means an appellant's or respondent's notice;

"appellant" means a person who brings or seeks to bring an appeal;

"lower court" means the court from which, or the person from whom, the appeal lies; and

"respondent" means—
 (a) a person other than the appellant who was a party to the proceedings in the lower court and who is affected by the appeal; and
 (b) a person who is permitted by the appeal court to be a party to the appeal.

(4) This Part is subject to any rule, enactment or practice direction which sets out special provisions with regard to any particular category of appeal.

30.2. Parties to comply with the practice direction

All parties to an appeal must comply with Practice Direction 30A.

30.3.— Permission

(1) An appellant or respondent requires permission to appeal—
 (a) against a decision in proceedings where the decision appealed against was made by a district judge or a costs judge, unless paragraph (2) applies; or
 (b) as provided by Practice Direction 30A.

(2) Permission to appeal is not required where the appeal is against—
 (a) a committal order; or
 (b) a secure accommodation order under section 25 of the 1989 Act.

(3) An application for permission to appeal may be made—
 (a) to the lower court at the hearing at which the decision to be appealed was made; or
 (b) to the appeal court in an appeal notice.

(Rule 30.4 sets out the time limits for filing an appellant's notice at the appeal court. Rule 30.5 sets out the time limits for filing a respondent's notice at the appeal court. Any application for permission to appeal to the appeal court must be made in the appeal notice (see rules 30.4(1) and 30.5(3).)

(4) Where the lower court refuses an application for permission to appeal, a further application for permission to appeal may be made to the appeal court.

(5) Where the appeal court, without a hearing, refuses permission to appeal, the person seeking permission may request the decision to be reconsidered at a hearing.

(6) A request under paragraph (5) must be filed within 7 days beginning with the date on which the notice that permission has been refused was served.

(7) Permission to appeal may be given only where—

(a) the court considers that the appeal would have a real prospect of success; or

(b) there is some other compelling reason why the appeal should be heard.

(8) An order giving permission may—

(a) limit the issues to be heard; and

(b) be made subject to conditions.

(9) In this rule "costs judge" means a taxing master of the Senior Courts.

30.4.— Appellant's notice

(1) Where the appellant seeks permission from the appeal court it must be requested in the appellant's notice.

(2) Subject to paragraph (3), the appellant must file the appellant's notice at the appeal court within —

(a) such period as may be directed by the lower court (which may be longer or shorter than the period referred to in sub-paragraph (b)); or

(b) where the court makes no such direction, 21 days after the date of the decision of the lower court against which the appellant wishes to appeal.

(3) Where the appeal is against an order under section 38(1) of the 1989 Act, the appellant must file the appellant's notice within 7 days beginning with the date of the decision of the lower court.

(4) Unless the appeal court orders otherwise, an appellant's notice must be served on each respondent and the persons referred to in paragraph (5)—

(a) as soon as practicable; and

(b) in any event not later than 7 days,

after it is filed.

(5) The persons referred to in paragraph (4) are—

(a) any children's guardian, welfare officer, or children and family reporter;

(b) a local authority who has prepared a report under section 14A(8) or (9) of the 1989 Act;

(c) an adoption agency or local authority which has prepared a report on the suitability of the applicant to adopt a child;

(d) a local authority which has prepared a report on the placement of the child for adoption; and

(e) where the appeal is from a magistrates' court, the court officer.

30.5.— Respondent's notice

(1) A respondent may file and serve a respondent's notice.

(2) A respondent who—

(a) is seeking permission to appeal from the appeal court; or

(b) wishes to ask the appeal court to uphold the order of the lower court for reasons different from or additional to those given by the lower court,

must file a respondent's notice.

(3) Where the respondent seeks permission from the appeal court it must be requested in the respondent's notice.

(4) A respondent's notice must be filed within—

(a) such period as may be directed by the lower court; or

(b) where the court makes no such direction, 14 days beginning with the date referred to in paragraph (5).

(5) The date referred to in paragraph (4) is—

(a) the date on which the respondent is served with the appellant's notice where—

(i) permission to appeal was given by the lower court; or

(ii) permission to appeal is not required;

(b) the date on which the respondent is served with notification that the appeal court has given the appellant permission to appeal; or
(c) the date on which the respondent is served with notification that the application for permission to appeal and the appeal itself are to be heard together.

(6) Unless the appeal court orders otherwise, a respondent's notice must be served on the appellant, any other respondent and the persons referred to in rule 30.4(5)—
(a) as soon as practicable; and
(b) in any event not later than 7 days,
after it is filed.

(7) Where there is an appeal against an order under section 38(1) of the 1989 Act—
(a) a respondent may not, in that appeal, bring an appeal from the order or ask the appeal court to uphold the order of the lower court for reasons different from or additional to those given by the lower court; and
(b) paragraphs (2) and (3) do not apply.

30.6. Grounds of appeal
The appeal notice must state the grounds of appeal.

30.7.— Variation of time
(1) An application to vary the time limit for filing an appeal notice must be made to the appeal court.
(2) The parties may not agree to extend any date or time limit set by—
(a) these rules;
(b) Practice Direction 30A; or
(c) an order of the appeal court or the lower court.

(Rule 4.1(3)(a) provides that the court may extend or shorten the time for compliance with a rule, practice direction or court order (even if an application for extension is made after the time for compliance has expired).)
(Rule 4.1(3)(c) provides that the court may adjourn or bring forward a hearing.)

30.8. Stay
Unless the appeal court or the lower court orders otherwise, an appeal does not operate as a stay$^{(GL)}$ of any order or decision of the lower court.

30.9. Amendment of appeal notice
An appeal notice may not be amended without the permission of the appeal court.

30.10.— Striking out appeal notices and setting aside or imposing conditions on permission to appeal
(1) The appeal court may—
(a) strike out$^{(GL)}$ the whole or part of an appeal notice;
(b) set aside$^{(GL)}$ permission to appeal in whole or in part;
(c) impose or vary conditions upon which an appeal may be brought.

(2) The court will only exercise its powers under paragraph (1) where there is a compelling reason for doing so.

(3) Where a party was present at the hearing at which permission was given that party may not subsequently apply for an order that the court exercise its powers under paragraphs (1)(b) or (1)(c).

30.11.— Appeal court's powers
(1) In relation to an appeal the appeal court has all the powers of the lower court.
(Rule 30.1(4) provides that this Part is subject to any enactment that sets out special provisions with regard to any particular category of appeal.)
(2) The appeal court has power to—
(a) affirm, set aside$^{(GL)}$ or vary any order or judgment made or given by the lower court;
(b) refer any application or issue for determination by the lower court;

(c) order a new hearing;
(d) make orders for the payment of interest;
(e) make a costs order.

(3) The appeal court may exercise its powers in relation to the whole or part of an order of the lower court.

(Rule 4.1 contains general rules about the court's case management powers.)

(4) If the appeal court—
   (a) refuses an application for permission to appeal;
   (b) strikes out an appellant's notice; or
   (c) dismisses an appeal,

and it considers that the application, the appellant's notice or the appeal is totally without merit, the provisions of paragraph (5) must be complied with.

(5) Where paragraph (4) applies—
   (a) the court's order must record the fact that it considers the application, the appellant's notice or the appeal to be totally without merit; and
   (b) the court must at the same time consider whether it is appropriate to make a civil restraint order.

30.12.— Hearing of appeals

(1) Every appeal will be limited to a review of the decision of the lower court unless—
   (a) an enactment or practice direction makes different provision for a particular category of appeal; or
   (b) the court considers that in the circumstances of an individual appeal it would be in the interests of justice to hold a re-hearing.

(2) Unless it orders otherwise, the appeal court will not receive—
   (a) oral evidence; or
   (b) evidence which was not before the lower court.

(3) The appeal court will allow an appeal where the decision of the lower court was—
   (a) wrong; or
   (b) unjust because of a serious procedural or other irregularity in the proceedings in the lower court.

(4) The appeal court may draw any inference of fact which it considers justified on the evidence.

(5) At the hearing of the appeal a party may not rely on a matter not contained in that party's appeal notice unless the appeal court gives permission.

30.13.— Assignment of appeals to the Court of Appeal

(1) Where the court from or to which an appeal is made or from which permission to appeal is sought ("the relevant court") considers that—
   (a) an appeal which is to be heard by a county court or the High Court would raise an important point of principle or practice; or
   (b) there is some other compelling reason for the Court of Appeal to hear it,

the relevant court may order the appeal to be transferred to the Court of Appeal.

(2) This rule does not apply to proceedings in a magistrates' court.

30.14.— Reopening of final appeals

(1) The High Court will not reopen a final determination of any appeal unless—
   (a) it is necessary to do so in order to avoid real injustice;
   (b) the circumstances are exceptional and make it appropriate to reopen the appeal; and
   (c) there is no alternative effective remedy.

(2) In paragraphs (1), (3), (4) and (6), "appeal" includes an application for permission to appeal.

(3) This rule does not apply to appeals to a county court.

(4) Permission is needed to make an application under this rule to reopen a final determination of an appeal.

(5) There is no right to an oral hearing of an application for permission unless, exceptionally, the judge so directs.

(6) The judge will not grant permission without directing the application to be served on the other party to the original appeal and giving that party an opportunity to make representations.

(7) There is no right of appeal or review from the decision of the judge on the application for permission, which is final.

(8) The procedure for making an application for permission is set out in Practice Direction 30A.

PART 30 COMMENTARY

Part 30 is supplemented by PD30A. This is a full practice direction setting out the manner in which appeals should be conducted. It provides at para 14.1 that the rules in Part 30 apply to appeals relating to orders made by consent in addition to orders which are not made by consent, and that an appeal is the only way to challenge a consent order. This is of a piece with the fact that there is no replacement of the old CCR Ord 37 r 1 (which gave a judge power to order a rehearing where no error of the court at the hearing is alleged). The only way to challenge a valid order, other than one made without notice, is by way of appeal.

Part 30 deals with appeals, except for appeals to the Court of Appeal and appeals to the Supreme Court, and appeals in detailed assessment proceedings (which are governed by the CPR). The rules are based on CPR Part 52.

Permission to appeal is required even from a decision of a district judge, save in relation to a committal order or a secure accommodation order. Permission may be sought from the lower court at the hearing of the decision which is being appealed or the appeal court. Where the lower court refuses permission a further application for permission may be made to the appeal court. Permission to appeal may only be given where either there is a real prospect of success, or there is some other compelling reason (r 30.3).

An appellant's notice must be filed at the appeal court within 21 days of the decision of the lower court against which the appellant wishes to appeal or such other period as may be directed by the lower court, save for interim care or supervision orders which must be appealed within seven days (r 30.4).

An appeal will be limited to a re-hearing unless an enactment or practice direction provides otherwise, or the court considers that in the particular circumstances of an appeal a re-hearing would be in the interests of justice (r 30.12).

The county court and High Court may order an appeal to be transferred to the Court of Appeal (r 30.13).

The relevant forms for Part 30 are N161–N164.

PRACTICE DIRECTION 30A – APPEALS

This Practice Direction supplements FPR Part 30

This Practice Direction is made by the President of the Family Division under the powers delegated to him by the Lord Chief Justice under Schedule 2, Part 1,

FPR 2010, Practice Direction 30A

paragraph 2(2) of the Constitutional Reform Act 2005, and is approved by the Parliamentary Under Secretary of State, by authority of the Lord Chancellor and comes into force on 6th April 2011

1.1 This practice direction applies to all appeals to which Part 30 applies.

ROUTES OF APPEAL

2.1 The following table sets out to which court or judge an appeal is to be made (subject to obtaining any necessary permission)—

Decision of:	Appeal made to:
Magistrates' Court	Circuit judge
District judge of a county court	Circuit judge
District judge of the High Court	High Court judge
District judge of the principal registry of the Family Division	High Court judge
Costs judge	High Court Judge
Circuit judge or recorder	Court of Appeal
High Court judge	Court of Appeal

(Provisions setting out routes of appeal include section 16(1) of the Senior Courts Act 1981 (as amended); section 77(1) of the County Courts Act 1984 (as amended) and the Access to Justice Act 1999 (Destination of Appeals) (Family Proceedings) Order 2009 (see paragraphs 9.1 to 9.12 below. The Family Proceedings (Allocation to Judiciary) (Appeals) Directions 2009 provide for an appeal from a magistrates' court to be heard by a Circuit judge.

The routes of appeal from an order or decision relating to contempt of court of a magistrates' court under section 63(3) of the Magistrates' Courts Act 1980 and of a county court and the High Court are set out in section 13(2) of the Administration of Justice Act 1960. Appeals under section 8(1) of the Gender Recognition Act 2004 lie to the High Court (see section 8 of the 2004 Act). The procedure for appeals to the Court of Appeal is governed by the Civil Procedure Rules 1998, in particular CPR Part 52.).

2.2 Where the decision to be appealed is a decision in a Part 19 (Alternative Procedure For Applications) application on a point of law in a case which did not involve any substantial dispute of fact, the court to which the appeal lies, where that court is the High Court or a county court and unless the appeal would lie to the Court of Appeal in any event, must consider whether to order the appeal to be transferred to the Court of Appeal under rule 30.13 (Assignment of Appeals to the Court of Appeal).

GROUNDS FOR APPEAL

3.1 Rule 30.12 (hearing of appeals) sets out the circumstances in which the appeal court will allow an appeal.

3.2 The grounds of appeal should—

(a) set out clearly the reasons why rule 30.12 (3)(a) or (b) is said to apply; and
(b) specify in respect of each ground, whether the ground raises an appeal on a point of law or is an appeal against a finding of fact.

PERMISSION TO APPEAL

4.1 Rule 30.3 (Permission) sets out the circumstances when permission to appeal is required. At present permission to appeal is required where the decision appealed against was made by a district judge or a costs judge. However, no permission is

The Family Procedure Rules 2010

required where rule 30.3(2) (appeals against a committal order or a secure accommodation order under section 25 of the Children Act 1989) applies.

(The requirement of permission to appeal may be imposed by a practice direction – see rule 30.3(1)(b) (Permission).).

Court to which permission to appeal application should be made

4.2 An application for permission should be made orally at the hearing at which the decision to be appealed against is made.

4.3 Where—

(a) no application for permission to appeal is made at the hearing; or
(b) the lower court refuses permission to appeal,

an application for permission to appeal may be made to the appeal court in accordance with rules 30.3(3) and (4) (Permission).

(Rule 30.1(3) defines 'lower court'.)

4.4 Where no application for permission to appeal has been made in accordance with rule 30.3(3)(a) (Permission) but a party requests further time to make such an application the court may adjourn the hearing to give that party an opportunity to do so.

4.5 There is no appeal from a decision of the appeal court to allow or refuse permission to appeal to that court (although where the appeal court, without a hearing, refuses permission to appeal, the person seeking permission may request that decision to be reconsidered at a hearing- see section 54(4) of the Access to Justice Act 1999 and rule 30.3 (5) (Permission)).

Material omission from a judgment of the lower court

4.6 Where a party's advocate considers that there is a material omission from a judgment of the lower court or, in a magistrates' court, the written reasons for the decision of the lower court (including inadequate reasons for the lower court's decision), the advocate should before the drawing of the order give the lower court which made the decision the opportunity of considering whether there is an omission and should not immediately use the omission as grounds for an application to appeal.

4.7 Paragraph 4.8 below applies where there is an application to the lower court for permission to appeal on the grounds of a material omission from a judgment of the lower court. Paragraph 4.9 below applies where there is an application for permission to appeal to the appeal court on the grounds of a material omission from a judgment of the lower court. Paragraphs 4.8 and 4.9 do not apply where the lower court is a magistrates' court.

4.8 Where the application for permission to appeal is made to the lower court, the court which made the decision must—

(a) consider whether there is a material omission and adjourn for that purpose if necessary; and
(b) where the conclusion is that there has been such an omission, provide additions to the judgment.

4.9 Where the application for permission to appeal is made to the appeal court, the appeal court—

(a) must consider whether there is a material omission; and
(b) where the conclusion is that there has been such an omission, may adjourn the application and remit the case to the lower court with an invitation to provide additions to the judgment.

Consideration of Permission without a hearing

4.10 An application for permission to appeal may be considered by the appeal court without a hearing.

4.11 If permission is granted without a hearing the parties will be notified of that decision and the procedure in paragraphs 6.1 to 6.8 will then apply.

4.12 If permission is refused without a hearing the parties will be notified of that decision with the reasons for it. The decision is subject to the appellant's right to have it reconsidered at an oral hearing. This may be before the same judge.

4.13 A request for the decision to be reconsidered at an oral hearing must be filed at the appeal court within 7 days after service of the notice that permission has been refused. A copy of the request must be served by the appellant on the respondent at the same time.

Permission hearing

4.14 Where an appellant, who is represented, makes a request for a decision to be reconsidered at an oral hearing, the appellant's advocate must, at least 4 days before the hearing, in a brief written statement—

(a) inform the court and the respondent of the points which the appellant proposes to raise at the hearing;
(b) set out the reasons why permission should be granted notwithstanding the reasons given for the refusal of permission; and
(c) confirm, where applicable, that the requirements of paragraph 4.17 have been complied with (appellant in receipt of services funded by the Legal Services Commission).

4.15 The respondent will be given notice of a permission hearing, but is not required to attend unless requested by the court to do so.

4.16 If the court requests the respondent's attendance at the permission hearing, the appellant must supply the respondent with a copy of the appeal bundle (see paragraph 5.9) within 7 days of being notified of the request, or such other period as the court may direct. The costs of providing that bundle shall be borne by the appellant initially, but will form part of the costs of the permission application.

Appellants in receipt of services funded by the Legal Services Commission applying for permission to appeal

4.17 Where the appellant is in receipt of services funded by the Legal Services Commission (or legally aided) and permission to appeal has been refused by the appeal court without a hearing, the appellant must send a copy of the reasons the appeal court gave for refusing permission to the relevant office of the Legal Services Commission as soon as it has been received from the court. The court will require confirmation that this has been done if a hearing is requested to re-consider the question of permission.

Limited permission

4.18 Where a court under rule 30.3 (Permission) gives permission to appeal on some issues only, it will—

(a) refuse permission on any remaining issues; or
(b) reserve the question of permission to appeal on any remaining issues to the court hearing the appeal.

4.19 If the court reserves the question of permission under paragraph 4.18(b), the appellant must, within 14 days after service of the court's order, inform the appeal court and the respondent in writing whether the appellant intends to pursue the reserved issues. If the appellant does intend to pursue the reserved issues, the parties must include in any time estimate for the appeal hearing, their time estimate for the reserved issues.

4.20 If the appeal court refuses permission to appeal on the remaining issues without a hearing and the applicant wishes to have that decision reconsidered at an oral hearing, the time limit in rule 30.3(6) (Permission) shall apply. Any application for an extension of this time limit should be made promptly. The court hearing the appeal on the issues for which permission has been granted will not normally grant, at the appeal hearing, an application to extend the time limit in rule 30.3 (6) for the remaining issues.

4.21 If the appeal court refuses permission to appeal on remaining issues at or after an oral hearing, the application for permission to appeal on those issues cannot be renewed at the appeal hearing (see section 54(4) of the Access to Justice Act 1999).

Respondents' costs of permission applications

4.22 In most cases, applications for permission to appeal will be determined without the court requesting—

(a) submissions from; or
(b) if there is an oral hearing, attendance by

the respondent.

4.23 Where the court does not request submissions from or attendance by the respondent, costs will not normally be allowed to a respondent who volunteers submissions or attendance.

4.24 Where the court does request—

(a) submissions from; or
(b) attendance by the respondent,

the court will normally allow the costs of the respondent if permission is refused.

APPELLANT'S NOTICE

5.1 An appellant's notice must be filed and served in all cases. Where an application for permission to appeal is made to the appeal court it must be applied for in the appellant's notice.

Human Rights

5.2 Where the appellant seeks—

(a) to rely on any issue under the Human Rights Act 1998; or
(b) a remedy available under that Act,

for the first time in an appeal the appellant must include in the appeal notice the information required by rule 29.5(2).

5.3 Practice Direction 29A (Human Rights, Joining the Crown) will apply as if references to the directions hearing were to the application for permission to appeal.

Extension of time for filing appellant's notice

5.4. If an extension of time is required for filing the appellant's notice the application must be made in that notice. The notice should state the reason for the delay and the steps taken prior to the application being made.

5.5 Where the appellant's notice includes an application for an extension of time and permission to appeal has been given or is not required the respondent has the right to be heard on that application and must be served with a copy of the appeal bundle (see paragraph 5.9). However, a respondent who unreasonably opposes an extension of time runs the risk of being ordered to pay the appellant's costs of that application.

5.6 If an extension of time is given following such an application the procedure at paragraphs 6.1 to 6.8 applies.

Applications

5.7 Notice of an application to be made to the appeal court for a remedy incidental to the appeal (e.g. an interim injunction under rule 20.2 (Orders for interim remedies))

FPR 2010, Practice Direction 30A

may be included in the appeal notice or in a Part 18 (Procedure For Other Applications in Proceedings) application notice.

(Paragraph 13 of this practice direction contains other provisions relating to applications.).

Documents

5.8 The appellant must file the following documents together with an appeal bundle (see paragraph 5.9) with his or her appellant's notice—

(a) two additional copies of the appellant's notice for the appeal court;
(b) one copy of the appellant's notice for each of the respondents;
(c) one copy of the appellant's skeleton argument for each copy of the appellant's notice that is filed;
(d) a sealed or stamped copy of the order being appealed or a copy of the notice of the making of an order;
(e) a copy of any order giving or refusing permission to appeal, together with a copy of the court's reasons for allowing or refusing permission to appeal;
(f) any witness statements or affidavits in support of any application included in the appellant's notice.

5.9 An appellant must include the following documents in his or her appeal bundle—

(a) a sealed or stamped copy of the appellant's notice;
(b) a sealed or stamped copy of the order being appealed, or a copy of the notice of the making of an order;
(c) a copy of any order giving or refusing permission to appeal, together with a copy of the court's reasons for allowing or refusing permission to appeal;
(d) any affidavit or witness statement filed in support of any application included in the appellant's notice;
(e) where the appeal is against a consent order, a statement setting out the change in circumstances since the order was agreed or other circumstances justifying a review or re-hearing;
(f) a copy of the appellant's skeleton argument;
(g) a transcript or note of judgment or, in a magistrates' court, written reasons for the court's decision (see paragraph 5.23), and in cases where permission to appeal was given by the lower court or is not required those parts of any transcript of evidence which are directly relevant to any question at issue on the appeal;
(h) the application form;
(i) any application notice (or case management documentation) relevant to the subject of the appeal;
(j) any other documents which the appellant reasonably considers necessary to enable the appeal court to reach its decision on the hearing of the application or appeal; and
(k) such other documents as the court may direct.

5.10 All documents that are extraneous to the issues to be considered on the application or the appeal must be excluded. The appeal bundle may include affidavits, witness statements, summaries, experts' reports and exhibits but only where these are directly relevant to the subject matter of the appeal.

5.11 Where the appellant is represented, the appeal bundle must contain a certificate signed by the appellant's solicitor, counsel or other representative to the effect that the appellant has read and understood paragraph 5.10 and that the composition of the appeal bundle complies with it.

5.12 Where it is not possible to file all the above documents, the appellant must indicate which documents have not yet been filed and the reasons why they are not currently available. The appellant must then provide a reasonable estimate of when the missing document or documents can be filed and file them as soon as reasonably practicable.

Skeleton arguments

5.13 The appellant's notice must, subject to paragraphs 5.14 and 5.15, be accompanied by a skeleton argument. Alternatively the skeleton argument may be included in the appellant's notice. Where the skeleton argument is so included it will not form part of the notice for the purposes of rule 30.9 (Amendment of appeal notice).

5.14 Where it is impracticable for the appellant's skeleton argument to accompany the appellant's notice it must be filed and served on all respondents within 14 days of filing the notice.

5.15 An appellant who is not represented need not file a skeleton argument but is encouraged to do so since this will be helpful to the court.

5.16 A skeleton argument must contain a numbered list of the points which the party wishes to make. These should both define and confine the areas of controversy. Each point should be stated as concisely as the nature of the case allows.

5.17 A numbered point must be followed by a reference to any document on which the party wishes to rely.

5.18 A skeleton argument must state, in respect of each authority cited –

(a) the proposition of law that the authority demonstrates; and
(b) the parts of the authority (identified by page or paragraph references) that support the proposition.

5.19 If more than one authority is cited in support of a given proposition, the skeleton argument must briefly state the reason for taking that course.

5.20 The statement referred to in paragraph 5.19 should not materially add to the length of the skeleton argument but should be sufficient to demonstrate, in the context of the argument –

(a) the relevance of the authority or authorities to that argument; and
(b) that the citation is necessary for a proper presentation of that argument.

5.21 The cost of preparing a skeleton argument which –

(a) does not comply with the requirements set out in this paragraph; or
(b) was not filed within the time limits provided by this Practice Direction (or any further time granted by the court),

will not be allowed on assessment except to the extent that the court otherwise directs.

5.22 The appellant should consider what other information the appeal court will need. This may include a list of persons who feature in the case or glossaries of technical terms. A chronology of relevant events will be necessary in most appeals.

Suitable record of the judgment

5.23 Where the judgment to be appealed has been officially recorded by the court, an approved transcript of that record should accompany the appellant's notice. Photocopies will not be accepted for this purpose. However, where there is no officially recorded judgment, the following documents will be acceptable—

<u>Written judgments</u> – Where the judgment was made in writing a copy of that judgment endorsed with the judge's signature.

<u>Written reasons</u> – in a magistrates' court, a copy of the written reasons for the court's decision.

<u>Note of judgment</u> – When judgment was not officially recorded or made in writing a note of the judgment (agreed between the appellant's and respondent's advocates) should be submitted for approval to the judge whose decision is being appealed. If the parties cannot agree on a single note of the judgment, both versions should be provided to that judge with an explanatory letter. For the purpose of an application for

permission to appeal the note need not be approved by the respondent or the lower court judge.

Advocates' notes of judgments where the appellant is unrepresented – When the appellant was unrepresented in the lower court it is the duty of any advocate for the respondent to make the advocate's note of judgment promptly available, free of charge to the appellant where there is no officially recorded judgment or if the court so directs. Where the appellant was represented in the lower court it is the duty of the appellant's own former advocate to make that advocate's note available in these circumstances. The appellant should submit the note of judgment to the appeal court.

5.24 An appellant may not be able to obtain an official transcript or other suitable record of the lower court's decision within the time within which the appellant's notice must be filed. In such cases the appellant's notice must still be completed to the best of the appellant's ability on the basis of the documentation available. However it may be amended subsequently with the permission of the appeal court in accordance with rule 30.9 (Amendment of appeal notice).

Advocates' notes of judgments

5.25 Advocates' brief (or, where appropriate, refresher) fee includes—

(a) remuneration for taking a note of the judgment of the court;
(b) having the note transcribed accurately;
(c) attempting to agree the note with the other side if represented;
(d) submitting the note to the judge for approval where appropriate;
(e) revising it if so requested by the judge,
(f) providing any copies required for the appeal court, instructing solicitors and lay client; and
(g) providing a copy of the note to an unrepresented appellant.

Appeals from decision made by a family proceedings court under Parts 4 and 4A of the Family Law Act 1996

5.26 Where the appeal is brought against the making of a hospital order or a guardianship order under the Mental Health Act 1983, the court officer for the court from which the appeal is brought must send a copy of any written evidence considered by the magistrates under section 37(1)(a) of that Act to the appeal court.

Appeals under section 8(1) of the Gender Recognition Act 2004

5.27 Paragraph 5.28 to 5.30 apply where the appeal is brought under section 8(1) of the Gender Recognition Act 2004 to the High Court on a point of law against a decision by the Gender Recognition Panel to reject the application under sections 1(1), 5(2), 5(A)(2) or 6(1) of the 2004 Act.

5.28 The appeal notice must be—

(a) filed in the principal registry of the Family Division; and
(b) served on the Secretary of State and the President of the Gender Recognition Panels.

5.29 The Secretary of State may appear and be heard in the proceedings on the appeal.

5.30 Where the High Court issues a gender recognition certificate under section 8(3)(a) of the Gender Recognition Act 2004, the court officer must send a copy of that certificate to the Secretary of State.

Transcripts or Notes of Evidence

5.31 When the evidence is relevant to the appeal an official transcript of the relevant evidence must be obtained. Transcripts or notes of evidence are generally not needed for

The Family Procedure Rules 2010

the purpose of determining an application for permission to appeal.

Notes of evidence

5.32 If evidence relevant to the appeal was not officially recorded, a typed version of the judge's (including a district judge (magistrates' courts) or justices' clerk's /assistant clerk's notes of evidence must be obtained.

Transcripts at public expense

5.33 Where the lower court or the appeal court is satisfied that—

(a) an unrepresented appellant; or
(b) an appellant whose legal representation is provided free of charge to the appellant and not funded by the Community Legal Service,

is in such poor financial circumstances that the cost of a transcript would be an excessive burden the court may certify that the cost of obtaining one official transcript should be borne at public expense.

5.34 In the case of a request for an official transcript of evidence or proceedings to be paid for at public expense, the court must also be satisfied that there are reasonable grounds for appeal. Whenever possible a request for a transcript at public expense should be made to the lower court when asking for permission to appeal.

Filing and service of appellant's notice

5.35 Rule 30.4 (Appellant's notice) sets out the procedure and time limits for filing and serving an appellant's notice. Subject to paragraph 5.36, the appellant must file the appellant's notice at the appeal court within such period as may be directed by the lower court, which should not normally exceed 14 days or, where the lower court directs no such period within 21 days of the date of the decision that the appellant wishes to appeal.

5.36 Rule 30.4(3) (Appellant's notice) provides that unless the appeal court orders otherwise, where the appeal is against an order under section 38(1) of the 1989 Act, the appellant must file the appellant's notice within 7 days beginning with the date of the decision of the lower court.

5.37 Where the lower court announces its decision and reserves the reasons for its judgment or order until a later date, it should, in the exercise of powers under rule 30.4 (2)(a)) (Appellant's notice), fix a period for filing the appellant's notice at the appeal court that takes this into account.

5.38 Except where the appeal court orders otherwise a sealed or stamped copy of the appellant's notice, including any skeleton arguments must be served on all respondents and other persons referred to in rule 30.4(5) (Appellant's notice) in accordance with the timetable prescribed by rule 30.4(4) (Appellant's notice) except where this requirement is modified by paragraph 5.14 in which case the skeleton argument should be served as soon as it is filed.

5.39 Where the appellant's notice is to be served on a child, then rule 6.33 (supplementary provision relating to service on children) applies and unless the appeal court orders otherwise a sealed or stamped copy of the appellant's notice, including any skeleton arguments must be served on the persons or bodies mentioned in rule 6.33(2). For example, the appeal notice must be served on any children's guardian, welfare officer or children and family reporter who is appointed in the proceedings.

5.40 Unless the court otherwise directs, a respondent need not take any action when served with an appellant's notice until such time as notification is given to the respondent that permission to appeal has been given.

5.41 The court may dispense with the requirement for service of the notice on a respondent.

5.42 Unless the appeal court directs otherwise, the appellant must serve on the respondent the appellant's notice and skeleton argument (but not the appeal bundle), where the appellant is applying for permission to appeal in the appellant's notice.

5.43 Where permission to appeal—

(a) has been given by the lower court; or
(b) is not required,

the appellant must serve the appeal bundle on the respondent and the persons mentioned in paragraph 5.39 with the appellant's notice.

Amendment of Appeal Notice

5.44 An appeal notice may be amended with permission. Such an application to amend and any application in opposition will normally be dealt with at the hearing unless that course would cause unnecessary expense or delay in which case a request should be made for the application to amend to be heard in advance.

PROCEDURE AFTER PERMISSION IS OBTAINED

6.1 This paragraph sets out the procedure where—

(a) permission to appeal is given by the appeal court; or
(b) the appellant's notice is filed in the appeal court and—
 (i) permission was given by the lower court; or
 (ii) permission is not required.

6.2 If the appeal court gives permission to appeal, the appeal bundle must be served on each of the respondents within 7 days of receiving the order giving permission to appeal.

6.3 The appeal court will send the parties—

(a) notification of the date of the hearing or the period of time (the 'listing window') during which the appeal is likely to be heard;
(b) where permission is granted by the appeal court a copy of the order giving permission to appeal; and
(c) any other directions given by the court.

6.4 Where the appeal court grants permission to appeal, the appellant must add the following documents to the appeal bundle—

(a) the respondent's notice and skeleton argument (if any);
(b) those parts of the transcripts of evidence which are directly relevant to any question at issue on the appeal;
(c) the order granting permission to appeal and, where permission to appeal was granted at an oral hearing, the transcript (or note) of any judgment which was given; and
(d) any document which the appellant and respondent have agreed to add to the appeal bundle in accordance with paragraph 7.16.

6.5 Where permission to appeal has been refused on a particular issue, the appellant must remove from the appeal bundle all documents that are relevant only to that issue.

Time estimates

6.6 If the appellant is legally represented, the appeal court must be notified, in writing, of the advocate's time estimate for the hearing of the appeal.

6.7 The time estimate must be that of the advocate who will argue the appeal. It should exclude the time required by the court to give judgment.

6.8 A court officer will notify the respondent of the appellant's time estimate and if the respondent disagrees with the time estimate the respondent must inform the court within 7 days of the notification. In the absence of such notification the respondent will be deemed to have accepted the estimate proposed on behalf of the appellant.

The Family Procedure Rules 2010

RESPONDENT

7.1 A respondent who wishes to ask the appeal court to vary the order of the lower court in any way must appeal and permission will be required on the same basis as for an appellant.

(Paragraph 3.2 applies to grounds of appeal by a respondent.).

7.2 A respondent who wishes to appeal or who wishes to ask the appeal court to uphold the order of the lower court for reasons different from or additional to those given by the lower court must file a respondent's notice.

7.3 A respondent who does not file a respondent's notice will not be entitled, except with the permission of the court, to rely on any reason not relied on in the lower court. This paragraph and paragraph 7.2 do not apply where the appeal is against an order under section 38(1) of the 1989 Act (see rule 30.5(7) (Respondent's notice)).

7.4 Paragraphs 5.3 (Human Rights and extension for time for filing appellant's notice) and 5.4 to 5.6 (extension of time for filing appellant's notice) of this practice direction also apply to a respondent and a respondent's notice.

Time limits

7.5 The time limits for filing a respondent's notice are set out in rule 30.5(4) and (5) (Respondent's notice).

7.6 Where an extension of time is required the extension must be requested in the respondent's notice and the reasons why the respondent failed to act within the specified time must be included.

7.7 Except where paragraphs 7.8 and 7.10 apply, the respondent must file a skeleton argument for the court in all cases where the respondent proposes to address arguments to the court. The respondent's skeleton argument may be included within a respondent's notice. Where a skeleton argument is included within a respondent's notice it will not form part of the notice for the purposes of rule 30.9 (Amendment of appeal notice).

7.8 A respondent who—

(a) files a respondent's notice; but
(b) does not include a skeleton argument with that notice,

must file the skeleton argument within 14 days of filing the notice.

7.9 A respondent who does not file a respondent's notice but who files a skeleton argument must file that skeleton argument at least 7 days before the appeal hearing.

(Rule 30.5(4) (Respondent's notice) sets out the period for filing a respondent's notice.).

7.10 A respondent who is not represented need not file a skeleton argument but is encouraged to do so in order to assist the court.

7.11 The respondent must serve the skeleton argument on—

(a) the appellant; and
(b) any other respondent;

at the same time as the skeleton argument is filed at court. Where a child is an appellant or respondent the skeleton argument must also be served on the persons listed in rule 6.33(2) unless the court directs otherwise.

7.12 A respondent's skeleton argument must conform to the directions at paragraphs 5.16 to 5.22 with any necessary modifications. It should, where appropriate, answer the arguments set out in the appellant's skeleton argument.

Applications within respondent's notices

7.13 A respondent may include an application within a respondent's notice in accordance with paragraph 5.7.

Filing respondent's notices and skeleton arguments

7.14 The respondent must file the following documents with the respondent's notice in every case—

(a) two additional copies of the respondent's notice for the appeal court; and
(b) one copy each for the appellant, any other respondents and any persons referred to in paragraph 5.39.

7.15 The respondent may file a skeleton argument with the respondent's notice and—

(a) where doing so must file two copies; and
(b) where not doing so must comply with paragraph 7.8.

7.16 If the respondent considers documents in addition to those filed by the appellant to be necessary to enable the appeal court to reach its decision on the appeal and wishes to rely on those documents, any amendments to the appeal bundle should be agreed with the appellant if possible.

7.17 If the representatives for the parties are unable to reach agreement, the respondent may prepare a supplemental bundle.

7.18 The respondent must file any supplemental bundle so prepared, together with the requisite number of copies for the appeal court, at the appeal court—

(a) with the respondent's notice; or
(b) if a respondent's notice is not filed, within 21 days after the respondent is served with the appeal bundle.

7.19 The respondent must serve—

(a) the respondent's notice;
(b) the skeleton argument (if any); and
(c) the supplemental bundle (if any),
on–
 (i) the appellant; and
 (ii) any other respondent;

at the same time as those documents are filed at the court. Where a child is an appellant or respondent the documents referred to in paragraphs (a) to (c) above must also be served on the persons listed in rule 6.33(2) unless the court directs otherwise.

APPEALS TO THE HIGH COURT

Application

8.1 The appellant's notice must be filed in—

(a) the principal registry of the Family Division; or
(b) the district registry which is nearest to the court from which the appeal lies.

8.2 A respondent's notice must be filed at the court where the appellant's notice was filed.

8.3 In the case of appeals from district judges of the High Court, applications for permission and any other applications in the appeal, appeals may be heard and directions in the appeal may be given by a High Court Judge or by any person authorised under section 9 of the Senior Courts Act 1981 to act as a judge of the High Court.

APPEALS TO A COUNTY COURT

Appeals to a judge of a county court from a district judge

9.1 The Designated Family Judge in consultation with the Family Division Liaison Judges has responsibility for the allocation of appeals from decisions of district judges to circuit judges.

The Family Procedure Rules 2010

Appeals to a county court from a magistrates' court

Appeals under section 111A of the Magistrates' Courts Act 1980 ("the 1980 Act") from a magistrates' court to a county court on the ground that the decision is wrong in law or in excess of jurisdiction

9.2 As a result of an amendment to section 111 of the 1980 Act by the Access to Justice Act 1999 (Destination of Appeals) (Family Proceedings) Order 2009 ("the Destination Order") an application to have a case stated for the opinion of the High Court under section 111 of that Act may not be made in relation to family proceedings. Family proceedings for those purposes are defined as—

(a) proceedings which, by virtue of section 65 of the 1980 Act, are or may be treated as family proceedings for the purposes of that Act; and
(b) proceedings under the Child Support Act 1991.

9.3 Section 111A of the 1980 Act, which is inserted by article 4(3) of the Destination Order, provides that in family proceedings as defined in paragraph 9.2 above a person may appeal to a county court on the ground that a decision is wrong in law or is in excess of jurisdiction; this appeal to a county court replaces the procedure for making an application to have a case stated. Section 111A(3)(a) provides that no appeal may be brought under section 111A if there is a right of appeal to a county court against the decision otherwise than under that section.

9.4 Subject to section 111A of the 1980 Act and any other enactment, the following rules in Part 30 apply to appeals under section 111A of the 1980 Act-

(a) 30.1 (scope and interpretation);
(b) 30.2 (parties to comply with the practice direction);
(c) 30.4 (appellant's notice);
(d) 30.6 (grounds of appeal);
(e) 30.8 (stay); and
(f) 30.9 (amendment of appeal notice).

9.5 Section 111A(4) of the 1980 Act provides that the notice of appeal must be filed within 21 days after the day on which the decision of the magistrates' court was given. The notice of appeal should also be served within this period of time. The time period for filing the appellant's notice in rule 30.4 (2) does not apply. There can be no extension of this 21 day time limit under rule 4.1(3)(a).

Other statutory rights of appeal from a magistrates' court and the court at which the appellant's notice is to be filed - provisions applying to those appeals and appeals under section 111A of the 1980 Act

9.6 The effect of the Destination Order is that appeals against decisions of magistrates' courts in family proceedings shall lie to a county court instead of to the High Court. In addition to replacing appeals by way of case stated by amending the 1980 Act as outlined above, the Destination Order amends the statutory provisions listed in paragraph 9.7 below to provide for the appeals under those provisions to lie to a county court instead of to the High Court Paragraph 9.7 also refers to the amendment to the 1980 Act for completeness.

9.7 Paragraph 9.8 and 9.9 below apply to appeals under-

(a) section 4(7) of the Maintenance Orders Act 1958;
(b) section 29 of the Domestic Proceedings and Magistrates' Courts Act 1978;
(c) section 60(5) of the Family Law 1986;
(d) section 94(1) to (9) of the Children Act 1989;
(e) section 61 of the Family Law Act 1996;
(f) sections 10(1)(a) to (3) and 13 (1) and (2) of the Crime and Disorder Act 1998; or
(g) section 111A of the 1980 Act.

9.8 Subject to any enactment or to any directions made by the President of the Family

FPR 2010, Practice Direction 30A

Division in exercise of the powers conferred on him under section 9 of the Courts and Legal Services Act 1990, a district judge may-

(a) dismiss an appeal;
 (i) for want of prosecution; or
 (ii) with the consent of the parties; or
(b) give leave for the appeal to be withdrawn,

and may deal with any question of costs arising out of the dismissal or withdrawal.

Unless the court directs otherwise, any interlocutory application in an appeal under the statutory provisions listed in paragraph 9.7 may be made to a district judge.

9.9 Subject to paragraph 9.10 below, the appellant's notice and other documents required to be filed by rule 30.4 and this practice direction shall where the appeal is against the making by a magistrates' court of any order or any refusal by a magistrates' court to make such an order—

(a) in proceedings listed in Schedule 1 to this Practice Direction, be filed in a care centre within the meaning of article 2 (b) of the Allocation and Transfer of Proceedings Order 2008;
(b) in proceedings under the Adoption and Children Act 2002, be filed in an adoption centre or an intercountry adoption centre within the meaning of article 2 (c) and (d) of the Allocation and Transfer of Proceedings Order 2008; and
(c) in any other case, be filed in a family hearing centre within the meaning of article 2(a) of that Order.

9.10 Where the appeal is an appeal from a decision of a magistrates' court under section 94 of the 1989 Act or section 61 of the Family Law Act 1996, the documents required to be filed by rule 30.4 and this practice direction may be filed in the principal registry of the Family Division of the High Court.

9.11 Article 11 of the Destination Order amends article 3 of the Allocation and Transfer of Proceedings Order 2008 to provide that the principal registry of the Family Division of the High Court is treated as a county court for the purposes of appeals from decisions of a magistrates' court under section 94 of the Children Act 1989 and section 61 of the Family Law Act 1996.

9.12 This practice direction applies to appeals under the statutory provisions listed in paragraph 9.7 with the following modifications and any other necessary modifications-

(a) after paragraph 5.6 insert-
 "5.6A Paragraphs 5.4 to 5.6 do not apply to an appeal to a county court under section 111A of the Magistrates' Courts Act 1980."
(b) in paragraph 5.35, insert "and 5.36A" after " subject to paragraph 5.36";
(c) after paragraph 5.36 insert-
 "5.36A Where the appeal is to a judge of a county court under section 111A of the Magistrates' Courts Act 1980, the appellant's notice must be filed and served within 21 days after the day on which the decision of the lower court was given.".

Appeals to a county court from the Child Maintenance and Enforcement Commission ("the Commission"): Deduction order appeals

9.13 A "deduction order appeal" is an appeal under regulation 25AB(1)(a) to (d) of the Child Support (Collection and Enforcement) Regulations 1992 (S.I. 1992/1989) ("the Collection and Enforcement Regulations"). A deduction order appeal is an appeal against -

(a) the making of a regular deduction order under section 32A of the Child Support Act 1991 ("the 1991 Act");
(b) a decision on an application to review a regular deduction order;
(c) a decision to withhold consent to the disapplication of sections 32G(1) and 32H(2)(b) of the 1991 Act which has the effect of unfreezing funds in the liable person's account; or

The Family Procedure Rules 2010

(d) the making of a final lump sum deduction order under section 32F of the 1991 Act.

A deduction order appeal lies to a county court from the Commission as a result of regulation 25AB(1) of the Collection and Enforcement Regulations.

9.14 The rules in Part 30 apply to deduction order appeals with the amendments set out in paragraphs 9.15 to 9.27 and 9.29 and 9.30 below. The rules in Part 30 also apply to appeals against the decision of a district judge in proceedings relating to a deduction order appeal with the amendments set out in paragraph 9.28 below.

9.15 "The respondent" means—

(a) the Commission and any person other than the appellant who was served with an order under section 32A(1), 32E(1) or 32F(1) of the 1991 Act; and
(b) a person who is permitted by the appeal court to be a party to the appeal.

9.16 The appellant will serve the appellant's notice on the Commission and any other respondent.

9.17 The appellant shall file and serve the appellant's notice, within 21 days of—

(a) where the appellant is a deposit-taker, service of the order;
(b) where the appellant is a liable person, receipt of the order; or
(c) where the appellant is either a deposit-taker or a liable person, the date of receipt of notification of the decision.

9.18 For the purposes of paragraph 9.17—

(a) references to "liable person" and "deposit-taker" are to be interpreted in accordance with section 32E of the 1991 Act and regulation 25A(2) of the Collection and Enforcement Regulations and section 54 of the 1991 Act, respectively; and
(b) the liable person is to be treated as having received the order or notification of the decision 2 days after it was posted by the Commission.

9.19 Rule 4.1(3)(a) (court's power to extend or shorten the time for compliance with a rule, practice direction or court order) does not apply to an appeal against the making of a lump sum deduction order under section 32F of the 1991 Act in so far as that rule gives the court power to extend the time set out in paragraph 9.17 for filing and serving an appellant's notice after the time for filing and serving the that notice set out in paragraph 9.17 has expired.

9.20 The Commission shall provide to the court and serve on all other parties to the appeal any information and evidence relevant to the making of the decision or order being appealed, within 14 days of receipt of the appellant's notice.

9.21 Subject to paragraph 9.23, a respondent who wishes to ask the appeal court to uphold the order or decision of the Commission for reasons different from or in additional to those given by the Commission must file a respondent's notice.

9.22 A respondent's notice must be filed within 14 days of receipt of the appellant's notice.

9.23 Where the Commission as a respondent, wishes to contend that its order or decision should be—

(a) varied, either in any event or in the event of the appeal being allowed in whole or in part; or
(b) affirmed on different grounds from those on which it relied when making the order or decision,

it shall, within 14 days of receipt of the appellant's notice, file and serve on all other parties to the appeal a respondent's notice.

9.24 In so far as rule 30.7 (Variation of time) may permit any application for variation of the time limit for filing an appellant's notice after the time for filing the appellant's notice has expired, that rule shall not apply to an appeal made against an order under section 32F(1) of the Act of 1991.

9.25 Rule 30.8 (stay) shall not apply to an appeal made against an order under section 32F(1) of the Act of 1991.

9.26 A district judge may hear a deduction order appeal.

9.27 Rule 30.11 (appeal court's powers) does not apply to deduction order appeals.

9.28 Rule 30.11(2)(d) (making orders for payment of interest) does not apply in the case of an appeal against a decision of a district judge in proceedings relating to a deduction order appeal.

9.29 In the case of a deduction order appeal—

(a) the appeal court has power to—
 (i) affirm or set aside the order or decision;
 (ii) remit the matter to the Commission for the order or decision to be reconsidered, with appropriate directions;
 (iii) refer any application or issue for determination by the Commission;
 (iv) make a costs order; and
(b) the appeal court may exercise its powers in relation to the whole or part of an order or decision of the Commission.

9.30 In rule 30.12 (Hearing of appeals)—

(a) at the beginning of paragraph (1), for "Every" substitute "Subject to paragraph (2A), every";
(b) at the beginning of paragraph (2), for "Unless" substitute "Subject to paragraph (2A), unless";
(c) after paragraph (2), insert—
 "(2A) In the case of a deduction order appeal, the appeal will be a re-hearing, unless the appeal court orders otherwise.";
(d) in paragraph (3), after "lower court" insert "or, in a deduction order appeal, the order or decision of the Commission"; and
(e) for sub-paragraph (b) of paragraph (3), substitute—
 "(b) unjust because of a serious procedural or other irregularity in—
 (i) the proceedings in the lower court; or
 (ii) the making of an order or decision by the Commission."

Information about the Commission's decision

9.31 In relation to the deduction order appeals listed in column 1 of the table in Schedule 2 to this Practice Direction-

(a) the documents to be filed and served by the appellant include the documents set out in Column 3; and
(b) the relevant information to be provided by the Commission in accordance with paragraph 9.20 above includes the information set out in Column 4.

The court at which the appeal notice is to be filed

9.32 In relation to a deduction order appeal, the appellant's notice and other documents required to be filed with that notice shall be filed in a county court (the Collection and Enforcement Regulations 25AB(1)).

The Commission's address for service

9.33 For the purposes of a deduction order appeal the Commission's address for service is-

The Family Procedure Rules 2010

Commission Legal Adviser
Deduction Order Team
Legal Enforcement (Civil)
Antonine House
Callendar Road
Falkirk FK1 1XT

All notices or other documents for CMEC relating to a deduction order appeal should be sent to the above address.

9.34 This practice direction applies to deduction order appeals and appeals against the decision of a district judge in proceedings relating to a deduction order appeal with the following modifications and any other necessary modifications-

(a) in paragraph 5.35, insert "and 5.36B" after " subject to paragraph 5.36A";
(b) after paragraph 5.36A insert-
"5.36A Where the appeal is a deduction order appeal, the appellant's notice must be filed and served within 21 days of –
   (a) where the appellant is a deposit-taker, service of the order;
   (b) where the appellant is a liable person, receipt of the order; or
   (c) where the appellant is either a deposit-taker or a liable person, the date of receipt of notification of the decision the lower court was given.".

Appeal against the court's decision under rules 31.10, 31.11 or 31.14

10.1 The rules in Part 30 apply to appeals against the court's decision under rules 31.10, 31.11 or 31.14 with the amendments set out in paragraphs 10.2 to 10.5 below. Rules 31.15 and 31.16 apply to these appeals. These modifications do not apply to appeals against the decision made on appeal under rule 31.15.

10.2 Rule 30.3 (permission to appeal) does not apply.

10.3 The time for filing an appellant's notice at the appeal court in rule 30.4(2) does not apply. Rule 31.15 sets out the time within which an appeal against the court's decision under rules 31.10, 31.11 or 31.14 must be made to a judge of the High Court.

10.4 Rule 4.1(3)(a) (court's power to extend or shorten the time for compliance with a rule, practice direction or court order) does not apply to an appeal against the court's decision under rules 31.10, 31.11 or 31.14 in so far as that rule gives the court power to extend the time set out in rule 31.15 for filing an appellant's notice.

10.5 Rules 30.7 (variation), 30.8 (stay of proceedings), 30.10 (striking out appeal notices, setting aside or imposing conditions on permission to appeal) and 30.12 (hearing of appeals) do not apply.

Appeals against pension orders and pension compensation sharing orders

11.1 Paragraph 11.2 below applies to appeals against-

(a) a pension sharing order under section 24B of the Matrimonial Causes Act 1973 or the variation of such an order under section 31 of that Act;
(b) a pension sharing order under Part 4 of Schedule 5 to the Civil Partnership Act 2004 or the variation of such an order under Part 11 of Schedule 5 to that Act;
(c) a pension compensation sharing order under section 24E of the Matrimonial Causes Act 1973 or a variation of such an order under section 31 of that Act; and
(d) a pension compensation sharing order under Part 4 of Schedule 5 to the Civil Partnership Act 2004 or a variation of such an order under Part 11 of Schedule 5 to that Act.

11.2 Rule 4.1(3)(a) (court's power to extend or shorten the time for compliance with a rule, practice direction or court order) does not apply to an appeal against the making of the orders referred to in paragraph 11.1 above in so far as that rule gives the court power to extend the time set out in rule 30.4 for filing and serving an appellant's notice after the time for filing and serving that notice has expired.

11.3 In so far as rule 30.7 (Variation of time) may permit any application for variation of the time limit for filing an appellant's notice after the time for filing the appellant's notice has expired, that rule shall not apply to an appeal made against the orders referred to in paragraph 11.1 above.

Appeals to a court under section 20 of the 1991 Act (appeals in respect of parentage determinations)

12.1 The rules in Chapters 1 and 5 of Part 8 will apply as appropriate to an appeal under section 20(1) of the 1991 Act where that appeal must be made to a court in accordance with the Child Support Appeals (Jurisdiction of Courts) Order 2002

12.2 The respondent to such an appeal will be the Child Maintenance and Enforcement Commission.

12.3 Where the justices' clerk or the court is considering whether or not to transfer appeal proceedings under section 20(1) of the 1991 Act, rules 12.9 to 12.11 will apply as appropriate.

Applications

13.1 Where a party to an appeal makes an application whether in an appeal notice or by Part 18 (Procedure For Other Applications in Proceedings) application notice, the provisions of Part 18 will apply.

13.2 The applicant must file the following documents with the notice—

(a) one additional copy of the application notice for the appeal court, one copy for each of the respondents and the persons referred to in paragraph 5.39;
(b) where applicable a sealed or stamped copy of the order which is the subject of the main appeal or a copy of the notice of the making of an order;
(c) a bundle of documents in support which should include—
  (i) the Part 18 application notice; and
  (ii) any witness statements and affidavits filed in support of the application notice.

Appeals against consent orders

14.1 The rules in Part 30 and the provisions of this Practice Direction apply to appeals relating to orders made by consent in addition to orders which are not made by consent. An appeal is the only way in which a consent order can be challenged.

Disposing of applications or appeals by consent

15.1 An appellant who does not wish to pursue an application or an appeal may request the appeal court for an order that the application or appeal be dismissed. Such a request must state whether the appellant is a child, or a protected person.

15.2 The request must be accompanied by a consent signed by the other parties stating whether the respondent is a child, or a protected person and consents to the dismissal of the application or appeal.

Allowing unopposed appeals or applications on paper

16.1 The appeal court will not normally make an order allowing an appeal unless satisfied that the decision of the lower court was wrong, but the appeal court may set aside or vary the order of the lower court with consent and without determining the merits of the appeal, if it is satisfied that there are good and sufficient reasons for doing so. Where the appeal court is requested by all parties to allow an application or an appeal the court may consider the request on the papers. The request should state whether any of the parties is a child, or protected person and set out the relevant history of the proceedings and the matters relied on as justifying the proposed order and be accompanied by a copy of the proposed order.

Summary assessment of costs

17.1 Costs are likely to be assessed by way of summary assessment at the following hearings—

(a) contested directions hearings;
(b) applications for permission to appeal at which the respondent is present;
(c) appeals from case management decisions or decisions made at directions hearings; and
(d) appeals listed for one day or less.

(Provision for summary assessment of costs is made by section 13 of the Practice Direction supplementing CPR Part 44)

17.2 Parties attending any of the hearings referred to in paragraph 17.1 should be prepared to deal with the summary assessment.

Reopening of final appeals

18.1 This paragraph applies to applications under rule 30.14 (Reopening of final appeals) for permission to reopen a final determination of an appeal.

18.2 In this paragraph, "appeal" includes an application for permission to appeal.

18.3 Permission must be sought from the court whose decision the applicant wishes to reopen.

18.4 The application for permission must be made by application notice and supported by written evidence, verified by a statement of truth.

18.5 A copy of the application for permission must not be served on any other party to the original appeal unless the court so directs.

18.6 Where the court directs that the application for permission is to be served on another party, that party may within 14 days of the service on him or her of the copy of the application file a written statement either supporting or opposing the application.

18.7 The application for permission, and any written statements supporting or opposing it, will be considered on paper by a single judge, and will be allowed to proceed only if the judge so directs.

SCHEDULE 1

Description of proceedings

(1) Proceedings under section 25 of the Children Act 1989;
(2) Proceedings under Parts IV and V of the Children Act 1989;
(3) Proceedings under Schedules 2 and 3 to the Children Act 1989;
(4) Applications for leave under section 91(14),(15) or (17) of the Children Act 1989;
(5) Proceedings under section 102 of the Children Act 1989 or section 79 of the Childcare Act 2006;
(6) Proceedings for a residence order under section 8 of the Children Act 1989 or for a special guardianship order under section 14A of the Children Act 1989 with respect to a child who is the subject of a care order.
(7) Proceedings for a residence order under section 8 of the Children Act 1989 where either section 28(1) (child placed for adoption) or 29(4) (placement order in force) of the Adoption and Children Act 2002 applies;
(8) Proceedings for a special guardianship order under section 14A of the Children Act 1989 where either section 28(1) (child placed for adoption) or section 29(5) (placement order in force) of the Adoption and Children Act 2002 applies.

FPR 2010, Practice Direction 30A

SCHEDULE 2

APPEAL	RELEVANT LEGISLATION	APPELLANT INFORMATION	COMMISSION INFORMATION
Appeal against the making of a regular deduction order (under section 32A of the 1991 Act)	Section 32C(4)(a) of the 1991 Act The Collection and Enforcement Regulations 25AB(1)(a) (appeals)	A copy of the order; A covering letter explaining that the order has been made and the reasons for the order namely that there are arrears of child maintenance and/or no other arrangements have been made for the payment of child maintenance, including arrears	The amount of the current maintenance calculation, the period of debt and the total amount of arrears (including account breakdown if appropriate) and the reasons for the Commission's decision, details of all previous attempts to negotiate payment i.e. phone calls and letters to the non resident parent, details of any previous enforcement action taken
Appeal against a decision on an application for a review of a regular deduction order	Sections 32C(4)(b) 32C(2)(k) of the 1991 Act The Collection and Enforcement Regulations 25G (review of a regular deduction order) and 25AB(1)(b) (appeals)	A decision notification setting out whether or not the review has been agreed by the Commission and the resulting action to be taken if agreed; with an enclosure setting out the specific reasons for the Commission's decision	The reasons for the Commission's decision in respect of the application for review and any evidence supporting that decision
Appeal against the withholding of consent to the disapplication of sections 32G(1) and 32H(2)(b) of the 1991 Act	Section 32I(4) of the 1991 Act	A decision notification setting out that either:	The reasons for the Commission's decision in respect of the application for consent and any evidence supporting that decision
	The Collection and Enforcement Regulations 25N (disapplication of sections 32G(1) and 32H(2)(b) of the 1991 Act) and 25AB(1)(c) (appeals)	a) consent has been refused; or b) consent has been given in relation to part of the application i.e. that only some of the funds which were requested to be released have been agreed to be released (the right of appeal will lie in respect of the part of the application which has been refused).	

633

The Family Procedure Rules 2010

APPEAL	RELEVANT LEGISLATION	APPELLANT INFORMATION	COMMISSION INFORMATION
		There will be an enclosure with the notification setting out the reasons for the decision on the application.	
Appeal against the making of a final lump sum deduction order (under section 32F of the 1991 Act)	Section 32J(5) of the 1991 Act The Collection and Enforcement Regulations 25AB(1)(d) (appeals)	A copy of the order; A covering letter explaining that the order has been made and the reasons for the order namely that there are arrears of child maintenance and/or no other arrangements have been made for the payment of child maintenance, including arrears	The amount of the current maintenance calculation (if applicable), the period of debt and the total amount of arrears (including account breakdown if appropriate) and the reasons for the Commission's decision, details of all previous attempts to negotiate payment i.e. phone calls and letters to the non resident parent, details of any previous enforcement action taken.

The Right Honourable

Sir Nicholas Wall

The President of the Family Division

Signed by authority of the Lord Chancellor:

[   ]

Parliamentary Under Secretary of State

Ministry of Justice

PART 31

REGISTRATION OF ORDERS UNDER THE COUNCIL REGULATION, THE CIVIL PARTNERSHIP (JURISDICTION AND RECOGNITION OF JUDGMENTS) REGULATIONS 2005 AND UNDER THE HAGUE CONVENTION 1996

31.1. Scope
This Part applies to proceedings for the recognition, non-recognition and registration of—
(a) judgments to which the Council Regulation applies;
(b) measures to which the 1996 Hague Convention applies; and
(c) judgments to which the Jurisdiction and Recognition of Judgments Regulations apply, and which relate to dissolution or annulment of overseas relationships entitled to be treated as a civil partnership, or legal separation of the same.

31.2.— Interpretation
(1) In this Part —

(a) "judgment" is to be construed —
 (i) in accordance with the definition in Article 2(4) of the Council Regulation where it applies;
 (ii) in accordance with regulation 6 of the Jurisdiction and Recognition of Judgments Regulations where those Regulations apply; or
 (iii) as meaning any measure taken by an authority with jurisdiction under Chapter II of the 1996 Hague Convention where that Convention applies;
(b) "the Jurisdiction and Recognition of Judgments Regulations" means the Civil Partnership (Jurisdiction and Recognition of Judgments) Regulations 2005;
(c) "Member State" means —
 (i) where registration, recognition or non-recognition is sought of a judgment under the Council Regulation, a Member State of the European Union which is bound by that Regulation or a country which has subsequently adopted it;
 (ii) where recognition is sought of a judgment to which the Jurisdiction and Recognition of Judgments Regulations apply, a Member State of the European Union to which Part II of those Regulations applies;
(d) "Contracting State" means a State, other than a Member State within the meaning of (c) above, in relation to which the 1996 Hague Convention is in force as between that State and the United Kingdom; and
(e) "parental responsibility" —
 (i) where the Council Regulation applies, has the meaning given in Article 2(7) of that Regulation; and
 (ii) where the 1996 Hague Convention applies, has the meaning given in Article 1(2) of that Convention.

(2) References in this Part to registration are to the registration of a judgment in accordance with the provisions of this Part.

31.3.— Where to start proceedings

(1) Every application under this Part, except for an application under rule 31.18 for a certified copy of a judgment, or under rule 31.20 for rectification of a certificate issued under Articles 41 or 42, must be made to the principal registry.

(2) Nothing in this rule prevents the determination of an issue of recognition as an incidental question by any court in proceedings, in accordance with Article 21(4) of the Council Regulation.

(3) Notwithstanding paragraph (1), where recognition of a judgment is raised as an incidental question in proceedings under the 1996 Hague Convention or the Jurisdiction and Recognition of Judgments Regulations the court hearing those proceedings may determine the question of recognition.

31.4.— Application for registration, recognition or non-recognition of a judgment

(1) Any interested person may apply to the court for an order that the judgment be registered, recognised or not recognised.

(2) Except for an application under rule 31.7, an application for registration, recognition or nonrecognition must be —
(a) made to a district judge of the principal registry; and
(b) in the form, and supported by the documents and the information required by a practice direction.

31.5.— Documents – supplementary

(1) Except as regards a copy of a judgment required by Article 37(1)(a) of the Council Regulation, where the person making an application under this Part does not produce the documents required by rule 31.4(2)(b) the court may —
(a) fix a time within which the documents are to be produced;
(b) accept equivalent documents; or

(c) dispense with production of the documents if the court considers it has sufficient information.

(2) This rule does not apply to applications under rule 31.7.

31.6.— Directions

(1) As soon as practicable after an application under this Part has been made, the court may (subject to the requirements of the Council Regulation) give such directions as it considers appropriate, including as regards the following matters —
- (a) whether service of the application may be dispensed with;
- (b) expedition of the proceedings or any part of the proceedings (and any direction for expedition may specify a date by which the court must give its decision);
- (c) the steps to be taken in the proceedings and the time by which each step is to be taken;
- (d) the service of documents; and
- (e) the filing of evidence.

(2) The court or court officer will —
- (a) record the giving, variation or revocation of directions under this rule; and
- (b) as soon as practicable serve a copy of the directions order on every party.

31.7.— Recognition and enforcement under the Council Regulation of a judgment given in another Member State relating to rights of access or under Article 11(8) for the return of the child to that State

(1) This rule applies where a judgment has been given in another Member State —
- (a) relating to rights of access: or
- (b) under Article 11(8) of the Council Regulation for the return of a child to that State,

which has been certified, in accordance with Article 41(2) or 42(2) as the case may be, by the judge in the court of origin.

(2) An application for recognition or enforcement of the judgment must be —
- (a) made in writing to a district judge of the principal registry; and
- (b) accompanied by a copy of the certificate issued by the judge in the court of origin.

(3) The application may be made without notice.

(4) Rules 31.5 and 31.8 to 31.17 do not apply to an application made under this rule.

(5) Nothing in this rule shall prevent a holder of parental responsibility from seeking recognition and enforcement of a judgment in accordance with the provisions of rules 31.8 to 31.17.

31.8.— Registration for enforcement or order for non-recognition of a judgment

(1) This rule applies where an application is made for an order that a judgment given in another Member State, or a Contracting State, should be registered, or should not be recognised, except where rule 31.7 applies.

(2) where the application is made for an order that the judgment should be registered —
- (a) upon receipt of the application, and subject to any direction given by the court under rule 31.6, the court officer will serve the application on the person against whom registration is sought;
- (b) the court will not accept submissions from either the person against whom registration is sought or any child in relation to whom the judgment was given.

(3) Where the application is for an order that the judgment should not be recognised —
- (a) upon receipt of the application, and subject to any direction given by the court under rule 31.6, the court officer will serve the application on the person in whose favour judgment was given;
- (b) the person in whose favour the judgment was given must file an answer to the application and serve it on the applicant —

(i) within 1 month of service of the application; or
(ii) if the applicant is habitually resident in another Member State, within two months of service of the application.

(4) In cases to which the 1996 Hague Convention applies and the Council Regulation does not apply, the court may extend the time set out in subparagraph (3)(b)(ii) on account of distance.

(5) The person in whose favour the judgment was given may request recognition or registration of the judgment in their answer, and in that event must comply with 31.4(2)(b), to the extent that such documents, information and evidence are not already contained in the application for non-recognition.

(6) If, in a case to which the Council Regulation applies, the person in whose favour the judgment was given fails to file an answer as required by paragraph (3), the court will act in accordance with the provisions of Article 18 of the Council Regulation.

(7) If, in a case to which the 1996 Hague Convention applies and the Service Regulation does not, the person in whose favour the judgment was given fails to file a answer as required by paragraph

(3) —
(a) where the Hague Convention of 15th November 1965 on the service abroad of judicial and extrajudicial documents in civil or commercial matters applies, the court shall apply Article 15 of that Convention; and
(b) in all other cases, the court will not consider the application unless —
(i) it is proved to the satisfaction of the court that the person in whose favour judgment was given was served with the application within a reasonable period of time to arrange his or her response; or
(ii) the court is satisfied that the circumstances of the case justify proceeding with consideration of the application.

(8) In a case to which the Jurisdiction and Recognition of Judgments Regulations apply, if the person in whose favour judgment was given fails to file an answer as required by paragraph (3), the court will apply the Service Regulation where that regulation applies, and if it does not —
(a) where the Hague Convention of 15th November 1965 on the service abroad of judicial and extrajudicial documents in civil or commercial matters applies, the court shall apply Article 15 of that Convention; and
(b) in all other cases, the court will apply the provisions of paragraph (7)(b).

31.9. Stay of recognition proceedings by reason of an appeal

Where recognition or non-recognition of a judgment given in another Member State or Contracting State is sought, or is raised as an incidental question in other proceedings, the court may stay the proceedings —
(a) if an ordinary appeal against the judgment has been lodged; or
(b) if the judgment was given in the Republic of Ireland, if enforcement of the judgment is suspended there by reason of an appeal.

31.10. Effect of refusal of application for a decision that a judgment should not be recognised

Where the court refuses an application for a decision that a judgment should not be recognised, the court may —
(a) direct that the decision to refuse the application is to be treated as a decision that the judgment be recognised; or
(b) treat the answer under paragraph (3)(b) of rule 31.8 as an application that the judgment be registered for enforcement if paragraph (5) of that rule is complied with and order that the judgment be registered for enforcement in accordance with rule 31.11.

31.11.— Notification of the court's decision on an application for registration or non-recognition

(1) Where the court has —

(a) made an order on an application for an order that a judgment should be registered for enforcement; or
(b) refused an application that a judgment should not be recognised and ordered under rule 31.10 that the judgment be registered for enforcement,

the court officer will as soon as practicable take the appropriate action under paragraph (2) or (3).

(2) If the court refuses the application for the judgment to be registered for enforcement, the court officer will serve the order on the applicant and the person against whom judgment was given in the state of origin.

(3) If the court orders that the judgment should be registered for enforcement, the court officer will —
(a) register the judgment in the central index of judgments kept by the principal registry;
(b) confirm on the order that the judgment has been registered; and
(c) serve on the parties the court's order endorsed with the court officer's confirmation that the judgment has been registered.

(4) A sealed order of the court endorsed in accordance with paragraph (3)(b) will constitute notification that the judgment has been registered under Article 28(2) of the Council Regulation or under Article 26 of the 1996 Hague Convention, as the case may be, and in this Part "notice of registration" means a sealed order so endorsed.

(5) The notice of registration must state —
(a) full particulars of the judgment registered and the order for registration;
(b) the name of the party making the application and his address for service within the jurisdiction;
(c) the right of the person against whom judgment was given to appeal against the order for registration; and
(d) the period within which an appeal against the order for registration may be made.

31.12. Effect of registration under rule 31.11

Registration of a judgment under rule 31.11 will serve for the purpose of Article 21(3) of the Council Regulation, Article 24 of the 1996 Hague Convention, or regulation 7 of the Jurisdiction and Recognition of Judgments Regulations (as the case may be) as a decision that the judgment is recognised.

31.13. The central index of judgments registered under rule 31.11

The central index of judgments registered under rule 31.11 will be kept by the principal registry.

31.14.— Decision on recognition of a judgment only

(1) Where an application is made seeking recognition of a judgment only, the provisions of rules 31.8 and 31.9 apply to that application as they do to an application for registration for enforcement.

(2) Where the court orders that the judgment should be recognised, the court officer will serve a copy of the order on each party as soon as practicable.

(3) A sealed order of the court will constitute notification that the judgment has been recognised under Article 21(3) of the Council Regulation, Article 24 of the 1996 Hague convention or regulation 7 of the Jurisdiction and Recognition of Judgments Regulations, as the case may be.

(4) The sealed order shall indicate —
(a) full particulars of the judgment recognised;
(b) the name of the party making the application and his address for service within the jurisdiction;
(c) the right of the person against whom judgment was given to appeal against the order for recognition; and
(d) the period within which an appeal against the order for recognition may be made.

31.15.—— Appeal against the court's decision under rules 31.10, 31.11 or 31.14

(1) An appeal against the court's decision under rules 31.10, 31.11 or 31.14 must be made to a judge of the High Court —
- (a) within one month of the date of service of the notice of registration; or
- (b) if the party bringing the appeal is habitually resident in another Member State, or a Contracting State, within two months of the date of service.

(2) The court may not extend time for an appeal on account of distance unless the matter is one to which the 1996 Hague Convention applies and the Council Regulation does not apply.

(3) If, in a case to which the 1996 Hague Convention applies and the Service Regulation does not, the appeal is brought by the applicant for a declaration of enforceability or registration and the respondent fails to appear —
- (a) where the Hague Convention of 15th November 1965 on the service abroad of judicial and extrajudicial documents in civil or commercial matters applies, the court shall apply Article 15 of that Convention; and
- (b) in all other cases, the court will not consider the appeal unless —
  - (i) it is proved to the satisfaction of the court that the respondent was served with notice of the appeal within a reasonable period of time to arrange his or her response; or
  - (ii) the court is satisfied that the circumstances of the case justify proceeding with consideration of the appeal.

(4) This rule is subject to rule 31.16. (The procedure for applications under rule 31.15 is set out in Practice Direction 30A (Appeals).)

31.16.—— Stay of enforcement where appeal pending in state of origin

(1) A party against whom enforcement is sought of a judgment which has been registered under rule 31.11 may apply to the court with which an appeal is lodged under rule 31.15 for the proceedings to be stayed where —
- (a) that party has lodged an ordinary appeal in the Member State or Contracting State of origin; or
- (b) the time for such an appeal has not yet expired.

(2) Where an application for a stay is filed in the circumstances described in paragraph (1)(b), the court may specify the time within which an appeal must be lodged.

31.17.—— Enforcement of judgments registered under rule 31.11

(1) The court will not enforce a judgment registered under rule 31.11 until after —
- (a) the expiration of any applicable period under rules 31.15 or 31.16; or
- (b) if that period has been extended by the court, the expiration of the period so extended.

(2) A party applying to the court for the enforcement of a registered judgment must produce to the court a certificate of service of —
- (a) the notice of registration of the judgment; and
- (b) any order made by the court in relation to the judgment.

(Service out of the jurisdiction, including service in accordance with the Service Regulation, is dealt with in chapter 4 of Part 6 and in Practice Direction 6B.)

31.18.—— Request for a certificate or a certified copy of a judgment

(1) An application for a certified copy of a judgment, or for a certificate under Articles 39, 41 or 42 of the Council Regulation, must be made to the court which made the order or judgment in respect of which certification is sought and without giving notice to any other party.

(2) The application must be made in the form, and supported by the documents and information required by a practice direction.

(3) The certified copy of the judgment will be an office copy sealed with the seal of the court and signed by the district judge, or by the court where the application is made to the Magistrates' Court.

It will be issued with a certified copy of any order which has varied any of the terms of the original order.

(4) Where the application is made for the purposes of applying for recognition or recognition and enforcement of the order in another Contracting State, the court must indicate on the certified copy of the judgment the grounds on which it based its jurisdiction to make the order, for the purposes of Article 23(2)(a) of the 1996 Hague Convention.

31.19. Certificates issued in England and Wales under Articles 41 and 42 of the Council Regulation

The court officer will serve —

      (a)   a certificate issued under Article 41 or 42; or

      (b)   a certificate rectified under rule 31.20,

on all parties and will transmit a copy to the Central Authority for England and Wales.

31.20.— Rectification of certificate issued under Article 41 or 42 of the Council Regulation

(1) Where there is an error in a certificate issued under Article 41 or 42, an application to rectify that error must be made to the court which issued the certificate.

(2) A rectification under paragraph (1) may be made —

      (a)   by the court of its own initiative; or

      (b)   on application by —

            (i)   any party to the proceedings; or

           (ii)   the court or Central Authority of another Member State.

(3) An application under paragraph (2)(b) may be made without notice being served on any other party.

31.21. Authentic instruments and agreements under Article 46 of the Council Regulation

This Chapter applies to an authentic instrument and an agreement to which Article 46 of the Council Regulation applies as it applies to a judgment.

31.22. Application for provisional, including protective measures.

An application for provisional, including protective, measures under Article 20 of the Council Regulation or Articles 11 or 12 of the 1996 Hague Convention may be made notwithstanding that the time for appealing against an order for registration of a judgment has not expired or that a final determination of any issue relating to enforcement of the judgment is pending.

PART 31 COMMENTARY

Part 31 is supplemented by PD31A, which sets out that Part 19 procedure applies to applications under this section, subject to the modifications provided in rr 31.8 to 31.14 to rr 19.4 to 19.9.

Part 31 relates to proceedings for the recognition, non-recognition and registration of judgments to which the Council Regulation (EC) No 2201/2003 on jurisdiction and the recognition and enforcement of judgments in matrimonial matters and in matters of parental responsibility apply, measures to which the 1996 Hague Convention on Jurisdiction, Applicable Law, Enforcement and Co-operation in Respect of Parental Responsibility and measures for the Protection of Children apply, and to judgments to which the Jurisdiction and Recognition of Judgments Regulations apply and which relate to the dissolution or annulment of overseas relationships entitled to be treated as a civil partnership. This had been provided for in Part VII of the FPR 1991, but there has been a comprehensive revision of the old rules.

Rule 31.3 sets out that proceedings must be started in the principal registry.

Relevant forms for Part 31 are: C60 to C62 – certificates referred to in Articles 39, 41(1), 42(1) of Council Regulation 2201/2001, and D180 – Concerning Judgments in matrimonial matters.

PRACTICE DIRECTION 31A – REGISTRATION OF ORDERS UNDER THE COUNCIL REGULATION, THE CIVIL PARTNERSHIP (JURISDICTION AND RECOGNITION OF JUDGMENTS) REGULATIONS 2005 AND UNDER THE 1996 HAGUE CONVENTION

This Practice Direction is made by the President of the Family Division under the powers delegated to him by the Lord Chief Justice under Schedule 2, Part 1, paragraph 2(2) of the Constitutional Reform Act 2005, and is approved by the Parliamentary Under Secretary of State, by authority of the Lord Chancellor and comes into force on 6th April 2011

This Practice Direction supplements FPR Part 31

FORM OF APPLICATION

1.1 An application under rule 31.4 must be made using the Part 19 procedure, except that the provisions of rules 31.8 to 31.14 and of this Practice Direction shall apply in place of rules 19.4 to 19.9.

1.2 Where the application is for recognition only of an order, it should be made clear that the application does not extend to registration for enforcement.

EVIDENCE IN SUPPORT OF ALL APPLICATIONS FOR REGISTRATION, RECOGNITION OR NON-RECOGNITION

2.1 The requirements for information and evidence for applications differ according to whether the application is made under the Council Regulation, the Jurisdiction and Recognition of Judgments Regulations, or the 1996 Hague Convention.

2.2 All applications to which rule 31.4(2) applies must be supported by a statement that is sworn to be true or an affidavit, exhibiting the judgment, or a verified, certified or otherwise duly authenticated copy of the judgment. In the case of an application under the Jurisdiction and Recognition of Judgments Regulations or under the 1996 Hague Convention, a translation of the judgment should be supplied.

2.3 Where any other document required by this Practice Direction or by direction of the court under rule 31.5 is not in English, the applicant must supply a translation of that document into English certified by a notary public or a person qualified for the purpose, or accompanied by witness statement or affidavit confirming that the translation is accurate.

EVIDENCE REQUIRED IN SUPPORT OF APPLICATION FOR REGISTRATION, RECOGNITION OR NON-RECOGNITION OF A JUDGMENT UNDER THE COUNCIL REGULATION

3.1 An application for a judgment to be registered, recognised or not recognised under the Council Regulation must be accompanied by a witness statement or an affidavit exhibiting the following documents and giving the information required by 3.2 or 3.3 below, as appropriate.

3.2 In the case of an application for recognition or registration —

(a) the certificate in the form set out in Annex I or Annex II of the Council Regulation, issued by the Member State in which judgment was given;
(b) in the case of a judgment given in default, the documents referred to in Article 37(2);
(c) whether the judgment provides for the payment of a sum or sums of money;

The Family Procedure Rules 2010

(d) whether interest is recoverable on the judgment or part of the judgment in accordance with the law of the State in which the judgment was given, and if that is the case, the rate of interest, the date from which interest is recoverable, and the date on which interest ceases to accrue;

(e) an address within the jurisdiction of the court for service of process on the party making the application and stating, in so far as is known to the applicant, the name and usual or last known address or place of business of the person against whom judgment was given; and

(f) where appropriate, whether Article 56 has been complied with, and the identity and address of the authority or authorities from whom consent has been obtained, together with evidence of that consent.

3.3 In the case of an application for an order that a judgment should not be recognised under Article 21(3) –

(a) the certificate referred to at paragraph 3.2 (a);

(b) in relation to the documents identified at paragraph 3.2 (b), those documents or a statement that no such service or acceptance occurred if that is the case;

(c) an address within the jurisdiction of the court for service of process on the applicant and stating, in so far as is known to the applicant, the name and usual or last known address or place of business of the person in whose favour judgment was given; and

(d) a statement of the ground or grounds under Articles 22 or 23 (as the case may be) on which it is requested that the judgment should not be recognised, the reasons why the applicant asserts that such ground or grounds is, or are, made out, and any documentary evidence on which the applicant relies.

EVIDENCE REQUIRED IN SUPPORT OF AN APPLICATION FOR REGISTRATION, RECOGNITION OR NON-RECOGNITION OF A JUDGMENT UNDER THE 1996 HAGUE CONVENTION.

4.1 An application for an order for a judgment to be registered under Article 26 or not recognised under Article 24 of the 1996 Hague Convention must be accompanied by a witness statement or affidavit exhibiting the following documents and giving the information required by 4.2, 4.3 or 4.4 below as appropriate.

4.2 In the case of an application for registration –

(a) those documents necessary to show that the judgment is enforceable according to the law of the Contracting State in which it was given;

(b) a description of the opportunities provided by the authority which gave the judgment in question for the child to be heard, except where that judgment was given in a case of urgency;

(c) where the judgment was given in a case of urgency, a statement as to the circumstances of the urgency that led to the child not having the opportunity to be heard;

(d) details of any measures taken in the non-Contracting State of the habitual residence of the child, if applicable, specifying the nature and effect of the measure, and the date on which it was taken;

(e) in as far as not apparent from the copy of the judgment provided, a statement of the grounds on which the authority which gave the judgment based its jurisdiction, together with any documentary evidence in support of that statement;

(f) where appropriate, a statement regarding whether Article 33 of the 1996 Hague Convention has been complied with, and the identity and address of the authority or authorities from which consent has been obtained, together with evidence of that consent; and

(g) the information referred to at 3.2 (c) to (e) above.

4.3 In the case of an application for an order that a judgment should not be recognised –

(a) a statement of the ground or grounds under Article 23 of the 1996 Hague Convention on which it is requested that the judgment be not recognised, the reasons

why the applicant asserts that such ground or grounds is or are made out, and any documentary evidence on which the Applicant relies; and
(b) an address within the jurisdiction of the court for service of process on the applicant and stating, in so far as is known to the applicant, the name and usual or last known address or place of business of the person in whose favour judgment was given.

4.4 Where is it sought to apply for recognition only of a judgment under the 1996 Hague Convention, the provisions of paragraph 4.2 apply with the exception that the applicant is not required to produce the document referred to in subparagraph 4.2 (a).

EVIDENCE REQUIRED IN SUPPORT OF AN APPLICATION FOR RECOGNITION OR NON-RECOGNITION OF A JUDGMENT UNDER THE JURISDICTION AND RECOGNITION OF JUDGMENTS REGULATIONS

5.1 An application for recognition of a judgment under regulation 7 of the Jurisdiction and Recognition of Judgments Regulations or for non-recognition of a judgment under regulation 8 must be accompanied by a witness statement or affidavit exhibiting the following documents and giving the information at 5.2 or 5.3 below, as appropriate.

5.2 In the case of an application for recognition of a judgment –

(a) where applicable, details of any decision determining the question of the substance or validity of the civil partnership previously given by a court of civil jurisdiction in England and Wales, or by a court elsewhere;
(b) where the judgment was obtained otherwise than by means of proceedings –
   (i) an official document certifying that the judgment is effective under the law of the country in which it was obtained;
   (ii) where either civil partner was domiciled in another country from that in which the judgment was obtained at the relevant date, an official document certifying that the judgment is recognised as valid under the law of that country; or
   (iii) a verified, certified or otherwise duly authenticated copy of the document at (i) or (ii) above, as appropriate;
(c) in relation to a judgment obtained by means of proceedings and given in default, the original or a certified true copy of the document which establishes that the party who did not respond was served with the document instituting the proceedings or with an equivalent document, or any document indicating that the respondent has accepted the judgment unequivocally; and
(d) the information referred to at paragraph 3.2 (c) to (e) above.

5.3 In the case of an application for non-recognition of a judgment –

(a) an address within the jurisdiction of the court for service of process on the applicant and stating, in so far as is known to the applicant, the name and usual or last known address or place of business of the person in whose favour judgment was given;
(b) a statement of the ground or grounds under regulation 8 of the Jurisdiction and Recognition of Judgments Regulations on which it is requested that the judgment should not be recognised together with any documentary evidence on which the applicant relies; and
(c) where the judgment was obtained by means of proceedings, the document referred to at paragraph 5.2(c) or a statement that no such service or acceptance occurred if that is the case.

EVIDENCE IN SUPPORT OF APPLICATION FOR A CERTIFICATE UNDER ARTICLES 39, 41 OR 42 OF THE COUNCIL REGULATION, OR FOR A CERTIFIED COPY OF A JUDGMENT

6.1 The procedure described in the following paragraphs should be used where the application for the certified copy of the judgment or relevant certificate under the Council Regulation has not been made at the conclusion of the proceedings to which it relates.

6.2 An application for a certified copy of a judgment, or for a certificate under Articles

The Family Procedure Rules 2010

39, 41 or 42 of the Council Regulation must be made by witness statement or affidavit, containing the information and attaching the documents required under paragraph 6.3, and paragraphs 6.4, 6.5 or 6.6 below, as appropriate.

6.3 All applications must –

(a) provide details of the proceedings in which the judgment was obtained;
(b) attach a copy of the application by which the proceedings were begun;
(c) attach a copy of all statements of case filed in the proceedings; and
(d) state –
  (i) whether the judgment provides for the payment of a sum of money; and
  (ii) whether interest is recoverable on the judgment or part of it and if so, the rate of interest, the date from which interest is recoverable, and the date on which interest ceases to accrue.

Further, where the application relates to the Council Regulation, the applicant must attach a document showing that he or she benefitted from legal aid in the proceedings to which the judgment relates, if that is the case.

6.4 An application for a certified copy of the judgment and a certificate under Article 41 or 42 of the Council Regulation must –

(a) contain a statement of whether the certificate is sought under Article 41 or Article 42;
(b) attach a document evidencing the service of the application by which the proceedings were begun on all respondents, and if no such service occurred, details of all opportunities provided to each respondent to put their case before the court;
(c) provide information regarding the age of the child at the time of the judgment and the opportunities given during the proceedings, if any, for the child's wishes and feelings to be ascertained;
(d) state the full names, addresses and dates and places of birth (where available) of all persons holding parental responsibility in relation to the child or children to whom the judgment relates; and
(e) state the full names and dates of birth of each child to whom the judgment relates.

6.5 An application for a certified copy of the judgment and a certificate under Article 39 of the Council Regulation must –

(a) state whether the certificate sought relates to a parental responsibility matter or a matrimonial matter;
(b) in relation to a parental responsibility matter, attach evidence that the judgment has been served on the respondent;
(c) in the case of a judgment given in default, attach a document which establishes that the respondent was served with the petition or application by which the proceedings were commenced, or a document indicating that the respondent accepted the judgment unequivocally;
(d) state that the time for appealing has expired, or give the date on which it will expire, as appropriate, and state whether a notice of appeal against the judgment has been given;
(e) in relation to a matrimonial matter, give the full name, address, country and place of birth, and date of birth of each party, and the country, place and date of the marriage;
(f) in relation to a parental responsibility matter, give the full name, address, place and date of birth of each person who holds parental responsibility;
(g) as appropriate, give the name, address, and date and place of birth of the person with access rights, or to whom the child is to be returned.

6.6 An application for a certified copy of a judgment for the purposes of recognition and enforcement of the judgment under the 1996 Hague Convention must –

(a) provide a statement of the grounds on which the court based its jurisdiction to make the orders in question;
(b) indicate the age of the child at the time of the judgment and the measures taken, if any, for the child's wishes and feelings to be ascertained; and

(c) indicate which persons were provided with notice of the proceedings and, where such persons were served with the proceedings, attach evidence of such service.

The Right Honourable

Sir Nicholas Wall

The President of the Family Division

Signed by authority of the Lord Chancellor:

[   ]

Parliamentary Under Secretary of State

Ministry of Justice

PART 32

REGISTRATION AND ENFORCEMENT OF ORDERS

CHAPTER 1

Scope and interpretation of this part

32.1.— Scope and interpretation

(1) This Part contains rules about the registration and enforcement of maintenance orders and custody orders.

(2) In this Part—

"the 1950 Act" means the Maintenance Orders Act 1950;

"the 1958 Act" means the Maintenance Orders Act 1958.

(3) Chapter 2 of this Part relates to—
- (a) the registration of a maintenance order, made in the High Court or a county court, in a court in Scotland or Northern Ireland in accordance with the 1950 Act; and
- (b) the registration of a maintenance order, made in Scotland or Northern Ireland, in the High Court in accordance with the 1950 Act.

(Provision in respect of proceedings in the magistrates' court under the 1950 Act is in rules made under section 144 of the Magistrates' Courts Act 1980).

(4) Chapter 3 of this Part contains rules to be applied in the High Court or a county court in relation—
- (a) The registration of a maintenance order, made in the High Court or a county court, in a magistrates' court in accordance with the 1958 Act; and
- (b) The registration of a maintenance order, made in a magistrates' court, in the High Court in accordance with the 1958 Act.

(Provision in respect of proceedings in the magistrates' court under the 1958 Act is in rules made under section 144 of the Magistrates' Courts Act 1980).

(5) Chapter 4 of this Part relates to the registration and enforcement of custody orders in accordance with the 1986 Act.

The Family Procedure Rules 2010

CHAPTER 2

REGISTRATION ETC. OF ORDERS UNDER THE 1950 ACT

SECTION 1

INTERPRETATION OF THIS CHAPTER

32.2. Interpretation
In this Chapter—
"the clerk of the Court of Session" means the deputy principal clerk in charge of the petition department of the Court of Session;
"county court order" means a maintenance order made in a county court;
"High Court order" means a maintenance order made in the High Court;
"maintenance order" means a maintenance order to which section 16 of the 1950 Act applies;
"Northern Irish order" means a maintenance order made by the Court of Judicature of Northern Ireland;
"the register" means the register kept for the purposes of the 1950 Act;
"the registrar in Northern Ireland" means the chief registrar of the Queen's Bench Division (Matrimonial) of the High Court of Justice in Northern Ireland;
"registration" means registration under Part 2 of the 1950 Act and "registered" is to be construed accordingly; and
"Scottish Order" means a maintenance order made by the Court of Session.

SECTION 2

REGISTRATION ETC OF HIGH COURT AND COUNTY COURT ORDERS

32.3.— Registration of a High Court order
(1) An application for the registration of a High Court order may be made by sending to a court officer at the court which made the order—
    (a) a certified copy of the order; and
    (b) a statement which—
        (i) contains the address in the United Kingdom, and the occupation, of the person liable to make payments under the order;
        (ii) contains the date on which the order was served on the person liable to make payments, or, if the order has not been served, the reason why service has not been effected;
        (iii) contains the reason why it is convenient for the order to be enforced in Scotland or Northern Ireland, as the case may be;
        (iv) contains the amount of any arrears due to the applicant under the order;
        (v) confirms that the order is not already registered; and
        (vi) is verified by a statement of truth.
(2) If it appears to the court that—
    (a) the person liable to make payments under the order resides in Scotland or Northern Ireland; and
    (b) it is convenient for the order to be enforced there,
the court officer will send the documents filed under paragraph (1) to the clerk of the Court of Session or to the registrar in Northern Ireland, as the case may be.
(3) On receipt of a notice of the registration of a High Court order in the Court of Session or the Court of Judicature of Northern Ireland, the court officer (who is the prescribed officer for the purposes of section 17(4) of the 1950 Act) will—
    (a) enter particulars of the notice of registration in the register;
    (b) note the fact of registration in the court records; and
    (c) send particulars of the notice to the principal registry.

FPR 2010

32.4.— Notice of Variation etc. of a High Court order

(1) This rule applies where a High Court order, which is registered in the Court of Session or the Court of Judicature of Northern Ireland, is discharged or varied.

(2) A court officer in the court where the order was discharged or varied will send a certified copy of that order to the clerk of the Court of Session or the registrar in Northern Ireland, as the case may be.

32.5.— Cancellation of registration of a High Court order

(1) This rule applies where—
   (a) the registration of a High Court order registered in the Court of Session or the Court of Judicature of Northern Ireland is cancelled under section 24(1) of the 1950 Act; and
   (b) notice of the cancellation is given to a court officer in the court in which the order was made (who is the prescribed officer for the purposes of section 24(3)(a) of the 1950 Act).

(2) On receipt of a notice of cancellation of registration, the court officer will enter particulars of the notice in Part 1 of the register.

32.6. Application of this Chapter to a county court order

Rules 32.3 to 32.5 apply to an application to register a county court order as if—
   (a) references to a High Court order were references to a county court order;
   (b) where the order is to be registered in Scotland, references to the Court of Session and the clerk of the Court of Session were references to the sheriff court and the sheriff-clerk of the sheriff court respectively; and
   (c) where the order is to be registered in Northern Ireland, references to the Court of Judicature of Northern Ireland and the registrar of Northern Ireland were references to the court of summary jurisdiction and the clerk of the court of summary jurisdiction respectively.

SECTION 3

REGISTRATION ETC. OF SCOTTISH AND NORTHERN IRISH ORDERS

32.7. Registration of Scottish and Northern Irish orders

On receipt of a certified copy of a Scottish order or a Northern Irish order for registration, a court officer in the principal registry (who is the prescribed officer for the purposes of section 17(2) of the 1950 Act) will—
   (a) enter particulars of the order in Part 2 of the register;
   (b) notify the clerk of the Court of Session or the registrar in Northern Ireland, as the case may be, that the order has been registered; and
   (c) file the certified copy of the order and any statutory declaration, affidavit[GL] or statement as to the amount of any arrears due under the order.

32.8. Application to adduce evidence before High Court

The Part 18 procedure applies to an application by a person liable to make payments under a Scottish order registered in the High Court to adduce before that court any evidence on which that person would be entitled to rely in any proceedings brought before the court by which the order was made for the variation or discharge of the order.

32.9.— Notice of variation etc. of Scottish and Northern Irish orders

(1) This rule applies where—
   (a) a Scottish order or a Northern Irish order, which is registered in the High Court, is discharged or varied; and
   (b) notice of the discharge or variation is given to a court officer in the High Court (who is the prescribed officer for the purposes of section 23(1)(a) of the 1950 Act).

(2) On receipt of a notice of discharge or variation, the court officer will enter particulars of the notice in Part 2 of the register.

The Family Procedure Rules 2010

32.10.— Cancellation of registration of Scottish and Northern Irish orders

(1) The Part 18 procedure applies to an application for the cancellation of the registration of a Scottish order or a Northern Irish order in the High Court.

(2) The application must be made without notice to the person liable to make payments under the order.

(3) If the registration of the order is cancelled, the court officer will—
  (a) note the cancellation in Part II of the register; and
  (b) send written notice of the cancellation to—
    (i) the clerk of the Court of Session or the registrar in Northern Ireland, as the case may be; and
    (ii) the court officer in any magistrates' court in which the order has been registered in accordance with section 2(5) of the 1958 Act.

32.11.— Enforcement

(1) The Part 18 procedure applies to an application for or with respect to the enforcement of a Scottish order or a Northern Irish order registered in the High Court.

(2) The application may be made without notice to the person liable to make payments under the order.

32.12. Inspection of register and copies of order

Any person—
  (a) who is entitled to receive, or liable to make, payments under a maintenance order made by the High Court, the Court of Session or the Court of Judicature of Northern Ireland; or
  (b) with the permission of the court,

may—
  (i) inspect the register; or
  (ii) request a copy of any order registered in the High Court under Part 2 of the 1950 Act and any statutory declaration, affidavit$^{(GL)}$ or statement filed with the order.

CHAPTER 3

Registration of maintenance orders under the 1958 act

32.13. Interpretation

In this Chapter "the register" means the register kept for the purposes of the 1958 Act.

32.14. Registration of orders – prescribed period

The prescribed period for the purpose of section 2(2) of the 1958 Act is 14 days.

(Section 2(2) sets out the period during which an order, which is to be registered in a magistrates' court, may not be enforced)

32.15.— Application for registration of a maintenance order in a magistrates' court

(1) An application under section 2(1) of the 1958 Act may be made by sending to the court officer at the court which made the order—
  (a) a certified copy of the maintenance order; and
  (b) two copies of the application.

(2) When, on the grant of an application, the court officer sends the certified copy of the maintenance order to the magistrates' court in accordance with section 2(2), the court officer must—
  (a) note on the order that the application for registration has been granted; and
  (b) send to the magistrates' court a copy of the application for registration of the order.

(3) On receiving notice that the magistrates' court has registered the order, the court officer must enter particulars of the registration in the court records.

32.16.— Registration in a magistrates' court of an order registered in the High Court
(1) This rule applies where—
  (a) a maintenance order is registered in the High Court in accordance with section 17(4) of the 1950 Act; and
  (b) the court officer receives notice that the magistrates' court has registered the order in accordance with section 2(5) of the 1958 Act.
(2) The court officer must enter particulars of the registration in Part II of the register.

32.17.— Registration in the High Court of a magistrates' court order
(1) This rule applies where a court officer receives a certified copy of a magistrates' court order for registration in accordance with section 2(4)(c) of the 1958 Act.
(2) The court officer must register the order in the High Court by—
  (a) filing the copy of the order; and
  (b) entering particulars in—
    (i) the register; or
    (ii) if the order is received in a district registry, the cause book or cause card.
(3) The court officer must notify the magistrates' court that the order has been registered.

32.18.— Registration in the High Court of an order registered in a magistrates' court
(1) This rule applies where—
  (a) an order has been registered in the magistrates' court in accordance with section 17(4) of the 1950 Act; and
  (b) a sheriff court in Scotland or a magistrates' court in Northern Ireland has—
    (i) made an order for the registration of that order in the High Court; and
    (ii) sent a certified copy of the maintenance order to the court officer of the High Court in accordance with section 2(4)(c) of the 1958 Act.
(2) The court officer must register the order in the High Court by—
  (a) filing the copy of the order; and
  (b) entering particulars in the register.
(3) The court officer must notify—
  (a) the court which made the order; and
  (b) the magistrates' court in which the order was registered in accordance with section 17(4) of the 1950 Act,
that the order has been registered in the High Court.

32.19.— Variation or discharge of an order registered in a magistrates' court
(1) This rule applies where a maintenance order is registered in a magistrates' court under Part 1 of the 1958 Act.
(2) If the court which made the order makes an order varying or discharging that order the court officer must send a certified copy of the order of variation or discharge to the magistrates' court.
(3) If the court officer receives from the magistrates' court a certified copy of an order varying the maintenance order the court officer must—
  (a) file the copy of the order; and
  (b) enter the particulars of the variation in the place where the details required by rule 32.15(3) were entered.

32.20.— Variation or discharge of an order registered in the High Court
(1) This rule applies where a maintenance order is registered in the High Court under Part 1 of the 1958 Act.
(2) If the court officer receives from the magistrates' court a certified copy of an order varying or discharging the maintenance order the court officer must—
  (a) file the copy of the order;
  (b) enter the particulars of the variation or discharge in—
    (i) the register; or

(ii) if the order is received in a district registry, the cause book or cause card; and
(c) send notice of the variation or discharge to the court officer of a county court—
  (i) who has notified the court officer of enforcement proceedings in that court relating to the maintenance order; or
  (ii) to whom a payment is to be made under an attachment of earnings order made by the High Court for the enforcement of the registered order.

32.21.— Cancellation of registration – orders registered in the High Court
(1) This rule applies where an order is registered in the High Court.
(2) A person giving notice under section 5(1) of the 1958 Act must give the notice to the court officer.
(3) The court officer must take the steps mentioned in paragraph (4) if—
  (a) notice is given under section 5 of the 1958 Act; and
  (b) the court officer is satisfied, by a witness statement by the person entitled to receive payments under the order that no enforcement proceedings in relation to the order, that were started before the giving of the notice, remain in force.
(4) The court officer must, if satisfied as mentioned in paragraph (3)—
  (a) cancel the registration by entering particulars of the notice in the register or cause book (or cause card) as the case may be; and
  (b) send notice of the cancellation to—
    (i) the court which made the order; and
    (ii) where applicable, to the magistrates' court in which the order was registered in accordance with section 17(4) of the 1950 Act.
(5) Where the cancellation results from a notice given under section 5(1) of the 1958 Act, the court officer must state that fact in the notice of cancellation sent in accordance with paragraph (4)(b).
(6) If notice is received from a magistrates' court that the registration in that court under the 1958 Act of an order registered in the High Court in accordance with section 17(4) of the 1950 Act has been cancelled, the court officer must note the cancellation in Part II of the register.

32.22.— Cancellation of registration – orders registered in a magistrates' court
(1) Where the court gives notice under section 5(2) of the 1958 Act, the court officer must endorse the notice on the certified copy of the order of variation or discharge sent to the magistrates' court in accordance with rule 32.19(2).
(2) Where notice is received from a magistrates' court that registration of an order made by the High Court or a county court under Part 1 of the 1958 Act has been cancelled, the court officer must enter particulars of the cancellation in the place where the details required by rule 32.15(3) were entered.

CHAPTER 4

REGISTRATION AND ENFORCEMENT OF CUSTODY ORDERS UNDER THE 1986 ACT

32.23. Interpretation
In this Chapter—
"appropriate court" means, in relation to—
  (a) Scotland, the Court of Session;
  (b) Northern Ireland, the High Court in Northern Ireland; and
  (c) a specified dependent territory, the corresponding court in that territory;
"appropriate officer" means, in relation to—
  (a) the Court of Session, the Deputy Principal Clerk of Session;

(b) the High Court in Northern Ireland, the Master (Care and Protection) of that court; and
(c) the appropriate court in a specified dependent territory, the corresponding officer of that court;

"Part 1 order" means an order under Part 1 of the 1986 Act;

"the register" means the register kept for the purposes of Part 1 of the 1986 Act; and

"specified dependent territory" means a dependent territory specified in column 1 of Schedule 1 to the Family Law Act 1986 (Specified Dependent Territories) Order 1991.

32.24.— Prescribed officer and functions of the court

(1) The prescribed officer for the purposes of sections 27(4) and 28(1) of the 1986 Act is the family proceedings department manager of the principal registry.

(2) The function of the court under sections 27(3) and 28(1) of the 1986 Act shall be performed by a court officer.

32.25.— Application for the registration of an order made by the High Court or a county court

(1) An application under section 27 of the 1986 Act for the registration of an order made in the High Court or a county court may be made by sending to a court officer at the court which made the order—
  (a) a certified copy of the order;
  (b) a copy of any order which has varied the terms of the original order;
  (c) a statement which—
    (i) contains the name and address of the applicant and the applicant's interest under the order;
    (ii) contains—
      (aa) the name and date of birth of the child in respect of whom the order was made;
      (bb) the whereabouts or suspected whereabouts of the child; and
      (cc) the name of any person with whom the child is alleged to be;
    (iii) contains the name and address of any other person who has an interest under the order and states whether the order has been served on that person;
    (iv) states in which of the jurisdictions of Scotland, Northern Ireland or a specified dependent territory the order is to be registered;
    (v) states that to the best of the applicant's information and belief, the order is in force;
    (vi) states whether, and if so where, the order is already registered;
    (vii) gives details of any order known to the applicant which affects the child and is in force in the jurisdiction in which the order is to be registered;
    (viii) annexes any document relevant to the application; and
    (ix) is verified by a statement of truth; and
  (d) a copy of the statement referred to in paragraph (c).

(2) On receipt of the documents referred to in paragraph (1), the court officer will, subject to paragraph (4)—
  (a) keep the original statement and send the other documents to the appropriate officer;
  (b) record in the court records the fact that the documents have been sent to the appropriate officer; and
  (c) file a copy of the documents.

(3) On receipt of a notice that the document has been registered in the appropriate court the court officer will record that fact in the court records.

(4) The court officer will not send the documents to the appropriate officer if it appears to the court officer that—
  (a) the order is no longer in force; or

The Family Procedure Rules 2010

   (b)   the child has reached the age of 16.
(5) Where paragraph (4) applies—
   (a)   the court officer must, within 14 days of the decision, notify the applicant of the decision of the court officer in paragraph (4) and the reasons for it; and
   (b)   the applicant may apply to a judge, but not a district judge, in private for an order that the documents be sent to the appropriate court.

32.26.— Registration of orders made in Scotland, Northern Ireland or a specified dependent territory

(1) This rule applies where the prescribed officer receives, for registration, a certified copy of an order made in Scotland, Northern Ireland or a specified dependent territory.
(2) The prescribed officer will—
   (a)   enter in the register—
      (i)   the name and address of the applicant and the applicant's interest under the order;
      (ii) the name and date of birth of the child and the date the child will attain the age of 16;
      (iii) the whereabouts or suspected whereabouts of the child; and
      (iv) the terms of the order, its date and the court which made it;
   (b)   file the certified copy and accompanying documents; and
   (c)   notify—
      (i)   the court which sent the order; and
      (ii) the applicant,
      that the order has been registered.

32.27.— Revocation and variation of an order made in the High Court or a county court

(1) Where a Part 1 order, registered in an appropriate court, is varied or revoked, the court officer of the court making the order of variation or revocation will—
   (a)   send a certified copy of the order of variation or revocation to—
      (i)   the appropriate officer; and
      (ii) if a different court, the court which made the Part 1 order;
   (b)   record in the court records the fact that a copy of the order has been sent; and
   (c)   file a copy of the order.
(2) On receipt of notice from the appropriate court that its register has been amended, this fact will be recorded by the court officer of—
   (a)   the court which made the order of variation or revocation; and
   (b)   if different, the court which made the Part 1 order.

32.28.— Registration of varied, revoked or recalled orders made in Scotland, Northern Ireland or a specified dependent territory

(1) This rule applies where the prescribed officer receives a certified copy of an order made in Scotland, Northern Ireland or a specified dependent territory which varies, revokes or recalls a registered Part 1 order.
(2) The prescribed officer shall enter particulars of the variation, revocation or recall in the register and give notice of the entry to—
   (a)   the court which sent the certified copy;
   (b)   if different, the court which made the Part 1 order;
   (c)   the applicant for registration; and
   (d)   if different, the applicant for the variation, revocation of recall of the order.
(3) An application under section 28(2) of the 1986 Act must be made in accordance with the Part 19 procedure.
(4) The applicant for the Part 1 order, if not the applicant under section 28(2) of the 1986 Act, must be made a defendant to the application.

(5) Where the court cancels a registration under section 28(2) of the 1986 Act, the court officer will amend the register and give notice of the amendment to the court which made the Part 1 order.

32.29. Interim directions

The following persons will be made parties to an application for interim directions under section 29 of the 1986 Act—
- (a) the parties to the proceedings for enforcement; and
- (b) if not a party to those proceedings, the applicant for the Part 1 order.

32.30.— Staying and dismissal of enforcement proceedings

(1) The following persons will be made parties to an application under section 30(1) or 31(1) of the 1986 Act—
- (a) the parties to the proceedings for enforcement which are sought to be stayed(GL); and
- (b) if not a party to those proceedings, the applicant for the Part 1 order.

(2) Where the court makes an order under section 30(2) or (3) or section 31(3) of the 1986 Act, the court officer will amend the register and give notice of the amendment to—
- (a) the court which made the Part 1 order; and
- (b) the applicants for—
  - (i) registration;
  - (ii) enforcement; and
  - (iii) stay(GL) or dismissal of the enforcement proceedings.

32.31. Particulars of other proceedings

A party to proceedings for or relating to a Part 1 order who knows of other proceedings which relate to the child concerned (including proceedings out of the jurisdiction and concluded proceedings) must file a witness statement which—
- (a) states in which jurisdiction and court the other proceedings were begun;
- (b) states the nature and current state of the proceedings and the relief claimed or granted;
- (c) sets out the names of the parties to the proceedings and their relationship to the child;
- (d) if applicable and if known, states the reasons why relief claimed in the proceedings for or relating to the Part 1 order was not claimed in the other proceedings; and
- (e) is verified by a statement of truth.

32.32. Inspection of register

The following persons may inspect any entry in the register relating to a Part 1 order and may request copies of the order any document relating to it—
- (a) the applicant for registration of the Part 1 order;
- (b) a person who, to the satisfaction of a district judge, has an interest under the Part 1 order; and
- (c) a person who obtains the permission of a district judge.

PART 32 COMMENTARY

Part 32 is not supplemented by a practice direction.

Part 32 relates to the registration and enforcement of UK maintenance and custody orders.

Chapter 2 deals with registration under the Maintenance Orders Act 1950 (registration of maintenance orders from Scotland and Northern Ireland).

Chapter 3 deals with registration under the Maintenance Orders Act 1958 (registration of county court or High Court maintenance orders in the magistrates' court, or magistrates' court orders in the High Court).

The Family Procedure Rules 2010

Chapter 4 deals with registration and enforcement under the Family Law Act 1986 (which deals with recognition, registration and enforcement of orders relating to children within the United Kingdom and Isle of Man).

The form relevant to Part 32 is D151 – Application for registration of a maintenance order in a magistrates' court.

PART 33

ENFORCEMENT

CHAPTER 1

GENERAL RULES

33.1.— Application
(1) The rules in this Part apply to an application made in the High Court and a county court to enforce an order made in family proceedings.
(2) Part 50 of, and Schedules 1 and 2 to, the CPR apply, as far as they are relevant and with necessary modification (including the modifications referred to in rule 33.7), to an application made in the High Court and a county court to enforce an order made in family proceedings.

SECTION 1

ENFORCEMENT OF ORDERS FOR THE PAYMENT OF MONEY

33.2. Application of the Civil Procedure Rules
Part 70 of the CPR applies to proceedings under this Section as if—
    (a) in rule 70.1, in paragraph (2)(d), "but does not include a judgment or order for the payment of money into court" is omitted; and
    (b) rule 70.5 is omitted.

33.3.— How to apply
(1) Except where a rule or practice direction otherwise requires, an application for an order to enforce an order for the payment of money must be made in a notice of application accompanied by a statement which must—
    (a) state the amount due under the order, showing how that amount is arrived at; and
    (b) be verified by a statement of truth.
(2) The notice of application may either—
    (a) apply for an order specifying the method of enforcement; or
    (b) apply for an order for such method of enforcement as the court may consider appropriate.
(3) If an application is made under paragraph (2)(b), an order to attend court will be issued and rule 71.2(6) and (7) of the CPR will apply as if the application had been made under that rule.

33.4.— Transfer of orders
(1) This rule applies to an application for the transfer—
    (a) to the High Court of an order made in a designated county court; and
    (b) to a designated county court of an order made in the High Court.
(2) The application must be—
    (a) made without notice; and
    (b) accompanied by a statement which complies with rule 33.3(1).
(3) The transfer will have effect upon the filing of the application.
(4) Where an order is transferred from a designated county court to the High Court—

(a) it will have the same force and effect; and
(b) the same proceedings may be taken on it,

as if it were an order of the High Court.

(5) This rule does not apply to the transfer of orders for periodical payments or for the recovery of arrears of periodical payments.

SECTION 2

COMMITTAL AND INJUNCTION

33.5.— General rule — committal hearings to be in public

(1) The general rule is that proceedings in the High Court for an order of committal will be heard in public.

(2) An order of committal may be heard in private where this is permitted by rule 6 of Order 52 of the RSC (cases in which a court may sit in private).

33.6.— Proceedings in the principal registry treated as pending in a designated county court

(1) This rule applies where an order for the warrant of committal of any person to prison has been made or issued in proceedings which are—
(a) in the principal registry; and
(b) treated as pending in a designated county court or a county court.

(2) The person subject to the order will, wherever located, be treated for the purposes of section 122 of the County Courts Act 1984 as being out of the jurisdiction of the principal registry.

(3) Where—
(a) a committal is for failure to comply with the terms of an injunction$^{(GL)}$; or
(b) an order or warrant for the arrest or committal of any person is made or issued in proceedings under Part 4 of the 1996 Act in the principal registry which are treated as pending in a county court,

the order or warrant may, if the court so directs, be executed by the tipstaff within any county court.

33.7.— Specific modifications of the CCR

(1) CCR Order 29, rule 1 (committal for breach of an order or undertaking) applies to—
(a) section 8 orders, except those referred to in paragraph (2)(a); and
(b) orders under the following sections of the 1989 Act—
(i) section 14A (special guardianship orders);
(ii) section 14B(2)(b) (granting of permission on making a special guardianship order to remove a child from the United Kingdom);
(iii) section 14C(3)(b) (granting of permission to remove from the United Kingdom a child who is subject to a special guardianship order); and
(iv) section 14D (variation or discharge of a special guardianship order),

as if paragraph (3) of that rule were substituted by the following paragraph—

"(3) In the case of a section 8 order (within the meaning of section 8(2) of the Children Act 1989) or an order under section 14A, 14B(2)(b), 14C(3)(b) or 14D of the Children Act 1989 enforceable by committal order under paragraph (1), the judge or the district judge may, on the application of the person entitled to enforce the order, direct that the proper officer issue a copy of the order, endorsed with or incorporating a notice as to the consequences of disobedience, for service in accordance with paragraph (2), and no copy of the order shall be issued with any such notice endorsed or incorporated save in accordance with such a direction.".

(2) CCR Order 29, rule 1 applies to—

The Family Procedure Rules 2010

    (a)   contact orders to which a notice has been attached under section 11I of the 1989 Act or under section 8(2) of the Children and Adoption Act 2006;
    (b)   orders under section 11J of the 1989 Act (enforcement orders); and
    (c)   orders under paragraph 9 of Schedule A1 to the 1989 Act (orders following breach of enforcement orders),

as if paragraph (3) were omitted.

33.8. Section 118 County Courts Act 1984 and the tipstaff

For the purposes of section 118 of the County Courts Act 1984 in its application to the hearing of family proceedings at the Royal Courts of Justice or the principal registry, the tipstaff is deemed to be an officer of the court.

CHAPTER 2

COMMITTAL BY WAY OF JUDGMENT SUMMONS

33.9. Interpretation

In this Chapter, unless the context requires otherwise—

"order" means an order made in family proceedings for the payment of money;

"judgment creditor" means a person entitled to enforce an order under section 5 of the Debtors Act 1869;

"debtor" means a person liable under an order; and

"judgment summons" means a summons under section 5 of the Debtor's Act 1869 requiring a debtor to attend court.

33.10.— Application

(1) An application for the issue of a judgment summons may be made—
    (a)   in the case of an order of the High Court—
        (i)   where the order was made in matrimonial proceedings, to the principal registry, a district registry or a divorce county court, whichever in the opinion of the judgment creditor is most convenient;
        (ii)   where the order was made in civil partnership proceedings, to the principal registry, a district registry or a civil partnership proceedings county court, whichever in the opinion of the judgment creditor is the most convenient; and
        (iii)   in any other case, to the principal registry, a district registry or a designated county court, whichever in the opinion of the judgment creditor is most convenient;
    (b)   in the case of an order of a divorce county court, to whichever divorce county court is in the opinion of the judgment creditor most convenient; and
    (c)   in the case of an order of a civil partnership proceedings county court, to whichever civil partnership proceedings county court is in the opinion of the judgment creditor most convenient,

having regard (in any case) to the place where the debtor resides or carries on business and irrespective of the court or registry in which the order was made.

(2) An application must be accompanied by a statement which—
    (a)   complies with rule 33.3(1);
    (b)   contains all the evidence on which the judgment creditor intends to rely; and
    (c)   has exhibited to it a copy of the order.

33.11.— Judgment summons

(1) If the debtor is in default under an order of committal made on a previous judgment summons in respect of the same order, a judgment summons must not be issued without the court's permission.

(2) A judgment summons must—
    (a)   be accompanied by the statement referred to in rule 33.10(2) and
    (b)   be served on the debtor personally not less than 14 days before the hearing.

(3) A debtor served with the judgment summons under paragraph (2)(b) must be paid or offered a sum reasonably sufficient to cover the expenses of travelling to and from the court at which the debtor is summoned to appear.

33.12. Successive judgment summonses

Subject to rule 33.11(1), successive judgment summonses may be issued even if the debtor has ceased to reside or carry on business at the address stated in the application for the issue of a judgment summons since the issue of the original judgment summons.

33.13. Requirement for personal service

In proceedings for committal by way of judgment summons, the following documents must be served personally on the debtor—

- (a) where the court has summonsed the debtor to attend and the debtor has failed to do so, the notice of the date and time fixed for the adjourned hearing; and
- (b) copies of the judgment summons and the documents mentioned in rule 33.10(2).

33.14.— Committal on application for judgment summons

(1) No person may be committed on an application for a judgment summons unless—

- (a) where the proceedings are in the High Court, the debtor has failed to attend both the hearing that the debtor was summonsed to attend and the adjourned hearing;
- (b) where the proceedings are in a county court, an order is made under section 110(2) of the County Courts Act 1984; or
- (c) the judgment creditor proves that the debtor—
    - (i) has, or has had, since the date of the order the means to pay the sum in respect of which the debtor has made default; and
    - (ii) has refused or neglected, or refuses or neglects, to pay that sum.

(2) The debtor may not be compelled to give evidence.

33.15. Orders for the benefit of different persons

Where an applicant has obtained one or more orders in the same application but for the benefit of different persons—

- (a) where the judgment creditor is a child, the applicant may apply for the issue of a judgment summons in respect of those orders on behalf of the judgment creditor without seeking permission to act as the child's litigation friend; and
- (b) only one judgment summons need be issued in respect of those orders.

33.16.— Hearing of judgment summons

(1) On the hearing of the judgment summons the court may—

- (a) where the order is for lump sum provision or costs; or
- (b) where the order is an order for maintenance pending suit, an order for maintenance pending outcome of proceedings or an order for other periodical payments and it appears to the court that the order would have been varied or suspended if the debtor had made an application for that purpose,

make a new order for payment of the amount due under the original order, together with the costs of the judgment summons, either at a specified time or by instalments.

(2) If the court makes an order of committal, it may direct its execution to be suspended on terms that the debtor pays to the judgment creditor—

- (a) the amount due;
- (b) the costs of the judgment summons; and
- (c) any sums accruing due under the original order,

either at a specified time or by instalments.

(3) All payments under a new order or an order of committal must be made to the judgment creditor unless the court directs otherwise.

(4) Where an order of committal is suspended on such terms as are mentioned in paragraph (2)—
- (a) all payments made under the suspended order will be deemed to be made—
  - (i) first, in or towards the discharge of any sums from time to time accruing due under the original order; and
  - (ii) secondly, in or towards the discharge of a debt in respect of which the judgment summons was issued and the costs of the summons; and
- (b) the suspended order must not be executed until the judgment creditor has filed a statement of default on the part of the debtor.

33.17.— Special provisions as to judgment summonses in the High Court

(1) The court may summons witnesses to give evidence to prove the means of the debtor and may issue a witness summons for that purpose.

(2) Where the debtor appears at the hearing, the court may direct that the travelling expenses paid to the debtor be allowed as expenses of a witness.

(3) Where the debtor appears at the hearing and no order of committal is made, the court may allow the debtor's proper costs including compensation for any loss of earnings.

(4) When the court makes—
- (a) a new order; or
- (b) an order of committal,

a court officer must send notice of the order to the debtor and, if the original order was made in another court, to that court.

(5) An order of committal must be directed—
- (a) where the order is to be executed by the tipstaff, to the tipstaff; or
- (b) where the order is to be executed by a deputy tipstaff, to the county court within the district of which the debtor is to be found.

33.18.— Special provisions as to judgment summonses in designated county courts

(1) Rules 1, 2, 3(2), 5, 7(3) and 9(2) of Order 28 of the CCR (which deal with the issue of a judgment summons in a county court and the subsequent procedure) do not apply to judgment summons issued in a designated county court.

(2) Rule 9(1) of Order 28 of the CCR (notification of order on judgment of High Court) applies to such a summons as if for the words "the High Court" there were substituted the words—
- (a) "any other court" where they first appear; and
- (b) "that other court" where they next appear.

(3) Rule 7(1) and (2) of Order 28 of the CCR (suspension of a committal order) apply to such a summons subject to rule 33.16(2) and (3).

CHAPTER 3

Attachment of earnings

33.19. Proceedings in the Principal Registry

The Attachment of Earnings Act 1971 and Order 27 of the CCR (attachment of earnings) apply to the enforcement of an order made in family proceedings in the principal registry which are treated as pending in a designated county court as if they were an order made by such a court.

CHAPTER 4

Warrant of execution

33.20. Applications to vary existing orders

Where an application is pending for a variation of—
- (a) a financial order;
- (b) an order under section 27 of the 1973 Act; or
- (c) an order under Part 9 of Schedule 5 to the 2004 Act,

no warrant of execution may be issued to enforce payment of any sum due under those orders, except with the permission of the district judge.

33.21. Section 103 County Courts Act 1984
Where a warrant of execution has been issued to enforce an order made in family proceedings pending in the principal registry which are treated as pending in a designated county court, the goods and chattels against which the warrant has been issued must, wherever they are located, be treated for the purposes of section 103 of the County Courts Act 1984 as being out of the jurisdiction of the principal registry.

CHAPTER 5

COURT'S POWER TO APPOINT A RECEIVER

33.22. Application of the CPR
Part 69 of the CPR applies to proceedings under this Part.

CHAPTER 6

ORDERS TO OBTAIN INFORMATION FROM JUDGMENT DEBTORS

33.23. Application of the CPR
Part 71 of the CPR applies to proceedings under this Part.

CHAPTER 7

THIRD PARTY DEBT ORDERS

33.24.— Application of the CPR
(1) Part 72 of the CPR applies to proceedings under this Part with the following modifications.
   (2) In rule 72.4—
      (a) in paragraph (1), for "a judge" there is substituted "the court"; and
      (b) in paragraph (2), for "judge" there is substituted "court".
(3) In rule 72.7, in paragraph (2)(a), after "the Royal Courts of Justice" insert ", or the principal registry".
   (4) Rule 72.10 is omitted.

CHAPTER 8

CHARGING ORDER, STOP ORDER, STOP NOTICE

33.25.— Application of the CPR
(1) Part 73 of the CPR applies to proceedings under this Part with the following modifications.
   (2) In rule 73.1, paragraph (2), sub-paragraphs (b) and (c) are omitted.
(3) For rule 73.2, there is substituted "This Section applies to an application by a judgment creditor for a charging order under section 1 of the 1979 Act.".
   (4) In rule 73.3, paragraph (2), sub-paragraphs (b) and (c) are omitted.
   (5) In rule 73.4—
      (a) in paragraph (1), for "a judge" there is substituted "the court,"; and
      (b) in paragraph (2), for "judge" there is substituted "court".
   (6) In rule 73.9, in the parenthesis after paragraph (1)—
      (a) "and regulation 51.4 of the 1992 Regulations" is omitted;
      (b) for "provides" there is substituted "provide", and
      (c) ", or (where the 1992 Regulations apply) of the authority," is omitted.
   (7) In rule 73.10—
      (a) in paragraph (1), for "a claim" there is substituted "an application";

The Family Procedure Rules 2010

- (b) in paragraph (2) and the parenthesis following it, for "A claim" each time it appears there is substituted "An application";
- (c) in paragraph (3), for "claimant" there is substituted "applicant";
- (d) in paragraph (4), for "claim form" there is substituted "application"; and
- (e) in paragraph (5), for "claimant's" there is substituted "applicant's".

(8) In rule 73.11, "funds in court or" is omitted.

(9) In rule 73.12—
- (a) paragraph (1)(a) is omitted;
- (b) in paragraph (1)(b) "other than securities held in court" is omitted;
- (c) in paragraph (2), in sub-paragraph (b), for "claim form" there is substituted "application notice"; and
- (d) in paragraph (3)—
  - (i) "or claim form" is omitted; and
  - (ii) for sub-paragraph (b) there is substituted "the person specified in rule 73.5(1)(d)".

(10) Rule 73.13 is omitted.

(11) In rule 73.14, in paragraph (1), "other than securities held in court" is omitted.

(12) In rule 73.16—
- (a) in paragraph (a) for "; and" there is substituted "."; and
- (b) paragraph (b) is omitted.

PART 33 COMMENTARY

Part 33 is supplemented by PD33A in relation to the enforcement of undertakings.

Part 33 makes provision for applications for the enforcement of orders in family proceedings.

Rule 33.1 applies Part 50 of the CPR and Schs 1 and 2 (containing provisions from the RSC 1965 and the CCR 1981) as far as they are relevant and with necessary modification to applications to enforce an order made in family proceedings.

Section 1 deals with the enforcement of orders for the payment of money.

Rule 33.2 applies with specified modifications Part 70 of the CPR which contains the General Rules about enforcement of Judgments and Orders.

Rule 33.3(2) contains a new provision for an application for an order for such method of enforcement as the court may consider appropriate. If that route is chosen then r 71.2(6) and (7) apply, requiring attendance at court and the provision of information.

Section 2 deals with committals, and injunctions, and provides, at r 33.7 specified amendments to CCR Order 29, r 1.

Chapter 2 deals with Committal by Judgment Summons.

Chapter 3 deals with Attachment of Earnings.

Chapter 4 deals with Warrant of Execution.

Chapter 5 deals with the Court's power to appoint a receiver, by way of applying Part 69 of the CPR.

Chapter 6 applies Part 71 of the CPR in relation to obtaining information from Judgment Debtors.

FPR 2010, Practice Direction 33A

Chapter 7 applies Part 72 of the CPR to applications for Third Party Debt Orders.

Chapter 8 applies Part 73 of the CPR to applications for a Charging order, Stop order, or Stop notice.

PD33A makes specific provision in relation to the enforcement of undertakings.

The form of an undertaking to do or abstain from doing any act must be endorsed with a notice as follows (PD33A, para 1.4):

> *'You may be sent to prison for contempt of court if you break the promises that you have given to the court.'*

And the person giving the undertaking must make a signed statement as follows (para 1.5):

> *'I understand the undertaking that I have given, and that if I break any of my promises to the court I may be sent to prison for contempt of court'.*

The statement need not be given before the court in person and may be endorsed on the court copy of the undertaking or filed in a separate document.

Specific provision is made about undertakings in financial remedy orders. It is directed that any undertaking for the payment of money in a financial remedy order may be enforced as if it were an order and Part 33 applies accordingly. Such an undertaking must be endorsed as follows (para 2.2):

> *'If you fail to pay any sum of money which you have promised the court that you would pay, a person entitled to enforce the undertaking may apply to the court for an order. If it is proved that you have had the means to pay the sum but you have refused or neglected to pay that sum, you may be sent to prison.'*

The person giving the undertaking must make a signed statement as follows (para 2.3):

> *'I understand the undertaking that I have given, and that if I break my promise to the court to pay any sum of money, I may be sent to prison.'*

Again, the statement need not be given in person before the court.

Forms relevant to Part 33 are D62 – request for issue of judgment summons, N56, N323, N336, N337, N349, N379, N380.

PRACTICE DIRECTION 33A – ENFORCEMENT OF UNDERTAKINGS

This Practice Direction supplements FPR Part 33

ENFORCEMENT OF UNDERTAKING TO DO OR ABSTAIN FROM DOING ANY ACT OTHER THAN THE PAYMENT OF MONEY

1.1 Rule 33.1(2) provides that Part 50 of, and Schedules 1 and 2 to, the CPR (which contain the Rules of the Supreme Court (RSC) and County Court Rules (CCR) respectively) apply, as far as they are relevant and with necessary modification, to an application made in the High Court and a county court to enforce an order made in family proceedings.

1.2 Subject to the Debtors Act 1869 (which makes provision in relation to orders for the payment of money), RSC Order 45.5 and CCR Order 29.1 enable a judgment or order to be enforced by committal for contempt of court where—

The Family Procedure Rules 2010

(a) a person who is required by a judgment or order to do an act has refused or neglected to do that act within the specified time; or
(b) a person disobeys a judgment or order requiring him to abstain from doing an act.

1.3 These Rules apply to undertakings as they apply to orders, with necessary modifications.

1.4 The form of an undertaking to do or abstain from doing any act must be endorsed with a notice setting out the consequences of disobedience, as follows:

"You may be sent to prison for contempt of court if you break the promises that you have given to the court".

1.5 The person giving the undertaking must make a signed statement to the effect that he or she understands the terms of the undertaking being given and the consequences of failure to comply with it, as follows:

"I understand the undertaking that I have given, and that if I break any of my promises to the court I may be sent to prison for contempt of court".

1.6 The statement need not be given before the court in person. It may be endorsed on the court copy of the undertaking or may be filed in a separate document such as a letter.

ENFORCEMENT OF UNDERTAKING FOR THE PAYMENT OF MONEY

2.1 Any undertaking for the payment of money that has effect as if it was an order made under Part 2 of the Matrimonial Causes Act 1973 may be enforced as if it was an order and Part 33 applies accordingly.

2.2 The form of an undertaking for the payment of money that has effect as if it were an order under Part 2 of the Matrimonial Causes Act 1973 must be endorsed with a notice setting out the consequences of disobedience, as follows:

"If you fail to pay any sum of money which you have promised the court that you would pay, a person entitled to enforce the undertaking may apply to the court for an order. If it is proved that you have had the means to pay the sum but you have refused or neglected to pay that sum, you may be sent to prison."

2.3 The person giving the undertaking must make a signed statement to the effect that he or she understands the terms of the undertaking being given and the consequences of failure to comply with it, as follows:

"I understand the undertaking that I have given, and that if I break my promise to the court to pay any sum of money, I may be sent to prison".

2.4 The statement need not be given before the court in person. It may be endorsed on the court copy of the undertaking or may be filed in a separate document such as a letter.

PART 34

RECIPROCAL ENFORCEMENT OF MAINTENANCE ORDERS

34.1.— Scope and interpretation of this Part
 (1) This Part contains rules about the reciprocal enforcement of maintenance orders.
 (2) In this Part—
"the 1920 Act" means the Maintenance Orders (Facilities for Enforcement) Act 1920;
"the 1972 Act" means the Maintenance Orders (Reciprocal Enforcement) Act 1972;
"the 1982 Act" means the Civil Jurisdiction and Judgments Act 1982;
"the 1988 Convention" means the Convention on jurisdiction and the enforcement of judgments in civil and commercial matters done at Lugano on 16th September 1988;

"the Judgments Regulation" means Council Regulation (EC) No. 44/2001 of 22nd December 2000 on jurisdiction and the recognition and enforcement of judgments in civil and commercial matters; and

"the Lugano Convention" means the Convention on jurisdiction and the recognition and enforcement of judgments in civil and commercial matters, between the European Community and the Republic of Iceland, the Kingdom of Norway, the Swiss Confederation and the Kingdom of Denmark signed on behalf of the European Community on 30th October 2007.

(3) Chapter 1 of this Part relates to the enforcement of maintenance orders in accordance with the 1920 Act.

(4) Chapter 2 of this Part relates to the enforcement of maintenance orders in accordance with Part 1 of the 1972 Act.

(5) Chapter 3 of this Part relates to the enforcement of maintenance orders in accordance with—

 (a)   the 1982 Act;
 (b)   the Judgments Regulation; and
 (c)   the Lugano Convention.

34.2.— Meaning of prescribed officer in a magistrates' court

(1) For the purposes of the 1920 Act, the prescribed officer in relation to a magistrates' court is the designated officer for that court.

(2) For the purposes of Part 1 of the 1972 Act and section 5(2) of the 1982 Act, the prescribed officer in relation to a magistrates' court is the justices' clerk for the local justice area in which the court is situated.

34.3. Registration of maintenance orders in magistrates' courts in England and Wales

Where a magistrates' court is required by any of the enactments referred to in rule 34.1(2) to register a foreign order the court officer must—

 (a)   enter and sign a memorandum of the order in the register kept in accordance with rules made under section 144 of the Magistrates' Courts Act 1980; and
 (b)   state on the memorandum the statutory provision under which the order is registered.

CHAPTER 1

Enforcement of maintenance orders under the Maintenance Orders (Facilities for Enforcement) Act 1920

34.4.— Interpretation

(1) In this Chapter—

"payer", in relation to a maintenance order, means the person liable to make the payments for which the order provides; and

"reciprocating country" means a country or territory to which the 1920 Act extends.

(2) In this Chapter, an expression defined in the 1920 Act has the meaning given to it in that Act.

34.5.— Confirmation of provisional orders made in a reciprocating country

(1) This rule applies where, in accordance with section 4(1) of the 1920 Act, the court officer receives a provisional maintenance order.

(2) The court must fix the date, time and place for a hearing.

(3) The court officer must register the order in accordance with rule 34.3.

(4) The court officer must serve on the payer—

 (a)   certified copies of the provisional order and accompanying documents; and
 (b)   a notice—
  (i)   specifying the time and date fixed for the hearing; and
  (ii)   stating that the payer may attend to show cause why the order should not be confirmed.

The Family Procedure Rules 2010

(5) The court officer must inform—
- (a) the court which made the provisional order; and
- (b) the Lord Chancellor,

whether the court confirms, with or without modification, or decides not to confirm, the order.

34.6. Payment of sums due under registered orders

Where an order made by a reciprocating country is registered in a magistrates' court, the court must order payments due to be made to the court officer.

(Practice Direction 34A contains further provisions relating to the payment of sums due under registered orders.)

34.7.— Enforcement of sums due under registered orders

(1) This rule applies to—
- (a) an order made in a reciprocating country which is registered in a magistrates' court; and
- (b) a provisional order made in a reciprocating country which has been confirmed by a magistrates' court.

(2) The court officer must—
- (a) collect the monies due under the order in the same way as for a magistrates' court maintenance order; and
- (b) send the monies collected to—
  - (i) the court in the reciprocating country which made the order; or
  - (ii) such other person or authority as that court or the Lord Chancellor may from time to time direct.

(3) The court officer may take proceedings in that officer's own name for enforcing payment of monies due under the order.

34.8.— Prescribed notice for the taking of further evidence

(1) This rule applies where a court in a reciprocating country has sent a provisional order to a magistrates' court for the purpose of taking further evidence.

(2) The court officer must send a notice to the person who applied for the provisional order specifying—
- (a) the further evidence required; and
- (b) the time and place fixed for taking the evidence.

34.9. Transmission of maintenance orders made in a reciprocating country to the High Court

A maintenance order to be sent by the Lord Chancellor to the High Court in accordance with section 1(1) of the 1920 Act will be—
- (a) sent to the senior district judge who will register it in the register kept for the purpose of the 1920 Act; and
- (b) filed in the principal registry.

34.10.— Transmission of maintenance orders made in the High Court to a reciprocating country

(1) This rule applies to maintenance orders made in the High Court.

(2) An application for a maintenance order to be sent to a reciprocating country under section 2 of the 1920 Act must be made in accordance with this rule.

(3) The application must be made to a district judge in the principal registry unless paragraph (4) applies.

(4) If the order was made in the course of proceedings in a district registry, the application may be made to a district judge in that district registry.

(5) The application must be—
- (a) accompanied by a certified copy of the order; and
- (b) supported by a record of the sworn written evidence.

(6) The written evidence must give—

(a) the applicant's reason for believing that the payer resides in the reciprocating country;
(b) such information as the applicant has as to the whereabouts of the payer; and
(c) such other information as may be set out in Practice Direction 34A.

34.11.— Inspection of the register in the High Court

(1) A person may inspect the register and request copies of a registered order and any document filed with it if the district judge is satisfied that that person is entitled to, or liable to make, payments under a maintenance order made in—
(a) the High Court; or
(b) a court in a reciprocating country.

(2) The right to inspect the register referred to in paragraph (1) may be exercised by—
(a) a solicitor acting on behalf of the person entitled to, or liable to make, the payments referred to in that paragraph; or
(b) with the permission of the district judge, any other person.

CHAPTER 2

Enforcement of maintenance orders under Part 1 of the 1972 Act

34.12.— Interpretation

(1) In this Chapter—
(a) "reciprocating country" means a country to which Part 1 of the 1972 Act extends; and
(b) 'relevant court in the reciprocating country' means, as the case may be—
  (i) the court which made the order which has been sent to England and Wales for confirmation;
  (ii) the court which made the order which has been registered in a court in England and Wales;
  (iii) the court to which an order made in England and Wales has been sent for registration; or
  (iv) the court to which a provisional order made in England and Wales has been sent for confirmation.

(2) In this Chapter, an expression defined in the 1972 Act has the meaning given to it in that Act.

(3) In this Chapter, "Hague Convention Countries" means the countries listed in Schedule 1 to the Reciprocal Enforcement of Maintenance Orders (Hague Convention Countries) Order 1973.

34.13.— Scope

(1) Section 1 of this Chapter contains rules relating to the reciprocal enforcement of maintenance orders under Part 1 of the 1972 Act.

(2) Section 2 of this Chapter modifies the rules contained in Section 1 of this Chapter in their application to—
(a) the Republic of Ireland;
(b) the Hague Convention Countries; and
(c) the United States of America.

(Practice Direction 34A sets out in full the rules for the Republic of Ireland, the Hague Convention Countries and the United States of America as modified by Section 2 of this Chapter.)

The Family Procedure Rules 2010

SECTION 1

RECIPROCAL ENFORCEMENT OF MAINTENANCE ORDERS UNDER PART 1 OF THE 1972 ACT

34.14. Application for transmission of maintenance order to reciprocating country
An application for a maintenance order to be sent to a reciprocating country under section 2 of the 1972 Act must be made in accordance with Practice Direction 34A.

34.15. Certification of evidence given on provisional orders
A document setting out or summarising evidence is authenticated by a court in England and Wales by a certificate signed, as the case may be, by—
    (a)   one of the justices; or
    (b)   the District Judge (Magistrates' Courts),
before whom that evidence was given.
(Section 3(5)(b), 5(4) and 9(5) of the 1972 Act require a document to be authenticated by the court.)

34.16.— Confirmation of a provisional order made in a reciprocating country
    (1)   This rule applies to proceedings for the confirmation of a provisional order made in a reciprocating country.
    (2)   Paragraph (3) applies on receipt by the court of—
        (a)   a certified copy of the order; and
        (b)   the documents required by the 1972 Act to accompany the order.
    (3)   On receipt of the documents referred to in paragraph (2)—
        (a)   the court must fix the date, time and place for a hearing or a directions appointment; and
        (b)   the court officer must send to the payer notice of the date, time and place fixed together with a copy of the order and accompanying documents.
    (4)   The date fixed for the hearing must be not less than 21 days beginning with the date on which the court officer sent the documents to the payer in accordance with paragraph (2).
    (5)   The court officer will send to the relevant court in the reciprocating country a certified copy of any order confirming or refusing to confirm the provisional order.
    (6)   This rule does not apply to the confirmation of a provisional order made in a reciprocating country varying a maintenance order to which sections 5(5) or 9(6) of the 1972 Act applies.
(Section 5(5) and 7 of the 1972 Act provide for proceedings for the confirmation of a provisional order.)
(Provision in respect of confirmation of a provisional order varying a maintenance order under the 1972 Act is in rules made under section 144 of the Magistrates' Courts Act 1980.)
(Rule 34.22 provides for the transmission of documents to a court in a reciprocating country.)

34.17.— Consideration of revocation of a provisional order made by a magistrates' court
    (1)   This rule applies where—
        (a)   a magistrates' court has made a provisional order by virtue of section 3 of the 1972 Act;
        (b)   before the order is confirmed, evidence is taken by the court or received by it as set out in section 5(9) of the 1972 Act; and
        (c)   on consideration of the evidence the court considers that the order ought not to have been made.
(Section 5(9) of the 1972 Act provides that a magistrates' court may revoke a provisional order made by it, before the order has been confirmed in a reciprocating country, if it receives new evidence.)
    (2)   The court officer must serve on the person who applied for the provisional order ("the applicant") a notice which must—

(a) set out the evidence taken or received by the court;
(b) inform the applicant that the court considers that the order ought not to have been made; and
(c) inform the applicant that the applicant may—
  (i) make representations in relation to that evidence either orally or in writing; and
  (ii) adduce further evidence.

(3) If an applicant wishes to adduce further evidence—
(a) the applicant must notify the court officer at the court which made the order;
(b) the court will fix a date for the hearing of the evidence; and
(c) the court officer will notify the applicant in writing of the date fixed.

34.18.— Notification of variation or revocation of a maintenance order by the High Court or a county court

(1) This rule applies where—
(a) a maintenance order has been sent to a reciprocating country in pursuance of section 2 of the 1972 Act; and
(b) the court makes an order, not being a provisional order, varying or revoking that order.

(2) The court officer must send a certified copy of the order of variation or revocation to the relevant court in the reciprocating country.

(Rule 34.22 provides for the transmission of documents to a court in a reciprocating country.)

34.19.— Notification of confirmation or revocation of a maintenance order by a magistrates' court

(1) This rule applies where a magistrates' court makes an order—
(a) not being a provisional order, revoking a maintenance order to which section 5 of the 1972 Act applies;
(b) under section 9 of the 1972 Act, revoking a registered order; or
(c) under section 7(2) of the 1972 Act, confirming an order to which section 7 of that Act applies.

(2) The court officer must send written notice of the making, revocation or confirmation of the order, as appropriate, to the relevant court in the reciprocating country.

(3) This rule does not apply to a provisional order varying a maintenance order to which sections 5 or 9 of the 1972 Act apply.

(Section 5 of the 1972 Act applies to a provisional order made by a magistrates' court in accordance with section 3 of that Act which has been confirmed by a court in a reciprocating country.)

(Provision in respect of notification of variation of a maintenance order by a magistrates' court under the 1972 Act is made in rules made under section 144 of the Magistrates' Courts Act 1980.)

(Rule 34.22 provides for the transmission of documents to a court in a reciprocating country.)

34.20.— Taking of evidence for court in reciprocating country

(1) This rule applies where a request is made by or on behalf of a court in a reciprocating country for the taking of evidence for the purpose of proceedings relating to a maintenance order to which Part 1 of the 1972 Act applies.

(Section 14 of the 1972 Act makes provision for the taking of evidence needed for the purpose of certain proceedings.)

(2) The High Court has power to take the evidence where—
(a) the request for evidence relates to a maintenance order made by a superior court in the United Kingdom; and
(b) the witness resides in England and Wales.

(3) The county court has power to take the evidence where—

The Family Procedure Rules 2010

      (a)   the request for evidence relates to a maintenance order made by a county court; and

      (b)   the maintenance order has not been registered in a magistrates' court under the 1958 Act.

(4) The following magistrates' courts have power to take the evidence, that is—

      (a)   where the proceedings in the reciprocating country relate to a maintenance order made by a magistrates' court, the court which made the order;

      (b)   where the proceedings relate to an order which is registered in a magistrates' court, the court in which the order is registered; and

      (c)   a magistrates' court to which the Secretary of State sends the request to take evidence.

(5) A magistrates' court not mentioned in paragraph (4) has power to take the evidence if the magistrates' court which would otherwise have that power consents because the evidence could be taken more conveniently.

(6) The evidence is to be taken in accordance with Part 22.

34.21.— Request for the taking of evidence by a court in a reciprocating country

(1) This rule applies where a request is made by a magistrates' court for the taking of evidence in a reciprocating country in accordance with section 14(5) of the 1972 Act.

(2) The request must be made in writing to the court in the reciprocating country.

(Rule 34.22 provides for the transmission of documents to a court in a reciprocating country.)

34.22.— Transmission of documents

(1) This rule applies to any document, including a notice or request, which is required to be sent to a court in a reciprocating country by—

      (a)   Part 1 of the 1972 Act; or

      (b)   Section 1 of Chapter 2 of this Part of these rules.

(2) The document must be sent to the Lord Chancellor for transmission to the court in the reciprocating country.

34.23.— Method of payment under registered orders

(1) Where an order is registered in a magistrates' court in accordance with section 6(3) of the 1972 Act, the court must order that the payment of sums due under the order be made—

      (a)   to the court officer for the registering court; and

      (b)   at such time and place as the court officer directs.

(Section 6(3) of the 1972 Act makes provision for the registration of maintenance orders made in a reciprocating country.)

(2) Where the court orders payments to be made to the court officer, whether in accordance with paragraph (1) or otherwise, the court officer must send the payments—

      (a)   by post to either—

            (i)   the court which made the order; or

            (ii)   such other person or authority as that court, or the Lord Chancellor, directs; or

      (b)   if the court which made the order is a country or territory specified in the Practice Direction 34A—

            (i)   to the Crown Agents for Overseas Governments and Administrations for transmission to the person to whom they are due; or

            (ii)   as the Lord Chancellor directs.

(Practice Direction 34A contains further provisions relating to the payment of sums due under registered orders.)

34.24.— Enforcement of payments under registered orders

(1) This rule applies where a court has ordered periodical payments under a registered maintenance order to be made to the court officer.

(2) The court officer must take reasonable steps to notify the payee of the means of enforcement available.

(3) Paragraph (4) applies where periodical payments due under a registered order are in arrears.

(4) The court officer, on that officer's own initiative—
- (a) may; or
- (b) if the sums due are more than 4 weeks in arrears, must,

proceed in that officer's own name for the recovery of the sums due unless of the view that it is unreasonable to do so.

34.25.— Notification of registration and cancellation

(1) The court officer must send written notice to the Lord Chancellor of the due registration of orders registered in accordance with section 6(3), 7(5), or 10(4) of the 1972 Act.

(2) The court officer must, when registering an order in accordance with section 6(3), 7(5), 9(10), 10(4) or (5) or 23(3) of the 1972 Act, send written notice to the payer stating—
- (a) that the order has been registered;
- (b) that payments under the order should be made to the court officer; and
- (c) the hours during which and the place at which the payments should be made.

(3) The court officer must, when cancelling the registration of an order in accordance with section 10(1) of the 1972 Act, send written notice of the cancellation to the payer.

SECTION 2

MODIFICATION OF RULES IN SECTION 1 OF THIS CHAPTER

SUB-SECTION 1

REPUBLIC OF IRELAND

34.26.— Application of Section 1 of this Chapter to the Republic of Ireland

(1) In relation to the Republic of Ireland, Section 1 of this Chapter has effect as modified by this rule.

(2) A reference in this rule and in any rule which has effect in relation to the Republic of Ireland by virtue of this rule to—
- (a) the 1972 Act is a reference to the 1972 Act as modified by Schedule 2 to the Reciprocal Enforcement of Maintenance Orders (Republic of Ireland) Order 1993; and
- (b) a section under the 1972 Act is a reference to the section so numbered in the 1972 Act as so modified.

(3) A reference to a reciprocating country in rule 34.12(1) and Section 1 of this Chapter is a reference to the Republic of Ireland.

(4) In the words in brackets at the end of rule 34.15 (certification of evidence given on provisional orders), for the sections mentioned substitute "section 3(5)(b) or 5(3)".

(5) Rules 34.16 (confirmation of provisional orders) and 34.21 (request for the taking of evidence by a court in a reciprocating country) do not apply.

(6) For rule 34.17 (consideration of revocation of a provisional order made by a magistrates' court) substitute—

34.17.— "Consideration of confirmation of a provisional order made by a magistrates' court

(1) This rule applies where—
- (a) a magistrates' court has made a provisional order by virtue of section 3 of the 1972 Act;
- (b) the payer has made representations or adduced evidence to the court; and

The Family Procedure Rules 2010

    (c) the court has fixed a date for the hearing at which it will consider confirmation of the order.
  (2) The court officer must serve on the applicant for the provisional order—
    (a) a copy of the representations or evidence; and
    (b) written notice of the date fixed for the hearing.".
 (7) For rules 34.18 and 34.19 (notification of variation or revocation) substitute—

34.18. "Notification of variation or revocation of a maintenance order by the High Court
 Where the High Court makes an order varying or revoking an order to which section 5 of the 1972 Act applies the court officer must send—
    (a) a certified copy of the order of variation or revocation; and
    (b) a statement as to the service on the payer of the documents mentioned in section 5(3) of the 1972 Act,
 to the court in the Republic of Ireland.
 (Rule 34.22 provides for the transmission of documents to a court in a reciprocating country.)

34.19. Notification of revocation of a maintenance order by a magistrates' court
 Where a magistrates' court makes an order revoking an order to which section 5 of the 1972 Act applies, the court officer must send written notice of the making of the order to the Lord Chancellor.
 (Section 5 of the 1972 Act applies to a maintenance order sent to the Republic of Ireland in accordance with section 2 of that Act and a provisional order made by a magistrates' court in accordance with section 3 of that Act which has been confirmed by such a court.)
 (Provision in respect of notification of variation of a maintenance order by magistrates' court under the 1972 Act is made in rules made under section 144 of the Magistrates' Courts Act 1980.)".
 (8) For rule 34.23(2) (method of payment under registered orders), substitute—
  "(2) Where the court orders payment to be made to the court officer, the court officer must send the payments by post—
    (a) to the payee under the order; or
    (b) where a public authority has been authorised by the payee to receive the payments, to that public authority.".
 (9) For rule 34.24 (enforcement of payments under registered orders), substitute—

34.24.— "Enforcement of payments under registered orders
  (1) This rule applies where periodical payments under a registered order are in arrears.
  (2) The court officer must, on the written request of the payee, proceed in that officer's own name for the recovery of the sums due unless of the view that it is unreasonable to do so.
  (3) If the sums due are more than 4 weeks in arrears the court officer must give the payee notice in writing of that fact stating the particulars of the arrears.".
 (10) For rule 34.25 (notification of registration and cancellation) substitute—

34.25. "Notification of registration and cancellation
 The court officer must send written notice to—
    (a) the Lord Chancellor, on the due registration of an order under section 6(3) or 10(4) of the 1972 Act; and
    (b) to the payer under the order, on—
      (i) the registration of an order under section 10(4) of the 1972 Act; or
      (ii) the cancellation of the registration of an order under section 10(1) of that Act. ".
 (11) After rule 34.25 insert—

34.25A.— "Other notices under section 6 of the 1972 Act
- (1) A notice required under section 6(6) or (10) of the 1972 Act must be in the form referred to in a practice direction.
- (2) Where a magistrates' court sets aside the registration of an order following an appeal under section 6(7) of the 1972 Act, the court officer must send written notice of the court's decision to the payee.

(Section 6(6) of the 1972 Act provides for notice of registration in a United Kingdom court of a maintenance order made in the Republic of Ireland, and section 6(10) of that Act for notice that a maintenance order made in the Republic of Ireland has not been registered in a United Kingdom court.)"

SUB-SECTION 2

HAGUE CONVENTION COUNTRIES

34.27.— Application of Section 1 of this Chapter to the Hague Convention Countries

(1) In relation to the Hague Convention Countries, Section 1 of this Chapter has effect as modified by this rule.

(2) A reference in this rule, and in any rule which has effect in relation to the Hague Convention Countries by virtue of this rule to—
- (a) the 1972 Act is a reference to the 1972 Act as modified by Schedule 2 to the Reciprocal Enforcement of Maintenance Orders (Hague Convention Countries) Order 1993; and
- (b) a section under the 1972 Act is a reference to the section so numbered in the 1972 Act as so modified.

(3) A reference to a reciprocating country in rule 34.12(1) and Section 1 of this Chapter is a reference to a Hague Convention Country.

(4) Rules 34.15 (certification of evidence given on provisional orders), 34.16 (confirmation of provisional orders), 34.19 (notification of confirmation or revocation of a maintenance order by a magistrates' court) and 34.21 (request for the taking of evidence by a court in a reciprocating country) do not apply.

(5) For rule 34.17 (consideration of revocation of a provisional order made by a magistrates' court) substitute—

34.17.— "Consideration of revocation of a maintenance order made by a magistrates' court
- (1) This rule applies where—
  - (a) an application has been made to a magistrates' court by a payee for the revocation of an order to which section 5 of the 1972 Act applies; and
  - (b) the payer resides in a Hague Convention Country.
- (2) The court officer must serve on the payee, by post, a copy of any representations or evidence adduced by or on behalf of the payer.

(Provision relating to consideration of variation of a maintenance order made by a magistrates' court to which section 5 of the 1972 Act applies is made in rules made under section 144 of the Magistrates' Courts Act 1980.)".

(6) For rule 34.18 (notification of variation or revocation of a maintenance order by the High Court or county court) substitute—

34.18.— "Notification of variation or revocation of a maintenance order by the High Court or a county court
- (1) This rule applies if the High Court or a county court makes an order varying or revoking a maintenance order to which section 5 of the 1972 Act applies.
- (2) If the time for appealing has expired without an appeal having been entered, the court officer will send to the Lord Chancellor—
  - (a) the documents required by section 5(8) of the 1972 Act; and
  - (b) a certificate signed by the district judge stating that the order of variation or revocation is enforceable and no longer subject to the ordinary forms of review.

The Family Procedure Rules 2010

(3) A party who enters an appeal against the order of variation or revocation must, at the same time, give written notice to the court officer.".

(7) For rule 34.23(2) (method of payment under registered orders) substitute—

"(2) Where the court orders payment to be made to the court officer, the court officer must send the payments by post to the payee under the order.".

(8) For rule 34.25 (notification of registration and cancellation) substitute—

34.25. "Notification of registration and cancellation

The court officer must send written notice to—

    (a) the Lord Chancellor, on the due registration of an order under section 10(4) of the 1972 Act; and

    (b) the payer under the order, on—

        (i) the registration of an order under section 10(4) of the 1972 Act; or

        (ii) the cancellation of the registration of an order under section 10(1) of the 1972 Act.".

(9) After rule 34.25 insert—

34.25A.— "General provisions as to notices

(1) A notice to a payer of the registration of an order in a magistrates' court in accordance with section 6(3) of the 1972 Act must be in the form referred to in a practice direction.

(Section 6(8) of the 1972 Act requires notice of registration to be given to the payer.)

(2) If the court sets aside the registration of a maintenance order following an appeal under section 6(9) of the 1972 Act, the court officer must send written notice of the decision to the Lord Chancellor.

(3) A notice to a payee that the court officer has refused to register an order must be in the form referred to in a practice direction.

(Section 6(11) of the 1972 Act requires notice of refusal of registration to be given to the payee.)

(4) Where, under any provision of Part 1 of the 1972 Act, a court officer serves a notice on a payer who resides in a Hague Convention Country, the court officer must send to the Lord Chancellor a certificate of service.".

SUB-SECTION 3

UNITED STATES OF AMERICA

34.28.— Application of Section 1 of this Chapter to the United States of America

(1) In relation to the United States of America, Section 1 of this Chapter has effect as modified by this rule.

(2) A reference in this rule and in any rule which has effect in relation to the United States of America by virtue of this rule to—

    (a) the 1972 Act is a reference to the 1972 Act as modified by Schedule 1 to the Reciprocal Enforcement of Maintenance Orders (United States of America) Order 2007; and

    (b) a section under the 1972 Act is a reference to the section so numbered in the 1972 Act as so modified.

(3) A reference to a reciprocating country in rule 34.12(1) and Section 1 of this Chapter is a reference to the United States of America.

(4) Rules 34.15 (certification of evidence given on provisional orders), 34.16 (confirmation of provisional orders), 34.19 (notification of confirmation or revocation of a maintenance order made by a magistrates' court) and 34.21 (request for the taking of evidence in a reciprocating country) do not apply.

(5) For rule 34.17 (consideration of revocation of a provisional order made by a magistrates' court) substitute—

34.17.— "Consideration of revocation of a maintenance order made by a magistrates' court

(1) This rule applies where—
  (a) an application has been made to a magistrates' court by a payee for the revocation of an order to which section 5 of the 1972 Act applies; and
  (b) the payer resides in the United States of America.
(2) The court officer must serve on the payee by post a copy of any representations or evidence adduced by or on behalf of the payer.

(Provision relating to consideration of variation of a maintenance order made by a magistrates' court to which section 5 of the 1972 Act applies is made in rules made under section 144 of the Magistrates' Courts Act 1980.)".

(6) For rule 34.18 (notification of variation or revocation), substitute—

34.18. "Notification of variation or revocation

If the High Court or a county court makes an order varying or revoking a maintenance order to which section 5 of the 1972 Act applies, the court officer will send to the Lord Chancellor the documents required by section 5(7) of that Act.".

(7) For rule 34.23(2) (method of payment under registered orders) substitute—
 "(2) Where the court orders payment to be made to the court officer, the court officer must send the payments by post to the payee under the order.".

(8) For rule 34.25 (notification of registration and cancellation) substitute—

34.25. "Notification of registration and cancellation

The court officer must send written notice to—
  (a) the Lord Chancellor, on the due registration of an order under section 10(4) of the 1972 Act; or
  (b) the payer under the order, on—
    (i) the registration of an order under section 10(4) of the 1972 Act; or
    (ii) the cancellation of the registration of an order under section 10(1) of that Act. "

CHAPTER 3

ENFORCEMENT OF MAINTENANCE ORDERS UNDER THE CIVIL JURISDICTION AND JUDGMENTS ACT 1982, THE JUDGMENTS REGULATION AND THE LUGANO CONVENTIO

SECTION 1

REGISTRATION AND ENFORCEMENT IN A MAGISTRATES' COURT OF MAINTENANCE ORDERS MADE IN A CONTRACTING STATE TO THE 1968 CONVENTION, A CONTRACTING STATE TO THE 1988 CONVENTION, A REGULATION STATE OR A STATE BOUND BY THE LUGANO CONVENTION

34.29. Interpretation

In this Section—
  (a) an expression defined in the 1982 Act has the meaning given to it in that Act; and
  (b) "the 1958 Act" means the Maintenance Orders Act 1958.

34.30.— Registration of maintenance orders

(1) In this rule, "assets to which the 1958 Act applies" means assets against which, after registration in the High Court, the maintenance order could be enforced under Part 1 of the 1958 Act.
(2) This rule applies where the court officer for a magistrates' court receives—
  (a) an application under Article 31 of the 1968 Convention for the enforcement of a maintenance order made in a Contracting State other than the United Kingdom;

The Family Procedure Rules 2010

   (b) an application under Article 31 of the 1988 Convention for the enforcement of a maintenance order made in a State bound by the 1988 Convention other than a Member State of the European Union;
   (c) an application under Article 38 of the Judgments Regulation for the enforcement of a maintenance order made in a Regulation State other than the United Kingdom; or
   (d) an application under Article 38 of the Lugano Convention for the enforcement of a maintenance order made in a State bound by the Lugano Convention other than a Member State of the European Union.

(3) The court officer must—
   (a) take such steps as appear appropriate for ascertaining whether the payer resides within the local justice area for which the court acts; and
   (b) consider any available information as to the nature and location of the payer's assets.

(4) If the court officer is satisfied that the payer—
   (a) does not reside within the local justice area for which the court acts; and
   (b) does not have assets to which the 1958 Act applies,

the court officer must refuse the application and return the application to the Lord Chancellor stating the information the court officer has as to the whereabouts of the payer and the nature and location of the payer's assets.

(5) If the court officer is satisfied that the payer—
   (a) does not reside within the local justice area for which the court acts; but
   (b) has assets to which the 1958 Act applies,

then either—
      (i) the court officer must register the order; or
      (ii) if the court officer believes that the payer is residing within the local justice area in which another magistrates' court acts, the court officer may refuse the application and return the documents to the Lord Chancellor with the information referred to in paragraph (4) above.

(6) Except where paragraphs (4) or (5) apply, the court officer must register the order unless—
   (a) in the case of an application under Article 31 of the 1968 Convention, Articles 27 or 28 of that Convention apply; and
   (b) in the case of an application under Article 31 of the 1988 Convention, Articles 27 or 28 of that Convention apply.

(7) If the court officer refuses to register an order to which this rule relates the court officer must notify the applicant.

(8) If the court officer registers an order the court officer must send written notice of that fact to—
   (a) the Lord Chancellor;
   (b) the payer; and
   (c) the applicant.

(9) If the court officer considers that it would be appropriate for all or part of a registered order to be enforced in the High Court the court officer must notify the applicant—
   (a) that the court officer so considers it appropriate; and
   (b) that the applicant may apply under the 1958 Act for the order to be registered in the High Court.

34.31.— Appeal from a decision relating to registration

(1) This rule applies to an appeal under—
   (a) Article 36 or Article 40 of the 1968 Convention;
   (b) Article 36 or Article 40 of the 1988 Convention;
   (c) Article 43 of the Judgments Regulation; or
   (d) Article 43 of the Lugano Convention.

(2) The appeal must be to the magistrates' court—

(a) in which the order is registered; or
(b) in which the application for registration has been refused,
as the case may be.

34.32.— Payment of sums due under a registered order

(1) Where an order is registered in accordance with section 5(3) of the 1982 Act or Article 38 of the Judgments Regulation or Article 38 of the Lugano Convention, the court must order that payment of sums due under the order be made—
(a) to the court officer for the registering court; and
(b) at such time and place as the court officer directs.

(2) Where the court orders payments to be made to the court officer, whether in accordance with paragraph (1) or otherwise, the court officer must send the payments by post either—
(a) to the court which made the order; or
(b) to such other person or authority as that court, or the Lord Chancellor, directs.

(Practice Direction 34A contains further provisions relating to the payment of sums due under registered orders.)

34.33.— Enforcement of payments under registered orders

(1) This rule applies where a court has ordered periodical payments under a registered maintenance order to be made to the court officer for a magistrates' court.

(2) The court officer must take reasonable steps to notify the payee of the means of enforcement available.

(3) Paragraph (4) applies where periodical payments due under a registered order are in arrears.

(4) The court officer, on that officer's own initiative—
(a) may; or
(b) if the sums due are more than 4 weeks in arrears, must,
proceed in that officer's own name for the recovery of the sums due unless of the view that it is unreasonable to do so.

34.34.— Variation and revocation of registered orders

(1) This rule applies where the court officer for a registering court receives notice that a registered maintenance order has been varied or revoked by a competent court in a Contracting State to the 1968 Convention, a Contracting State to the 1988 Convention (other than a Member State of the European Union), a Regulation State or a State bound by the Lugano Convention, other than a Member State of the European Union.

(2) The court officer for the registering court must—
(a) register the order of variation or revocation; and
(b) send notice of the registration by post to the payer and payee under the order.

34.35.— Transfer of registered order

(1) This rule applies where the court officer for the court where an order is registered considers that the payer is residing within the local justice area in England and Wales for which another magistrates' court acts.

(2) Subject to paragraph (4), the court officer must transfer the order to the other court by sending to that court—
(a) the information and documents relating to the registration;
(b) a certificate of arrears, if applicable, signed by the court officer;
(c) a statement giving such information as the court officer possesses as to the whereabouts of the payer and the nature and location of the payer's assets; and
(d) any other relevant documents which the court officer has relating to the case.

(3) The information and documents referred to in paragraph (2)(a) are those required, as appropriate, under—

The Family Procedure Rules 2010

    (a)   Articles 46 and 47 of the 1968 Convention;
    (b)   Articles 46 and 47 of the 1988 Convention;
    (c)   Article 53 of the Judgments Regulation; or
    (d)   Article 53 of the Lugano Convention.

(4) If an application is pending in the registering court for the registration of the whole or part of the order in the High Court under Part 1 of the 1958 Act, the court officer must not transfer the order, or the part to which the application relates, under paragraph (2).

(5) The court officer must give notice of the transfer of an order to—
    (a)   the payee; and
    (b)   the Lord Chancellor.

(6) If an order is transferred, the court officer for the court to which it is transferred must register the order.

34.36.— Cancellation of registered orders

(1) Where the court officer for the registering court—
    (a)   has no reason to transfer a registered order under rule 34.35; and
    (b)   considers that the payer under the registered order is not residing within the local justice area for which the court acts and has no assets to which the 1958 Act applies,

the court officer must cancel the registration of the order.

(2) The court officer must—
    (a)   give notice of cancellation to the payee; and
    (b)   send the information and documents relating to the registration and the other documents referred to in rule 34.35(2) to the Lord Chancellor.

SECTION 2

RECIPROCAL ENFORCEMENT IN A CONTRACTING STATE OR REGULATION STATE OF ORDERS OF A COURT IN ENGLAND AND WALES

34.37.— Application in a magistrates' court for a maintenance order, or revocation of a maintenance order, to which the 1982 Act, the Judgments Regulations or the Lugano Convention applies

(1) This rule applies where a person applies to a magistrates' court for a maintenance order, or for the revocation of a maintenance order, in relation to which the court has jurisdiction by virtue of the 1982 Act, the Judgments Regulation or the Lugano Convention, and the respondent is outside the United Kingdom.

(2) On the making of the application the court officer shall send the following documents to the Lord Chancellor—
    (a)   notice of the proceedings, including a statement of the grounds of the application;
    (b)   a statement signed by the court officer giving such information as he has regarding the whereabouts of, and information to assist in identifying, the respondent; and
    (c)   where available, a photograph of the respondent.

(3) In considering whether or not to make a maintenance order pursuant to an application to which paragraph (1) applies, where the respondent does not appear and is not represented at the hearing the court shall take into account any written representations made and any evidence given by the respondent under these rules.

(Part 27 makes provision relating to attendance at hearings and directions appointments.)
(Part 9 makes provision for applications relating to financial remedies including those under Schedule 1 to the 1989 Act, Part 1 of the 1978 Act, and Schedule 6 to the 2004 Act.)
(Rules made under section 144 of the Magistrates' Courts Act 1980 make provision for applications to vary maintenance orders made in magistrates' courts.)

34.38.— Admissibility of Documents

(1) This rule applies to a document, referred to in paragraph (2) and authenticated in accordance with paragraph (3), which comprises, records or summarises evidence given in, or information relating to, proceedings in a court in another part of the UK, another Contracting State to the 1968 Convention or the 1988 Convention, Regulation State or State bound by the Lugano Convention, and any reference in this rule to "the court", without more, is a reference to that court.

(2) The documents referred to at paragraph (1) are documents which purport to—
- (a) set out or summarise evidence given in the court;
- (b) have been received in evidence the court;
- (c) set out or summarise evidence taken in the court for the purpose of proceedings in a court in England and Wales to which the 1982 Act applies; or
- (d) record information relating to payments made under an order of the court.

(3) A document to which paragraph (1) applies shall, in any proceedings in a magistrates' court in England and Wales relating to a maintenance order to which the 1982 Act applies, be admissible as evidence of any fact stated in it to the same extent as oral evidence of that fact is admissible in those proceedings.

(4) A document to which paragraph (1) applies shall be deemed to be authenticated—
- (a) in relation to the documents listed at paragraph 2(a) or (c), if the document purports to be—
  - (i) certified by the judge or official before whom the evidence was given or taken; or
  - (ii) the original document recording or summarising the evidence, or a true copy of that document;
- (b) in relation to a document listed at paragraph (2)(b), if the document purports to be certified by a judge or official of the court to be, or to be a true copy of, the document received in evidence; and
- (c) in relation to the document listed at paragraph (2)(d), if the document purports to be certified by a judge or official of the court as a true record of the payments made under the order.

(5) It shall not be necessary in any proceedings in which evidence is to be received under this rule to prove the signature or official position of the person appearing to have given the certificate referred to in paragraph (4).

(6) Nothing in this rule shall prejudice the admission in evidence of any document which is admissible in evidence apart from this rule.

(7) Any request by a magistrates' court in England and Wales for the taking or providing of evidence by a court in another part of the United Kingdom or in another Contracting State to the 1968 Convention or the 1988 Convention or the Lugano Convention (other than a Member State of the European Union) for the purpose of proceedings to which the 1982 Act applies shall be communicated in writing to the court in question.

(Chapter 2 of Part 24 makes provision for taking of evidence by a court in another Regulation State).

34.39.— Enforcement of orders of a magistrates' court

(1) This rule applies to applications to a magistrates' court under—
- (a) section 12 of the 1982 Act;
- (b) article 54 of the Judgments Regulation; or
- (c) article 54 of the Lugano Convention.

(2) A person who wishes to enforce in a Contracting State to the 1968 Convention, a Contracting State to the 1988 Convention (other than a Member State of the European Union), a Regulation State or a State bound by the Lugano Convention (other than a Member State of the European Union) a maintenance order obtained in a magistrates' court must apply for a certified copy of the order.

(3) An application under this rule must be made in writing to the court officer and must specify—

The Family Procedure Rules 2010

  (a) the names of the parties to the proceedings;
  (b) the date, or approximate date, of the proceedings in which the maintenance order was made and the nature of those proceedings;
  (c) the Contracting State or Regulation State in which the application for recognition or enforcement has been made or is to be made; and
  (d) the postal address of the applicant.

(4) The court officer must, on receipt of the application, send a copy of the order to the applicant certified in accordance with a practice direction.

(5) Paragraph (6) applies where—
  (a) a maintenance order is registered in a magistrates' court in England and Wales; and
  (b) a person wishes to obtain a certificate giving details of any payments made or arrears accrued under the order while it has been registered, for the purposes of an application made or to be made in connection with that order in—
    (i) another Contracting State to the 1968 Convention;
    (ii) another Contracting State to the 1988 Convention (other than a Member State of the European Union);
    (iii) another Regulation State;
    (iv) another State bound by the Lugano Convention (other than a Member State of the European Union); or
    (v) another part of the United Kingdom.

(6) The person wishing to obtain the certificate referred to in paragraph (5) may make a written application to the court officer for the registering court.

(7) On receipt of an application under paragraph (6) the court officer must send to the applicant a certificate giving the information requested.

(Rule 74.12 (application for certified copy of a judgment) and 74.13 (evidence in support) of the CPR apply in relation to the application for a certified copy of a judgment obtained in the High Court or a county court.)

PART 34 COMMENTARY

Part 34 is supplemented by PD34A - Reciprocal Enforcement of Maintenance Orders and PD34B. PD34A contains at Annex 1 modification to the rules in relation to the Republic of Ireland, at Annex 2, modification of the rules in relation to Hague Convention Countries, and at Annex 3, modification of the rules in relation to specified states of the Unites States of America. (It is anticipated that there will be amending order in May 2011 to reflect the EU Maintenance Regulation which will bring about changes to PD34A). PD34B is a pre existing Practice Note, *Tracing Payers Overseas* (10 February 1976) which has survived by virtue of the *Practice Direction – Practice Directions Relating to Family Proceedings in Force before 6th April 2011 which support the Family Procedure Rules 2010.*

Part 34 makes detailed provisions about the reciprocal enforcement of maintenance orders under the relevant statutes and international instruments. The applicable procedures for enforcement under the various enactments or instruments are set out in separate Chapters as follows:

Chapter 1 deals with the Maintenance Orders (Facilities for Enforcement) Act 1920 (which provides for enforcement in England of orders made in Guernsey, Jersey and certain other dependant territories and Commonwealth countries).

Chapter 2 deals with Part 1 of the Maintenance Orders (Reciprocal Enforcement) Act 1972 (which makes provision for the reciprocal enforcement of maintenance orders between different jurisdictions of the United Kingdom on the one hand, and reciprocating countries on the other).

Section 1 deals with applications to be sent to a reciprocating country; Section 2, subsection 1 modifies the rules in section 1 in relation to the Republic of Ireland, subsection 2 modifies the rules in relation to the Hague Convention countries, subsection 3 modifies the rules in relation to the United States of America.

Chapter 3 deals with enforcement of maintenance orders under the Civil Jurisdiction and Judgment Act 1982, the Judgments Regulation (which means Council Regulation (EC) No 44/2001 of 22nd December 2000) and the Lugano Convention.

Section 1 deals with registration and enforcement in a magistrates' court of maintenance orders made in a contracting state to the 1968 Convention, a contracting state to the 1988 Convention, a regulation state, or a state bound by the Lugano convention. Section 2 deals with reciprocal enforcement in a contracting state of an order of a court in England and Wales.

Provision is to be made in a new Chapter 4 in relation to the Maintenance Regulation (Council Regulation (EC) No 4/2009 of 18 December 2008 on jurisdiction, applicable law, recognition and enforcement of decision and cooperation relating to maintenance obligations) which is expected to come into effect on 18 June 2011.

Forms relevant to Part 34 are REMO 1 and 2 – Notice of Registration and Notice of Refusal of Registration.

PRACTICE DIRECTION 34A – RECIPROCAL ENFORCEMENT OF MAINTENANCE ORDERS

This Practice Direction is made by the President of the Family Division under the powers delegated to him by the Lord Chief Justice under Schedule 2, Part 1, paragraph 2(2) of the Constitutional Reform Act 2005, and is approved by the Parliamentary Under Secretary of State, by authority of the Lord Chancellor and comes into force on 6th April 2011

This Practice Direction supplements FPR Part 34

NOTING RECORD OF MEANS OF PAYMENT

1.1 Where a magistrates' court orders payments under a maintenance order to which Part 34 applies to be made in a particular way, the court must record that on a copy of the order.

1.2 If the court orders payment to be made to the court officer of a magistrates' court by a method referred to in section 59(6) of the Magistrates' Courts Act 1980, the court may vary the method of payment on the application of an interested party and where it does so the court must record the variation on a copy of the order.

(Section 59(6) refers to payment by standing order or other methods which require transfer between accounts of a specific amount on a specific date during the period for which the authority to make the payment is in force.)

The Family Procedure Rules 2010

NOTIFICATION BY COURT OFFICER

2.1 The court officer must, as soon as practicable, notify in writing the person liable to make the payments of the method by which they must be made.

2.2 If the court orders payment to be made to the court officer of a magistrates' court by a method referred to in section 59(6) of the Magistrates' Courts Act 1980 the court officer must inform the person liable to make the payments of the number and location of the account to which the payments must be made.

2.3 If the court varies the method of payment on the application of an interested party the court officer must, as soon as practicable, notify all interested parties in writing of the result of an application (including a decision to refer it to the court).

APPLICATIONS UNDER SECTION 2 OF THE 1920 ACT

3.1 This paragraph refers to an application for the transmission of a maintenance order to a reciprocating country under section 2 of the 1920 Act in accordance with rule 34.10.

3.2 The applicant's written evidence must include such information as may be required by the law of the reciprocating country for the purpose of enforcement of the order.

3.3 If, in accordance with section 2 of the 1920 Act, the court sends a maintenance order to the Lord Chancellor for transmission to a reciprocating country, it shall record the fact in the court records.

APPLICATIONS UNDER SECTION 2 OF THE 1972 ACT (RULE 34.14)

Introduction

4.1 An application for a maintenance order to be sent to a reciprocating country under section 2 of the 1972 Act is made by lodging specified documents with the court. The documents to be lodged vary according to which country it is intended that the maintenance order is be sent and the requirements are set out in this paragraph.

General provision

4.2 The general requirement is that the following documents should be lodged with the court—

(a) an affidavit by the applicant stating—
  (i) the reason that the applicant has for believing that the payer under the maintenance order is residing in the reciprocating country; and
  (ii) the amount of any arrears due to the applicant under the order, the date to which those arrears have been calculated and the date on which the next payment under the order falls due;
(b) a certified copy of the maintenance order;
(c) a statement giving such information as the applicant has as to the whereabouts of the payer;
(d) a statement giving such information as the applicant has for facilitating the identification of the payer, (including, if known to the applicant, the name and address of any employer of the payer, his occupation and the date and place of issue of any passport of the payer); and
(e) if available to the applicant, a photograph of the payer.

Republic of Ireland

4.3 If the country to which it is intended to send the maintenance order is the Republic of Ireland, then the following changes to the general requirements apply.

4.4 The applicant must lodge the following documents with the court in addition to those set out in paragraph 4.2—.

(a) a statement as to whether or not the payer appeared in the proceedings in which the maintenance order was made;
(b) if the payer did not so appear—
  (i) the original of a document which establishes that notice of the institution of proceedings was served on the payer; or
  (ii) a copy of such a document certified by the applicant or the applicant's solicitor to be a true copy;
(c) a document which establishes that notice of the order was sent to the payer; and
(d) if the payee received legal aid in the proceedings in which the order was made, a copy certified by the applicant or the applicant's solicitor to be a true copy of the legal aid certificate.

Hague Convention Country

4.5 If the country to which it is intended to send the maintenance order is a Hague Convention country, then the following changes to the general requirements apply.

4.6 In addition to the matters stated in that paragraph, the affidavit referred to in paragraph 4.2(a) must also state whether the time for appealing against the maintenance order has expired and whether an appeal is pending.

4.7 The applicant must lodge the following documents with the court in addition to those set out in paragraph 4.2—

(a) a statement as to whether or not the payer appeared in the proceedings in which the maintenance order was made;
(b) if the payer did not so appear—
  (i) the original of a document which establishes that notice of the institution of proceedings, including notice of the substance of the claim, was served on the payer; or
  (ii) a copy of such a document certified by the applicant or the applicant's solicitor to be a true copy;
(c) a document which establishes that notice of the order was sent to the payer;
(d) a written statement as to whether or not the payee received legal aid in the proceedings in which the order was made, or in connection with the application under section 2 of the 1972 Act; and
(e) if the payee did receive legal aid, a copy certified by the applicant or the applicant's solicitor to be a true copy of the legal aid certificate.

United States of America

4.8 If the country to which it is intended to send the maintenance order is a specified State of the United States of America, then the following changes to the general requirements apply.

4.9 There is no requirement to lodge a statement giving information as to the whereabouts of the payer since this information must be contained in the affidavit as mentioned in paragraph 4.10.

4.10 In addition to the matters stated in that paragraph, the affidavit referred to in paragraph 4.2(a) must also state—

(a) the address of the payee;
(b) such information as is known as to the whereabouts of the payer; and
(c) a description, so far as is known, of the nature and location of any assets of the payer available for execution.

4.11 The applicant must lodge three certified copies of the maintenance order.

NOTIFICATION TO THE LORD CHANCELLOR

5.1 Where, in accordance with Part 1 of the 1972 Act, a magistrates' court registers a maintenance order sent to it from a Hague Convention Country, the court officer

The Family Procedure Rules 2010

must sent written notice of the registration to the Lord Chancellor.

NOTIFICATION OF MEANS OF ENFORCEMENT

6.1 The court officer of a magistrates' court must take reasonable steps to notify the person to whom payments are due under a registered order of the means of enforcement available in respect of it.

6.2 Notification of the means of enforcement includes, where appropriate, notification of the possibility of registration of the order in the High Court under Part I of the Maintenance Orders Act 1958.

CERTIFIED COPIES OF ORDERS ISSUED UNDER RULE 34.39

7.1 In an application under rule 34.39 by a person wishing to enforce abroad a maintenance order obtained in a magistrates' court, the certified copy of the order will be a sealed copy and will be accompanied by a certificate signed by the court officer.

7.2 In an application under the 1982 Act, the certificate signed by the court officer must state that it is a true copy of the order concerned and must give particulars of the proceedings in which it was made.

7.3 In an application under the Judgments Regulation, the certificate will be in the form of Annex V to the Regulation.

7.4 In an application under the Lugano Convention, the certificate will be in the form of Annex V to the Convention.

COUNTRIES AND TERRITORIES IN WHICH SUMS ARE PAYABLE THROUGH CROWN AGENTS FOR OVERSEAS GOVERNMENTS AND TERRITORIES (RULE 34.23)

8.1 Gibraltar, Barbados, Bermuda, Ghana, Kenya, Fiji, Hong Kong, Singapore, Turks and Caicos Islands, United Republic of Tanzania (except Zanzibar), Anguilla, Falkland Islands and Dependencies, St Helena.

PART 1 OF THE 1972 ACT – MODIFIED RULES

9.1 The annexes to this Practice Direction set out rules 34.14 to 34.25 as they are modified—

(a) in relation to the Republic of Ireland, by rule 34.26 (Annex 1);
(b) in relation to the Hague Convention Countries, by rule 34.27 (Annex 2); and
(c) in relation to Specified States of the United States of America, by rule 34.28 (Annex 3).

9.2 The statutory references in the annexes are construed in accordance with rule 34.26(2), 34.27(2) or 34.28(2) as the case may be.

ANNEX 1
APPLICATION OF SECTION 1 OF CHAPTER 2 OF PART 34 TO THE REPUBLIC OF IRELAND

Application for transmission of maintenance order to the Republic of Ireland

34.14 An application for a maintenance order to be sent to the Republic of Ireland under section 2 of the 1972 Act must be made in accordance with Practice Direction 34A.

Certification of evidence given on provisional orders

34.15 A document setting out or summarising evidence is authenticated by a court in England and Wales by a certificate signed, as appropriate, by—

(a) one of the justices; or
(b) the District Judge (Magistrates' Courts),

before whom that evidence was given.

(Section 3(5)(b) or 5(3) of the 1972 Act require a document to be authenticated by the court.)

Confirmation of a provisional order . . . ..

34.16 [This rule does not apply to the Republic of Ireland]

Consideration of confirmation of a provisional order made by a magistrates' court

34.17. —

(1) This rule applies where—
   (a) a magistrates' court has made a provisional order by virtue of section 3 of the 1972 Act;
   (b) the payer has made representations or adduced evidence to the court; and
   (c) the court has fixed a date for the hearing at which it will consider confirmation of the order.
(2) The court officer must serve on the applicant for the provisional order—
   (a) a copy of the representations or evidence; and
   (b) written notice of the date fixed for the hearing.

Notification of variation or revocation of a maintenance order by the High Court

34.18 Where the High Court makes an order varying or revoking an order to which section 5 of the 1972 Act applies the court officer must send—

(a) a certified copy of the order of variation or revocation; and
(b) a statement as to the service on the payer of the documents mentioned in section 5(3) of the 1972 Act;

to the court in the Republic of Ireland.

(Rule 34.22 provides for the transmission of documents to a court in a reciprocating country.)

Notification of revocation of a maintenance order by a magistrates' court

34.19 Where a magistrates' court makes an order revoking an order to which section 5 of the 1972 Act applies, the court officer must send written notice of the making of the order to the Lord Chancellor.

(Section 5 of the 1972 Act applies to a maintenance order sent to the Republic of Ireland in accordance with section 2 of that Act and a provisional order made by a magistrates' court in accordance with section 3 of that Act which has been confirmed by such a court.)

(Provision in respect of notification of variation of a maintenance order by a magistrates' court under the 1972 Act is made in Rules made under section 144 of the Magistrates' Courts Act 1980.)

Taking of evidence for court in the Republic of Ireland

34.20 —

(1) This rule applies where a request is made by or on behalf of a court in the Republic of Ireland for the taking of evidence for the purpose of proceedings relating to a maintenance order to which Part 1 of the 1972 Act applies.

(Section 14 of the 1972 Act makes provision for the taking of evidence needed for the purpose of certain proceedings.)

The Family Procedure Rules 2010

(2) The High Court has power to take the evidence where—
  (a) the request for evidence relates to a maintenance order made by a superior court in the United Kingdom; and
  (b) the witness resides in England and Wales.
(3) The county court has power to take the evidence where—
  (a) the request for evidence relates to a maintenance order made by a county court; and
  (b) the maintenance order has not been registered in a magistrates' court under the 1958 Act.
(4) The following magistrates' courts have power to take the evidence, that is—
  (a) where the proceedings in the Republic of Ireland relate to a maintenance order made by a magistrates' court, the court which made the order;
  (b) where the proceedings relate to an order which is registered in a magistrates' court, the court in which the order is registered; and
  (c) a magistrates' court to which the Secretary of State sends the request to take evidence.
(5) A magistrates' court not mentioned in paragraph (4) has power to take the evidence if the magistrates' court which would otherwise have that power consents because the evidence could be taken more conveniently.
(6) The evidence is to be taken in accordance with Part 22.

Request for the taking of evidence by a court . . . ..

34.21 [This rule does not apply to the Republic of Ireland]

Transmission of documents

34.22 —

(1) This rule applies to any document, including a notice or request, which is required to be sent to a court in the Republic of Ireland by—
  (a) Part 1 of the 1972 Act; or
  (b) Section1 of Chapter 2 of this Part of these Rules.
(2) The document must be sent to the Lord Chancellor for transmission to the court in the Republic of Ireland.

Method of payment under registered orders

34.23 —

(1) Where an order is registered in a magistrates' court in accordance with section 6(3) of the 1972 Act, the court must order that the payment of sums due under the order be made—
  (a) to the court officer for the registering court; and
  (b) at such time and place as the court officer directs.

(Section 6(3) of the 1972 Act makes provision for the registration of maintenance orders made in the Republic of Ireland.)

(2) Where the court orders payment to be made to the court officer, the court officer must send the payments by post—
  (a) to the payee under the order; or
  (b) where a public authority has been authorised by the payee to receive the payments, to that public authority.

(Practice Direction 34A contains further provisions relating to the payment of sums due under registered orders.)

Enforcement of payments under registered orders

34.24 —

(1) This rule applies where periodical payments under a registered order are in arrears.
(2) The court officer must, on the written request of the payee, proceed in that officer's own name for the recovery of the sums due unless of the view that it is unreasonable to do so.
(3) If the sums due are more than 4 weeks in arrears the court officer must give the payee notice in writing of that fact stating the particulars of the arrears.

Notification of registration and cancellation

34.25 The court officer must send written notice to—

(a) the Lord Chancellor, on the due registration of an order under section 6(3) or 10(4) of the 1972 Act; and
(b) to the payer under the order, on—
    (i) the registration of an order under section 10(4) of the 1972 Act; or
    (ii) the cancellation of the registration of an order under section 10(1) of that Act.

Other notices under section 6 of the 1972 Act

34.25A —

(1) A notice required under section 6(6) or (10) of the 1972 Act must be in the form referred to in a practice direction.
(2) Where a magistrates' court sets aside the registration of an order following an appeal under section 6(7) of the 1972 Act, the court officer must send written notice of the court's decision to the payee.

(Section 6(6) of the 1972 Act provides for notice of registration in a United Kingdom court of a maintenance order made in the Republic of Ireland, and section 6(10) of that Act for notice that a maintenance order made in the Republic of Ireland has not been registered in a United Kingdom court.)

ANNEX 2
APPLICATION OF SECTION 1 OF CHAPTER 2 OF PART 34 TO THE HAGUE CONVENTION COUNTRIES

Application for transmission of maintenance order to a Hague Convention Country

34.14 An application for a maintenance order to be sent to a Hague Convention Country under section 2 of the 1972 Act must be made in accordance with Practice Direction 34A.

Certification of evidence given on provisional orders

34.15 [This rule does not apply to the Hague Convention Countries]

Confirmation of a provisional order made in a reciprocating country

34.16 [This rule does not apply to the Hague Convention Countries]

Consideration of revocation of a maintenance order made by a magistrates' court

34.17 —

(1) This rule applies where—
    (a) an application has been made to a magistrates' court by a payee for the revocation of an order to which section 5 of the 1972 Act applies; and
    (b) the payer resides in a Hague Convention Country.
(2) The court officer must serve on the payee, by post, a copy of any representations or evidence adduced by or on behalf of the payer.

(Provision relating to consideration of variation of a maintenance order made by a

The Family Procedure Rules 2010

magistrates' court to which section 5 of the 1972 Act applies is made in Rules made under section 144 of the Magistrates' Courts Act 1980.)

Notification of variation or revocation of a maintenance order by the High Court or a county court

34.18 —

(1) This rule applies if the High Court or a county court makes an order varying or revoking a maintenance order to which section 5 of the 1972 Act applies.
(2) If the time for appealing has expired without an appeal having been entered, the court officer will send to the Lord Chancellor—
    (a) the documents required by section 5(8) of the 1972 Act; and
    (b) a certificate signed by the district judge stating that the order of variation or revocation is enforceable and no longer subject to the ordinary forms of review.
(3) A party who enters an appeal against the order of variation or revocation must, at the same time, give written notice to the court officer.

Notification of confirmation or revocation of a maintenance order by a magistrates' court

34.19 [This rule does not apply to the Hague Convention Countries]

Taking of evidence for court in a Hague Convention Country

34.20 —

(1) This rule applies where a request is made by or on behalf of a court in a Hague Convention Country for the taking of evidence for the purpose of proceedings relating to a maintenance order to which Part 1 of the 1972 Act applies.

(Section 14 of the 1972 Act makes provision for the taking of evidence needed for the purpose of certain proceedings.)

(2) The High court has power to take the evidence where—
    (a) the request for evidence relates to a maintenance order made by a superior court in the United Kingdom: and
    (b) the witness resides in England and Wales.
(3) The county court has power to take the evidence where—
    (a) the request for evidence relates to a maintenance order made by a county court; and
    (b) the maintenance order has not been registered in a magistrates' court under the 1958 Act.
(4) The following magistrates' courts have power to take the evidence, that is—
    (a) where the proceedings in the Hague Convention Country relate to a maintenance order made by a magistrates' court, the court which made the order;
    (b) where the proceedings relate to an order which is registered in a magistrates' court, the court in which the order is registered; and
    (c) a magistrates' court to which the Secretary of State sends the request to take evidence.
(5) A magistrates' court not mentioned in paragraph (4) has power to take the evidence if the magistrates' court which would otherwise have that power consents because the evidence could be taken more conveniently.
(6) The evidence is to be taken in accordance with Part 22.

Request for the taking of evidence by a court in a Hague Convention country

34.21 [This rule does not apply to the Hague Convention countries.]

FPR 2010, Practice Direction 34A

Transmission of documents

34.22 —

(1) This rule applies to any document, including a notice or request, which is required to be sent to a court in a Hague Convention country by—
   (a) Part 1 of the 1972 Act; or
   (b) Section1 of Chapter 2 of this Part of these Rules.
(2) The document must be sent to the Lord Chancellor for transmission to the court in the Hague Convention country.

Method of payment under registered orders

34.23 —

(1) Where an order is registered in a magistrates' court in accordance with section 6(3) of the 1972 Act, the court must order that the payment of sums due under the order be made—
   (a) to the court officer for the registering court; and
   (b) at such time and place as the court officer directs.

(Section 6(3) of the 1972 Act makes provision for the registration of maintenance orders made in a Hague Convention country.)

(2) Where the court orders payment to be made to the court officer, the court officer must send the payments by post to the payee under the order.

(Practice Direction 34A contains further provision relating to the payment of sums due under registered orders.)

Enforcement of payments under registered orders

34.24 —

(1) This rule applies where a court has ordered periodical payments under a registered maintenance order to be made to the court officer.
(2) The court officer must take reasonable steps to notify the payee of the means of enforcement available.
(3) Paragraph (4) applies where periodical payments due under a registered order are in arrears.
(4) The court officer, on that officer's own initiative—
   (a) may; or
   (b) if the sums due are more than 4 weeks in arrears, must,
proceed in that officer's own name for the recovery of the sums due unless of the view that it is unreasonable to do so.

Notification of registration and cancellation

34.25 The court officer must send written notice to—

(a) the Lord Chancellor, on the due registration of an order under section 10(4) of the 1972 Act; and
(b) the payer under the order, on—
   (i) the registration of an order under section 10(4) of the 1972 Act; or
   (ii) the cancellation of the registration of an order under section 10(1) of the 1972 Act.

General provisions as to notices

34.25A —

(1) A notice to a payer of the registration of an order in a magistrates' court in accordance with section 6(3) of the 1972 Act must be in the form referred to in a practice direction.

(Section 6(8) of the 1972 Act requires notice of registration to be given to the payer.)

(2) If the court sets aside the registration of a maintenance order following an appeal under section 6(9) of the 1972 Act, the court officer must send written notice of the decision to the Lord Chancellor.

(3) A notice to a payee that the court officer has refused to register an order must be in the form referred to in a practice direction.

(Section 6(11) of the 1972 Act requires notice of refusal of registration to be given to the payee.)

(4) Where, under any provision of Part 1 of the 1972 Act, a court officer serves a notice on a payer who resides in a Hague Convention Country, the court officer must send to the Lord Chancellor a certificate of service.

ANNEX 3
APPLICATION OF SECTION 1 OF CHAPTER 2 OF PART 34 TO THE UNITED STATES OF AMERICA

Application for transmission of maintenance order to the United States of America

34.14 An application for a maintenance order to be sent to the United States of America under section 2 of the 1972 Act must be made in accordance with Practice Direction 34A.

Certification of evidence given on provisional orders

34.15 [This rule does not apply to the United States of America]

Confirmation of a provisional order made in a reciprocating country

34.16 [This rule does not apply to the United States of America]

Consideration of revocation of a maintenance order made by a magistrates' court

34.17 —

(1) This rule applies where—
  (a) an application has been made to a magistrates' court by a payee for the revocation of an order to which section 5 of the 1972 Act applies; and
  (b) the payer resides in the United States of America.
(2) The court officer must serve on the payee by post a copy of any representations or evidence adduced by or on behalf of the payer.

(Provision relating to consideration of variation of a maintenance order made by a magistrates' court to which section 5 of the 1972 Act applies is made in rules made under section 144 of the Magistrates' Courts Act 1980.)

Notification of variation or revocation

34.18 If the High Court or a county court makes an order varying or revoking a maintenance order to which section 5 of the 1972 Act applies, the court officer will send to the Lord Chancellor the documents required by section 5(7) of that Act.

Notification of confirmation or revocation of a maintenance order by a magistrates' court

34.19 [This rule does not apply to the United States of America]

Taking of evidence for court in United States of America

34.20 —

(1) This rule applies where a request is made by or on behalf of a court in the United States of America for the taking of evidence for the purpose of proceedings relating to a maintenance order to which Part 1 of the 1972 Act applies.

(Section 14 of the 1972 Act makes provision for the taking of evidence needed for the purpose of certain proceedings.)

(2) The High Court has power to take the evidence where—
    (a) the request for evidence relates to a maintenance order made by a superior court in the United Kingdom; and
    (b) the witness resides in England and Wales.
(3) The county court has power to take the evidence where—
    (a) the request for evidence relates to a maintenance order made by a county court; and
    (b) the maintenance order has not been registered in a magistrates' court under the 1958 Act.
(4) The following magistrates' courts have power to take the evidence, that is—
    (a) where the proceedings in the United States of America relate to a maintenance order made by a magistrates' court, the court which made the order;
    (b) where the proceedings relate to an order which is registered in a magistrates' court, the court in which the order is registered; and
    (c) a magistrates' court to which the Secretary of State sends the request to take evidence.
(5) A magistrates' court not mentioned in paragraph (4) has power to take the evidence if the magistrates' court which would otherwise have that power consents because the evidence could be taken more conveniently.
(6) The evidence is to be taken in accordance with Part 22.

Request for the taking of evidence by a court in a reciprocating country

34.21 [This rule does not apply to the United States of America]

Transmission of documents

34.22 —

(1) This rule applies to any document, including a notice or request, which is required to be sent to a court in the United States of America by—
    (a) Part 1 of the 1972 Act; or
    (b) Section1 of Chapter 2 of this Part of these Rules.
(2) The document must be sent to the Lord Chancellor for transmission to the court in the United States of America.

Method of payment under registered orders

34.23 —

(1) Where an order is registered in a magistrates' court in accordance with section 6(3) of the 1972 Act, the court must order that the payment of sums due under the order be made—
    (a) to the court officer for the registering court; and
    (b) at such time and place as the court officer directs.

(Section 6(3) of the 1972 Act makes provision for the registration of maintenance orders made in the United States of America.)

The Family Procedure Rules 2010

(2) Where the court orders payment to be made to the court officer, the court officer must send the payments by post to the payee under the order.

(Practice Direction 34A contains further provisions relating to the payment of sums due under registered orders.)

Enforcement of payments under registered orders

34.24 —

(1) This rule applies where a court has ordered periodical payments under a registered maintenance order to be made to the court officer.
(2) The court officer must take reasonable steps to notify the payee of the means of enforcement available.
(3) Paragraph (4) applies where periodical payments due under a registered order are in arrears.
(4) The court officer, on that officer's own initiative—
    (a) may; or
    (b) if the sums due are more than 4 weeks in arrears, must,
proceed in that officer's own name for the recovery of the sums due unless of the view that it is unreasonable to do so.

Notification of registration and cancellation

34.25 The court officer must send written notice to—

(a) the Lord Chancellor, on the due registration of an order under section 10(4) of the 1972 Act; or
(b) the payer under the order, on—
    (i) the registration of an order under section 10(4) of the 1972 Act; or
    (ii) the cancellation of the registration of an order under section 10(1) of that Act.

The Right Honourable

Sir Nicholas Wall

The President of the Family Division

Signed by authority of the Lord Chancellor:

[   ]

Parliamentary Under Secretary of State

Ministry of Justice

PRACTICE DIRECTION 34B – PRACTICE NOTE TRACING PAYERS OVERSEAS

10 February 1976

FAMILY DIVISION

Difficulties can arise where a person in this country wishes to take proceedings under the Maintenance Orders (Facilities for Enforcement) Act 1920 or Part I of the Maintenance Orders (Reciprocal Enforcement) Act 1972 to obtain or enforce a maintenance order against a payer living overseas whose address is unknown to the applicant.

To mitigate these difficulties, arrangements have now been made with the appropriate authorities in Australia, Canada, New Zealand and South Africa, whereby the court may on request ask the authorities in those countries to make enquiries with a view to tracing the whereabouts of the payer. The following procedure should be followed.

On or before an application is made for a provisional maintenance order, or for transmission of an absolute maintenance order under the above Acts by an applicant who does not know the payer's actual address in either Australia, Canada, New Zealand or South Africa, there should be completed and lodged with the district judge a questionnaire, in duplicate, (Principal Registry Form D312 or county court Form D85 as appropriate) obtainable from the registry or court office, together with a written undertaking from the solicitor (or from the applicant if acting in person) that any address of the payer received in response to the enquiries will not be disclosed or used except for the purpose of the proceedings.

PART 35

MEDIATION DIRECTIVE

35.1.— Scope and Interpretation
(1) This Part applies to mediated cross-border disputes that are subject to Directive 2008/52/EC of the European Parliament and of the Council of 21 May 2008 on certain aspects of mediation in civil and commercial matters ("the Mediation Directive").
(2) In this Part—
"cross-border dispute" has the meaning given by article 2 of the Mediation Directive;
"mediation" has the meaning given by article 3(a) of the Mediation Directive;
"mediation administrator" means a person involved in the administration of the mediation process;
"mediation evidence" means evidence regarding information arising out of or in connection with a mediation process;
"mediator" has the meaning given by article 3(b) of the Mediation Directive; and
"relevant dispute" means a cross-border dispute that is subject to the Mediation Directive.

35.2.— Relevant disputes: applications for consent orders in respect of financial remedies
(1) This rule applies in relation to proceedings for a financial remedy where the applicant, with the explicit consent of the respondent, wishes to make an application that the content of a written agreement resulting from mediation of a relevant dispute be made enforceable by being made the subject of a consent order.
(2) The court will not include in a consent order any matter which is contrary to the law of England and Wales or which is not enforceable under that law.
(3) The applicant must file two copies of a draft of the order in the terms sought.
(4) Subject to paragraph (5), the application must be supported by evidence of the explicit consent of the respondent.
(5) Where the respondent has written to the court consenting to the making of the order sought, the respondent is deemed to have given explicit consent to the order and paragraph (4) does not apply.
(6) Paragraphs (1)(b) and (2) to (6) of rule 9.26 apply to an application to which this rule applies.

35.3.— Mediation evidence: disclosure and inspection
(1) Where a party to proceedings seeks disclosure or inspection of mediation evidence that is in the control of a mediator or mediation administrator, that party must first obtain the court's permission to seek the disclosure or inspection, by an application made in accordance with Part 18.
(2) The mediator or mediation administrator who has control of the mediation evidence must be named as a respondent to the application and must be served with a copy of the application notice.

The Family Procedure Rules 2010

(3) Evidence in support of the application must include evidence that—
    (a) all parties to the mediation agree to the disclosure or inspection of the mediation evidence;
    (b) disclosure or inspection of the mediation evidence is necessary for overriding considerations of public policy, in accordance with article 7(1)(a) of the Mediation Directive; or
    (c) the disclosure of the content of an agreement resulting from mediation is necessary to implement or enforce that agreement.

(4) Where this rule applies, Parts 21 to 24 apply to the extent they are consistent with this rule.

35.4.— Mediation evidence: witnesses and depositions

(1) This rule applies where a party wishes to obtain mediation evidence from a mediator or mediation administrator by–
    (a) a witness summons;
    (b) cross-examination with permission of the court under rule 22.8 or 23.4;
    (c) an order under rule 24.7 (evidence by deposition);
    (d) an order under rule 24.9 (enforcing attendance of witness);
    (e) an order under rule 24.10(4) (deponent's evidence to be given orally); or
    (f) an order under rule 24.12 (order for the issue of a letter of request).

(2) When applying for a witness summons, permission under rule 22.8 or 23.4 or order under rule 24.7, 24.9, 24.10(4) or 24.12, the party must provide the court with evidence that-
    (a) all parties to the mediation agree to the obtaining of the mediation evidence;
    (b) obtaining the mediation evidence is necessary for overriding considerations of public policy in accordance with article 7(1)(a) of the Mediation Directive; or
    (c) the disclosure of the content of an agreement resulting from mediation is necessary to implement or enforce that agreement.

(3) When considering a request for a witness summons, permission under rule 22.8 or 23.4 or order under rule 24.7, 24.9, 24.10(4) or 24.12, the court may invite any person, whether or not a party, to make representations.

(4) Where this rule applies, Parts 21 to 24 apply to the extent they are consistent with this rule.

PART 35 COMMENTARY

Part 35 is supplemented by PD35A.

Part 35, contains entirely new provisions for family proceedings, relates to mediated cross-border disputes which are subject to the Mediation Directive (Directive 2008/52/EC of the European Parliament and of the Council of 21 May 2008 on certain aspects of mediation in civil and commercial matters ('the Mediation Directive').

The Directive, which is directly applicable in the UK with effect from 6 April 2011, concerns mediation in cross-border disputes within the European Union and the rules make consequential provisions for questions arising out of the operation of the Directive.

Rule 35.2 applies where an application is made for the content of a written agreement resulting from mediation within the Directive to be made enforceable by being made the subject of a consent order for a financial remedy and is designed to ensure that the order includes only those terms which are within the court's powers. In such a case, the court will not include in the consent order any matter which is contrary to the law of England and Wales or which is not enforceable under that law: r 35.2(2).

Rules 35.3 and 35.4 make provision for applications for disclosure of mediation evidence or to obtain mediation evidence in accordance with the Directive.

Practice Direction 35A provides for an application to which r 35.2 applies, or any necessary written consent, to be in English or accompanied by a translation into English.

PRACTICE DIRECTION 35A – MEDIATION DIRECTIVE

This Practice Direction supplements FPR rule 35.2 (Relevant disputes: applications for consent orders in respect of financial remedies)

1.1 An application for an order to which rule 35.2 applies must be completed in English or accompanied by a translation into English.

1.2. Where the application is supported by evidence of explicit consent to the application by a party, the evidence must also be in English or accompanied by a translation into English.

1.3. Where a party chooses to write to the court consenting to the making of the order the correspondence must be in English or accompanied by a translation into English.

PART 36

TRANSITIONAL ARRANGEMENTS AND PILOT SCHEMES

36.1. Transitional provisions
Practice Direction 36A shall make provision for the extent to which these rules shall apply to proceedings started before the day on which they come into force.

36.2. Pilot schemes
Practice directions may modify or disapply any provision of these rules—
- (a) for specified periods; and
- (b) in relation to proceedings in specified courts,

during the operation of pilot schemes for assessing the use of new practices and procedures in connection with proceedings.

PART 36 COMMENTARY

Part 36 is supplemented by PD36A.

Part 36 deals with transitional arrangements, which are set out in the Practice Direction and provides for the modification or disapplication of the rules for the purpose of pilot schemes.

The general scheme set out in the Practice Direction (para 2.1) is to apply the new rules to existing proceedings (ie proceedings commenced before 6 April 2011) so far as is practicable, but where it is not, to apply the previous rules.

Where an initiating step has been taken or a case begun using an old type of form or originating process, the previous rules normally apply to any step to be taken in response. Otherwise, where a new step is to be taken in existing proceedings on or after 6 April 2011, the new rules apply.

When proceedings come before the court for the first time on or after 6 April 2011, the court may direct how the new rules are to apply; the general

The Family Procedure Rules 2010

presumption will be that the new rules apply from then on, unless otherwise directed.

The overriding objective applies to all existing proceedings from 6 April 2011.

PRACTICE DIRECTION 36A — TRANSITIONAL ARRANGEMENTS

This Practice Direction supplements FPR Part 36

CONTENT OF THIS PRACTICE DIRECTION

1.1 This Practice Direction deals with the application of the FPR to proceedings started before 6th April 2011 ("existing proceedings").

1.2 In this Practice Direction "the previous rules" means, as appropriate, the Rules of the Supreme Court 1965 and County Court Rules 1981 as in force immediately before 26 April 1999, and—

the Maintenance Orders (Facilities for Enforcement) Rules 1922;
the Magistrates' Courts (Guardianship of Minors) Rules 1974;
the Magistrates' Courts (Reciprocal Enforcement of Maintenance Orders) Rules 1974;
the Magistrates' Courts (Reciprocal Enforcement of Maintenance Orders) (Republic of Ireland) Rules 1975;
the Magistrates' Courts (Reciprocal Enforcement of Maintenance Orders) (Hague Convention Countries) Rules 1980;
the Magistrates' Courts (Child Abduction and Custody) Rules 1986;
the Magistrates' Courts (Civil Jurisdiction and Judgments Act 1982) Rules 1986;
the Family Proceedings Rules 1991;
the Family Proceedings Courts (Children Act 1989) Rules 1991;
the Family Proceedings Courts (Matrimonial Proceedings etc.) Rules 1991 (in so far as those rules do not relate to enforcement or variation of orders);
the Magistrates' Courts (Costs Against Legal Representatives in Civil Proceedings) Rules 1991 (in so far as those rules relate to family proceedings);
the Family Proceedings Courts (Child Support Act 1991) Rules 1993;
the Magistrates' Courts (Reciprocal Enforcement of Maintenance Orders) (United States of America) Rules 1995 (subject to the saving in paragraph 3.6 of this Practice Direction);
the Magistrates' Courts (Hearsay Evidence in Civil Proceedings) Rules 1999 (in so far as those rules relate to family proceedings); and
the Family Procedure (Adoption) Rules 2005,

as in force immediately before 6th April 2011.

GENERAL SCHEME OF TRANSITIONAL ARRANGEMENTS

2.1 The general scheme is—

(a) to apply the FPR to existing proceedings so far as is practicable; but
(b) where this is not practicable, to apply the previous rules to such proceedings.

WHERE THE PREVIOUS RULES WILL NORMALLY APPLY

General principle

3.1 Where an initiating step has been taken in a case before 6th April 2011, in particular a step using forms or other documentation required by the previous rules, the case will proceed in the first instance under the previous rules. Where a party must take a step in response to something done by another party in accordance with the previous

Responding to old process

3.2 A party who is served with an old type of originating process (for example, an originating summons) on or after 6th April 2011 must respond in accordance with the previous rules and the instructions on any forms received.

Filing and service of pleadings where old process served

3.3 Where a case has been begun by an old type of originating process (whether served before or after 6th April 2011), filing and service of pleadings will continue according to the previous rules.

Pre-commencement order inconsistent with FPR

3.4 Where a court order has been made before 6th April 2011, that order must still be complied with on or after that date.

Steps taken before commencement

3.5 Where a party has, before 6th April 2011, taken any step in the proceedings in accordance with the previous rules, that step will remain valid on or after that date, and a party will not normally be required to take any action that would amount to taking such a step again under the FPR.

Saving – Reciprocal enforcement of maintenance orders (United States of America)

3.6 Where, by virtue of article 6(2) of the Reciprocal Enforcement of Maintenance Orders (United States of America) Order 2007, the Reciprocal Enforcement of Maintenance (United States of America) Order 1995 continues in full force and effect, the Magistrates' Courts (Reciprocal Enforcement of Maintenance Orders) (United States of America) Rules 1995 shall, notwithstanding any provision in the FPR, continue to apply as if they had not been amended by the Magistrates' Courts (Reciprocal Enforcement of Maintenance Orders) (Miscellaneous Amendment) Rules 2007.

WHERE THE FPR WILL NORMALLY APPLY

General principle

4.1 Where a new step is to be taken in any existing proceedings on or after 6th April 2011, it is to be taken under the FPR.

Part 1 (Overriding objective) to apply

4.2 Part 1 of the FPR (Overriding objective) will apply to all existing proceedings from 6th April 2011 onwards.

Issuing of application forms after the FPR come into force

4.3

(1) The general rule is that—
    (a) only application forms under the FPR will be issued by the court on or after 6th April 2011; and
    (b) if a request to issue an old type of form or originating process (summons, etc.) is received at the court on or after 6th April 2011, it will be returned unissued.
(2) By way of exception to the general rule, the court may in cases of urgency direct that the form or process is to be issued as if the request to issue it had been a

The Family Procedure Rules 2010

request to issue an application form under the FPR and, if it does so, the court may make such supplementary directions as it considers appropriate.

First time before a court on or after 6th April 2011

4.4

(1) When proceedings come before a court (whether at a hearing or on paper) for the first time on or after 6th April 2011, the court may direct how the FPR are to apply to the proceedings and may disapply certain provisions of the FPR. The court may also give case management directions.
(2) The general presumption will be that the FPR will apply to the proceedings from then on unless the court directs or this practice direction provides otherwise.
(3) If an application has been issued before 6th April 2011 and the hearing of the application has been set on or after that date, the general presumption is that the application will be decided having regard to the FPR.
(4) When the first occasion on which existing proceedings are before a court on or after 6th April 2011 is a hearing of a substantive issue, the general presumption is that the hearing will be conducted according to the FPR.

Costs

4.5

(1) Any assessment of costs that takes place on or after 6th April 2011 will be in accordance with FPR Part 28 and the provisions of the Civil Procedure Rules as applied by that Part.
(2) However, the general presumption is that no costs for work undertaken before 6th April 2011 will be disallowed if those costs would have been allowed on detailed assessment before that date.
(3) The decision as to whether to allow costs for work undertaken on or after 6th April 2011 will generally be taken in accordance with FPR Part 28 and the provisions of the Civil Procedure Rules as applied by that Part.

PRACTICE DIRECTION – PRACTICE DIRECTIONS RELATING TO FAMILY PROCEEDINGS IN FORCE BEFORE 6TH APRIL 2011 WHICH SUPPORT THE FAMILY PROCEDURE RULES 2010

This Practice Direction is made by the President of the Family Division under the powers delegated to him by the Lord Chief Justice under Schedule 2, Part 1, paragraph 2(2) of the Constitutional Reform Act 2005, and is approved by the Parliamentary Under Secretary of State, by authority of the Lord Chancellor and comes into force on 6th April 2011

INTRODUCTION AND THE EXISTING PRACTICE DIRECTIONS

1.1 The Family Procedure Rules 2010 ("the FPR 2010") come into force on 6th April 2011. The purpose of this practice direction is to inform court users of the practice directions relating (only) to family proceedings which date from before 6th April 2011 ("existing Practice Directions") but will continue to apply after that date.

1.2 The table in the Annex to this practice direction lists those existing Practice Directions which will continue to apply. The listed existing Practice Directions will apply to family proceedings on and after 6th April 2011 –

(a) with the modifications outlined in the Annex (in particular that the numbering of the existing Practice Directions will be as set out in column one of the table in the Annex) and any other modifications necessary in consequence of the FPR 2010 coming into force; and
(b) subject to the FPR 2010 and any other practice directions supporting those rules.

APPLICATION OF PRACTICE DIRECTION 23B OF THE CIVIL PROCEDURE RULES 1998

2.1 Paragraphs 1.1, 1.2, 1.4 and 1.5 of CPR Practice Direction 23B apply to applications under Part III of the Family Law Reform Act 1969 for the use of scientific tests to determine parentage. These applications will be made using the procedure in Part 18 of the FPR 2010 (Procedure for Other Applications in Proceedings).

ANNEX

Number	TITLE	DATE	COURT	UPDATED Rule References
Practice Direction 6C	Practice Direction (Disclosure of Addresses by Government Departments) (amending Practice Direction of 13th February 1989) (NB this practice direction does not apply to requests for disclosure from HMRC and related agencies which are covered by "Disclosure Orders against the Inland Revenue- Guidance from the President's Office (November 2003)"	20 July 1995	High Court, county court and magistrates' court	
Practice Direction 7D	Gender Recognition Act 2004	5th April 2005	High Court and county court	
Practice Direction 12A	Public Law Proceedings Guide to Case Management: April 2010	April 2010	High Court, county court and magistrates' court	
Practice Direction 12B	The Revised Private Law Programme	April 2010	High Court, county court and magistrates' court	
Practice Direction 12I	Applications for Reporting Restriction Orders (nb this practice direction applies to information about children and protected parties)	18 March 2005	High Court	

The Family Procedure Rules 2010

Number	TITLE	DATE	COURT	UPDATED Rule References
Practice Direction 12J	Residence and Contact Orders: Domestic Violence and Harm	14th January 2009	High Court, county court and magistrates' court	In paragraph 10, for "the Family Proceedings Rules 1991, rule 4.17AA and by the Family Proceedings Courts (Children Act 1989) Rules 1991, rule 17AA", substitute, "rule 12.34 of the Family Procedure Rules 2010"
Practice Direction 12K	President's Direction (Children Act 1989: Exclusion Requirement)	17th December 1997	High Court, county court and magistrates' court	
Practice Direction 12L	Children Act 1989: Risk Assessments under Section 16A	3rd September 2007	High Court, county court and magistrates' court	
Practice Direction 12M	Family Assistance Orders: Consultation	3rd September 2007	High Court, county court and magistrates' court	
Practice Direction 12N	Enforcement of Children Act 1989 Contact Orders: Disclosure of Information to Officers of the National Probation Service (High Court and county court)	6th November 2008	High Court and county court (The Lord Chief Justice issued a Practice Direction on this subject for the magistrates' courts mirroring the one for the High Court and county courts)	
Practice Direction 12O	Practice Direction (Arrival of Child in England by Air)	18th January 1980	High Court and county court	
Practice Direction 12P	Registrar's Direction (Removal from jurisdiction: issue of Passports)	15th May 1987	High Court and county court	

FPR 2010, PDs relating to family proceedings etc

Number	TITLE	DATE	COURT	UPDATED Rule References
Practice Direction 14A	Who Receives a Copy of the Application Form for Orders in Proceedings		High Court, county court and magistrates' court	In the heading, for "Part 5, rule 24(1)(b)(ii) of the Family Procedure (Adoption) Rules 2005", substitute "Part 14, rule14.6(1)(b)(ii) of the Family Procedure Rules 2010"
Practice Direction 14B	The First Directions Hearing-Adoptions with a Foreign Element		High Court, county court and magistrates' court	In the heading, for "Part 5, rule 26(3) of the Family Procedure (Adoption) Rules 2005", substitute "Part 14, rule 14.8(3) of the Family Procedure Rules 2010"; and in paragraph 2,for "rule 26(1)", substitute "rule 14.8(1)"
Practice Direction 14C	Reports by the Adoption Agency or Local Authority		High Court, county court and magistrates' court	In the heading for "Part 5, rule 29(3) of the Family Procedure (Adoption) Rules 2005", substitute "Part 14, rule 14.11(3) of the Family Procedure Rules 2010"
Practice Direction 14D	Reports by a Registered Medical Practitioner ("Health Reports")		High Court, county court and magistrates' court	In the heading for "Part 5, rule 30(2) of the Family Procedure (Adoption) Rules 2005", substitute "Part 14, rule 14.12(2) of the Family Procedure Rules 2010"; and in paragraph 1.1, for "rule 30(1)", substitute "rule 14.12(1)"
Practice Direction 14E	Communication of Information Relating to the Proceedings		High Court, county court and magistrates' court	In the heading for "Part 8, rule 78(1)(b) of the Family Procedure (Adoption) Rules 2005", substitute "Part 14, rule 14.14(b) of the Family Procedure Rules 2010"; and in paragraph 1.1, for "rule 78", substitute "rule 14.14"

The Family Procedure Rules 2010

Number	TITLE	DATE	COURT	UPDATED Rule References
Practice Direction 14F	Disclosing Information to an Adopted Adult		High Court, county court and magistrates' court	In the heading for "Part 8, rule 84(1)(d) of the Family Procedure (Adoption) Rules 2005", substitute "Part 14, rule 14.18(1)(d) of the Family Procedure Rules 2010"; in paragraphs 1,1 and 1.2, for "rule 84", substitute "rule 14.18"; and in paragraph 1.2, for "rule 17", substitute "rule 5"
Practice Direction 27A	Family Proceedings: Court Bundles (Universal Practice to be applied in All Courts other than the Family Proceedings Court)	27th July 2006	High Court and county court	
Practice Direction 27B	Attendance of Media Representatives at Hearings in Family Proceedings (High Court and county courts) (This practice direction should be read as if amended by Re X (a child) (residence and contact: rights of media attendance) (2009) EWHC 1728 (Fam) [87])	20 April 2009	High Court and county courts	For references to "rule 10.28 of the Family Proceedings Rules 1991", substitute "rule 27.11 of the Family Procedure Rules 2010"; in paragraph 2.2 for "paragraphs (4) to (6)", substitute "paragraphs (3) to (5)"; in paragraph 2.3, for "Part 11 of the Family Proceedings Rules 1991", substitute "Part 12, Chapter 7 of the Family Procedure Rules 2010 and Practice Direction 12G"; in paragraph 4.2, for "paragraph (8)",substitute "paragraph (7)";

Number	TITLE	DATE	COURT	UPDATED Rule References
				in paragraph 4.3, for "paragraph (3)(f)", substitute "paragraph 2(f)" and for "paragraph 3(g)", substitute "paragraph (2)(g)"; in paragraph 5.1, for paragraph (4), substitute paragraph (3); in paragraph 5.2, for "paragraph (4)", substitute "paragraph (3)" and for "paragraph (4)(a)", substitute "paragraph 3(a)"; in paragraph 5.3, for "paragraph 4(a)(iii)", substitute "paragraph 3(a)(iii)"; in paragraph 5.4, for "paragraph 4(b)", substitute "paragraph 3(b)"; and in paragraph 6.1, for "paragraph (6)" substitute "paragraph (5)"
Practice Direction 27C	Attendance of Media Representatives at Hearings in Family Proceedings (Family Proceedings Court) (This practice direction should be read as if amended by Re X (a child) (residence and contact: rights of media attendance) (2009) EWHC 1728 (Fam) at [87]	20 April 2009	Magistrates' courts	In paragraph 1.1, for "rule 16A of the Family Proceedings Courts (Children Act 1989) Rules 1991 ("the Rules")", substitute "rule 27.11 of the Family Procedure Rules 2010 ("the Rules")"; In paragraph 2.1, for references to "rule 16A(2)" where it occurs, substitute "rule 27.11(1)" and for "paragraphs (3) to (5) of rule 16A", substitute; "paragraphs (3) to (5) of rule 27.11";

701

The Family Procedure Rules 2010

Number	TITLE	DATE	COURT	UPDATED Rule References
				in paragraph 2.2, for "rule 16A(2)", substitute "rule 27.11(1)"; in paragraph 2.3 for "Part 11C (rules relating to disclosure to third parties)", substitute "Part 12, Chapter 7 of the Family Procedure Rules 2010 and Practice Direction 12G"; in paragraph 2.4, for "rule 16A", substitute "rule 27.11"; and in paragraph 4.3, for "paragraph (1)(f)", substitute "paragraph 2(f)" and for "paragraph (1)(g)" substitute "paragraph 2(g)"
Practice Direction 29B	Human Rights Act 1998	24th July 2000	High Court, county court and magistrates' court	
Practice Direction 34B	Practice Note Tracing Payers Overseas	10 February 1976	High Court and county court	

The Right Honourable

Sir Nicholas Wall

The President of the Family Division

Signed by authority of the Lord Chancellor:

[   ]

Parliamentary Under Secretary of State

Ministry of Justice

GLOSSARY

SCOPE

This glossary is a guide to the meaning of certain legal expressions as used in these rules, but it does not give the expressions any meaning in the rules which they do not otherwise have in the law.

Expression	Meaning
Affidavit	A written, sworn, statement of evidence.
Cross-examination	Questioning of a witness by a party other than the party who called the witness.
Evidence in chief	The evidence given by a witness for the party who called him.
Injunction	A court order prohibiting a person from doing something or requiring a person to do something.
Official copy	A copy of an official document, supplied and marked as such by the office which issued the original.
Pre-action protocol	Statements of best practice about pre-action conduct which have been approved by the President of the Family Division and which are annexed to a Practice Direction.
Privilege	The right of a party to refuse to disclose a document or produce a document or to refuse to answer questions on the ground of some special interest recognised by law.
Seal	A seal is a mark which the court puts on document to indicate that the document has been issued by the court.
Service	Steps required by rules of court to bring documents used in court proceedings to a person's attention.
Set aside	Cancelling a judgment or order or a step taken by a party in the proceedings.
Stay	A stay imposes a halt on proceedings, apart from the taking of any steps allowed by the rules or the terms of the stay. Proceedings can be continued if a stay is lifted.
Strike out	Striking out means the court ordering written material to be deleted so that it may no longer be relied upon.
Without prejudice	Negotiations with a view to settlement are usually conducted "without prejudice" which means that the circumstances in which the content of those negotiations may be revealed to the court are very restricted.

Nicholas Wall, P
Philip Waller
Duncan Adam
John Baker
Timothy Becker
Paul Carr
Martyn Cook

The Family Procedure Rules 2010

Bruce Edgington
Angela Finnerty
Mike Hinchliffe
Ruth Lindley-Glover
David Salter
John Wilson

I allow these Rules

Signed by authority of the Lord Chancellor

13th December 2010

J Djanogly
Parliamentary Under Secretary of State

Ministry of Justice

Index

Absence of parties
  financial remedy applications, and, 2.44
  Part 18 applications, and, 5.132
Accounts and inquiries
  generally, 6.2
Acknowledgment of service
  service out of the jurisdiction, and, 5.31
  statements of truth, and, 5.54
Address for service
  service of documents, and, 5.22
Adjournments
  case management, and, 1.4
Adoption applications
  children proceedings, and, 4.8
Adoption effected overseas
  declarations, and, 5.158
Affidavits
  See also **Witness statements**
  exhibiting documents, 5.68
  filing, 5.69
  format, 5.66
  forms
    general, 2.10
    request to dispense with service of petition on respondent, 2.8
  swearing, 5.67
  use, 5.65
Alteration of maintenance agreement after death of one party
  Part 8 applications, and, 5.142
Alternative dispute resolution
  generally, 1.7
  mediation exceptions, 1.9
  protocol requirements, 1.8
Alternative method of service
  documents, and, 5.28
  petition, and, 5.17
Alternative place of service
  documents, and, 5.28
  petition, and, 5.17
Alternative service providers
  service of documents, and, 5.24
Amendments to application or answer
  generally, 2.12
Ancillary relief
  change in nomenclature, and, 1.3

Answers
  amendments, 2.12
  form, 2.7
  further information about contents, 2.14
  replies, 2.13
  supplemental answers, 2.13
Anton Piller orders
  generally, 6.2
Appeals
  general, 6.22
  grounds, 6.25
  'internal appeals', 6.22
  notices of appeal, 6.24
  permission, 6.23
Applications
  See also **Financial remedy applications**
  alteration of maintenance agreement after death of one party, for, 5.142
  consent to marriage of child, for, 5.172
  corrected gender recognition certificate, for, 5.141
  costs, and, 6.16
  declarations, for
    adoption effected overseas, as to, 5.158
    Attorney General's role, 5.154
    case management, 5.153
    civil partnership status, as to, 5.155
    introduction, 5.149
    legitimacy, of, 5.157
    legitimation, of, 5.157
    marital status, as to, 5.155
    parentage, of, 5.156
    parties, 5.151
    relevant court, 5.150
    response, 5.152
  enforcement, and
    attachment of earnings orders, 6.37
    committal by way of judgment summons, 6.32
    form, 6.29
    generally, 6.27
    obtaining information from a judgment debtor, 6.42
    relevant court, 6.28
    third party debt orders, 6.47
  generally, 2.2

705

Index

Applications – *cont.*
  interim remedies, and
    evidence in support, 6.6
    generally, 6.5
    urgent cases, 6.7
    without notice, 6.7
  nomenclature, and, 1.3
  orders preventing avoidance under Child Support Act 1991, s 32L, for, 5.171
  Part 8, under
    alteration of maintenance agreement after death of one party, for, 5.142
    conversion table, 5.140
    consent to marriage of child, for, 5.172
    corrected gender recognition certificate, for, 5.141
    declarations of status, for, 5.149–5.158
    financial remedy after overseas proceedings, for, 5.159–5.163
    introduction, 5.139
    orders preventing avoidance under CSA 1991, s 32L, for, 5.171
    overview, 5.123
    question as to property to be decided in summary way, for, 5.143–5.148
    registration of civil partnership of child, for, 5.172
    transfer of tenancy, for, 5.164–5.170
  Part 18, under
    absent parties, 5.132
    evidence in support, 5.128
    filing notice, 5.126
    general procedure, 5.126
    hearings, 5.129
    introduction, 5.124
    overview, 5.123
    relevant proceedings, 5.125
    scope, 5.125
    service, 5.127
    telephone hearings, 5.130
    video conferencing, 5.130
    without merit, 5.132
    without notice orders, 5.131
  Part 19, under
    case management, 5.138
    evidence, 5.137
    filing notice, 5.135
    general procedure, 5.135
    hearings, 5.138
    introduction, 5.133
    overview, 5.123
    relevant proceedings, 5.134
    response, 5.136
    scope, 5.134
  permission to apply for financial remedy after overseas proceedings, for

Applications – *cont.*
  permission to apply for financial remedy after overseas proceedings, for – *cont.*
    hearings, 5.162
    introduction, 5.159
    procedure, 5.160
    relevant court, 5.161
    substantive application, 5.163
  publicity, 5.173
  question as to property to be decided in summary way, for
    case management, 5.148
    general, 5.146
    hearings, 5.148
    introduction, 5.143
    overview, 5.123
    procedure, 5.144
    relevant court, 5.145
    response, 5.147
  registration of civil partnership of child, for, 5.172
  transfer of tenancy under FLA 1996, s 53 and Sch 7, for
    case management, 5.169
    injunctions, 5.170
    introduction, 5.164
    procedure, 5.165
    relevant court, 5.166
    response, 5.168
    service, 5.167
  withdrawal, 5.46
Appointment of receivers
  generally, 6.30
Armed forces
  service out of the jurisdiction, and, 5.36
Assessors
  appointment, 5.122
  comparison table, 5.99
  introduction, 5.98
Attachment of earnings orders
  applications, 6.37
  case management, 6.40
  generally, 6.36
  hearings, 6.40
  introduction, 6.30
  relevant court, 6.38
  service, 6.39
Attendance at court
  case management, and, 1.4
  expert evidence, and, 5.120
Attorney General
  declarations, and, 5.154
Avoidance under Child Support Act 1991, s 32L
  Part 8 applications, and, 5.171

Index

Bailiffs
service of documents, and, 5.11
British consular authorities
service out of the jurisdiction, and, 5.34
Bundles
financial remedy applications, and, 2.45
Case management
attachment of earnings orders, and, 6.40
declarations, and, 5.153
generally, 1.4
obtaining information from a judgment debtor, and, 6.45
Part 19 applications, and, 5.138
principles of FPR 2010, and, 1.2
question as to property to be decided in summary way, and, 5.148
transfer of tenancy under FLA 1996, s 53 and Sch 7, and, 5.169
Case management hearings
generally, 2.15
Certificates of service
generally, 5.5
statements of truth, and, 5.54
Change of solicitor
introduction, 5.38
notice, 5.39
order that solicitor has ceased to act, 5.40
removal of solicitor who ceased to act on application of another party, 5.41
Charging orders
applications, 6.53
further evidence, 6.56
generally, 6.52
hearings, 6.56
introduction, 6.30
relevant court, 6.54
service, 6.55
statements of truth, and, 5.54
Child abduction
children proceedings, and, 4.5
Child Support Act 1991
applications for relief precluded, 5.48
disclosure, 5.44
Part 8 applications for orders preventing avoidance, and, 5.171
Children proceedings
adoption applications, 4.8
child abduction, 4.5
communication of information to third parties, 4.6
expert evidence, and
draft order, 5.114
information to be filed and served, 5.113
initial enquiries of proposed experts, 5.111

Children proceedings – *cont.*
expert evidence, and – *cont.*
introduction, 5.110
letter of instruction, 5.115
proposal to instruct, 5.113
response to inquiries, 5.112
general, 4.1
Human Fertilisation and Embryology Act 2008, s 54, and, 4.7
inherent jurisdiction, 4.4
international child abduction, 4.5
legal representation, 4.10
parental orders, 4.7
placement applications, 4.8
practice directions, 4.1
private law, 4.3
public law, 4.2
relevant proceedings, 4.1
representation, 4.10
service of documents, and, 5.26
wardship, 4.4
Civil Partnership (Jurisdiction and Recognition of Judgments) Regulations 2005, under
forms, 6.60
introduction, 6.58
procedure, 6.61
relevant court, 6.59
Civil partnership orders
meaning, 2.2
Civil partnership proceedings
amendments to application or answer, 2.12
applications, 2.2
case management hearing, 2.15
comparison table, 2.3
costs, 2.18
declarations as to status, and, 5.155
decree absolute
expedition, 2.20
separation grounds, on, 2.19
disclosure, 2.16
forms and documents
affidavit in support of request to dispense with service of petition on respondent, 2.8
affidavits in support, 2.10
application for decree nisi or conditional order, 2.9
generally, 2.4
statement of arrangements for children, 2.6
statement of reconciliation, 2.5
further information about contents of application and answer, 2.14
inspection, 2.16
overview, 2.1

707

Index

Civil partnership proceedings – *cont.*
  proof of civil partnership, 2.11
  replies to answers, 2.13
  supplemental petitions and answers, 2.13
Civil Procedure Rules 1998
  costs, and
    generally, 6.17
    introduction, 6.16
  harmonisation with FPR 2010, and, 1.1
Civil restraint orders
  generally, 1.5
  principles of FPR 2010, and, 1.2
  types, 1.6
Committal
  generally, 6.30
Committal by way of judgment summons
  applications, 6.32
  committal, 6.35
  generally, 6.31
  introduction, 6.30
  relevant court, 6.33
  service, 6.34
Communication of information to third parties
  children proceedings, and, 4.6
Computation of time
  principles of FPR 2010, and, 1.2
Consent of trustee to act
  evidence, and, 5.83
Consent orders
  financial remedy applications, and, 2.31
  principles of FPR 2010, and, 1.2
Consent to marriage of child
  Part 8 applications, and, 5.172
Consolidation of proceedings
  case management, and, 1.4
Corrected gender recognition certificate
  Part 8 applications, and, 5.141
Costs
  applications, 6.16
  Civil Procedure Rules, and
    generally, 6.17
    introduction, 6.16
  financial remedy applications, and
    'financial remedy proceedings', 6.19
    generally, 6.18
    interim orders, 6.20
    introduction, 6.16
    overview, 2.48
    relevant factors, 6.21
  general principle, 6.16
  generally, 2.18
  overview, 6.15
  transitional provisions, 1.14
  wasted costs orders, 6.16

Costs estimates
  case management, and, 1.4
Cross examination
  generally, 5.71
Custody orders
  registration of orders, and, 6.65
Declarations
  adoption effected overseas, as to, 5.158
  Attorney General's role, 5.154
  case management, 5.153
  civil partnership status, as to, 5.155
  introduction, 5.149
  legitimacy, of, 5.157
  legitimation, of, 5.157
  marital status, as to, 5.155
  parentage, of, 5.156
  parties, 5.151
  relevant court, 5.150
  response, 5.152
Decree absolute
  expedition, 2.20
  separation grounds, on, 2.19
Decree nisi
  application form, 2.9
Deemed service
  documents, and, 5.27
  petition, and, 5.15
Delivery up
  generally, 6.11
  introduction, 6.2
Depositions
  examination, 5.91
  examiners of the court, 5.93
  generally, 5.89
  order for examination, 5.90
  persons out of the jurisdiction, from
    introduction, 5.94
    member states, 5.96
    non member states, 5.95
  use at hearing, 5.92
Detention, custody or preservation of property
  generally, 6.2
Disclosure
  case management, and, 1.4
  Child Support Act 1991, under, 5.44
  financial remedy applications, and
    forms, 2.27–2.30
    non-parties, against, 2.49–2.52
    voluntary, 2.34
  generally, 2.16
Dispensing with service
  affidavit in support of request, 2.8
  documents, and, 5.29
  petition, and, 5.18

Index

Dissolution orders
civil partnership orders, and, 2.2
Divorce decrees
matrimonial orders, and, 2.2
Documents
gender recognition, and, 5.49
sealing, 5.50
service, and
  address for service, 5.22
  alternative method, by, 5.28
  alternative place, at, 5.28
  alternative service provider, by, 5.24
  children, on, 5.26
  deemed service, 5.27
  dispensing with service, 5.29
  DX, by, 5.23–5.24
  email, by, 5.25
  fax, by, 5.25
  generally, 5.19
  methods, 5.20
  person, in, 5.21
  post, by, 5.24
  protected parties, on, 5.26
DX service
documents, and, 5.23–5.24
petition, and, 5.12
Email
service of documents, and, 5.25
Emergency cases
expert evidence, and, 5.105
Enforcement
applications
  attachment of earnings orders, 6.37
  committal by way of judgment summons, 6.32
  form, 6.29
  generally, 6.27
  obtaining information from a judgment debtor, 6.42
  relevant court, 6.28
  third party debt orders, 6.47
appointment of receiver, 6.30
attachment of earnings orders
  applications, 6.37
  case management, 6.40
  generally, 6.36
  hearings, 6.40
  introduction, 6.30
  relevant court, 6.38
  service, 6.39
case management
  attachment of earnings orders, 6.40
  obtaining information from a judgment debtor, 6.45
charging orders
  applications, 6.53

Enforcement – *cont.*
charging orders – *cont.*
  further evidence, 6.56
  generally, 6.52
  hearings, 6.56
  introduction, 6.30
  relevant court, 6.54
  service, 6.55
committal, 6.30
committal by way of judgment summons
  applications, 6.32
  committal, 6.35
  generally, 6.31
  introduction, 6.30
  relevant court, 6.33
  service, 6.34
Form D50K, 6.29
garnishee orders, 6.30
generally, 6.26
hardship orders, 6.50
hearings
  attachment of earnings orders, 6.40
  obtaining information from a judgment debtor, 6.45
  third party debt orders, 6.51
methods, 6.30
obtaining information from a judgment debtor
  applications, 6.42
  case management, 6.45
  generally, 6.41
  hearings, 6.45
  introduction, 6.30
  relevant court, 6.43
  service, 6.44
principles of FPR 2010, and, 1.2
service
  attachment of earnings orders, 6.39
  committal by way of judgment summons, 6.34
  obtaining information from a judgment debtor, 6.44
  third party debt orders, 6.49
stop notices, 6.30
stop orders, 6.30
third party debt orders
  applications, 6.47
  further evidence, 6.51
  generally, 6.46
  hardship orders, 6.50
  hearings, 6.51
  introduction, 6.30
  relevant court, 6.48
  service, 6.49
undertakings, and, 6.57

Index

Enforcement – *cont.*
  venue for proceedings
    attachment of earnings orders, 6.38
    committal by way of judgment summons, 6.33
    generally, 6.28
    obtaining information from a judgment debtor, 6.43
    third party debt orders, 6.48
  warrants of execution, 6.30

Entry to land or buildings
  interim remedies, and, 6.2

Evidence
  affidavits
    exhibiting documents, 5.68
    filing, 5.69
    format, 5.66
    swearing, 5.67
    use, 5.65
  assessors, and
    appointment, 5.122
    comparison table, 5.99
  consent of trustee to act, of, 5.83
  court's powers, 5.62
  cross examination, 5.71
  depositions
    examination, 5.91
    examiners of the court, 5.93
    generally, 5.89
    order for examination, 5.90
    persons out of the jurisdiction, from, 5.94–5.96
    use at hearing, 5.92
  depositions from persons out of the jurisdiction
    introduction, 5.94
    member states, 5.96
    non member states, 5.95
  experts, and
    See also **Expert evidence**
    adult protected parties, 5.107
    attendance at court, 5.120
    children proceedings, 5.110–5.115
    comparison table, 5.99
    content of report, 5.109
    discussions between experts, 5.118
    duties, 5.108
    emergency cases, 5.105
    instructions to give evidence, 5.120
    meetings between experts, 5.118
    non-children proceedings, 5.116
    overview, 5.98
    permission to instruct, 5.102–5.104
    post-final hearing action, 5.121
    practice direction, 5.100–5.122
    pre-application instruction, 5.104

Evidence – *cont.*
  experts, and – *cont.*
    questions to experts, 5.117
    refusal by party to be bound by experts' agreement, 5.119
    service of orders upon experts, 5.106
    urgent cases, 5.105
  foreign law, on, 5.82
  general rule, 5.63
  hearsay, 5.80
  introduction, 5.61
  magistrates' court, in, 5.84
  models, 5.80
  notice to admit facts, 5.73
  notice to admit or procure documents, 5.74
  Part 18 applications, and, 5.128
  Part 19 applications, and, 5.137
  photographs, 5.80
  plans, 5.80
  statements of truth
    consequences of failure to verify, 5.58
    documents requiring verification, 5.54
    false statements, 5.59
    introduction, 5.53
    nature, 5.55
    persons entitled to sign, 5.56
    persons unable to read or sign, 5.57
    relevant documents, 5.54
    summary, 5.60
  summary, 5.78
  video link, by, 5.77
  witness statements
    exhibiting documents, 5.68
    filing, 5.69
    format, 5.66
    generally, 5.64
    introduction, 5.63
    Part 7 proceedings, in, 5.76
    service for use at final hearing, 5.70
    use in other proceedings, 5.65
    verification, 5.67
  witness summary, 5.72
  witness summonses
    compensation for loss of time, 5.87
    generally, 5.86
    magistrates' court, in, 5.88
    travelling expenses, 5.87
  witnesses, 5.85

Ex parte
  change in nomenclature, and, 1.3

Examiners of the court
  depositions, and, 5.93

Exhibits
  witness statements, and, 5.68

Index

Experiments on or with property
  generally, 6.2
Expert evidence
  adult protected parties, 5.107
  attendance at court, 5.120
  children proceedings, in
    draft order, 5.114
    information to be filed and served, 5.113
    initial enquiries of proposed experts, 5.111
    introduction, 5.110
    letter of instruction, 5.115
    proposal to instruct, 5.113
    response to inquiries, 5.112
  comparison table, 5.99
  content of report, 5.109
  discussions between experts, 5.118
  duties, 5.108
  emergency cases, 5.105
  instructions to give evidence, 5.120
  meetings between experts, 5.118
  non-children proceedings, 5.116
  overview, 5.98
  permission to instruct
    generally, 5.102
    pre-application, 5.104
    relevant proceedings, 5.103
  post-final hearing action, 5.121
  practice direction
    generally, 5.100
    introduction, 5.101
    permission to instruct, 5.102–5.104
  pre-application instruction, 5.104
  questions to experts, 5.117
  refusal by party to be bound by experts' agreement, 5.119
  reports
    contents, 5.109
    statements of truth, 5.54
  service of orders upon experts, 5.106
  urgent cases, 5.105
Extended civil restraint orders
  generally, 1.5
  types, 1.6
Extension of time
  case management, and, 1.4
False statements
  statements of truth, and, 5.59
Family Law Act 1996
  Part 4 applications, and, 3.1
  Part 4A applications, and, 3.2
  registration of orders, and, 6.65
Family Procedure Rules 2010
  alternative dispute resolution, and, 1.7–1.9
  background, 1.1–1.6

Family Procedure Rules 2010 – *cont.*
  case management powers, 1.4
  changes in nomenclature, 1.3
  Civil Procedure Rules, and, 1.1
  civil restraint orders, and, 1.5–1.6
  general philosophy, 1.1
  nomenclature, 1.3
  objectives, 1.1
  philosophy, 1.1
  principles, 1.2
  transitional provisions, 1.10–1.14
  underlying principles, 1.2
Fax
  service of documents, and, 5.25
Filing
  affidavits, and, 5.69
  Part 18 applications, and, 5.126
  Part 19 applications, and, 5.135
  witness statements, and, 5.69
Financial Dispute Resolution (FDR)
  financial remedy applications, and, 2.42
Financial orders
  nomenclature, and, 1.3
Financial remedy
  See also **Financial remedy applications**
  meaning, 2.22
  nomenclature, and, 1.3
Financial remedy applications
  absence of parties, 2.44
  bundles, 2.45
  comparison table, 2.23
  consent orders, 2.31
  costs
    'financial remedy proceedings', 6.19
    generally, 6.18
    interim orders, 6.20
    introduction, 6.16
    overview, 2.48
    relevant factors, 6.21
  disclosure
    forms, 2.27–2.30
    non-parties, against, 2.49–2.52
    voluntary, 2.34
  Financial Dispute Resolution (FDR), 2.42
  'financial remedy', 2.22
  first appointment, 2.41
  forms and documents
    consent orders, 2.31
    disclosure, 2.27–2.30
    Form A, 2.24
    Form A1, 2.25
    Form A2, 2.26
    Form E, 2.27
    Form E1, 2.28
    Form E2, 2.29
    replies, 2.30

Index

Financial remedy applications – *cont.*
  generally, 2.22
  hearings
    absent parties, 2.44
    bundles, 2.45
    introduction, 2.43
  inspection appointments
    application, 2.50
    further guidance, 2.52
    generally, 2.49
    response, 2.51
  interim provision, 2.47
  introduction, 2.21
  magistrates' court proceedings, and, 2.46
  maintenance pending suit, 2.47
  non-party disclosure
    application, 2.50
    further guidance, 2.52
    generally, 2.49
    response, 2.51
  overseas proceedings, after
    application, 2.55
    generally, 2.53
    permission to apply, 5.159–5.163
    procedure, 2.56
    venue for proceedings, 2.54
  pensions
    attachment orders, 2.37
    generally, 2.35
    implementation, 2.38
    PPF compensation, 2.39
    sharing orders, 2.36
  place of proceedings
    generally, 2.40
    overseas proceedings, after, 2.54
  pre-application protocol, 2.21
  replies, 2.30
  statements of information, 2.33
  undertakings, 2.32
  venue for proceedings
    generally, 2.40
    overseas proceedings, after, 2.54
  voluntary disclosure, 2.34
First appointment
  financial remedy applications, and, 2.41
Forced marriage
  Family Law Act 1996, Part 4A, and, 3.2
Foreign government
  service out of the jurisdiction, and, 5.34
Foreign law
  evidence, and, 5.82
Forms
  affidavits in support
    general, 2.10
    request to dispense with service of petition on respondent, 2.8

Forms – *cont.*
  application for decree nisi or conditional order, 2.9
  answer, 2.7
  enforcement, and, 6.29
  financial remedy applications, and
    consent orders, 2.31
    disclosure, 2.27–2.30
    Form A, 2.24
    Form A1, 2.25
    Form A2, 2.26
    Form E, 2.27
    Form E1, 2.28
    Form E2, 2.29
    replies, 2.30
  generally, 5.1
  introduction, 2.4
  service, and
    D89, 5.6
    FP6, 5.5
    introduction, 5.4
  start of proceedings, and, 5.2
  statement of arrangements for children, 2.6
  statement of reconciliation, 2.5
Freezing injunctions
  content, 6.9
  generally, 6.2
Further information
  contents of application and answer, 2.14
Garnishee orders
  generally, 6.30
Gender recognition
  application for corrected certificate, 5.141
  documents, 5.49
Glossary
  principles of FPR 2010, and, 1.2
Hague Convention 1996
  forms, 6.60
  introduction, 6.58
  procedure, 6.61
  relevant court, 6.59
Hardship orders
  third party debt orders, and, 6.50
Hardship payments orders
  statements of truth, and, 5.54
Hearings
  attachment of earnings orders, and, 6.40
  financial remedy applications, and
    absent parties, 2.44
    bundles, 2.45
    introduction, 2.43
  obtaining information from a judgment debtor, and, 6.45
  Part 18 applications, and, 5.129
  Part 19 applications, and, 5.138

Hearings – *cont.*
permission to apply for financial remedy after overseas proceedings, and, 5.162
question as to property to be decided in summary way, and, 5.148
third party debt orders, and, 6.51
Hearsay evidence
generally, 5.80
Human Fertilisation and Embryology Act 2008, s 54
children proceedings, and, 4.7
Human Rights Act 1998
generally, 5.47
Information from a judgment debtor
applications, 6.42
case management, 6.45
generally, 6.41
hearings, 6.45
introduction, 6.30
relevant court, 6.43
service, 6.44
Inherent jurisdiction
children proceedings, and, 4.4
Injunctions
Family Law Act 1996, Part 4, under, 3.1
Inspection
case management, and, 1.4
generally, 2.16
Inspection appointments
application, 2.50
further guidance, 2.52
generally, 2.49
response, 2.51
Inspection of property
generally, 6.2
Instructions to give evidence
expert evidence, and, 5.120
Interim declarations
generally, 6.2
Interim injunctions
cessation if application stayed, 6.8
generally, 6.9
introduction, 6.2
third parties, against, 6.12
Interim provision
financial remedy applications, and, 2.47
Interim remedies
accounts and inquiries, 6.2
Anton Piller orders, 6.2
applications
evidence in support, 6.6
generally, 6.5
urgent cases, 6.7
without notice, 6.7
available orders, 6.2

Interim remedies – *cont.*
delivery up
generally, 6.11
introduction, 6.2
detention, custody or preservation of property, 6.2
entry to land or buildings, 6.2
evidence in support, 6.6
experiments on or with property, 6.2
freezing injunctions
content, 6.9
generally, 6.2
inspection of property, 6.2
interim declarations, 6.2
interim injunctions
cessation if application stayed, 6.8
generally, 6.9
introduction, 6.2
third parties, against, 6.12
jurisdiction, 6.3
location of property or assets, 6.2
Mareva injunctions, 6.2
non-party disclosure, 6.2
overview, 6.1
payment into court, 6.2
payment of income from property, 6.2
payment of specified fund into court, 6.2
practice direction
introduction, 6.1
jurisdiction, 6.3
scope, 6.3
preparation and filing of accounts, 6.2
procedure, 6.5
sale of perishable property, 6.2
search orders
generally, 6.10
introduction, 6.2
taking of sample of property, 6.2
time for making, 6.4
urgent applications, 6.7
without notice applications, 6.7
International child abduction
children proceedings, and, 4.5
Judgments and orders
generally, 5.51
Judicial authorities
service out of the jurisdiction, and, 5.34
Judicial separation decrees
matrimonial orders, and, 2.2
Leave to appeal
change in nomenclature, and, 1.3
Legal representation
children proceedings, and, 4.10
Legitimacy
declarations, and, 5.157

Index

Legitimation
  declarations, and, 5.157
Limited civil restraint orders
  generally, 1.5
  types, 1.6
Magistrates' court proceedings
  evidence, and, 5.84
  financial remedy applications, and, 2.46
  registration of maintenance orders, and, 6.64
Maintenance orders
  Maintenance Orders Act 1950, under, 6.63
  Maintenance Orders Act 1958, under, 6.64
  reciprocal arrangements, 6.66
Maintenance pending suit
  financial remedy applications, and, 2.47
Mareva injunctions
  generally, 6.2
Marital status
  declarations, and, 5.155
Matrimonial order
  meaning, 2.2
Matrimonial proceedings
  amendments to application or answer, 2.12
  applications, 2.2
  case management hearing, 2.15
  comparison table. 2.3
  costs, 2.18
  decree absolute
    expedition, 2.20
    separation grounds, on, 2.19
  disclosure, 2.16
  forms and documents
    affidavit in support of request to dispense with service of petition on respondent, 2.8
    affidavits in support, 2.10
    application for decree nisi or conditional order, 2.9
    answer, 2.7
    generally, 2.4
    statement of arrangements for children, 2.6
    statement of reconciliation, 2.5
  further information about contents of application and answer, 2.14
  inspection, 2.16
  medical examination in nullity proceedings, 2.17
  overview, 2.1
  replies to answers, 2.13
  supplemental petitions and answers, 2.13
Medical examinations
  nullity proceedings, 2.17
Meetings between experts
  expert evidence, and, 5.118

Models
  evidence, and, 5.80
Non-molestation orders
  Family Law Act 1996, Part 4, under, 3.1
Non-party disclosure
  financial remedy applications, and
    application, 2.50
    further guidance, 2.52
    generally, 2.49
    response, 2.51
  generally, 6.2
Notice
  change of solicitor, and, 5.39
  generally, 5.45
Notice of appeal
  generally, 6.25
Notice to admit facts
  generally, 5.73
Notice to admit or procure documents
  generally, 5.74
Nullity proceedings
  civil partnership orders, and, 2.2
  matrimonial orders, and, 2.2
  medical examination, 2.17
Obtaining information from a judgment debtor
  applications, 6.42
  case management, 6.45
  generally, 6.41
  hearings, 6.45
  introduction, 6.30
  relevant court, 6.43
  service, 6.44
Occupation orders
  Family Law Act 1996, Part 4, under, 3.1
Order of proceedings
  case management, and, 1.4
Orders
  generally, 5.51
Overriding objective
  case management, and, 1.4
  philosophy of FPR 2010, and, 1.1
Overseas proceedings (financial remedy applications)
  application, 2.55
  generally, 2.53
  permission to apply
    hearings, 5.162
    introduction, 5.159
    procedure, 5.160
    relevant court, 5.161
    substantive application, 5.163
  procedure, 2.56
  venue for proceedings, 2.54
Parentage
  declarations, and, 5.156

Index

Parental orders
children proceedings, and, 4.7
Part 7 proceedings
witness statements, and, 5.76
Part 8 applications
alteration of maintenance agreement after death of one party, for, 5.142
consent to marriage of child, for, 5.172
conversion table, 5.140
corrected gender recognition certificate, for, 5.141
declarations, for
 adoption effected overseas, as to, 5.158
 Attorney General's role, 5.154
 case management, 5.153
 civil partnership status, as to, 5.155
 introduction, 5.149
 legitimacy, of, 5.157
 legitimation, of, 5.157
 marital status, as to, 5.155
 parentage, of, 5.156
 parties, 5.151
 relevant court, 5.150
 response, 5.152
introduction, 5.139
orders preventing avoidance under Child Support Act 1991, s 32L, for, 5.171
overview, 5.123
permission to apply for financial remedy after overseas proceedings, for
 hearings, 5.162
 introduction, 5.159
 procedure, 5.160
 relevant court, 5.161
 substantive application, 5.163
publicity, 5.173
question as to property to be decided in summary way, for
 case management, 5.148
 general, 5.146
 hearings, 5.148
 introduction, 5.143
 overview, 5.123
 procedure, 5.144
 relevant court, 5.145
 response, 5.147
registration of civil partnership of child, for, 5.172
transfer of tenancy under FLA 1996, s 53 and Sch 7, for
 case management, 5.169
 injunctions, 5.170
 introduction, 5.164
 procedure, 5.165
 relevant court, 5.166
 response, 5.168

Part 8 applications – *cont.*
transfer of tenancy under FLA 1996, s 53 and Sch 7, for – *cont.*
 service, 5.167
withdrawal, 5.46
Part 18 applications
absent parties, 5.132
evidence in support, 5.128
filing notice, 5.126
general procedure, 5.126
hearings, 5.129
introduction, 5.124
overview, 5.123
relevant proceedings, 5.125
scope, 5.125
service, 5.127
telephone hearings, 5.130
video conferencing, 5.130
without merit, 5.132
without notice orders, 5.131
Part 19 applications
case management, 5.138
evidence, 5.137
filing notice, 5.135
general procedure, 5.135
hearings, 5.138
introduction, 5.133
overview, 5.123
relevant proceedings, 5.134
response, 5.136
scope, 5.134
Payment into court
generally, 6.2
Payment of income from property
generally, 6.2
Payment of specified fund into court
generally, 6.2
Pensions
financial remedy applications, and
 attachment orders, 2.37
 generally, 2.35
 implementation, 2.38
 PPF compensation, 2.39
 sharing orders, 2.36
Periodical payments orders
registration, and, 6.64
Permission to appeal
nomenclature, and, 1.3
Permission to instruct experts
generally, 5.102
pre-application, 5.104
relevant proceedings, 5.103
Personal details
generally, 5.43
Personal service
documents, and, 5.21

Index

Personal service – *cont.*
  petition, and, 5.16
Petitions
  change in nomenclature, and, 1.3
  service, and
    alternative address, 5.10
    alternative method, by, 5.17
    alternative place, at, 5.17
    bailiff, by, 5.11
    children, on, 5.14
    deemed service, 5.15
    dispensing with service, 5.18
    DX, by, 5.12
    generally, 5.8
    methods, 5.9
    no address given by respondent, where, 5.13
    proof of personal service, 5.16
    protected parties, on, 5.14
    solicitor, on, 5.12
    substituted method, by, 5.17
Photographs
  evidence, and, 5.80
Place of proceedings
  financial remedy applications, and
    generally, 2.40
    overseas proceedings, after, 2.54
Placement applications
  children proceedings, and, 4.8
Plans
  evidence, and, 5.80
Postal service
  documents, and, 5.24
Practice directions
  children proceedings, and, 4.1
  expert evidence, and
    generally, 5.100
    introduction, 5.101
    permission to instruct, 5.102–5.104
  interim remedies, and
    introduction, 6.1
    jurisdiction, 6.3
    scope, 6.3
  philosophy of FPR 2010, and, 1.1
Pre-application protocols
  financial remedy applications, and, 2.21
Preliminary issues
  case management, and, 1.4
Preparation and filing of accounts
  generally, 6.2
Presumption of death decrees
  matrimonial orders, and, 2.2
Presumption of death orders
  civil partnership orders, and, 2.2
Private law proceedings
  children, and, 4.34

Proof of civil partnership
  generally, 2.11
Proportionality
  principles of FPR 2010, and, 1.2
Protected parties
  See also **Children proceedings**
  representation, 4.9
  service
    documents, 5.26
    petition, 5.14
Protection of individuals
  forced marriage, 3.2
  injunctions under Part 4 of FLA 1996, 3.1
Public law proceedings
  children, and, 4.2
Publicity
  applications, and, 5.173
Question as to property to be decided in summary way
  case management, 5.148
  general, 5.146
  hearings, 5.148
  introduction, 5.143
  overview, 5.123
  procedure, 5.144
  relevant court, 5.145
  response, 5.147
Questions to experts
  expert evidence, and, 5.117
Reciprocal enforcement
  registration of orders, and, 6.66
Registration of civil partnership of child
  Part 8 applications, and, 5.172
Registration of orders
  Civil Partnership (Jurisdiction and Recognition of Judgments) Regulations 2005, under
    forms, 6.60
    introduction, 6.58
    procedure, 6.61
    relevant court, 6.59
  Council Regulation, under
    forms, 6.60
    introduction, 6.58
    procedure, 6.61
    relevant court, 6.59
  custody orders, 6.65
  Family Law Act 1986, under, 6.65
  Hague Convention 1996, under
    forms, 6.60
    introduction, 6.58
    procedure, 6.61
    relevant court, 6.59
  magistrates' court, in, 6.64

Index

Registration of orders – *cont.*
  maintenance orders
    Maintenance Orders Act 1950, under, 6.63
    Maintenance Orders Act 1958, under, 6.64
    reciprocal arrangements, 6.66
  Part 32, under
    custody orders, 6.65
    maintenance orders, 6.63– 6.64
    scope, 6.62
  periodical payments orders, 6.64
  reciprocal enforcement, 6.66
Replies
  financial remedy applications, and, 2.30
Replies to answers
  generally, 2.13
Representation
  children, 4.10
  protected parties, 4.9
Sale of perishable property
  generally, 6.2
Sample of property
  generally, 6.2
Sealing
  documents, and, 5.50
Search orders
  generally, 6.10
  introduction, 6.2
Security for costs
  background, 6.13
  generally, 6.14
Separate orders
  civil partnership orders, and, 2.2
Separate proceedings
  case management, and, 1.4
Service
  alternative means, 5.7
  attachment of earnings orders, 6.39
  certificate of service, 5.5
  committal by way of judgment summons, 6.34
  documents, of
    address for service, 5.22
    alternative method, by, 5.28
    alternative place, at, 5.28
    alternative service provider, by, 5.24
    children, on, 5.26
    deemed service, 5.27
    dispensing with service, 5.29
    DX, by, 5.23–5.24
    email, by, 5.25
    fax, by, 5.25
    generally, 5.19
    methods, 5.20
    person, in, 5.21

Service – *cont.*
  documents, of – *cont.*
    post, by, 5.24
    protected parties, on, 5.26
  enforcement, and
    attachment of earnings orders, 6.39
    committal by way of judgment summons, 6.34
    obtaining information from a judgment debtor, 6.44
    third party debt orders, 6.49
  forms
    D89, 5.6
    FP6, 5.5
    introduction, 5.4
  generally, 5.3
  obtaining information from a judgment debtor, 6.44
  orders upon experts, of, 5.106
  out of the jurisdiction
    See also **Service out of the jurisdiction**
    generally, 5.30–5.36
  Part 18 applications, and, 5.127
  petition, of
    alternative address, 5.10
    alternative method, by, 5.17
    alternative place, at, 5.17
    bailiff, by, 5.11
    children, on, 5.14
    deemed service, 5.15
    dispensing with service, 5.18
    DX, by, 5.12
    generally, 5.8
    methods, 5.9
    no address given by respondent, where, 5.13
    proof of personal service, 5.16
    protected parties, on, 5.14
    solicitor, on, 5.12
    substituted method, by, 5.17
  request for personal service by court bailiff, 5.6
  summary, 5.37
  third party debt orders, 6.49
  transfer of tenancy under FLA 1996, s 53 and Sch 7, and, 5.167
  witness statements, and, 5.70
Service out of the jurisdiction
  acknowledgment of service, 5.31
  British consular authorities, through, 5.34
  foreign government, through, 5.34
  introduction, 5.30
  judicial authorities, through, 5.34
  members of regular forces, 5.36
  methods, 5.32
  responding to application, 5.31

Index

Service out of the jurisdiction – *cont.*
  Service Regulation, in accordance with, 5.33
  translations, 5.35
  USAF members, 5.36
Shorten time
  case management, and, 1.4
Specific disclosure
  case management, and, 1.4
Start of proceedings
  generally, 5.2
Statements of arrangements for children
  form, 2.6
  statements of truth, and, 5.54
Statements of case
  statements of truth, and, 5.54
Statements of information
  generally, 2.33
  statements of truth, and, 5.54
Statements of reconciliation
  form, 2.5
Statements of truth
  consequences of failure to verify, 5.58
  documents requiring verification, 5.54
  false statements, 5.59
  introduction, 5.53
  nature, 5.55
  persons entitled to sign, 5.56
  persons unable to read or sign, 5.57
  relevant documents, 5.54
  summary, 5.60
Stay of proceedings
  case management, and, 1.4
Stop notices
  generally, 6.30
Stop orders
  generally, 6.30
Substituted service
  documents, and,, 5.17
Supplemental petitions and answers
  generally, 2.13
Swearing
  affidavits, and, 5.67
Taking of sample of property
  generally, 6.2
Telephone hearings
  case management, and, 1.4
  Part 18 applications, and, 5.130
Third party debt orders
  applications, 6.47
  further evidence, 6.51
  generally, 6.46
  hardship orders, 6.50
  hearings, 6.51
  introduction, 6.30
  relevant court, 6.48

Third party debt orders – *cont.*
  service, 6.49
  statements of truth, and, 5.54
Transfer of tenancy applications under FLA 1996, s 53 and Sch 7
  case management, 5.169
  injunctions, 5.170
  introduction, 5.164
  procedure, 5.165
  relevant court, 5.166
  response, 5.168
  service, 5.167
Transitional provisions
  costs, 1.14
  existing proceedings, 1.11–1.12
  introduction, 1.10
  new proceedings, 1.13
Translations
  service out of the jurisdiction, and, 5.35
Travelling expenses
  witness summonses, an, 5.87
Undertakings
  financial remedy applications, and, 2.32
  generally, 6.57
'Unless' orders
  case management, and, 1.4
Urgent applications
  interim remedies, and, 6.7
Urgent cases
  expert evidence, and, 5.105
USAF personnel
  service out of the jurisdiction, and, 5.36
Venue for proceedings
  attachment of earnings orders, and, 6.38
  committal by way of judgment summons, and, 6.33
  declarations as to status, and, 5.150
  enforcement, and
    attachment of earnings orders, 6.38
    committal by way of judgment summons, 6.33
    generally, 6.28
    obtaining information from a judgment debtor, 6.43
    third party debt orders, 6.48
  financial remedy applications, and
    generally, 2.40
    overseas proceedings, after, 2.54
  obtaining information from a judgment debtor, and, 6.43
  Part 18 applications, 5.125
  Part 19 applications, and, 5.134
  permission to apply for financial remedy after overseas proceedings, and, 5.161
  question as to property to be decided in summary way, and, 5.145

Index

Venue for proceedings – *cont.*
  third party debt orders, and, 6.48
  transfer of tenancy under FLA 1996, s 53 and Sch 7, and, 5.166
Video conferencing
  Part 18 applications, and, 5.130
Video link evidence
  generally, 5.77
Voluntary disclosure
  financial remedy applications, and, 2.34
Wardship
  children proceedings, and, 4.4
Warrants of execution
  generally, 6.30
Withdrawal of applications
  generally, 5.46
Without merit applications
  Part 18 applications, and, 5.132
Without notice
  interim remedies, and, 6.7
  nomenclature, and, 1.3
  Part 18 applications, and, 5.131

Witness statements
  exhibiting documents, 5.68
  filing, 5.69
  format, 5.66
  generally, 5.64
  introduction, 5.63
  Part 7 proceedings, in, 5.76
  service for use at final hearing, 5.70
  statements of truth, and, 5.54
  use in other proceedings, 5.65
  verification, 5.67
Witness summaries
  generally, 5.72
Witness summonses
  compensation for loss of time, 5.87
  generally, 5.86
  magistrates' court, in, 5.88
  travelling expenses, 5.87
Witnesses
  evidence, and, 5.85